An Economic History of Imperial Madagascar, 1750–1895

The first comprehensive economic history of precolonial Madagascar, this study examines the island's role from 1750 to 1895 in the context of a burgeoning international economy and the rise of modern European imperialism. Challenging conventional portrayals of nineteenth-century Madagascar as a unified and progressive kingdom, this study reveals that the Merina of the central highlands attempted to found an island empire and through the exploitation of its human and natural resources build the economic and military might to challenge British and French pretensions in the region. Ultimately, the Merina failed due to imperial forced labor policies and natural disasters, the nefarious consequences of which (disease, depopulation, ethnic enmity) have in traditional histories been imputed to external capitalist and French colonial policies. Although by 1890, Madagascar was firmly integrated into a regional trade network stretching from South Africa to India, dominated by British Indians, Britain acknowledged French claims to Madagascar. France took 13 years to conquer Madagascar, finally succeeding only due to the internal collapse of Merina power.

GWYN CAMPBELL is a professor in the Department of History at McGill University. He is the editor of *Southern Africa and Regional Cooperation in the Indian Ocean Regions* (2003) and *The Structure of Slavery in Indian Ocean Africa and Asia* (2004). He is also the author of numerous articles, in such scholarly journals as the *Journal of African History* and *International Journal of African Historical Studies.*

African Studies Series 106
Editorial Board

(continued after the Index)

An Economic History of Imperial Madagascar, 1750–1895

The Rise and Fall of an Island Empire

Gwyn Campbell
McGill University

CAMBRIDGE
UNIVERSITY PRESS

CAMBRIDGE UNIVERSITY PRESS
Cambridge, New York, Melbourne, Madrid, Cape Town, Singapore, São Paulo

Cambridge University Press
40 West 20th Street, New York, NY 10011-4211, USA

www.cambridge.org
Information on this title: www.cambridge.org/9780521839358

First published 2005

Printed in the United States of America

A catalog record for this book is available from the British Library.

Library of Congress Cataloging in Publication Data
Campbell, Gwyn, 1952–

    An economic history of Imperial Madagascar 1750–1895, or, The rise and fall of an island
empire / Gwyn Campbell.

      p.   cm. – (African studies series ; 106)

    Includes bibliographical references and index.

    ISBN 0-521-83935-1

    1. Madagascar – Economic conditions.   2. Madagascar – History.
3. Madagascar – Colonization.   4. Merina (Malagasy people) – History.
I. Title : Rise and fall of an island empire. II. Title. III. Series.
HC895.C36   2004
330.9691′01 – dc22   2003069667

ISBN-13   978-0-521-83935-8 hardback
ISBN-10   0-521-83935-1 hardback

TO MY MOTHER, EILEEN
AND THE MEMORY OF MY FATHER, JOHN

Contents

Appendices

Tables, Figures, and Maps

Tables

Figures

Maps

Illustrations

Acknowledgments

I owe a debt of gratitude to many colleagues and students, past and present, who have helped to shape the structure of this book. Also to the Leverhulme Trust, the British Academy, Ernest Oppenheimer Foundation, DAAD (Deutscher Akademischer Austausch Dienst – German Academic Exchange Service), the International Institute for Asian Studies (Leiden), and the University of the Witwatersrand for research grants, and finally to Marianne for her steadfast support and editorial skills.

Introduction

The Context

Until recently, the history of Madagascar has been a well-guarded Gallic secret. France held long-established colonial claims to the island, which is the size of France, Belgium, and the Netherlands combined. Following a period of early French settlement (1642–74), Madagascar was incorporated into the French empire (1896–1960) and subsequently into membership in *la Francophonie* – the association of Francophone countries. French influence there is still strong. Francophone scholars have dominated the historiography of Madagascar, their views expressed through two broad schools of thought, the Colonial and Nationalist. These have focused on political and cultural, at the expense of economic, history – a relatively undeveloped discipline in France. The predominant themes of study are French historical claims to Madagascar; European political, social, and religious relations with the precolonial Merina state; and the French colonial era. While the two schools disagree on issues such as the justification for, and impact of, French colonialism, they concur that the history of Madagascar is an anomaly in the western Indian Ocean–Africa region because the island's peoples speak dialects and hold to cultural practices that are predominantly Austronesian in origin. Consequently, most historians have considered Madagascar in historical isolation, an island museum largely unrelated to its immediate region – the western Indian Ocean and Indian Ocean Africa (IOA).

Historians of mainland Africa and of other Indian Ocean countries have largely respected the Gallic tradition. Consequently, they have excluded Madagascar from the scope of their research and publications. Influenced by the British colonial tradition, Anglophone scholars segmented the areas of Africa bordered by the Indian Ocean and its Red Sea extension into northeast, east, and southern Africa. Each of these became home to specialist scholars who rarely, if ever, alluded to Madagascar. Since the early 1970s, a small number of Anglophone scholars have broken into the field of Malagasy studies.[1] They have tempered the Francophone vision, notably with allusions to the African affinities of the first Malagasy and the role of predominantly British Protestant missions in the island. However, such studies have largely been set within the framework of the mainstream Francophone historical tradition that they have strengthened rather than challenged.

This volume breaks with the dominant tradition. It constitutes the first comprehensive study of the economic history of precolonial Madagascar during the period of Merina ascendancy.[2] Moreover, it places Madagascar within a regional economy that linked all countries lapped by the western Indian Ocean and, in doing so, reveals the basic structural unity of the regional economy.

---

[1] P. M. Mutibwa, *The Malagasy and the Europeans* (London: Longman, 1974); Bonar A. Gow, *Madagascar and the Protestant Impact. The work of the British missions, 1818–1895* (London: Longman & Dalhousie University Press, 1979); Stephen Ellis, *The Rising of the Red Shawls: A Revolt in Madagascar, 1895–1899* (Cambridge: Cambridge University Press, 1985); Pier Larson, *History and Memory in the Age of Enslavement* (Portsmouth: Heinemann, 2000).

An exception is Raymond Kent, who, on grounds largely rejected by other scholars, argued for a major African historical influence in Madagascar – see his *Early Kingdoms in Madagascar, 1500–1700* (New York: Holt, Rinehart & Winston, 1970).

[2] A number of important studies relating to aspects of the economic history of Madagascar – but limited in scope, include Raymond Decary and Rémy Castel, *Études démographiques. Modalités et conséquences des migrations intérieures récentes des populations malgaches* (Tananarive, 1941); Hubert Deschamps, *Les migrations intérieures à Madagascar* (Paris, 1959); Paul Ottino, *Les économies paysannes malgaches du Bas-Mangoky* (Paris, 1963); Micheline Rasoamiara-manana, *Aspects économiques et sociaux de la vie à Majunga entre 1862 et 1881* (Antananarivo, 1983); Yves Feugeas, *Le marché du riz pendant la période coloniale à Madagascar (1905–1940)* (Antananarivo, 1979); Albert Ralaikoa, *Fiscalité, administration et pression coloniales dans le sud Betsileo (1895–1918)* (Antananarivo, 1987); Jacques Dez, "Développement économique et tradition à Madagascar" *Cahiers de l' institut de science économique appliquée* supplément 129, série V.4 (1962); idem, "Considération sur les prix pratiqués à Tananarive en 1870," *BAM* 40 (1962); idem, "Éléments pour une étude de l'économie agro-sylvo-pastorale de l'Imerina ancienne" *Université de Madagascar: École nationale supérieure agronomique* 8 (1970); idem, "Monnaie et structure traditionnelle à Madagascar" *Cahiers Vuilfredo Pareto – Revue européenne des sciences sociales* (1970); idem, "Éléments pour une étude sur les prix et les échanges de biens dans l'économie mérina ancienne" *BAM* 48/ 1–2 (1970); idem, "La monarchie mérina et le développement agricole" *Terre Malgache* 10 (1971); Jean Fremigacci, "Mise en valeur coloniale et travail forcé: la construction du chemin de fer Tananarive-Antsirabe (1911–1923)" *Omaly sy Anio* 1–2 (1975); idem, "La colonisation à Vatomandry-Mahanoro – Espérances et désillusions (1895–1910)" *Omaly sy Anio* 3–4 (1976); idem, "Les colons de la côte est centrale de Madagascar, de la prospérité à la crise (1924–1939)" *Omaly sy Anio* 15 (1982); idem, "Les difficultés d'une politique coloniale: le café de Madagascar à la conquête du marché français (1930–1938)" *Omaly sy Anio* 21–22 (1985); also see works by present author cited in bibliography.

It also dispels the myth of the creation in the nineteenth century of a unified and civilized Malagasy nation state possessing a single cohesive economy. As significantly, it argues that the colonization of Madagascar is explicable less in terms of French historical claims to the island, or to the forces of French capitalism, than to a combination of two other factors. These are, first, the forces impelling the British forward movement in IOA from the 1870s and, second, the autarkic policies and mismanagement of the indigenous Merina regime that triggered the implosion of the Merina empire in Madagascar.

Historiographical Traditions: The Particularity of Madagascar

The historical particularity of Madagascar was central to the perspective of the French Colonial School, centered on the works of Alfred and Guillaume Grandidier whose arguments dominated the historiography of the island for most of the twentieth century.[3] From the early 1970s, a new Nationalist School emerged, which currently dominates the field. Members of the Nationalist School accept an ancient African influence on Madagascar and reject the Colonial School's justification for the imposition of French rule in the island. Nevertheless, they have maintained the emphasis on the historical distinctiveness of the island. Of key importance here is the view that from c.1790–1810, the Merina of the central highlands forged of the different peoples of the island a single and progressive nation-state, unique in nineteenth-century Africa, and fondly referred to in the Nationalist School literature as "The Kingdom" ("Le Royaume").[4]

The Nationalist School's interpretation of nineteenth-century Malagasy history runs approximately as follows: The founding father of the Malagasy nation, Andrianampoinimerina (r. c.1795–1810), united the central highland province of Imerina and gave to his people the first ever sense of a Malagasy identity. Radama I (r.1810–28) continued where his father left off. In the 1820s, he concluded an alliance with the British who provided him with the personnel and equipment to build a modern standing army and education system. He also banned the slave trade and admitted Christian missionaries into the country.

---

[3] Alfred et Guillaume Grandidier, esp. *GH*.

[4] Françoise Raison-Jourde, "Introduction" in *idem* (ed.), *Les souverains de Madagasar* (Paris, 1983), 7–68; Raymond K. Kent (ed.), *Madagascar in History. Essays from the 1970s* (Berkeley, 1979); Hubert Deschamps, *L' histoire de Madagascar* (Paris, 1972); Ellis, *Rising of the Red Shawls*; Guy Jacob, "Influences occidentales en Imerina et déséquilibres économiques avant la conquête française," *Omaly sy Anio* 5–6 (1977), 223–31; *idem*, "La révolution industrielle et l'Imerina au XIXe siècle ou l'impossible transfert," Colloque International d'histoire malgache (Antananarivo, 31 juillet - 5 août 1989); Larson, *History and Memory*.

Radama I's wife and successor, Ranavalona I (1828–61), was a traditionalist who expelled the missionaries, persecuted indigenous Christians, and generally adopted anti-Western policies. She also permitted a handful of commoners to accede to the top posts in government and the army, whose control was consolidated in a coup d'etat in 1863, during which Radama II, Ranavalona I's son and successor, was killed. The effective ruler of Madagascar was subsequently Rainilaiarivony, who, as prime minister, married a succession of Malagasy queens. During his reign Rainilaiarivony performed a complex political juggling act, balancing policies designed to assuage Western demands for modernization with others aimed at keeping Westerners at bay and preserving Malagasy independence. He maintained a largely open door policy, encouraging foreign investment. He adopted Christianity as the state religion and, with missionary assistance, founded a compulsory national education system. He also instituted a constitutional monarchy, reformed the judiciary, and took the first steps toward the abolition of slavery.

Despite these evident signs of a progressive regime, the French asserted ancient colonial claims to Madagascar. These were backed up by the French Navy (which harbored enormous resentment at having suffered defeat in the Napoleonic and Prussian Wars), by the land-thirsty Francophone community of the neighboring Mascarene islands (Réunion and Mauritius), and from the 1870s, by the new belligerent imperialism espoused by capitalist forces in France. The Franco-Merina War of 1883–5 established a nominal French protectorate over Madagascar, but the Merina government ignored French pretensions to govern external policy. Their cause was supported by British missionaries and some British army officers. However, the British government remained aloof and in 1890 agreed to give the French a free hand in Madagascar in return for French recognition of British dominance in Zanzibar. The fate of Madagascar was sealed. In 1895, French forces overran the island. By that time, the Nationalist School argues, the Malagasy formed a united and progressive nation-state, the first in Africa, and responded with fury in a massive nationalist uprising. Although largely suppressed by 1897, the embers of revolt smoldered on into the first years of the twentieth century.

For a New Historical Context: The Indian Ocean World and Indian Ocean Africa

The present study challenges both the Colonialist and the Nationalist schools of thought, first by seeking to situate Madagascar historically as an integral part of the wider Indian Ocean world (IOW), a term that requires some explanation. For those who place Europe at the center of the development of world systems of trade and production, the Indian Ocean world is probably associated with Asian cultures, which in conventional Eurocentric histories are portrayed as archaic monoliths, characterized by intractable social and political structures utterly resistant to the forces of change and modernization. From this perspective, economic development, where it occurred in the Asian region, was a result of external, specifically European, forces.

However, a revisionist school has recently developed that argues that Asia, not Europe, forged the first global economy, which in turn emerged at a considerably earlier date than was previously thought. Adapting Ferdinand Braudel's concept of a Mediterranean maritime economy, K. N. Chaudhuri, and later André Brink, argued that an Asia–Indian Ocean global economy emerged alongside Islam from the seventh century and that Europeans achieved global dominance only in the eighteenth century. Others date the start of the Asia–Indian Ocean global economy to between the tenth and thirteenth centuries. Andre Gunder Frank considers that it may well have arisen much earlier and that European dominance was achieved only in the nineteenth century with industrialization and the emergence of a truly international economy.[5] These revisionists largely omitted Africa from their analysis. Nevertheless, southern, eastern and northeastern Africa, and the offshore islands, possessed strong historical linkages to the Middle East, South and Southeast Asia, and the Far East. All formed an integral part of the Asia–Indian Ocean economy.[6] Therefore, the entire area from the Cape to Cairo to Calcutta to Canton and beyond forms what is here termed the Indian Ocean world.

---

[5] K. N. Chaudhuri, *Trade and Civilisation in the Indian Ocean. An Economic History from the Rise of Islam to 1750* (Cambridge, Cambridge University Press, 1985); *idem, Asia Before Europe. Economy and Civilisation of the Indian Ocean from the Rise of Islam to 1750* (Cambridge: Cambridge University Press, 1992); André Wink, *Al-Hind. The Making of the Indo-Islamic World* 2 vols. (Leiden, New York, Köln, 1996 and 1997); Janet L. Abu-Lughod, *Before European Hegemony. The World System A.D. 1250–1350* (New York & Oxford: Oxford University Press, 1989); George Modelski and William R. Thompson, *Leading Sectors and World Powers. The Coevolution of Global Economics and Politics* (Columbia: University of South Carolina, 1996), esp. pp. 142–5, 156; Andre Gunder Frank, *ReORIENT: Global Economy in the Asian Age* (Berkeley, Los Angeles, London: Berkeley University Press, 1998); see also P. J. Cain & A. G. Hopkins, "Gentlemanly Capitalism and British Expansion Overseas I. The Old Colonial System, 1688–1850," *Economic History Review* 39.4 (1986).

[6] Peter Boomgaard, "Human Capital, Slavery and Low Rates of Economic and Population Growth in Indonesia, 1600–1910," in Gwyn Campbell (ed.), *The Structure of Slavery in Indian Ocean Africa and Asia* (London: Frank Cass, 2004), 83–96; Abdul Sheriff, "The Slave Trade and its Fallout in the Persian Gulf" and Nigel Worden, "Indian Ocean Slavery and Its Demise in the Cape Colony" – in Gwyn Campbell (ed.), *Abolition and Its Aftermath in Indian Ocean Africa and Asia* (London: Routledge, forthcoming 2004/5).

While possessing some unique features, Madagascar was historically part of an IOW that included IOA. The first human settlers of Madagascar were of Austronesian and African (Bantu-speaking) origin.[7] They imported plants and economic techniques from both Indonesia and Africa and at first maintained links with both regions. In time, relations with Africa grew and those with Indonesia diminished, notably with the rise of Portuguese maritime activity in the IOW during the sixteenth century.

The rise of a plantation economy on the French Mascarene islands of Réunion and Mauritius from the mid-eighteenth century inaugurated a new phase in the island's economic history as it was by far the closest source of provisions and slaves for the plantations. In the late eighteenth century, a French commercial empire was proposed, stretching from the Mascarenes to the Swahili and Mozambique coasts, in which Madagascar would play a central role. The island was critically important as a supplier of provisions and plantation workers for the Masacarenes, and its trade "is so linked to that of the coast of Africa that we believe it impossible to separate them."[8] The following century, Madagascar played a critical part in the east African slave trade, developed commercial ties with South Africa, and became steadily incorporated, alongside other countries in the region, into the burgeoning international economy.

There is a cogent argument that the major economic changes in West Africa resulted mainly from its integration into the international economy during the nineteenth century.[9] The catalyst for this change was the industrial revolution, not colonialism. Industrialization and the concomitant rise of the international economy led to the demise of the slave trade and the rise of free commodity trade. These in turn laid the basis for European colonial takeover. Growing integration of West African regions into the international economy increased their vulnerability to world market fluctuations. This first became evident in the severe and protracted depression of the 1880s. The depression strained Afro–European commercial relations to the extent that European traders called upon their home governments to secure their commercial interests through political intervention in West Africa. Until that time, indigenous elites had largely

---

[7] The uniquely Austronesian origin of the Malagasy people has been convincingly disproved as DNA analysis has for the first time demonstrated that the Malagasy are overwhelmingly of mixed African and Austronesian origin – see, R. Hewitt, A. Krause, A. Goldman G. Campbell, T. Jenkins, "ß-Globin Haplotype Analysis Suggests that a Major Source of Malagasy Ancestry is Derived from Bantu-Speaking Negroids," *American Society of Human Genetics* 58 (1996), 1303–8.

[8] Morice, "Mémoire sur la côte oriental d'Afrique" (Isle de France, 15 juin 1777) – ed. de Cossigny 1790, *BL.* Add.18126.

[9] See, e.g., A. G. Hopkins, *An Economic History of West Africa* (London, 1977), esp. Ch. 4.

possessed sufficient political, economic, and military power to repel outside intervention. However, by the 1880s, European intervention in Africa was facilitated by a number of factors. First, the slave export trade, upon which rested the power of dominant West African elites, had been critically undermined by the 1860s. Second, powerful imperialist pressure groups in Europe, such as the French Navy, backed demands for intervention by their nationals trading in Africa. Finally, by the late nineteenth century, key technological spin-offs of the industrial revolution, notably the application of steam power to transport, the invention of the Gatling gun, and the medical application of quinine as a malarial antidote, enabled Europeans to settle and survive in tropical Africa for the first time.

Different economic forces were at work in IOA, from the Cape to Cairo to Madagascar to the Mascarenes. Conventionally, it has been argued that the traditional staples of foreign trade – slaves, gold, and ivory exchanged for arms, cloth, alcohol, and ironmongery – were similar but directed toward Muslim countries to the north rather than to North America or Europe.[10] This critically delayed the impact of the European-based industrial revolution upon the region, prolonging the traditional nature of foreign trade. The rise of the Mascarene plantation economy from the late eighteenth century, and the demands of the Atlantic slave trade from c.1810–50, greatly stimulated slave exports from Mozambique and Madagascar. Also, Middle Eastern and Indian demand sustained a vigorous slave and ivory export trade from the Swahili coast.[11] For Ralph Austen, Abdul Sheriff, and more recently William Clarence-Smith, the Islamic commercial nexus based on Zanzibar is the central issue in the story of the integration of East Africa into the international economy.[12] However, the basis of colonialism was laid not by the 1880s depression, for the price of slaves and ivory remained buoyant, but by the growing abolitionist pressure placed upon the Zanzibar court by the British. Europeans optimistic about the economic potential of the interior backed calls for colonization of East Africa and Madagascar, often justified by demands for the abolition of slavery. Such pressures had by the 1880s undermined the power of local elites, laying the way open for growing European commercial and political intervention.

The case of Madagascar is somewhat different. The island possessed two overlapping precolonial economies, that of the Merina empire and that of the

[10] Ralph Austen, *African Economic History* (London, 1987), 101.

[11] Abdul Sheriff, *Slaves, Spices and Ivory in Zanzibar* (London, 1987).

[12] W. G. Clarence-Smith, "The Economics of the Indian Ocean and Red Sea Slave Trades in the 19th Century: An Overview," in *idem* (ed.), *The Economics of the Indian Ocean Slave Trade* (London, 1989), 1–20; see also articles by Austen and Sheriff in same volume.

independent south and west. Staple exports from the Merina empire comprised cash crops, forest products, cattle, and, from the 1880s, gold. Staple imports comprised not only cloth and arms, but also slaves. Indeed, Malagasy slave imports sustained the east African slave export trade after the eclipse of Brazilian and Cuban demand by 1860 and British suppression of the Swahili coast trade by the 1880s. The same pattern of foreign trade applied to areas of the island independent of Merina rule, with the important exception that they also exported slaves, mostly captured from within the Merina empire.

The Rise and Fall of a Secondary Empire

A central theme of this study is secondary imperialism. Like Egypt under Mohammed Ali and Thailand under progressive monarchies, the nineteenth-century Merina crown in Madagascar attempted to counter the menace of European colonial intervention through secondary imperialism and economic modernization. Within this context, the conventional view of a progressive nation-state emerging in precolonial Madagascar is a major historical distortion. Rather, the precolonial Merina regime was a polity built on imperial expansion, successive nineteenth-century Merina states being motivated by the drive to create and exploit an island empire.

The Origins of Merina Imperialism

This study commences by examining the economic basis for the rise of the Merina state. The expansion of hydraulic riziculture in the eighteenth century enabled the build-up of grain surpluses, which in turn fueled demographic growth and permitted the development of a specialist artisan sector. Division of labor promoted trade, whereby agricultural and artisanal products traveled along local and long distance domestic trade networks. This overlapped with foreign trade networks, a traditional one involving the export of slaves, food, and other tropical produce from the west coast into the predominantly Muslim maritime network of the western Indian Ocean, and the other, from the mid-eighteenth century, exporting slaves and produce to the Mascarene plantations.

The rise of the Mascarene plantation economy from c.1750 was the major stimulus for the development of the Merina state. It established a large demand for provisions and slaves from Madagascar, which rapidly grew with conversion to sugar monoculture in the early nineteenth century. This provoked internecine battles in Madagascar over sources and trade routes. Civil wars in the highly populated central plateau provided Merina princes with slaves who they sold to foreign traders for cash and arms. However, from the 1790s when central Imerina became unified, Merina armies increasingly subjected and enslaved neighboring peoples. At the same time, they sought to eradicate middlemen and impose direct control over trade routes. The state that Andrianampoinimerina had militarily carved out of a number of small competing highland polities by 1810 was founded on control of the slave export and arms import trades.

The boom in foreign trade promoted the development of a market economy in Imerina. At the same time, advances in riziculture techniques permitted the growth in Imerina of large grain surpluses. In conjunction with commercial profits, these encouraged the emergence of a small number of full-time craftsmen and professional middlemen.[13] Supply and demand strongly affected foreign trade, as well as the iron and textile manufacturing sectors, notably in Imerina where money, market speculators, and usurers developed. However, the allocation of resources, incomes, and outputs continued to be heavily influenced by nonmarket factors such as caste,[14] kinship, and political patronage. Moreover, indigenous political authorities maintained tight control over land and free labor, which they exchanged on a redistributive basis. They also largely dominated the external trade in arms and slaves, the possession of which underpinned their economic and political power.

It was on this basis that the Merina emerged as the predominant Malagasy polity. From c.1810, Radama I pursued Andrianampoinimerina's policy, creating a small empire by expanding to seize control of further slave sources and trade routes to the coast. The 1820 British alliance earned him international recognition as king of all Madagascar, although he was then ruler of only a small area of the island, comprising part of the central plateau and a narrow corridor connecting it to the main east coast port of Toamasina. However, in return for a ban on slave exports, the British promised the Merina crown military, artisanal, and educational aid with which to effect the conquest of the entire island and build a new enlarged economy in which cash crops and manufactures would replace slaves as Madagascar's staple exports.

Autarky: Origins and Impact

By 1825, Merina armies had subjugated most of the eastern littoral of Madagascar and forged an outlet to the major west coast port of Mahajanga. However, British agricultural and artisanal techniques proved ill-adapted to local

---

[13] See Paul Bohannan and George Dalton, "Introduction" to *idem* (eds.), *Markets in Africa* (Evanston, 1962); Marshall Sahlins, *Stone Age Economics* (London, 1974), 277–314.

[14] For fuller explanation of caste in Madagascar, see Chapter 6.

conditions and, with the ban on slave exports, foreign trade revenues slumped. At the same time, British imperial pretensions to the island competed with those of the Merina. As a result, the Merina court rejected the British alliance and free trade and adopted autarkic policies, the three main pillars of which were state monopolies, *fanompoana* (unremunerated forced labor for state ends[15]), and the creation and exploitation of an island empire. Moreover, contrary to the conventional historical viewpoint, Ranavalona I adopted and expanded Radama I's autarkic policies, pursuing them with vigor.

Autarkic policies were initially successful. By 1836, a major industrial center had been created, possibly the first in Africa and contemporaneous with similar projects in Europe, producing manufactures ranging from cannon to glass. Moreover, Malagasy apprentices had by then mastered the techniques of industrial production from European personnel. Also, missionaries had through schools inculcated in local youth a loyalty to the Merina crown and empire and a basic literacy and numeracy. Most scholars were drafted into the industrial workshops and factories, or into the ranks of the army, but some received a more elaborate education before being drawn into the imperial bureaucracy. Finally, a newly formed British-trained standing army launched unceasing campaigns into non-Merina regions of Madagascar. They subjugated and enslaved local populations, seized their cattle and land, and established military colonies protected by Merina forts.

However, by mid-century, the autarkic impulse had run out of steam. Attempted industrialization failed. So did efforts to develop large-scale plantation and craft production for export. The internal transport and communications system remained rudimentary and costly. Court monopolies imposed limits on the growth of manufacture and trade. In addition, Merina armies failed to establish effective Merina rule over more than one third of the island, the southern and western reaches of which remained largely independent. Moreover, anti-Merina uprisings characterized conquered areas, while in disputed regions Merina convoys were harried and their outposts attacked. Guerrilla tactics deprived Merina armies of provisions, while the malaria prevalent in lowland regions so decimated highland troops that increasing numbers deserted. Soldiers and workers reacted to *fanompoana* and harsh work conditions by flight – many joining brigand bands – and protest (industrial workers sabotaged machinery). By the mid-1850s, the industrial experiment had failed, and Merina hopes of establishing an island empire had evaporated.

---

[15] For fuller explanation of *fanompoana*, see Chapter 6.

The Scramble for Colonies and the French Takeover of Madagascar

The conventional viewpoint is that the French takeover of Madagascar in 1895 was largely due to external forces, notably a combination of traditional pro-imperial groups in France joined, in the late nineteenth century, by expansionist French capitalist forces. This interpretation overestimates the strength of French influence in nineteenth-century Madagascar. It also underestimates the importance of British influence there and the role played by internal factors in facilitating the French conquest.

Pax Britannica

British Imperial Interests   The priority for Britain, the chief imperial player in the region, was to secure the route to India, the jewel of its empire. This it largely secured through direct and informal control of much of southern and eastern Africa and Mauritius. Madagascar was of peripheral interest to Britain, especially following the advent of steamships and the 1869 opening of the Suez Canal.

Regional British Forces   The economy of Madagascar revived in the 1860s and 1870s, benefiting from an expanding international and regional economy. Many aspects of regional economic development have been hidden from official statistics, but there is growing evidence of vibrant and expanding trade in slaves and contract labor and commodities such as ivory, cowries, precious woods, gum copal, rubber, hides, sugar, and gold, with a vigorous return trade in cottons and other cloth, arms, and alcohol. This trade was greatly facilitated by the opening of the Suez Canal in 1869 and the parallel development of steam transport, in the form of both railways and riverine and oceanic steamships. However, possibly the major factor underlying the unity and promoting the expansion of an economy that linked all IOA regions including Madagascar was the role of Indians financiers and middlemen. Backed by large family firms in Bombay and Gujarat, and benefiting as British subjects from the *Pax Britannica* established in the region from 1815, they played a vital commercial function, extending credit to local producers and European agents. Their network, with its African headquarters at Zanzibar, provided a commercial structure that facilitated the growing involvement in regional trade of other British subjects, notably from Natal and Mauritius, thus helping to establish an economic basis, hitherto underestimated, for a British forward movement in the region spearheaded by men such as Donald Currie and William Mackinnon. Unlike West

Africa, the staples of Indian Ocean Africa remained buoyant in price throughout the 1880s, thus giving those with commercial stakes in the region optimism for future growth.

Official Disinterest   British trading and political influence was thus stronger in Madagascar, as in most of IOA, than that of the French and other Westerners.

However, Britain's traditional naval and economic supremacy was by the 1880s being undermined by its rivals, and the British government felt the need to establish a new status quo to protect its interests. It also wished to placate French sentiments about the British forward movement in other regions of Africa more pertinent to its imperial interests, such as Egypt and Zanzibar. French annexation of the Comoros and the 1883–5 Franco–Merina War convinced the British government that the French possessed a real desire to colonize Madagascar. Thus in 1890, as part of a flurry of international treaties designed to clarify its hold over most of southern and eastern Africa, Britain recognized French claims to Madagascar in return for renewed French acceptance of British influence over Zanzibar.

The French Imperial Movement: A Reassessment

The role of imperialist forces in promoting the French conquest of Madagascar has been overrated in the conventional historiography. France was the European power with the strongest historical colonial claims to Madagascar. The French Navy and a Réunionnais population desperate for access to Malagasy labor and land vociferously backed these claims. They were also acknowledged, first tacitly, then openly, by a British government eager to placate France over areas more pertinent to British imperial interests. Despite this, the French took twenty years to conquer the island, and this imperial success was due more to a collapse of the Merina regime from within than to French military prowess or capitalist aggression.

The above demonstrates the need to question the conventional scholarly approach to precolonial Madagascar. From 1815, the foreign policy of France was characterized by a desire to accommodate British interests overseas. This was confirmed from 1845 by French acceptance of British dominance in IOA and of Merina sovereignty in Madagascar – reiterated in treaties signed in the 1860s. French military adventures in Madagascar occurred rarely, at moments when the goals of the Ministry of the Marine briefly dominated foreign policy. The 1883–5 Franco–Merina War was a rare example of successful political opportunism by the French Navy and Réunionnais deputies. However, the conflict served to bolster British and undermine French influence in Madagascar and soured the French government from further involvement in the island. French colonization, a decade later, can be explained only partially by the rise of the colonial grouping in France as the latter showed little interest in Madagascar until the eve of the conquest. The major focus of French interest in Africa was rather in creating an imperial sphere in West and North Africa where they faced intense competition from Britain.

British recognition in 1890 of French colonial priority over Madagascar proved embarrassing to the French, who had little real authority in Madagascar. They delayed enforcing their colonial rights to the island for another five years and, even then, their expeditionary force was almost defeated by a combination of military incompetence and disease.

Capitalist Forces and the French Takeover

Some historians have argued that European missionaries, traders, and planters in Madagascar were the harbingers of Western capitalist forces that rendered the Merina economy increasingly dependent on the West, thus paving the way for the eventual French conquest of the island. However, there is very little evidence to support such assertions.[16]

The few large Western firms there were kept firmly in check by the Merina court, which constituted their major commercial competitor. Foreign investment in Madagascar was small, and imports, notably of cottons, supplemented rather than undermined indigenous cloth production. At the same time, neither the Franco–Merina War nor the 1880s depression had a significant negative impact on the economy of Madagascar as a whole. Indeed, the indications are that the terms of trade were in the Madagascar's favor for much of the period.

The vast majority of foreign traders comprised Mascarene Creoles on the east coast and, on the west coast, British Indians and Swahili Muslims (locally termed *Karana/Karany* and *Antalaotra* respectively – and collectively known as *Silamo*). Generally impoverished, the Creoles were an economically backward rather than modern capitalist force. The Indians mostly represented the Zanzibar branches of major trading firms from Western India. However, like the Swahili with whom they were linked, their heavy involvement in the slave trade

---

[16] Jacob, "Influences occidentales"; Bernard Schlemmer, *Le Menabe, histoire d'une colonisation* (Paris: ORSTOM, 1983), 35; see also F. V. Esoavelomandroso, "Rainilaiarivony and the Defence of Malagasy Independence at the End of the Nineteenth Century" in Kent (ed.) *Madagascar in History* (Albany, CA, 1979), 232–3; Stephen Ellis, "The Malagasy Background II: The nineteenth century" in Finn Fuglestad & Jarle Simensen (eds.), *Norwegian Missions in African History vol. 2: Madagascar* (Oslo, 1986), 37–42; Pierre Vérin, *Madagascar* (Paris, 1990), 146–8.

meant that for most of the nineteenth century they represented an essentially preindustrial form of capitalism.

The Merina court also controlled British missionaries, considered by the Nationalist School to have been the main harbingers of Western capitalism in Madagascar. During the two periods of missionary activity from 1820–35 and again from 1869 (they were expelled from 1835/6–62), the missionaries were subordinated to crown control. Indeed, instead of transmitting Western capitalist values, they acted as imperial Merina agents. Notably, they helped draft and supervise *fanompoana*, the backbone of the autarkic imperial Merina economy.

Internal Factors: The Implosion of the Merina Empire

The Merina empire was built on solid foundations. Hydraulic riziculture produced agricultural surpluses that encouraged demographic expansion, division of labor, the rise of a specialist craft sector, and trade at a time when the rise of the Mascarene economy also stimulated foreign trade. However, an alliance with the British in which a ban on slave exports would be compensated for by European technical assistance to promote commercial agriculture and manufacturing, and by military aid to help establish an island empire, failed to produce the desired results. In consequence, the Merina regime adopted autarkic policies designed to forge an industrial revolution and to rapidly effect the conquest, colonization, and commercial exploitation of the island.

In the event, autarkic policies were the most important contributory factors to the French takeover of Madagascar, for they directly undermined the economy. The refusal to improve overland routes ensured that domestic freight rates remained high during the second half of the nineteenth century when, because of the investment in steam transport, rates elsewhere in the region were tumbling. More damaging were the effects of the Merina imperialism and its labor policies. A century of Merina imperial expansion, colonization, and exploitation created an enduring enmity to the Merina among non-Merina peoples of Madagascar, both in subjugated areas such as Betsimisaraka and in largely unsubjugated regions such as Sakalava land and Ibara.

Also, the failure to establish control over more than one third of the island's territory by the 1850s, when the Merina court abandoned its expansionist policies, effectively created two competing economies in the island: the imperial Merina economy, which governed the central and eastern regions from which tenuous links extended to other pockets of Merina control, notably at Mahajanga and Tolanaro, and the economy of the largely independent reaches of western and southern Madagascar. Both participated from the 1860s in the substantial growth in regional trade, the structure and dimensions of which have been underestimated by the traditional historical schools.

The Franco–Merina War gave a considerable fillip to the foreign trade of independent Madagascar, where the expanding Indian commercial frontier provided considerable credit and middleman services for both Malagasy and European traders. The latter included large European concerns such as O'Swald and regional firms such as McCubbin of Natal, all of whom, like the Indians, possessed wide-ranging interests that linked Madagascar to the Swahili coast, Mozambique, South Africa, and Mauritius.

The growth of external trade in independent Madagascar fueled the ability of the Sakalava, Bara, and groups of refugees from Merina rule to purchase foreign arms. These they used initially to resist Merina economic and military interests in the lowlands and, increasingly from the mid-1880s, to launch raids into the imperial Merina heartland. By the early 1890s, even central Imerina was menaced. The inability of the imperial Merina army to repel such attacks and the presence of bands of refugees from imperial rule were in turn linked to *fanompoana*, the most critical factor in the collapse of the imperial economy. *Fanompoana*, the institution of unremunerated forced labor for the Merina state, formed one of the pillars of the imperial Merina economy under autarky from the 1820s, and its role was reinforced from 1869 when the Merina court created a state church whereby it imposed control over all mission churches and schools, transforming them into institutions for the registration, recruitment, and, increasingly, supervision of state *fanompoana* units.

The opportunity costs of *fanompoana* critically undermined the imperial Merina economy and regime. Specialist artisans, practicing both traditional Malagasy and imported European crafts, and skilled industrial workers formed during the industrial experiment were the most valued for *fanompoana*. However, their reaction to being subjected to a regime of permanent forced labor was to abandon their craft and flee. Protest against imperial *fanompoana* was a root cause of the failure of the industrial experiment. Unskilled labor was summoned on a periodic basis, but in accord with imperial imperatives rather than those of the agricultural cycle. The result was periodic harvest shortfalls, famine, and growing vulnerability to disease. These were gravely aggravated when the French conflict and the 1880s depression caused the Merina regime to intensify its exploitation of imperial subjects through taxation and *fanompoana*.

The impact of forced labor was initially concentrated in colonized regions, notably Betsimisaraka land, but with the opening up of state goldfields from the mid-1880s, it also affected the plateau. There, *fanompoana* and flight from it drew the able-bodied away from the land, undermining the intricate system of labor-intensive hydraulic riziculture that had underpinned the original development of the Merina economy. The collapse of plateau agriculture, far more than the intrusion of Western capitalist forces, was responsible for the huge increase in famine and disease, notably of malaria, in the plateau interior in the late nineteenth century.

By the early 1890s, the imperial Merina economy was in terminal decline. In an ever-growing cycle of forced labor, flight, impoverishment, and disease, growing numbers of ordinary Merina fled to join brigand bands, while disenchantment with the imperial regime became general. This largely explains not only rampant brigandry and the ability of Sakalava and Bara raiders to penetrate with growing impunity the imperial heartland, but also the success of the lackluster French expeditionary force in 1895. Unsalaried *fanompoaned* Merina soldiers preferred flight to possibility of death or injury in defense of what had by then become a universally unpopular regime. Ultimately the opportunity costs of *fanompoana*, expressed chiefly in terms of abandonment of crafts and agriculture, sabotage, flight, and rebellion, doomed the imperial Merina economy to failure and guaranteed the success of the 1895 French assault where all previous attacks on the island by foreign powers had failed. Moreover, when the French declared a protectorate that maintained the existing Merina administrative structure, a widespread revolt erupted in which mission institutions and personnel, seen as responsible for recruiting imperial forced labor, were the primary targets.

In sum, this work presents an alternative history of precolonial Madagascar. It is primarily an economic history – the first general economic history of Madagascar. As such, it highlights historical issues largely absent from the Gallic tradition. These include the imperial rivalry of three powers (France, Britain, and Imerina) in Madagascar; the creation in the island of a Merina empire; the adoption of autarkic policies; the attempt to forge an industrial revolution, contemporaneous with similar industrial experiments in nineteenth-century Europe; the division of the island into two economies; the central role of Madagascar in maintaining the east African slave trade up to the close of the nineteenth century; the incorporation of Madagascar into regional trading networks emanating from Western India, the Swahili coast, and South Africa; and the predominant role played by internal factors in the collapse of the Merina empire and establishment of French colonial rule.

These issues clearly indicate that Madagascar historically formed an integral part of southern and eastern Africa. Also, contrary to the conventional Nationalist School perspective, the precolonial Merina regime forged an empire that largely collapsed due to internal mismanagement and exploitative imperial policies – thus facilitating the French conquest of 1895. Hence the subtitle of this book – *The Rise and Fall of an Island Empire*. Madagascar was part of a wider IOW economy and should be studied as such. Reversing the comparison, it is also evident that the histories of regions, from South Africa to Zanzibar to the Middle East and India, are incomplete without consideration of Madagascar. This volume is an attempt to provide a preliminary basis for reevaluating the history of Madagascar in the context of the regional, IOW, and international economies.

1 The Traditional Economy, 1750–1820: Industry and Agriculture

Introduction

Two major factors underpinned traditional economic activity in Madagascar: the natural environment and the knowledge, skills, and preferences of the island's human colonizers. Madagascar possessed no indigenous human population prior to the major and economically decisive phase of immigration and settlement during the first millennium C.E. Moreover, the island's topography ensured that human settlements were scattered and developed distinctive economies adapted to their specific geographical and climatic environments. In this sense, the natural environment in Madagascar was a much stronger force than in countries of new European settlement, such as North America, Australia, or New Zealand, which possessed preexisting indigenous populations.

The Natural Environment

The geography and climate of Madagascar established the framework within which economic activity occurred. The island lies in the Indian Ocean between 12° and 25° latitude south, separated from mainland Africa by some 350 kilometers (km) of ocean (the Mozambique Channel). With a total land surface of 587,041 km^2, it is the world's fourth largest island, approximately 2.4 times larger than the British Isles. Madagascar comprises three major geographical regions. Its most distinctive topographical feature is the indented central plateau, 800 to 2,800 meters high, which runs on a north–south axis almost the

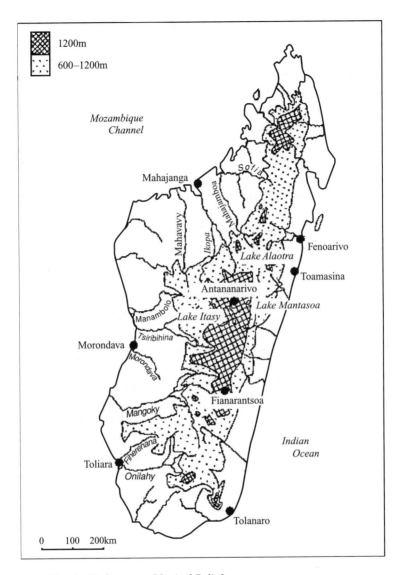

Map 1. *Madagascar: Physical Relief*

entire 1,592-km length of the island (Map 1). To the east, an escarpment drops abruptly to a coastal plain averaging 50 km in width, along which run a series of lagoons. The east coast is generally rectilinear, with few sheltered harbors. Westward, the plateau descends more gradually to a wide plain and indented coastline characterized by coral reefs and a number of good harbors, notably in the northwest. Two important subregions exist: the extreme north and extreme south, isolated from other regions by respectively the Tsaratanana massif and the sterile Horombe plateau and a desert plain.[1]

Madagascar's climate (Map 2) varies according to latitude and the influence of the dominant eastern trade winds. On the east coast, tropical conditions prevail: wet and humid throughout the year, it experiences an average annual rainfall of 2,950 millimeters (mm) – almost double that at Antananarivo on the central plateau – and temperatures varying from an average of 24.3° in the north (Vohimara) to 22.8° in the south (Tolanaro).[2] It possesses extensive marshland to the immediate hinterland and, on the interior escarpment, supports a tropical rainforest.[3]

The high central plateau, 1,300 to 1,700 meters above sea level, experiences two distinct seasons: hot and humid from November to March and dry from April to November. July and August are particularly cool and windy. South-east trade winds prevail, although north- and southwesterlies are not unknown. Plateau temperature and rainfall are well below those of the east coast. The plateau is hit often by hailstorms and occasionally, between November and March, by cyclones traveling inland from the east coast.[4]

The island's wide western reaches are drier than the center and east and, as on the plateau, humidity falls progressively as one moves south. Three climatic belts affect the west. The northwest is strongly influenced by the northern monsoon from October to March and is also occasionally visited by a cyclone from the east. Because of this, its average annual rainfall and temperature are slightly below those of the east coast, although, in contrast, it experiences a hot dry season from April to September. The midwest, less affected by the northern monsoon and by eastern cyclones, experiences two distinct seasons: hot and dry from April to October and hot and wet from November to March. The temperature there is higher by an annual average of 3° in the north and 2° in the south than at similar altitudes in the east of the island. Average annual rainfall varies from near that of the east coast, in the north, to about 492.5 mm

[1] Deschamps, *migrations intérieures*, 13; Samuel Pasfield Oliver, *Madagascar. An Historical and Descriptive Account* 2 vols. (London, 1886) vol. I, 178.
[2] Oliver, *Madagascar* vol. I, 285, 451–2; James Sibree, *A Naturalist in Madagascar* (London: Seeley, 1915), 53; Charles Robequain, *Madagascar et les bases dispersées de l'union française* (Paris, 1958), 50–1.
[3] Deschamps, *migrations intérieures*, 13, 15.
[4] Hugon, "Aperçu de mon dernier voyage à ancova de l'an 1808," *BL*.Add.18137, 11; Le Sage, "Mission to Madagascar" (1816), 102 – *PRO*. CO.167/34; Oliver, *Madagascar* vol. I, 450 and vol. II, 3; *GH* (1928), 6–8, 30–9.

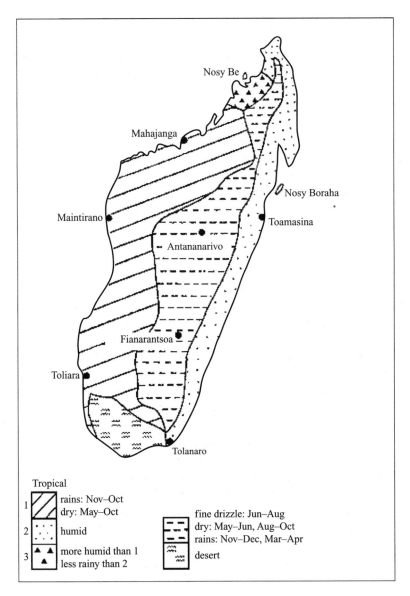

Map 2. *Madagascar: Climatic Zones*

close to Toliara, in the south. To the south and interior of Toliara lies a vast plain, a semidesert that frequently experiences no rainfall. However, within this region may occur wide climatic variations, the southwest coastal belt being more vulnerable to drought than, to select an exceptional example, the eastern-facing escarpment near Tsivoty, which has an annual average rainfall of almost 9,550 mm.[5]

As few natural pathways linked east to west, communication between the regions was difficult. On the coasts, the sea afforded the most convenient means of travel, while passage to the plateau interior was easiest by river from the west coast – although rapids obliged travelers to make the final stage overland. The ascent from the east coast was far more difficult due to the steep and forested escarpment. The least strenuous routes followed the Onive, Maningony, and Moramanga valleys. On the plateau, travel was relatively easy. However, passage through the mountains and desert of the south and in the mountains of the extreme north was very difficult.[6]

Agriculture and Fishing

These basic climatic and topographical factors provided the initial framework for economic activity in Madagascar. However, humans have radically altered the original environment, adding new and imposing constraints upon the economy. The debate over indigenous versus external catalysts for economic change in mainland Africa is not applicable to Madagascar, where the first immigrants arrived late in the first millennium C.E. They imported plants and agricultural techniques of predominantly Indonesian origin, as well as zebu cattle from East Africa. Geographical barriers to travel meant that, as late as 1700, the island possessed a pattern of dispersed human settlements, save in the well-populated valleys of the southeast coast and on the central plateau. Possibly the main human impact upon the environment prior to the eighteenth century was the destruction by fire of savannah belts, bush, and woodlands – in the center and east to create agricultural plots and in the south and west to create pasture.[7] Some of the remaining forests supported a small population of hunter-gatherers, such as the Mikea and Behosy, although the Mikea also cultivated patches of land and raised some cattle. However, the peoples of the dense eastern forest, and other smaller forest groups, including the Vakinankaratra Merina, practiced

[5] Oliver, *Madagascar* vol. I, 465; Robequain, *Madagascar*, 58–9; Deschamps, *migrations intérieures*, 13, 15.

[6] Deschamps, *migrations intérieures*, 15.

[7] For a review of the current environment in Madagascar, see Gwyn Campbell, "Madagascar" in *Encyclopaedia of World Environmental History* (London: Routledge, 2004), 796–8.

swidden agriculture (*tavy*), turning to full-time foraging only when crops failed.[8]

Riziculture formed the basis of the swidden economy in eastern Madagascar. Forest on level or gently sloping land was selected to ensure that, after firing, much of the resultant ash would remain to enhance soil fertility. From August to October, forest plots were cleared with axes. An average of four to five hours of collective labor was required to burn one hectare of cleared ground, the undergrowth being fired in the cool of the night, and from top to bottom, in order to control the flames. Women sowed: One would use an iron rod to prod small holes between the charred tree stumps; another followed, dropping seeds into the holes, which she then closed by pressing the soil down with her feet. The same plot was sown, using identical methods, with supplementary crops, maize or haricot, and its borders planted with *saonjo* (an edible arum that took three years to mature). Wherever possible, banana and plantain were also cultivated; additional crops might include sugar cane, sweet potatoes, and manioc (cassava).[9]

In the first year of cultivation, no weeding was necessary, although in January and February guards were posted to protect the maturing plants against the ravages of birds and wild hogs. Maize and haricots were harvested from December to March and rice from March to April. Among the Zafimaniry, the average family worked 22 days to produce from 800 to 1,200 kg of rice from one hectare of land, an area generally sufficient to support a family in rice. The stubble remained in the fields until September, when women and children rooted out all new vegetable growth and laid it out to dry. The plot was fired and replanted with rice successively for five to six years, although yields steadily diminished. After the fourth year, the soil frequently proved too infertile to support maize and haricots, which were then replaced by sweet potato or manioc.[10]

Following the abandonment of an exhausted plot, another was cleared at a higher level. In principle this ensured that sufficient soil nutrients from the new plot would seep into the abandoned field to renew its fertility and enable

---

[8] Mayeur, "Voyage au pays d'ancove, autrement dit des hovas ou Amboilamba dans l'intérieur des terres, Isle de Madagascar" (1777), *BL*.Add.18128, 170; Anon, "Mémoire historique et politique sur l'Isle de Madagascar" [1790], *BL*.Add.18126, 74–5; Daniel Couland, *Les Zafimaniry, un groupe ethnique de Madagascar à la poursuite de la forêt* (Tananarive, 1973); *GH* (1908), 364–5.

[9] Couland, *Les Zafimaniry*, 159–60, 161–3, 169; Chapelier, "manuscrits" (ed. Henri Poisson) in Académie Malgache, *Collection de documents concernant Madagascar et les pays voisins* vol. II (Tananarive, 1940), 51; Louis Michel, *Moeurs et coutumes des Bara* (Tananarive, 1957), 166–7; Le Sage, "Mission" (1816), 36.

[10] Couland, *Les Zafimaniry*, 163–5; *GH* (1928), 51.

recultivation after five fallow years. In reality, many nutrients washed away during the rainy season and the depleted soil could bear only one or two additional harvests of credible yield. Moreover, removal of vegetation from the cleared plot and frequent accidental burning of adjacent forest exposed increasing areas of thin topsoil to erosion by rain and to the tropical sun that bleached the ground, killing the humus essential to continued soil fertility.[11]

Wet rice was extensively cultivated on the fertile mud flats and riverine marshes of the east, southeast, and west coasts and in the central highlands. On the coastal plains from June to July, seeds were scattered over the mud of exposed riverbeds or riverine marshlands. No other labor was required until the crop was harvested the following November. In northwestern Madagascar, accumulated silt guaranteed fertility sufficient to produce a yield, superior to that of swidden, of up to 5,000 kg per hectare.[12] On the plateau, marshland riziculture was most likely introduced from the early 1600s, first in Betsileo and Antsihanaka and subsequently in Imerina. This led to progressive deforestation.[13] During the 1700s, hydraulic riziculture brought hillsides under cultivation, and dykes built in lowland areas enabled marshland to be converted into rice fields – a technique of Indonesian origin that Malagasy highland peoples adopted in response to demographic pressure. The most spectacular example was the conversion to rice fields of the Betsimitatatra marshes, west of Antananarivo, in the early 1700s, in response to the *Tsimiofy*, a seven-year famine in which hundreds perished. King Andriamasinavalona (c.1675–1710) organized a *Hova* caste[14] *fanompoana* that in seven years constructed the dyke (termed *Vakok' Andriamasinavalona*), several meters deep and wide, flanking the river Ikopa for some 26 km of its course between Alasora and Andriantavy. Similar projects independently adopted in Betsileo resulted in irrigated riziculture expanding up hillsides, in spectacular tiered rice terraces covering both convex and concave mountain slopes. In Imerina, riziculture was limited to valleys and plains until c.1790 when, due to population pressure, and possibly the introduction of more sophisticated techniques from Betsileo, lower concave hillside slopes were increasingly brought under cultivation (see Table 1.1).[15]

[11] Couland, *Les Zafimaniry*, 155, 165–7, 172; *GH* (1928), 13–14, 16; Hugon, "Aperçu" (1808), 9.
[12] Mayeur, "Voyage au pays des Séclaves, côte de Madagascar" (1774), *BL*.Add.18128, 99; Lescalier, "Voyage à l'isle de Madagascar" (1792), *BL*.Add.18128, 321; *GH* (1908), 300–1 and (1928), 37–9, 42–3, 51; Oliver, *Madagascar* vol. I, 269–70.
[13] *RH*, 18–19.
[14] For fuller explanation of caste in Madagascar, see Chapter 5.
[15] Mayeur, "Voyage au pays d'ancove" (1777), 162–3, 171–2; *GH* (1908), 79–80 and (1928), 3, 5, 9, 30–1, 40; Robequain, *Madagascar*, 275; *RH*, 24, 26–7; Oliver, *Madagascar* vol. I, 250–1 and vol. II, 53; Raymond Decary, "La population de Madagascar," *BAM* 28 (1947–8), 36–7.

TABLE 1.1. *Agricultural Fanompoana Units under Andrianampoinimerina*

A Construction and maintenance of Dykes	
Fanompoana (District)	*Dykes*
Avaradrano	Ankosy, Andranomasina, the Mamba
Marovatana	Moriandro, Kelialina
Ambodirano	Ampitantafika, Hiarandandriana, Anoaimanjaka, Andrombo, Katsoaka
Vakinisisaony	Ampitantafika, Hiarandandriana, Anoaimanjaka, Kisaony
Vakinankaratra	west of Antsirabe, and south of Betafo
All districts	Vahilava
B Rice cultivation	
Fanompoana (District)	*Rice fields*
Mandiavato	Mandiavato
Tsimiamboholahy	Masombahiny (west of Ilafy)
Tsiarondahy	Ambohimanga

Source: *RH*, 27, 35; *HR* III, 749, 754.

In mainland Africa, cattle were rarely utilized as draft animals. By contrast, zebu were used on the Malagasy plateau to trample water into the broken soil, although they were barred from the Betsimitatatra plain in c.1800 because of the damage they could inflict upon its complex dyke system.[16] Improved agricultural techniques boosted productivity and enabled the Merina to build up surpluses, an insurance against lean years. Nicolas Mayeur[17] stated in 1777 that Andriantsimarofy, king of Antananarivo, possessed a granary containing eight to ten "milliers" (4,000 to 5,000 kg) of rice.[18]

The development of irrigated riziculture in Imerina and Betsileo necessitated enormous inputs of labor. Mayeur noted in 1785:

The continual attention, toil and vigilance of the cultivator, his skill in channelling the water necessary to irrigate the soil...his unshakeable perseverance, his incredible industry...and the large number of workers permits the cultivation of the greater part of the land; and this labour, although unceasing, and however thankless and laborious, ultimately reaps a reward.[19]

---

[16] Mayeur, "Voyage au pays d'ancove" (1777), 172; *idem*, "Voyage au pays d'ancove, par le pays d'ancaye autrement dit des Baizangouzangoux" (1785), 223 – BL.Add.18128; *GH* (1908), 375 and (1928), 12, 43; Adolphe Razafintsalama, "Les funérailles royales en Isandra d'après les sources du XIXe siècle" in Raison-Jourde (ed.), *Les souverains de Madagascar*, 195; Gwyn Campbell, "The Role of the London Missionary Society in the Rise of the Merina Empire, 1810–1861" Ph.D. University of Wales (1985) vol. I, 43.

[17] A French commercial agent active in Madagascar in the late 1700s.

[18] Mayeur, "Voyage au pays d'ancove" (1777), 156–7, 171.

[19] Mayeur, "Voyage au pays d'ancove" (1785), 224.

According to estimates, an average Merina family of four to five people, working 330 days a year on one hectare of land, produced from 2,000 to 2,500 kg of rice. Despite a comparatively heavy investment in terms of human and animal labor, yields in plateau riziculture were inferior to those of coastal wet rice and of swidden because of low soil fertility, low temperatures, wind and hail, and locust attacks.[20] It was essential for rice seeds and shoots to be nurtured in water, for not only did the topsoil harden, crack, and crumble during the dry season, exposing the roots to a quick death in the sun, but also plateau soil, devoid of phosphoric acid, chalk, potassium, and nitrogen, was low in fertility. Long-standing marshland contained a residue of fertility, but dry land needed to be assiduously broken, oxygenized, irrigated, and fertilized with humus or human or animal excrement before a reasonable yield could be expected.[21] Nevertheless, plateau soil was cultivated with such assiduity that, by 1800, two rice crops, the *vary vaky ambiaty* and the *vary aloha*, were being annually produced in Imerina.[22]

The agricultural cycle in the highlands was dominated by riziculture. In May and June, the topsoil was turned with an *angady*, a long-handled iron spade, which produced clods approximately 300-mm square and 130-mm thick (see Illustration 2). Also, irrigation and drainage channels were repaired. In September, the rice nurseries (*tanin-ketsa*) of Betsileo and Imerina were flooded (to a height of about 50 mm) and well manured, before being planted with rice seeds. The resulting shoots were carefully tended until they stood 125 to 150 mm above the water's surface. With the onset of the wet season in October, the main fields were flooded. On smaller plots, two or three men driving between 20 and 30 cattle, and in larger fields up to 30 men with 50 to 100 cattle, within a day trampled the broken clay sods into liquid mud. In Antsihanaka, where productive land was more freely available, rice seeds were subsequently broadcast and left until harvest time. In Betsileo and Imerina, women replanted every shoot, at the rate of two to three per second, 150 to 225 mm apart, in the larger fields.[23]

---

[20] Hugon, "Aperçu" (1808), 11; Dumaine, "Voyage à la côte de l'ouest, autrement dite pays des Séclaves" (janvier 1793), 302 – BL.Add.18128; Le Sage, "Mission" (1816), 102; *GH* (1908), 363 and (1928), 6–7, 30–9, 51, 342; Oliver, *Madagascar* vol. II, 3, 6; Maurice Bloch, *Placing the Dead: Tombs, Ancestral Villages and Kinship Organisation in Madagascar* (London, 1971), 92–3; G. S. Chapus & G. Mondain, "Un chapitre inconnu. Des rapports de Maurice et de Madagascar," *BAM* 30 (1951–2), 3–8; Raymond Decary, "Poids et mesures d'autrefois," *BAM* 35 (1957), 130; Alain Delivré, *L'histoire des rois d'Imerina. Interprétation d'une tradition orale* (Paris, 1974), 201; Couland, *Les Zafimaniry*, 164.

[21] Mayeur, "Voyage au pays d'ancove" (1785), 224; James Hastie, "Diary" (1817), 187– *PRO.CO.*167/34; *GH* (1928), 3–7, 11.

[22] H. M. Dubois, *Monographie des Betsileo (Madagascar)* (Paris, 1938), 429.

[23] Lescalier, "Voyage" (1792), 320; *GH* (1928), 31; Oliver, *Madagascar* vol. II, 4–5, 53; Hastie, "Diary" (1817), 187; Bloch, *Placing the Dead*, 75–6, 93–4.

2. Turning the Topsoil (by Rainimaharosoa)

The entire community helped to harvest the main *vary vaky ambiaty* crop from May to June. In Imerina, a smaller amount of *vary aloha*, or "first rice," was sown at the end of the rainy season, often in riverbeds, replanted from July to September, and harvested from December to February, during the rainy season. Men cut the stalks with long knives and laid the stem on the stubble for women to collect, tie in bundles, and store. Both sexes helped in threshing the rice once it had dried. After the harvest, fields were flooded afresh to

3. Pounding Rice circa 1880

accelerate the decomposition of the stubble in preparation for the succeeding season.[24]

Secondary crops in the highlands were, as in the forest, maize, haricot beans, manioc, sugar cane, sweet potato, and *saonjo*. *Tavo* (another edible arum), sorghum, and *voanemba* (a species of bean) were also cultivated. Maize, probably introduced by the Portuguese during the sixteenth or seventeenth century, had reached the central plateau by c.1750.[25] Secondary crops contributed greatly to the plateau diet from November to March, when rice was scarce. However,

[24] Mayeur, "Voyage au pays d'ancove" (1785), 223; Oliver, *Madagascar* vol. II, 5–6; *GH* (1928), 20, 42; Bloch, *Placing the Dead*, 94; Dubois, *Monographie des Betsileo*, 429.

[25] Mayeur, "Voyage au pays d'ancove" (1777), 172–3, 175; *idem*, "Voyage au pays d'ancove" (1785), 223–4; *GH* (1928), 3, 54–5, 57–8; Couland, *Les Zafimaniry*, 168–71; *RH*, 24; Oliver, *Madagascar* vol. II, 13; H. T. Johnson, "Betsileo, Past and Present, a twenty years' review," *AAMM* 24 (1900), 482.

yields were comparatively poor because of the low fertility of plateau soil; for each hectare of cultivated land, an average of between 20,000 and 25,000 kg of manioc was produced on the east coast compared to only 8,000 to 12,000 kg on the plateau.[26]

Animal husbandry was widespread in Madagascar. The main grazing lands were the southern and western plains, where cattle raising was the chief occupation of the pastoral Bara, Mahafaly, Antandroy, and Sakalava peoples and the northern highland region occupied by the Tsimihety. The cattle were of two breeds: a humpless European type and the more common zebu. The Grandidiers claimed that Arabs introduced zebu directly from Asia, in the ninth century, although James Sibree considered them to have come via East Africa.[27] Cattle were let free to roam, although night stockades were occasionally built, and the savannah was fired each dry season to encourage the growth of fresh grass. Despite the hazards of drought and lack of fodder, which resulted in the death of 25 to 33 percent of newly born calves, total herd numbers were large. Cattle were deemed a source of wealth rather than of meat, while cow milk consumption was uncommon except among the northern Sakalava.[28] By 1810, cattle raising had spread to Antsihanaka, the Ankay, parts of the east coast, and the uncultivated hilltops of Imerina and Betsileo. However, in Imerina, firing the grass resulted in such erosion "as to leave many acres totally inaccessible to cattle."[29] Therefore, while sheep, goats, pigs, and fowl were a common sight in Imerina, cattle were relatively rare and valuable. To encourage the growth of cattle herds, King Andriantsimitovy (c.1650–70) forbade the slaughter of more than 15 cattle per market in central Imerina.[30]

In the mainly cattle-raising regions, crop cultivation was an important secondary, and chiefly female, activity. Rice, maize, millet, haricot beans, coconut palms, manioc, and *saonjo* were grown in riverine areas fertile from the

---

[26] *GH* (1928), 56.

[27] See Mayeur, "Voyage au pays d'ancove" (1785), 205; Rondeaux, "Mémoire" (1809) in Jean Valette, "Un mémoire de Rondeaux sur Madagascar (1809)," *BAM* 44-II (1966), 120; Oliver, *Madagascar* vol. I, 501 and vol. II, 36; Samuel Copland, *A History of Madagascar* (London, 1822), 17–18; *GH* (1908), 231–4, 358, 360–1 and (1928), 14–15, 94, 111, 114, 116, 122–3, 127, 129, 131; Sibree, *A Naturalist*, 35; Michel, *Moeurs*, 15–19, 129–30; Deschamps, *histoire*, 35–6; 170; Dez, "Eléments pour une étude sur les prix," 21–2; Couland, *Les Zafimaniry*, 175; Dumaine, "Voyage à la côte de l'ouest," 256–7.

[28] *MT* II.42 (22 Oct. 1884), 385.

[29] James Hastie, "Diary" (1824–5), *PRO.CO*.167/78, 11; see also Razafintsalama, "funérailles royales," 195.

[30] Mayeur, "Voyage au pays d'ancove" (1777), 166, 175; see also Hugon, "Aperçu" (1808), 11; Chardenoux, "Journal du voyage fait dans l'intérieur" (1816), *BL*.Add.18129, 174; *GH* (1928), 117, 119, 127, 139–41, 143–4.

sediments washed down from the plateau. As James Hastie[31] remarked of the Maniendy Sakalava in 1824, "I think them a hardy race and am certain that their daily provisions are far superior to those of the people of Ovah [Imerina], even of a respectable clan."[32] As on the eastern littoral and escarpment, peoples of western Madagascar resorted to foraging whenever harvests failed or a community was forced to uproot and relocate.[33]

Certain coastal communities, such as the Vezo Sakalava, Antankarana, Betsimisaraka of Nosy Boraha (Sainte Marie) and the Andriambakara, Vohilakatra, and Antaisaka of the southeast, were predominantly fishermen, as were the peoples living near large inland lakes, like Itasy and Alaotra.[34] Groups of men would trample through small inland streams; the mud they stirred up forced eels to the surface, where they were either caught from the bank with poles or hooked from rock pools. In larger west coast rivers, nets were stretched between poles stuck in the river beds about 20 meters apart, toward which fish were driven by canoe parties who thrashed the water some 100 meters out with bamboo poles. However, fish and nets were frequently lost to the crocodiles that infested coastal rivers. Turtles and whales, as well as fish, were caught at sea. Turtles were hunted on the north and northwest coasts from April to November. Marine hunters (*mpirehy rano,* lit. "rowers on water") generally landed 10 turtles a season, but prospects for shore hunters (*mpiambinjia,* lit. "watchers on the sand") were more speculative; catches varied from 1 to 20 turtles per season. The Betsimisaraka of Nosy Boraha and the Sakalava also hunted whales and sharks for oil and meat. Whaling canoes carrying seven or eight men were particularly active in August and generally chased young whales. Hunters harpooned the whale in the juncture between the head and spine, clung to the attached rope until the animal was exhausted, and then speared it to death at close range and towed it ashore.[35]

---

[31] Chief British negotiator of the Britanno–Merina treaties of 1816, 1817, and 1820 and the resident British agent at the Merina court from 1820 to 1826.

[32] Hastie, "Diary" (1824–5).

[33] *GH* (1908), 225 and (1928), 9, 11, 15, 21, 29–30, 36–9, 42, 53, 58–9; Michel, *Moeurs,* 143, 145–9, 151–2, 165–7.

[34] Lescalier, "Voyage" (1792), 323; Oliver, *Madagascar* vol. II, 54; *GH* (1908), 205–6, 214, 229, 234, 378, 381–2.

[35] Anon, "Essai sur Madagascar" [1816], *BL*.Add.18135; De La Salle, "Notes sur Madagascar" (1816) 123, *BL*.Add.18135; Sémerville, "Souvenirs de Sainte-Marie" (1824) (Raymond Decary ed.) in *BAM* 16 (1933), 46–7; Chapelier, "Manuscrits," 41; Oliver, *Madagascar* vol. II, 54, 100–102; *GH* (1908), 375–6, 381–2 and (1928), 242, 245–6, 248, 251; Raymond Decary, *Coutumes guerrières et organisation militaire chez les anciens malgaches* (Paris, 1966) vol. I, 24. For a detailed description of turtle hunting, see *MT* II.41 (15 Oct. 1884), 377 and II.42 (22 Oct. 1884), 384–5.

Industry

By 1820, a considerable craft industry had developed in Madagascar. The chief products were cloth, mats and baskets, pottery, iron implements, alcohol, and, in some regions, boats and canoes. Cloth manufacture was a ubiquitous and mainly part-time female occupation, except among the Zanadoria and Zanadralambo clans of northern Imerina where the weaving of the highly valuable red silk shrouds used to wrap the dead of noble castes was a male prerogative.[36] Cloth was woven from tree bark, leaves, raffia, hemp, cotton, and silk, all of which grew wild and required little human attention. Raffia cloth, which one foreign observer compared favorably to French Lyonnais cloth, was produced mainly in the raffia palm regions of the west, Antsihanaka, the Ankay, and the east coast as far south as the river Matitatana.[37] The east coast was the main center of bark and leaf cloth manufacture, although banana tree fiber was also manufactured into cloth on the plateau. A coarse fabric was likewise woven from marshland reeds (*zozoro* and *hazondrano*) and from hemp, which flourished in fertile terrain, such as the volcanic soil found near Betafo in southern Vakinankaratra and around Tolanaro.[38]

Cotton grew best in regions experiencing a sharp climatic contrast between wet and dry seasons, notably the west (especially the northwest), although S. P. Oliver claimed that the finest Malagasy cotton, of silk-like quality, came from Anosy in the southeast. It was also cultivated with assiduity on the plateau.[39] Silkworm, an important element in human diet in Ibara and Imerina, were raised on the leaves of two main species of shrub, the *tapia* and *ambatry*, although neither the cultivation of the plants nor silkworm rearing received more than cursory human attention. *Tapia* was grown by the Ankandrarezina Bara and in Imerina, particularly in western Imamo, and by the Antehiroka of Marovatana, where silk manufacture probably started toward the close of the seventeenth century, later than in other regions of the island.[40] The *ambatry/amberivatry*,

[36] Mayeur, "Voyage au pays d'ancove" (1777), 183; *idem*, "Voyage au pays d'ancove" (1785), 208; Anon, "Mémoire historique" [1790], 62; *GH* (1908), 243–6, 250 and (1928), 167.

[37] Anon, "Mémoire historique" [1790], 63; Chapelier, "Manuscrits," 82–3; Oliver, *Madagascar* vol. II, 82; *GH* (1928), 169.

[38] Mayeur, "Voyage au pays d'ancove" (1777), 161, 165–6, 173; *idem*, "Voyage au pays d'ancove" (1785), 220–1; Oliver, *Madagascar* vol. II, 11, 79, 82–3; *GH* (1928), 5, 86, 168; G. S. Chapus et Dandouau, "Les anciennes industries malgaches" *BAM* 30 (1951–2), 49–50.

[39] Mayeur, "Voyage au pays d'ancove" (1785), 226; Oliver, *Madagascar* vol. II, 11, 79; *GH* (1928), 84–5, 168.

[40] Hastie, "Diary" (1817), 168–70; Chapelier, "lettres adressées au citoyen préfet de l'ile de France, de décembre 1803 en mai 1805," *BAM* IV (1905–6), 38–9; Chardenoux, "Journal" (1816), 175; Raombana, "texts" in Simon Ayache (ed.), *Raombana (1809–1855) l'Historien* II (Fianarantsoa,

4. Weaving

found in some Merina locations, such as Andramasina and Ambohitromby, was more common in Betsileo, the Andrantsay valley, on the Tsienimparihy plain, and in Ibara. *Ambatry* silk was finer, less fatty, and more valued than *tapia*.[41]

Cloth manufacture was technically simple. Raw silk, for instance, was doubled, compressed and baked, and then softened in water, washed, dried, and threaded by hand or spindle before being reeled out on a bobbin. Subsequently, it was wound round two stakes and the threads counted, separated, and dyed. After being dried it was again soaked, this time in rice water, blackened with mud, rewound, and woven on a simple loom (see Illustration 4). At least five different types of indigenous silk cloth were produced, frequently interwoven

1976), 13; Oliver, *Madagascar* vol. I, 343, 387 and vol. II, 13; Chapus et Dandouau, "anciennes industries malgaches," 49–50.

For comparisons of silkworm and caterpillar-eating on mainland Africa and elswhere, see P. J. Quin, *Foods and Feeding Habits of the Pedi* (Johannesburg, 1959), 114–16.

[41] Anon, "Mémoire historique" [1790], 87–9; Mayeur, "Voyage au pays d'ancove" (1777), 165, 172–3; *idem*, "Voyage au pays d'ancove" (1785), 224; Chapelier, "lettres adressées," 38–9; Oliver, *Madagascar* vol. II, 13, 191; *GH* (1928), 91; Anon, "Natural history notes," *AAMM* 22 (1898), 251–2; Chapus et Dandouau, "anciennes industries malgaches," 50.

with other fibers and even tin.[42] Oliver provides a description of traditional weaving techniques in Imerina:

Two strong pieces of wood, rounded on the side, over which the threads of the warp are passed . . . are made of the branches of the rofia [raffia], and are put through the warp in order to stretch it out at both ends. One of these pieces of wood is passed through the warp at each end and fastened to posts in the floor. They are drawn together or removed further apart by cords tied to posts, two of which are driven firmly into the ground at each end. By this means, the weaver can tighten or slacken the warp, drawing up towards her what is done and bringing the remainder nearer as the progress of the work may require.

The shuttle . . . is a piece of round stick, pointed at one end for the purpose of being passed more easily between the threads. The knocker of the weft . . . is made of wood and resembles a scythe. The woman . . . puts this between the threads of the warp in order to open them, and then, after throwing in the shuttle, knocks the threads two or three times before she draws it out; and in this manner, with the assistance of a moving rod in the warp to open the threads, and the pressure of her left hand, the process of weaving is continued.[43]

In Imerina, the loom sat low, 100 to 125 mm separating the warp from the ground, but on the east coast foot treadles were used in European fashion. Both types of loom produced a maximum cloth size of about 3 by 0.8 meters.[44]

An associated, ubiquitous, and exclusively female cottage industry was the manufacture of mats and baskets, fashioned from a huge variety of grasses and vegetable fibers.[45] For these, as for cloth, dyes were produced. Red and blue dyes, extracted respectively from ochre and indigo or *somangy* bark, were the most popular, but many other dyes were produced from a range of different vegetable and mineral sources. Indigo, probably introduced from the East and cultivated in furrows along Chinese lines, required constant weeding, but could produce four harvests a year.[46]

Pottery manufacture was also widespread and mainly a part-time female occupation, although specialist potter villages existed among the Antambahoaka

[42] Mayeur, "Voyage au pays d'ancove" (1777), 165–6, 173, 175; *idem*, "Voyage au pays d'ancove" (1785), 223; Chardenoux, "Journal" (1816), 175; Oliver, *Madagascar* vol. II, 80–1; Chapus et Dandouau, "anciennes industries malgaches," 48, 50–1.

[43] Oliver, *Madagascar* vol. II, 81; see also *ibid*, 82; Chapus et Dandouau, "anciennes industries malgaches," 50–1.

[44] Oliver, *Madagascar* vol. II, 80–1; *GH* (1928), 168.

[45] Mayeur, "Voyage au pays d'ancove" (1785), 220; Hastie, "Diary" (1817), 167; Edmont Samat, "Notes: La côte ouest de Madagascar en 1852," *BAM* 15 (1932), 65; Chapus et Dandouau, "anciennes industries malgaches," 50–1, 59; R. Baron, "Notes on the economic plants of Madagascar," *AAMM* 22 (1898), 218–23.

[46] Mayeur, "Voyage au pays d'ancove" (1777), 165–6; Hastie, "Diary" (1817), 167; Chapelier, "Manuscrits," 3–6, 54; Oliver, *Madagascar* vol. I, 492–3 and vol. II, 11–12; Baron, "Notes on the economic plants," 218–23; *GH* (1928), 167–8.

5. Iron Smelting, Forge, and Blacksmiths on the Plateau

and Antimanaza of the southeast. In all cases, crude kilns were fashioned in circular earthen pits, lined with stone, and plastered with clay. Rice husks were generally used as tinder. Most pottery was coarse, although good earthenware was produced in East Avaradrano, in Imerina, where an excellent kaolin (*tany ravo*) was found, and in Betsileo, which possessed a fine blue clay.[47]

As important as weaving was iron manufacturing, a male preserve, the techniques of which were probably introduced into Madagascar from the East prior to 1540 (see Illustration 5). Skilled ironworkers were found throughout the island, except among the Bezanozano and Antaimoro (see Map 3). In the south and west, most iron was obtained from shipwrecks and imported barrels or iron bars. The Merina, the most renowned ironworkers in the island, possessed local deposits of good quality ore. In western Imerina, mines reached depths of up to 7 meters, but lack of wood for fuel drove the industry east, to the border of the great rainforest, where surface deposits were worked in pits averaging 1 meter square and 1.6 meters deep.[48] Mayeur, who visited the eastern region in 1785, found:

[47] Mayeur, "Voyage au pays d'ancove" (1785), 220; Oliver, *Madagascar* vol. I, 504 and vol. II, 87; *GH* (1908), 203–4 and (1928), 218–19.

[48] Mayeur, "Voyage dans le nord de Madagascar" (1775), *BL*.Add.18128, 36; *idem*, "Voyage au pays d'ancove" (1785), 210; Hastie, "Diary" (1817), 169–70, 182–3; Sémerville, "Souvenirs" (1824), 28; William Ellis, *History of Madagascar* vol. I (London, 1838), 307–9; Oliver, *Madagascar* vol. I, 343, 488, 492 and vol. II, 88–9; *RH*, 15; *GH* (1928), 179, 181; Decary, *Coutumes guerrières* vol. I, 29.

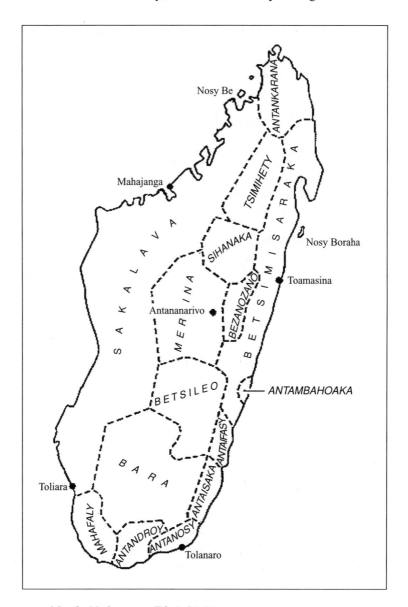

Map 3. *Madagascar: Ethnic Divisions*

almost all were engaged in work. Some open up iron ore mines, others construct furnaces of sandstone, built on good foundations and faced with clay, two feet in diameter and four feet deep. [There exist] two bellows to fan the charcoal fire that has been lit below. The Merina start by placing a thick bed of charcoal on the bottom of the furnace, followed by a thinner layer of well-washed iron ore, upon which another layer of charcoal is laid and so on until it is full. They then work the bellows, continuously and energetically, until the ore has melted. This procedure lasts about four or five hours and regularly produces approximately forty to fifty pounds of iron. Once the mass has cooled sufficiently, they select the purest iron for forging; it is of high quality. The rest, they pour back into the crucible a second time in order to fully eradicate the impurities.[49]

In 1817, Hastie noted one site comprising two workshops containing 18 and 32 forges respectively.[50] He commented that the bellows comprised,

two upright cylinders (butts of trees hollowed) three and a half feet [1.06 meters] high and thirteen inches [325 mm] in diameter. The valve is formed by a hoop-padding one inch [25 mm] thick that fits tight in each cylinder and is suspended half an inch below a cover three quarters of an inch less in diameter than the cylinder. The cover has a staff handle four feet [1.3 meters] long.[51]

Five men and two boy apprentices working a furnace similar to that described by Mayeur produced on average 18 to 25 kg of iron per session, although up to 408 kg has been recorded. The Grandidiers claimed that traditional methods permitted 40 percent of worked iron to be transformed into pure iron, although this figure was based on only 25 percent of the original mineral, the rest of which was lost during the smelting process.[52]

Some workshops on the eastern ore field combined all the processes of production; Hastie commented of one of these workshops that "five men and two boys can convert ore into 48 pounds [21.8 kg] of iron and the iron into eight spades per day." Each spade weighed 2.27 kg, measured 150 mm in width and 225 mm in length, and was completed by a 3.3-meter-long handle of hard red wood. Smelted iron was also transported to market; it was purchased by smiths whose forges, comprising an anvil the size of a sledgehammer and a furnace similar to but smaller than the original smelting furnace, were located in their homes.

Chapelier[53] claimed in 1803 that Malagasy ironwork was comparable in quality to that of Europe. Comprising mainly tools and weapons, it included anvils, spades, axes, hammers, chisels, planes, scissors, knives, needles, hinges, square nails, awls, tripods, scales, railings, slave irons and chains, pots, bayonets, and spearheads. In five months in 1817, one ironsmith produced 180 bayonets. Ironsmiths from the Antandroy, the Bekily, and Bekitro from the

---

[49] Mayeur, "Voyage au pays d'ancove" (1785), 210; see also *idem*, "Voyage au pays d'ancove" (1777), 174; Lescalier, "Voyage" (1792), 327–8; Oliver, *Madagascar* vol. II, 88–9; *GH* (1928), 179.

[50] Hastie, "Diary" (1817), 169–70; *GH* (1908), 368–9.

[51] Hastie, "Diary" (1817), 181–2.

[52] Mayeur, "Voyage au pays d'ancove" (1777), 174; *GH* (1928), 182–3.

[53] A French naturalist who visited Madagascar in the early 1800s.

southeast, from Mahavelona (Foulepointe), and from the Merina Andrianando caste were renowned for their skill in repairing foreign musketry and those of the Andrianando for manufacturing musket balls. However, indigenous muskets were too heavy for actual use (while Malagasy gunpowder was a distinctly inferior adulteration of imported European powder).[54]

Other mineral workers included gold, silver, tin, brass and copper smiths, and manufacturers of bitumen and salt. Little indigenously produced gold, silver, and brass circulated in Madagascar. Smiths, most likely using Arabian and South Asian techniques (adopted from Swahili and Indian smiths), worked imported precious metals into high-quality jewelry and weapon ornamentation.[55] In Imerina in 1817, it was claimed that most silver chains were produced by three men and all gold chains by one smith. The Sakalava worked copper deposits near Lake Kinkony. They also manufactured marine salt, notably at Belo, on the west coast; it was similarly produced by the Antankarana Ampanira in north Madagascar and by the Antaimoro Ampanira at the mouths of the rivers Namorona and Mananara on the east coast. Salt was also extracted from plants, particularly in the eastern forest and Ankay basin.[56]

Alcohol was produced island-wide. It was made chiefly from sugar cane,[57] of which at least 20 different varieties exist, but also from honey, a vast range of berries and fruit, *satrana* palm seed, and some tree barks (e.g., the Sakalava wild coconut palm).[58] Distillation methods varied widely, but the most common was on the lines of that used on the east coast. The cane was first laid on a log along whose length a groove had been chiseled. Another log was rolled over the cane, crushing it and causing its juice to flow along the groove into a collecting pan, where it was left to ferment. Occasionally, the juice was consumed following the initial fermentation. More often, the fermented liquid was boiled in a large vessel and sealed save for a bamboo reed or iron pipe and fixed in a cask of

[54] Chapelier (1803) in *GH* (1908), 185, 313 and (1928), 185, 216, 294; Mayeur, "Voyage au pays d'ancove" (1777), 165, 171, 175; *idem*, "Voyage au pays d'ancove" (1785), 210, 228; Anon, "Mémoire historique" [1790], 58–9; Lescalier, "Voyage" (1792), 327; Chapelier, "Lettres adressées"; Chardenoux, "Journal" (1816), 174; Oliver, *Madagascar* vol. II, 90–1; Chapus et Dandouau, "anciennes industries malgaches," 64; Decary, *Coutumes guerrières* vol. I, 22–7, 31–2, 37, 49, 53–5.

[55] Hastie, "Diary" (1817), 186; Oliver, *Madagascar* vol. I, 504; *GH* (1908), 368 and (1928), 166; Decary, *Coutumes guerrières* vol. I, 59.

[56] Mayeur, "Voyage au pays d'ancove" (1777), 176; Chapelier, "Manuscrits," 81; *GH* (1908), 361, 366 and (1928), 199–200, 214–15, 295; G. S. Chapus et E. Birkeli, "Historique d'Antsirabe jusqu'en l'année 1905," *BAM* 26 (1944–5), 69.

[57] It was also eaten raw.

[58] Mayeur, "Voyage au pays d'ancove" (1785), 223–4; Chapelier, "Manuscrits," 48; Hastie, "Diary" (1820), *PRO.CO.*167/50, 471; Oliver, *Madagascar* vol. II, 8, 95; Michel, *Moeurs*, 152; Copland, *History of Madagascar*, 12–13.

cool water, which carried the condensed spirit to another pan. Imported opium equipment was also sometimes adapted to distill alcohol.[59]

There also existed a number of regional or local craft industries. Many peoples, particularly fishing communities, used a variety of boats and canoes, small ones for inland waterways and larger ones for sea fishing. Lake and river canoes, varying in size from tiny children's dugouts to craft up to 7 meters long, were generally fashioned from the hollowed-out *varongy* tree trunk. The sea-going Antankarana and Betsimisaraka fishing canoes, similarly made from a single trunk, averaged 5.3 meters long by 337.5 mm wide – sufficient to hold two men. Along the west coast, the Sakalava and Antankarana utilized a more sophisticated double, or increasingly a single, outrigger canoe, fashioned from thin planks. By far the largest canoes, measuring up to 10 by 1.2 meters and carrying up to 60 warriors, were those used from 1790 to 1820 in Betsimisaraka raids on the Comoro Islands, Zanzibar, and the Mozambique coast.[60] In common use on the southeast coast were rafts built from planks lashed together with raffia cord and caulked with strips of bamboo. Similar to boats used in Madras, they were used primarily as ferries to cross rivers and meet craft anchored offshore.[61] Finally, in yards on the northwest coast, the Swahili constructed dhows of up to 200 tons to carry their coastal and trans-Mozambique Channel trade.[62] Associated activities included the manufacture of sails, hemp or bark fiber rope, whale and sawfish oil, harpoons, and a wide range of fishing baskets and nets. In addition, the Sakalava mined Mount Ambohitsosy (16°46'S) for bitumen, used by the Swahili to caulk their boats.[63]

Another important regional industry was woodcraft. The most renowned wood craftsmen were forest peoples such as the Zafimaniry of Ivohitrambo, the Tanala of Mahasita and Anjolobato, and the Antanosy Roandriana castes, as well as the southeastern Betsileo. A traditional carpenter's tools included

---

[59] Mayeur, "Voyage au pays d'ancove" (1785), 212; Dumaine, "Voyage au pays d'ancaye, autrement dit des Bezounzouns, Isle de Madagascar" (1790), *BL*.Add.18128, 256; Chapelier, "Manuscrits," 48; Hastie, "Diary" (1824–5); Oliver, *Madagascar* vol. II, 9, 95; Michel, *Moeurs*, 152.

[60] Anon, "Mémoire historique" [1790], 60; Mayeur, "Voyage au pays d'ancove" (1775), 54; Grégoire Avine, "Voyages aux isles de France d'Anjouan de Madagascar, de Mosambique, de Zanzibar et de la côte Coromondel" (1802), *Mauritius Archives Publications* 5 (Paris, 1961), 26–7; Oliver, *Madagascar* vol. I, 38, 433, 435 and vol. II, 38, 54, 101–2; *GH* (1908), 380–1.

[61] Mayeur, "Voyage au pays d'ancove" (1775), 54; Oliver, *Madagascar* vol. I, 434–5; *GH* (1908), 205–6.

[62] Dumaine, "Voyage à la côte de l'ouest" (1793), 297; Avine, "Voyages" (1802), 25; *GH* (1928), 372.

[63] Anon, "Mémoire historique" [1790], 60–1; Samat, "Notes" (1852), 65; Oliver, *Madagascar* vol. II, 83; *GH* (1928), 214–5, 372; Campbell, "Role of the London Missionary Society" vol. I, 46.

axes, hatchets, chisels, planes, wooden mallets, drills, and a rule, but not the saw, which was introduced by Europeans. Products included dishes, winnowing pans, spade handles, furniture, and houses. For example, houses in the eastern forest were constructed of planks, each of which comprised half a tree trunk hacked to size with a hatchet and held together by rope. By contrast, on the denuded plateau only the rich could afford timber houses; most people lived in huts of stone and wattle covered in thatch. Rope and glue were used to cement wood to wood or metal.[64]

Although most hide was consumed with the meat, another significant activity was the manufacture of products from slaughtered cattle: cattle-horn holders (for powder and tobacco) and kitchen utensils, bone buttons, tallow candles, and leather sandals and drum and shield covers.[65]

In all, by the mid eighteenth century, Madagascar possessed sufficient natural resources, productive capacity and demand (domestic and foreign) to sustain an expanding structure of commercial exchange – the subject of the next chapter.

---

[64] Mayeur, "Voyage au pays d'ancove" (1777), 174; Chapelier, "Lettres adressées," 16, 23; RH, 6; Oliver, Madagascar vol. II, 83, 91, 96–7; GH (1908), 369 and (1928), 104, 133; Couland, Les Zafimaniry, 137–42.

[65] Le Sage, "Mission" (1816), 107; HR vol. I, 147, 158, 162, 171–2, 204–19, 454, 644–6; Oliver, Madagascar vol. II, 84; GH (1928), 133–5; Jacques Lombard, La royauté Sakalava: Formation, développement et effondrement du XVIIe au XXe siècle (Tananarive, 1973), 73–4.

2   The Traditional Economy, 1750–1820: Commerce

Introduction

All communities need to produce agricultural surpluses in order to survive periods of harvest shortfall. Also, natural endowment leads to regional specialization in craft production. Both factors encouraged the early development of trade within Madagascar. This chapter analyzes the nature and structure of long distance trade, defined as the exchange of goods and services over distances of more than 50 km (approximately 30 miles), prior to the rise of the Merina empire from the close of the eighteenth century.

Domestic Trade

By the mid-eighteenth century, considerable regional economic specialization and interregional trade existed in Madagascar. In the west, cattle herders supplied the Vezo Sakalava and Antankarana fishermen with cattle, rice, and maize in return for fish and salt; and the Vezo accepted maize and dried manioc from the Sakalava and Mahafaly of Menabe and Fiherenana hinterland, in return for orchil.

The Merina imported cattle, salt, raw silk, and raffia from the pastoral Sakalava, in exchange for piastres and Merina staple trade goods – slaves, cotton cloth, and especially iron goods. Cotton cloth, ironware, dried manioc, and pottery were also traded with the Antsihanaka for *zozoro* reed, rice, and dried or smoked fish and with the peoples to the east for timber, charcoal, raffia, tree and leaf fiber, honey, and both sea and vegetable salt.[1] Except for ironware, the Betsileo produced a similar, but often superior range of products to the Merina, albeit in lesser quantity. These they sent east to the forest and south to the Bara, from whom they obtained cattle and some silk. Through Betsileo from the south flowed raw hemp, cotton, and silk to Imerina where weavers transformed them into cloth that was subsequently redistributed, along with iron manufactures, throughout the island. By 1820, few communities were untouched by internal long distance commerce. Even small, isolated, forest hunter-gatherer groups generally exchanged honey and brush wood for the iron implements and cloth of outside peoples (see Table 2.1).[2]

Cattle raiding and the kidnapping of humans for ransom or sale may be included under the ambit of internal long distance trade.[3] Cattle raiding was a highly discriminate and organized activity endemic among the pastoral peoples of the west and southwest. It formed part of commercial exchange because its frequency and reciprocity was such that, although there was no immediate and balanced exchange of goods, there was a long-term, unbalanced, and delayed exchange, with cattle in constant circulation. The more cattle someone possessed, the greater his perceived wealth, status, and influence, but also the more prone he became to attack from cattle thieves. Cattle raiding, considered an honorable pursuit, was immaculately planned, with gangs of up to 100 men seizing herds of 200 to 300 cattle. Whereas most other long distance commercial activities were confined to the dry season (April to October), when routes were passable, cattle raiding occurred mostly during the summer, when rains could obliterate the tracks of thieves.[4]

Kidnapping assumed various forms. One was traditional warfare, usually a speculative dry season activity that followed conventional rules. Combatants,

---

[1] Mayeur, "Voyage au pays d'ancove" (1777), 176, 183; *idem*, "Voyage au pays d'ancove" (1785), 208, 223, 226; Hugon, "Aperçu" (1808), 13; Dumaine, "Voyage au pays d'ancaye" (1790), 258, 263, 266–7, 269, 276; *idem*, "Voyage à la côte de l'ouest" (1793), 299, 306–7; Rondeaux, "Mémoire" (1809), 122; Hastie, "Diary" (1817), 145–6; Oliver, *Madagascar* vol. I, 216, 229, 251, 256 and vol. II, 54, 91; *GH* (1908), 214 and (1928), 16, 181, 216, 229, 253, 256, 297, 307, 338; Sibree, *A Naturalist*, 56; Chapus et Dandouau, "anciennes industries malgaches," 47, 64; Charles Robequain, "Une capitale montagnarde en pays tropical: Tananarive," *Revue de géographie alpine* 37. 2 (1949), 285; Delivré, *L'histoire des rois*, 341, 343.
[2] Mayeur, "Voyage au pays d'ancove" (1777), 166; *idem*, "Voyage au pays d'ancove" (1785), 226; Hugon, "Aperçu" (1808), 16; Rondeaux, "Mémoire" (1809), 123; Oliver, *Madagascar* vol. I, 387 and vol. II, 191; Chapus et Dandouau, "anciennes industries malgaches," 47; *GH* (1908), 218, 223, 258 and (1928), 169.
[3] See Lars Sundström, *The Exchange Economy of Pre-Colonial Tropical Africa* (London, 1974), 19; *GH* (1908), 362.
[4] *GH* (1908), 225; Copland, *History of Madagascar*, 17–18; Michel, *Moeurs*, 129, 137–41.

TABLE 2.1. *Market Produce in Imerina, 1777–90*

			Manufactures	
Foodstuffs	Raw Materials	Livestock	Domestic	Foreign
Fresh beef	Iron	Oxen	Silk cloth	Surat cottons
Roast beef	Construction	Sheep	Raffia cloth	Surat silk
Rice	timber	Pigs	Banana fiber cloth	
Red haricot	Firewood	Geese	Crucibles	
White haricot	Raffia	Ducks	Axes	
Sugar cane	Cotton	Chickens	Railings	
Ambrevade peas	Bark	Pigeons	Spades	
Sweet potato	Indigo	Slaves	Slave irons	
Banana	Peat		Scales	
Lemon	Vegetable salt		Spears	
	Marine salt		Hammers	
	Tangena nut[a]		Scissors	
	Coral		Knives	
	Tin		Needles	
	Yellow copper		Silver jewelry	
	Borax		Copper jewelry	
	Soldering iron			
	Silk cocoons			

[a] The tangena nut was used to produce poison – for fuller details, see Chapter 7.
Source: Mayeur, 'Voyage au pays d'ancove' (1777), 176; Dumaine, 'Voyage au pays d'ancaye' (1790), 270–1.

comprising spearmen and musketry, assisted by noncombatants, mostly relatives and slaves of the warriors, aimed to outmaneuver and kidnap enemy fighters. Compared to European engagements involving similar forces and weapons, very few combatants were killed or wounded. Indeed, fighting was suspended should a crisis arise, such as the arrival of a plague of locusts, which might threaten common agricultural interests.[5] Kidnap victims were held in the expectation of reclamation by relatives for, as Mayeur noted in Imerina in 1785, "it rarely happens that a prisoner of war is not redeemed by his family, once they hear about his capture." In the rare instance of a captive not being reclaimed, or of his relatives being too poor to pay the demanded fee, his captor retained or sold him as a slave. The emphasis placed on burial in the ancestral tomb also meant that corpses of slain warriors could be similarly sold; indeed, they were

[5] Mayeur, "Voyage au pays d'ancove" (1785), 214–15; Anon, "Mémoire historique" [1790], 73; Avine, "Voyages" (1802), 55; Decary, *Coutumes guerrières* vols. I and II.

cut up and the parts bargained for separately in the hope of gaining a greater profit.[6]

Specialist slave raiders were also active. For example, until 1820, the inhabitants of Vohimbohitra, near the confluence of the rivers Mananara and Betsiboka, regularly raided Imerina for slaves to sell on the west coast. In Imerina, numerous bands operated, kidnapping individuals or even the entire population of a village. The Betsimisaraka sea raids of 1790–1820 against the Comoro islands and the east African coast were of a different order, proving so serious that in August 1809 a British ship was stationed off the Mozambique coast in an attempt to ward off the raiders, and in 1817 the Supreme Court of Calcutta petitioned Robert Farquhar, the British governor of Mauritius, to end them.[7]

The Role of Imerina

By 1800, Imerina had emerged as the island's main distributive center. Straddling the central portion of the high plateau, Imerina offered easy access to most other regions. It was also the chief domestic producer of cotton and iron goods, among the most prized of long distance trading commodities. Specialized traders and markets emerged to cater for long distance commerce. Salt, a relatively rare and valuable mineral, was handled mainly by the Ampanira Antankarana or the Belo Sakalava, who established a Friday salt market at "Antaismammou" in Imerina. Similarly, special markets developed in Imerina at Asabotsy-Tsiafahy (for hemp), Angavo (wood), Alahadinilanifasana (cotton), Antanjombato (slaves), and at an unnamed location 19 km south of Antananarivo for silk.[8] Markets for regional products developed closer to the region of origin. Thus, the Sunday market at Ambatomanga, in eastern Imerina, catering for Imerina-Ankay commercial exchange, was noted by Hastie in 1817 for its "Great quantities of raw and boiled manioc and potatoes, rice, zozoura [*zozoro*] and hayrana [*herana* – a sedge commonly used for thatching roofs], wood for

---

[6] Mayeur, "Voyage au pays d'ancove" (1775), 62; *idem*, "Voyage" (1785), 215, 229.

[7] Mayeur, "Voyage au pays de Séclaves" (1774), 91, 97; *idem*, "Voyage au pays d'ancove" (1777), 153, 167, 180, 183; *idem*, "Voyage au pays d'ancove" (1785), 211, 216, 229; Dumaine, "Voyage à la côte de l'ouest" (1793), 299; Rondeaux, "Mémoire" (1809), 119; *RH*, 75; Farquhar to Radama, Port Louis, 9 Aug. 1817; *idem* to Stanfell, Port Louis, 22 Aug. 1817; Blanc to Pye, Port Louis, 20 Sept. 1817, *PRO.CO.*167/34, 84, 105–6, 121; Hastie, "Diary" (1824–5); Decary, *Coutumes guerrières* vol. I, 87–8; see also Sundström, *Exchange Economy*, 19.

[8] Mayeur, "Voyage au pays d'ancove" (1777), 176; *idem*, "Voyage au pays d'ancove," (1785), 212–4; Hastie, "Diary" (1817), 170–1; Oliver, *Madagascar* vol. II, 91; *GH* (1928), 295; Sibree, *A Naturalist*, 56; Chapus et Birkeli, "Historique d'Antsirabe," 69; Chapus et Dandouau, "anciennes industries malgaches," 49–50.

building and burning, grass for burning a little ginger, saffron, iron work and rofia [raffia]."[9]

The Merina market system, which existed from at least the mid-seventeenth century, was first organized on a permanent basis by Andrianamboatsimarofy (c.1773–95). By 1800, it constituted the largest and most complex permanent market system in the island. Each province possessed rotational markets that interlinked with those of neighboring provinces. Originally termed *fihaonana*, or meeting place, these markets served as centers both of commercial exchange and of public address where royal edicts were published. Andrianamboatsimarofy renamed them *tsena* (originally meaning "meeting place") and enacted severe laws against fraud and theft, backed by the appointment of the Tsiarondahy, a caste[10] of royal slaves, as market stewards. However, traditional weights and measures were initially crude. Thus, *azo sakelehina* (lit. "that which could be easily carried under one arm") indicated a weight of between 2 and 3 kg, while the traditional *refy* ("arm's length") varied from 137.5 to 150 mm. Nevertheless, the use of scales, probably introduced by the Swahili, spread rapidly in the major commercial centers, as did the piastre of the Spanish Union. Gunpowder and piastres were generally the only commodities to be measured on scales for which the standard weight was the piastre or Malagasy dollar (*ariary*), or its weight equivalent of 720 grains of moist rice. The scales were incapable of weighing anything over two piastres, or 54 grams, with any accuracy, but under that limit they were highly accurate. The use of false weights, or loaded scales, was widespread until the reforms of Andrianamboatsimarofy. Following the end of the Merina Civil Wars in the late 1790s, Andrianampoinimerina further regularized a widening market network.[11] He enforced five standard iron weights, possessing a fixed equivalent weight in piastres and fractions (1/2, 1/4, 1/8, and 1/12) thereof. For example, the standard weight of a *loso*, equivalent to half a piastre, was 13.5 grams. Measurements of length and volume were also standardized. The *refy* was made the equivalent of one meter, already a standard measure on the east coast, the *vary iray/ vata* (the traditional measurement of volume based on rice) was standardized at about 120 liters, and the smaller *vata menalefona* ("the measurement of the red spear") at 22 liters. By 1810, the established unit of weight for most goods in foreign trade was the British 100 pounds (45.36 kg), although there existed some regional variations;

[9] Hastie, "Diary" (1817), 147.

[10] For fuller explanation of caste in Madagascar, see Chapter 5.

[11] Mayeur, "Voyage au pays d'ancove" (1777), 172, 175–6, 181–2; *idem*, "Voyage au pays d'ancove" (1785), 213, 226–7; Hugon, "Aperçu" (1808), 18; Decary, *Coutumes guerrières* vol. 1, 128. For comparative role of market stewards on mainland Africa, see Sundström, *Exchange Economy*, 20–1.

6. Moneychanging at the Meat Market (by Rainimaharosoa)

for instance, the standard in the northeast was the *farasila*, equivalent to about 16 kg, and on the west coast was the *manampaka*, approximately equal to 34 kg[12] (see Illustration 6 and Map 4).

---

[12] Mayeur, "Voyage au pays d'ancove" (1777), 177; *GH* (1928), 266, 340, 518; Oliver, *Madagascar* vol. II, 114–15, 212; Alfred Grandidier, "Souvenirs de voyages, 1865–1870," *Documents anciens sur Madagascar* VI (Tananarive, n.d.), 35; Decary, *Coutumes guerrières* vol. I, 125–30; J. et S. Chauvicourt, "Les premières monnaies de Madagascar," *BdM* 261 (1968), 106–7, 165.

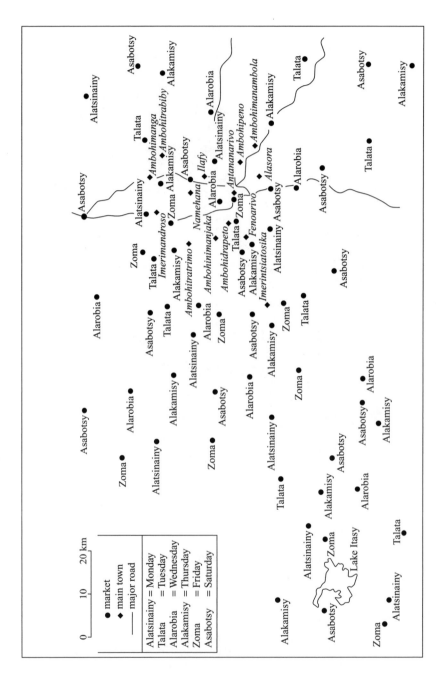

Map 4. *Markets in Nineteenth-Century Imerina*

46

By 1800, slaves, cattle, iron bars, muskets, flints, cartridges, knives, scissors, razors, mirrors, coral and other beads, earrings, thimbles, seeds, and salt all enjoyed occasional use as currencies in Madagascar. Coinage, probably introduced by Arabs into northern Madagascar from the tenth century, was supplemented from the 1500s by European coinage. Gunpowder, cloth, and coins formed a distinct category in that they could be subdivided to represent the value of the smallest purchase and were generally accepted in payment for goods, taxes, and fines throughout the island.

Coins were usually consumed locally (as jewelry or hoarded) or passed immediately to west coast Swahili merchants in payment for imported textiles and muskets.[13] The failure of coins to flow back to European traders prompted Colbert to insist that French East India Company agents in Madagascar practice barter exchange. However, the strong bargaining position of the Malagasy allowed them to insist on payment in coin. Hence, during the seventeenth century, foreign money – notably the Spanish *de plata* silver piastre (minted in Mexico and valued at eight *reales*) – became common currency in the island's main commercial centers. Coins first reached Imerina in the early seventeenth century and by 1650 lubricated much long distance trade in the interior. A mint was established in Imerina under Andriambelomasina (c.1730–70) that printed *tavaiky* coins, but the venture quickly collapsed. Due to the volume of imported coin – to pay for the slaves and provisions required by the burgeoning plantation economy on the Mascarenes – coins became the predominant currency in the foreign trade of Madagascar and, alongside gunpowder and cloth, one of the main forms of domestic currency. This is confirmed by the steady inflation of prices in late eighteenth-century Madagascar.[14]

---

[13] Morice, "Plan of Operation for the Trade of the coast of East Africa" (n.d.) and *idem*, "Plan for a Trading Centre on the East Coast of Africa" (Île de France, 24 Sept. 1777) – in G. S. P. Freeman-Grenville, *The French at Kilwa Island* (Oxford, 1965), 190, 196; Campbell, "Role of the London Missionary Society" vol. I, Chs. 2 and 3; *idem*, "Madagascar and the Slave Trade, 1810–1895," *JAH* 22 (1981).

[14] Le Sage, "Mission" (1816), 99; *RH*, 19, 24; Oliver, *Madagascar* vol. II, 205, 209; L.Dahle, "The Influence of Arabs on the Malagasy Language," *AAMM* II (1876), 84, 105–13; P. Taix, "Extrait du diaire de Tamatave" (14 janvier 1885) in *idem*, "Tamatave: notes historiques" (1908), *AHVP*; Chauvicourt, "premières monnaies," 146–52; *GH* (1928), 268; E. A. Alpers, "The French Slave Trade," *Historical Association of Tanzania paper* 3 (1967), 87, 101–4; Sundström, *Exchange Economy*, 96–8; Micheline Rasoamiaramanana, "Aspects économiques et sociaux de la vie à Majunga entre 1862 et 1881" (thèse, Université de Madagascar, 1973), 55; Campbell, "Role of the London Missionary Society" vol. I, 66–7; for an Ethiopian comparison, see Richard Pankhurst, *Economic History of Ethiopia, 1800–1935* (Addis Ababa, 1968), 460–8.

Foreign Trade

As indicated above, foreign trade contributed significantly to Madagascar's domestic market system. From the initial human colonization of the island, contacts were maintained with East Africa and by the ninth and tenth centuries, Swahili colonies had formed on the northwest coast, notably at Langany (in Mahajamba Bay) and Sahadia (at the mouth of the river Manambolo), and the northeast coast, at Vohimara, Mahanara, Sahambava, Lokoho, and Antalaha. By 1800, they comprised two groups, the *Hounzati*, originally from Malindi and living in Iboina, and the *Mozanghi* of Mahajanga (Bombetoc). Indians, mostly Khoja or Bohra Shia Muslims from western India, probably started settling Madagascar from about the twelfth century.[15] Bartle Frere wrote of them in 1873:

In Madagascar and elsewhere the Indians assured me that though their oldest house was not more than sixty years standing, their caste had traded to the coast for ages previous.... In Madagascar they assert that they have been, for at least a century, settled at Nosi Beh [Nosy Be] and other ports, and that they [i.e., the Bohras and Khojas] preceded the Hindoos on the African Coast.[16]

Indian and Swahili trading communities suffered with the arrival of Europeans in the IOW; the Portuguese destroyed their main entrepôts at the close of the fifteenth and start of the sixteenth centuries, as from 1680–1720 did European pirates who made Madagascar a base for raids on merchant ships in the western Indian Ocean.[17] Thereafter, their fortunes recovered, reaching a zenith in the 1790s when Mahajanga boasted a population of 6,000 Indian and Swahili traders and their families.[18]

Recovery was due to three factors: suppression of piracy, economic development on the Mascarenes, and alliance with the Sakalava. The suppression

---

[15] Rasoamiaramanana, "Aspects économiques," 10–11, 35, 54; Vincent Noel, "Ile de Madagascar: Recherches sur les Sakalava," *Bulletin de la société de géographie* (1843), 19, 27–38, 93, 99; *GH* (1908), 106, 119–39, 143–60, 163–70, 315–16; Grandidier, "Souvenirs," 28; Gabriel Rantoandro, "Une communauté mercantile du nord-ouest: Les Antalaotra," *Colloque d'histoire de l' Université de Madagascar* (Mahajanga, 1981), 8; Ottino, *économies paysannes*, 187; *idem, Madagascar, les comores, et le sud-ouest de l' Océan Indien* (Tananarive, 1974).

[16] Frere, "memo regarding the Banians . . . in East Africa," incl.1 in Frere to Granville, Gulf of Oman, 16 April 1873, and "Memo," 31 Mar. 1873, in *CFM*; see also N. Hafkin, "Trade, Society and Politics in Northern Mozambique c.1753–1913" (Ph.D. Boston University, 1973), 85–8; R. Coupland, *East Africa and Its Invaders* (Oxford, 1956), Chs. 5, 8–9; *GH* (1928), 39, 249, 299, 304, 317; Samat, "Notes" (1852), 57–8, 61–2.

[17] For a full history of the pirates, see Hubert Deschamps, *Les pirates à Madagascar* (Paris, 1949).

[18] Rasoamiaramanana, "Aspects économiques," 10–11, 35, 54; Noel, "Ile de Madagascar" (1843), 19, 27–38, 93, 99; Grandidier, "Souvenirs," 28.

of the pirates from 1720 enabled Indian and Swahili merchant ships to sail again in security, regular direct contact being reestablished with Arabia and India; this encouraged, for instance, an annual merchant fleet to sail from Surat to northwest Madagascar.[19] Second, Bernard-François Mahé de la Bourdonnais, governor of the Mascarenes, inaugurated a program of rapid economic development based upon cultivation of plantation crops for export. Previously, Malagasy slaves, rice, live cattle, and smoked or salted meat had been exported by Indian and Swahili traders to the Portuguese at Mozambique and through Zanzibar to the markets of Arabia and northwest India.[20] European ships also occasionally exported the same commodities.[21]

From 1750, Mascarene demand for slave labor and provisions (chiefly cattle and rice) was such that Swahili merchants redirected sizeable quantities of slaves, cattle, rice, and maize from the west coast hinterland, overland to the east coast ports of Mahavelona and Toamasina (Tamatave), for sale to Mascarene merchants.[22] In 1803, all slaves for sale on Nosy Boraha (a French-held island off the northeast coast of Madagascar) hailed from Anjouan, in the Comoro group.[23] Large quantities of cattle and meat and about 500 tons of rice were also annually exported from Madagascar to the Mascarenes.[24]

---

[19] Dumaine, "Voyage à la côte de l'ouest" (1793), 297; *GH* (1908), 106 and (1928), 261.

[20] *GH* (1908), 324 and (1928), 298, 302–3.

[21] Charles Nordhoff, *Stories of the Island World* (New York, 1857), 44.

[22] Mayeur, "Voyage au pays de Séclaves" (1774), 86, 92–3, 97, 101, 103–5, 115, 121, 123; *idem*, "Voyage dans le nord" (1775), 34, 37, 46; *idem*, "Voyage au pays d'ancove" (1777), 176, 180; *idem*, "Voyage au pays d'ancove" (1785), 221–2, 227, 233; Morice, "Mémoire" (1777), 100–6; Anon, "Mémoire historique" [1790], 95; Dumaine, "Voyage au pays d'ancaye" (1790), 278; *idem*, "Voyage à la côte de l'ouest" (1793), 295, 297; Mayeur to Froberville, 4 avril 1806, in Jean Valette (ed.), "Documents pour servir à l'étude des relations entre Froberville et Mayeur," *BAM* 46 I–II (1968), 89; Rondeaux, "Mémoire" (1809), 121–2; Copland, *History of Madagascar*, 12, 18; Samat, "Notes" (1852), 61, 64; Duroche, "note sur Madagascar" (15 mars 1816), *BL*.Add.18135; Hastie, "Diary" (1824–5); Noel, "Ile de Madagascar" (1843); Guillain, *Documents sur l'histoire, la géographie et le commerce de la partie occidentale de Madagascar* 2 vols. (Paris, 1845); Prud'homme, "Considérations sur les Sakalaves," *Notes, reconnaissances et explorations* 6 (1900), 413–14; Lombard, *La royauté Sakalava*; Oliver, *Madagascar* vol. I, 272, 291, 323–4, 423; *GH* (1908), 160, 165, 315–16, 324 and (1928), 260–2, 308; Alfred Horn, *The Waters of Africa* (London, 1932), 97.

[23] J. M. Filliot, *La traite des esclaves vers les Mascareignes* (Paris, 1974), 153–4; Gill Shepherd, "The Comorians and the East African Slave Trade," in James L. Watson (ed.), *Asian and African Systems of Slavery* (Oxford, 1980), 74–6; see also James Walvin, *Slavery and the Slave Trade* (London, 1983), 66, 69.

[24] Mayeur, "Voyage au pays de Séclaves" (1774), 123; *idem*, "Voyage dans le nord" (1775), 62; Grégoire Avine, "Notes de voyage à Fort Dauphin" (1804) in Raymond Decary, "Le voyage d'un chirurgien philosophe à Madagascar," *BAM* 36 (1958), 326; Rondeaux, "Mémoire" (1809),

Third, the revival in Indian and Swahili trading fortunes was assisted by their alliance with the Sakalava, whose empire, based on foreign trade, reached its height in the early eighteenth century when it covered possibly one-third of the island. The Antsihanaka, Antankarana, and Merina, excluded from the formal empire, nevertheless paid tribute to the Sakalava court and protected Sakalava emissaries and traders. The Sakalava alliance confirmed the Indian and Swahili monopoly of foreign trade over much of the west coast and enabled them to extend their commercial network from their base at Mahajanga. By 1810, their 5- to 10-ton dhows (trans-Mozambique Channel dhows ranged from 30 to 80 tons) engaged in coastal and riverine trade in the north and west; the Manambolo and Betsiboka were navigable inland for 96 and 144 km respectively. Indian and Swahili caravans, often led by hired Sakalava armed with muskets, swords, and even bows and barbed arrows,[25] traveled throughout the north of the island and as far south as Imerina and the Ankay.

From the 1500s, Europeans, who regarded Madagascar mainly as a reprovisioning base on the route to India and the East,[26] established coastal posts in the island, notably in St. Augustin Bay, around Tolanaro, and in Antongil Bay. They also ventured inland, first reaching Imerina in the reign of Andrianjaka (c.1610–30). Imerina, one of the most populous regions, became the major supply center of slaves. As Mayeur remarked in 1777, "the flow of both Malagasy and strangers in these markets is amazing; one sees individuals from every province and region who visit the markets to both buy and sell."[27] By the close of the eighteenth century, planters and merchants, mainly Mascarenes Creoles, started to settle the northeast coast in small numbers.[28]

91–108; *GH* (1908), 171 and (1928), 38–9, 297; P. D. Curtin, *The Atlantic Slave Trade* (Madison, 1970), 229; Rantoandro, "communauté mercantile," 9–10.

[25] Hastie, "Diary" (1824–5); *GH* (1908), 165.

[26] Madagascar lay on the chief sea-lanes that passed either through the Mozambique Channel or followed the east coast of Madagascar. Nearing the equator ships sailed before the southwest monsoon to India, returning on the northeast monsoon on the return trip – Oliver, *Madagascar* vol. I, 404–5; *GH* (1908), 172–5; René Sédillot, *Histoire des colonisations* (Paris, 1958), 490, 519; Edward Berman, "Salem and Zanzibar: 1825–1850. Twenty-five years of Commercial Relations," *Essex Institute of Historical Collections* 105.4 (1969), 339–43; Christian G. Mantaux, "Journal de Berube-Dudemene Capitaine du Bougainville à Madagascar en 1774," *BAM* 49 II (1971), 89.

[27] Mayeur, "Voyage au pays d'ancove" (1777), 166; see also *idem*, "Voyage au pays d'ancove" (1785), 226; Hugon, "Aperçu" (1808), 16; Rondeaux, "Mémoire" (1809), 123; Oliver, *Madagascar* vol. I, 387 and vol. II, 191; Chapus et Dandouau, "anciennes industries malgaches," 47; *GH* (1908), 218, 223, 258 and (1928), 169.

[28] Mayeur, "Voyage au pays d'ancove" (1777), 153; Lescalier, "Voyage" (1792), 317; Avine, "Notes de voyage" (1804), 326; Chapelier, "Manuscrits," 49–50; Nourse to Farquhar, HMS Andromarche, Mozambique Channel, 17 Nov. 1822, *PRO.CO*.167/66; *RH*, 19–20; Oliver, *Madagascar* vol. I, 9–21; Jully, "Mission en extrême-orient," *BAM* II.2 (1903), 75; *GH* (1908), 171–86, 198 and (1928), 263; Deschamps, *histoire*, 63–91; Decary, *Coutumes guerrières* vol. I, 50–1.

Following the American War of Independence, North Americans increasingly visited Malagasy waters, for whaling and in order to reprovision East Indiamen that by the 1790s had transformed Salem, Massachusetts, into the world's premier pepper emporium. Mauritius, the major market for goods seized by French privateers from British Indiamen in the Indian Ocean during the Napoleonic Wars, attracted more American merchants who subsequently started to explore Madagascar's commercial potential.[29]

On the northwest coast, Europeans and Americans (collectively referred to as *Vazaha* a term for "white foreigners") were obliged to trade through Indian and Swahili traders; these controlled the commerce of all major ports in the northwest – including Ampasindava, Mahajanga, Tambohorana, Marovoay, Baly Bay, Makomba (in Boina Bay), Mahajamba Bay, Anorotsanga (in Rafaralahy Bay), and Ambavatoby Bay.[30] South of Tambohorana, notably at St. Augustin, Morondava, Tsimanandrafozana (a delta port at the mouth of the Tsiribihina), and Maintirano, Westerners generally traded directly with Sakalava chiefs. However, this southern trade was less organized, less secure, and less profitable than the northern trade.[31] By far the most important east coast port frequented by European traders by 1810 was Mahavelona (Marofototra), followed by Maroantsetra, Mananara, Manoro, Nosy Boraha, Takotainga (Tintingue), Masindrano, Fenoarivo, Matitatana, Mahambo, Vohimara, Mahanoro, Mahela, Tolanaro, Vatomandry, Ste. Luce, Mananjary, and Ranofotsy. Of these, only the last five and Mahavelona offered relatively safe anchorage.[32]

The structure of trade on the east coast was similar to that of the southern Sakalava coast. As an American sailor commented when his ship visited the Malagasy coast [Ste. Luce?] in 1792:

At Our Landing the Natives met us all of them was Armed with Muskets Knifs and Spers and Conducted us to the Forte ware the wite man was he Informed us that the King Did

---

[29] Berman, "Salem and Zanzibar," 339–40.

[30] Mayeur, "Voyage au pays de Séclaves" (1774); *idem*, "Voyage dans le nord" (1775), 48; Rondeaux, "Mémoire" (1809), 121; Samat, "Notes" (1852); *GH* (1928), 263, 297; Mantaux, "Journal de Berube-Dudemene," 91–108.

[31] Avine, "Notes de voyage" (1804), 326; Oliver, *Madagascar* vol. I, 421–30; Edward Ives, "extract" from "A Voyage to India" (1754), *AAMM* 22 (1898), 241–4; *GH* (1908), 315–6; Decary, *Coutumes guerrières* vol. I, 17; Campbell, "Madagascar and the Slave Trade," 220–2; Rantoandro, "communauté mercantile," 8.

[32] Mayeur, "Voyage au pays d'ancove" (1785); *idem*, "Réflexions sur l'établissement et l'amélioration du commerce de Madagascar" (1802), *BL*.Add.18136, 42–3; Lescalier, "Voyage" (1792), 323; Chapelier, "Manuscrits," 49–50; Avine, "Notes de voyage" (1804), 326; Schneider, Archives Coloniales (1818) in *GH* (1928), 280; Frappaz, "Notice sur les vents, les courans, et les atterrages de la côte sud-est de l'ile de Madagascar," *Annales maritimes et coloniales* (1820) II, 692–3; Copland, *History of Madagascar*, 14–15; Oliver, *Madagascar* vol. I, 408, 410–18; Decary, *Coutumes guerrières* vol. I, 50–1.

Live four Mile [6.4 km] in the Country and would be Down the Nex Day and he Tould us that we must Give the King a Present for with Out that we Should not be Able to Git Aney Rice of him.[33]

Mascarene trading ships were often condemned "bullockers," considered good for a few short trips to the east coast of Madagascar to pick up live cattle, as well as slaves, rice, and other produce.[34] In the 1810s, 30,000 cattle were exported to the Mascarenes annually from the coast between Vohimara and Cape Amber. However, following the 1817–25 Merina conquest of the east coast, the larger cattle herders migrated to the western plains, and cattle exports dropped dramatically. Mascarene merchants shipped some cattle from the extreme northeast coast to Maroantsetra and Angontsy at the start of the cyclone season, when variable winds offered the chance of a comparatively short passage, as voyages during the dry season, against the southwest monsoon, took much longer.[35]

European traders were initially content to remain in coastal trading posts. However, internecine disputes, among the Betsimisaraka and other hinterland peoples, over control of foreign trade disrupted supplies to such a degree that they attempted to establish direct contact with suppliers in the hinterland.[36] Unlike the Indians and Swahili, European traders usually hired *maromita*, or local free labor, to carry imported goods to the interior and to escort slaves or cattle back to the east coast. Porterage was a largely seasonal occupation restricted, like most long distance trade, to the dry season, when routes up the eastern escarpment to the central plateau were passable. The hirer paid for canoes, provisions, and, whenever necessary, arms, for the porters. However, should a porter fall ill, he was obliged to find a replacement or forfeit his salary.[37]

Because of their long residence in Madagascar, Indian and Swahili traders had no need of interpreters, but most European traders required an agent who

[33] John Bartlett, "Journal to the N. W.Coast and China 1790 on the ship Massachusetts," M.656 1790M, *PM*.

[34] Mayeur, "Voyage au pays d'ancove" (1777), 153; *idem*, "Voyage au pays d'ancove" (1785), 205; Copland, *History of Madagascar*, 15; Nils Bergsten, "Mémoire sur les moyens d'augmenter à Madagascar les revenus du gouvernement" (1825), (Jean Valette, ed.), *BAM* 44 (1966), 16; Oliver, *Madagascar* vol. I, 265, 412, 414; Anon, "Some Betsimisaraka folk-tales and superstitions" (trans. J. Sibree), *AAMM* 22 (1898), 217; Sibree, *A Naturalist*, 20, 22–3, 35; *GH* (1928), 297; Robequain, "capitale montagnarde," 287; Jean Valette, "Nouvelle note pour servir à l'étude des exportations de boeufs de Fort-Dauphin à Bourbon (1820)," *BAM* 50 II (1972), 33–6.

[35] *MT* II.41 (15 Oct. 1884), 376.

[36] Mayeur, "Voyage au pays d'ancove" (1777); *idem*, "Réflexions" (1802).

[37] Mayeur, "Voyage dans le nord" (1775), 48, 60; *idem*, "Voyage au pays d'ancove," (1785), 198–202; Dumaine, "Voyage au pays d'ancaye" (1790), 259; Hugon, "Aperçu" (1808), 2, 6, 11; Le Sage, "Mission" (1816), 10, 38–9, 44–5; Hastie, "Diary" (1820), 470, 504; Gwyn Campbell, "Labour and the Transport Problem in Imperial Madagascar, 1810–1895," *JAH* 21 (1980).

could cope with local dialects and traditions. Traders representing a large firm, or the government in the Mascarenes, usually hired someone who had been raised in Madagascar as the son of a Creole or European trader. Thus, Maurice Benyowski, in French government pay, hired Mayeur, son of a French merchant, who had lived in Madagascar since the age of four.[38] Smaller traders, unable to afford such professionals, took advantage of the Malagasy custom of offering their daughters to foreigners to fulfill their sexual and commercial needs. Ambitious parents solicited foreign traders to take on their daughters, Hastie commenting in 1817 that "a mother with fifty dollars worth of trinkets on her person will recommend and display the charms of her daughter to a stranger."[39] The advantages to the girl were considerable: higher living standards and status and, as she gained greater commercial and linguistic expertise, the prospect of regular employment on a similar basis, with a wealthier merchant. For the duration of the trading season, she performed the functions of wife, companion, and commercial agent, it being usual for European traders on the east coast to send "Native women that they kept" into the interior "to trade for them."[40] Such contractual relationships were also commonly sought by indigenous long distance traders who, however, "married" both adult and infant females along their trading routes, for to them the commercial skill of their "spouses" was less important than the familial bond of trust and mutual assistance such alliances engendered.[41]

A common code of commercial behavior existed for foreign traders in Madagascar. They contracted with the chief of the port they wished to use as a base, for authority to erect, and protection for, a warehouse.[42] Safe passage across internal political boundaries was secured by concluding a *fatidra*, or blood brotherhood ceremony, with each local paramount chief. The *fatidra* bound the initiates in closer than familial bonds, it even being expected that they share wives. An observer noted in 1790 that

It joins forever two individuals or two families, who thereafter and on all occasions offer mutual protection and assistance, as if they were related by blood. . . . In front of

[38] Mayeur, "Voyage au pays d'ancove" (1785), 209; Dumaine, "Voyage au pays d'ancaye" (1790), 253; Le Sage, "Mission" (1816), 103; Sundström, *Exchange Economy*, 58.

[39] Hastie, "Diary" (1817), 185.

[40] Hastie, "Dairy" (1820), 482; see also Lescalier, "Voyage" (1792), 329; Avine, "Voyages" (1802), 55; Capmartin, "Notes sur la Baye St. Augustin (Côte occidentale de Madagascar)" [1815], 13, BL.Add.18135; Le Sage, "Mission" (1816), 64; Oliver, *Madagascar* vol. I, 454.

[41] Dumaine, "Voyage au pays d'ancaye" (1790), 274.

[42] Mayeur, "Voyage au pays de Séclaves" (1774), 87, 100–1; *idem*, "Voyage dans le nord" (1775), 17; *idem*, "Voyage au pays d'ancove" (1785), 210; Dumaine, "Voyage au pays d'ancaye" (1790), 264.

witnesses, the two parties make reciprocal oaths [of allegiance] . . . following which each makes a small incision in his chest – enough to give one or two drops of blood. They staunch the blood with a small portion of ginger. They are subsequently given and eat the ginger stained by the blood of their "brother." It is considered infamy for anyone to break this oath.[43]

Swahili traders traveling largely in west Madagascar required few *fatidra* due to the extent of the hegemony of their Sakalava allies, many leaders of whom in addition converted to Islam. By contrast, Europeans in politically fragmented eastern Madagascar were obliged to conclude numerous *fatidra*. For example, Dumaine, a leading French trader to Madagascar in the late eighteenth century, negotiated up to twenty *fatidra* to secure his commercial interests.[44] Once the authority of the trader was recognized, all villages through which he traveled were obliged, whenever demanded, to furnish him and his cortege with food and lodging. The merchant was custom-bound to present the villagers with a gift, but its value reflected the status of the trader rather than that of the service provided.[45]

Foreign merchants pour-parleyed in order to fix the terms of exchange. As the value of gifts presented by the trader, required both to open and to lubricate commercial negotiations, was traditionally greater than that presented by the supplier, this initial process could prove costly to the former. In major commercial centers, such as Imerina, this "tax" could be kept down because preliminary negotiations followed a standard procedure and might last only a few days. Indeed, by 1800, most foreign traders visiting Imerina were restricted to centers and markets designated for foreign trade. In remoter regions, the desired produce was usually not at hand and was sought for only after the terms of exchange had been settled. The delay involved, frequently amounting to several months, laid the foreign trader open to pressure from suppliers to renegotiate the terms of sale. In addition, traders had to negotiate in advance the price to be

[43] Anon, "Mémoire historique" [1790]; see also Mayeur, "Voyage dans le nord" (1775), 35; *idem*, "Voyage au pays d'ancove" (1777), 160, 168, 180; *idem*, "Voyage au pays d'ancove" (1785), 208–9; Dumaine, "Voyage au pays d'ancaye" (1790), 280, 284; Lescalier, "Voyage" (1792), 318–19; Chardenoux, "Journal" (1816), 170; *GH* (1928), 266.

[44] Mayeur, "Voyage dans le nord" (1775), 35; *idem*, "Voyage au pays d'ancove" (1777), 160, 168, 180; *idem*, "Voyage au pays d'ancove" (1785), 208–9; Dumaine, "Voyage au pays d'ancaye" (1790), 280; Hugon, "Aperçu" (1808), 7; Le Sage, "Mission" (1816), 65.

[45] Hastie, "Diary" (1822), *PRO.CO.*167/63; Mayeur, "Voyage au pays de Séclaves" (1774); *idem*, "Voyage dans le nord" (1775), 30; *idem*, "Voyage au pays d'ancove" (1785), 203; Dumaine, "Voyage au pays d'ancaye" (1790), 262–3, 267; Lescalier, "Voyage" (1792), 322; Hugon, "Aperçu" (1808), 12, 19; Le Sage, "Mission" (1816), 46–7, 57, 79; for mainland African comparisons, see Sundström, *Exchange Economy*, 2, 13.

paid for the return of any slaves or cattle that might escape his custody between the moment of purchase and embarkation.[46]

Indian and Swahili imports included Surat raw silk and cotton and Surat cloths, muskets, musket balls, flint stones, gunpowder, glass, jewelry, salt, and even ostrich eggs. The Sakalava paid for these in slaves, cattle, hides, rice, precious woods, gum copal, and ambergris; the Antankarana in tortoise shell; and the Merina, Antsihanaka, and Bezanozano in slaves and piastres. Of the estimated 120,000 piastres annually imported by European traders on the east coast to purchase export goods, the Malagasy transferred some 80 percent to Indian and Swahili traders in payment for imports from the west coast. As Hastie remarked of Radama I of Imerina in 1817, "He exchanges chains [of silver] with the Arabs as they are stocked with slaves, and slaves with all European merchants."[47]

The Western products most in demand were quality goods, mainly cotton cloth, printed and plain handkerchiefs, arms, and ammunition, as well as ironware, liquor, and silver piastres. There was a considerable Mascarene market for slaves (from Imerina, Anosy, and, to a lesser extent, Betsimisaraka) and for live cattle, salted beef, rice, and construction timber (from Betsimisaraka, the Ankay, and the Antaimoro). The Mascarenes imported an estimated annual average of 1,350 Malagasy cattle from 1775 to 1800 and, by the latter date, between 2,000 and 2,500 metric tons of rice from Mahavelona alone. Salted beef sold on Réunion for 2.5 to 2.9 times its purchase price in Toamasina.

Slaves may have constituted the main eighteenth-century export. By 1790, some 3,000 slaves were imported annually into Mauritius, mostly from the Malagasy east coast. Mascarene demand for slaves grew dramatically following the revitalization of the islands from the 1730s. Madagascar, its closest and cheapest source, supplied 45 percent of the 160,000 slaves imported into the Mascarenes from 1610 to 1810. This compared to 40 percent from East Africa. In the Malagasy interior, the Merina, Antsihanaka, Bezanozano, Antaimoro,

[46] Mayeur, "Voyage dans le nord" (1775), 18, 35; idem, "Voyage au pays d'ancove" (1777), 153, 161–2; idem, "Voyage au pays d'ancove" (1785), 208–9; Des Milices, "Mémoire sur les moyens de former pour le Roi dans l'isle de Madagascar un établissement de culture, de commerce, et d'entrepôt général pour l'Europe, l'Asie, et l'Afrique" (1780), 21 – BL.Add.18136; Dumaine, "Voyage au pays d'ancaye" (1790), 282, 285; Hugon, "Aperçu" (1808), 15; Capmartin, "Notes" [1815], 12; Hastie, "Diary" (1817), 171.

[47] Hastie, "Diary" (1817), 188; see also ibid, 157; idem, "Diary" (1824–5); Copland, History of Madagascar, 12–18; Oliver, Madagascar vol. II, 16–17; GH (1908), 106, 160, 162, 171 and (1928), 260, 302–3, 322–3, 327, 332; Horn, Waters of Africa, 97; Mayeur, "Voyage dans le nord" (1775), 86; idem, "Voyage au pays d'ancove" (1785), 227; Anon, "Mémoire historique" [1790], 55; Dumaine, "Voyage à la côte de l'ouest" (1793), 294–7; Chapelier, "Lettres adressées," 34.

Betsileo, Bara, and Sakalava launched slave raids in the dry winter months. From the 1770s, French and, increasingly, Merina traders dominated the traffic in slaves from Imerina, which from 1802 to 1808 exported to the east coast 1,500 to 1,800 slaves annually.[48] Pier Larson has claimed that the overwhelming bulk of slaves exported was of Merina origin.[49] However, from c.1795 most were Sakalava and Betsileo enslaved by the Merina, who sold them for export either in Imerina or on the east coast.[50]

Profits could be considerable; slaves costing between 20 and 25 piastres could resell on the Mascarenes for 90 piastres, "depending on their sex, age, strength and beauty."[51] The French preferred east coast Malagasy markets; they were the nearest center of supply for the Mascarenes, were close to inland slave marts, and possessed a rice-producing hinterland. Mahavelona, the major entrepôt in the late eighteenth century, was replaced by Toamasina from 1801.[52] However, the disruption of trade routes to Imerina, due to internecine strife and commercial disputes, encouraged middlemen – notably Swahili (from the northwest) and Betsimisaraka (from the northeast) – to search for alternative sources of slaves. These included, from 1785 to 1820, the Comoro islands (notably Anjouan) and east African ports, including Ibo, Kilwa, Querimba, and Mozambique Island.[53]

There also existed a much smaller, traditional slave export trade from western Madagascar to Middle Eastern and Indian markets and to occasional European ships supplying markets as widely dispersed as the Mascarenes, the Cape of Good Hope, and the Americas. Merina and Swahili traders sold slaves from the interior to Muslim merchants on the northwest coast, while European slavers

---

[48] Filliot, *La traite des esclaves*, 157–9; Anon, "Etat de l'approvisionnement des marchandises de France destinées à faciliter les traites de nègres à l'isle de Madagascar," ms. (1768) in Decary, *Coutumes guerrières* vol. I, 50; Mayeur, "Voyage au pays de Séclaves" (1774), 87, 92, 101–5, 123, 212–14; *idem*, "Voyage au pays d'ancove" (1777), 176, 186; *idem*, "Voyage au pays d'ancove" (1785), 221–2; *idem*, "Réflexions" (1802), 45; Morice, "Mémoire" (1777), 116; Des Milices, "Mémoire" (1780), 20; Anon, "Mémoire historique" [1790], 85–7; Dumaine, "Voyage au pays d'ancaye" (1790), 261, 270–1; *idem*, "Voyage à la côte de l'ouest" (1793), 300; Lescalier, "Voyage" (1792), 326–7; Chapelier, "Lettres" (1803–5), 30; Hugon, "Aperçu" (1808), 5, 17; Rondeaux, "Mémoire" (1809), 121, 173; *GH* (1928), 293, 297, 303; Rantoandro, "communauté mercantile," 10.

[49] Pier Larson, *History and Memory in the Age of Enslavement* (Portsmouth, 2000).

[50] Gwyn Campbell, "Larceny in the Highlands of Madagascar" review article *Slavery & Abolition* 23.1 (2002), 137–46.

[51] Mayeur, "Voyage dans le nord" (1775), 18; see also *ibid*, 60–1; Des Milices, "Mémoire" (1780), 20; Hastie, "Diary" (1817), 170; *GH* (1928), 298; Sundström, *Exchange Economy*, 76–7.

[52] Filliot, *La traite des esclaves*, 129–41; Earl of Caledon to Nicholas Vansittart, Cape of Good Hope, 27 June 1810; Moorson to Commodore Christian, HMS Andromarche, 24 May 1825 – in George Theal, *Records of South-Eastern Africa* IX (Cape Town, 1964), 13, 50–2.

[53] Earl of Caledon to Nicholas Vansittart, Cape of Good Hope, 27 June 1810, in Theal, *Records* IX (1964), 13; Filliot, *La traite des esclaves*, 160–1.

were supplied chiefly by the Bara and Sakalava of the southwest coast.[54] By 1820, five main slave supply routes had developed in Madagascar: Betsileo–Morondava, Ibara–St.Augustin, Imerina–Iboina (notably Mahajanga), Iboina–Antongil Bay (via the river Sofia), and Imerina–northeast coast (Mahavelona and Toamasina). All channeled Malagasy slaves for export, while the fourth also fed African slaves imported through ports in the northwest, via overland routes, to the northeast coast.[55]

Less valuable products sold to passing vessels and Mascarene traders included yams, coconuts, banana and other fruit, sheep, poultry, hogs, milk, salt, purslane, sweet potatoes, fish, lances, beeswax, loincloths (*salaka*), and matting. More localized exports comprised, from the west and northwest coasts, tortoise meat and shells – including cowry shells shipped to West Africa and Asia to be used as a currency; from the west coast, maize and ambergris (exported to Europe to be used in cooking and in the manufacture of perfumes); from the southwest, orchil and cassis shell (used in the production of dye and of cameo and porcelain respectively) and sea-slugs (*Holothuria*) (exported to Chinese markets as a soup delicacy).[56] Finally, by the early 1800s, Europeans on the east coast were beginning to exploit rubber and other forest products and to cultivate export crops such as tea and coffee.[57]

By 1820, long distance trade possessed a standard code of commercial practice, widespread usage of coinage, and a well-developed market system. The security that followed the end of the Merina Civil Wars in the 1790s and the development of a highly regulated market system ensured Imerina's preeminence in the domestic commercial network. The variety of produce sold on Merina markets increased markedly.[58] A Betsimisaraka song recorded in 1803 exalted the benefits of such commerce:

> O Fortunate East, fortunate East, fortunate East,
> You, from where the sun appears, and the White man comes,
> The source of silver, and of cotton cloth,
> The source of firearms, and of gunpowder,

[54] Filliot, *La traite des esclaves*, 157–9.

[55] *Ibid*, 155–6.

[56] Ives, "extract" (1754), 241–4; Mayeur, "Voyage au pays de Séclaves" (1774), 85; Chapelier, "Manuscrits," 50; Copland, *History of Madagascar*, 15; Oliver, *Madagascar* vol. I, 272; *GH* (1908), 376–7 and (1928), 93, 208, 263, 308, 316, 318–19, 323; Decary, *Coutumes guerrières* vol. I, 52.

[57] Gwyn Campbell, "Coffee Production in Madagascar" in Steven Topik & William Gervase Clarence-Smith. (eds.), *Coffee under Colonialism and Post-Colonialism: The Global Coffee Economy in Africa, Asia, and Latin America, c1800–c1960* (Cambridge, 2002). Chapelier, "lettres adressées," 3, 16–18, 20, 23; *GH* (1928), 105, 314–15.

[58] See Tables 1 and 3.1.

The source of flint stones, and of lead shot,
The source of the fire that illuminates the earth,
[And from which] one fashions the billhook and axe,
Which has enabled man to work and to eat his fill!
O Fortunate East, that lies yonder!

O Fortunate West, fortunate West, fortunate West, fortunate West,
You, against whom the moon breaks, whence comes silk,
The source of girdles, and of the loincloth,
The source of the *angady* [spade], and of the Hova [Merina],
Who serves the Betsimisaraka?
The source of cattle!
O Fortunate West, that lies yonder![59]

[59] Chapelier, "lettres adressées," 30.

3   Empire and the Adoption of Autarky, 1810–1826

Introduction

Most historians of Madagascar claim that in the nineteenth century its peoples were united under Merina sovereigns who, except for Ranavalona I (1828–61), were benign and progressive. This view derives from the writings of the London Missionary Society (LMS) agents active in the island from 1821 to 1835 and again after 1862. William Ellis, compiler of the "authorized" LMS *History of Madagascar* (1838), praised Radama I (1810–28) for "his superiority to many of the puerile superstitions of his country, his firmness in adhering to plans calculated to elevate the physical and moral condition of his own people, and his faithfulness in maintaining his treaties."[1]

The historical consensus to date is that Radama I was a profoundly sage monarch who concluded an alliance with Britain in 1820, but directed European influence to his own advantage.[2] By contrast, his successor, Ranavalona I, is portrayed as having usurped the imperial throne with the aid of conservative counselors who induced her to adopt autarkic policies. She rejected the British alliance, proscribed Christianity, and expelled most foreigners, thus plunging the island into a quarter of a century of isolation.[3] Hubert Deschamps, author of the standard *Histoire de Madagascar*, states of Radama I:

---

[1] Ellis, *History of Madagascar* vol. II, 403.

[2] Valette has indicated that the Merina economy was in serious difficulty by the last years of Radama I's reign, but the reference is brief and not elaborated – see Jean Valette, "Radama I, the Unification of Madagascar and the Modernisation of Imerina (1810–1828)," in Kent (ed.), *Madagascar in History*, 194.

[3] Ellis, *History of Madagascar* vol. II, 411, 416.

Realising the superiority of European technology, and desirous of acquiring it in order to promote his own power, he knew how to introduce it, without either jeopardising his independence, or losing the loyalty of his subjects, maintaining throughout his control over everything. His reign, brief and extraordinarily charged with events, marked a turning point and inaugurated in Madagascar a nineteenth century characterised to the end by three elements: Anglo-French rivalry, the conquest of the greater part of the island by the Merina, and the intrusion of European influence.[4]

However, he describes Ranavalona I as "ignorant, credulous and malleable," considering that her reign was characterized by "A: the seizure of power by a plutocratic oligarchy, B: a break with European influence, C: the adoption of isolationism, D: the fight against Christianity."[5] Thus, in Deschamps' as in Ellis' view, autarky was a product of Ranavalona I's reign. The difference is that whereas Ellis held that the height of autarky was reached with the mass expulsion of Europeans and Americans in 1835, for Deschamps it climaxed with the 1845 Franco–British naval bombardment of Toamasina.[6]

This traditional interpretation has been partially challenged by Simon Ayache and Mervyn Brown, who argue for some continuity between the reigns of Radama I and Ranavalona I in terms of willingness to accept innovation and European influence that did not compromise Merina sovereignty. However, both reiterate the argument that, whereas Radama I coped with the forces of change, the increase in tempo of those forces after 1828, combined with deficiency of character, rendered Ranavalona I increasingly incapable of controlling change. Her reaction was to defy the outside world and adopt autarkic policies.[7]

It is here argued that Radama I, not his successor, was the first to adopt autarkic policies and that his decision was linked to Britanno–Merina imperial rivalry. Far from promoting the economic welfare of the Merina crown, the British alliance weakened it, threatening to make the Merina crown a vassal of Mauritius. Consequently, Radama I rejected the British alliance and adopted autarkic policies. There was thus both economic and political continuity between the reigns of Radama I and Ranavalona I. Rather than undermining a progressive regime by introducing reactionary government, the latter adopted and developed her predecessor's autarkic policies in a rational and systematic manner.

---

[4] Deschamps, *histoire*, 151.

[5] *Idem*, 163.

[6] *Idem*, 165; Ellis, *History of Madagascar* vol. II, 486.

[7] Simon Ayache, "Esquisse pour le portrait d'une reine: Ranavalona 1ère," *Omaly sy Anio*, I–II (1975), 251–70; Mervyn Brown, "Ranavalona I and the Missionaries, 1828–1840," *Omaly sy Anio*, V–VI (1977), 107–39.

The British Alliance, 1810–1820

The Napoleonic Wars initially boosted the economy of the French Mascarenes, whose privateers launched devastating raids upon British East Indiamen. Their booty, an estimated £2.5 million worth of goods and bullion – £300,000 of which was seized in two months alone in 1808 – transformed Port Louis into a major emporium. However, stung by their losses, the British captured Réunion (then called Bourbon) in 1809 and Mauritius (Ile de France) in 1810. Réunion was restored to France under the Treaty of Paris (1814), but Britain retained Mauritius, which possessed an excellent harbor (Port Louis) and was of primary strategic importance in safeguarding the route to India via the Cape of Good Hope.[8] Farquhar, the first British governor of Mauritius, quickly realized that to fulfill a role in British global strategy, Mauritius should also secure Madagascar, its main source of provisions. After British troops had seized former French trading stations on the Malagasy east coast in 1810–11, Farquhar declared Madagascar to be under British sovereignty. He installed British agents in the island and commissioned research to facilitate the establishment of a British settlement.

As a colony, Madagascar might serve several key purposes. First, it would relieve the chronic overpopulation of Mauritius, for as Chazal noted,

> The Isle de France [Mauritius] is glutted by a superfluous population which lacks in food.... [S]oon, the new and overabundant generation will not know where to work. This generation, [if] prepared [for the task] with forethought by a benevolent government, could be destined to make its fortune, and that of France, in this large island [i.e., Madagascar].[9]

It would also guarantee provisions for Mauritius, help secure the route to India, and assist British industrial development through supplying raw materials in return for British manufactures. In sum, British predominance in Madagascar was vital for

---

[8] Anon, "Instructions sommaires qu'il est convenable d'adresser aux agens du gouvernement à Tamatave et à foulepointe, Isle de Madagascar" (1811), *BL*.Add.18136, 64–7; Raymond Decary, "La reddition de Tamatave à l'Angleterre en 1811," *BAM* 15 (1932), 489; Valette, "Documents," 84; Sémerville, "Souvenirs de Sainte-Marie," in Raymond Decary, "Le voyage du lieutenant de vaisseau de Sémerville à l'Île Sainte-Marie en 1824," *BAM* 16 (1933), 17–20; J. Anderson, *Descriptive Account of Mauritius, Its Scenery, Statistics, etc., with a brief Historical Sketch* (Mauritius, 1858), 119; North-Coombes, *The Island of Rodrigues* (Mauritius, 1971), 63–72; J. P. et J. Durand, *L'Île Maurice et ses populations* (Bruxelles, 1978), 36–9; Sédillot, *Histoire des colonisations*, 490, 519.

[9] Chazal, "Réflexions ... sur Madagascar et autres mémoires" [c.1815], *BL*.Add.18135, 31; see also *idem*, "Notes sur Madagascar" (1816), *BL*.Add.18135.

the safety of intercourse, and facility of trade, with a country on which this island [i.e., Mauritius] depends for its subsistence, and which has arrived at that point of civilisation that affords a growing and extensive market for bartering its valuable produce, the richest articles of tropical growth, for the manufactures of England and British India.[10]

However, London rejected Farquhar's arguments for colonizing Madagascar, arguing that possession of the Cape and Mauritius was sufficient to preserve British interests in the region. Indeed, in order to placate a French government outraged by Farquhar's actions in Madagascar, London tacitly recognized French claims to the island.[11] Farquhar was undaunted. A plantation owner himself, he was convinced that without securing Madagascar the Mauritian economy would be threatened and with it British interests in the IOW. As the British government had ruled out a formal protectorate, Farquhar maneuvered to render Madagascar an informal dependency of Mauritius. In 1814 and 1816, colonists were dispatched to northeast Madagascar, where Benyowski had established a French colony in the late 1700s. When attempts at settlement foundered due mainly to hostility from local peoples and to the prevalence of malaria,[12] Farquhar turned his attention to the high plateau interior. It was reportedly healthy and inhabited by a more civilized, fair-skinned, people, and its central location would enable a British settlement there to dominate the entire island.

Emissaries to the highland kingdom of Imerina in 1816 confirmed the substance of earlier reports, which in February 1817 led to a treaty designed to incorporate Imerina into the British imperial sphere. Imerina was a small land-locked country, but the treaty envisaged that Creole soldiers would quickly forge a trade outlet to east coast ports where British naval depots would be established. Soldier colonists would develop cash crops for export – commerce with Britain being on a free trade basis. Pacification of other regions of Madagascar would

---

[10] Farquhar to Earl Bathurst, Port Louis, 18 Nov. 1817, quoted in Ellis, *History of Madagascar* vol. II, 193; see also Thompson to Telfair, 31 Oct. 1814, "Archives de Port Louis," *PRO.CO*.167 Bk.50, 70; *The Missionary Register* (1818), 10; Anon, *Notices statistiques sur les colonies françaises. IV: Madagascar* (Paris, 1840), 2; Raymond Decary, *L'établissement de Sainte-Marie sous la Restauration et le rôle de Sylvain Roux* (Paris, 1937), 5–11; Jean Valette (ed.), *Le préfet Legèr à Madagascar* (Tananarive, 1966), 7–17; Samuel Pasfield Oliver, "Sir Robert Townsend Farquhar and the Malagasy Slave Trade," *AAMM* 15 (1891), 319; G. S. Graham, *Great Britain in the Indian Ocean, 1815–50* (Oxford, 1967); R. E. P. Wastell, "British Imperial Policy in Relation to Madagascar, 1810–1896," Ph.D. (London, 1944), 50.

[11] Wastell, "British Imperial Policy"; Graham, *Great Britain*, 3–4; see also G. N. Sanderson, "The European Partition of Africa: Coincidence or Conjecture?" *Journal of Imperial and Commonwealth History* 3.1 (1974).

[12] Excerpt from the "Gazette du Maurice" and from Farquhar's "Instructions to Lieutenant Le Sage," 20 April 1816, Archives de Port Louis, F. 7 no. 2; James Hastie, "Journal," in James Sibree and A. Jully (eds.), "Le voyage de Tananarive en 1817–18 – manuscrits de James Hastie," *BAM* II (1902), 92; *The Missionary Register* (1821), 345; Graham, *Great Britain*, 3–4, 55–6.

be gradual, giving Farquhar sufficient time to select and train British agents needed to administer an enlarged Merina empire under the nominal leadership of Radama I. By then, the Creole trailbreakers would have laid the basis for a second and much larger influx from Mauritius, comprising civilian colonists and their families.[13]

Radama I welcomed the British initiative. As a landlocked power, Imerina was highly vulnerable to any pressure upon its external trade links, particularly via the northeast coast. The end of the *Compagnie* monopoly in 1769 had resulted in a rush of Mascarene merchants to northeast Madagascar, where they refused to be limited either by locality or by previous price agreements. The resultant competition caused export prices to rise sharply; at Mahavelona in 1787, the price of a slave leapt from 52 to 77 piastres. Moreover, the Malagasy demand for payment in piastres, which the *Compagnie* monopoly had restricted, was generally satisfied.[14] However, enhanced demand and rising export prices also undermined security in the politically fragmented regions of east and central Madagascar, leading minor chiefs into fierce struggles for control of supply centers and slave routes from the interior. As one such chief explained to Mayeur in 1777, "There exist hardly any kings in this country who do not owe to you their authority, riches and power, for because of you we possess men to defend us, muskets, ammunition, and the sharp weapons which we lacked."[15] Internecine rivalry and pillaging of trade caravans reached such a pitch that, from the 1780s, routes linking Imerina to the northeast coast were regularly blocked. The French concluded treaties with coastal chiefs, but none of these had sufficient power to impose commercial peace upon hinterland authorities.[16] European traders subsequently attempted to bypass the middlemen and establish direct contact with Malagasy producers in the interior. New supply centers were opened up in hitherto unexplored parts of the east coast, and trade routes were forged into the interior. However, great difficulties were encountered in the highlands, despite a general eagerness to trade. The Betsileo could not guarantee a regular supply

---

[13] Chazal, Réflexions [c.1815], 30–2; *idem*, "Notes" (1816); Farquhar, "Instructions to Cochet," Port Louis, 23 May 1813, and *idem*, "Instructions pour M.Charenoux," 4 avril 1816, – in G. S. Chapus (ed.), "Nouveaux documents sur l'époque de Radama I et Ranavalona I," 325, *AM*; Chardenoux, "Journal" (1816); Le Sage, "Mission" (1816), 121–2; *RH*, 81, 86–8; Ellis, *History of Madagascar* vol. I, 217–18 and vol. II, 158–65.

[14] Mayeur, "Voyage dans le nord" (1775), 60–3; *idem*, "Voyage au pays d'ancove" (1777), 22; *idem*, "Réflexions" (1802); Morice, "Mémoire" (1777), 107–13; [Jouette], "Mémoire sur Madagascar" (1 juin 1806), *BL*.Add.18135; Hugon, "Aperçu" (1808), 15, 17, 22; GH (1928), 336; Delivré, *L'histoire des rois*, 224.

[15] Mayeur, "Voyage au pays d'ancove" (1777), 164.

[16] Mayeur, "Voyage au pays d'ancove" (1777), 167, 180, 186; *idem*, "Voyage au pays d'ancove" (1785), 204–5, 207–8, 212–16; *idem*, "Réflexions" (1802), 42; Morice, "Mémoire" (1777), 114; Dumaine, "Voyage au pays d'ancaye" (1790), 254–5, 257–9; Hugon, "Aperçu" (1808), 15, 20; Delivré, *L'histoire des rois*, 217.

of slaves, while the Merina, who could, were embroiled in internecine warfare until the 1790s and in wars of expansion thereafter. They also demanded high prices. As a French commentator remarked in 1806,

Continuously for almost eight months of the year, expeditions can be seen leaving Tamatave [Toamasina] for the country of the Ovas [Hova – i.e., the Merina]. This people . . . is incessantly at war, every prisoner being enslaved. Before, they sent them [the slaves] to Tamatave where they were sold. Today, we [merchants] go to their country [i.e., Imerina], where we compete with one another. This is entirely to our disadvantage, for when the ova leader, who has a number of slaves to sell, sends them to Tamatave, they are there sold at a reasonable price fixed by the merchants. However, as their country is reached only after a long, arduous and costly trip, a journey one does want to undertake at a loss, one is obliged to accept their terms.[17]

Moreover, plateau authorities proved incapable of stemming brigand attacks on trade caravans.[18]

Frustrated, Mascarene merchants turned to the west coast. However, attempts, such as Mayeur's in 1774–5, to forge trade routes across the island, from west to east, were frustrated by the Boina Sakalava court's insistence that European merchants trade through Indian and Swahili intermediaries[19] – whose counterparts in East Africa similarly hindered French efforts to tap slave sources there. Even when direct contact was established with east African producers, uncertainties of supply and the extra distance involved slashed profit margins.[20] In desperation, Mascarene merchants formed projects to directly annex Madagascar. In 1790, Jean François Charpentier de Cossigny revived Morice's (1777) proposal for a French commercial empire that would embrace Madagascar, the Comoro islands, and the Swahili coast from Zanzibar south to Mozambique. In the event, any possibility of French colonization of Madagascar was thwarted by the outbreak of war in Europe.[21]

[17] [Jouette], "Mémoire" (1806), 157; see also Mayeur, "Voyage au pays d'ancove" (1777), 161–2.
[18] Mayeur, "Voyage au pays d'ancove" (1777), 167, 180, 186; idem, "Voyage au pays d'ancove" (1785), 204–5, 207–8, 212–16; idem, "Réflexions" (1802), 42; Morice, "Mémoire" (1777), 114; Dumaine, "Voyage au pays d'ancaye" (1790), 254–5, 257–9; Hugon, "Aperçu" (1808), 15, 20; Delivré, L'histoire des rois, 217.
[19] Mayeur, "Voyage au pays des Séclaves" (1774); idem, "Voyage dans le nord" (1775); see also [Jouette], "Mémoire" (1806); Hugon, "Aperçu" (1808).
[20] André Scherer, Histoire de la Réunion (Paris, 1966), 27; Mayeur, "Voyage au pays de Séclaves" (1774), 101–5, 115–22; idem, "Voyage dans le nord" (1775), 48; Benyowsky (1774) in GH (1928), 263; Morice, "Mémoire" (1777), 106; Anon, "Mémoire historique" [1790], 95–6; Dumaine, "Voyage au pays d'ancaye" (1790), 270–1, 281; idem, "Voyage à la côte de l'ouest autrement dite pays des Séclaves" (janvier 1793) BL.Add.18128, 308.
[21] Morice, "Mémoire" (1777), 99–107, 114, 117, 127; Dumaine, "Voyage à la côte de l'ouest" (1793), 293; De Cossigny, "Réflexions sur l'Isle de Madagascar" (1800) BL.Add.18126, 148–62; see also Oliver, Madagascar vol. I, 16–17; Freeman-Grenville, The French at Kilwa Island (Oxford, 1965); Gwyn Campbell, "Imperial Rivalry in the Western Indian Ocean and Schemes to

The Merina were alarmed by French attempts to locate alternative slave supplies and by Bezanozano and Betsimisaraka disruption of trade routes. They felt further threatened when Swahili traders succeeded in enhancing their share of Malagasy–Mascarene commerce through establishing overland routes from Iboina to the northeast coast. Thomas Pye, an appointed British agent to the Malagasy east coast in 1811, spoke of

The relations of friendship and commerce for many years subsisting between this Chief [Similaza of Mahavelona] and the Arabs, who by the payment of certain duties in return for the privilege of his Port, furnished him with the greater part of his revenue and added to this strong tie of interests the commanding influence the Arabs had obtained in that part of the island of Madagascar . . . by their numbers and superior courage.[22]

By 1820, through their alliance with Jean René, the most powerful regional chief, the Swahili had gained paramount interest in Toamasina – which by then had surpassed Mahavelona as the chief port in northeast Madagascar – and were supplying Mascarene merchants there with large numbers of *Masombika* (a generic term for slaves imported from Africa).[23] The resulting Swahili–Merina friction was accentuated by Merina payment for Swahili imports in adulterated coinage – a practice that undermined "good" money and helped fuel inflation in Imerina.[24]

The final major blow to Merina commerce was occasioned by the 1809–11 British blockade and occupation of the Mascarenes. These actions severely disrupted foreign trade. Although the variety of produce sold on Merina markets continued to increase (see Table 3.1), this belied a crisis in external trade reflected in sharp falls from 1810 both in the domestic money supply and in domestic slave prices – which from 1810 to 1817 halved from $90 to $45.[25] In addition, the death of Andrianampoinimerina in 1810 provoked uprisings in recently conquered Merina territory and renewed attacks upon Merina trade

Colonise Madagascar, 1769–1826" in Lawrence Marjaing & Brigitte Reinwald (eds.), *African-isch Beziehungen, Netzwerke und Räume* (Münster, 2001), 111–30.

[22] Thomas Pye, "A summary of the Proceedings at Madagascar" from the 6th June to the 14th June 1817, *PRO.CO*.167/34, 90; see also Mayeur, "Voyage au pays d'ancove" (1777), 171; *idem*, "Imerina and Antananarivo" (James Sibree, ed.), *AAMM* 20 (1896), 392; Dumaine, "Voyage au pays d'ancaye" (1790), 279, 285; *idem*, "Voyage à la côte de l'ouest" (1793), 298, 308; Hastie, "Diary" (1817), 147; *idem*, "Diary" (1822); *GH* (1928), 297.

[23] Farquhar to Stanfell, Port Louis, Mauritius, 28 Sept. 1817, *PRO.CO*.167/34, 112; Hastie, "Diary" (1820), 500–1.

[24] Mayeur, "Voyage au pays d'ancove" (1777), 176–7.

[25] Le Sage, "Mission" (1816), 121–2; Hastie, "Diary" (1817), 150; A.Toussaint, *La route des Îles – contribution à l'histoire maritime des Mascareignes* (Paris, 1967); Filliot, *La traite des esclaves*; Campbell, "Madagascar and the Slave Trade," 203–8; *idem*, "Role of the London Missionary Society" vol. I, Ch. 2.

TABLE 3.1. *Market Produce in Imerina, 1816–17*

| Foodstuffs | Raw Materials | Livestock | Manufactures | |
			Domestic	Foreign
Beef	Construction timber	Oxen	Silk thread (red, green, & blue)	European cloth shawls (white & blue)
Mutton	Firewood	Sheep	Spun silk	Palampore printed cottons
Fresh fish	Raffia thread	Pigs	Spun silk	Other printed cottons
Dried fish	Bark of red wood	Geese	Silk cloth	Arab coarse colored silks
Silkworm	Somangy bark (for blue dye)	Ducks	Spun cotton	Beads
Eggs	Peat	Fowl	Cotton cloth (red, yellow, & blue)	Earrings
Milk	Raw silk	Fighting bulls	Fine raffia	Necklaces
Red rice	Zozoro cane	Slaves	Dyes	Arab trinkets
White rice	Split zozoro		Grid iron	Scissors
Beans	Dried zozoro		Iron pots	European cutlery
Sugarcane	Grass fuel		Axes	Arab cutlery
Sweet potato	Rice straw		Spades	European salt
Potato	Herana rushes (for brooms)		Handcuffs	
Boiled potato	Blue earth (for finishing pottery)		Chains	
Raw yam	Tobacco		Tripods	
Boiled yam	Oil		Spears	
Manioc	Grease		Knives	
Plantain	Ambrevade		Chisels	
Lemon	Ginger		Planes	
Pineapple	Saffron		Bayonets	
Maize	Tarminic		Silver chains	
Honey			Trinkets	
Garlic			Earthenware	
Chilies			Talismans	

Source: Chardenoux, "Journal" (1816), 174; Hastie, "Diary" (1817).

routes by the Bezanozano and Betsimisaraka. Radama I, the new king, faced a major dilemma. His father's victory in the civil wars that had raged in Imerina in the late 1700s was due to his capture of major domestic markets and trade routes. Subsequent earnings from slave exports paid for the imported arms and ammunition necessary to dispose of his rivals. Military might enabled him to consolidate his position through seizing further slave supply centers, like Vakinankaratra, and rival trade routes, such as the one forged by the Swahili from Iboina via Antsihanaka to the northeast coast.[26]

Radama I pursued his father's policy of military expansion. He immediately launched devastating attacks upon the Bezanozano of the Ankay "in order to eliminate any intermediary between him and the European traders" on the northeast coast and annexed the neighboring plateau regions of Imamo, Valalafotsy, and the populous cattle-country of Vonizongo. Further, he conquered and established Merina soldier colonies (*voanjo*) on the rich agricultural lands of north Betsileo and the Lake Alaotra region of Antsihanaka. By 1814, Merina-ruled territory had quadrupled in extent and the core of the future Merina empire been created. From it, a series of cattle and slave raids were launched on other peoples. In 1816, one such expedition returned from southwest Madagascar with a booty of 2,000 slaves and 4,000 cattle.[27] By 1816, Radama I had gained control over major slave sources to the south and west and seized sufficient cattle-grazing land to become an exporter of cattle. Also, in possible reaction to the attempt on his life in 1815, allegedly by a member of the eastern middleman groups, Radama I ordered his army to "completely destroy" the Ankay – a region that had formerly controlled the trade route to the east coast. However, the destruction wrought created famine conditions, further undermining security in the region.[28]

The British alliance thus came at an opportune moment. At first, Radama I rebuffed British pressure to ban slave exports, which financed the court and its expansionist policies. It was also the chief source of revenue of the Merina elite, leading slave traders whose support had been critical to

[26] Delivré, *L'histoire des rois*, 225–6; *GH* (1928), 268, 335; Daniel Couland, *Les Zafimaniry, un groupe éthnique de Madagascar à la poursuite de la forêt* (Tananarive, 1973), 106–14.

[27] Hastie, "Diary" (1817), 147, 211; *RH*, 21, 67; Raombana, "texts," 13; Oliver, *Madagascar* vol. I, 221–2, 227–9; *HR* vol. I, 441–2; vol. II, 658; vol. III, 120; Prud'homme, "Considérations sur les Sakalaves" *Notes, reconnaissances et explorations* 6 (1900), 414; *GH* (1908), 233, 235, 249–52, 268 and (1928), 235, 268, 335; C. Savaron, "Contribution à l'histoire de l'Imerina" in "Notes d'histoire malgache," *BAM* 14 (1931); G. S. Chapus, "le soin du bien-être du peuple sous le règne d'Andrianampoinimerina," *BAM* 30 (1951–2), 1; Jean Valette, *Études sur le règne de Radama I* (Tananarive, 1962), 19; Delivré, *L'histoire des rois*, 208, 225.

[28] Chazal, "Notes" (1816) *BL*.Add.18135, 24; Le Sage, "Mission" (1816), esp. 61–2, 85, 91–139; see also Chardenoux, "Journal du voyage fait dans l'intérieure" (Tamatave, 17 août).

Andrianampoinimerina's success in the civil wars and who comprised the most important segment of Radama I's own council.[29]

Nevertheless, Radama I felt members of the council to be too powerful and wished to increase the crown's power at their expense. A ban on slave exports would fundamentally weaken his councilors. In order to avoid it similarly undermining royal revenues, it was imperative that Imerina develop alternative export staples and secure an immediate outlet to the coast. In June 1817, a 40,000-strong Merina force marched on Toamasina, whose ruler, Jean René, had already accepted informal British protection. Only the arrival of the British navy deterred Radama I from annexing the entire northeastern littoral. Instead, the British agent Pye arranged a "Treaty of Amity and Alliance offensive and defensive between His Majesty RADAMA King of Ova [i.e., Imerina] and Dependencies on the one part and His Elder Brother JOHN RENE King of TAMATAVE and Dependencies on the other part."[30]

Radama I's boldness impressed Farquhar, who altered his conception of the Merina role within the envisaged British colonization of Madagascar. Thus, Farquhar announced Radama I to be "a most powerful and intelligent, but still semi barbarous and superstitious Monarch" who might hold "the destinies of the vast, populous, and fertile, but ill-treated Island of Madagascar entirely in his hands."[31] In a second treaty, signed in October 1817, Farquhar upgraded Radama I, naming him king of all Madagascar. Further, he promised him military aid to subjugate the rest of the island, technical assistance to promote the development of legitimate exports, and compensation for the ban on slave exports. He nevertheless impressed upon Radama, still ruler of a very small portion of Madagascar, his protectorate status. Insisting that Radama accept a resident British resident agent at the Merina court, he emphasized that

this happy and powerful and flourishing island of Mauritius is but as one drop of rain compared with the great ocean, when considered as a part of the wealth and power and glory of my Sovereign, whose friendship I will obtain for you.[32]

---

[29] Campbell, "Role of the London Missionary Society" vol. I, Ch. 4; Ludvig Munthe, Simon Ayache, and Charles Ravoajanahary, "Radama I et les Anglais. Les négociations de 1817 d'après les sources malgaches ("sorabe" inédits)," *Omaly sy Anio*, 3–4 (1976).

[30] *RH*, 89; see also Pye, "A summary (6–14 June 1817)," *PRO.CO*.167/34, 90–5; Hastie, "Diary" (1817); Le Sage, "Mission" (1816), 33.

[31] Farquhar to Stanfell, Port Louis, 7 and 22 Aug. 1817, *PRO.CO*.167/34, 97–9, 103–4.

[32] Farquhar to Radama I, Port Louis, 9 Aug. 1817, *PRO.CO*.167/34, 85; see also *idem* to Stanfell, 22 Aug. 1817; "Treaty between Radama and Governor Farquhar," Tamatave, 23 Oct. 1817, in *Papers relating to the Abolition of the Slave Trade in the Mauritius, 1817–1829* 18, *HCPP* (1821), 356–7; "Correspondance de Jean René et Sir Robert Farquhar" (Jean Valette, ed.), *BAM* 45 (1967), 71–98; Ellis, *History of Madagascar* vol. II, 140–2, 163–5, 243; "Registre de Rabezandrina," 7 – *ANM*.

When Farquhar took the treaty to Britain for ratification, Gage John Hall, his temporary replacement, repudiated the Merina alliance and downscaled the importance of Madagascar in Mauritian foreign policy. This had two main repercussions: the slave export trade broke out afresh, and René negotiated a French alliance and quickly conquered Betsimisaraka, Betanimena, and the Ankay, gaining effective control of the main trade routes between the highland interior and the northeast coast. Hastie estimated that, as a result of the renewed slave trade, Toamasina quadrupled in size from 1818 to 1820, eventually housing 60 European slave traders.[33]

For Radama I, this was a catastrophe. The 1817 expedition to Toamasina had created a foreign trade outlet for Imerina, with immediately beneficial results – the average price of foreign imports fell by more than one-third. Similarly, conquest of the Ankay plain gave the Merina a major source of cattle, an alternative export to slaves. Initially, too, the resurgence of slave exports that followed Hall's refusal to honor the treaty benefited the crown. In 1817, Radama raised the slave export tax from $1 to $2.50, a head without provoking the indignation of the slave trading elite, which was relieved that the ban on slave exports had not been maintained. However, René's campaigns blocked Imerina's newly won outlet to the coast and severely disrupted its foreign trade. The influx of foreign currency was again curtailed as export earnings fell from approximately $200,000 in 1810 and $22,500 in 1817 to a low of $1,500 by 1820, a movement reflected in average individual slave prices on the Merina market which plummeted from $45 in 1817 to only $3 in 1820.[34]

The British Alliance and Economic Crisis in Imerina, 1820–1825

In 1820, following Farquhar's return to Mauritius, the Britanno–Merina treaty was renewed. Radama I believed that, despite the slave export ban, the treaty

[33] Le Sage, "Mission" (1816), 26–7, 61–2; Hastie, "Diary" (1817), 130; idem, "Diary" (1820), 466–7; Samuel Pasfield Oliver, "General Hall and the export slave trade from Madagascar. A Statement and a Vindication," AAMM 12 (1888); Decary, "La reddition de Tamatave," 59–60; L. Aujas, "Notes sur l'histoire des Betsimisaraka," BAM 4 (1905–6), 108–11; Jean Valette, "Rainandriamampandry, historien de Jean René," BAM 48/I-II (1970), 1–3.

[34] Chapelier, "Lettres en mission à Madagascar de décembre 1803 en mai 1805" (ed. M. Jully), BAM (1904), 34; Chazal, "notes" (1816), 24; Chardenoux, "Journal" (1816), 163; N. Leminier, "Notes sur une excursion faite dans l'intérieur de l'Île de Madagascar en 1825," BdM 292 (1970), 797; Hastie, "Diary" (1817), 137, 147, 157, 164, 170, 177, 188–9, 197, 211; idem, "Diary" (1820), 489; RH, 21, 67, 82, 93–4; Raombana, "texts," 13; Ellis, History of Madagascar vol. II, 16, 198; Chapus & Mondain, "Un chapitre inconnu," 117; HR vol. I, 441–2; vol. II, 658; vol. III, 120; Prud'homme, "Contribution à l'histoire de l'Imerina" in "Notes d'histoire malgache," BAM 14 (1931); Chapus, "Le soin du bien être," 1; Jean Valette, Études, 19; Oliver, Madagascar vol. I, 221–2, 227–9, 252–3; idem, "General Hall," 678; GH (1908), 113, 233, 235, 249–52, 268 and (1928), 113, 235, 268, 297, 335; Campbell, "Madagascar and the Slave Trade," 206, 208.

would benefit him. First, Farquhar promised the Merina crown compensation for lost slave export earnings of $20,000 per annum in goods and cash ($1,000 in gold and $1,000 in silver coins). British technical assistance would generate rapid economic expansion. British military aid would secure for the Merina a permanent outlet to the coast and assist in subjugating other Malagasy peoples. The result would be an island empire, the natural resources and trade of which would become a Merina monopoly.[35] Severe discontent among the elite erupted in the female revolt of 1822, which Radama ruthlessly suppressed.[36] Subsequently, he promised those who served him honor and wealth from imperial expansion in the form of battle booty, fertile land, and captives who, instead of being sold, could support their masters in a life of luxury.[37]

By 1822, cash crop plantations, workshops (manufacturing furniture, clothes, and leather goods), and schools had all been established. A sound basis appeared to have been laid for the growth of export alternatives to slaves, with the associated prospect of a strong positive balance of trade and a plentiful money supply. Nevertheless, by 1825 it was obvious to the Merina crown that the Britanno–Merina treaty had failed to fulfill its promise, and Radama I moved decisively toward autarky. For this there were five main reasons, all related to the British alliance: the transfer of foreign trade to areas independent of Merina rule; insufficient compensation for the slave export ban; failure to develop alternative exports; the cost of empire; and the threat of British free trade imperialism.

By 1825, Merina garrisons were installed in all major east coast ports, but on the west coast only at Mahajanga. All foreign traders, except the British, who under the terms of the 1820 treaty paid 5 percent (ad valorem), were required to pay 10 percent customs duties in Merina-held ports. This was deeply resented because foreign merchants had before the Merina invasion negotiated invariably lower duties separately with individual east coast chiefs. In addition, demand for slaves grew with the wholesale switch to monoculture sugar production on the Mascarenes in the 1820s.

In consequence, foreign traders transferred their activity from Merina ports to East Africa and to independent west coast ports of Madagascar, where duties were cheaper and slaves available. The proportion of the Réunionnais merchant fleet trading in non-Merina ports increased from 42 percent in 1819 to a peak of 61 percent in 1823. Moreover, they were followed by Mauritian merchants

---

[35] Farquhar, "Minute" on Madagascar (Port Louis, Aug. 1822), *PRO.CO*.167/63; Campbell, "Role of the London Missionary Society" vol. I, 115.

[36] Gwyn Campbell, "Larcency in the Highlands of Madagascar" review article in *Slavery & Abolition* 23.1 (2002), 137–46.

[37] *RH* in Munthe et al., "Radama I et les Anglais," 33.

("British" from 1810) incapable of meeting Merina demands for export duty payments in cash because of a severe currency crisis on Mauritius. Commodities were cheaper on the west coast and could also be purchased by barter. One consequence was that slave imports into the Mascarenes grew, from between 8,700 and 12,200 slaves annually from 1815 to 1817 to between 13,300 and 16,800 a year by 1830. Most were shipped to Réunion, but many were smuggled from there to Mauritius.[38]

After the slave export ban, Merina royal revenue slumped dramatically, from $32,927 in 1821 to $22,360 in 1822. By 1824 it had increased to $50,000, but still fell far short of crown requirements.[39] Farquhar had promised an annual compensation valued at $20,000. However, from 1820 to 1826, Radama received in cash $18,000, with the rest comprising military and other goods. Total compensation amounted to $104,853 worth of specie and goods, $35,147 short of that promised (see Table 3.2). Had the ban not been imposed, royal revenue, raised mostly in cash from the slave export tax for the period 1820–6, would probably have totaled between $198,310 and $204,680.[40]

In addition, the treaty failed to compensate Radama for the profit that would have accrued from the export of royal slaves, estimated at a minimum of $1,049,580 for the period 1820–6. The compensation may also be calculated in terms of the value of gunpowder, a royal monopoly, which Radama I imported in exchange for slaves. The domestic retail value of gunpowder obtained in · exchange for potential royal slave exports from 1820–6 would have amounted to at least $10 million (although in reality most of the powder would have been stockpiled in imperial arsenals). Under treaty compensation, Radama I received a maximum of $1,760 worth of gunpowder up to 1823. Thereafter, he was obliged to pay for additional imports in cash.[41] Furthermore, no Merina slave dealer other than the king received compensation for loss of slave export earnings, which over the period 1820–6 would probably have totaled about $2.5 million. The slave export ban inevitably reduced incomes, the money

[38] Despite assertions – based on Réunionnais records – to the contrary – Claude Wanquet, *Fragments pour une histoire des économies et sociétés de plantation à la Réunion* (Université de la Réunion, 1989), 205; see Campbell, "Madagascar and the Slave Trade," 206, 208; *idem*, "Role of the London Missionary Society" vol. I, 174–6, 189–90.

[39] Campbell, "Role of the London Missionary Society" vol. I, 172–7; Duhaut-Cilly, "Notices sur le royaume d'Emirne, sur la capitale de Tananarivou et sur le gouvernement de Rhadama" (1825), in Jean Valette, "Deux documents français sur Madagascar en 1825; les rapports Duhaut-Cilly et Frère," *BAM* 16/I–II (1968), 238–9.

[40] Farquhar, "Minute" (1822); "Expenses incurred by the Government on Mauritius on account of Madagascar," *HCPP* 26 (1828), 72–82; Farquhar to Earl Bathurst, Port Louis, 29 July 1822, *PRO.CO*.167/63; Campbell, "Madagascar and the Slave Trade," 206, 208.

[41] Hastie, "Diary" (1817), 188; *idem*, "Diary" (1820), 472.

TABLE 3.2. *Financial Compensation for the Merina Ban on Slave Exports 1820–6*

Currency	1820	1821	1822	1823	1824	1825	1826
Gold Mohurs	750						
$ Spanish	1,250		4,000	2,000		4,000	
$ Currency		5,851	37,000	9,070	6,430	12,785	
£ Sterling							3,667
Total equivalent in $ Spanish at current exchange rates	8,000	3,433	26,932	9,490	5,841	15,762	15,717

Source: Calculations based on data from "Expenses incurred" (1828), 72–82; Hastie, "Diary" (1817), 493.

supply, and demand for imports.[42] The Merina crown lost not only slave export earnings (sale and tax) but also, as commerce stagnated, general trade duty revenue: Domestic market levies comprised 20 percent of declared Merina trader profits, $4 per slave sold, and 2 percent of the price of goods purchased from Indian and Swahili merchants[43].

Radama I had realized at the outset that a ban on slave exports from Imerina would weaken his position and strengthen that of non-Merina competitors. He had not foreseen the further threat to his position posed by inadequate treaty compensation and the transfer of foreign trade from the Merina-controlled east coast to the independent reaches of the west coast. There remained two other potentially beneficial outcomes of the British alliance: the growth of alternative exports to replace slaves and the subjection of political and commercial rivals through the rapid creation of an island empire under British-backed Merina rule.

To assist in the development of an alternative export sector, Farquhar despatched to Madagascar agricultural experts and artisans equipped with seeds and tools. Nevertheless, by 1825 attempts to promote legitimate exports had largely collapsed. In 1823, Radama I wrote in desperation to Farquhar that "we are doing all in our power, neglecting nothing; we do not lack the manpower, but we do lack people capable of instructing us. . . . [P]lanting wheat is easy, but knowing how to utilise it is another thing altogether."[44]

---

[42] This probably underpinned the 1822, female protest against the pro-British policies of the Merina crown – see Campbell, "Larceny in the Highlands of Madagascar."

[43] Jones and Griffiths to LMS, Antananarivo, 2 June 1824, *SOAS/LMS-MIL*, B2.F1.JA; Hastie, "Diary" (1817), 143, 148, 188; *idem*, "Diary" (1820), 484, 493, 496; *idem*, "Diary" (1822); Hastie to Barry, Antananarivo, 22 April 1824, *PRO.CO*.167/78, pt.I, 43; Mayeur, "Voyage au pays d'ancove" (1777), 177–80; Duhaut-Cilly, "Notice sur le royaume d'Emirne," 238–9; Alfred Grandidier, "Property among the Malagasy" (trans. James Sibree), *AAMM* 22 (1898), 228, 230.

[44] Radama I to Farquhar, Antananarivo, 13 May 1823, *PRO.CO*.167/66.

The agricultural projects foundered chiefly because of a failure by the "British" agents to appreciate Malagasy conditions. In the temperate central highlands, which were characterized by sharp climatic contrasts and poor soil, efforts to grow a variety of vegetables and wheat and oats in European fashion failed.[45] The other main attempt from 1822 to introduce cash crops, particularly wheat and oats, at Mahavelona, on the northeast coast, was initially promising. Farquhar noted in 1823 that they "have already introduced the use of the plough and have succeeded in disciplining their oxen to freight work and carrying."[46] However, that venture also foundered due to a failure to account for and adapt to local circumstances. Tropical conditions prevailed at Mahavelona, where temperatures were too high and daylight hours too few for essentially temperate climate plants. In addition, the misty rain characteristic of the east coast encouraged fungal infections to which wheat and oats were prone. Crops on the east coast were also more vulnerable to destruction by insects, animals, and cyclones than those grown on the plateau. The failure of the first year's crop at Mahavelona was blamed on the destruction wrought by wild boars, although reputedly the soil was too saline to cultivate due to cyclones and other storms that caused frequent oceanic inundations.[47]

Craft production for export also met with little success, despite the influx of a number of skilled European and Creole artisans. Supplies were a major problem. For instance, John Canham, an LMS artisan, was initially prevented from tanning by the lack of lime and leather. As a substitute for lime, he sought bark, the nearest reliable sources of which were in the eastern forest, some 48 km from his workshop in Antananarivo.[48] A more ludicrous arrangement was made concerning leather. The Malagasy possessed vast herds of bullocks, a staple export, on hoof or salted, to the Mascarenes. However, no domestic skinning industry existed, and the Malagasy ate beef with the hide attached. Consequently, Canham had to import from Mauritius leather taken from Malagasy cattle exported there.[49] By contrast, Thomas Rowlands, an LMS weaver, did locate plentiful supplies of locally spun cotton. However, as Malagasy spinners

---

[45] Mayeur, "Voyage au pays d'ancove" (1785), 224; Hastie, "Diary" (1817), 160, 187; see also GH (1928), 3–7, 11, 53, 60–1.

[46] Farquhar quoted in *RH*, 14–15; see also *RH*, 161, 178, 403, 406, 456.

[47] Sémerville, "Souvenirs de Sainte-Marie," 50–1; Hastie, "Diary" (1822); *idem*, "Diary" (1822–3), *PRO.CO*.167/66; Oliver, *Madagascar* vol. I, 285, 451–2; Sibree, *A Naturalist*, 53; Robequain, *Madagascar*, 50–1.

[48] Hastie, "Extract" in "Report of the Examination of the Schools" (17 March 1825), *SOAS/LMS-MIL*, B2.F2.JA; GH (1908), 256.

[49] Hastie, "Diary" (1817), 128; Jones and Griffiths to LMS (n.d.), *SOAS/LMS-MIL*, B1.F5.JA; Canham to Burder, Ifenoarivo, 5 Nov. 1824, *SOAS/LMS-MIL*, B2.F1.JC; *RH*, 16–17; *HR* vols. III–IV, 927.

worked on a seasonal basis, they could not provide him with a regular supply. As a result, Rowland's two looms were running at only 25 percent of capacity by early 1824.[50]

Most raw materials had to be imported or, if found within Madagascar, transported a considerable distance. Apart from a few kilometers of paved road in Antananarivo, routes in Madagascar were primitive: horses, mules, and wheeled carts were largely unknown, and human porterage was the sole means for the carriage of people and freight. In consequence, transport costs were staggering. Brigandry, endemic in the eastern forest, entailed further losses, through both theft and protection costs.[51]

In part, the price of European artisan production also reflected the living costs of foreigners in Madagascar. The artisans initially received a Mauritius government subsidy, but this steadily diminished, the expectation being that they would become self-supporting within a few years. They lived more modestly than the clerical missionaries, one of whom commented that whereas the most respectable Merina family could live comfortably on $120 a year, a white missionary family would require a minimum of $1,000. Nevertheless, when artisan wages were added to the costs of production, the price of the finished product was beyond the reach of ordinary Merina. For example, at $2 a pair, Canham's shoes were effectively restricted to rich Malagasy, who preferred to purchase imported luxury shoes. Moreover, sale in foreign markets was precluded by high transport costs to the coast. Success attended only artisans possessing an elite clientele or crown contracts.[52]

Sale of local European-made goods was also limited by indigenous competition. Overhead costs were lower for the Malagasy, who employed simple, labor-intensive production methods in their own homes. Sufficient local demand existed for some crafts, such as ironwork, to sustain full-time specialists. However, production costs for indigenous craftsmen were comparatively so low that George Chick, the LMS blacksmith, made profits only on fancy ironwork for the local luxury market.[53] Cotton and silk cloth weaving was a ubiquitous

[50] Jones and Griffiths to LMS (n.d.), *SOAS/LMS-MIL*, B2.F1.JB; William Ellis, *Three Visits to Madagascar during the years 1853–1854–1856* (London, 1859), 341–2; Keturah Jeffreys, *The Widowed Missionary's Journal* (Southampton, 1827), 173–6.

[51] See Chapters 8 and 10.

[52] Hastie, "Diary" (1817); *idem*, "Diary" (1820); Canham to Burder, Ifenoarivo, 5 Nov. 1824, *SOAS/LMS-MIL*, B2.F1.JC; Oliver, *Madagascar* vol. I, 307, 318–19; GH (1928), 33; Campbell, "Role of the London Missionary Society" vol. I, 183; for transport see *idem*, "Labour and the Transport Problem," 341–56; for brigandage, see *idem*, *Forced Labour* (forthcoming).

[53] Jones and Griffiths to LMS (May 1823), *SOAS/LMS-MIL*, B1.F5.JA; *idem* to Burder, Antananarivo, 16 Dec. 1825, *SOAS/LMS-MIL*, B2.F2.JC; Rowlands to Jones and Griffiths, Amparibe, 15 May 1827, *SOAS/LMS-MIL*, B2.F4.JA; "Extracts of the Minutes of the Madagascar Mission" (4 May–8 July 1829), *SOAS/LMS-MIL*, B3.F3.JA; Oliver, *Madagascar* vol. II, 82, 91; Ellis,

female activity practiced from June to August, in the off-peak agricultural (dry) season, when most festivals were held and demand for new clothes peaked. Rowlands simply could not compete with indigenous weavers who had significantly lower production costs. As Hastie commented, "The demand for native growth and manufactures, which is sold at a price materially lower than the purchaser of the raw article can afford, does not admit of his attempting a competition in weaving."[54] The same problems were encountered from 1821 to 1823 by Savigny (Savinery), a Mauritian weaver, and by Raolombelona, one of the nine Merina youths dispatched to Britain in 1820, who on his return could not profitably adapt Manchester techniques of weaving and dyeing to Malagasy conditions.[55] Moreover, unlike their counterparts in metalwork, European weavers failed to corner any of the domestic luxury market. Elite demand was met by Indian, Swahili, British, and American importers, whose fine velvets, silks, and printed and plain cottons were cheaper, despite transport costs. For example, Manchester cottons fetched from $3.50 to $4 a piece in Antananarivo, compared to $6 a piece that was the cheapest of Rowland's range.[56]

Domestic sales were also limited by "the great poverty of these people since the slave traffic is stopped."[57] Because of the ban on slave exports, the slave population of Imerina increased to constitute 33 percent of the total population by 1830, sometimes reaching 66 percent (around 30,000) in Antananarivo. These slaves had little purchasing power. The majority of Merina was little better off for, as Canham stated in 1824, "The fact is there is no money in the country, nor any channel to bring it. I am often told by the people that when they sold slaves they had plenty of money, but since the slave trade ceased they are become impoverished."[58]

History of Madagascar vol. I, 311–13; G. S. Chapus, *Quatre-vingts années d'influences européennes en Imerina (1815–1895)* (Tananarive, 1925), 80.

[54] Hastie, "Report on Missionary Instruction in Ovah" (17 March 1824), and *idem*, "Report on the Schools superintended by the Missionaries at Tananarive" (19 April 1824), *PRO.CO.*167/78, pt. II; see also Campbell, "Role of the London Missionary Society" vol. I, 186; for West African comparisons of the relative costs of low- and high-technology cloth production see J. Bray, "The economics of traditional cloth production in Iseyin, Nigeria," *Economic Development and Cultural Change* 17 (1969), and M. Johnson, "Technology, Competition and African Crafts," in C. Dewey and A. G. Hopkins (eds.), *The Imperial Impact: Studies in the Economic History of Africa and India* (London, 1978).

[55] *RH*, 96–7; *RA*, 297, 300; Barry to Hastie, Port Louis, 12 May 1823, *PRO.CO.*167/77; Freeman to Burder, Antananarivo, 23 Oct. 1827, *SOAS/LMS-MIL*, B2.F5.

[56] *RH*, 6–7; Jones and Griffiths to LMS, Antananarivo, 2 June 1824, *SOAS/LMS-MIL*, B2.F1.JA; Rowlands to Burder, Antananarivo, 17 June 1824, *SOAS/LMS-MIL*, B2.F1.JB; Rowlands to LMS, Antsahadinta, 13 June 1826, *SOAS/LMS-MIL*, B2.F3.JA; Jones and Griffiths to Burder, Antananarivo, 30 May 1827, *SOAS/LMS-MIL*, B2.F3.JA.

[57] Jones and Griffiths to LMS, Antananarivo, 2 June 1824, *SOAS/LMS-MIL*, B2.F1.JA.

[58] Canham to Burder, Ifenoarivo, 5 Nov. 1824, *SOAS/LMS-MIL*, B2.F1.JD; see also Campbell, "Role of the London Missionary Society" vol. I, 171–88.

The cost of imperial expansion was the fourth major contributory factor to the economic crisis of the mid-1820s. The crown was entitled to about 25 percent of all booty seized during military campaigns. However, Radama I had promised the Merina elite compensation for the slave export ban in the form of battle booty, and they determined to reap immediate benefits from imperial expansion, even at the crown's expense. Senior army officers led campaigns that devastated conquered provinces, plundering and laying waste much fertile territory. Thus, it was remarked of the northeast coast in 1825, "Many of the conquered provinces are almost depopulated because of destruction or flight by the vanquished."[59] Consequently, rather than boost royal coffers with booty and additional tax revenue, campaigns of imperial expansion emptied them of money to pay for armaments and other military equipment. As Louis Blancard explained, "As his Majesty Radama, having subjugated almost all Madagascar, has been obliged to greatly expand his army and to maintain it continually on a war footing, this has incurred a growth in expenditure which has forced him to increase his revenues."[60]

In addition, Blancard's estimation of Merina military progress was too sanguine. Merina forces had by 1825 imposed firm military rule over only about one-third of Madagascar. Moreover, military expansion was also costly in human terms. Recruitment for imperial campaigns was initially restricted to Merina conscripts, up to half of whom perished annually, mainly through malaria and starvation. They had to be replaced to keep army numbers from falling, but such was Radama's determination to create an island empire that between 1822 and 1824, he increased the size of his standing army from 12,000 to 17,500 men. It was a vicious circle in which soldiers were drawn from the small farmer class who also paid a special tax to support the army, yet while serving under imperial colors, remained unsalaried. As recruitment intensified, from approximately 6,000 soldiers per annum in 1822 to 14,250 in 1824, and 8,750 a year thereafter, the number of cultivators dwindled. Those who remained were increasingly the older and less able-bodied. Consequently, farmers first channeled slave labor into subsistence agriculture – instead of into cash crop cultivation, as had been envisaged at the time of the 1820 treaty. However, as their impoverishment grew, cultivators were obliged to sell their slaves, who were thus increasingly transferred into the hands of the court elite.[61]

Older Merina commented that their country was even more depopulated in 1825 than during the Merina civil wars of the late 1700s, a fact that had grave

---

[59] Duhaut-Cilly, "Notice sur le royaume d'Emirne," 237.

[60] Louis Blancard to Governor of Mauritius, in Chapus & Mondain, "Un chapitre inconnu," 117; see also Duhaut-Cilly, "Notice sur le royaume d'Emirne," 238–9.

[61] See Chapters 7 and 9.

implications for the fragile agricultural base of the economy. In addition, Merina craftsmen were drafted into the army in order to maintain weaponry and to build roads, bridges, and forts. Demand for labor by the military alone was such that Radama I could not contemplate acquiescing to the request from Mascarene planters for Malagasy contract workers, even though such migrants would have earned badly needed foreign exchange and helped stem the shift in foreign trade to the independent west coast.[62]

Finally, Radama I became convinced that the British wished to colonize Madagascar. The first draft of the unratified 1817 treaty clearly revealed Farquhar's designs to systematically colonize Madagascar with British Mauritian settlers.[63] The free trade clauses of 1817, reiterated in the 1820 treaty, threatened Radama I's sovereignty in a more insidious manner. In 1822, European traders and artisans refused to pay the king a 20 percent tax on their profits and the newly established LMS mission erupted in internal disputes. All this raised considerable doubts for Radama as to his ability to control the activity of British residents in his domains, particularly as they claimed extraterritorial rights under the British treaty. Such apprehension appeared confirmed by Farquhar's order to the British agent at the Merina court in 1822 to "request of Radama to transmit to me copies of all communications which he may make to, or receive from other Governments, relative to the sovereignty of Madagascar or other public matters of transcendent interest to its prosperity."[64] Indeed, Farquhar intimated that he might use force should British interests in Madagascar be threatened:

The establishment [i.e., the British colony] in Madagascar is yet comparatively small and in its infancy. It is but the seed and germ that time will develop and extend, and it is necessary to look forward and provide against contingencies, so liable to occur, and which, unless prudently met, might prove highly disadvantageous, if not fatal to the British interests in that island.[65]

Free trade as envisaged by the British treaty would thus lead to the colonization of Madagascar by Mauritians. This implied a foreign economic and political domination deeply offensive to Merina tradition and pride. It would also dash Radama I's dreams of using the British alliance as a springboard to create an island empire, which might eventually gain mastery over the western Indian

---

[62] Hastie, "Diary" (1820); *idem* to Barry, Antananarivo, 22 April 1824, *PRO.CO.*167/77; Oliver, *Madagascar* vol. II, 160; GH (1908), 371; Bojer, "Journal," in Jean Valette (ed.), "L'Imerina en 1822–1825 d'après les journaux de Bojer et d'Hilsenburg," extrait du *BdM* (avril-mai, 1963), 23; Ellis, *History of Madagascar* vol. I, 119; James Cameron, *Recollections of Mission Life in Madagascar in the early days of the LMS Mission* (Antananarivo, 1874), 24–6.

[63] Campbell, "Role of the London Missionary Society" vol. I, 103–9.

[64] Farquhar to Hastie, Mauritius, 30 April 1822, *PRO.CO.*167/34.

[65] *Ibid.*

Ocean and stand as an equal beside Britain and France.[66] It is possible that Radama I had decided to break with the British treaty as early as 1824. However, only in 1826, following the death of Hastie, the British agent, did the Merina monarch radically revise imperial plans, reject free trade, and adopt an autarkic economic policy. Ranavalona I, after ascending to the Merina throne in 1828, extended her predecessor's autarkic policies with the same end in mind: the fostering of national economic growth and the promotion of imperial Merina power.

This change in Merina policy clashed with British imperial and free trade interests in the region. From the outset, Radama I had refused extraterritorial judicial rights for Europeans residing in his territories. In 1823, in Betsimisaraka province, and in 1824, in Imerina, he infringed the British treaty by upholding the traditional Merina law that no foreigner might gain freehold property in the island. In 1825, he imposed 10-year residence permits on foreigners living in Imerina, including the LMS missionaries who were considered part of the official British presence in Madagascar. At the same time, restrictions were placed upon the freedom of movement of resident and visiting foreigners, all of whom were closely surveilled. The Merina court instructed missionaries where to reside and rejected their plans to evangelize distant provinces. Foreigners wishing to travel any distance had to apply to the court for passports that were subject to regular inspections en route.[67]

However, more central to autarkic plans were state regulation of foreign trade, promotion of industry, and the creation of an island empire whose resources were to form the basis of autarkic economic development – issues explored in subsequent chapters.

---

[66] Farquhar (1821) in A Resident, *Madagascar Past and Present* (London, 1847), 196, 198; Farquhar to Bathurst, Port Louis, 20 May 1823, and Darling to Bathurst, Mauritius, 16 June 1823, *PRO.CO*.167/66; for the imperial ambitions of Radama I see Daniel Tyerman and George Bennet, *Journal of Voyages and Travels, 1821–1829* (ed. James Montgomery) II (London, 1831), 531; *RH*, 79–95; Hastie, "Diary" (1817); Munthe et al., "Radama I et les Anglais," 9–104; Deschamps, *histoire*, 151.

[67] Jean René to Farquhar, 4 Dec. 1821, in "Correspondance de Jean René à Sir R. T. Farquhar," 83; Raymond Decary, "Documents historiques relatifs à l'établissement française de Sainte-Marie sous la restauration, *BAM* 13 (1930), 65; *RA*, 295; Ellis, *History of Madagascar* vol. I, 377–8; *idem, Madagascar Revisited* (London, 1867), 247–8; copies of correspondence between Freeman and Johns, and Ranavalona I, *SOAS/LMS-MIL*, B4.F3.JC and B4.F3.JD; Rabary, *Ny Daty Malaza* vol. I (Tananarive, 1930), 23, 26–7; *HR* vols. III–IV, 928; Campbell, "Labour and the Transport Problem," 341–3.

4   Industry and Agriculture, 1820–1895

Introduction

The imperial Merina era witnessed an industrial experiment, which was arguably unique in Tropical Africa for four main reasons: It occurred in the precolonial era; was contemporaneous with industrial experiments in Western Europe and North America; was largely a result of local enterprise; and involved concentrated, large-scale, and machine-based production. The attempt to industrialize failed by mid-century, industrial efforts thereafter concentrating on gold mining. This chapter examines development in the industrial and agricultural sectors between 1820 and 1895.

The First Industrial Phase, 1820–1861

Proto-industrialization?

The industrial experiment in nineteenth-century Madagascar is possibly best analyzed in the context of *proto-industrialization*, described by Franklin Mendels as a necessary transitory phase between a traditional rural and modern industrial economy. Some neo-Marxists have even identified a proto-industrial "mode of production" defined by Mendels as "the simultaneous occurrence of three ingredients within the framework of a region: rural industries, external destinations, and symbiosis of rural industry within the regional development of a commercial agriculture."[1]

---

[1] Quoted in D.C. Coleman, "Proto-Industrialization: A Concept Too Many," *Economic History Review* 36.3 (1983), 437; see also Peter Kriedte, Hans Medick and Jurgen Schlumbohm, *Industrialization Before Industrialization* (Cambridge, 1981), 4.

In focusing upon export orientated woolen, linen, and hemp textiles in Europe from 1780 to 1820, the proto-industrialization school posits a critical role for rural handicrafts in preparing the path to full industrialization. The development of a domestic textile industry led to uncontrolled population growth within the rural handicraft sector and interregional specialization. It also facilitated the entry of capitalist forces into a feudal agrarian structure. However, the tendency for the population of rural handicraft workers to rise irrespective of the state of the manufacturing industry, and the obstacle their traditional value system presented to the growth of large-scale modern industry, meant that the agrarian manufacturing system was doomed to failure. It either transformed itself into a capital-intensive modern manufacturing sector or experienced pauperization and deindustrialization. The proto-industrialization school has attracted severe criticism, notably for neglecting the role of other rural industries, the dynamics of urban industry, and regional and international differences in the structure of industries and for overlooking the complexities of demographic trends in the immediate preindustrial era.[2]

The concept of proto-industrialization provides a useful context within which to discuss industrial experiments in the non-European world, including Madagascar, provided that major criticisms of the theory are considered. Mendels' definition of proto-industrialization may at first appear of potentially great relevance to precolonial Africa, which was overwhelmingly rural and characterized by an almost total absence of urban industry. Peter Kriedte et al. posit that proto-industrialization was more likely to develop in infertile mountainous areas where an inability to earn a livelihood from agriculture obliged the small farmer to supplement the family income through recourse to handicraft industry.[3] This focuses attention on regions such as highland Ethiopia and Madagascar. However, claims that Ethiopia attempted industrialization have long been discredited.[4] By contrast, nineteenth-century Madagascar witnessed a serious attempt at large-scale industrial production that fundamentally marked the subsequent history of the island.

In late eighteenth-century Madagascar, rural industry was most concentrated and developed in Imerina. Due to a temperate climate, infertile soil, and

---

[2] Coleman, "Proto-Industrialization," 435–48; Pierre Jeannin, "La proto-industrialization: développement ou impasse? (Note critique)," *Annales – économies – sociétés – civilisations* 35.1 (1980), 52–65.

[3] Coleman, "Proto-Industrialization," 438, 440–1.

[4] See, e.g., Charles W. McClellan, "Land, Labor, and Coffee: The South's Role in Ethiopian Self-Reliance, 1889–1935," *African Economic History* 9 (1980), 69–77; Timothy Derek Fernyhough, "Serfs, Slaves and Shefta: Modes of Production in Southern Ethiopia from the late nineteenth century to 1941" Ph.D., University of Illinois at Urbana-Champaign, 1986.

mountainous terrain, the small cultivator there was obliged to be versatile within agricultural production. At the same time, the seasonal nature of agricultural effort permitted the practice of other tasks during the slack season. A considerable sexual division of craft labor developed. The male was skilled with the ax, hammer, and chisel; could fell, shape, and carry trees for lumber and fuel; join timber; construct and thatch houses; quarry, shape, and transport large stones; and build tombs. Females wove silk, cotton, and vegetable fibers into cloth, mats and baskets, and manufactured pottery, utilizing in both cases a number of designs and dyes. Both sexes constructed stills and produced alcohol, primarily from sugarcane.[5]

Mendels argues that the more time a family devoted to handicrafts, the greater its premium upon children as human capital investment and the greater its dependence upon external provisions – hence the development of a symbiotic relationship between rural industry and agriculture leading to regional specialization.[6] The number of people engaged in major or full-time handicraft production in Imerina cannot be quantified. However, by the late eighteenth century, agricultural production was sufficient to sustain a substantial nonagricultural population. This in turn led to intra- and interregional specialization, characterized by considerable commercialization of agriculture and the sale of rural Merina craftwork outside the province. Unlike Russia in its proto-industrial stage, a well-developed market network served domestic demand in Imerina at the start of the nineteenth century.[7]

The Role of the State

The proto-industrialization school has largely relied on the British model of successful transition from rural textile handicraft to modern factory machine production. However, Pierre Jeannin and D. C. Coleman have underscored the importance of other industries, notably mining and metalworking, which involved a greater concentration of capital.[8] Christian Vandenbroeke, reconsidering the issue of proto-industrialization in eighteenth-century Flanders, the region upon which Mendels based his theory, identifies 10 variables as decisive in the transition to modern industry: the state of domestic industry, the

---

[5] See Chapters 1 and 2.

[6] Mendels, "Proto-industrialization," 245.

[7] Gwyn Campbell, "Slavery and *Fanompoana*: The Structure of Forced Labour in Imerina (Madagascar), 1790–1861" *JAH* 29 (1988), 467; see also introduction.

[8] Jeannin, "La proto-industrialization," 61–2; Coleman, "Proto-Industrialization," 443.

state of the agricultural sector, the importance and growth of foreign trade, economic policy, the economic infrastructure, demographic structure and growth, human capital, the activity rate, domestic demand, and wage costs. The relative importance of these factors varied according to the socioeconomic structure of each individual country. Recent revisionist work on late eighteenth-century and early nineteenth-century western Europe indicates that the engine of economic growth in Flanders might have been lower wage costs. In France, technological and economic innovations (involving, among other factors, factories and market strategy) preceded those of Britain, whose own motor of growth was less nascent industry than a progressive agricultural sector allied to the expanding financial muscle of the city and other parts of the service sector.[9]

Although a rural basis for economic development existed, the catalyst for growth in Imerina, as in seventeenth-century Russia, was the state, which was pushed into the role of entrepreneur by the failure of the British alliance.[10] When in 1825–6, Radama I rejected the British free trade alliance and adopted autarkic policies,[11] his priority was to garner indigenous resources and adopt and adapt Western technology in order to stimulate industrial self-sufficiency, notably in textiles and armaments. The long-term aim was to produce textiles, cash crops, and forest products such as wax and rubber for export as well as to increase the traditional export of provisions (namely bullocks, meat, and rice) and animal products (especially hides).[12]

Economic progress and higher government revenue would be achieved through the implementation of high tariffs and the regulation of industry and

---

[9] Thus, Vandenbroeke argues that lower wage costs were the engine of economic growth of Flanders; Robert Aldrich supports François Crouzet's contention that technological and economic innovations, preceding those adopted in Britain, fomented French development; while for Britain, Peter Cain and A. G. Hopkins stress the rising productivity of an agricultural sector reformed by a progressive and commercially orientated landed class in alliance with a service sector of growing importance: Christian Vandenbroeke, "The Regional Economy of Flanders and Industrial Modernization in the Eighteenth Century: a Discussion," *Journal of European Economic History* 16.1 (1987), 163–70; Robert Aldrich, "Late-Comer or Early-Starter? New Views on French Economic History," *Journal of European Economic History* 16.1 (1987), 91, 95–6; N. F. R. Crafts, "British Economic Growth, 1700–1831: A Review of the Evidence," *Economic History Review* 36.2 (1983), 177–99; P. J. Cain and A. G. Hopkins, "Gentlemanly Capitalism and British Expansion Overseas I. The Old Colonial System, 1688–1850," *Economic History Review* 39.4 (1986), 504, 510–11.

[10] For a comparison of the role of the Russian state in fostering industrial growth, see Olga Crisp, "Labour and Industrialization in Russia," in *Cambridge Economic History of Europe* (Cambridge, 1978), Ch. 7; for early developments in agriculture, see Chapter 1.

[11] See Chapter 3.

[12] Gwyn Campbell, "The Adoption of Autarky in Imperial Madagascar, 1820–1835," *JAH* 28 (1987), 400.

commerce through state monopolies. From 1826 to 1834, customs duties were generally raised from 5 to between 20 and 25 percent ad valorem, were again lowered to 5 percent in 1834, but from 1842 were doubled. To ensure compliance with the new duties, foreign commerce was restricted to 12 ports.[13] Moreover, from 1824 to 1837, the Merina crown entered into monopolistic foreign trade contracts with about five Mascarene individuals or syndicates and into industrial contracts with about 20 European or Mauritian artisans.[14]

Human Capital

The substitution of fixed for circulating capital is considered a key element in the transition from rural handicraft to modern industry in Europe. The labor-intensive nature of cottage industry kept costs low and profits high for the merchant entrepreneur controlling the industry, enabling him to accumulate capital funds that subsequently could be invested in the factory plant characteristic of modern industry.[15] However, because Madagascar lacked domestic capital formation, and autarky precluded the raising of foreign loans, economic growth depended upon the investment of human capital. Nevertheless, while the central plateau was relatively densely populated, only certain valleys in the southeast suffered from overpopulation.

The Merina crown therefore declared a monopoly on labor and summoned free subjects for *fanompoana* (unremunerated forced labor) (see Tables 4.1 and 4.2). For example, the carriage of raw materials to industrial centers was generally allocated to *fanompoana* units of conquered provincial peoples, notably the Bezanozano, Betsimisaraka, Sihanaka, and Betsileo[16]. The second

---

[13] All on the eastern seaboard except for Mahajanga, located on the northwest coast – see Campbell, "Role of the London Missionary Society" vol. I, 206.

[14] The commercial contracts were with a Mauritius consortium headed by the Blancard brothers (1827–8), Samuel Shipton (1834), and captain Garnot (1836–7). From 1837, foreign trade was largely monopolized on the northwest coast by William Marks, an agent for Boston merchants, and on the east coast by de Rontaunay. The foreign specialists involved in state contracts included five Bengali cultivators and silkworm workers, three Mauritian and one English carpenter, one Mauritian tailor, a Mauritian tinsmith, one Mauritian and one Welsh weaver, an English cobbler, an English and one French blacksmith, an English tanner, and two master artisans, one French and the other Scottish, who could perform a wide range of skilled work from carpentry to founding cannon: – Campbell, "Role of the London Missionary Society" vol. I, Ch. 5 and vol. II, Chs. 7 and 9.

[15] Mendels, "Proto-industrialization," 243–5, 255–6.

[16] Campbell, "Slavery and *Fanompoana*," 468–70, 484; for forced labor see also the next chapter.

TABLE 4.1. *Permanent Skilled Fanompoana Units in Imerina, 1790–1883*

Sector	Andrianampoinimerina (c.1790–1810)		Radama I (1810–28)		Ranavalona I (1828–61)	
	Number	% Total	Number	% Total	Number	% Total
Agriculture	394	77.87	424	6.46	630	6.54
Extractive	0	0	27	0.41	73	0.76
Textile	0	0	57	0.87	222	2.31
Metal	0	0	4,406	67.16	4,509	46.82
Military	86	17.00	370	5.64	2,747	28.53
Building	26	5.14	1,276	19.45	1,276	13.25
Other	0	0	0	0	175	1.82
Total	506	100.00	6,560	100.00	9,630	100.00

Source: Hastie, "Journal" (1817–18), 231; Freeman to Hankey, Antananarivo, 12 Oct. 1831 and Johns, Freeman and Canham to Ellis, Antananarivo, 28 May 1833, *SOAS/LMS MIL,* Bx.4 F.1 J.C.; *HR* V, 1158; Chapus, *Quatre-vingts années,* 230; GH V (1928), 134, 166, 370; J. J. Freeman and David Johns, *A Narrative of the Persecution of the Christians in Madagascar* (London, 1840), 25–6, 42, 107; Claude Rey, "A propos d'une lettre de Jean Laborde" *ORSTOM* 25 (1965), 167–90; J. Chauvin, "Jean Laborde, 1805–1878," *Mémoires de l'Académie Malgache* 29 (Tananarive, 1939), 8–9, 29, 43; Ida Pfieffer, *The Last Travels of Ida Pfieffer* (London, 1861), 222, 267; Ellis, *History of Madagascar* I, 196–7, 282, 311–13 and II, 293–4; Cameron, *Recollections of Mission Life,* 230; M. Cheffaud, "L'artisanat indigène à Madagascar" *Exposition coloniale internationale de Paris* (1931), 7.

source of labor was slaves, who by 1817 formed approximately one third of the population of Imerina. Following the ban on slave exports from 1820, Radama I counseled his subjects to use their slaves to produce legitimate exports: "Let my subjects, them who have slaves, employ them in planting rice, and

TABLE 4.2. *Workforce of Crown Plantations on East Coast, 1825–61*

	Designation	Origin	Comments
Fanompoana:	Antaimoro	Southeast	Forcibly resettled
	Antaifasy	Southeast	Forcibly resettled
Slaves:	Tsimanoa	Vorimo & Andiamahakiry	Captured in 1823–4
	Moromaniry	Tanala	Captives – served Lastelle
	Maroratsy	Soamandrakizay	Served Arnoux
	Antaisoa	Soamandrakizay	Served Orieux
	Maromiasa		Captured 1853 – served Orieux
	Telovohitra		Slaves of Rainizanamanga (son of Rainilaiarivony)

Source: Fontoynont et Nicol *Les traitants français de la côte est de Madagascar de Ranavalona I à Radama II* (Tananarive, 1940), 11–12, 29–30.

other provisions, and in taking care of their flocks – in collecting bees-wax and gums, and in manufacturing cloths and other articles which they can sell."[17]

However, slave ownership increasingly became a prerogative of the ruling elite for whom, as occurred with elites across the IOW, slaves often constituted status symbols rather than units of production.[18] There are few indications of slaves servicing the commodity export trade and industrial sectors until the 1830s, after which some provincial captives were directed into east coast plantations and sugar factories. Nevertheless, the largest slave labor force comprised the porters who, from the 1830s, increasingly monopolized transport between Antananarivo and Toamasina. Their initial numbers are unknown, but they probably totalled about 60,000 in the late nineteenth century.[19] The Merina court also conscripted into public works *gadralava*, people of free status convicted for crime, debt, sorcery, and sedition (e.g., Christians in the reign of Ranavalona I), in addition to vagabonds and other floating elements of the population.[20] The crown further appealed for voluntary labor from the destitute, in return for food rations, hoping that this would remove "the necessity of any person committing a theft to satisfy the wants of nature, as his labour would thus secure him subsistence."[21]

Finally, Radama I had access to skilled labor in the form of foreign technical personnel and Malagasy trained in Western techniques. From 1816 to 1830, 27 Merina youths, some of them metal workers, were sent abroad – five to Britain, the remainder to Mauritius – to learn the arts of gun and gunpowder manufacture; factory textile production; machine technology; gold, silver, and iron working; carpentry; shoe mending; and painting. Another 50 were trained as sailors aboard a British warship.[22] Radama I also assigned to each foreign artisan in Imerina an average of two Malagasy apprentices (about 40 in total), with instructions that their training be completed in as short a time as possible.[23]

[17] Radama I, quoted in David Jones, "Journal," *Quarterly Chronicle* (1821–4), 127; see also Campbell, "Madagascar and the Slave Trade," 203–27.
[18] Gwyn Campbell (ed.), The Structure of Slavery in Indian Ocean Africa and Asia (London: Frank Cass, 2004); *idem* (ed.), Abolition and its Aftermath in Indian Ocean Africa and Asia (London: Routledge, forthcoming).
[19] Campbell, "Labour and the Transport Problem," 341–56; see also Chapter 10.
[20] Chapus, *Quatre-vingts années*, 207.
[21] Hastie, "Diary" (1822–23); see also *HR* vol. V, 1103; Ellis, *History of Madagascar* vol. II, 303.
[22] Miller to Arundel, 2 May 1823; Miller to Arundel, Austin Friars, 17 June 1824; Barry to Hastie, Port Louis, 6 June 1825; Clunie to Arundel, Manchester, 21 June 1825 – in Ayache, *Raombana l'historien*, 268, 270, 272; Campbell, "Role of the London Missionary Society" vol. I, 128.
[23] Canham to Burder, Antananarivo, 30 June 1822, *SOAS/LMS-MIL*, B1.F4.JA; Ellis, *History of Madagascar* vol. II, 275.

Education

Education plays a key role in economic growth. It enhances the value of human capital, for literacy is considered vital to the ease and speed of worker adaptation to industrial employment (it has been estimated for nineteenth-century Russia that four years of schooling raised the industrial productivity of an individual worker by 40 percent). Indeed, a sufficiently high correlation exists between literacy and industrial development to make it an accepted precondition of industrial takeoff.[24]

In Imerina, a formal educational system was established in 1822, under the auspices of Welsh missionaries. It remained limited to three schools until 1824 when, in anticipation of the move to autarky, Radama I imposed state control.[25] He opened a further 30 schools, housing over 200 students. By 1828, schools numbered 100 and students 5,000. In 1829, the educational system was extended: Schools were founded in Betsileo and Antsihanaka and a boarding school for provincial pupils planned for Antananarivo.[26] To facilitate this expansion, the crown used its theoretical right over land and labor to order local leaders (*amboninzato*) to apportion land and, where necessary, local *fanompoana*, to construct schools and conscript students.[27] Radama I subsequently

[24] See Crisp, "Labour and Industrialization," 387–8.

[25] In c.1800–4, a school was established at the Merina court in which by 1817 five to six children of royal blood had been taught *sorabe*, or Malagasy written in Arabic script, by Andriamazanoro, an Antaimoro from the southeast of the island. However, the Arabic characters used in *sorabe* failed adequately to express the rich range of vowel sounds in Malagasy. In addition, the Antaimoro tradition of education was highly elitist, and *sorabe* writing was considered to have powerful sacerdotal and magical powers. This hindered the expansion of education required for the effective running of the economy and administration of the Merina empire. Radama I therefore sought European teachers. In 1817, Hastie was appointed as British agent and tutor to royal princes at the Merina court, but the same year the British treaty was negated by Hall, acting governor of Mauritius, and in 1819 Radama I appointed a Frenchman, Robin, as royal tutor: see Hastie, "Diary" (1817), 153, 188–9; Jones and Griffiths to Burder, Antananarivo, 30 May 1827, *SOAS/LMS-MIL*, B2.F4.JA; Ludvig Munthe, *La bible à Madagascar. Les deux premières traductions du Nouveau Testament Malgache* (Oslo, 1969), 8–15, 23; *idem*, "La tradition Arabico-Malgache" *CRASOM* 37. 2 (1977), 265; Raharijaona and Raveloson, "Andriamazanoro, prince Antaimoro de Vohipeno," *BAM* 32 (1954), 31–6; Jacques Dez, "Le temps et le pouvoir; l'usage du calendrier divinatoire antaimoro" in Raison-Jourde (ed.) *Les souverains de Madagascar*, 110–11, 119–20; GH (1928), 387; Ellis, *History of Madagascar* vol. I, 292, 402–3; James Hastie, "Report" (March 1825); Jones and Griffiths to Phillips, Antananarivo, 30 April 1823, *ALGC* 19157E no. 3; Campbell, "Role of the London Missionary Society" vol. I, 149–51.

[26] David Griffiths, *Hanes Madagascar* (Machynlleth, 1843), 41; Johns to LMS, Antananarivo, 8 Nov. 1826, *SOAS/LMS-MIL*, B2.F3.JC; "Second Report of the Madagascar Missionary School Society" (1828), *SOAS/LMS-MIL*, B2.F4. JC; "Report of the Madagascar Mission School Society, March 1828–December 1829," *SOAS/LMS-MIL*, B3; Betsileo District Committee to LMS Deputation, Fianarantsoa, 19 Oct. 1920, *SOAS/LMS* "Madagascar Personal" B1 (1920).

[27] Jeffrey to Burder, Ambatomanga, 24 May 1824, *SOAS/LMS-MIL*, B2.F1.JA; Jones to Hankey, Antananarivo, 29 July 1829, *SOAS/LMS-MIL*, B3.F2.JA.

fashioned the schools into the chief institution for the recruitment and rudimentary education of soldiers, administrators, and master artisans. In 1824, he proclaimed that no subject entering "his service, either military or civil, after a limited defined period, should be promoted if not found capable of writing"[28] and in 1825 replaced oral with written instruction in the administration. Consequently, the schools were highly successful. From 1827 to 1835, the number of literate school graduates rose from 4,000 to 15,000. As late as 1897, the literacy rate in Russia was only 21 percent;[29] by comparison, in Imerina as early as 1835, it was probably over 7 percent, prompting Raombana to note in 1853 that "had no schools been established in IMERINA, no important business or affair could have been transmitted to the Garrisons"[30] (see Map 5).

In a country without developed urban centers, schools also helped instill a sense of discipline, deemed essential in transforming an agricultural into an industrial workforce. The core of a number of LMS directives to missionary teachers,[31] this message was also impressed on LMS artisans who from the outset schooled their indigenous apprentices, albeit on an irregular basis. An attempt was made to formalize craft education in 1826, when the first graduates were attached as *fanompoana* apprentices to foreign artisans.[32] In 1831, the first formal worker education program was launched by James Cameron in an evening school for 560 of his Analakely factory workers. This initiative, followed by Chick, proved a success. In 1840, it was reported of all mission education:

new scenes have been visited; new energies created; and a new kind of life instituted; new ranks and orders in society established; and in a word, a new physical aspect given to the condition of society.... [R]ude and unwieldy masses have been brought under European discipline.[33]

---

[28] Hastie, "Report" (April 1824).

[29] Crisp, "Labour and Industrialization," 388, 391.

[30] *RH*, 134; see also Rabary, *Daty Malaza* vol. I, 58; Mrs. Ellis, *Madagascar: its Social and Religious Progress* (London, 1863), 28; Ellis, *History of Madagascar* vol. II, 470–1; N. B. Leminier, "Notes sur une excursion faites dans l'intérieur de l'île de Madagascar en 1825" *BdM* 292 (1970), 796; Joseph Freeman and David Johns, *A Narrative of the Persecution of the Christians in Madagascar* (London, 1840), 75.

[31] See, e.g., Anon, "Instruction of the Rising Generation" in *The Missionary Register* (1826), 208.

[32] Jones and Griffiths to LMS, *SOAS/LMS-MIL*, B1.F5.JA; "School Report" (1826), *SOAS/LMS-MIL*, B2.F3.JE; "Second Report of the Madagascar Mission School Society" (1828), *SOAS/LMS-MIL*, B2.F4.JD.

[33] Freeman and Johns, *A Narrative*, 83; see also *ibid*, 78; Baker to Arundel, Antananarivo, 5 April 1831, and Johns to Arundel, Antananarivo, 12 April 1831 – *SOAS/LMS-MIL*, B4.F1.JA; Ellis, *History of Madagascar* vol. I, 103–4, 308; for a Russian comparison see Crisp, "Labour and Industrialization," 375–6.

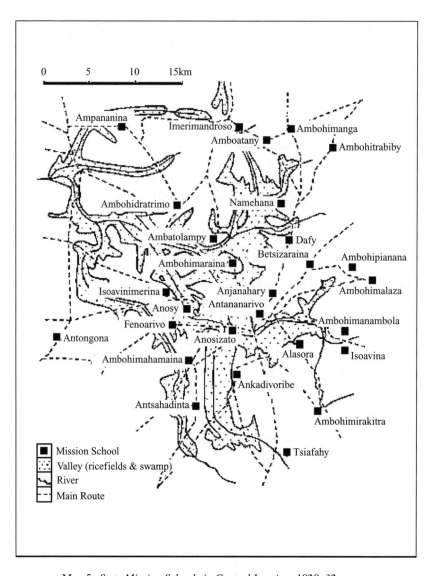

Map 5. *State Mission Schools in Central Imerina, 1828–32.*
Source: Gwyn Campbell, "An Industrial Experiment in Pre-colonial Africa: The Case of Imperial Madagascar, 1825–1861," *Journal of Southern African Studies* 17.3 (1991), 542.

Finally, the schools instilled personal loyalty to the crown and empire. Thus when Carayon visited Ambatomanga school in 1826, he had the following passage written on the board for him by a child as proof of its schooling: "Radama has no equal amongst the princes. He is superior to all chiefs in the island. All the land of Madagascar belongs to him alone."[34] This mission school ideology was of immense importance for economic development in the form of crown monopolies, and it complemented caste ideology[35] by helping to shape a docile and disciplined workforce.

The 1835–6 expulsion of missionaries ended formal public education. How-ever, informal education continued and by mid-century had probably generated greater literacy than the formal system. Informal Western education started in the chapels, established in 1821. It was generally avoided by the Merina until 1827, when large numbers of military conscripts attended as listeners. Their numbers fell after Radama I's death in mid-1828, until the new sovereign in-dicated her approval of chapels in May 1829. Thereafter, such eagerness was expressed for the *taratasy*, or ability to read the Scriptures, that by 1832, two new LMS chapels had opened and a number of Malagasy-run prayer meetings instituted, mainly in Antananarivo, its suburbs, military camps, and garrison towns.[36]

Slaves were also strongly affected. Missionaries compelled their slave ser-vants or apprentices to attend both chapel and evening schools. Slaves proved eager to learn, as conversion to Christianity and an ability to read and discuss the Christian scriptures gave them a status within the Christian community impossible to attain in the caste stratified ancestral society outside. Proselytiza-tion within the slave community spread rapidly, slave literacy accelerating from December 1831 when the missionaries, barred from baptizing and conferring church membership upon free Merina subjects, concentrated their efforts upon the slaves. Court proscription of slave education in May 1832 and of Christian-ity in February 1835 came too late to prevent the continued spread of literacy through an indigenous clandestine church that flourished despite bouts of state persecution. All social ranks were affected by the thirst for the *taratasy*. The few books to escape the mass burning of 1835 were copied and circulated and a voracious demand established for Christian literature smuggled into the island by the LMS.[37]

---

[34] Quoted in Françoise Raison, "L'échange inégal de la langue. La pénétration des techniques linguistiques au sein d'une civilisation de l'oral (Imerina, début du XIXe siècle), *Revues annales ESC* (février 1976), 5.

[35] For fuller explanation of caste in Madagascar, see Chapter 5.

[36] Campbell, "Role of the London Missionary Society" vol. II, 274–6.

[37] Campbell, "Role of the London Missionary Society" vol. II, 277–8 and Ch. 8.

Wage Costs

A further early economic advantage for the Merina crown was wage costs, a factor Vandenbroeke considers to have been vital for the success of the economy of eighteenth-century Flanders:

the cost of wages form one of the most essential components in the final level of prices. In a society where labour-saving devices are few and where therefore few differences in productivity were possible, it is logical that the relative importance of the costs of wages will be great.[38]

In Imerina, a brief experiment with wage labor in the 1820s ended because it threatened the institution of *fanompoana* upon which the crown's autarkic policies rested. As LMS missionary Joseph Freeman observed in 1829, "a regular monthly payment ... to a large body of teachers might excite some jealousy – and dissatisfaction" among unremunerated industrial workers and soldiers.[39] Thereafter, free labor could theoretically be hired at $0.04 per day for an unskilled workman, and $0.08 for a skilled craftsman, but in practice was monopolized by the state so that foreigners were obliged either to hire slave labor from the court syndicate or to request forced labor from the crown.[40]

All *fanompoana* and slave labor for state projects was unremunerated, conscripted workers even having to provision themselves. Indeed, through a system of fines and royal tribute (*hasina*), there was a net cash transfer from workers to the court. Reliance upon human porterage, again comprising slave or forced labor, also represented a considerable saving in wages for the crown. For example, from July to October 1817, at the height of the commercial season, 1,000 porter loads reached Antananarivo from the east coast. Representing to foreign hirers a wage cost of $12,000, this would have entailed for the crown a net gain of $1,000 from *hasina*.[41]

In addition, the LMS and the Mauritian government initially provided educational goods, financed Merina youths trained abroad, and paid the salaries of British personnel working in Imerina. Most school equipment, comprising imported books and slates, was donated by churches in North Wales, the foreign community in Antananarivo, and the LMS in London – which alone spent

---

[38] Vandenbroeke, "The Regional Economy of Flanders," 164; see also *ibid*, 165–70.
[39] Freeman to Hankey, Antananarivo, 10 Feb. 1829, *SOAS/LMS-MIL*, B3.F1.JA; see also Griffiths to Arundel, "private," Antananarivo, 20 Dec. 1825, *SOAS/LMS-MIL*, B2.F2.JC.
[40] Jones and Griffiths to Burder, Antananarivo, 30 May 1827, *SOAS/LMS-MIL*, B2.F4.JA; see also Campbell, "Role of the London Missionary Society" vol. II, 266.
[41] Campbell, "Role of the London Missionary Society" vol. II, 244.

from $9,000 to $13,000 on imported educational goods from 1820 to 1835.[42] The crown also saved $443,227 (at $1,000 per annum for clerics and $360 for artisans) in salaries for missionaries from 1820 to 1826.[43] In December 1824, most foreign craftsmen, at least half of whom were missionary artisans, signed royal contracts, generally for five years, to manufacture skilled articles. In return, they were provided with apprentice labor and a salary.[44] This established a pattern of royal control of missionary industry in which priority was given to the production of military goods.

Under autarky, the Merina crown assumed responsibility for the salaries, lodging, and provisioning of all foreign artisans. Housing, servants, and food were all provided through *fanompoana*, and artisans were paid in part with a proportion of the goods they produced. For the crown, this reduced most artisan wages to an annual minimum of $900 from 1826 to 1828, although exceptionally valued craftsmen like Cameron and Jean Laborde earned far more: In 1833, for instance, Laborde signed a two-year contract for $4,500.[45]

The crown defrayed such wage and other industrial costs through extraordinary taxation. In 1837, two levies were imposed. The first, $1 on every slave owned, was earmarked for the $31,800 owed to Napoléon de Lastelle for imported European muskets. The second, an additional poll tax of $0.25, raised $70,000. This prompted the crown to impose a second extraordinary levy which yielded the $100,000 required to finance the construction by Laborde of the Mantasoa (Isoatsimanampiovana) cannon foundry in 1837–9. To pay these additional taxes, many subjects were forced to borrow at an exorbitant interest rate from or sell cattle to members of the court. Their monopoly of cattle exports enabled the latter to dictate a sale price of $0.071 a bullock, which they resold to foreign merchants on the coast for $15.[46]

[42] LMS to Jones, "Account Sheet," *SOAS/LMS-MIL*, B2.F1.JC; Griffiths, *Hanes Madagascar*, 48; Campbell, "Role of the London Missionary Society" vol. II, 221, 245.

[43] "Expenses incurred by the Government of Mauritius on account of Madagascar" in "Papers Relating to Slavery in Mauritius" (26 Nov. 1827), *HCPP* 36 (1828), 72–82; Griffiths to Burder, Antananarivo, 6 Nov. 1821, *SOAS/LMS-MIL*, B1.F2.JC; Jones and Griffiths to LMS, Antananarivo, 2 June 1824, *SOAS/LMS-MIL*, B2.F1.JA; Griffiths to Burder, 24 Dec. 1825, and Rowlands to Burder, 26 Dec. 1825, *SOAS/LMS-MIL*, B2.F2.JC.

[44] Chick to Burder, Antananarivo, 16 Dec. 1825, *SOAS/LMS-MIL*, B2.F2.JC; *ibid*, 6 June 1826, *SOAS/LMS-MIL*, B2.F3.JA; Robert Lyall, "Journal" (eds. Chapus, G. S. & Mondain, G.) in Académie Malgache, *Collection de documents concernant Madagascar et les pays voisins* 5 (Tananarive, 1954), 171; *HR* vol. V, 1062–3, 1066; Chapus, *Quatre-vingts années*, 201–2; Ellis, *Three Visits*, 262–3; Oliver, *Madagascar* vol. II, 91; Campbell, "Slavery and Fanompoana."

[45] Campbell, "Role of the London Missionary Society" vol. II, 245, 259, 262.

[46] Oliver, *Madagascar* vol. II, 196.

The Industrial Experiment

Autarky aimed to promote industrial self-sufficiency and exports. The proto-industrialization school has emphasized the importance of developments within textile manufacturing for the emergence of modern industry. Despite having an important domestic textile industry, Imerina imported cheap Indian and Lancashire pieces as well as luxury cloth. Import substitution was first achieved in luxury cloth, demand for which was largely restricted to the Merina. In 1824, a factory was established where from 40 to 50 females (missionary sewing group members) produced European-style small overcoats of twilled calico and bordered woollen cloth, as well as gowns, trousers, shirts, and kerchiefs. These products sold well in the mission shop operating from 1825 to 1829 in Antananarivo.[47]

However, as noted in Chapter 3, ordinary household production proved more cost effective and generated a surplus effectively undermining factory produced goods intended for local mass consumption – as LMS weaver Rowlands found to his cost:

> Every woman in the country from the King's wives to the Slaves are weavers. They will sit upon their heels weaving from morning 'til night a month together for 1/8 of a Spanish dollar. Most families spin and weave the whole of their own clothing. The markets are stocked with home made clothes. No cloth meets with a rapid sale . . . if it be not superior to their own in whiteness, fineness, brilliance of colours etc.[48]

Factory cloth produced by expensive imported machinery and craftsmen simply could not compete.[49] In 1827, Radama I tried to promote domestic factory production in two ways. First, he imposed protective barriers against imports by altering the payment for cattle exports, traditionally made in cloth, to cash.[50] Second, to benefit from economies of scale, he planned a water-powered factory, equipped with British machines, with the capacity to produce 5,000 cotton pieces a year. Cameron was contracted to build the water mill, supplied by canal

[47] Jones to Farquhar, Antananarivo, 25 March 1822, *PRO.CO.*167/63; Griffiths, *Hanes Madagascar*, 29; Ellis, *History of Madagascar* vol. I, 277–8; Valette, *Etudes*, 321; Rabary, *Daty Malaza* vol. I, 24, 41; Campbell, "Role of the London Missionary Society" vol. II, 247–9.

[48] Rowlands to LMS, Antsahadinta, 13 June 1826, *SOAS/LMS-MIL*, B2.F3.JA.

[49] Hastie, "Diary" (1817), 143, 167–8; *idem*, "Report" (March 1824) and "Report" (April 1824); Bojer, "Journal," 24; Rowlands to Jones and Griffiths, Amparibe, 15 May 1827; Jones and Griffiths to Burder, Antananarivo, 30 May 1827 – *SOAS/LMS-MIL*, B2.F4.JA; J. A.Wills, "Native Products used in Malagasy Industries" *AAMM* 9 (1885), 124–5; Ellis, *History of Madagascar* vol. I, 324–7; *idem, Three Visits*, 151; Keturah Jeffreys, *The Widowed Missionary's Journal* (Southampton, 1827), 173–6; J. Dez, "Développement économique et tradition à Madagascar," *Cahiers de l'institut de science économique appliquée* supplt. 5.129 (1962), 4, 92–3.

[50] Campbell, "Role of the London Missionary Society" vol. I, 205.

from the river Ikopa,[51] and the LMS offered half the required investment – in return for 50 percent of profits until repaid by the crown. The factory was to be managed by Rowlands and by Raolombelona, one of the Merina trained in Manchester where in 1825 he was reported to be "a very good workman and far better acquainted with the principles of the art and preparation of the work, than many who earn their livelihood by weaving."[52] However, the project was delayed by the deaths of Rowlands and Radama I and, following the 1829 French invasion of the northeast coast, Ranavalona I substituted for textiles the idea of an armaments factory. Thereafter, the textile machinery was worked on a small scale by government weavers producing *lamba*, a kind of Malagasy toga.[53]

Armaments production was a royal priority. Radama I instructed Canham, while on furlough in Britain from 1825 to 1827, to study the latest British armament techniques. To promote import substitution, the king prohibited French arms imports and insisted that British merchants pay cash for Malagasy exports – although from 1827, in recognition of Imerina's continued dependence upon imports, foreign armaments were allowed in at a nominal duty of 5 percent.[54] After Radama I's death in 1828, Ranavalona I maintained the emphasis on arms production, establishing four factories in the vicinity of Antananarivo: a gunpowder mill at Isoraka (the site formerly earmarked for textile production), under the direction of Cameron and Rainimanana/Ravarika (Verkey) – a Merina trained at the Walthamstow gunpowder factory; a sword and bayonet factory at Amparibe under Chick; a musket factory and cannon foundry at Ilafy, under Frenchmen Droit and Laborde; and three tanneries under Canham at Ambohimandroso, Andoharano, and Vodivato for the manufacture of military boots, belts, saddles, and pouches[55] (see Map 6).

[51] Robin to Missionaries, 24 Jan.–14 Feb.1827; Rowlands to Jones and Griffiths, Amparibe, 15 May 1827; Cummins to Jones and Griffiths, Amparibe, 17 May 1827; Cameron to J. & G. Brighton, 19 May 1827; Jones and Griffiths to Burder, Antananarivo, 30 May 1827; Cameron to Arundel, 19 May 1827, *SOAS/LMS-MIL*, B2.F4.JA; Campbell, "Role of the London Missionary Society" vol. II, 248.

[52] Clunie to Arundel, Manchester, 21 June 1825, in Ayache, *Raombana l'historien*, 272.

[53] Rabary, *Daty Malaza* vol. I, 50, 59, 66; Valette, *Études*, 30; "Extracts of the Minutes of the Madagascar Mission" (4 May–8 July 1829), *SOAS/LMS-MIL*, B3.F2.JA; Campbell, "Role of the London Missionary Society" vol. I, 206–7, 259–62.

[54] Munthe *et al.* "Radama I et les Anglais," 56; Leminier, "Notes" (1825), 797; Jones and Griffiths to LMS, Antananarivo, 9 Nov. 1826, *SOAS/LMS-MIL*, B2.F3.JD; Canham to Burder, Ifenoarivo, 3 Oct. 1827, *SOAS/LMS-MIL*, B2.F4.JC; Lyall, "Journal," 11–13, 33; Chapus et Mondain, "Un chapitre inconnu. Des rapports de Maurice et de Madagascar" *BAM* 30 (1951–2), 111–13, 118; Campbell, "Role of the London Missionary Society" vol. I, 205.

[55] Campbell, "Slavery and Fanompoana."

94

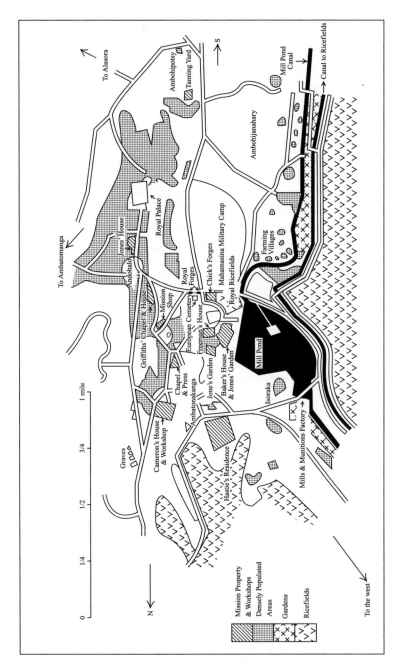

Map 6. *Antananarivo: Mission Property and Workshops, 1828–35*

Only the tanneries and the Amparibe factory were in full production by 1830. Cattle, the most ubiquitous form of wealth in precolonial Madagascar, were traditionally considered sacred. During the military expansionism of the first half of the nineteenth century, the Merina oligarchy accumulated large numbers of cattle, supplemented in later years with purchases, mainly from the cattle marts of Fianarantsoa and Antsenasabotsy in Betsileo, Mahabo in Sakalava land, and Imerimandroso in Antsihanaka. Their herds were grazed on the vast plains of Vonizongo and the Ankay. Outside traditional festivals, there existed little domestic demand for meat, but the Mascarene market (for draught animals on the plantations and to feed a burgeoning population) and an emerging domestic hides industry encouraged commercialization.[56] The court ordered the hides, suet, and neat's-foot oil of all slaughtered cattle to be sent to Canham – over 16,500 hides being surrendered in 1828 alone.[57] Tannin was initially obtained from bark, notably from *nanto*, a hard red mahogany-like wood that grew in abundance in the northeastern forests. As the gathering and transport of bark was time- and labor-consuming, alternatives were sought. By 1830, Cameron was being supplied with both lime and sulfur from the Sirabe plain in Betsileo, from six to seven days (72 km) south of Antananarivo.[58] In addition, by 1830, a few specialist ironsmith villages around Antananarivo were producing bayonets and spearheads for the state,[59] supplementing output from the Amparibe factory, which from 1832 to 1835, produced possibly 48,000 quality bayonets and swords annually.[60]

By the end of 1834, the crown considered that it had attained self-sufficiency in armaments production. Sufficient numbers of indigenous apprentices – 250 under Chick – had been trained for the manufacture of bayonets, swords, and military leather ware to replace foreign supervisors.[61] By 1828, Cameron had successfully produced niter and sulphur from local resources.[62] Despite doubts

---

[56] Campbell, "Role of the London Missionary Society" vol. II, 297–9.

[57] Canham to Burder, Ifenoarivo, 13 Dec. 1825, *SOAS/LMS-MIL*, B2.F2.JC; Griffiths, *Hanes Madagascar*, 38; Oliver, *Madagascar* vol. II, 84–5; *MT* II.46 (19 Nov. 1884), 415; *GH* (1928), 133–4.

[58] *MT* II.41 (15 Oct. 1884), 376; Campbell, "Slavery and Fanompoana."

[59] Oliver, *Madagascar* vol. I, 228–9 and vol. II, 86, 90; Chapus et Birkeli, "Historique d'Antsirabe," 59–82; James Sibree, "Industrial Progress in Madagascar" *AAMM* 22 (1898), 129–32.

[60] Hastie, "Diary" (1817), 182; Campbell, "Slavery and Fanompoana."

[61] Canham to Ellis, Ambohimandroso, 20 July 1833, *SOAS/LMS-MIL*, B4.F4.JB; "Minutes of the Madagascar Mission" (Dec. 1833–May 1834), *SOAS/LMS-MIL*, B5.F1.JC; Wills "Native Products," 123.

[62] From the lixiviation of decayed gneiss located to the northwest of Lake Itasy and to the south of the Vakinankaratra range, and from the blood and offal of slaughtered bullocks – Campbell, "Role of the London Missionary Society," 206–7, 259–62.

about the lack of elements (glass, indigo, copper, alum, acids, salt, and heating apparatus) needed to conduct full chemical and mineral tests, he successfully manufactured gunpowder. His factory, described as being "on an immense scale," was in full production by February 1835. A contemporary noted,

One of the principal native gunsmiths, and one of the superintendents of the powder mill, then made an oration in praise of their own ability, and assured the Queen, through her officers, that they would faithfully retain and improve the knowledge of these arts, which they had received from the Europeans.[63]

At the same time, at Ilafy, Laborde had succeeded in "manufacturing exceptionally good gunpowder and muskets," at one stage at a rate of one a day, as well as a cannon and bullets cast from an impure lead extracted from indigenous galena.[64] Thus in 1835, when the political stance of the missionary clerics made the continued presence of the LMS contingent untenable to the Merina court, the latter was confident of its industrial future.[65] Plans had been drawn up for a paper mill and a cannon foundry,[66] and a factory constructed by Cameron in 1832 was successfully producing cheap soap for the home market[67] (see Illustration 7).

Indigenous personnel took over the running of all except the Ilafy site, which lacked the necessary water and fuel to expand or even maintain production.[68] In 1837, Laborde relocated to Mantasoa, situated close to a series of lakes in the eastern forest, some 40 km from Antananarivo (see Map 7). Following the technical manuals published by N. E. Roret, he constructed "a true industrial centre,

---

[63] Freeman and Johns, *A Narrative*, 118; see also Freeman to Hankey, Antananarivo, 18 June 1832, *SOAS/LMS-MIL*, B4.F2.JD; George & Mary Chick to Ellis, Antananarivo, 11 Nov. 1833, *SOAS/LMS-MIL*, B4.F4.JC; Freeman to Philip, Ambohimandroso, 24 Sept. 1834, *SOAS/LMS-MIL*, B5.F1.JD; see also Rafaralahy to Arundel, Antananarivo, 1 Dec. 1830; Rahaniraka to Hankey, Antananarivo, 5 Dec. 1830 – *SOAS/LMS-MIL*, B3.F4.JC; Ayache, *Raombana l'historien*, 313; Campbell, "Role of the London Missionary Society" vol. I, 206–7 and vol. II, 259–62.

[64] Chapus, *Quatre-vingts années*, 203.

[65] Canham received a final injunction to leave in May 1834 from which time Merina tanners produced leather shoes, boots, hat linings, belts, bags, and saddles from the skins of bullocks, sheep, goats, and dogs – Canham to Ellis, Ambohimandroso, 20 July 1833, *SOAS/LMS-MIL*, B4.F4.JB; "Minutes of the Madagascar Mission" (Dec. 1833–May 1834), *SOAS/LMS-MIL*, B5.F1.JC; Wills, "Native Products," 123. Cameron was invited to remain in the island, but chose to follow his colleagues into exile – Cameron to Ellis, Antananarivo, 3 Oct. 1834, *SOAS/LMS-MIL*, B5.F1.JD; Griffiths, *Hanes Madagascar*, 65.

[66] Geo. & Mary Chick to Ellis, Antananarivo, 11 Nov. 1833, *SOAS/LMS-MIL*, B4.F4.JC; Freeman to Philip, Ambohimandroso, 24 Sept. 1834, *SOAS/LMS-MIL*, B5.F1.JD; see also Rafaralahy to Arundel, Antananarivo, 1 Dec. 1830; Rahaniraka to Hankey, Antananarivo, 5 Dec. 1830 – *SOAS/LMS-MIL*, B3.F4.JC; Ayache, *Raombana l'historien*, 313; Campbell, "Role of the London Missionary Society" vol. I, 206–7 and vol. II, 259–62.

[67] Campbell, "Role of the London Missionary Society" vol. II, 259.

[68] Chapus, *Quatre-vingts années*, 203.

7. Lake Anosy – Location of Gunpowder Mills and Arsenal, with Royal Palace
in Background

a kind of Malagasy Creusot."[69] An aqueduct was built to convey water to the
complex where, in June 1843, the first blast furnace was lit; 13 months later, the
first cannon was completed.[70] In 1849, plans were laid for the construction of
19 new buildings. At its height, Mantasoa comprised five factories containing
blast furnaces – that smelted iron ore in far larger quantities and more ef-
ficiently than the traditional small-scale bellow furnaces,[71] forges, hydraulic
machines, and numerous craft shops. The complex specialized in musket and
cannon manufacture, but also produced swords, gunpowder, grapeshot, copper,
steel, lightening conductors, glass, pottery, bricks, tiles, silk, a variety of cloths,
candles, lime, dye, white soap, paper potassium, processed sugar into sweets
and alcohol, and tanned leather.[72]

Although industrial activity was concentrated on the plateau and its margins,
there were also attempts under autarky to process mineral and agricultural products in conquered lowland provinces. For example, on the east coast from 1840
to 1845, ironsmiths under the direction of Lastelle manufactured pickaxes, axes,
and shovels for export to Réunion, thus realizing an enterprise first conceived by
Bourdonnais in the mid-eighteenth century. Lastelle also established a shipyard

---

[69] *Ibid*, 204. The manuals were part of a series published in Paris from 1824 as the 'Librarie
Encyclopédique de Roret'. Le Creosot was a major industrial site created in Burgandy, France,
by Eugène Schnoider from 1836
[70] *Ibid*.
[71] In the latter, an estimated 75 percent of ore was lost – *GH* (1928), 182–3.
[72] Raombana B2 Livre 13, 18, *AM*; Oliver, *Madagascar* vol. II, 107; Chapus, *Quatre-vingts années*,
204–5.

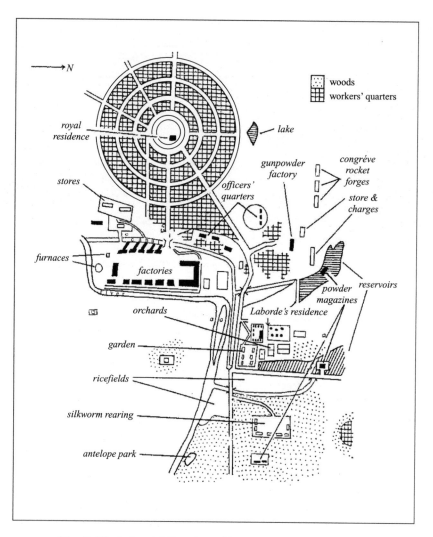

Map 7. *The Industrial Complex at Mantasoa, circa 1850*
Source: Campbell, "An Industrial Experiment," 550.

at Mahela where 150 Malagasy carpenters, ironsmiths, and coopers "are occupied all year round building and repairing our boats, to be employed on inland waters, on the rivers, and on the coast."[73] More importantly, military expansion into Iboina, in the northwest of the island, in the early 1820s secured

---

[73] Campbell, "Role of the London Missionary Society" vol. II, 297; Fontoynont et Nicol, *Les traitants français de la côte est de Madagascar de Ranavalona I à Radama II* (Tananarive, 1940), 25; see also *MT* I.9 (17 June 1882), 52.

for the Merina vast herds of Sakalava cattle. Consequently, a large industry producing raw and salted hides for export soon developed.[74]

Plantations

The Merina court also formed associations with foreigners for cash crop plantations on the east coast. From the adoption of autarky, the crown provided the land and labor while the foreign associate provided the necessary machinery and European skills – the produce being split between the two parties.[75] As noted, the first such project established at Mahavelona in 1822, in collaboration with the government of Mauritius, failed due to a combination of inappropriate European farming techniques and crops, a turbulent climate, and saline soil.[76] In 1825, the Réunionnais merchants Arnoux and Lastelle were engaged to create coffee (150,000 bushes), vanilla (50,000 feet), and sugarcane plantations, as well as distilleries.[77] The arabica coffee tree was imported from Réunion to which, in the early 1700s, it had been brought from Mocha, in Arabia. Much valued on the world market, it was in Madagascar initially termed *small coffee* because of its small-sized grains.[78]

By the early 1830s, following Arnoux's death, the large Réunionnais firm of Rontaunay, with which Laborde was associated, became the dominant foreign interest. After the 1833 abolition of slavery in British colonies created major problems for the British sugarcane industry, the Merina court became interested in sugar production. The first large sugarcane plantation was created by Laborde at Tsarahafatra on the banks of the river Mananara in 1834. Others followed, at Bakoro, also on the Mananara, in 1842 and at Soamandrakizay, on the river Ivondrona, in 1843. In 1846, Lastelle constructed two sugar refineries, one on each river. In all, Rontaunay invested over $400,000 in sugarcane cuttings, machinery, and skilled foreign personnel to establish and run these concerns, which, by the late 1840s, had an average annual output of 500 tons of sugar

[74] Thompson to Hathorne, Majunga, 27 Nov. 1878, encl.1 in Hathorne to Bertram, Zanzibar, 11 Dec. 1878, "Letterbook" of H. Hathorne, agent of Arnold, Hines & Co., New York and John Bertram, Salem, and U.S. consul at Zanzibar, 1878–80, *PM* acc.11.584.

[75] Tentor de Ravis, "Projet de système de conquête, colonisation et civilisation de l'Île de Madagascar," St Denis, 15 août 1852, Carton dossier 11e, *AHVP*; Robequain, "Une capitale montagnarde," 288; *GH* (1928), 70, 228.

[76] See Chapter 3.

[77] Manassé Esoavelomandroso, *La province maritime orientale du "Royaume de Madagascar" à la fin du XIXe siècle (1882–1895)* (Antananarivo, 1979), 87.

[78] Albert Lougnon, *L'Ile Bourbon pendant la Régence – Desforges Boucher. Les Débuts du Café* (Nevac: Imprimerie Couderc, 1956); F. Ciolina, "Café" in Marcel de Coppet (ed.), *Madagascar* vol. I (Paris: Encyclopédie de l'Empire Française, 1947), 299.

and 2,000 barrels of rum. In addition, Laborde created sugarcane plantations at Lohasoa and introduced cigar manufacturing.[79]

Clove and spice plantations were also established. Cloves, first introduced from Mauritius in 1803, were from 1835 cultivated extensively by Laborde at Rianambo near Mahela. Within a decade, 6,610 kg of cloves, worth $1,983, had been exported to France. Vanilla, brought from Réunion, was in 1840 planted at Mahela by Lastelle. He also planted 50,000 coconut palms (to produce oil) and cultivated and exported to France 200,000 black currants. In addition, in 1840, Nicol signed an eight-year crown contract for a coffee plantation and manufactory at Mananjary.[80]

Further, Radama I wished to develop silk cloth exports. Two of the five convict Bengali cultivators, who accompanied the British embassy to Imerina in 1816, devoted themselves to raising imported Indian silkworm. They also discouraged the indigenous practice of eating silkworm. From 1820, Radama I distributed mulberry bush cuttings to community leaders (the *ambonizato*), urging them to follow the example of the Bengalis whose endeavors were, by 1823, described as highly successful.[81] Outside the plateau, a mulberry bush plantation was established in 1825 to the south of Mahavelona,[82] and in the 1830s white mulberries were cultivated by Lastelle at Mananjary and red mulberries by Laborde at Mantasoa – where a rearing house for silkworm produced annually 200 kg of raw silk.[83]

Plantations were also started on the west coast by Merina colonists and Indian and Swahili traders. By 1846, for example, Mohammed Desharee, a wealthy trader from Johanna, possessed near Mahajanga slave-run plantations of coconuts, mangroves, oranges, plums, rice, maize, and plantains.[84] Merina soldiers, totaling 3,000 by 1845, assigned to garrisons in Iboina and Menabe,

---

[79] *GH* (1928), 70, 228; J. H. Galloway, *The Sugar Cane Industry. An historical geography from its origins to 1914* (Cambridge, 1989), 131.

[80] The crown donated the land and 30 laborers to Nicol who paid a European artisan to maintain his "machine." The produce was to be divided equally between Nicol and the court – "contract," Antananarivo, 25 and 26 Alakarabo, in Ayache, *Raombana l'historien*, 321, 323.

[81] Le Sage, "Mission" (1816) and Hastie, "Diary" (1817), 159, 173; Hastie, "Diary" in Tyerman and Bennett, *Journal*, 189–90; Farquhar to Wilmott, Madagascar, 6 June 1823, *PRO.CO*.167/66; Bojer, "Journal," 24; Leminier, "Notes" (1825), 778; W. F. W. Owen, *Narrative of Voyages to . . . Africa, Arabia, and Madagascar* II (London, 1833), 171; Cameron, *Recollections of Mission Life*, 28.

[82] Hastie, "Diary" (2 April 1825), *PRO.CO*.167/78 pt. II.

[83] *GH* (1928), 171.

[84] J. Ross Browne, *Etchings of a Whaling Cruise with notes of a sojourn on the island of Zanzibar* (New York, 1846), 251, 254.

were obliged to cultivate in order to ensure self-sufficiency. Also, some imperial officers, such as Ratrimo at Mahatombo, started plantations of cash crops such as cotton. However, the surplus agricultural produce of both Merina soldier-colonists and Indian and Swahili planters was consumed locally rather than exported.[85]

Construction

Autarky directly stimulated the construction industry. Carpenters, ironworkers, and masons were mobilized for construction projects of the crown and, by extension, of the Merina elite. In the early 1820s, Radama I summoned massive *fanompoana* to level sites at Ambohijanary, Fiadanana,[86] and Soanierana, near Antananarivo, for the construction of palaces. For years, 60 carpenters and apprentices under Louis Gros were employed building the palace at Soanierana; timber was obtained (each trunk required from 10 to 40 porters) from the forest 80 km to the east.[87] In 1827, Radama I also drafted large numbers of Betsimisaraka to improve and extend the east coast canal system.[88] In 1834 and 1847, in response to rumors of a French assault, a massive Betsimisaraka *fanompoana* was summoned to construct batteries at Toamasina and Mahavelona and in an unsuccessful bid to erect a barrage across the entrance to Toamasina harbor. Again in 1846, in preparation for a possible French invasion, a large *fanompoana* fortified Ambohimanga.[89] Missionaries, who were considered court agents, also had the right to forced labor. In 1822, a 2,000-strong *fanompoana* leveled the ground for missionary houses in Antananarivo,[90] David Johns was in 1830 granted 15 carpenters to help build a chapel, and in 1834 Freeman was granted forced labor to construct a publishing house.[91]

[85] Browne, *Etchings of a Whaling Cruise*, 251, 254; Campbell, "Slavery and Fanompoana," 477.

[86] *HR* vol. V, 111–12, 1114.

[87] Ellis, *History of Madagascar* vol. I, 107–8.

[88] *RA*, 263.

[89] Johns to LMS, Tamatave, 6 Aug. 1838, *SOAS/LMS-MIL*, B5.F3.JB; Cartier, "notes sur Madagascar" (1839–40), p. 12, Clla, *AHVP*; Campbell, "Slavery and Fanompoana."

[90] Canham to Burder, Antananarivo, 30 June 1822, *SOAS/LMS-MIL*, B1.F2.JB; Freeman to Hankey, Antananarivo, 10 Feb. 1829, *SOAS/LMS-MIL*, B3.F1.JA; Baker to Arundel, Antananarivo, 29 March 1829, *SOAS/LMS-MIL*, B3.F1.JB; "Expenses from November 1st 1831 to April 30th 1832," *SOAS/LMS-MIL*, B4.F3.JB.

[91] Johns to Phillip, Antananarivo, 11 April 1831, *ALGC* 19157E; Baker to Arundel, Antananarivo, 5 April 1831; Johns to Hankey, Antananarivo, 12 April 1831, *SOAS/LMS-MIL*, B4.F1.JA; Freeman to Ellis, Antananarivo, 19 Aug. 1834, *SOAS/LMS-MIL*, B5.F1.JC.

A Failed Experiment

The proto-industrialization school argues that key conditions for a successful transition from rural handicraft to modern factory industry include a division of labor that entails the demise of the household work unit, separation of the workplace from the home, and widespread literacy. Of particular importance was the opportunity cost of transferring labor from the agricultural to the industrial sector. Through forced labor, the Merina state formed permanent and occasional unskilled work units and a number of full-time specialist groups that operated away from home whenever necessary. Mission schools ensured a literate core of workers. In addition, the agricultural sector initially produced regular surpluses. Nevertheless, the industrial experiment failed. Arms production could not satisfy state demand, which continued to be met through imports.[92] Finally, in November 1853, the Isoraka powder mills exploded[93] and with Laborde's expulsion from the island in 1859 for political intrigue, production at Mantasoa ended.[94] Of the foreign industrial techniques introduced onto the plateau, only soap manufacture succeeded, spreading steadily from the mid-1830s, but on a handicraft rather than factory basis.[95] Also, despite minimal wage costs, the coastal plantations proved disappointing. Malagasy produce secured a peripheral and generally temporary niche on the world market.[96] However, the greatest single reason for the failure of the industrial experiment and cash crop production for exports was the imperial forced labor policy – a subject fully explored in the next chapter.

Gold – The Second Industrial Phase, 1880–1895

From the 1850s, the Merina court abandoned hopes of a domestic industrial revolution. Subsequently, it reverted to the concept – intrinsic to the

---

[92] From Marks (the U.S. commercial agent at Mahajanga on the west coast) and Lastelle (on the east coast) in later 1830s and 1840s."contract," Antananarivo, 1 Adalo 1840; Marks to Raombana, Majunga, 6 Sept. 1852 – Ayache, *Raombana l'historien*, 323, 325, 329.

[93] The explosion killed instantly nine workers, including Rainimanana, and wounded 47, some of them fatally – Raombana "Manuscrit écrit à Tananarive (1853–1854)" trans. J. F. Radley, *BAM* 13 (1930), 4.

[94] Although 2,000 plus workers still remained theoretically assigned to the works until 1861 when they were dismissed by Radama II – Hewlett, "Mantasoa," 378, 381; Raombana B2 Livre 13, 18.

[95] Raombana, B2 Livre 13, 29; [Finaz], "Tananarive, Capitale de Madagascar. Séjour d'un missionnaire Catholique en 1855, 56 et 57," p. 109, sect.II Diaires no.20, *AHVP*.

[96] See Chapter 8.

Britanno–Merina alliance (1817–25) – of promoting economic development through the export of raw materials in exchange for manufactured goods from Europe and the United States. Domestic arms manufacture was limited to a small factory near Ambohimanga, where output was restricted in range and quantity until the 1883–5 Franco–Merina War: By late 1884, the factory was producing guns, cannon, breech-loading cartridges, and several thousand shells a week. Also, tons of iron went into the production of spears for the war effort.[97] However, the declaration by the U.S. consul in Toamasina, in September 1885, that the Merina had attained self-sufficiency in armaments, was premature. The Merina regime continued to rely heavily on imported armaments.[98] To pay for these and other imports, the largely bankrupt Merina court decided to exploit its gold fields.[99] The second major industrial phase in Madagascar thus focused on the extraction and export of raw materials, notably gold (see Map 8).

Conventional accounts of African gold production largely exclude Madagascar. Nevertheless, gold is present over much of the island. Gold-bearing seams occur in belts of gneiss, mica shale, quartzite, and, more rarely, in the crystalline massif, but were rarely substantial enough to bear the cost of mining. It thus proved easier to exploit alluvial deposits at the base of hillsides and along crevices and riverbeds.[100] The main gold fields lay along the river Onive (in Vakinankaratra), in the eastern forests bordering Betsileo, the Ampasay and Sakaleona basins, and the Fisakana region. In the nineteenth century, the Merina court initially prohibited gold exploitation, which however continued to be illicitly worked on a small scale.[101] In 1884, impelled by the financial exigencies of the Franco–Merina conflict, the court legalized gold mining under a crown monopoly.[102] From 1886, crown concessions were offered to foreign investors and a scramble ensued. However, the only gold working with significant capital investment was that of Suberbie at Maevatanana – and even there the

---

[97] Raombana B2 Livre 13, 18; Oliver, *Madagascar* vol. I, 228–9 and vol. II, 86, 90; Chapus et Birkeli, "Historique d'Antsirabe," 59–82; Sibree, "Industrial Progress," 129–32; *MT* II.24 (18 June 1884), 229 and II.50 (17 Dec. 1884), 452.

[98] Robinson to Contre-Admiral Miot, Tamatave, 21 Sept. 1885, *REC/CR-MZL*.

[99] Bachelder to Ropes, Emmerton & Co., Antananarivo, 20 June 1884, *REC/CR-MZL*.

[100] Hugh Marriot, "Report on the Golf Resources of Madagascar with special reference to the properties of the Lecompte Madagascar Gold, Hanning's Concessions, Harrison Smith's Concessions, Cie. Coloniale, Cie. Lyonnaise" (Johannesburg, 22 September 1905), HE Record Department F.10, No.9, "Private Papers," 10–11, 14–15 – *BRA*.

[101] Raymond Decary, "L'ancien régime de l'or à Madagascar," *BAM* 40 (1962); Gwyn Campbell, "Gold Mining and the French Takeover of Madagascar, 1883–1914," *African Economic History* 17 (1988), 99–126.

[102] Decary, "L'ancien régime de l'or"; *MT* II.35 (3 Sept. 1884), 328; Campbell, "Gold Mining."

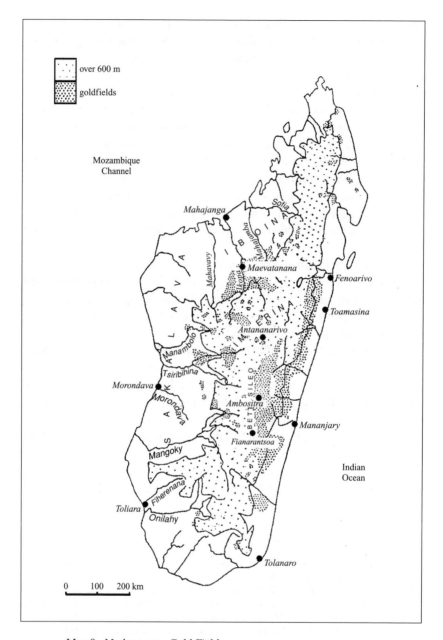

Map 8. *Madagascar: Gold Fields*
Source: Gwyn Campbell, "Gold Mining and the French Takeover of Madagascar,"
African Economic History 17 (1988), 101.

TABLE 4.3. *Location of Main Gold Fields in Madagascar, 1882–96 (Indicating Year of Commencement)*

1. Merina Government		2. Main Foreign Concessions			
Year	Region	Year	Region	Holder	Nationality
1884	Ambositra	1886	Maevatanana	Suberbie	French
1885	Boina	1888	Ankavandra & Analabe	Talbot	Mauritian
1885	Betsiriry	1889	Befandriana & Mandritsara	Abraham Kingdon	British
1885	Tsinjoarivo (SE Vakinankaratra)	1889	Ialatsara (Ambositra)	Guinard	French
1885	east Betsileo	1891	Vakinankaratra	Rigaud	French
1885	Maevatanana	1893	Antsihanaka	Harrison-Smith	British
1888	Ankavandra	1894	Amboanana (Arivonimamo)	Shervington	British

Source: Raymond Decary, "L'ancien régime de l'or à Madagascar," *BAM* 40 (1962), 83–96; Devred, "Les mines," 63; see also Agence économique du gouvernement général de Madagascar, *Madagascar "La Grande Ile"* (Paris, n.d.), 77, 79.

gold fields were predominantly labor intensive, worked by *fanompoana*[103] (see Table 4.3).

Most alluvial exploitation commenced in the dry season. A barrage was built across a gold-bearing river. Male workers subsequently excavated the riverbed, occasionally to a depth of 4.6 meters, gold deposits tending to be richer on the bedrock. Women removed and washed the excavated soil in which nuggets several ounces in weight were sometimes found. Any veins discovered were prospected and exploited in every direction until all traces of ore had vanished. Men occasionally worked shoulder deep in water during the rainy season; as gold was then being actively deposited, they rarely needed to dig deep. Pits were frequently reexcavated following a flood or heavy rain, but the fresh silt rarely yielded much gold. Overall, gold working proved harsher than most other forms of *fanompoana*. In 1905, a South African mining expert described a typical alluvial working at Ambaravarambato, 19 km east of Antsirabe:

> The natives had evidently been keen on recovering rock immediately on either side of and under the creek bed, and with this object in view they had dammed the creek on one side and were, at the time of my visit still endeavouring to cope with the continual rush of mud and slush in their workings.... The open cut ... has reached a depth of about six feet [1.8 meters] below the water level. The sides were a soft decomposed earth and at the bottom

[103] Louis Catat, *Voyage à Madagascar* (Paris, 1895), 178; Devred, "Les mines" in de Coppet (ed), *Madagascar* vol. II, 64; Anon, "Travaux du service géologique," *BdM*, 97 (1954), 558.

was the quartz stringer. The method of working was to empty the hole every morning by throwing out the water in wooden pans and handing up the slush as fast as possible. . . . As soon as the bottom was reached a few small pieces of gold bearing quartz were gauged out from under the water by means of a primitive spade. These pieces were then crushed between two stones and the resultant panning constituted the total output for the day.[104]

An estimated 50 percent of all gold (measured in Malagasy ounces, represented by the weight of a Mexican dollar – approximately 0.958 of a troy ounce)[105] was produced illegally. This indicates that, had the royal monopoly been effective, imperial gold deposits might have enabled the Merina court to avoid bankruptcy. Tight supervision of alluvial workings, which often spread for a number of Kilometers along a multitude of minor creeks and were illicitly exploited even by foreigners, was impossible. Detection of smuggled ore also proved difficult. Most gold was ground to dust and sealed in the hollow of bamboo, used as porters' shoulder poles and in the manufacture of cases and *filanzana* (palanquin). Consequently, unlike specie and in contrast to the Gold Coast, where gold in transit was an easy target for highwaymen,[106] gold transport in Madagascar was secure: An American agent reported in March 1893 that there had been no known losses of gold in transit between Antananarivo and Toamasina.[107] Consequently, as early as 1884 it was noted:

Gold-dust is now becoming more and more plentiful in Madagascar, and there is not a foreigner in Antananarivo but will tell you that the Malagasy are daily bringing it in to him for sale. Some bring in as much as 2000 dollars worth at a time.[108]

In the northwest, large-scale smuggling caused the court to declare it a capital offence. Gold spies were employed in the main commercial centers and, from 1890, all Malagasy entering Indian or European shops in Mahajanga were searched. It was commented of the neighboring gold town of Maevatanana:

People working steal the gold, sell it, and, if caught, their heads are cut off and stuck on poles. It is reported that there are dozens of heads of gold-stealers and so-called robbers stuck up like this at Maevatanarivo [Maevatanana]. . . . Lately I have heard that

---

[104] Marriot, "Report" (1905); see also Jaques de Saint-Ours, 'Étude des feuilles Tsaratanana et Marovato, *BdM* 107 (1955), 362; Zélie Colville, *Around the Black Man's Garden* (Edinburgh, 1893), 205–6.

[105] Raymond Decary, "L'ancien régime de l'or à Madagascar," *BAM* 40 (1962), 83–96; *MT* II.35 (3 Sept. 1884), 328; Gwyn Campbell, "Gold Mining and the French Takeover of Madagascar, 1883–1914," *African Economic History* 17 (1988), 99–126.

[106] Ray A. Kea, " 'I am here to plunder on the general road': Bandits and banditry in the pre-nineteenth century Gold Coast," in Donald Crummey (ed.), *Banditry, Rebellion and Social Protest in Africa* (London, 1986), 109–32.

[107] Ryder to Ropes Emmerton & Co, Tamatave, 27 March 1893, B46.F1 (Jan.–July 1893) – *REC/CR-MZL*.

[108] *MT* (3 Sept. 1884).

a young girl of twelve or thirteen years, along with a young man, were caught with a small quantity of gold on them at Maeratanarivo [Maevatanana] and their heads were sawn off by a spear-head, taking hours over it.[109]

Plantation and Forest Exploitation, 1861–1895

The rise in the world price of tropical produce in the late 1860s and 1870s led to a rush of foreign investment in Madagascar. This concentrated in the Toamasina region, in coffee (also around Mananjary and Vatomandry), tobacco, and sugarcane and to a lesser extent in manila and Fijian cotton. Mascarene settlers also planted cocoa and British investors planted tea 900 meters up in the Mangoro valley and on the plateau.[110] Such investment in turn encouraged some industry. For instance, by the 1880s, locally cut cigars were selling in Antananarivo at $0.75 per 1,000.[111] There was also considerable interest in forest products such as rubber and gum – immediately declared a crown monopoly and exploited by *fanompoana*.[112]

However, significant obstacles existed to the development of cash crops and forest products. Prices declined from 1877, due to the onset of the great depression from the late 1870s. Prices recovered slightly in 1879, but potential investors – mainly poor Mascarene Creoles fleeing poverty at home – remained wary. As a result, few new plantations or commercial ventures were established.[113] Plantations suffered further during the Franco–Merina conflict – some due to the initial French bombardment, all because of the subsequent flight of labor and Merina ban on exports. By contrast, indigenous coffee producers, who had on average only four to five trees, survived due to smaller overheads and the ability to retreat for some years into subsistence farming.[114]

Natural disasters posed a major problem. Cyclones regularly devastated parts of the east coast: One was the probable cause of the 1884 sugarcane crop

---

[109] Anon, "Gold in Madagascar," in *ASR* (March and April 1890), 69–70.

[110] Finkelmeier to Secretary of the U.S. Treasury, Tamatave, 5 Jan.1870; *idem* to Davis, 5 Oct. 1870; "7th Annual Report on Commercial Relations with Madagascar" (Oct.1872); "8th Annual Report" (24 Oct. 1873); Finkelmeier to Hunter, 30 Dec. 1874; Robinson to Hunter, 1 Oct. 1877 – *US*; Ciolina, "Café," 299; G. Foucart, "L'Etat du commerce à Madagascar" in E. Caustier, A. Milne-Edwards, De Faymoreau, L. Suberbie, G. Foucart, Lacaze and L. Olivier (eds.), *Ce qu'il faut connaître de Madagascar* (Paris: Paul Ollendorf, [1897?]), 87.

[111] *MT* II.39 (1 Oct. 1884), 364 and I.6 (27 May 1882), 5.

[112] *MT* II.41 (15 Oct. 1884), 376.

[113] Robinson to Hunter, 1 Oct. 1877; Robinson to Hankey, 29 Oct. 1879; Finkelmeier to Payson, 20 May 1880; Robinson to Payson, 2 Oct. 1880; *idem* to Third Assistant Secretary of State, 13 Feb.1882 – US; *CdM* 34 (23 août 1892).

[114] *MT* II.13 (2 April 1884), 115.

failure on some northeastern estates.[115] Also, when in 1878 settlers imported from Réunion *Liberia*, a West African variety of coffee reputedly hardier than arabica, they brought with it *Hemileia vastatrix* – a coffee disease that had come to Réunion from Ceylon (Sri Lanka). By 1881, the disease had virtually wiped out coffee plantations on land below 270 meters and, in the 1881–2 season, caused the destruction of hundreds of tons of coffee.[116] By the mid-1880s, only a few isolated plantations of *arabica* existed on the northeast coast. By contrast, plantations survived unscathed on the high plateau – hence the name *café de l'Emyrne* (Imerina coffee) applied to Malagasy *arabica*.[117] Most surviving plantations of *arabica* were in indigenous hands:

The small indigenous plantations found in the vicinity of certain villages on the route from Tamatave to Tananarive regularly produce good harvests, which are due also to the care lavished on them and the application of manure.

As is demonstrated by a large plantation of 350,000 bushes, established a few years ago at Ivato, at about 1,400 metres above sea-level, the coffee bush thrives even on the central plateau. Nevertheless, at this altitude, the full development of the bushes is inhibited and they produce fewer beans.[118]

A few foreign planters subsequently followed the example of the Dutch in Java by experimenting with Congolese coffee varieties, first *Kouilou* and later *robusta*. These yielded on average 0.5 kg of coffee per tree, but harvests were negligible prior to the French takeover in 1895.[119]

Others abandoned coffee and switched to growing cocoa. In 1883, from 5,000 to 6,000 trees were planted in eastern Madagascar, around Toamasina and on the offshore island of Nosy Boraha. Despite being abandoned during the 1883–5 conflict, many cocoa trees continued to flourish, encouraging renewed investment. From 1885 to 1888, cultivation increased from 39 to 49 hectares, and by the end of the 1880s, over 20 cocoa plantations, comprising more than 150,000 trees, had been established on the east coast.[120] From 1888, as fertile

---

[115] *MT* II.41 (15 Oct. 1884), 878.

[116] Robinson to Payson, 7 Aug.1880; *idem* to Third Assistant Secratary of State, 3 July 1885; Campbell to Porter, 6 Oct. 1888; *idem* to Wharton, 23 Dec. 1889; Wetter to Uhl, 8 Oct. 1894 – US; Oliver, *Madagascar* vol. II, 200–3; William Woodruff, *The Rise of the British Rubber Industry during the Nineteenth Century* (Liverpool, 1958), 39–40, 63–7; Ciolina, "Café," 299; B. B. Keale, *Coffee from Grower to Consumer* (London: Isaac Pitman, [1924/5]), 13.

[117] Ciolina, "Café," 299.

[118] Foucart, "L'Etat du commerce à Madagascar," 87.

[119] Jean Thorel, *La mise en valeur des richesses économiques de Madagascar* (Paris: Les Presses Modernes, 1927), 17–18; A. de Faymoreau D'Arquistade, "Les Grandes Cultures à Madagascar in E.Caustier et al. (eds.), *Ce qu'il faut connaître de Madagasca*, 65; Foucart, "L'Etat du commerce à Madagascar," 87.

[120] Anon, "Les études de colonisation (province de Tamatave)," *Notes, reconnaissances et explorations* 3 (1897), 506, 523, 527; H. Jumelle, *Le cacaoyer, sa culture et son exploitation dans tous les pays de production* (Paris: Augustin Challamel, 1900), 189–90; Boucabeille,

land was quickly occupied around Toamasina, the cocoa frontier moved outward. By the end of the nineteenth century, there were three distinct zones of cocoa cultivation dispersed over a 1,100-km stretch of the eastern littoral: in the northeast (Sambava and Vohimara), along the Ivoloina and Ivondrona rivers (10 to 15 km to the north and south of Toamasina respectively), and on the mideast coast (Mahanoro and Mananjary). Of Mananjary, it was reported in 1897 that "Of all crops tried up to now, that of the cocoa plant would appear to give the most excellent results."[121] Some cocoa trees were also planted on Nosy Be, off the northwest coast, from the mid-1880s.[122]

The exploitation of forest products was, from the outset, characterized by poor techniques and adulteration. This affected particularly rubber, the sole commodity subject to intense competition from 1875 to 1900. Rubber was extracted from vines by cutting a slit in the stem through which the juice flowed into a receptacle. Traditionally, the milk was coagulated in the cool of evening by adding salt water and kneading the mixture into balls or by cooking the milk over a fire. From the 1880s, sulphuric acid was also used, notably on the northwest coast, where it was imported at $1.25 a pint. In contrast to vines, trees were bled morning and evening, the juice coagulating in the sun through natural evaporation.[123] However, demand was so great that as early as 1870 an observer remarked "unless the number of trees in Madagascar is unlimited it will soon run out as the natives in collecting cut them down instead of tapping them as customary."[124] The emergence by 1884 of both Antananarivo and Marovoay as rubber markets reflects this prolific expansion of supply.[125]

A further obstacle to foreign investment was the Merina refusal to grant foreigners freedom of travel or freehold property. The 1865 and 1868 treaties acknowledged the right of respectively British and French nationals to freehold ownership, but omitted details as to procedure. Subsequent treaties reasserted the traditional policy of inalienability. The Merina regime stressed that since land could be let on long (99-year) leases, inalienability posed no threat to

"De Tananarive à Diego-Suarez (suite et fin)," *Notes, reconnaissances et explorations* 2 (1897), 285; Esoavelomandroso, *La province maritime orientale*, 183.

[121] Anon, "Les études de colonisation, district de Mahanoro, district de Vatomandry," *Notes, reconnaissances et explorations* 2 (1897), 303; see also *ibid*, 972; Nèple, *Guide de l'Immigrant à Madagascar* II (Paris, 1899), 96, 359; Anon, "Les études de colonisation (province de Tamatave)," 523, 527; Jumelle, *Le cacaoyer*, 190.

[122] R.Decary, *L'île de Nosy Bé de Madagascar: histoire d'une colonisation* (Paris: Editions Maritimes et d'Outre-Mer, 1960), 159–60.

[123] *MT* II.41 (15 Oct. 1884), 377.

[124] J. Orme Ryder to Bertram, Tamatave, 4 March 1870, John Bertram Papers B2.F5, Agency Records – Tamatave. Correspondence and Accounts, 1867–1870, *EI*.

[125] Dawson to Ropes, Emmerton & Co, and Arnold, Hines & Co, Port Louis, Mauritius, 29 Jan. 1884; Ryder to Ropes, Emmerton & Co, and Arnold, Hines & Co, Nossi B, 11 Feb.1884 – *REC/CR-MZL*.

commercial investment. Protestant missions and foreign traders, whose combined demand for leasehold property forced up the average price of a plot of land in and around Antananarivo from $192.50 in 1862–3 to $1,000 by 1890, gave credibility to their claim.[126]

Nevertheless, wealthier foreign planters were deterred, so that most plantations were started by impoverished Réunionnais Creoles.[127] Successive sugar crop failures on Réunion in the late 1870s and early 1880s, and the takeover of the French market by beet sugar, led the value of Réunion sugar exports to drop by a third between 1876 and 1882 (from $4,615,735 to $3,056,705). The slump caused many mortgages to be abandoned, and Réunionnais pressure mounted for access to land and labor in Madagascar.[128] Unable to compete for concessions alongside the larger European concerns, they established small plantations and entered petty commerce – bypassing formal obstacles to alienation through liaisons with local women in whose names they purchased houses, land, and slave labor. As was noted in 1884, "Frenchmen could not do business in Madagascar without living with native women."[129] The 1887 Merina ban on concubinage proved impossible to enforce. Nevertheless, few planters were able through their Malagasy "wives" to gain a workforce sufficient for their needs, while court hostility, the imposition of arbitrary judgments, and especially official Merina manipulation of plantation labor through state *fanompoana* were sufficient to create rank insecurity among Creoles. In consequence, Creole appeals for a French takeover of Madagascar grew increasingly strident from the mid-1880s.[130]

In summary, the Merina court failed in its attempts to found a modern industrial sector, develop cash crop plantations, and exploit mineral and forest resources. This was in part due to natural factors, such as weather and disease.

---

[126] Peake to PM, Isoavina, 26 Aug.1879, HH2, 887–8, ANM; Procter to PM, Tamatave, 24 June 1880, DD21, 8–10, *ANM*; Oliver, *Madagascar* vol. II, 273–8; see also land contracts in HH9-HH11, *ANM*.

[127] "7th Annual report" (Oct.1872); Finkelmeier to Hunter, 3 Nov. and 30 Dec. 1874; Robinson to Hunter, Tamatave, 1 and 11 Aug.1876; PM to Robinson, Antananarivo, 22 Sep.1876; Street to Robinson, 14 Oct. 1876; Robinson to Hankey, Tamatave, 1 Oct. 1878; *idem* to Hunter, 21 July 1879 and 12 Jan.1880; Andrews to Robinson, Majunga, 30 May 1882, "US Consular Correspondence from Majunga" – *US*; Cameron, "Newspaper Cuttings describing Recent Events in Madagascar"(1883), 60, File X, *FJKM*; Campbell, "Madagascar and the Slave Trade," 213–14.

[128] *MT* II.44 (5 Nov.1884), 404.

[129] Quoted in *MT* II.9 (5 March 1884), 71; see also *ibid* II.15 (16 April 1884), 133.

[130] Noel Deerr, *The History of Sugar* I (London, 1949), 21, 28, 241–2; Lacombe, "Histoire de la mission de Tamatave," *AHVP* II, 1; G. S. Chapus & G.Mondain, *Rainilaiarivony: un homme d'état malgache* (Paris, 1953), 237–8; Manasse Esoavelomandroso, *Problèmes de police et de justice dans le gouvernement de Tamatave à l'époque de Rainandriamampandry, 1882–1895* (Antananarivo, 1974), 29, 42–3, 45–6.

In the main, however, it was a result of state policies. A major state-induced constraint on the competitiveness of Malagasy products was high transport costs (see Chapter 10), which to some degree canceled out low wage costs. More important was the imperial Merina regime's labor policy, a subject to which the next chapter is devoted.

5   Labor, 1820–1895

Introduction

The economy of Imperial Madagascar was critically dependent on manpower. This reflected the balance of factors of production. In Madagascar, as in most IOW economies, land was abundant, labor and capital relatively scant (in contrast to Western Europe where labor and capital were plentiful and land scarce). A few IOW countries, such as Egypt, borrowed heavily from European sources to finance modernization programs. However, most experienced difficulty securing European capital or, for nationalist reasons, repudiated foreign investment. Most commonly, IOW authorities attempted to promote modernization and expand their political power through labor intensive means, which in turn entailed control over labor resources.

Martin Klein argues that the labor requirements of Middle Eastern and precolonial African state building were met by an increased use of slaves.[1] However, many slaves were tied up in private ownership. Thus a common state response to manpower shortages in the nineteenth-century IOW, from Korea to Thailand to Egypt and Imerina, was the imposition of massive forced labor schemes. In precolonial Asia and Madagascar, neither the slave trade nor forced labor impositions satisfied state manpower requirements. Consequently, some governments sought to transfer slave labor resources from private to state control through attacks on private slave holding.[2] In Korea, this occurred from the

---

[1] Martin Klein, "Introduction: Modern European Expansion and Traditional Servitude in Africa and Asia" in *idem* (ed.), *Breaking the Chains. Slavery, Bondage and Emancipation in Modern Africa and Asia* (Madison, Wisconsin: University of Wisconsin Press, 1993), 8.

[2] Gwyn Campbell, "Introduction" to *idem* (ed.), *Abolition and Its Aftermath in Indian Ocean Africa and Asia*.

late 1700s[3] and in Thailand and imperial Madagascar during the nineteenth century. Western historians have generally interpreted such measures as reflective of progressive regimes, which accepted abolitionist arguments. However, rulers were often motivated by the desire to monopolize domestic labor resources and liberated slaves immediately became subject to state imposed corvées.

The nature of forced labor is critical to an understanding of the economy of imperial Madagascar where the Crown lacked domestic capital resources, had limited foreign investment until 1862, and failed in its subsequent bid to attract significant amounts of external capital. Maximization of its labor resources was therefore essential. This posed considerable difficulty because of the scattered nature of the population. The average population density in nineteenth-century Madagascar was under eight people per km^2.[4] On the southern and western plains where a pastoral system evolved, or the fertile littoral, the lack of labor posed few problems. However, irrigated plateau riziculture required a heavy, concentrated, and constant input of labor. Moreover, in the nineteenth century, demand for labor increased dramatically in Imerina. This was due to the establishment of a large standing army, frequent warfare against non-Merina peoples, attempted industrialization, the creation of plantations, and finally the rapid development of mining. Political control of manpower, required to preserve scarce labor resources, was achieved through the institutions of slavery and *fanompoana*.[5] This chapter examines the rise and impact of these institutions.[6]

Slavery

Slavery is here defined according to the 1926 Slavery Convention as "the status or condition of a person over whom any or all of the powers attaching to the right of ownership are exercised."[7] No comprehensive study of slavery in Madagascar has been undertaken since the classic studies by J. B. Piolet and

---

[3] Kim Bok Rae, "'Nobi,' a Korean Slave System" in Gwyn Campbell (ed.), *The Structure of Slavery in Indian Ocean Africa and Asia* (London: Frank Cass, 2004), 155–68.

[4] Madagascar has an area of 587,041 km and in the early nineteenth century possessed a population estimated at between two million and 4,500,000. See *GH* (1908), 291–3; James Sibree, *Madagascar and Its People. Notes of a Four Years' Residence* (London, 1870), 272–3.

[5] Maurice Bloch, "Modes of production and slavery in Madagascar," in James L. Watson (ed.), *Asian and African Systems of Slavery* (Oxford, 1980), 104; Campbell, "Role of the London Missionary Society" vol. 1, Ch. 2; *idem*, "Madagascar and the Slave Trade"; *HR* vol. I, 139–40.

[6] Chapter 6 analyzes the demographic regime and Chapter 9 the slave trade.

[7] Quoted in Léonie Archer (ed.), *Slavery and Other Forms of Unfree Labour* (London & New York: Routledge, 1988), 21–2.

E. C. André at the end of the nineteenth century. Nevertheless, a certain consensus on precolonial Malagasy slavery has emerged, based on the writings of Maurice Bloch.[8] Bloch holds that the economy of Madagascar was transformed from the mid-1700s as a result of two factors. First, the reforms of Andrianampoinimerina led to the creation of extensive labor-intensive hydraulic riziculture and a vast imperial army and administration. Second, the rise of the Mascarene plantation economy created a massive demand for Malagasy slaves. Imerina developed rapidly as the chief slave mart in Madagascar, and by the early 1800s, domestic slavery was so widespread that many free Merina were released from productive activity to perform forced labor in essentially unproductive occupations. This process accelerated following the prohibition on slave exports in 1820. Thereafter, Bloch argues, domestic slave markets were glutted: "By the mid-nineteenth century... most Merina had slaves, and most of the productive work was done by them for the benefit of their masters, who were preoccupied by the military and administrative needs of the kingdom."[9] Freed from ties to the land, the Merina increasingly left their ancestral villages to become petty administrators and teachers elsewhere, particularly in newly colonized territories: "While before the nineteenth century freemen had been primary agricultural producers, by the mid-nineteenth century they had become an administrative and military class, even in some cases a trading class, removed from the primary processes of production."[10] Most scholars have followed Bloch in assuming that the economy of nineteenth-century Imerina depended on slave labor. It is here argued, to the contrary, that forced labor for free subjects was more crucial for most of the period.

---

[8] Bloch, "Modes of production"; *idem*, "La séparation du pouvoir et du rang comme processus d'évolution. Une esquisse du développement des royautés dans le centre de Madagascar," in Raison Jourde (ed.), *Les souverains de Madagascar*, 273–6; *idem, From Blessing to Violence* (Cambridge, 1986), 14–16, 36; Bloch's views have become incorporated into some of the major secondary literature; see, e.g., Paul E. Lovejoy, *Transformations in Slavery. A History of Slavery in Africa* (Cambridge, 1983), 234, 238–9; P. D. Curtin et al., *African History* (London, 1984), 414; for the slave trade see Campbell, "Madagascar and the Slave Trade"; *idem*, "The East African Slave Trade, 1861–1895: The 'Southern' Complex," *International Journal of Southern African Studies* 21.4 (1988), 1–27; *idem*, "Madagascar and Mozambique in the Slave Trade of the Western Indian Ocean, 1800–1861," *Slavery and Abolition* (1989), 166–93. See also J. B. Piolet, *De l'escalavage à Madagascar* (Paris, 1896) and E. C. André, *De l'escalavage à Madagascar* (Paris, 1899); B. Domenichini-Ramiaramanana and J. P. Domenichi, "Questions relatives à l'esclavage en Imerina d'après les édits des souverains," paper presented at the *Colloque d'Histoire*, Université de Madagascar (Mantasoa, 1980).

[9] Bloch, "Modes of production," 110.

[10] *Ibid*, 111; see also *ibid*, 112; Lovejoy follows Bloch: Lovejoy, *Transformations in Slavery*, 234, 238–9.

At the start of the nineteenth century, slaves did, as Bloch states, form the basis of the imperial Merina workforce.[11] As Andrianampoinimerina advised his subjects:

The kingdom is powerful when supported by large numbers; sometimes when their "parents" neglect them, slaves are given to destruction. Do not give free rein to your slaves, for they are both a legacy and possession; they are like six hundred measures of rice stored in a granary; they cannot be eaten either by women or by children ... they are like jewels passed down to us by the ancestors, like a thick *lamba* [toga] that protects us against the cold and frost; in hot weather, they are like a velvet bed upon which one enjoys tranquillity, they are an adornment and a source of pride.[12]

In 1817, Hastie estimated 33 percent of the population of Imerina to be slaves, one-half of whom comprised inherited slaves and the other half war captives. They had become sufficiently numerous to enable the adult free male Merina (but not women and children) to avoid agricultural labor altogether. The re-modeling of the army into a regular, well-trained and equipped slave-raiding organization in the 1820s might appear to confirm Bloch's thesis. Provincial captives initially glutted the domestic Merina market, where the average price of a slave plummeted from $90 in 1810 to $3 or less by 1820. So dramatically did slave numbers grow that, fearing a slave revolt, the court instructed army commanders to retain only female and child captives and to execute male captives.[13]

Following the 1820 ban on slave exports, Radama I ruled "that as no more slaves are to be exported, they are to be employed in husbandry for the future."[14] Ellis, reflecting missionary observations of the 1820s, stated that most slaves in Imerina were employed in riziculture. However, some tended cattle, gathered fuel and roots, or were engaged in textile production and (if female) the fetching of water.[15] At first, it appeared as if the investment in slave labor was bearing fruit. LMS missionary David Griffiths commented in 1821 that "All the country around [Antananarivo] is thickly inhabited and well-cultivated the lowland produces excellent rice in great abundance and the high land is

---

[11] Bloch, "Modes of production," 110–11.

[12] Quoted in Malzac "Dernières recommandations d'Andrianampoinimerina (1810) d'après un manuscrit du P. Callet" *BAM* I (1902), 71.

[13] Campbell, "Madagascar and the Slave Trade," 209.

[14] *RH*, 95; see also Ellis, *History of Madagascar* vol. I, 138; Campbell, "Role of the London Missionary Society" vol. I, 119; Hastie, "Journal" (1817), 184, 250–1.

[15] Ellis, *History of Madagascar* vol. I, 194.

made to produce Manioc, Indian corn, sweet potatoes, sugar canes &c., &c. and pastures for cattle."[16]

However, as noted in Chapter 3, a progressive impoverishment of the Merina farmer followed the slave export ban. Thus, Griffiths in 1825 remarked how depopulated Imerina had become, while by 1832 Freeman noted, "The main body of the people is miserably poor perhaps not five dollars a year pass through their hands. Their whole dress you would not give a shilling for and a little patch of ground supplies them with rice or manioc."[17]

In such circumstances, the poor were forced to sell or pawn their slaves. Consequently, slave ownership passed increasingly to the court elite. This process was accelerated by a number of factors. First, the *tangena* poison ordeal, which had fallen into disuse in the 1820s, was from 1828 revived by the elite as a judicial instrument to systematically deprive potential rivals of their wealth.[18] They also retained most campaign booty in the form of slaves and cattle. In 1800, few Merina owned more than 40 slaves but, by the late 1820s, members of the imperial court possessed several thousand. For instance, on his death in 1828, prince Ratefy owned 2,000 slaves while, in the 1830s, royal favorites Rainiharo and Rainimaharo each amassed thousands of slaves from military expeditions in the provinces.[19] As a result, by 1869, at least one-third of the free Merina population owned no slaves. However, contrary to Bloch's claim,[20] the evidence, analyzed in Chapter 6, suggests that total slave numbers grew only until the mid-1830s and then remained fairly stationary.[21]

These factors, and competition from the Mascarene islands for provincial slaves, had a number of results. First, while the impact of the poison ordeal is impossible to gauge with precision, Raombana states that it depopulated the countryside. Second, a stagnant slave population, at a time of voracious demand for both slave and forced labor to fuel autarkic policies, led to a sharp

---

[16] David Griffiths, letter to William Griffiths [1821], *ALGC* 19157E.

[17] Freeman to Philip, Antananarivo, 19 April 1832, *SOAS/LMS-MIL*, B4.F2.JC; see also Griffiths to Arundel, Antananarivo, 20 Dec. 1825, *SOAS/LMS-MIL*, B2.F2.JC; Johns to Arundel, Antananarivo, 15 April 1832, *SOAS/LMS-MIL*, B4.F2.JC; see also Gwyn Campbell, "The monetary and financial crisis of the Merina empire, 1810–1826" *South African Journal of Economic History* I.1 (1986), 99–118.

[18] For fuller details of the tangena poison ordeal, see Chapter 6.

[19] *RA*, 186, 198–9, 277–8, 285, 291, 294, 302–5, 315, 373, 390–3; Raombana vol. 8 B1, 8, *AM*; Griffiths, *Hanes Madagascar*, 131; Grandidier, "Souvenirs," 32; Piolet, *De l'esclavage*, 452–3.

[20] Bloch appears to follow Raison, who states that in the period 1833–62 there occurred a fivefold increase in the number of slaves in Imerina where, by the latter date they formed 66 percent of the population, dropping to 50 percent by 1896: Françoise Raison, "Les Ramanenjana. Une mise en cause populaire du christianisme en Imerina, 1863" *ASEMI* 7/ 23 (1976), 284; Bloch, *Placing the Dead*, 71; *idem*, "Modes of production," 110.

[21] [Finaz], "Tananarive" (1855–7), 112–13.

rise in slave prices. The average price of a slave on the Merina market grew from \$3 in 1820 to \$37.50 by 1840, at which level it hovered for the next quarter of a century. Consequently, only the wealthy could afford to purchase slaves, and labor in subsistence agriculture reverted from slave to freeman – a situation briefly reversed from c.1865–77. Indeed, the shortage of agricultural labor encouraged polygamy and the development of *wife markets*, like that at Ilafy, to the north of Antananarivo. By mid-century, wives sold for \$20 to \$30 each, far less than female slaves who, depending on their skills, strength, age, and beauty, could command a price of up to \$100. Also, increasing demand stimulated a sharp rise in East African slave imports, notably from around 1840, although there had been a steady influx from at least 1824.[22]

A shift in the nature of slave labor resulted from the concentration of slave ownership. The court elite, whose quasi-monopoly of slave supplies quickly satisfied their own need for domestic servants and agricultural workers, formed a syndicate that hired out some surplus slaves to foreigners for cash, establishing others as traders to whom they advanced credit. The former, who generally remitted between one-third and two-thirds of their earnings to their masters, constituted virtually the only wage labor sector under autarky. Most slaves for hire entered the porterage system where, by the mid-1830s, they had largely replaced free Betsimisaraka, a move facilitated by the onerous forced labor allocated to the latter. By 1896, the number of slave porters is estimated to have been about 60,000.[23] Thus, contrary to Bloch's assertion that the imperial momentum was primarily to capture slaves to relieve the pressure of increased forced labor,[24] the enslaved were largely monopolized by the Merina elite, so that from the mid-1820s the influx of slaves in no way relieved the burden of *fanompoana* for the ordinary Merina farmer upon whom the brunt of autarkic projects fell. Indeed, the lot of a slave was generally considered to be better

[22] *RH*, 111, 131–3; *RA*, 246, 276, 473; Raombana Livre 13 B2, 34–6; A Resident, *Madagascar*, 34; *GH* (1908), 310, 337, 342–3; G. Mondain "Notes sur la condition sociale de la femme hova" *BAM* 4 (1906), 85–91; Joseph Sewell, *Remarks on Slavery in Madagascar* (London, 1876), 11; Campbell, "Role of the London Missionary Society" vol. I, 213 and vol. II, 335–6; *idem*, "Madagascar and the slave trade"; *idem*, "Madagascar and Mozambique"; *idem*, "East African Slave Trade"; *idem*, "The Adoption of Autarky"; the slave trade is analyzed in Chapter 9.

[23] Hastie to Griffiths, Port Louis, 18 Feb. 1821, *ALGC* 19157E; Baker to Arundel, Antananarivo, 1 July 1830, *SOAS/LMS-MIL*, B3.F3.JC; Baker to Ellis, Ivohitsara, 30 July 1834, *SOAS/LMS-MIL*, B5.F1.JC; Charles Mackensie Campbell, "Journal" (1840), in Jean Valette (ed.), "Le Journal de Campbell," *Studia* II (1963), 470, 476; Guillain, M, *Documents sur l'Histoire, la géographie et le commerce de la partie occidentale de Madagascar* I (Paris, 1845), 64; Joseph Mullens, *Twelve Months in Madagascar* (London, 1875), 324; *GH* (1928), 351, 353–4; for the porterage system in imperial Madagascar see Campbell, "Labour and the transport problem," 341–56 and Chapter 10 of this volume.

[24] Bloch, "La séparation du pouvoir," 273.

than that of the freeman who was subject to the rigors of the imperial forced labor system. As was commented in 1857, "The great and the small tyrants take more care of their slaves, who constitute their property, than of the ordinary people whom they bleed white."[25]

Moreover, the Merina hold on labor in the empire was increasingly challenged by Mascarene planters desperate for a cheap workforce in the face of the Merina ban on slave exports, high slave mortality, emancipation measures, and the aversion of liberated slaves to plantation labor. The failure in 1840 of a labor recruiting mission from Mauritius to the Merina court led Mauritian planters to procure contract labor from India. The planters of Réunion, denied access by the British and Merina to Indian and Malagasy labor respectively, intensified the trade in slaves and contract migrant labor from independent areas of Madagascar, notably the south and west. This rendered the Merina court even more dependent upon forced labor, prompting it to strengthen coastal garrisons and intensify imperial campaigns against provincial peoples.[26]

From 1861 to 1863, Radama II adopted an ambiguous attitude to slavery. His release of some, notably Sakalava, male slaves was more a reflection of his new imperial policies than a first step toward abolition.[27] In 1862, he even authorized the purchase of East African slaves at Mahajanga.[28] Nevertheless, the king's liberal, pro-European stance and his personal pro-abolition sentiments made the court elite suspicious that he might succumb to abolitionist pressure. This undoubtedly played a major role in the regicide of 1863.[29]

Rainilaiarivony, Merina prime minister and effective imperial dictator from 1864, played a dual game, making nominal gestures to assuage growing abolitionist pressure from Europe while simultaneously reinforcing and expanding

[25] [Finaz], "Tananarive" (1855–7), 31.

[26] Richard B. Allen, "Licentious and Unbridled Proceedings: The Illegal Slave Trade to Mauritius and the Seychelles during the early Nineteenth Century," *JAH* 42 (2001), 91–116; *idem*, Slaves, Freedmen and Indentured Laborers in Colonial Mauritius (Cambridge: Cambridge University Press, 1999), 13, 15–16, 41, 55–6; Keller, *Madagascar*, 187; Daniel Lefevre, *SaintPierre de la Réunion* (Réunion, 1975), 22, 24–6, 31, 34; Campbell, "Role of the London Missionary Society" vol. II, 317–18; Campbell, "Madagascar and the slave trade"; R. W. Beachey, *The Slave Trade of Eastern Africa* (London, 1976); Guillain, *Documents* II, 273–82; Lovejoy, *Transformations in Slavery*; Campbell, "Journal" (1840), 463–5, 481–3; Scherer, *Histoire*, de la Réunion 62; A Resident, *Madagascar*; Samuel Shipton, "Madagascar" in *Sentinelle de Madagascar* (9 June 1848).

[27] Mrs Ellis, *Madagascar*, 157, 174.

[28] Rasoamiaramana, "Aspects économiques" (1973), 83. When questioned by Ellis, who received a letter dated August 1862 from David Livingstone reporting a large trade in east African slaves to the west coast of Madagascar, the king pleaded ignorance – see Ellis, *Madagascar Revisited*, 22, 34.

[29] Henri Rahamefy, "L'Église du Palais à Madagascar" *Le monde nonchrétienne* 32 (1954), 392–3.

the state system of forced labor. In 1877, he ordered the emancipation of all slaves imported into the island from Africa since 1865 in a measure designed to replenish a dwindling state labor supply without cost to the imperial treasury. No compensation was paid to former owners: At a stroke, the private sector was deprived of an estimated 150,000 slaves, a considerable portion of its labor reserve. The liberated slaves, herded into special camps and grouped into imperial *corvée* units, became "simply the appropriation on the part of the Government of so much private though stolen property."[30] In consequence, the price of hired labor rose sharply, rendering slave owners more dependent upon *fanompoana*, which nevertheless proved insufficient for their needs, triggering a resurgence of slave imports in the 1880s. In 1884, the court banned the sale of slaves outside Imerina and exempted slaves and soldiers from the terms of the "labor" clause of foreign treaties.[31] The principle of payment for carrier services was proclaimed for the first time. However, it was only widely applied in 1885, when it was extended to imperial soldiers, and then only for a brief period. Thereafter, state *fanompoana* was enforced with greater rigor.[32]

Fanompoana

While slave labor was significant, *fanompoana* was of greater importance to the imperial Merina economy.[33] Generally translated as *corvée*, or unremunerated forced labor for the state, *fanompoana* involved more than this. John Houlder defined *fanompoana* in three ways: (1) unpaid labor exacted in lieu of tax, (2) unrequited compulsory service rendered to a superior, and (3) the service of a slave for a master.[34] Joseph Sewell, a Quaker missionary, gave a wider definition of the term in 1870:

The government here, as in all eastern monarchies, is essentially despotic. By an elaborate process, in some respects similar to the old feudal system formerly current in Europe, and in other respects very different, every individual, from the lowest slave up to the

---

[30] Robinson to Hunter, Tamatave, 28 June 1877, *US*; Campbell, "Labour and the Transport Problem," 353; *idem*, "Madagascar and the Slave Trade," 213–14.

[31] "Letter," Antananarivo, 7 April 1884, *MT* II.14 (9 April 1884), 122; and II.15 (16 April 1884), 126.

[32] Robinson to Hunter, Tamatave, 28 June 1877, *US*.

[33] *Fanompoana* is virtually ignored by Deschamps and Valette, who have written standard works on precolonial Madagascar. Before an earlier version of this chapter appeared in the *JAH*, the most detailed account was that given by Chapus, although that was inadequate. See Deschamps, *Histoire*, 162, 167–8, 211; *idem*, "Tradition and change in Madagascar, 1790–1870," *Cambridge History of Africa* V (Cambridge, 1976), 400; Valette, *Études*; *idem*, "Radama I," 179–80, 188–9; Chapus, *Quatre-vingts années*, Chs. 10 and 13.

[34] J. A. Houlder, *Ohabolana or Malagasy Proverbs* II (Antananarivo, 1930), 39.

Prime Minister, becomes the servant of someone else above him in rank, who can claim from him a large amount of unpaid labour, and not unfrequently money and property too. Service of this nature is called *fanompoana*.[35]

Although Bloch ascribes to Andrianampoinimerina the application of large-scale *fanompoana* to convert the marshlands of central Imerina into rice fields, Andrianampoinimerina neither created nor expanded it dramatically during his reign. The specific notion of supreme kingship and vassalage[36] with which *fanompoana* is linked, emerged in early sixteenth-century Imerina under Andriandranolava. Succeeding sovereigns expanded the concept. Andrianjaka (c.1610–30) restricted clans to certain localities, and his example was followed by his successors, notably by Andriamasinavalona.

The territorially based groupings, termed *foko*, were each ascribed a specific status in the caste hierarchy. This requires some explanation, as the conventional assumption is that *caste* was unique to Hindu India. The essence of caste was not occupation but a ritual distinction between *purity* and *pollution*. For example, such distinctions were upheld in South China, among the Nyiuba of Tibet, and in Imperial Madagascar: Slaves formed an outcaste that, unlike real people, did not possess ancestors, was regarded as impure and generally treated as "polluting pariahs."[37] In Madagascar, slaves were termed *mainty* (black) and *maloto* (impure) as opposed to the *fotsy* (white and pure) nonslave.[38] In both India and Madagascar, ritually impure tasks were conferred on members of the slave caste, with whom much social contact, including sexual relations, was taboo for nonslaves.[39] Moreover, in Imperial Madagascar, India, and South China, the outsider status of ex-slaves was institutionalized in structures that, in theory at least, ensured them a permanent and hereditary outcaste status

---

[35] Joseph Sewell, in *Friends' Monthly Review* (Suppl.) (15 November 1870), quoted in LMS, *A Brief Review of the LMS Mission in Madagascar from 1861 to 1870* (Antananarivo, 1871), 27.

[36] Termed *fanjakana ifanoavana*.

[37] For China and Tibet, see James Watson, "Transactions in People: The Chinese Market in Slaves, Servants, and Heirs" and "Introduction. Slavery as an Institution, Open and Closed Systems" in *idem* (ed.), *Asian and African Systems of Slavery*, 10, 237–8.

[38] Gwyn Campbell, "Unfree Labour and the Significance of Abolition in Madagascar, circa 1825–1897" in *idem* (ed.). 2004/5. *Abolition and Its Aftermath in Indian Ocean Africa and Asia* (London), Ch. 4; see also Sandra Evers, "Solidarity and Antagonism in Migrant Societies on the Southern Highlands" in François Rajaoson (ed.), *Fanandevozana ou Esclavage* (Antananarivo: Université d'Antananarivo, 1996), 565–71.

[39] Utsa Patnaik, "Introduction" to *idem* and Manjari Dingwaney (eds.), *Chains of Servitude, Bondage and Slavery in India* (Hyderabad: Sangam Books, 1985), 4; Martin Klein, "Introduction: Modern European Expansion and Traditional Servitude in Africa and Asia" in *idem* (ed.), *Breaking the Chains. Slavery, Bondage and Emancipation in Modern Africa and Asia* (Madison, Wisconsin: University of Wisconsin Press, 1993), 14.

that was maintained into the postabolition era. Frequently the ex-slave-holding group continued to use traditional terms for slave when referring to ex-slaves, whom they considered impure and polluting.[40]

Internally, caste ascriptions, focusing upon the cult of the ancestors, regulated the *foko* and ensured a high degree of caste endogamy. Externally, the system was maintained by the top *Andriana* caste through force of arms. The organization of the population, and the territorial restriction placed upon it, gave the king a control over scarce manpower resources, essential in a sparsely populated and largely infertile plateau region where agriculture was labor intensive and where the foreign trade of the period was largely dependent upon the export of slaves.[41]

Fanompoana, derived from the principle of obligatory service to the sovereign, was initially an honor for the caste and individuals chosen to perform a particular ritual task.[42] However, under Andriamasinavalona, such ritual services were extended to include all "first fruits." Their collection was made the *fanompoana* of a group called *mpanantatra* also responsible for the extension of ritual services to the provision by freemen of labor for state constructions – notably the creation and maintenance of river dykes and irrigated rice fields.[43] Ralambo (c.1575–1610) is traditionally considered the first Merina king to have commenced drainage and irrigation projects to promote riziculture. Such schemes were rapidly extended following two major famines in c.1708–16 and c.1747–70. The first famine prompted Andriamasinavalona to erect dykes to prevent the river Ikopa from overflowing, drain the surrounding Betsimitatatra marshland, and convert it to rice fields.

[40] Omar Eno, "The Abolition of Slavery and the Aftermath Stigma: the Case of the Bantu/Jareer People on the Benadir Coast of Southern Somalia" in Campbell (ed.), *Slave Systems* vol. 2; Sandra Evers, "Stigmatization as a Self-Perpetuating Process" in *idem* and Mare Spindler (eds.), *Cultures of Madagascar* (Leiden: IIAS, 1995), 137–56; Watson, "Transactions in People," 237–8, 246–7.

[41] *HR* vol. I, 14, 258, 304, 306, 360–1; André, *De l'esclavage*, 121; J. P. Raison "Perception et réalisation de l'espace dans la société merina" *Annales, économies, sociétés, civilisations* 32 (1977), 416–17, 423–5; Bloch, *Placing the Dead*, 14–25, Ch. 2; *idem*, "La séparation du pouvoir," 267–71; Deschamps "Tradition and change," 399–400; *idem, Histoire*, 167–8, 190, 203; Dez "Développement économique et tradition à Madagascar," 856, 889; *idem*, "Le fokonolona malgache: institution désuète ou cellule de développement?" *Cahiers de l'ISEA: économie et sociologie rurales* (avril, 1963), 189–252; *idem*, "Éléments pour une étude de l'économie," 367.

[42] Called a *santatra* – see Jean-François Baré, "Remarques sur le vocabulaire monarchique sakalava du nord" in Raison-Jourde (ed.) *Les souverains de Madagascar*, 167; Ellis, *History of Madagascar* vol. I, 175, 177–9.

[43] *HR* vol. I, 49, 303; see also *ibid*, 9, 489, 252–4, 256, 260, 262–3, 307, 313–14; vol. II, 596; vols. III–IV, 362, 737, 812, 885; vol. V, 1109; Campbell, "Role of the London Missionary Society" vol. I, 28.

To this end, he altered the organization of *fanompoana*: The entire Merina male population was divided into caste-based units and mobilized for the construction of the Ikopa dyke. Andriamasinavalona then applied *fanompoana* to drain marshes over much of central Imerina.[44] *Fanompoana* units were also used to build defenses around towns containing strategic stores of grain. These granary towns attracted ordinary cultivators seeking both protection and, in times of dearth, provisions. The subsequent concentration of population facilitated the imposition by rulers of further limits on the geographical mobility of the population in order to control their labor for *fanompoana* purposes.[45]

On this base, Andrianampoinimerina built. He incorporated the territorially restricted population groups, or *foko*, into larger regional units called *toko*, six of which formed greater Imerina: Avaradrano, Marovatana, Ambodirano, Vakinisisaony, Vonizongo, and Vakinankaratra. The inherently passive nature of the caste structure facilitated the transmission of royal orders concerning *fanompoana*, through the *mpanantatra* to the people via the local village councils.[46] The king claimed the labor of each male subject for six days each season (a total of 24 days a year) for public works, notably in agriculture. The application of *fanompoana* augmented food production by expanding rice cultivation, from one to two crops annually, thereby guaranteeing a regular agricultural surplus for the first time in Imerina's history. The same system was practiced in Betsileo.[47] Ordinary cultivators ultimately gained considerable benefits from large-scale agricultural improvements – although this does not constitute evidence that the village councils formed the basis for a democratic society or for an authoritarian socialism, as some historians claim.[48]

Labor and the Industrial Experiment, 1825–1861

A radical change in the nature of *fanompoana* occurred as a result of the adoption of autarky in the mid-1820s. Thereafter, the dual aim of the Merina regime was to effect a swift military conquest of the entire island and generate economic

---

[44] *GH* (1908), 846; *HR* vol. I, 238–9, 275–6, 279–80, 282, 297–8; *RH*, 247; Grandidier, "Souvenirs," 33; C. Keller, *Madagascar, Mauritius and the Other East African Islands* (London, 1901), 123; Dez "Éléments," 39, 41.

[45] *HR* vol. I, 304; see also previous note.

[46] Termed "*fokon'olona*."

[47] Dubois, *Monographie des Betsileo*, 429.

[48] *RH*, 69; *HR* vol. I, 276–7, 288, vols. III–IV, 823–7; vol. V, 1111; Léon Ozoux, *Vieux principes d'économie rurale malgache* (Paris, 1926), 5; Raison, "Perception et réalisation," 417; Deschamps, "Tradition and Change," 400–2; *idem, Histoire*, 204, 209; Dez, "le fokonolona malgache," 201; see also Bloch, "La séparation du pouvoir," 269.

growth through the exploitation of domestic resources. As attempts to stimulate alternative exports to slaves failed, and foreign investment was negligible, the Merina court based its bid for military and economic power on forced labor, notably *fanompoana*.[49]

In the early 1820s, Radama I conducted a population census with the express purpose of forming *fanompoana* units, each comprising between 10 and 1,000 men, on a territorial caste rather than clan basis.[50] To enforce participation, a royal edict of January 1823 obliged anyone who claimed to be ill, upon recovery, to spend a time corresponding to the length of their illness in public works *fanompoana*[51] (Tables 5.1 and 5.2). The crown also adopted and adapted European institutions, notably the school and army, to recruit and organize a new and radically enlarged *fanompoana* system. In 1823, Radama I established direct control over the LMS mission, transforming it into a machine for the recruitment of forced labor. Rather than be expelled from the country, the missionaries – comprising clerics, whose primary function was education, and artisans, who practiced European craft skills – complied.[52] Until they were expelled in 1835–6, the school system – itself a new aspect of *fanompoana* – gave Merina youth basic literacy before channeling them into the imperial army/administration. Such military personnel[53] formed a permanent *fanompoana* category, as distinct from nonmilitary subjects[54] who were theoretically subject to irregular civilian forced labor.[55]

The new *fanompoana* similarly underpinned attempted industrialization in the period 1820–61. Some industrial forced labor units had formed prior to 1820, notably for the manufacture of military goods. Also, in December 1824, most foreign artisans (at least half were LMS agents) signed royal contracts to promote craft production. Merina apprentices to missionary artisans subsequently formed specialist craft *fanompoana* units.[56] The attempt, following

[49] Campbell, "Adoption of Autarky."
[50] *HR* vol. V, 1109, 1111–12, 1114, 1123; *RH*, 96; Hastie "Journal" (1817–18), 241; A Resident, *Madagascar*, 57; Canham to Burder, Antananarivo, 30 June 1822, *SOAS/LMS-MIL*, B1.F2.JB; Freeman to Hankey, Antananarivo, 10 Feb. 1829, *SOAS/LMS-MIL*, B3.F1.JA; Baker to Arundel, Antananarivo, 29 March 1829, *SOAS/LMS-MIL*, B3.F1.JB; "Expenses from November 1st 1831 to April 30th 1832," *SOAS/LMS-MIL*, B4.F3.JB; Munthe, *La bible à Madagascar*, 84, 112–13; Campbell, "Role of the London Missionary Society" vol. I, Ch. 5 and vol. II, Ch. 6; *GH* (1908), 248, 371.
[51] Hastie, "Diary" (1822–3).
[52] Freeman to Hankey, Antananarivo, 12 March 1829, *SOAS/LMS-MIL*, B3.F5; *HR* vol. V, 1075.
[53] Termed *sorondany*.
[54] Termed *borizano*.
[55] *GH* (1908), 248, 371.
[56] Campbell, "Slavery and Fanompoana."

TABLE 5.1. *Permanent Skilled Fanompoana in Imerina, 1790–1883, by Era*

A. Under Andrianampoinimerina (c. 1790–1810)	Fanompoana	Number	% Total 1790–1810	% Total 1790–1883
Fitonjatolahy	Butchers	272	53.75	2.38
Mpiandry omby	Cattle herders	122	24.11	1.07
Manjakaray	Gunpowder manufacturers	86	17.00	0.75
Mpanety trano	Thatchers	26	5.14	0.23
Total 1790–1810	4 units	506	100.00	4.42
B. Under Radama I (1810–28)	**Fanompoana**	**Number**	**% Total 1790–1828**	**% Total 1790–1883**
Amparibe	Ironworkers	4,167	63.57	36.41
Tambato	Hewers and stonemasons	786	11.99	6.87
Mpandrafitra	Carpenters	463	7.06	4.05
Mpanefy vifotsy	Tin and zinc smiths	128	1.95	1.12
Ambohimandroso	Tanners	124	1.89	1.08
Fehin'Andrianambo	Copper workers	111	1.69	0.97
Andoharano	Makers of leather goods	83	1.27	0.73
Tsarahonenana	Cotton spinners and weavers	57	0.87	0.50
Deka Borigedry	Maintain iron tools and missiles	43	0.66	0.38
Mpanao kitrontsoavaly	Farriers	34	0.52	0.30
Fehin'dRainimandrato	Silkworm breeders	30	0.46	0.26
Mpamaky hazo	Sawers (using long saw)	27	0.41	0.24
Total 1810–28	12 units	6,049	92.28	52.85
Total 1790–1828	16 units	6,555	100.00	57.27
C. Under Ranavalona I (1828–61)	**Fanompoana**	**Number**	**% Total 1790–1861**	**% Total 1790–1883**
Analakely	Makers of cartridges and gunpowder	1,621	14.89	14.16
Alijinery	Crown porters	1,200	11.03	10.48
Avaratr'Ilafy	Gunsmiths	303	2.78	2.65
Mantasoa	Cannon founders	287	2.64	2.51
Mpanjaitra	Makers of military flags and clothes	165	1.52	1.44
Antranombasy	Makers of watches and precision parts	139	1.28	1.21
Mpanao ampongabe	Makers of crates and boxes	133	1.22	1.16

C. Under Ranavalona I (1828–61)	Fanompoana	Number	% Total 1790–1861	% Total 1790–1883
Vodivato	Makers of gunpowder and explosives	124	1.14	1.08
Mpamboly rongony	Hemp cultivators	106	0.97	0.93
Mpanefy volamena	Gold and silversmiths	69	0.63	0.60
Mpanao solika	Neat's-foot oil extractors	46	0.42	0.40
Fehin' dRamarosambaina	Machine-gun manufacturers	42	0.39	0.37
Mpanao tsorahy	Wire makers	30	0.28	0.26
Amboalefoka	Makers of blue dye/paint	21	0.19	0.18
Mpampiasa omby	Trainers of draught oxen	18	0.17	0.16
Mpanao sotro	Makers of zebu horn utensils	15	0.14	0.13
Mpamboly vary	Cultivators of royal rice fields	100	0.09	0.09
Total 1828–61	17 units	4,329	39.77	37.82
Total 1790–1861	33 units	10,884	100.00	95.10

D. Under Rasoherina (1863–8)	Fanompoana	Number	% Total 1790–1868	% Total 1790–1883
Mpanamalona	Fishermen (notably of eel)	89	0.81	0.78
Mpamono omby	Cattle butchers	70	0.63	0.61
Total 1863–8	2 units	159	1.44	1.39
Total 1790–1868	35 units	11,043	100.00	96.49

E. Under Ranavalona II (1868–83)	Fanompoana	Number	% Total 1790–1883
Manjakamandroso	Dynamite manufacturers	138	1.21
Antsahandriana	Forge workers	107	0.93
Mpandalotra	Pebble dashers, plasterers, and scaffolders	43	0.38
Mpandatsabiriky	Tile and brick makers	39	0.34
Fehin'dRamangetrika	Makers of machine-guns and precision parts	39	0.34
Fehin'Andrianavy	Makers of machine-guns and precision parts	36	0.31
Total 1868–83	6 units	402	3.51
Total 1790–1883	41 units	11,445	100.00

Source: Hastie, "Journal" (1817–18), 231; Freeman to Hankey, Antananarivo, 12 Oct. 1831 SOAS/LMS-MIL, B4.F1.JC; Johns, Freeman and Canham to Ellis, Antananarivo, 28 May 1833, SOAS/LMS-MIL, B4.F1.JC; HR vol. V, 1158; Chapus, Quatre-vingts années, 230; GH (1928), 134, 166, 370; Freeman and Johns, A Narrative, 256, 42, 107; Rey, "A propos d'une lettre," 16790; Chauvin, "Jean Laborde," 89, 29, 43; Pfieffer, Last Travels, 222, 276; Ellis, History of Madagascar vol. I, 196–7, 282, 311–13 and vol. II, 293–4; Cameron, Recollections of Mission Life, 230; Dez "Eléments"; Cheffaud, "L'artisanat indigène à Madagascar," 7.

TABLE 5.2. *Imerina: Permanent Skilled Fanompoana, 1790–1883, by Sector (% of Total)*

Era	Units	Members	% 1790–1810	% 1790–1828	% 1790–1861	% 1790–1868	% 1790–1883
A. Agriculture and the extractive industries							
1790–1810	2	394	77.87				3.44
1810–1828	1	30		0.46			0.26
1828–1861	4	180			1.65		1.57
1863–1868	2	159				1.44	1.39
1868–1883	–	–					–
1790–1883	9	673					6.66
B. Military and Armaments							
1790–1810	1	86	17.00				0.7
1810–1828	8	4,747		72.42			41.4
1828–1861	7	2,681			24.63		23.4
1863–1868	–	–					–
1868–1883	4	320					2.8
1790–1883	20	7,834					68.4
C. Construction							
1790–1810	1	26	5.14				0.23
1810–1828	3	1,276		19.47			11.15
1828–1861	–	–					–
1863–1868	–	–					–
1868–1883	2	82					0.72
1790–1883	6	1,384					12.10
D. Other							
1790–1810	–	–					–
1810–1828	–	–					–
1828–1861	6	1,468			13.49		12.8
1863–1868	–	–					–
1868–1883	–	–					–
1790–1883	6	1,468					12.8

Source: Hastie, "Journal" (1817–18), 231; Freeman to Hankey, Antananarivo, 12 Oct. 1831 *SOAS/LMS-MIL*, B4.F1.JC; Johns, Freeman and Canham to Ellis, Antananarivo, 28 May 1833, *SOAS/LMS-MIL*, B4.F1.JC; Callet, *Histoire des Rois* vol. V, 1158; Chapus, *Quatre-vingts années*, 230; *GH* (1928), 134, 166, 370; Freeman and Johns, *A Narrative*, 25–6, 42, 107; Rey, "A propos d'une lettre," 167–90; Chauvin, "Jean Laborde," 89, 29, 43; Pfieffer, *Last Travels*, 222, 276; Ellis, *History of Madagascar* vol. I, 196–7, 282, 311–13 and vol. II, 293–4; Cameron, *Recollections of Mission Life*, 230; Dez, "Eléments"; Cheffaud, "L'artisanat indigène à Madagascar," 7.

the adoption of autarky in the mid-1820s, to forge an industrial revolution greatly expanded *fanompoana*. It functioned on both a permanent and an intermittent basis, utilizing a new core of factory workers, traditional artisans, and general *fanompoana* to extract and supply raw materials. The concentration of labor was considerable. Cameron supervised 700 men in his Analakely factory.[57] The Mantasoa industrial complex possessed a permanent workforce of 5,000[58] who comprised condemned Christians as well as military and civilian *fanompoana*.[59]

The construction industry was another important employer of skilled *fanompoana*. Traditionally, labor for the construction of royal houses had been reserved for high status groups, although general *fanompoana* was used for defensive earthworks. As Mayeur noted in 1777, *fanompoana* could be utilized for work of national importance, including the erection of fortifications and royal residences.[60] Whereas this labor was both periodic and honorific, the huge expansion of *fanompoana* under autarky was applied to all projects desired by the court elite, whether or not in the national interest.

Industrial production and construction involved far greater numbers of unskilled than skilled *fanompoana*. Mantasoa was built by 20,000 workers, equivalent to about 5 percent of the adult Merina male population, registered for *fanompoana*. In 1830, a Betsileo forced labor pool of 21,000 men was formed. The industrial village of Soamalaza comprised chiefly unskilled *fanompoana*, including 200 convicts supplemented occasionally by skilled labor dispatched from Imerina. A penal workforce, first formed to lay a stone road between Radama I's palace and the former Zoma market in Antananarivo, from 1836 included condemned Christians. Convicts were employed in the harshest varieties of industrial work.[61] Felling and porterage of construction timber also involved great numbers of unskilled *fanompoana*, as did construction itself. For instance, it took workers 12 days to erect a 39-meter-high tree trunk on the site of Manjakamiadana palace. The job was assigned to a large *fanompoana* unit formed in Vakinandiana, a district east of Antananarivo, specifically to erect and square construction timber for royal buildings.[62] Thousands of additional

---

[57] Baker to Arundel, Antananarivo, 5 April 1831, *SOAS/LMS-MIL*, B4.F1.JB; Freeman to Ellis, Antananarivo, 15 Feb. 1834, *SOAS/LMS-MIL*, B5.F1.JA.

[58] Called *zazamadinika* ("little children") by Laborde.

[59] Raombana B2 Livre 13, 18; also see Chapter 4.

[60] See, e.g., Mayeur, "Voyage au pays d'ancove" (1777), 1778.

[61] E. Prout, *Madagascar: Its Mission and Its Martyrs* (London, 1863), 79; Hewlett, "Mantasoa," 381; Cameron to Arundel, Antananarivo, 25 Sept. 1829, *SOAS/LMS-MIL*, B3.F2.JB; Shipton to LMS, Tamatave, 10 Aug. 1834, *SOAS/LMS-MIL*, B5.F2.JA; Campbell, "Role of the London Missionary Society" vol. I, 208–10 and vol. II, 301; *HR* vol. V, 1103, 1114; *RA*, 256–7; Freeman and Johns, *A Narrative*, 48; Echalier "Betsileo et ses habitants," *Conférence de l'école coloniale* (15 fèvrier 1909), 48; Dubois, *Monographie des Betsileo*, 604–5; John A. Nilsen, "Ny tantaran'ny distry Fianarantsoa, 1878–1943," ms. *FLM/NMS* 57H, 1; Oliver *Madagascar* vol. I, 503; Chapus, *Quatre-vingts années*, 197, 206; *Les Missions Catholiques*, 153 (1872), 334; Chapus et Birkeli, "Historique d'Antsirabe," 59–82; Sibree, "Industrial Progress," 129–32; Oliver, *Madagascar* vol. I, 228–9 and vol. II, 86.

[62] This unit was called *fitonjatolahy* (lit. the "seven hundred") – Campbell, "Slavery and Fanompoana."

unskilled laborers were drafted for general manual labor on state construction projects.[63]

Although fewer than those involved in industrial work on the plateau, considerable numbers of *fanompoana* were also employed in the east coast plantations and factories. For example, in April 1825, a 2,000-strong Betanimena or Betsimisaraka workforce was summoned to help Hastie create a 4 hectare mulberry bush plantation near "Vonitzar[y]," on the Antananarivo–Andevoranto route.[64]

The Relaxation of *Fanompoana*, 1861–1877

In 1861, after announcing his intention to abolish *fanompoana*, Radama II dismissed the 2,000-plus workforce at Mantasoa.[65] The specter of him doing likewise to the army greatly alarmed the Merina elite whose commercial interests it served (see Chapter 7). Their fears were temporarily assuaged when, within three months of Radama II's assumption of power, up to 6,000 new soldiers were drafted to maintain the 40,000-strong imperial army.[66] The institution of *fanompoana* was confirmed following Radama II's death. In November 1864, Rainilaiarivony prohibited the civilian population from wearing hats and commanded them to tie up their hair in small knots (to distinguish them from the military who cut their hair short and wore hats) and to register for *fanompoana*.[67] Such were the levels of nonmilitary forced labor that LMS missionaries had their imported goods transported free of charge and, following the 1868–9 creation of a state church, missionaries stationed outside central Imerina summoned *fanompoana* at will for their own porterage needs.[68]

The commercial boom in the 1860s led to an appreciable rise in the standard of living of most Merina, to the extent that slave ownership again became common for the first time since the early 1820s. For about a decade, this enabled many Merina summoned for *fanompoana* to substitute slave labor for their own. The boom was accompanied by a burst of private, missionary, and government

---

[63] *RA*, 263.

[64] Hastie, "Diary" (April 1825).

[65] Hewlett, "Mantasoa," 378, 381.

[66] However, leading Merina officers were again alarmed when the king substantially reduced the force at Mahajanga; Boy au Jouen, Tananarive, 29 Oct. 1861, in "Correspondance P. Jouen, 1859–1869" C52 *AHVP*; Bee Jordaan, *Splintered Crucifix. Early Pioneers for Christendom on Madagascar and the Cape of Good Hope* (Cape Town, 1969), 235; Rasoamiramana "Aspects économiques" (1973), 15; Campbell, "Slavery and Fanompoana."

[67] Ellis, *Madagascar Revisited*, 455.

[68] *Ibid*, 424–5.

construction in Antananarivo. The limited supply of stone hewers, masons, carpenters, and roofers resulted in fierce competition for skilled *fanompoana*. The Merina court, which summarily siphoned skilled workers away from private and missionary building sites, had to be bribed to release workers for private employers. For example, according to Françoise Raison, the four LMS Memorial churches in Antananarivo were constructed only because the foremen of missionary builders Sibree and Cameron paid members of the court elite to release workers from state *fanompoana*.[69]

Ellis described *fanompoana* recruitment in 1865 to construct a royal building under Cameron's supervision. All eligible males from Voromahery were summoned and directed to their different tasks by Rainilaiarivony and his aides, as were full-time *fanompoana* units of masons. In addition, all imperial officers were required to provide about 36 liters of lime. For those already involved in building work this demand proved easy to satisfy. The rest had to send their slaves to quarry or purchased lime – which increased sixfold in price as a result of subsequent demand. A similar process of requisition applied to stones and timber. Ellis commented of such building *fanompoana*:

The obtaining of the timber was the most laborious work connected with the building. [*Fanompoana*] Chiefs went away with their men, in numbers of ten to fifty or more, to the forests north, east, or south, to a distance of twenty, thirty, or more miles [32 to 48 km or more], and when they had felled the trees, and obtained the required amount and kind of timber, the bringing or dragging it over the hill and valley, up steep, rugged, and precipitous places, where the ascent is difficult, often appeared to me the severest work the slaves ever had to perform. The largest trees, stripped of all their branches, are dragged by ropes. Sometimes rollers are used. . . . The heavier kinds of planks, made out of a tree split by wedges down the centre, and reduced by the hatchet, are carried by two or four men on their shoulders. Lighter planks are carried by a single individual. If there is a large number of planks to be conveyed, the noble or chief goes with his men to show his own loyalty, and also to encourage them. . . . [I] never saw them [i.e., *fanompoana* labor] either dragging or carrying their timber without great commiseration, as I noticed some of them lame, footsore, and often stretched on the roadside quite exhausted. . . . To the large trees the people attach ropes, or strongly twisted creepers, to both ends, and proceed in one or two rows, pulling with all their might, and singing or shouting as they pull. I have sometimes seen more than one hundred men dragging a single tree past my house.[70]

Ellis noted two alleviatory aspects of this *fanompoana*: Their wives, who cooked and sometimes helped with the load, often accompanied men who were also

[69] François Raison, "Un tournant dans l'histoire religieuse Merina du XIXe siècle: La fondation des temples protestantes à Tananarive entre 1861 et 1869" *Annales de l'Université de Madagascar. Série lettres et sciences humaines* XI, 35.

[70] Ellis, *Madagascar Revisited*, 477–8.

permitted to play the guitar both during work, to maintain spirits, and at night for entertainment and relaxation.[71]

Female slave labor supplemented such *fanompoana*. Some transported earth in baskets, while 100 royal slaves carried water, used to prepare mortar, from a pond near the top of the ridge on which Antananarivo was situated. Of the latter, Ellis commented, "About once every hour, for two or three days, I saw them pass in unbroken single line, each woman with a jar of water on her head."[72]

The Intensification of *Fanompoana*, 1877–1895

The burden of forced labor was renewed from the late 1870s. First, a commercial slump and the 1877 emancipation measure combined to dramatically narrow slave ownership, so that the full burden of *fanompoana* again fell upon ordinary freemen. Second, the 1883–5 Franco–Merina War virtually bankrupted the imperial regime, increasing its reliance on forced labor. Thereafter, *fanompoana* was also applied to the gold fields.[73]

Initially, the court summoned civilian *fanompoana* (in theory on an irregular basis) and permanent *fanompoana* units. The latter included woodcutters[74] who by the mid-1880s had grown from their original number of 1,200 to 2,000, 500 to 600 charcoal burners, and 400 smiths and general iron workers, as well as smaller numbers of gunsmiths, spear makers, gunpowder manufacturers, carpenters, seamstresses, tailors, tanners, curriers, and soap boilers. Oliver comments that Ellis's observation that these units were "a sort of Government slaves," confined to their villages and occupations for life, were as valid for the 1880s as when made in the 1830s.[75] Similarly, governors of Fianarantsoa, the chief Merina garrison in Betsileo, maintained a permanent forced labor pool of 900 men, comprising 100 carpenters, 100 guards and jailers, and 700 woodcutters.[76]

The system was abused by imperial officers who summoned forced labor on a semipermanent basis. For instance, it was noted in the late 1880s and early 1890s that whenever *fanompoana* was conscripted to fell and transport timber, five times the required amount of wood, and therefore of workers, was ordered

---

[71] This was a specific Malagasy instrument called a "*lokanga*" – *ibid*, 478.
[72] *Ibid*, 476; see also *ibid*, 475.
[73] Campbell, "Gold Mining and the French Takeover."
[74] Termed "*foloroazato*" (lit. "the 1,200").
[75] Oliver, *Madagascar* vol. II, 89, 192–3; *GH* (1908), 370.
[76] Nilsen "tantaran'ny distry Fianarantsoa," 7.

TABLE 5.3. *Fanompoana Quotas in Imerina, 1869*

Province	Quota	Province	Quota
Avaradrano	19,100	Marovatana	8,000
Vakinankaratra	18,000	Ambodirano	7,000
Vakinisisaony	9,000	Voromahery	3,100
Vonizongo	8,550	Total	72,750

Source: GH (1908), 260–1.

by the commanding officers, who subsequently sold the surplus wood for their own profit.[77]

To finance the war, the Merina crown started systematic exploitation of the island's gold fields. Failure to attract substantial foreign capital and skill meant that almost all gold was produced by slow and arduous labor-intensive methods. Hitherto, traditional civilian *fanompoana* had usually satisfied imperial needs. However, from the mid-1880s, the combined labor requirements of the army and gold mines outstripped the ability of the existing administrative apparatus to summon forced labor. In consequence, the imperial court resurrected the idea, employed from 1820–36, of recruiting *fanompoana* through missionary institutions. In 1869, it had created a state church that controlled all foreign missions. From the outbreak of war, it used mission churches and schools specifically to recruit *fanompoana*, with missionary and other state church agents playing increasingly significant roles both in drawing up forced labor quotas and in overseeing forced labor units.[78]

By July 1886, in response to the intensification of gold exploitation, the Merina court had formed a permanent *fanompoana* of between 600 and 700 miners. Foreign prospectors were also offered *fanompoana* in 1886–7. For example, Suberbie was allocated 4,000, many of them *Masombika* (slaves recently imported from East Africa, notably Mozambique) supposedly liberated from slavery in 1877, but in reality maintained as imperial *fanompoana*.[79] However, as most workings were alluvial, gold *fanompoana* was generally drawn on

---

[77] Francis Maude, *Five Years in Madagascar* (London, 1895), 103.

[78] "Minute Book of the English Church Mission in Madagascar" (28 June 1884); Gwyn Campbell, "Missionaries, Fanompoana and the Menalamba Revolt in late nineteeenth century Madagascar," *Journal of Southern African Studies* 15.1 (1988); see also Chapter 4.

[79] Robinson to Hunter, Tamatave, 28 June 1877, *US*; see also Robinson to Porter, Tamatave, 20 July 1886, *US*; Devred, "Les mines," 64; Decary, "L'ancien régime," 90; Jacqueline Ravelomanana, "La vie religieuse à Ambositra, 1880–1895," thèse (Université de Madagascar, 1971), 29; E. Defoort, *Étude historique et ethnologique sur le secteur d'AmbatoBoeni (cercle de Maevatanana)* (Tananarive, 1905), 78; Campbell, "Madagascar and the Slave Trade."

TABLE 5.4. *Fanompoana Draft Centers in Ambodirano and Vakinankaratra*

Ambodirano		Vakinankaratra	
Arivonimamo	Antsahadinta	Antoby	Antsirabe
Fenoarivo	Kingony	Ambositra	Antanamalza
Ambohijafy	Ambohimanga	Manandriana	
Ambohimasina	Ambohimahandry	Iaraivo	
Androhibe	Miantsoarivo	Betafo	

Source: GH (1908), 249–61.

a seasonal basis from missionary chapels and schools. In the northern Betsileo region of Mananadona, Norwegian Missionary Society (NMS) affiliated state churches were interrupted as early as 1887 by the imposition of a 400-strong gold *fanompoana* comprising both sexes[80].

In addition, children were drafted for the first time. By 1888, child labor had become so widespread in the gold fields that the *Madagascar Times* declared, in December that year,

> by forced labour, into which even evangelists and school children are pressed, the Prime Minister is washing for gold on his own account. It is said that more than a thousand labourers are daily employed on this work.[81]

Child exploitation in the gold fields, notably in Betsileo, intensified from the late 1880s with the renewed threat of French intervention. In general, the predominantly Protestant Merina officials obliged pupils from Jesuit supervised schools to undertake the heaviest *fanompoana*. However, in 1889, LMS-affiliated schools in the Ambohibeloma district (where military drill was instituted by the local missionary) were being drafted into gold *fanompoana*. The same year, the entire free population of the Ambositra region (from Behenjy to Ambositra – but excluding Antankaratra) was summoned.[82] In 1890, the government ordered all scholars aged over 16 into the gold fields, while in

[80] A. J. & G. Crosfield, *A Man in Shining Armour. The Story of the Life of William Wilson, M.R.C.S. and L.R.C.P., Missionary in Madagascar, Secretary of the Friends' Foreign Missionary Association* (Antananarivo, n.d.), 96.

[81] *The Madagascar Times* (8 Dec. 1888); see also Borchgrevink to PM, Antsahamanitra, 19 Oct. 1887, HH6, *ANM*; Borgrevink to PM, n.d, Boks 270G.

[82] C. Savaron, "notes d'histoire malgache" *BAM* 14 (1931), 72; Haile to PM, Ambohibeloma, 23 Aug. 1889, HH1, 529–30; Ranaivo to Selmer, Ambohipo, 15 Feb. 1894, HH7, 756–7; Berbezier to PM, Antananarivo, 26 juin 1893 and *idem* to Radoava, 7 May 1894, HH9, 218, 229–30 *ANM*; Anon, "Gold in Madagascar," 68.

some districts, such as Fisakana, all pupils were drafted regardless of sex or age.[83]

Thus by the eve of the French takeover in 1895, the economy of imperial Madagascar was almost entirely dependent upon *fanompoana* – the specifically Merina system of forced and unremunerated labour. This had dire consequences for the future of the imperial regime and economy. Its impact on demography is discussed in the following chapter.

---

[83] Borchgrevink to [PM] [c.1891], Boks 270G, *NMS/FLM*; Ravelomanana, "La vie religieuse à Ambositra," 58–63, 90.

6   Population, 1820–1895

Introduction

African historical demography has generated considerable debate between sup-
porters and critics of the demographic transition theory, which assumes that
precolonial Tropical Africa experienced high rates of both fertility and mortality, due primarily to internecine tribal warfare and disease. Consequently,
population growth remained largely stagnant until the colonial era, when security and medical services provided by Europeans induced population growth
by simultaneously raising birth rates and depressing mortality rates.[1] Critics
of the theory consider it was applicable to pre-industrial Europe, but less relevant to precolonial Tropical Africa. They assert that in Africa, minor climatic
changes, blights, drought, and epidemics formed part of a normal 5- to 10-year
cycle that occasionally had an adverse impact on food supplies, but not on
long-term population growth. Thus natural causes alone tended to leave a long-
term margin of births over deaths.[2] Moreover, conflict over land – which in
contrast to Europe was abundant in precolonial Africa – was minimal and thus
did not act as a powerful constraint on population growth.[3] Only when severe
social dislocation caused by human factors imposed upon this natural rhythm
might famine occur and population growth be retarded. Therefore, critics of the

---

[1] J. C. Caldwell, "Major Questions in African Demographic History" in *AHD* vol. I, 7–8; see also
John Iliffe, "The Origins of African Population Growth," *JAH* 30.1 (1989), 165–6; Joseph C.
Miller, "Demographic History Revisited," *JAH* 25 (1984), 94.

[2] Caldwell, "Major Questions," 10; J. E. Inikori, "Under-Population in nineteenth century West
Africa: the role of the export slave trade" in *AHD* vol. II, 297–9.

[3] Gavin Kitching, "Proto-industrialisation and Demographic Change: a Thesis and some possible
African Implications" *JAH* 24.2 (1983), 230.

134

demographic transition theory argue, the slave export trade drained many African societies of their youngest and fittest members and created such economic and social dislocation as to raise death rates and depress fertility rates.[4]

More serious was the imposition of colonial rule, which rather than raise birth rates and lower death rates[5] involved unprecedented levels of violence and social dislocation. These so upset the ecological balance that a catastrophic series of human and animal diseases occurred. Only from the 1920s did colonial health measures and security induce rapid population growth.[6]

The Role of the State

Central to the debate is the relative importance of natural and human factors upon the demographic regime. It could be argued that due predominantly to natural factors, Madagascar was by 1800 suffering from overpopulation – defined by the ability of the land under the existing technology to support a given population. The fishing, swidden, and pastoral economies of the lowlands set far greater demographic limits than did the labor-intensive riziculture of the central highlands. Like the irrigated terraces of some Lake Victoria islands and some cultivated hilltops of the northern Cameroons and Northeast Nigeria, the Malagasy highlands was one of the few areas of sub-Saharan Africa capable of sustaining very dense populations.[7] Indeed, early colonial censuses reveal that 6 to 16 people per km^2 inhabited the central plateau, compared to

[4] J. D. Fage, "Slavery and the slave trade in the context of West African History" *JAH* 10.3 (1969), 393–404; see also Helge Kjekshus, "The Population Trends of East African History: A Critical Review" and R. G. Willis, "Comment on Dr. Kjekshus' paper" in *AHD* vol. I, 358–60, 363–4; Patrick Manning, "Contours of Slavery and Social Change in Africa," *American Historical Review* 88.4 (1983), 838; see also *ibid*, 835–57; Inikori, "Under-Population," 283–314 and 371–84; for East Africa, see J-P. Chrétien, "Démographie et écologie en Afrique orientale à la fin du XIXe siècle: une crise exceptionnelle?," *Cahiers d'Études Africaines* 27.105–6 (1987), 46–7; Kjekshus, "Population Trends" and R. W. Beachey, "Some Observations on the Volume of the Slave Trade of Eastern Africa in the Nineteenth Century" – in *AHD* vol. I, 352–62, 365–73.
[5] Kitching, "Proto-industrialisation," 221–3; Caldwell, "Major Questions," 11–12, 16; Dennis D. Cordell, Joel W. Gregory, and Victor Pich, "African Historical Demography. The Search for a Theoretical Framework" in Dennis D. Cordell and Joel W. Gregory (eds.), *African Population and Capitalism* (Boulder, 1987), 14–15.
[6] Christopher Wrigley, "Population and History: Some Innumerate Reflexions," *AHD* vol. II, 17–18; Chrétien, "Démographie et écologie," 47–50; Kjekshus, "Population Trends," 352–62; Cordell et al., "African Historical Demography," 14–32; Gregory & Pich, "Démographie," 11–46; Dennis D. Cordell and Joel W. Gregory, "Historical Demography and Demographic History in Africa: Theoretical and Methodological Considerations," *Canadian Journal of African Studies* 14.3 (1980), 389–416; Inikori, "Under-Population," 293.
[7] Caldwell, "Major Questions," 12–13.

1 to 6 people per km^2 for the lowlands – except for the fertile valleys of the southeast, with 10 people per km^2.[8]

An indication that maximum densities had been reached in both lowland and upland Madagascar by the early 1800s was the island-wide practice of infanticide, a ritual associated with perennial problems of overpopulation. In lowland regions, it was common for three days of the week to be taboo for births, babies born on those days being left to die, while in some societies, such as the Tanala, entire months were taboo. However, the taboo against twins was also widespread on the plateau, which, in addition, had suffered two major famines in the early and mid-eighteenth century.[9]

The conventional historical view is that natural impediments to population growth were overcome in the nineteenth century by a strong indigenous Merina state, which provided internal security and progressive health and education facilities.[10] Thus, most would accept the McEvedy and Jones estimate of a Malagasy population steadily rising from 1.5 million in 1800 to 2 million in 1850 and 2.75 million in 1900.[11] Indeed, Yvan-Georges Paillard and Charles Robequain hold that, by 1900, the real population was, for a number of reasons, considerably higher: French colonial officials were untrained in census techniques, the unsettled political state of the country and evasion of tax officials by the Malagasy made statistics gathering extremely difficult, and French officials had a vested interest in underestimating the population in order to excuse low tax returns and above all to disguise the negative demographic impact of the colonial regime.[12] Despite its relative isolation, Madagascar shared with mainland Africa a heightened mortality after colonization due to the 1895 French conquest, the 1895–7 suppression of the *Menalamba* revolt, and the disturbances that followed abolition of slavery in 1896.[13]

Thus, the Malagasy population on the eve of colonization might well have been closer to the 3.3 million recorded in 1921, when the first comprehensive census

---

[8]   However, there existed sharp regional variations within Imerina, with two people per km^2 in the extreme north, 11 in Vakinankaratra, 18 in the west, 20 in the east, and 90 in and around the capital city of Antananarivo – *GH* (1908), 322; see also J. Vansina, "Long-Term Population History in the African Rain Forest," in *AHD* vol. II, 757.

[9]   Louis Molet, "Le boeuf dans l'Ankaizinana: son importance sociale et économique," *Mémoire de l'institut scientifique de Madagascar* série C, T.II (1953), 61–2; J. Richardson, "Tanala Customs, Superstitions and Beliefs," *AAMM* 2 (1876), 99–100; *GH* (1908), 97; Avine, "notes de voyage," 324.

[10] See, e.g., Deschamps, *Histoire*, 213–15.

[11] Colin McEvedy and Richard Jones, *Atlas of World Population History* (London, 1978), 265.

[12] Rebellions continued until 1913; see Robequain, *Madagascar*, 110; Yvan-Georges Paillard, "Les recherches démographiques sur Madagascar au début de l'époque coloniale et les documents de l'AMI" *Cahiers d'Études Africaines* 27 (1987), 20–1.

[13] Paillard, "recherches démographiques," 19–20.

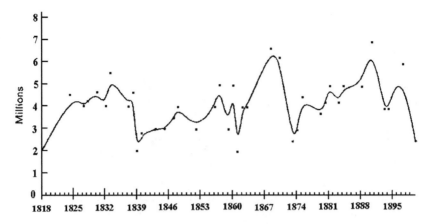

Figure 1. *Madagascar: Population Estimates, 1818–1900*
Source: see Appendix C

was completed. Moreover, whereas most of sub-Saharan Africa experienced significant population growth from the 1920s, this occurred in Madagascar only from the late 1940s.[14] Therefore, the consensus is that the state played a crucial but contrasting demographic role, the precolonial Merina state removing natural obstacles to population growth, and the succeeding colonial state imposing drastic artificial constraints that largely curtailed such expansion.

Estimates assembled from a large number of precolonial sources, both speculative and informed, suggest a different demographic trend.[15] They indicate the possibility that the total Malagasy population remained stagnant during the nineteenth century at between two million and three million, while that of Imerina, and the Merina capital of Antananarivo, grew: the population of Imerina from approximately 100,000 to 500,000 in the 1820s, at which level it remained, albeit with sharp fluctuations in the 1830s, until the late 1870s when it again increased to about 800,000, and the population of Antananarivo rising between 1820 and 1860 from about 17,000 to 50,000, in the subsequent decade reaching 100,000 at which level it remained despite sharp fluctuations. The first French censuses suggest that these figures are less reliable for Madagascar and Imerina than for Antananarivo, which alone appears to reflect the impact of major killer diseases, such as the smallpox epidemics of 1875–81 and 1884–9[16] (see Figures 1–3). As these population estimates have no sound statistical basis, they

---

[14] Wrigley, "Population and History," 17–18; for Madagascar see, e.g., Ralinoro, "Le problème démographique dans la circonscription médicale de Fianarantsoa," *BdM* 99 (1954), 732–40.

[15] See Appendix A.

[16] See Table 6.1.

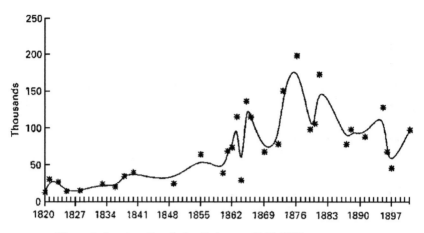

Figure 2. *Imerina: Population Estimates, 1817–1900*
Source: see Appendix C

must be treated warily, but in the absence of concrete evidence, do warrant serious consideration.[17] As such, they raise doubts as to the traditional assumption of a steady demographic expansion and suggest the existence of serious obstacles to population growth in nineteenth-century Madagascar. Attention falls upon the role of the precolonial state which, it is here argued, had a primary but *negative* demographic impact.

Cordell et al. contend that the colonial state was a paramount influence on demographic trends in Africa, where it shaped the mechanisms for the production

---

[17] The estimates are both speculative and derived from informed sources such as Merina court officials. The estimates with the soundest statistical basis are those that attempt to calculate the number of inhabitants per house. These generally fall within the range of 3.5–5.2 people per African rural household, revealed by a 1967 UN survey (quoted in Jack Goody, "The evolution of the family" in Peter Laslett and Richard Wall (eds.), *Household and Family in Past Time* [Cambridge, 1974], 115). In 1816, Le Sage estimated households on the northeast coast to average 10 members, although in the 1820s, it was claimed that Andevoranto had 4.8 inhabitants per house, close to the 1838 estimate of 4.5 for Toamasina. Estimates for Antananarivo also varied considerably: Duhaut-Cilly in 1825 and LMS missionaries in the early 1830s worked on the basis of three inhabitants per house, in comparison to Andrew Davidson's 1860s estimate of four per house, James Richardson's of 8.25 in the 1870s, and the Merina government's estimate of seven. It is possible that the variations were a reflection of whether the nuclear family alone was counted or the household, as most houses in Antananarivo possessed at least one slave and frequently accommodated nonnuclear relatives: Le Sage, "Mission" (1816), 60; Ellis, *History of Madagascar* vol. I, 18, 67, 96–7; Duhaut-Cilly, "Notice sur le royaume d'Emirne," 237; J. Richardson, "Dr Mullens and the Population of Antananarivo" *AAMM* 2 (1876), 72–4.

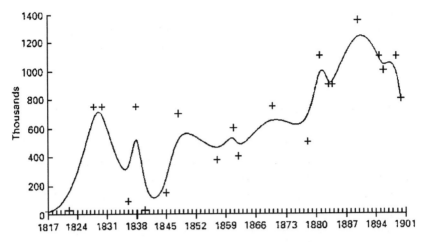

Figure 3. *Antananarivo: Population Estimates, 1820–1901*
Source: see Appendix C

and reproduction of labor through two broad strategies: first, forced labor, characterized by the use of a head tax, military conscription, and direct forced labor, and second the formation of a reserve army of voluntary workers.[18] Such measures had vital demographic consequences, but neither was unique to the colonial era. As in most of Africa, production in nineteenth-century Madagascar was critically dependent upon labor, so population size, growth, and density were as important to the precolonial state as they were to most colonial regimes.

Initially, the Merina state played a positive role. Following the major drought-induced famines of the early and mid-eighteenth century, it eliminated food scarcity by organizing the draining and cultivation of the vast Betsimitatatra marshland of central Imerina.[19] However, as noted in Chapter 5, autarkic policies from the 1820s involved oppressive labor regimes that had strongly negative demographic effects. The Merina crown restricted both free and slave labor geographically and manipulated it to serve state ends. Also, through the 1877 emancipation decree, it created a huge reserve state army of nominally free and voluntary workers.[20] Merina expansion under autarky was primarily at the

---

[18] Cordell et al., "African Historical Demography," 27–8.

[19] Campbell, "Slavery and Fanompoana," 465–7.

[20] Campbell, "Madagascar and the Slave Trade," 203–27; *idem*, "Adoption of Autarky," 395–409; *idem*, "Slavery and Fanompoana," 463–86.

demographic expense of subjected provinces, notably on the east coast, until the 1870s. Thereafter, the failure of autarky led to an intensification of state pressure upon the labor resources of the imperial heartland.[21]

Fertility and the Birth Rate

Christopher Wrigley and Gavin Kitching highlight fertility and the birth rate as possibly the primary demographic influences in precolonial Africa. However, whereas Wrigley argues that, besides natural disasters, "subtle and largely unconscious social forces" operated on the birth and infant/child mortality rates, Kitching posits political power holders, shaping factors bearing directly upon fertility, as the most critical influence.[22] Certainly in nineteenth-century Madagascar, the policies of the Merina state had a major impact upon such rates.

Like most mainland African communities,[23] the Malagasy placed a premium on children. Social mores encouraged early sexual experience, and few obstacles existed to divorce and remarriage or to extramarital sexual relations, except between lower-caste men and higher-caste females.[24] Caste proscriptions did not generally include foreigners. Most foreign males formed sexual liaisons with Malagasy women,[25] mostly short-lived, as Europeans were generally absent from Madagascar during the malarial, hurricane months from December to March. However, some endured, especially after the widespread adoption of quinine in the late nineteenth century permitted Europeans to reside permanently in malarial regions. By 1895, Toamasina boasted 2,000 foreign

---

[21] Campbell, "Slavery and Fanompoana"; *idem*, "Missionaries, Fanompoana and the Menalamba Revolt"; *idem*, "Gold Mining and the French Takeover."

[22] Wrigley, "Population and History," 23–4; Kitching, "Proto-industrialisation," 230–1; see also Cordell et al., "African Historical Demography," 22–4.

[23] David Voas, "Subfertility and Disruption in the Congo Basin" in *AHD* vol. II, 785–6; Pool, "A Framework," 49.

[24] Wolf, "Analysis" of "Narrative of Voyages to Explore the Shores of Africa, Arabia, and Madagascar," *Journal of the Royal Geographical Society* III, 203; *HR* vol. I, 333; Mondain, "Notes sur la condition sociale de la femme hova," 85, 91. It is uncertain what effect polygamy, which was practiced in Imerina during the first half of the nineteenth century, had upon the birth rate. British missionaries to Imerina commented in 1833, "Polygamy is common in this part of Madagascar, if not throughout the island, to all who can afford the expense. . . . To be able to maintain several wives, to have a numerous offspring – to hoard wealth, – and to build a commodious and handsome tomb, – these are the objects of desire and ambition in the breast of a Malagasy" – Johns and Freeman to Ellis, Antananarivo, 29 May 1833, *SOAS/LMS-MIL*, B4.F4.JB.

[25] See, e.g., Hastie, "Diary" (1820), 482.

residents.[26] A sizeable Creole community arose in the island. It was noted in 1902, for example, that Bullen, a resident of Toliara since the early 1880s, had "married the usual Malagash princess, and has a numerous family."[27] This indication of a high fertility rate in Madagascar is backed by LMS statistics revealing that, in 1825, 14 percent of girl pupils in Antananarivo were obliged to leave school because they fell pregnant.[28] It is therefore quite possible that the birth rate in Madagascar in the early 1800s equaled if not surpassed the 48 per 1,000 average postulated for precolonial sub-Saharan Africa.[29]

A high natural birth rate could explain the infanticide, which was widespread except in Imerina where, in 1823, it was banned in all provinces save Imamo, from where expectant mothers were encouraged to cross into central Imerina for delivery. Usually considered the result of humanitarian pleading by Hastie, the British agent,[30] the measure was probably a response to the enhanced labor needs of the imperial Merina economy under autarky.[31]

Indeed, any natural promotion of high fertility rates was profoundly upset from the mid-1820s by the adoption of autarkic policies, especially the new enlarged *fanompoana* system. First, *fanompoana* was unremunerated and so, in contrast to the era of proto-industrialization in Europe – where the advent of wage labor might have resulted in a lowering of the average age of marriage and in enhanced fertility – it decreased income opportunities for young adults. This probably resulted in a rise in the average age of marriage and in depressed fertility. The only significant body of wage earners were the slave porters, who were predominantly young and unattached.[32] Kitching argues that in Africa, in contrast to Europe, responsibility for child rearing rested with the extended rather than the nuclear family, so that parental income may not have influenced family size to a parallel degree.[33] However, the scale of *fanompoana* in imperial

---

[26] Avine, "Voyages," 55; Capmartin, "Notes" [1815], 13; Oliver, *Madagascar* vol. I, 454; *GH* (1908), 320–1.

[27] C. G. Smith, "Journal," Tulear, Madagascar, 5 Sept. 1902, in "Notes Taken by C.G.S. on Trip to Madagascar in 1902," ms, *BRA*. For White–Malagasy social relations in Toamasina, see Esoavelomandroso, *province maritime*, 145.

[28] Jones and Griffiths to Burder, Antananarivo, 4 Aug. 1825, *SOAS/LMS* -MIL, B2.F2.JB; "School Report" (1825), *SOAS/LMS-MIL*, B2.F3.JG.

[29] Iliffe, "Origins of African Population Growth," 168.

[30] Hastie, "Diary" (1822–3).

[31] See Thurstan Shaw, "Questions in the Holocene Demography of West Africa" in *AHD* vol. I, 107.

[32] Campbell, "Labour and the Transport Problem," 341–56; *idem*, Slavery and Fanompoana,' 463–86; Kitching, "Proto-industrialisation," 221–40.

[33] *Ibid.*, 234.

Madagascar steadily undermined the ability of the extended family to sustain its own members, notably the very young and old.[34]

Second, *fanompoana* involved long periods of harsh physical labor and inadequate rations. In women, this delayed puberty and altered ovulatory cycles – depressing fertility and increasing the incidence of miscarriages.[35] Traditionally, women worked harder than men in Imerina, who, from the late 1700s until 1820, were relieved of much of their labor due to a massive influx of slaves. Thus, in 1817, Hastie commented that "Many of the women are much stouter in person than the men. . . . When the males arrive to manhood the greater part of their labour ceases. The women work till age overcomes them."[36] The adoption of autarky in the 1820s and subsequent intensification of *fanompoana* further increased labor for females as slave ownership narrowed to elite circles and ordinary Merina farmers were conscripted for military and other state *fanompoana*, obliging plateau women to fulfill agricultural tasks normally executed by males. In addition, the exploitation of female labor for *fanompoana* steadily increased, peaking after the 1883–5 Franco–Merina War, notably in the gold fields.[37]

Third, conception rates were reduced as husband and wife were often separated for long periods under *fanompoana* schemes and, in the case of wives of absent soldiers, draconian punishments restricted adultery. Fourth, *fanompoana* inspired such fear that some people mutilated themselves and parents commonly hid their children to avoid conscription.[38] Decary and Sibree estimate that infanticide caused the deaths of 14.29 and 25 percent respectively of Malagasy babies,[39] figures that fall within the 15 to 50 percent infanticide rate calculated by Birdsell for aborigines in Pleistocene Australia – although there is no comparable indication that in Madagascar more female than male babies were affected.[40]

State labor policies also assisted the spread of venereal diseases, which contributed initially to lower fertility and to miscarriages. Voas and Brothwell date

---

[34] Campbell, "Slavery and Fanompoana."

[35] G. T. Nurse, J. S. Weiner, and T. Jenkins, *The Peoples of Southern Africa and their Affinities* (Oxford, 1985), 253–4.

[36] Hastie, "Diary" (1817).

[37] Campbell, "Slavery and Fanompoana," 463–86; *idem*, "Gold Mining," 99–126; *idem*, "Missionaries, Fanompoana and the Menalamba Revolt," 54–73.

[38] To spare the future generation from *fanompoana*, some couples probably limited their family size through practicing abortion and, despite the royal ban, infanticide – Campbell, "Role of the London Missionary Society" vol. II, 225–6, 265–6, 337; *idem*, "Missionaries, Fanompoana and the Menalamba Revolt," 54–73.

[39] James Sibree, *Fifty Years in Madagascar* (London, 1924), 253; Decary, "La population de Madagascar," 30; *idem*, "voyage d'un chirurgien," 326.

[40] See Thurstan Shaw, "Towards a Prehistoric Demography of Africa" in *AHD* vol. II, 586.

the arrival of venereal syphilis in sub-Saharan Africa to the start of the colonial era.[41] However, it probably reached Madagascar by the late 1700s due to commercial contact with Europeans and with the Swahili who, like the Arabic groups on the Comoros and Swahili coast, experienced lower birth rates than the surrounding indigenous population – probably due to syphilis.[42] Except for Imerina, which attracted numbers of foreign traders from the mid-1700s, most of the plateau interior was largely protected until 1862, when foreigners were for the first time permitted unrestricted entry into the Merina empire.[43]

In 1865, an estimated 10 percent of clinic patients in Antananarivo had syphilis. A decade later, 70 percent of LMS dispensary patients in Imerina, 20 percent in Betsileo, and most in Menabe were reported to be suffering from syphilis-related complaints.[44] Again, the early French colonial administration considered venereal diseases to be responsible for the large number of stillbirths in Madagascar.[45] However, the increase in venereal disease may have reflected better reporting due to the growth from 1861 in the number of foreign medical staff. Moreover, it is impossible in early medical reports to distinguish between cases of venereal disease and *farasisa* – the Malagasy term for all chronic diseases with cutaneous symptoms.[46] Nevertheless the venereal variety probably spread rapidly in the late 1800s. This was due partly to the increased influx of foreigners and the relaxed sexual mores of the Malagasy,[47] but mostly to the increased tempo of *fanompoana* from the late 1870s.

As in the Congo Basin under the exploitative Arab slave raiding and colonial rubber system of the late nineteenth and early twentieth centuries, *fanompoana* in Madagascar seriously disrupted social life. It caused the disintegration of families, undermined monogamy, and promoted the growth of promiscuity and prostitution, women infected with venereal diseases circulating widely in

[41] See Miller, "Demographic History Revisited," 96. A nonvenereal disease of the treponemal group appears to have been widespread in pre-nineteenth-century Africa, including Madagascar. Syphilis in mainland Africa was often confused with yaws; other treponematoses include pinta, bejel, and irkinja – see Juhani Koponen, "War, Famine and Pestilence in Late Precolonial Tanzania: A Case for a Heightened Mortality," *International Journal of African Historical Studies* 21.4 (1988), 656; T. Aidan Cockburn, "Infectious Diseases in Ancient Populations" in David Landy (ed.), *Culture, Diseases and Healing* (New York, 1977), 84–5.
[42] See Carol M. Eastman, "Women, Slaves and Foreigners: African Cultural Influences and Group Processes in the Formation of Northern Swahili Coastal Society," *International Journal of African Historical Studies* 21.1 (1988), 13.
[43] *RH*, 74; Hastie, "Diary" (1817).
[44] George A. Shaw, "The Betsileo: Country and People," *AAMM* 3 (1877), 79; *GH* (1908), 330; Joseph Sewell, *The Sakalava. Being Notes of a Journey made from Antananarivo to some Towns on the Border of the Sakalava Territory, in June and July 1875* (Antananarivo, 1875), 12, 17.
[45] Paillard, "recherches démographiques," 23.
[46] *Ibid*, 37.
[47] Pool, "A Framework," 53; Dubois, *Monographie des Betsileo*, 665–6.

both a geographical and a social sense.[48] Such was the barrenness of plateau women by the late 1800s that many made votive offerings to phallic-shaped standing stones in an attempt to regain fertility.[49] Numerous taboos also existed in nonplateau regions to enhance fertility and the chances of a successful birth.[50]

Despite having long enjoyed the best medical and administrative services in the island, by the end of the nineteenth century Imerina had the lowest fertility and highest infant mortality rates.[51] French surveys between 1899 and 1905 indicate that an estimated 40 percent of all deaths in Imerina occurred within the 0 to 5 year age range, one-third of all children born alive dying before the age of three – a figure close to the upper range of infant mortality estimates (25 to 30 percent) in modern times for parts of Tropical Africa least affected by medical and administrative services.[52] This led to a skewed demographic age profile for Madagascar. In 1853, for example, Ellis estimated that the average number of children per household was 3.5 on the east coast compared to 2.5 in Imerina.[53] These are lower than the average of between 4.9 and 5.25 children per household estimated for sub-Saharan Africa in general during precolonial and recent times. In early colonial Madagascar, 23.99 percent of the coastal population and 37.1 percent of the plateau population were aged under 16 years of age – compared to an African average closer to 55 percent.[54] In overall terms, low rates of fertility, birth, and infant survival meant that the reproduction rate on the plateau was just sufficient to enable the region to maintain or possibly permit a slight natural increase in population.[55]

---

[48] Voas, "Subfertility and Disruption," 786–96; see also Nancy Rose Hunt, "'La Bebe En Brousse': European Women, African Birth Spacing and Colonial Intervention in Breast Feeding in the Belgium Congo," *International Journal of African Historical Studies* 21.3 (1988), 403–4; see also David Birmingham and Phyllis M. Martin (eds.), *History of Central Africa* vol. II (London, 1986), 20.

[49] Shaw, "The Betsileo," 4; Sibree, *Fifty Years*, 41.

[50] For instance, pregnant Antanosy women and their husbands were forbidden extramarital sexual intercourse until the birth of the child – see Jorgen Ruud, *Taboo. A Study of Malagasy Customs and Beliefs* (Oslo, 1960), 244–5.

[51] Jean Valette, "Notes sur la géographie médicale de l'Imerina à la fin de la monarchie (1889–1893)" *BdM* 246 (1966), 1143–5; Paillard, "recherches démographiques," 25.

[52] *GH* (1908), 343; Paillard, "recherches démographiques," 34; Caldwell, "Major Questions," 10.

[53] *GH* (1908), 337.

[54] Paillard, "recherches démographiques," 33; For estimates of African averages, see Patrick Manning, "A Demographic Model of African Slavery" in *AHD* vol. II, 374, and for a mainland African example of a skewed age structure, see John Thornton, "The Slave Trade in Eighteenth Century Angola: Effects on Demographic Structure" *Canadian Journal of African Studies* 14.3 (1980), 421–2.

[55] Caldwell, "Major Questions," 9; Pool, "A Framework," 52.

Mortality and the Death Rate

In 1826, at the start of autarky, a British visitor claimed that most Merina survived their 80th year,[56] while almost 100 years later a Frenchman wrote:

An old centenarian from Isotry, who recently died, was born two years prior to the death of Andrianampoinimerina. In my presence, he brought together his children, grand children, sons- and daughters-in-law – a total of 154 people. [Again], two years ago, 84 women were counted in the family line of Ramba, the sister of Rainilaiarivony. Moreover the Hova [i.e., Merina] were polygamous.[57]

However, the overwhelming bulk of evidence points to a low life expectancy from birth in nineteenth-century Madagascar and for a major and direct state impact upon the death rate, which J. Caldwell, in contrast to Wrigley, posits instead of fertility as an independent variable in determining population change.[58]

Disease

Geographical isolation spared Madagascar some of the more serious diseases, such as trypanosomiasis and rinderpest, which directly and indirectly affected the demography of mainland Africa.[59] Nevertheless, the incidence of disease in Madagascar increased sharply from the mid-eighteenth century, associated with the growth of trade – notably from the 1870s, when steamships facilitated the rapid movement of disease to the island from other regions of the globe. Its spread has also been linked to concentrated settlements of population. Thus, the more sparsely populated regions of the island, such as the vast cattle-grazing plains of Sakalava land, were incapable of sustaining infectious diseases in endemic form, unlike the main ports, the densely settled valleys of the southeast, and the valleys and marshlands of the plateau interior.[60] The last and probably most important element influencing the spread of infectious diseases was imperial *fanompoana*.

---

[56] Locke Lewis, "An Account of the Ovahs, a race of people residing in the Interior of Madagascar: with a Sketch of their Country, Appearance, Dress, Language, &c," *Journal of the Royal Geographical Society* 5 (1835), 236.

[57] Baudin to Dubois, 25 août 1918, quoted in H. M. Dubois, "Les Origines des Malgaches" *Anthropos* 22 (1927), 96.

[58] Caldwell, "Major Questions, 11; Wrigley, "Population and History."

[59] Rinderpest, for example, devastated cattle stocks and game over much of southern and eastern Africa from 1892, thereby significantly reducing food supplies and lowering resistance to disease. See Swanzie Agnew, "Factors Affecting the Demographic Situation in Malawi in Precolonial and Colonial Times" in *AHD* vol. I, 378; Marc H. Dawson, "Disease and Population Decline of the Kikuyu of Kenya, 1890–1925" in *AHD* vol. II, 126.

[60] As among the pastoral Maasai – see Dawson, "Disease and Population Decline," 126.

The most important diseases to affect nineteenth-century Madagascar were malaria, transmitted to humans via the anopheles mosquito, and smallpox, syphilis, and tuberculosis, all of which were transmitted directly. Any disease could devastate a community previously untouched by that disease or which had lost previously acquired resistance. Resistance could be built up after exposure to malaria, smallpox, and tuberculosis, but not to venereal infections. Malaria presented a special case in that resistance could also be inherited with the sickle cell trait.[61]

As on mainland Africa, malaria – endemic in most tropical areas and regions of high rainfall – was the major fatal disease of all age groups in the Malagasy highlands.[62] The malarial cycle generally commenced from the start of the rains in November, which afforded the female anopheles mosquito ideal sites to lay eggs. Clinical symptoms of the disease usually started to show in the victim from one to four weeks after the onset of the rains and peaked in July. It was of particular demographic importance that a pregnant woman's acquired resistance to malaria decreases with the length of the pregnancy, heightening the risk of anemia, which was a frequent cause of neonatal death. Surviving babies were, up to their fourth month, generally protected from the disease by fetal hemoglobin and antibodies from the mother. Hence, malaria most seriously affected infants aged three to five, notably between the end of the rainy and the start of the winter season, when their physiological defences were often weakened by nutritional deficiency. However, it could seriously affect all age groups, especially when several years of poor rains and low malarial incidence, reducing the body's natural defences against infection, were followed by a protracted rainy season.[63]

Smallpox (*variola minor* or the more severe *variola major*) most likely first hit southern Africa, including Madagascar, during the eighteenth century. Dawson quotes Leakey's estimate of a 5 to 10 percent mortality in an epidemic that hit the pastoral Maasai in the early 1890s, although Ross put the rate in an unvaccinated population at 40 percent and Chrétien at from 50 to 70 percent. Indeed, Chrétien argues that in East Africa the demographic impact of smallpox and cholera

---

[61] William H. McNeill, *Plagues and People* (New York, 1976), 3–12; Leonard Jan Bruce-Chwatt, *Essential Malariology* (London, 1980), 58–67; Jean Delmont, "Paludisme et variations clima-tiques saisonnieres en savane soudanienne d'Afrique de l'Ouest," *Cahiers d'Études africaines* 22.85–86 (1982), 117–34.

[62] Nurse *et al.*, *Peoples of Southern Africa*, 19, 278–9; Ellis, *History of Madagascar* vol. I, 215, 217–19. Outbreaks of measles in Imerina in 1822–3 and 1884 resulted in some infant deaths, although whooping cough did not appear to have affected Madagascar in the same way as it did mainland Africa. See, e.g., Agnew, "Factors," 378.

[63] Delmont, "Paludisme," 117–34; Paillard, "recherches démographiques," 39.

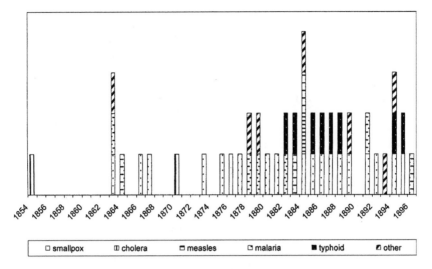

Figure 4. *Madagascar: Frequency of Disease, 1854–96*
Source: Gwyn Campbell, "Crisis of Faith and Colonial Conquest: The Impact of Famine and Disease in Late Nineteenth-Century Madagascar," *Cahiers d'Études Africaines* 32 (3) 127 (1992).

combined was probably far greater than that of the slave trade, especially when they coincided with periods of famine.[64] Such was the fear of smallpox in Imerina that its victims were initially driven from their villages and either stoned to death or forced into an open grave and left to die. Increasing familiarity with the disease, notably a realization that survivors gained immunity to it, brought about a more enlightened official attitude to victims. From the 1820s, they were obliged to retire to isolated huts until they had either succumbed to the disease or recovered[65] (see Figure 4). A series of smallpox epidemics from 1833 to 1835 effectively depopulated some central provinces. Nevertheless, attempts to introduce vaccination were opposed due to fear in court circles that Europeans wished thereby to infect the Malagasy with smallpox.[66]

---

[64] Dawson, "Disease and Population Decline," 127–8; Robert Ross, "Smallpox at the Cape of Good Hope in the Eighteenth Century" in *AHD* vol. I, 416–28; see also Beachey, "Some Observations," 369; Chrétien, "Démographie et écologie," 51, 55; Koponen, "War, Famine and Pestilence," 663–5; Nurse et al., *Peoples of Southern Africa*, 18.

[65] Although this was still considered harsh because the Malagasy, like mainland Africans, incorporated their ill within a tight familial or community network. For a comparison of isolating the ill, see Maryinez Lyons, "'From Death Camps to Cordon Sanitaire': The Development of Sleeping Sickness Policy in the Uele District of the Belgian Congo, 1903–1914," *JAH* 26.1 (1985), 69–91.

[66] Freeman to Ellis, Tamatave, 3 Oct. 1833 and Vohitsara, 11 Oct. 1833 – *SOAS/LMS-MIL*, B4.F4.JC.

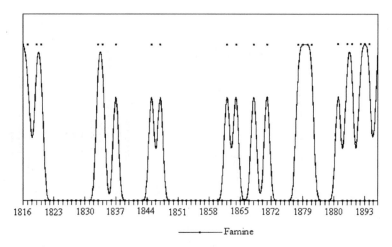

Figure 5. *Madagascar: Frequency of Famine, 1816–96*
Source: Campbell, "Crisis of Faith."

All diseases appear to have increased in proportion to the extent and severity of *fanompoana* and other exploitative policies of the Merina state. A high incidence of the sickle cell trait and resistance gained through exposure offered some protection against malaria to coastal peoples, although it entailed high child mortality.[67] By contrast, the peoples of the traditionally malaria-free highlands possessed no acquired resistance or genetic defense against the disease so that the increasing numbers, who from 1817, due to Merina expansionism, traveled to coastal regions, proved almost as vulnerable as Europeans to the disease. An estimated 25 to 50 percent of Merina soldiers in lowland provinces died each year, mostly of malaria, as did about 160,000 Merina soldiers (close to Raombana's estimate of 150,000 for the years 1820–53) in imperial campaigns from 1816–53 – giving an average of about 4,500 soldier deaths a year (possibly 0.8 to 4.5 percent of the Merina population).[68] The pace of military campaigning fell off radically from the early 1850s, so that a total of 235,000 Merina military dead, mostly from malaria and famine, for the entire period 1800–95 would appear reasonable[69].

Although the incidence of malaria among Merina troops in the provinces may have declined from 1850, it increased on the plateau. Paillard asserts that only after 1895 was the plateau was affected by malaria epidemics, which were due to

[67] Bruce-Chwatt, *Essential Malariology*, 58–61.

[68] Although a staggering 72 percent of the French expeditionary troops died of malaria in the Malagasy campaign of 1895 – William B. Cohen, "Malaria and French Imperialism," *JAH* 24.1 (1983), 24–5; see also Campbell, "Slavery and Fanompoana," 468–9.

[69] Campbell, "Slavery and Fanompoana."

the social upheaval that followed the implantation of colonial rule.[70] Certainly
by 1905, the only malaria-free area of the plateau was Antsirabe. However, missionary records demonstrate that epidemics of malaria and unspecified diseases
that caused hot fever and other symptoms characteristic of malarial infection
regularly afflicted the highlands from the late 1870s – a decade and a half before the French conquest.[71] The major reason for the spread of malaria to the
plateau was increased state *fanompoana*, which resulted in the mass circulation of forced labor units – a feature often ascribed only to European colonial
regimes – between the plateau and the forest and other malarial areas.[72]

Second, the imposition of security by the Merina state, from the end of the
Merina Civil Wars in the 1790s in Imerina and from about 1820 in Betsileo,
induced plateau peoples to evacuate their fortified hilltop encampments and
settle the cultivated valley bottoms.[73] This move from a theoretically hostile
environment to one friendly to mosquitoes (see Table 6.1) was of little importance until the late 1870s, when absorption into, or flight from, *fanompoana*
led to the abandonment of large stretches of the irrigated riziculture network.[74]
Following the rice harvest, it was customary in plateau regions to drain flooded
fields. However, from the late 1870s, due to labor shortages, water was increasingly left to stagnate. As a result, a putrid environment developed, attracting
the anopheles malaria vector from March to April until the fields were finally
drained in July, in the middle of the dry season.[75] It is also significant that
the incidence of malaria and similar unspecified diseases[76] increased sharply
from 1884 to 1894, when Madagascar experienced unusually wet weather –
often associated with malarial infection (which in 1895 caused 25 percent
mortality).[77]

[70] Paillard, "recherches démographiques," 38, 40.

[71] Campbell, "Gold Mining," 99–126; Marriot, "Report" (1905), 6; also see Table 6.1.

[72] Campbell, "Gold Mining"; *idem*, "Missionaries, Fanompoana and the Menalamba Revolt."

[73] Dubois, *Monographie des Betsileo*, 623.

[74] Maude, *Five Years in Madagascar*, 103; Campbell, "Missionaries, Fanompoana and the
Menalamba Revolt."

[75] See Paillard, "recherches démographiques," 39.

[76] Like *safo-tany*, which afflicted chiefly Betsileo in the late nineteenth century – although its
victims apparently failed to respond to quinine – see Anon, "Dr Forsyth Major's Expedition in
Madagascar," *AAMM* 20 (1896), 493; D. M. Rees, "Y 'Safo-tany' na 'Raporapo,'" *Y Cronicl*
(1898), 178–80.

[77] Ryder to Ropes, Emmerton & Co, and Arnold Hines & Co, Nossi Bé, 28 Feb. 1885, B44.F4,
18 Oct. 1887, B45.F6; Laborde to Whitney, Antananarivo, 22 Jan. 1887, B44.F2; Whitney to
Ropes, Emmerton & Co, Tamatave, 26 Jan. and 26 Feb. 1889, B45.F2; Trumball to Ropes,
Emmerton & Co, Tamatave, 26 March 1890, B46.F5; Duder to Dawson, [Antananarivo], 28
June 1890, B46.F5; Whitney to Ropes, Emmerton & Co, Tamatave, 27 March 1891, B46.F4;
Ryder to Ropes Emmerton & Co, Tamatave, 28 July and 27 Aug. 1893, B45.F7; Ryder to
Ropes, Emmerton & Co, Tamatave, 6 April 1894, B45.F7 – *REC/CR-MZL*; Paillard, "recherches
démographiques," 38, 40.

TABLE 6.1. *Famine and Disease in Madagascar, 1816–96*

Year	Event
1816	– Betanimena (northeast coast): famine (December)
1817	– Northeast coast: cyclone destroys harvest; Imerina: smallpox outbreak
1819–20	– Cholera [?]
1822–3	– Imerina: measles outbreak – several children die
1826	– Imerina: "A very extensive, and, in many instances, fatal malady, prevailed, both in the capital and in the neighbouring villages"
1833	– North Madagascar and Imerina: smallpox epidemic (peak in November)
1833–4	– Imerina: rainfall highest in living memory – rice harvest spoiled (November–February)
1834	– Imerina: smallpox – causes great turmoil
	– Northeast coast (Toamasina and Mahavelona) and Imerina: famine (September)
1835	– Imerina: smallpox – causes great turmoil (January–February)
	– Eastern forest: ban on swidden; imperial ports kept filthy (imperial Merina policy)
1845	– Northeast coast: famine
1847	– Northeast coast: famine
1854	– Cholera [?]
1862	– North Imerina (Ambohimanga): drought, crops fail, and famine anticipated
1863	– Imerina: smallpox, malaria, choreomania
1864	– Imerina: malaria
1866–7	– Imerina: mild form of smallpox
1870	– Mahajanga: cholera epidemic – 2,000 die (October–December)
1873	– Betsileo: smallpox
1875–7	– Toamasina: smallpox – over 800 die: communications cut with the interior
	– Vonizongo, Vakinankaratra, Ambohimara, and Betsileo: smallpox
1878–9	– Plateau: epidemic of aretin'olona (and/or malaria) – kills many
	– Betsileo: smallpox epidemic
1879	– Avaradrano: malaria epidemic
1880–1	– Smallpox epidemic
1882	– Toamasina: typhoid
1882–3	– Imerina: severe outbreak of typhoid and malaria
1884	– Smallpox epidemic and outbreak of measles
	– Severe outbreak of malaria after wettest rainy season for years
	– Marovatana province: choreomania – to appease the ancestors
1885–8	– Smallpox epidemic and typhoid
1889	– Smallpox epidemic
	– Imerina: river Ikopa threatens to flood Betsimitatatra rice plain (March)
	– Toamasina, Mahajanga, and Antseranana: the plague

1890	– Imerina: harvest shortfall – acute rice shortages
1891	– Mandridrano region: malaria and "other diseases" widespread
	– Smallpox outbreak
1892	– Anonibe (Betsimisaraka): smallpox epidemic – fields abandoned; famine ensues
1892	– Maroantsetra, Mananara, and Antongil Bay: floods destroy rice crop
1893	– Imerina: influenza epidemic – hundreds die
	– Toamasina region: cyclone
1894	– Imerina: influenza epidemic, "nervous fever" and (in Antananarivo) typhoid epidemic
	– Northeast coast: cyclone destroys rice and banana crop; and (in Vohimara) smallpox – famine ensues
1895	– Toamasina: smallpox
	– Toamasina: typhoid
1896	– East coast: French hostilities – flight and famine
	– Plateau: malaria

Sources: Campbell, "Crisis of Faith."

The incidence of all diseases increased dramatically with stress, malnourishment, and extreme fatigue, common under *fanompoana*, which upset the internal physiological balance, permitting low-grade infections to become fatal.[78] The body's defenses against disease were also undermined by alcohol consumption, which increased rapidly from the 1870s. This reflected both the immense social dislocation caused by forced labor and the influx – into all regions save Imerina – of cheap Mascarene rum, which foreign merchants frequently insisted upon as payment for Malagasy cattle exports. Imported rum supplemented the ubiquitous locally produced *toaka-gasy* variety.[79]

From the 1820s, the state also played a major causative role in food shortages, which in turn lowered resistance to disease. During the early 1800s, the impact of *fanompoana*, and subsequently of impoverishment and famine, was felt more in subjected forest and coastal provinces than on the plateau.[80] This changed from the 1870s, when food shortages became frequent on the plateau

---

[78] McNeill, *Plagues and People*, 16; see also Campbell, "Adoption of Autarky," 405; *GH* (1908), 339; Paillard, "recherches démographiques," 38.

[79] By 1880, Mascarene rum was retailing for $0.25 per quart on the east coast and $0.50 in the interior – Johnson to PM, Faravohitra, 19 Oct. 1889, HH4, ANM; LMS, *Ten Years' Review (1880–90)*, 114; see also Birmingham and Martin (eds.), *History of Central Africa* II, 167, 174; Anon, "Ny Toaka avy tany Morosy" in *Ny Gazety Malagasy* I.4 (2 Aug. 1876), 13; LMS, *Ten Years' Review of Mission Work in Madagascar 1870–1880* (Antananarivo, 1880), 31–4.

[80] See, e.g., *RA*, 263, 322 and *RH*, 136–7.

where, as in the early colonial Congo Free State and French Congo, increasingly unremitting forced labor resulted in insufficient time being devoted to subsistence agriculture. As a British visitor commented of *fanompoana*, "the result is always the same. The Queen honours 'Raini-bé' or 'Bootoo' by taking him away from his rice fields just at the season when his labour and supervision are most required for his crop."[81]

Especially significant was the large-scale drafting of women, the backbone of the agricultural labor force, into state gold fields from the early 1880s. The situation was complicated in Betsileo, where bankrupt farmers indebted to Merina usurers faced enslavement and thus fled to join brigand bands. These comprised mainly refugees from *fanompoana*, who survived largely by raiding – thus completing a vicious cycle of exploitation and abandonment of cultivation. Unlike the fishing, pastoral, and swidden economies of lowland regions, plateau agriculture was based upon a highly sophisticated and labor-intensive system of hydraulic riziculture that required a minimum production unit to ensure its viability. Although granaries might help withstand short-term dearth, that system was rendered increasingly untenable from the late 1870s through being deprived of labor.[82]

Impoverishment and famine were complicated on the plateau by cold winters and inadequate clothing. This made ordinary people, notably the very young and old, highly susceptible to influenza, bronchitis, and related diseases: Hundreds perished in the influenza epidemic of 1894–5, and it is possible that nineteenth-century rates were similar to those of the early colonial era – for example, in Antananarivo between April 1900 and March 1901, 13.1 percent of deaths were flu-related and 33.29 percent bronchial, in comparison to 7.51 percent that were malaria-related.[83]

Also, on the largely unforested plateau, ordinary people lacked the variety of fruits and roots common in wooded lowland regions.[84] This combination of

---

[81] Maude, *Five Years in Madagascar*, 103.

[82] Campbell, "Missionaries, Fanompoana and the Menalamba Revolt"; *idem*, "Gold Mining"; Dubois, *Monographie des Betsileo*; see also Koponen, "War, Famine and Pestilence," 644–7; Joseph C. Miller, "The Significance of Drought, Disease and Famine in the agriculturally marginal zones of West-Central Africa," *JAH* 23.1 (1982), 17–32.

[83] Paillard, "recherches démographiques," 36. In the Fianarantsoa region of Betsileo from 1932 to 1946, respiratory diseases accounted for 33.28 percent of all hospitalised patients (behind malaria at 43.80 percent) once the plague, which only became a serious affliction during the colonial era, is discounted (bronchial pneumonia and pneumonia accounted for 53 percent of all respiratory cases) – Ralinoro, "Le problème démographique," 733–4; Dubois, *Monographie des Betsileo*, 1041–2; see also Shaw, "Towards a Prehistoric Demography of Africa," 584–5.

[84] Oliver, *Madagascar* vol. I, 459; R. Toy, "Remarks on the Meteorology of Antananarivo and the Neighbourhood," *AAMM* (1878), 73ii, 74ii.

climatic and dietary factors, accentuated in *fanompoana* camps by unsanitary conditions, facilitated the spread of disease. Only in the case of smallpox did the state take preventative action: At the start of the second smallpox pandemic of 1884–9, which followed that of 1875–81 in which thousands of plateau people died, parents were ordered to present their children to be vaccinated on pain of a $0.025 fine.[85] However, smallpox continued to spread, with epidemics in Betsileo in 1886 and on the northeast coast from 1892. Moreover, impoverishment, coupled with the state ban on sanitary measures in order to cultivate an environment that might help deter any projected European invasion, led to the appearance of cholera and typhoid in the main towns. Cholera, first noted in 1819–20 and again in 1854, only had a drastic demographic impact from 1870 when an epidemic swept in from the Swahili coast to kill between one-third and one-half of the population of Mahajanga.[86] Also, from 1882, the two largest towns of Toamasina and Antananarivo were regularly hit by typhoid. In the midst of a particularly vicious outbreak in Antananarivo in 1894, S. B. Fenn, a Friends Foreign Mission Association (FFMA) doctor, commented:

I do not exagerate when I say that hundreds die of Typhoid fever every year, many, perhaps most, of whom might be saved if the city were cleaner, less crowded and the killing of oxen were prohibited within the limits of the town.[87]

Warfare and the Tangena

In 1860, the Catholic Mission noted a falling population, due largely to the ravages of imperial Merina campaigns and the state-sanctioned *tangena* poison ordeal.[88] Traditional warfare had little direct demographic importance. It affected only males, who are biologically expendable,[89] and normally took the form of a ritual game in which few lives were lost – despite the influx of European musketry in the eighteenth century.[90] From 1820, the Merina state

---

[85] Ellis, *History of Madagascar* vol. I, 215, 217–19, 227; Griffiths, *Hanes Madagascar*, 64–5; *MT* II.41 (15 Oct. 1884), 379.

[86] Koponen, "War, Famine and Pestilence," 661–2, 671.

[87] Fenn to PM, Isoavinandriana, Antananarivo, 23 Feb 1894, HH8, 552–3, *ANM*; see also Maude, *Five Years in Madagascar*, 28; *MT* (16 April 1884).

[88] Anon, "Madagascar et côte orientale d'Afrique," 6 – *AHVP*; see also Dalmond, "Mission Apostolique" (1837–47); Robequain, *Madagascar*, 110.

[89] Wrigley, "Population and History," 23; the same applied to the slave export trade to the Americas in which three males were exported to every female – see John Thornton, "The Demographic Effect of the Slave Trade on Western Africa, 1500–1850" in *AHD* vol. II.

[90] See Dubois, *Monographie des Betsileo*, 616; Gerald M. Berg, "Sacred Acquisition: Andrianampoinimerina at Ambohimanga, 1777–1790," *JAH* 29 (1988), 208–9; see also Koponen, "War, Famine and Pestilence," 650–1, 654.

altered the pattern as their adoption of European military techniques and weapons, and their program of imperial expansion, increased battle fatalities – until 1852 when their expansionism waned. From 1816–53, possibly 60,000 non-Merina (on average 1,622 per annum) were killed by Merina troops, whose own casualties were low because of their immense military and numerical superiority. However, indirect military mortality from famine was high, resulting from a combination of the enemies' scorched earth tactics, the refusal of the Merina state to provision its troops, and the spread of disease – facilitated by malnutrition and unsanitary conditions in army camps (see figure 6).[91]

Alain Delivré claims that the *tangena* poison ordeal was introduced into Imerina in the late 1700s, probably from Sakalava land, and that except for a few years in the late 1820s it was used until 1861 as the chief means by which the ruling elite dispensed justice and eradicated rivals in politics and wealth.[92] Raombana stated that the *tangena*

was but partially administered as a matter of state policy, that the people may reverence their Kings by making them suppose that they are in possession of a Divine or sacred Thing capable of finding out those who commits the most heinous crimes, and indeed so convinced were then the people of the sacredness of the Tangena ordeal . . . that in Law-suits they prefer their cases to be decided by it, than to be judged by the Testimonies of eye witnesses, and even those who losses their cases, although they are evidently in the right, shows no signs of disgust at the Tangena ordeal for having judged unjustly, but ascribe their defeat to some just hidden mysteries unknown to them and which are only known to the Tangena ordeal.[93]

In Imerina, the impact of the *tangena*, which was generally given to suspects of free status only after fowl and dog substitutes for the accused had already succumbed to it, varied according to the amount of poison given. This in turn depended upon the discretion of the court administrator. It was mainly applied in cases of suspected witchcraft and sorcery.

For Wrigley, witch manias reflected the rage of a male-dominated power structure against women and procreation and were a device to limit population growth.[94] However, in Madagascar, both females (witches) and males (sorcerers) were persecuted. For Patrick Manning, witch manias were an "example of both the declining value of humans and the psychic pressures on societies facing conquest."[95] Many *tangena* victims, like the Christians from 1835 to 1861, were accused of undermining Merina sovereignty and promoting

---

[91] Campbell, "Adoption of Autarky."

[92] Delivré, L'*Histoire des rois*, 188, 387; Raymond Delval, *Radama II: prince de la renaissance malgache 1861–1863* (Paris, 1972), 43–5, 431, 892–3; Griffiths, *Hanes Madagascar*, 24–5.

[93] *RH*, 42.

[94] Wrigley, "Population and History," 24.

[95] Manning, "Contours of Slavery," 856.

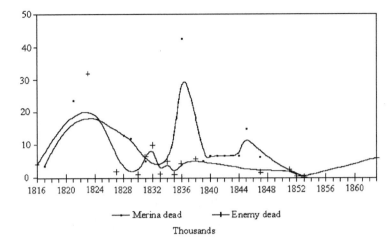

Figure 6. *Merina Military Campaigns: Estimated Gains and Losses, 1816–63*
Source: see Appendix C

European interests in Madagascar.[96] However, this was untrue of slaves, owned chiefly by the Merina elite, who constituted the major victims of the *tangena*. Should misfortune befall a master, there was cause for suspicion. Thus, when Andriantsovatra, Ranavalona I's niece, died of whooping cough, large numbers of her slaves were accused of witchcraft, subjected to the *tangena*, and consequently perished. Most slaves of the elite were subjected to the *tangena* (see Figure 7); in 1854 it was estimated that all slaves who had served Ranavalona I since the commencement of her reign in 1828 had survived at least seven such ordeals.[97]

Griffiths claimed an average fatality rate of 33 to 50 percent from *tangena*,[98] which, it is estimated, killed an average of 1,000 people annually (possibly 0.44 percent of the population) in the early 1820s, rising to 3,000 from 1828 to 1861. Its effect in individual cases and years could be much greater; in 1838 it killed an estimated 20 percent of Imerina's population (possibly 100,000 people)[99] and 85 percent of the 163 Tantsaha subjected to the ordeal in one case in 1853.[100] If three-quarters of the victims were slaves, *tangena*

[96] Campbell, "Role of the London Missionary Society" vol. II, 344–64.
[97] Griffiths, *Hanes Madagascar*, 24–5; Ellis, *History of Madagascar* vol. I, 114; Sibree, *Madagascar and its People*, 384.
[98] Griffiths, *Hanes Madagascar*, 24–5.
[99] Tyerman and Bennet, *Journal*, 515; Johns to Jones, Antananarivo, 1 July 1830, 19157E – *ALGC*; Sibree, *Fifty Years*, 35; Decary, "La population de Madagascar," 30; *GH* (1908), 327; J. A. Lloyd, "Memoir on Madagascar," *Journal of the Royal Geographical Society* 20 (1851), 66.
[100] Raombana, "Manuscrit," 6, 15.

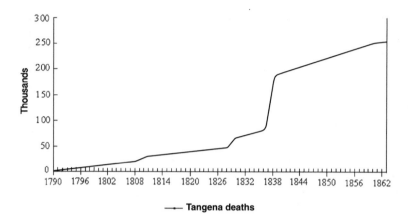

Figure 7. *Imerina: Estimated Tangena Deaths, 1790–1863 (Cumulative)*
Source: see Appendix C

deaths would have accounted for about 1 to 4.5 per cent of the slave population of Imerina annually.[101] Officially abolished in 1863, the *tangena* ordeal continued to be practiced secretly in some Merina regions and openly elsewhere in the island.[102]

All the above factors contributed to a death rate for imperial Madagascar that was probably higher than that of the early colonial era when, in 1905, it averaged 26.3 per thousand for Madagascar (35.0 per thousand for central Imerina). Nevertheless, this was significantly lower than the crude death rate of 45 per thousand posited by Caldwell for precolonial Tropical Africa and may indicate that in Madagascar the crude birth rate was of greater demographic significance than the crude death rate.[103]

Immigration and Emigration

The state also greatly influenced migration. Much immigration and emigration was accounted for by the slave trade (analyzed in closer detail in Chapter 9).

---

[101] Griffiths, *Hanes Madagascar*, 24–5; Ellis, *History of Madagascar* vol. I, 114; Sibree, *Madagascar and its People*, 384.

[102] Dumaine, "Voyage au pays d'ancaye" (1790), 275; Chapelier, "lettres adressés," 53; Richardson, "Tanala Customs," 95, 97; Raombana B2 Livre 13, 27; LMS, *Ten Years' Review (1870–80)*, 34–5.

[103] *GH* (1908), 342–3 – Caldwell posits a life expectancy of 22 years for precolonial tropical Africa, higher than Pool's figure of 20 years, but significantly lower than the 27.5 years incorporated in the "South" model of Coale and Demeny, adopted by Thornton: Caldwell, "Major Questions, 10; Pool, "A Framework," 53–4; Thornton, "The Slave Trade," 420.

From 1801 to 1891, about 290,000 slaves were exported from the island – an annual average of 3,222 (possibly 0.161 to 0.051 percent of the population).[104] It is unlikely that, as in many mainland African regions, drought and famine reduced families to selling members into slavery. However, it did force migration to areas where they became more vulnerable to capture. Impoverishment also reduced the defensive capabilities of rural communities and increased the flow of men into brigandry, in which slaving was a key activity.[105]

The Merina state respected the 1820 ban on slave exports, but played a major role in importing African slaves into Madagascar. From 1820–91, slave imports for the Malagasy market and for re-export totaled approximately 400,000. Fluctuations in slave imports, which peaked in the periods 1826–40 and 1863–90 (averaging approximately 7,326 and 9,264 per annum, respectively), were greater than for slave exports. From the early 1870s, estimates indicate a significant divergence between the cumulative numbers involved in the two trades although the actual gap was smaller as a considerable proportion of African slave imports were re-exported as "contract labor" to the French plantation islands. Nonslaves also emigrated: From 1824–46, some 15,000 Malagasy, mainly Sakalava, fled to Nosy Be and other islands off the northwest coast; while from 1831-51, an estimated 8,750 Betsimisaraka migrated to Nosy Boraha, off the northeast coast.[106]

Deaths also occurred in slave raiding. If Manning's 1983 (16.67 percent mortality for enslavement in the West African Atlantic trade) rather than 1981 estimates (10 percent mortality) are applied proportionately to Madagascar, approximately 48,343 people, averaging 681 annually, would have died during enslavement and export to the coast from 1820 to 1891.[107] On this basis, the net annual population gain for Madagascar from the external slave trade would have been small; possibly 1,750 in the late 1860s, rising to 2,500 in the 1870s and peaking at 7,000 in the 1880s (i.e., discounting enslavement losses). To these figures must be added a proportion of the 150,000 *Masombika* liberated from private into state ownership in 1877.[108]

---

[104] Campbell, "Madagascar and Mozambique," 185; *idem*, "East African Slave Trade," 25.

[105] Manning, "Contours of Slavery," 850; Miller, "Significance of Drought," 30; Campbell, "Missionaries, Fanompoana and the Menalamba Revolt," 54–73.

[106] *RA*, 263; Raombanara B2 Livre 13, 22; Campbell, "Role of the London Missionary Society" vol. II, 338–9; Wolf, "Analysis," 203; *MT* (5 Nov. 1884); *GH* (1908), 297; Horace P. Putnam, "A Cruise to the Indies and a Life on Shore" in La Plata, Bark, Seaman's Journal (Dec. 1848–Jan. 1850), Log 1847 W3 (B15), *EI*; A. Smith, "From Zanzibar to Nosibe" *AAMM* 7 (1883), 41; Dalmond à son frère, Madagascar, 1 fèvrier 1840, in "Lettres de M Dalmond à ses parents entre 1826 et 1846," C47, *AHVP*; Finaz au Jouen, Nossi-bé, 20 juillet 1846, Correspondance C35, *AHVP*; Nourse to Farquhar, HMS Andromarche, 17 Nov. 1822, *PRO.CO*.167/66.

[107] Manning, "Demographic Model," 371–84; *idem*, "Contours of Slavery," 850.

[108] Campbell, "Madagascar and the Slave Trade."

Imerina received approximately 120,000 non-Merina captives enslaved in military expeditions from 1816 to 1863, after which imperial slave raiding virtually ceased. Most such slaves were held by the Merina state and elite, notably in Antananarivo, where enslaved provincial and imported African slaves formed up to two-thirds of the population. Their numbers dropped sharply in the dry season as many porters and slaves, accompanying their masters on commercial and military expeditions, left town.[109] Such seasonal variations help explain heavy fluctuations in observers' estimates of Antananarivo's population. As relatively small numbers of Merina migrated permanently to nonplateau regions, Imerina's population gained about 250,000 through forced immigration up to 1850, notably from 1823 to 1837, and about 112,500 from 1850 to 1895.

The slave influx did not necessarily boost the rate of natural population increase within the Merina empire. First, some African slaves carried deadly diseases. They were, for example, the origin of the 1888 smallpox outbreak in Maintirano.[110] Second, slaves in Madagascar – as elsewhere outside the United States and possibly West Africa from the mid-nineteenth century – experienced a low birth and a high mortality rate and failed to reproduce themselves.[111] From 1820, the Merina court, fearing revolt, ordered the execution of all provincial male captives aged 10 and over. The resulting sexual imbalance in Imerina's slave population was partially redressed from the 1840s when the measure appears to have lapsed, but parity was never attained, especially in towns, due to the urban elite demand for female domestic slaves.[112]

Female slaves were sexually isolated: A sharp sexual division of slave labor existed throughout Madagascar and, contrary to most of Tropical Africa,[113] a rigid caste system prohibited sexual relations between slaves and free subjects. Thus, in December 1855, Ranavalona I had a servant girl stoned to death for sleeping with a *Masombika* slave.[114] Some free Merina males took slave concubines, but the latter's incentive to reproduce was limited. Resultant offspring were ascribed slave status and, after death, a slave's property passed to the owner.[115] Also, sexual unions between slaves could not gain the legitimacy of

[109] Campbell, "Labour and the Transport Problem," 341–56; *idem*, "Slavery and Fanompoana," 468–73.
[110] Knott to Aitken, Mojanga, 21 March 1888, in *ASR* (Nov. & Dec. 1888), 217.
[111] Manning, "Contours of Slavery," 853–4; Martin A. Klein, "The Demography of Slavery in Western Soudan. The Late Nineteenth Century" in Cordell & Gregory (eds.), *African Population and Capitalism*, 56–7.
[112] Finaz, "Journal" II, p. 12 – section II, Diaires 21, *AHVP*.
[113] See, e.g., Manning, "Contours of Slavery," 847–8.
[114] [Finaz], "Tananarive" (1855–7), 110.
[115] Dubois, *Monographie des Betsileo*, 585, 718.

a marriage contract and were thus inherently unstable: reflected in a popular saying concerning slaves – "*Hivady tsy toinana, ary hisaraka anio hiany*" ("It's not their concern to get married for they could be separated the very same day"). Moreover, when presented with the choice, most slaves rejected manumission for fear of being subjected to the state forced labor scheme.[116] Such factors inevitably limited slave reproduction, slaves sometimes preferring to invest in slaves rather than in children.[117] As noted, slaves were also the greatest victims of the *tangena* poison ordeal. Slave mortality may in addition have been affected in Betsileo by the tradition of burying royal slaves alive when their masters died, although the persistence of this custom into the nineteenth century is uncertain.[118]

Contrary to Bloch's claim that slave numbers increased from the 1820s to reach 50 percent of the population by the late 1800s, the evidence suggests that slave numbers grew only until the mid-1830s and then remained fairly stationary. It is probable that about one-third of the population of Imerina were slaves – although the proportion might have been temporarily high when large numbers of free subjects were conscripted into, or fled from, *fanompoana*.[119] Of the 500,000 slaves liberated in 1896, 43.6 percent lived in Imerina, where they formed 20 to 26 percent of the population – half the unsubstantiated figure claimed by Bloch.[120]

Most male slaves exported from Madagascar originated either from west coast societies or from Mozambique, and the majority passed via west coast entrepôts to the French plantation islands of the Indian Ocean. Female slaves, mostly of highland origin, would have been in greatest demand in the Muslim Comoros, with some possibly finding their way to the Middle East. For West Africa, J. E. Inikori estimates a 33:67 and 60:40 male-to-female slave export ratio to Muslim countries and the New World respectively,[121] and this may have been mirrored in the Malagasy trade to Muslim and French markets. However, on the plateau where a significant number of young adult males were either conscripted into forced labor units or became brigands, slave raiding by the Sakalava and Bara is likely to have resulted in an efflux from the highlands of

---

[116] Campbell, "Slavery and Fanompoana," 463–86; see also Klein, "Demography of Slavery," 56–7.

[117] Klein, "Demography of Slavery," 59–60.

[118] Dubois, *Monographie des Betsileo*, 571.

[119] See Chapter 5.

[120] See previous note; see also Grandidier, "Souvenirs," 32; Hastie, "Diary" (1817), 250–1; Campbell, "Madagascar and the Slave Trade," 209; André, *De l'esclavage*, 186; Berthier "La tribu des Hova" *Conférence à l'école coloniale* (Paris, d, c. 1908), 3; *GH* (1908), 333; *Le Journal* (8 octobre 1895).

[121] Inikori, "Under-Population," 304.

mostly young adolescent and women captives aged between 14 and 30, young children being excluded because of the slave raiders' need for mobility and speed.[122] Female slave exports would have lessened the sexual imbalance in Imerina, so that polygamy, still common in the 1820s, decreased from mid-century even without the influence of missionary teaching.[123] In addition, it would have reduced the birth rate among the free population, thus heightening labor shortages and the demand for slave imports and further impoverishing the traditional agricultural sector.[124]

The impact of the slave export trade would have been different for the island as a whole. As the Sakalava retained many highland female captives as slaves, men formed the majority of slaves exported. Hence, the slave trade would have skewed the sex ratio in the island as a whole in favor of women. This was a contributory factor in the imbalance reflected in the 1899 French census, which showed a sexual ratio of 778 males for every 1,000 females.[125]

Critics of the demographic transition theory blame what Kitching terms the African "crisis mortality" in the late 1800s and early 1900s[126] on the military and economic forces of European colonization. However, it is clear that in Madagascar, the demographic crisis started much earlier and the largest single contributory factor was the policies of the imperial Merina regime. This is not to deny natural forces. In imperial Madagascar, the forces of state and nature influenced one another considerably. Whereas in the late 1700s and early 1800s, the state mitigated the harmful demographic effects of droughts and disease, autarkic policies from the mid-1820s served to compound natural disasters. It is against this background that the traditional emphasis on the disruptive demographic impact of the early French colonial regime in Madagascar should be judged.

---

[122] Campbell, "Madagascar and the Slave Trade."

[123] Some evidence suggests that polygamy possibly depressed fertility slightly, except in cases where postpartum abstinence was the rule – Hunt, "'La Bebe En Brousse,'" 407; see also Pool, "A Framework," 53; Kitching, "Proto-industrialisation," 229–30; Manning, "Demographic Model," 379; Kenneth Swindell, "Domestic Production, labour mobility and population change in West Africa, 1900–1980" in *AHD* vol. II, 682; Ellis, *History of Madagascar* vol. I, 167–8.

[124] Campbell, "Madagascar and Mozambique"; *idem*, "East African Slave Trade."

[125] Paillard, "recherches démographiques," 33.

[126] Kitching, "Proto-industrialisation," 233.

7   The Trading Structure, 1820–1895

Introduction

Two forces shaped the trading structure of nineteenth-century Madagascar: the development of the international economy and the foundation of a Merina empire based on autarkic policies. The first resulted in enormously enhanced commercial opportunities in the IOW, including Madagascar, taken up by a number of groups, indigenous and foreign. However, the policies adopted by the Merina regime largely negated the advantages presented within the Merina empire upon which most historical attention has focused. However, as the Merina imposed firm imperial rule over only one-third of the island, notably the central and eastern provinces, a rival and independent trading network sprung up incorporating two regions, respectively north and south of Cape St. André. To the south, trade was initially largely unorganized, foreign traders negotiating directly with local chiefs; while in the northern commercial sector, foreign Indian and Swahili traders whose center of operations was Mahajanga dominated trade. This chapter compares and contrasts the trading structures of imperial Imerina and the independent regions of Madagascar, as well as analyzing the changes they underwent within the context of the rise of the international economy.

The Merina Empire

The Merina court early appreciated the benefits accruing from trade. In the eighteenth century, it standardized weights and monies, regulated markets, and declared a large degree of state control over the export of slaves and import of arms. Under autarky, the Merina crown declared monopolies over all valuable commodities and molded the imperial army into a commercial rather than a military institution. Because of the enormous technical superiority that from the mid-1820s its British trained army possessed over opposing forces, the Merina court viewed armed expeditions as primarily commercial ventures. An integral part of *fanompoana*, military service was unremunerated, but officers were encouraged to both trade and plunder.[1] Moreover, from 1822 to 1840, a network of Merina garrisons was erected along most major trade routes, simultaneously establishing a Merina military presence and control over long distance commerce. Some garrisons, like Mahabo and Malaimbandy, en route to Morondava, maintained Merina commercial influence well beyond its effective military sway (see Table 7.2).[2] The Merina elite vied for control of the commercially most important garrisons with, by mid-century, members of the powerful Tsimiamboholahy and Tsimahafotsy clans gaining the governorships of the chief east coast ports as well as of Mahajanga, the chief entrepôt in northwest Madagascar. Each port governor shared the customs revenue with the imperial treasury and his patron at court.[3]

The army constituted one of the pillars of *fanompoana* under autarky. Rank and file soldiers were recruited directly through village-level conscription, and *deka* (aides-de-camp) via the mission schools. Both categories immediately became camp followers of senior army officers who competed for the most gifted junior recruits, notably the mission-educated, who became their *deka*. Four thousand of the estimated 15,000 mission school graduates from 1821 to 1835 became *deka*; their literacy ensured accurate transempire communication, while those mastering foreign languages, notably English, became secretaries at court or to governors of the major ports. As the missionaries remarked,

The military Officers here, have not only their "Aides du camp," but their Writers. These are numerous, have many of them been brought up in the Schools and form a Class of respectable and intelligent young men ... many of whom may probably rise to occupy important and influential stations in the country.[4]

The crown could in theory summon as royal *deka* all officers and soldiers. In practice, it waived this right, both because alternative sources of forced labor

---

[1] Gabriel Rantoandro, "Le gouvernement de Tamatave de 1845 à 1865; développement économique," thèse (Université de Madagascar, 1973), 83–6; Campbell, "Slavery and Fanompoana," 472–4.

[2] Prud"homme, "Considérations," 419; Oliver, *Madagascar* vol. I, 251, 323–4; Émile F. Gautier, "Western Madagascar: its geology and physical geography" *AAMM* 22 (1898), 140–4.

[3] Rantoandro, "gouvernement de Tamatave," 83–6, 188–9; *RA*, 325–7; *GH* (1928), 264.

[4] Johns, Freeman, and Canham to Ellis, Antananarivo, 18 Nov. 1833, *SOAS/LM-MIL* B4.F4.JC; see also Finaz, "Journal" (1855–7), 69; Raombana, "Manuscrit," Freeman & Johns, *A Narrative*, 156; Ellis, *History of Madagascar* vol. II, 479; *idem*, *Three Visits*, 2–3, 119, 279; *HR* vol. V, 1127–8.

TABLE 7.1. *Estimated Growth of Imperial Merina Army, 1820–52*

Year	Soldiers	Recruits	Year	Soldiers	Recruits
1820	1,000	n.a.	1831	30,000	n.a.
1821	12,000	n.a.	1832	25,000	n.a.
1822	13,000	6,000	1833	30,000	n.a.
1823	14,000	6,000	1834	30,000	n.a.
1824	14,250	n.a.	1835	45,000	n.a.
1826	n.a.	8,750	1837	n.a.	2,228
1827	n.a.	8,750	1838	n.a.	45,000
1828	12,000	15,000	1840	20,000	40,000
1829	13,800	15,790	1845	n.a.	11,750
1830	30,000	n.a.	1852	100,000	n.a.

Source: Campbell, "Slavery and Fanompoana," 470.

were generally to be found and to avoid alienating top officials who considered army personnel their prerogative.[5] The number of *deka* permitted each rank of officer rose steadily under Ranavalona I; by 1857 Raharo possessed 800, his father, the commander of the imperial army, 1,500. This changed in the 1860s when effective government passed from the crown to the commander of the imperial army. To undermine his political rivals, Rainilaiarivony in the mid-1860s limited *deka* numbers to between one for an officer of nine honors and 30 for an officer of 16 honors. As his own patronage system remained unlimited, a considerable anti-Rainilaiarivony faction developed at court.[6]

The system benefited both *deka* and their superiors. The former used the status of their patron to advantage when dealing with those of lesser status and in order to protect themselves from harassment by *deka* serving rival patrons. Moreover, new *deka* immediately started recruiting their own *deka* following. Competition for *deka* ensured that talented new recruits were quickly rewarded with lucrative posts; there was considerable opportunity for upward mobility in an army, 50 percent of whose members were officers and where the turnover was great due to a high death rate.[7] *Deka* obligations could entail military service, but few Merina soldiers ever engaged in combat (see Table 7.1). Through their *deka*, court officials speculated in commercial ventures, purloining crown booty and exploiting both common soldiers and the subjugated provinces.[8] The system ensured that each member of the court oligarchy gained, in effect, a

[5] *HR* vol. I, 57.

[6] Griffiths, *Hanes Madagascar*, 35; *HR* vol. V, 1076; Raombana, B2 Livre 13, 4, 34; Ida Pfeiffer, *Voyage à Madagascar* (1857) (Paris, 1981), 180; Grandidier, "Souvenirs," 37.

[7] Due primarily to malaria – see Chapter 6.

[8] Rantoandro, "gouvernement de Tamatave," 83–6; Campbell, "Slavery and Fanompoana," 472–4; also see Chapter 3.

TABLE 7.2. *Merina Garrisons Established, 1822–34*

Year	Garrison	Region	Year	Garrison	Region
1822	Janjina	Menabe	1825	Manerinerina	Iboina
	Malaimbandy	”		Tolanaro	Southeast
	Bondrony	”	1826	Ankavandra	West
	Mahabo	”		Bevato	”
1823	Toamasina	East coast		Tsiroamandidy	”
	Maroantsetra	”	1834	Andranovana	Menabe
	Hiarambazaha	”		Inanga	”
	Ambatondrazaka	Antsihanaka		Kabevana	”
1824	Mahajanga	Iboina		Maneva	”
	Marovoay	”		Ranomafana	Betsimisaraka

Source: HR vol. V, 1062, 1083, 1088–91, 1095–6, 1158–9.

private army – or what one Malagasy historian has termed "a political party of merchants"[9] – which was used to further his private commercial and other interests:

> Dekana...attach themselves, as adherents, to any particular chief, and are considered devoted to the interests of such chiefs. Their number appeared to be limited only by the popularity of the chief or the prospects of advantage to his followers. Thus, when a young man was spoken of as Dekana to any chief, it seemed to mean that he was devoted to his interests, and to be engaged in his service.[10]

Garrison soldiers also traded on their own account. Indeed, after military expansion was curtailed in the early 1850s, most *deka* posted to Merina military garrisons became virtually full-time traders. One foreigner observed that they traveled from one fort to the next, "bartering the products of local industry, fabrics and some luxury or fancy items for gold dust or cattle,"[11] while Grandidier noted in 1869:

> At Ambohinomé [*sic*] I witnessed the arrival of officers of 10 Vtr and 11 Vtr [rank] respectively, who announced themselves to be *irak' Andriana* [i.e., officials of the Merina court]. Hardly had they arrived, than they hung a rope in the house where they had been

[9] Finaz noted of the *deka*: "They comprise the household and personnel of their patron, some being secretaries, some looking after his properties, or fulfilling commissions; whilst yet others are despatched to the coast to trade for their patron" – Finaz, "Journal" (1855–7); see also *HR* vol. I, 57.

[10] Ellis, *Three Visits*, 279; for comparisons with mainland Africa, see Sundström, *Exchange Economy*, 15, 60.

[11] Prud'homme, "Considérations," 21; According to Lacombe – an unreliable source – Radama I authorized ordinary soldiers one week in four to trade when not involved in military maneuvers – Leguéval de Lacombe, *Voyage à Madagascar et aux Îles Comores 1823 à 1830* (Paris, 1840), 142.

received, and there displayed some of the merchandise they had brought with them, as well as placing on their hands the rings they wished to sell: they were, despite their high rank, but lowly colporteurs who shared with their patron – one of the leading government ministers who furnished them with their wares – the profits they gleaned from their activity. The transport of their goods did not cost them much given that they used *corvée* labour which was fed at the expense of the inhabitants of the villages through which they passed and which, at they end of each trip, received in payment [from the colporteurs] a *Veloma hianareo hotahin Andriamanitra* ["Goodbye and may God keep you"].[12]

Deka traders, who were regulated by passport inspections in all garrisons on their route,[13] used slaves as colporteurs. Thus Joseph Mullens commented in 1873 of Merina forts along the Mahajanga–Antananarivo corridor: "the number of masters of various grades, doing nothing, living without pay, and living on what they can squeeze out of slaves and clients below them is countless."[14] The commercial significance of garrisons is underlined by the fact that *deka* comprised a majority in most Merina forts. For instance, in 1869, 500 of the 800-strong Andevoranto garrison, on the Antananarivo–Toamasina route, were *deka*. Moreover, garrison *deka* were frequently absent on trading ventures; in 1877, James Richardson found 144, or 96 percent, of the personnel of the Ihosy garrison so missing.[15]

The *deka* system excluded non-Merina from the most valuable aspects of trade in imperial Madagascar. On the east coast, for example, local Betsimisaraka were obliged to sell export commodities to court *deka* at low prices. As Coignet commented in 1863:

The population of the northeast coast may not conduct any trade with foreigners without the accord of the commander of the entire coast. . . . [I]n the majority of cases he conducts trade on his own account, purchasing at a cheap price from the locals and selling at a very high profit. It is only when a village chief, through giving the commander presents, has gained his favour, that he is authorised to sell his cattle and rice on the same terms as his superior. Commerce is totally in the hands of the [imperial Merina] governors and officers.[16]

The Merina court also formed monopolies with a few select foreigners. Threat of bankruptcy led Radama I in 1825 to seriously contemplate the advice of Nils

12 Grandidier, "Notes" (1869) in *GH* (1928), 264; see also *RA*, 325–7; Rantoandro, "gouvernement de Tamatave," 188–9; Rasoamiaramanana, "Aspects économiques" (1973), 21–4, 46–8.
13 Rasoamiaramanana, "Aspects économiques" (1973), 48; Ravelomanana, "La vie religieuse à Ambositra," 43.
14 Mullens, *Twelve Months in Madagascar*, 318.
15 Richardson, *Lights and Shadows*, 13; Grandidier, "Souvenirs," 49; Ravelomanana, "La vie religieuse à Ambositra," 40.
16 Coignet (1863) quoted in *GH* (1928), 274.

Bergsten, a Swedish doctor resident on Mauritius, that a foreign trade monopoly would enable the Merina crown to bypass middlemen and raise significantly the price of staple exports – thus augmenting royal revenue.[17] From 1826 to 1828, Radama I granted a virtual monopoly of foreign trade on the east coast to the Blancard consortium. This, and an augmentation of duties, led excluded merchants to transfer to independent ports. Many returned after 1828, when duties were lowered to 10 percent ad valorem. Moreover, the monopoly was annulled after Blancard, who accused Radama I of supplying inferior quality cattle, refused to advance more than a third of the promised $30,000 payment. Thus, the proportion of Réunionnais ships trading through imperial, as opposed to independent, Malagasy ports rose from a low of 30 percent in 1823 to 64 percent by 1828. Several other trade contracts were aborted before, in 1837, a monopoly over east coast exports of beeswax, gum copal, ebony, and hides was granted to Lastelle (an associate of the Réunionnais firm of Rontaunay) after he had paid several thousand dollars to Rainimaharavo, a leading member of the imperial oligarchy. In 1843, Rontaunay also obtained a monopoly of the foreign trade of Mahela, Mananjary, and Mahanoro, in exchange for an annual payment of $6,000 to the Merina crown.[18] For his Malagasy–Mascarene operations, Rontaunay engaged a personal fleet of 19 ships, supplemented by 47 chartered boats, and over 1,000 crew.[19]

Foreigners were banned from imperial ports in 1845, in reprisal for a Franco–British naval attack upon Toamasina. In 1853, Mascarene merchants and planters paid the Merina crown an indemnity to reopen the ports. However, relations remained strained until 1861, when the liberalization of foreign trade[20] attracted to the east coast large numbers of foreign traders. These comprised mainly Mascarene Creoles or British Indians who, unlike west coast Indians, originated from Madras. The handful of respectable foreign companies trading in Madagascar from the 1860s included Procter Brothers (London), John Bertram (Salem) – which merged into Ropes, Emmerton & Co. from 1865 – George Ropes (Boston), O'Swald (Hamburg), and Roux de Fraissinet (Marseille). De Fraissinet's interests, following bankruptcy in 1883, were taken

---

[17] Bergsten unsuccessfully applied for monopolistic trading rights on the east coast. Bergsten, "Mémoire" (1825), 5; Robequain, "Une capitale montagnarde," 287.

[18] Rontaunay had in 1826 tried and failed to secure a monopoly over the foreign trade of Mahela and Mananjary. Chapus & Mondain, "Un chapitre inconnu," 118; Campbell, "Role of the London Missionary Society," vol. II, 294, 301.

[19] Campbell, "Role of the London Missionary Society" vol. II, 301.

[20] Razi, "Sources d'histoire," 12, 23; Jackson to West, c.1845–51, in Bennett and Brooks (eds.), *New England Merchants*, 439–50; Raymond K. Kent, "How France acquired Madagascar" *Tarikh* 2.4 (1969), 16.

over by another Marseille concern, "Registe" (possibly a reference to Vidal Régis, who was consolidating trading interests centered on the Swahili coast[21]) – although the U.S. consul asserted in 1894 that the sole reputable French firm in Toamasina was Rebut et Savatile.[22] These firms dominated the most valuable commerce, notably hide exports and cotton imports.[23] Unlike American companies that from 1865 concentrated their factors in Toamasina and Nosy Be and maintained a strictly bilateral U.S.–Madagascar trade, the larger European concerns operated numerous small coastal agencies and engaged in regional trade. Thus, Procter Brothers was reported in 1885 as doing "a large business in rice, coffee, empty straw bags and Bees Wax with the Mauritius."[24]

All foreign trade was fiercely contested.[25] During the American Civil War (1861–5) when Confederate ships patrolled even the route to East Africa, U.S. trade in the region suffered.[26] However, it recovered quickly from 1865, assisted from 1866 by the establishment in Toamasina of a U.S. commercial agency, upgraded in 1871 to a consulate.[27] U.S. traders reasserted a dominance in cottons, the most valuable "legitimate" import and, by 1878, the two U.S. firms then operating in imperial Madagascar claimed to have captured over half of foreign commerce by value passing through Toamasina.[28] Nevertheless, the European share of the trade gradually increased. This was due in part to the opening of the Suez Canal in 1869, which permitted the establishment of Europe–East Africa steamship services, steamships proving far faster and more regular than

---

[21] Patrick Harries, *Work, Culture, and Identity. Migrant Laborers in Mozambique and South Africa, c.1860–1910* (Portsmouth, NH: Heinemann; Johannesburg: Witwatersrand University Press; London: James Currey), 86–8.

[22] Gwyn Campbell, "Toamasina (Tamatave) and the Growth of Foreign Trade in Imperial Madagascar, 1862–1895" in G. Liesegang, H. Pasch & A. Jones (eds.), *Figuring African Trade* (Berlin, 1986), 528–9; Finkelmeier to Seward, 12 Dec.1865 and 11 April 1867; Robinson to Hankey, 29 Oct.1877; *idem* to Payson, 7 Aug.1880; Wetter to Uhl, 26 Sept. 1894 – *US*; Pakenham to Granville, Tamatave, 3 Jan.1883, in "Correspondence Respecting Madagascar Relating to the Mission of Hova Envoys to Europe in 1882–1883," no. 67, *Africa* 1, *HCPP* (1883); Kellenbenz, "Zanzibar et Madagascar"; Fairburn, *Merchant Sail* V, 3014; Ropes, Emmerton & Co, to J. Orme Ryder, Salem, 30 April 1883 and 7 May 1883; *idem* to Whitney, Salem, 21 Dec. 1883 – *REC/CR–MZL*.

[23] Fontoynont et Nicol, *Les traitants français*; A Resident, *Madagascar*; Finkelmeier to Hunter, 30 Dec. 1879; Robinson to Third Assistant Secretary of State, Tamatave, 2 June 1865; Wetter to Uhl, Tamatave, 7 Nov. 1894 – *US*; A. Martineau, *Madagascar en 1894* (Paris, 1894), 278; Kessler Vrocker to John Bertram, Tamatave, 11 July 1867, John Bertram Papers B2.F5, Agency Records – Tamatave. Correspondence and Accounts, 1867–1870, *EI*.

[24] Dawson to Ropes, Emmerton & Co, and Arnold, Hines & Co, Tamatave, 24 Sept. 1885, *REC/C-MZL*.

[25] Kessler Vrocker to John Bertram, Tamatave, 11 July 1867, John Bertram Papers B2.F5, Agency Records – Tamatave. Correspondence and Accounts, 1867–1870, *EI*.

[26] Razi, "Sources d'histoire," 25; Fairburn, *Merchant Sail* V, 3014.

[27] Razi, "Sources d'histoire," 23–4.

[28] Quoted in Bennett, "Americans in Zanzibar," 37.

TABLE 7.3. *Merina Dealers of Imported American Cotton Piece Goods, 1885–90*

Rasaheno	Rainizanaka	Rainimanana "&c of Zoma"
Rajoely	Ramanangodra	Rainialidera (brother of Razafimbelo)
Ramanana	Ramanananjohn	Andriampatra/Andriampatsa
Raoelina	Razafimbelo	Andri[an]vonzato
F. H. Rama	Ratofarilana	Razafindrintsoa
Andrianisa	Randriamihary	Randriantsolo/a
Ravoavahy	Randriantaola	Ramanajoharo
Andriansolo	Ratsimanohatra	

Source: Bachelder to Dawson, Vatomandry, 9 Jan. 1885 and Antananarivo, 17 July 1885; Laborde to Ropes, Emmerton & Co, and Arnold, Hines & Co, Tamatave, 17 Jan. 1885; Laborde to Whitney, Antananarivo, 22 Jan. 1887; Dawson to Whitney, Antananarivo, 19 May 1888; Edward P. Duder to Whitney, Antananarivo, 10 Aug. 1889; Duder to Dawson, Antananarivo, 21 & 27 Dec. 1889, 28 June & 9 Aug. 1890 – *REC/CR-MZL.*

the sailing ships still used by Americans.[29] By 1882, British traders had drawn level with the Americans. Thereafter, the British dominated exports (with about 35 percent by value of all exports shipped through Toamasina) while Americans dominated imports (about 37.5 percent).[30]

To compete more effectively with foreign merchants, primarily in the import and distribution of cottons and the collection and export of hides, the Merina court established in the 1880s a civilian middlemen group – the Ambohimalaza cartel – comprising five Antananarivo-based houses.[31] In 1888, the cartel's two leading dealers, Raoelina and Andriampatra/Andriampatsa, were described as "very solid men . . . certainly the largest buyers of American cottons."[32] Much to the chagrin of foreign dealers, the Ambohimalaza cartel largely controlled the price and distribution of major legitimate commodities in the interior.[33] For instance, from June to July 1885, Malagasy exporters accounted for 16.86 to 31.85 percent of hide shipments to the coast (see Table 7.3 and Illustration 8). This percentage rose when hide prices fell because, unlike foreign traders, they

[29] Bennett, "Americans in Zanzibar," 44.

[30] Oliver, *Madagascar* vol. II, 173–4; Robinson to Hankey, Tamatave, 1 Oct. 1878, *US.*

[31] Laborde to Dawson, Vatomandry, 20 June 1885, *REC/CR MEL.* In December 1889 a leading member, Andrianisa, was arrested probably because of great indebtedness to Rainilaiarivony. It was reported that he owed his creditors $40,000, for which his property and wife were seized and sold – realizing 20 percent of the debt, the remainder of which he was to pay off at a rate of imprisonment calculated at $0.125 a day – which would give a prison term of 700 years. See Duder to Dawson, Antananarivo, 21 & 27 December 1889, *REC/CR-MZL.*

[32] Whitney to Ropes, Emmerton & Co, Tamatave, 1 May 1888; Dawson to Ropes, Emmerton & Co, Tamatave, 27 April 1890, *REC/CR-MZL.*

[33] Laborde to Whitney, Vatomandry, 28 June 1886 and Vatomandry, 1 Nov. 1886; Whitney to Ropes Emmerton & Co, Tamatave, 2 April 1888; Edward P. Duder to Whitney, Antananarivo, 10 Aug. 1889 – *REC/CR-MZL.*

8. Andohalo Market circa 1880

enjoyed privileged access to cheap porterage.[34] Money shortages could also dramatically alter the bargaining power of the parties engaged in foreign trade. Thus a U.S. commercial agent in Toamasina commented in December 1886:

Cloth buyers from the Capital will no doubt appear in this market in a short time, but the prospect of our obtaining better prices than has ruled during the last five months is poor, as the buyers comprehend the great demand for money that exists, and will make us pay for their dollars – One large buyer now here offers only $65 per 1000 yards [914 meters] for 100 Bales of Bangor and Lyman Mills Sheetings (1/2 each) and $55 for Mass. Shirtings.[35]

The Ambohimalaza cartel used their quasi-monopoly over domestic distribution to effect: In April 1888, in the midst of a cottons glut, they stockpiled imported cottons in Toamasina in order to maintain prices in Antananarivo.[36] Again, in June 1890, they held out for such high hide prices that foreign purchasers attempted to go directly to the sellers, one U.S. firm complaining that "for two weeks past [Duder] has been obliged to go into the weekly market to

[34] Bachelder to Dawson, Antananarivo, 20 June, 10 and 17 July 1885, *REC/CR-MZL*.
[35] Whitney to Ropes, Emmerton & Co, and Arnold, Hines & Co, Tamatave, 4 Dec.1886, *REC/CR-MZL*.
[36] Whitney to Ropes, Emmerton & Co, Tamatave, 1 May 1888, *REC/CR-MZL*.

buy direct from the hide dealers in order to break up a 'boycott' of the Antø middle men."[37]

The Independent Zones

The 1820 Britanno–Merina treaty banning slave exports led to a significant transfer of Swahili and Mascarene commerce to the independent regions of Madagascar. However, the 1824 Merina conquest of Mahajanga, the predominant west coast port, resulted in a dispersal of Indian and Swahili agents to neighboring independent ports, which also attracted Mascarene traders as their duties were cheaper than those of Merina-controlled ports. From 1824 to 1833, Americans dominated the foreign trade of Mahajanga, which served as their chief transhipment center for east African ivory and copal. Nevertheless, the Merina quickly came to depend upon the political and commercial expertise of Indian and Swahili traders. From 1830, they started to return to Mahajanga, which thereafter served both as the major west coast port of the Merina empire and as headquarters of commercial operations on the independent west coast.[38]

The return of Indian and Swahili agents helped induce American traders to transfer from Mahajanga to Zanzibar, their main east African entrepôt after the 1833 U.S.–Zanzibar treaty.[39] Nevertheless, Mahajanga remained important to U.S. trade: Of the 45 U.S. vessels that sailed from specified Malagasy ports to Zanzibar between September 1832 and September 1844, 82 percent sailed from Mahajanga, 8.9 percent from Nosy Be, and 4.4 percent from other bays on the northwest coast. Only two ships sailed from ports not on the northwest coast (St Augustin, and Vohimara – the latter being the only east coast port specified). As whalers account for Nosy Be, St. Augustin, and Passandava as ports-of-call, Mahajanga remained the sole Malagasy entrepôt for U.S. traders in this period.[40]

In June 1840, a crown monopoly of the foreign commerce of Mahajanga was granted to Marks, from 1840 to 1842 the representative for a number of Salem merchants;[41] by 1842 he and two other American agents were collecting

[37] Dawson to to Ropes, Emmerton & Co, Tamatave, 8 June 1890, *REC/CR-MZL*.

[38] Rasoamiaramanana,'Aspects économiques' (1973), 10–11, 35, 54; Noel, "Ile de Madagascar" (1843), 19, 27–38, 93, 99; Grandidier, "Souvenirs," 28.

[39] They thereafter shipped Malagasy exports either directly from Mahajanga or indirectly via Zanzibar where a U.S. consul was appointed in 1837; Bennett and Brooks (eds.), *New England Merchants*, xxvii.

[40] Razi, "Sources d'Histoire."

[41] Lyall, "Journal," 89; Chapus & Mondain, "Un chapitre inconnu," 127–8; *RA*, 327–30, 378–85, 435–6, 458–9; Alvin Thompson, "The role of firearms and the development of military

goods for brigs that called every four months.[42] For a brief period in 1843–4, Americans were prohibited from trading in Mahajanga, but such was the volume of trade when this ban was lifted that Salem merchants considered placing a vessel permanently in Malagasy waters. In 1846, Marks, who worked for a 2.5 percent commission,[43] had $12,000 worth of goods on hand for Bertram alone.[44] Indeed, Norman Bennet and George Brooks contend that,

Through this system the New England traders largely controlled the trade of northwestern Madagascar in the period before the American Civil War, with the commerce in hides providing a limited but profitable return for vessels trading with Zanzibar and Arabian-Persian ports.[45]

However, Marks' control was limited, as Swahili traders largely retained their monopoly of commerce on the northwest coast, including Mahajanga. Their dominance was secured through their alliance with the Indians who financed all aspects of commerce along the western littoral and much of interior Madagascar. The Indians also maintained close ties with large Bombay-based companies and cooperated closely with other Indian traders in East Africa, including Jairam Sewji, whose agents farmed the Omani customs.[46] The Swahili, themselves part of the Omani trading empire based on Zanzibar, had strong links with Muslim trading colonies on the Comoro Islands and the east African coast. Regular dhow sailings connected Madagascar with the Comoros, Mauritius, Mozambique, Delagoa Bay, and Bombay.[47] Political and commercial ties with both imperial and independent Madagascar reinforced the Swahili position.

techniques in Merina warfare c.1785–1828," *Revue française d'histoire d'outre-mer* LXI.224 (1974), 422; Guillain, *Documents* II, 214; Rasoamiaramanana "Aspects économiques" (1973), 31, 70; Bennett and Brooks (eds.), *New England Merchants*, xxvi.

[42] William Fairburn, *Merchant Sail* V (Lovell, 1945–55), 3014. Marks lived in Mahajanga from the early 1830s until his death in 1869 and received his orders from Richard Waters, merchant and U.S. consul at Zanzibar. The other two agents, Cyrus Hood and Ebenezer Tibbits, represented Salem merchants Joseph Cheever and Michael Shepherd. See Razi, "Sources d'histoire," 12–13.

[43] Bennett and Brooks (eds.), *New England Merchants*, xxvi.

[44] John Waters to Richard Waters, New York, 9 June 1844; Ephraim Emmerton, "A Visit to Eastern Africa, 1843–4"; and Ward to Romain-Desfossés, Zanzibar, 12 Feb. 1846 – in Bennett and Brooks (eds.), *New England Merchants*, 250, 259, 352.

[45] Bennett and Brooks (eds.), *New England Merchants*, xxvii–xxvii.

[46] Thompson to Hathorne, Majunga, 27 Nov. 1878, encl.1 in Hathorne to Bertram, Zanzibar, 11 Dec. 1878; Thompson to Hathorne, Mahajanga, 26 Dec. 1878, encl. in Hathorne to Bertram, Zanzibar, 8 Jan. 1879 – *PM*.

[47] Browne, *Etchings*, 274; Ward to State Department, Zanzibar, 21 March 1847; Hines to Seward, Zanzibar, 25 Oct. 1864 – in Norman R. Bennett and George E. Brooks (eds.), *New England Merchants in Africa* (Boston, 1965), 387, 532, 539; Rasoamiaramanana, "Aspects," 19, 23, 25, 77–8; Grandidier, "Souvenirs," 28; Guillain, *Documents* I, 89–100; Hafkin, "Trade, Society and Politics," 233–54; see also Alpers, *Ivory and Slaves*, 214–15.

Thus, Ramanetaka, the first Merina governor of Mahajanga, cultivated the friendship of Mose Sama, a local Swahili dignitary, while simultaneously, the Swahili forged marital links with local Sakalava chiefs whom they influenced to adopt Islamic customs.[48]

Such a web of alliances enabled the Swahili to dominate the foreign trade of Mahajanga, it being noted in 1843 that "The wealthiest residents are descendants of the Arabs, from Johanna, Zanzibar, and the coast of Africa."[49] The Swahili merchant, Mohammed Desharee, possessed "four wives, two hundred slaves, five hundred head of cattle, two plantations near Majunga, and one in Johanna" while his house, "a large bamboo building thatched with palmetto, and whitewashed outside" had its interior walls "covered with Chinese plates, American looking-glasses, Arabian fans, flags of different nations, Chinese pictures, old copper plates with inscriptions, Egyptian relics and charms, and various other curiosities."[50] Comparatively few Indians settled permanently in Madagascar, though many claimed Merina in addition to British citizenship.[51]

In 1845, when Merina ports were closed to the French and British, American merchants were also barred lest they act as middlemen for the Europeans. In consequence, foreign trade slumped: An American sailor commented in 1849 that "The town [Mahajanga] has not much the appearance of thrift or business. . . . We sold but little cargo here."[52] However, the Indian–Swahili grip on trade remained elsewhere in the northwest. Thus in 1850, when an American crew tried to purchase turtle shell and hides directly from the Sakalava of Boina Bay, two days' sail from Mahajanga, they succeeded in buying only a few hides

---

[48] Campbell, "Madagascar and the slave trade."

[49] Browne, *Etchings*, 256.

[50] Browne, *Etchings*, 251–2, 254, 256.

[51] By the late 1880s all Indians trading on the Malagasy west coast claimed to be British subjects – McMahon, "The Sakalava"; Bousserand, "Notice sur les tribus," 130; CdM 134 (13 March 1894); Kirk to Granville, Zanzibar, 3 April 1872, no. 8 in "Correspondence Respecting the Slave Trade" (1873); Frere to Granville, Mozambique Channel, 27 Feb, 12 March, and 7 May 1873 - CFM; Graves to Granville, 22 March 1884, no. 26, *English Blue Book*; Rostvig, *Sakalaverne*, 244; S.Pickersgill, "North Sakalava-land," AAMM 8 (1893), 29–43; Robinson to Adee, 29 Oct. 1884; Stanwood to Robinson (incl. in Stanwood to Bayard), Andakabe, 31 Oct. 1886; Stanwood to Campbell, Andakabe, 25 Aug., 19 Sep., and 21 Dec. 1887; Campbell to Razafindrazaka, 26 May 1890 - US; Knott to British Foreign Secretary, Mahajanga, 29 March 1895, "Correspondence of the British Vice Consulate in Majunga" (1894–7), AM; Esoavelomandroso, "La region du Fiheregna"; Prud'homme, "Considérations," 29; Liesegang, "First Look," 451–523; Jose Capela, "The Mujojos Slave Trade in Moçambique, 1830–1902" paper presented at the *Workshop on the Long-Distance Trade in Slaves across the Indian Ocean and Red Sea*, SOAS, London (December, 1987), 4–5.

[52] Putnam, "A Cruise" (1848–50).

and 150 pounds of "bad wax."[53] Following the reopening of imperial ports in 1853, Mahajanga largely recovered its former position and Daosa, the Indian leader there in the 1860s, followed the example of Indian traders working under Omani rule by financing the construction of a customs house.[54]

The 1845 ban together with the entrenched position of the Indians and Swahili led American and European merchants on the west coast to transfer their local agencies to Nosy Be, an island off the northwest coast of Madagascar occupied by the French in 1842. Nosy Be possessed considerable advantages. The prices of export staples there were half those of Mahajanga, where, in September 1842, export duties doubled to 10 percent ad valorem to equal east coast rates.[55] Also, Nosy Be lay on the direct maritime route via the Comoros to Zanzibar, 450 km to the northeast, and had excellent anchorage. A visiting American seaman commented in 1849: "The location is one of the finest that I have ever yet seen, the anchorage good and sheltered by high ranges of mountains that prevent the Monsoons from blowing with there [sic] full force."[56]

The 1848–9 Sakalava revolt against the French attempt to abolish slavery and the French ban on the import of muskets and gunpowder, major items of U.S. trade, temporarily undermined Nosy Be's position.[57] Zanzibar, where foreign trade was taxed at 5 percent, was a possible alternative, but from mid-century was flooded by foreign firms. Established companies included Bertram, Arnold Hines, O'Swald, and Hertz (Hamburg). They were joined in the early 1850s by Hansing (Hamburg), Vidal Régis, and Rabau frères (Marseille), and in 1867

---

[53] Horace B. Putnam, "Private Journal on the bark "Emily Wilder," McFarland master, voyage from Salem to the East Indies," m.656 184 E, *EI*.

[54] Rasoamiaramanana, "Aspects," 62.

[55] Cattle, for instance, cost $10–11 each in Mahajanga, twice their price on Nosy Be: Valette, "Quelques renseignements," 688; Campbell, "The Role of the London Missionary Society" vol. I, 189–91, vol. II, 319; see also Guillain à M. L'Ordinateur de l'Île Bourbon, Nosy-Be, 1842, C8e, *AHVP*; Prud'homme, "Observations," 424; Wastell, "British Imperial Policy," 271; Putnam, "A Cruise" (1848–50); McFarland, "List of goods suitable for Nos Beh, Mayotta, &c," in Bennett and Brooks (eds.), *New England Merchants*, 439.

[56] Putnam, "A Cruise to the Indies"; see also Raminosoa, "La Maison 'Wm. O'Swald & Co,'" 16.

[57] Ward to Buchanana, Zanzibar, 27 July 1847; *idem* to Shepard, Zanzibar, 26 March 1850; McFarland to Shepard, Zanzibar, 15 Sept. 1848; McFarland, "List," 439; Bates to Bertram, Nosy B, 11 Jan. 1849; Gregg to Shepard, Zanzibar, 12 May 1849; Jelly to West, Zanzibar, 26 Sept. 1849 and 23 March 1850; Ward to Abbot, Kennebunkport, 13 March 1851 – in Bennett and Brooks (eds.), *New England Merchants*, 389, 391, 437, 442–3, 450, 453, 879; Razi, "Sources d'histoire," 17–18; Putnam, "A Cruise" (1848–50); *MT* II.44 (5 Nov. 1884), 404.

The uprising of Sakalava on Nosy Be followed the 1848 emancipation of slaves by the French – see Ephraim Emmerton, "Journal: A Visit to Eastern Africa, 1848," in Bennett and Brooks (eds.), *New England Merchants*, 406; Razi, "Sources d'histoire," 19–20.

Roux de Fraissinet.[58] Increased foreign competition in East Africa resulted in the search for collection points for Malagasy exports closer to source. One possibility was Mozambique, which, however, like Mahajanga, was plagued by the imposition of high duties: In 1845, duties were 15 percent at Mozambique Island and 46.5 percent at other Mozambique ports.[59] Consequently some foreign traders recommenced trading with Mahajanga via Indian and Swahili middlemen. Thus, Sheik Adam bin Ibriheme (son and namesake of the former Indian agent for Bertram and Arnold Hines) was by 1878 the Mahajanga·agent for O'Swald, purchasing chiefly wax and rubber for a 5 percent commission (2.5 percent each on sales and purchases). He was willing to work on the same basis for the U.S. firms.[60] However, the need to deal through Swahili and Indian middlemen continued to frustrate Western merchants, an American agent in Mahajanga commenting in late 1878 of the Indians: "those 'Bohoras' . . . seem to be one family, and it would be cheaper, and better in every way to have our own man here."[61]

In order to lure back traders who had fled Nosy Be following the 1848–9 revolt, the French authorities declared the island a free port. Consequently, O'Swald and other large foreign firms reestablished agencies there.[62] By contrast, smaller Creole traders attempted to bypass Swahili traders by moving southward beyond Cape St. André. Some, like Desmorels, had been active in the southwest since the early 1800s, but the real expansion in the foreign trade of the area started in the 1830s and 1840s with the arrival on the mid- and lower west coast of the Samat and Rossier brothers, Achille Lemerle, and César Pepin.[63]

[58] Hieke, *Zur Geschichte des deutschen Handels*, 114–15, 139–40, 209; Evers, "Das Hamburger Zanzibarhandelshaus Wm. O'Swald," 18.

[59] William Bates, "Journal and Observations, 8th Voyage, Brig Richmond, 1845," in Bennett and Brooks (eds.), *New England Merchants*, 264–5; see also *idem*, xxviii.

[60] Thompson to Hathorne, Majunga, 27 Nov. 1878, encl.1 in Hathorne to Bertram, Zanzibar, 11 Dec. 1878; Thompson to Hathorne, Mahajanga, 26 Dec. 1878, encl. in Hathorne to Bertram, Zanzibar, 8 Jan. 1879 – *PM*.

[61] Thompson to Hathorne, Majunga, 26 Dec. 1878, encl. in Hathorne to Bertram and Arnold, Hines, Zanzibar, 8 Jan. 1879, "letter book" of H. Hathorne, agent for Arnold, Hines & Co, New York and John Bertram, Salem, and U.S. consul in Zanzibar (1878–80), Bk.II, *PM*.

[62] Hathorne to Thompson, Zanzibar, 10 Dec. 1878; Thompson to Hathorn, Majunga, 27 Nov. 1878, encl. 1 in Hathorne to Bertram, Zanzibar, 11 Dec. 1878 – Hathorne, "Letterbook" (1878–80). Mozambique was approximately 560 km from Mahajanga and Zanzibar was approximately eight days sail from Toamasina. Richard Waters, "Journals" (1836–44), in Bennett and Brooks (eds.), *New England Merchants*, 191; Edward D. Ropes to [parents], Tamatave, 24 March 1882, B1 (1882–1886) Zanzibar Acc.11840 and 11884: Letters 1882, Papers of Edward D. Ropes Jr, *PM*; Razi, "Sources d'Histoire Malgache," 19–20.

[63] Stanwood to Robinson, Morondava, 1 Dec. 1880, US3; encl. 2 (1882) in Stanwood to Campbell, Andakabe, 19 Sept. 1887, US5; R. L. Ader, "Les traitants de Nosy-Vé, Tulear à la fin du XIXe

Western commercial interest in the independent west coast increased from the mid-1870s. First, direct commercial links were forged between South Africa, notably Natal, and the southwest of the island. Some Natal merchants – seven in the period 1878–81 – led by Mc Cubbin, established trading posts in and around St. Augustin Bay.[64] Second, there was a marked rise in foreign competition on the mid- and northwest coasts. From the late 1870s, steamship lines established services linking Toamasina, Antseranana (Diego Suarez), Nosy Be, Nosy Ve, and Mayotta, encouraging Western traders to settle or establish agencies in those ports.[65] From 1881 to 1885, for example, the number of German firms in the region increased from two to five.[66] Competition was fierce: In mid-1884, the efforts of O'Swald and Ropes, Emmerton and Co. to force down the price of Malagasy export staples collapsed when O'Swald raised its steamer freight rates,[67] while Registe, expanding from Mozambique to assume the Malagasy business of Roux de Fraissinet, from 1883, started a price war with his European and U.S. competitors.[68] However, traders soon became disenchanted with the steamship ports-of-call. In northern Madagascar all such ports were, at the start of the 1883–5 Franco–Merina War, occupied by the French, who imposed taxes on non-French subjects and removed Nosy Be's status as a free port: In mid-1886, one U.S. firm was ordered to pay $1,500 a year to the French authorities on Nosy Be.[69]

The result was an exodus of non-French traders[70] whose decision to establish agencies on the independent west coast was facilitated by the decline there in Indian and Swahili influence following the 1878–9 cholera epidemic that devastated successively Zanzibar, Nosy Be, and Mahajanga, precipitating the

---

siècle," *Etudes Tuléariennes* vol. II (décembre 1970); Campbell, "Madagascar and the Slave Trade."

[64] Natal Archives: ms.722/4521 (1879); 723/4636 (1879); 723/4679 (1879); 724/4750 (1879); 726/4955 (1879); 733/5626 (1879); 1236/5851 (1889); 1352/6003 (1892); *Third Report of the Commission on Scale and Stock Diseases, 1894–95* (Pietermaritzburg, 1895), 5; Natal Blue Books.

[65] Néple, *Guide de l'Immigrant à Madagascar* II (Paris, 1899), 269.

[66] Ryder to Ropes, Emmerton & Co, and Arnold, Hines & Co, Nossi Bé, 15 March 1884, Partner and Agency Records. Madagascar Agencies. Correspondence Sent (Letterbook, 1884–7), Feb.–May 1884, B44.F6, *EI.*

[67] Ropes, Emmerton & Co, to J.Orme Ryder, Salem, 30 April 1883 and 7 May 1883; *idem* to Whitney, Salem, 21 Dec. 1883 – *REC/CR-MZL.*

[68] Ryder to Ropes, Emmerton & Co, and Arnold, Hines & Co, Nossi B, 15 March 1884, *REC/CR-MZL.*

[69] Payable in French francs – Ryder to Ropes, Emmerton & Co, and Arnold, Hines & Co, Nosy Be, 6 and 27 Aug. 1886, *REC/CR-MZL.*

[70] Ryder to Ropes, Emmerton & Co, and Arnold, Hines & Co, Nossi Bé, 1 Oct. 1884 and 6 and 27 Aug. 1886 – Partner and Agency Records. Madagascar Agencies: Correspondence Sent. Letterbook (1884–7), Ropes, Emmerton & Co. ms.103, B44.F2 and F5, *EI.*

bankruptcy of a number of Bombay-based firms.[71] As early as 1878, George Ropes opened agencies at "Menai Be" (Menabe province – the chief ports of which were Belo and Morondava) and "Metrano" (Maintirano).[72] Other large European and U.S. firms such as O'Swald, Hines, and Roux de Fraissinet, Cape Town merchants, and agents of the main steamer lines serving East Africa, followed his example, attracted notably by the trade in precious woods.[73]

However, the absence on the coast south of Maintirano of an organized body of middlemen such as the Swahili frequently obstructed trade. On the one hand, this led to visiting crews, notably of whalers, exploiting the local and relatively commercially unsophisticated Sakalava.[74] On the other hand, foreign traders were subject to arbitrary taxes and delays. Contracts varied with each individual chief, took months to conclude, and were often broken. Also, lack of credit rendered suppliers almost totally dependent upon fluctuations in demand. In addition, Sakalava tradition considered ships in distress to be fair game for plunder.[75]

Nevertheless, commerce on the southwest coast remained buoyant for most of the 1880s due to the maintenance of a fragile trading structure based on three groups: Mascarene, Malagasy, and Indian. The first stabilizing influence was provided by the presence of traders such as the Samat and Rossier brothers, who, by virtue of their initial control over the import of gunpowder and firearms and their influence with European officials, attained positions as political advisers to, and protectors of, local chiefs. Like their Indian and Swahili counterparts to the north, they frequently forged close ties with Merina provincial governors. They also petitioned the authorities to appoint sympathizers to their cause to official posts on the west coast. For example, in 1887, they successfully agitated for the replacement of an anti-slave trade governor at Andakabe, near Morondava, by Rainizafindrazaka who had by mid-1888, in collaboration with Mascarene and

---

[71] Hathorne to [Machan] Morris & Co, Zanzibar, 6 Feb. 1879 – Hathorne, "Letterbook" (1878–80).

[72] Thompson to Hathorne, Majunga, 27 Nov. 1878, encl.1 in Hathorne to Bertram, Zanzibar, 11 Dec. 1878 – Hathorne, "Letterbook" (1878–80).

[73] Indian and Swahili agents from Zanzibar working in Madagascar sold their ebony in Maintirano to de Fraissinet rather than ship it to Hathorne, the Zanzibar agent for Hines and Bertram, who offered lower prices – Hathorne to Arnold, Hines & Co, Zanzibar, 24 and 29 Aug., 17 Oct., and 14 Nov. 1877, 16 Oct. 1878 – 'Letterbook of William H. Hathorne, Zanzibar (1877–79), acc.11.584, *PM*.

[74] "Log of the Bark 'Reaper,' 1838–9"; Ward to Clayton, Zanzibar, 4 July 1850 – in Bennett and Brooks (eds.), *New England Merchants*, 185, 455; Browne, *Etchings*, 263; Nordhoff, *Stories*, 58.

[75] Grandidier, "Souvenirs," 24–5; Stanwood to Robinson, Morondava, 1 Dec. 1880, *US*; *GH* (1928), 272; Campbell, "Madagascar and the Slave Trade," 220–4; see also Sundström, *Exchange Economy*, 17; Beachey, *Slave Trade*, 60; Pankhurst, *Economic History of Ethiopia*, 884–9; Browne, *Etchings*, 218, 224.

Indian allies, gained a near monopoly of arms imports in exchange for slave exports along the coast between Ranopas and Maintirano. Slave traders such as Norden at Toliara and Govea at Maintirano also gained quasi-consular status.[76] Large foreign firms active in West Madagascar used such agents regularly until the late 1880s. For instance, George Ropes employed a certain Henry Smith, who was married to a daughter of Leo Samat, to smuggle into Sakalava land large arms consignments.[77]

A second stabilizing factor was provided by two communities of refugees from Merina rule that emerged after 1885 as major slave traders. The Antanosy of the southwest operated a two-way trade, selling captives for export and importing slaves for the Merina market. The Betsiriry to their north, who specialized in exports, raided the entire west-central plateau for slaves, from Mandridrano in the north to Fanjakana in the south. Indeed, most Merina governors in the western provinces were obliged to cooperate with the Betsiriry, described as "the most powerful confederacy in Menabe."[78] The Betsiriry army, 10,000-strong under Ratoera, was equipped with modern Snider and Remington rifles obtained in return for slaves from the Indian "Dalakeimo," whose boats cruised the Tsiribihina from his base at Tsimanandrafozana.[79]

The Indians constituted the final stabilizing element. In the course of the 1880s, they and their Swahili allies recovered to catch up with and impose their dominance over Western traders. Seizing advantage of the chaos caused by the 1883–5 conflict, the Indians moved south beyond Maintirano. Whereas prior to the 1883–5 war there were no non-Christian traders in the Toliara region, soon after its conclusion in 1885 Indians came to dominate trade along the entire west coast, notably in cloth, gunpowder, and slaves.[80] There were a number of reasons for this. First, Indian and Swahili traders collaborated while Western

[76] Robinson to Adee, 22 Oct. 1884; Campbell to Porter, 23 Aug. 1887; Campbell to Rives, 10 Feb. 1888; Stanwood to Andriamifidy, 1 Sept. 1888 – *US*; Grandidier, "Souvenirs," 27.

[77] Stanwood to Bayard, Andakabe, 31 Oct. 1886; Stanwood to Campbell, Andakabe, 19 Sept. 1887; *idem* to Wharton, 9 Sept. 1889 – *US*.

[78] Bousserand, "Notice sur les tribus Tanala et Sakalava" in M. E. Fagereng, "Histoire des Maroserana du Menabe," *BAM* 28 (1947–8), 130.

[79] Fagereng, "Histoire des Maroserana," 129; E. O. McMahon, "First Visit of a European to the Betsiriry Tribe," *AAMM* 15 (1891), 280; J. Richardson, *Lights and Shadows* (Antananarivo, 1877), 40; Grandidier, "Souvenirs," 10–11.

[80] Memos, 31 March and 7 May 1873 (incl. 1, no. 52), CFM; Hafkin, "Trade, Society and Politics," 232–52; Kirk to Granville, 25 Jan. and 5 March 1872, "Correspondence Respecting the Slave Trade" c.867, *HCPP* LXI (1873); Mable V. Jackson, *European Powers and Southeast Africa, 1796–1856* (London, 1967), Chs. 3 and 6; L. Rostvig, *Sakalaverne og deres land* (Stavanger, 1886), 244; Pickersgill, "North Sakalava-land"; Stanwood to Robinson, incl. in Stanwood to Bayard, 31 Oct. 1886, *US4*; Manassé Esoavelomandroso, "La region du Fiheregna à la veille de la conquête française," *Colloque d' histoire* (Université de Madagascar, 1979); Prud'homme,

merchants competed.[81] Second, steamships could not compete regionally with the freight rates offered by dhows, while contact with steamship agents freed the Indian and Swahili traders from the necessity of conducting their European and American business through resident foreign agents.[82] Finally, the Indians and Swahili were largely protected from attack by local Malagasy due to their marital alliances with the Sakalava. For these reasons, Western merchants continued to use their services; by 1888, for example, all of George Ropes's agents were Indians.[83]

However, from the late 1880s, security and trade deteriorated on the west coast. This stemmed largely from a steady collapse from 1882 of Merina authority on the imperial periphery that induced the Sakalava and Bara to launch increasingly daring slave and cattle raids onto the plateau.[84] Such fierce rivalry developed between suppliers of slaves for export that all contemporary accounts refer to a state of perpetual internecine warfare in central, southern, and western Madagascar from the late 1880s[85] and a rise in the number of Sakalava/Vezo attacks on foreign merchants on the coast.[86]

Consequently, trade suffered and foreign merchants left the Malagasy mainland. Larger concerns switched to Mozambique, 320 to 560 km away, where

---

"Considérations," 29; Campbell, "Madagascar and the Slave Trade," 223–4; *GH* (1928), 39, 249, 299, 304, 317; Samat, "Notes" (1852), 57–8, 61–2.

[81] Ropes, Emmerton & Co, to Cheney, Salem, 25 Sept. 1883, *REC/CR-MZL*.

[82] Norman R. Bennett, "Americans in Zanzibar: 1865–1915" *Essex Institue Historical Collection* 98 (1962), 44; Ropes, Emmerton & Co, to J. Orme Ryder, Salem, 30 April and 7 May 1883, ms.103, Ropes, Emmerton & Co. Records (1873–1902) B42.F4: Correspondence Received. Madagascar and Zanzibar Letterbook, 1883–85, *EI*; Raminosoa, "La Maison 'Wm. O'Swald & Co,'" 31.

[83] McMahon, "The Sakalava"; Bousserand, "Notice sur les tribus," 130; *CdM* 134 (13 March 1894); Kirk to Granville, Zanzibar, 3 April 1872, no. 8 in "Correspondence Respecting the Slave Trade" (1873); Frere to Granville, Mozambique Channel, 27 Feb. and 12 March 1873 – *CFM*; Graves to Granville, 22 March 1884, no. 26, *English Blue Book*; Rostvig, *Sakalaverne*, 244; Pickersgill, "North Sakalava-land"; Robinson to Adee, 29 Oct. 1884; Stanwood to Robinson (incl. in Stanwood to Bayard), Andakabe, 31 Oct. 1886; Stanwood to Campbell, Andakabe, 25 Aug., 19 Sept., and 21 Dec. 1887; Campbell to Razafindrazaka, 26 May 1890 – *US*; Knott to British Foreign Secretary, Mahajanga, 29 March 1895, "Correspondence of the British Vice Consulate in Majunga" (1894–7), *AM*; Esoavelomandroso, "La region du Fiheregna"; Prud'homme, "Considérations," 29; Liesegang, "First Look," 451–523; Jose Capela, "The Mujojos Slave Trade in Moçambique, 1830–1902" paper presented at the *Workshop on the Long-Distance Trade*, SOAS (December, 1987), 4–5.

[84] Campbell, *Unfree Labour*, Ch. 8.

[85] *ASR* (July and Aug.1888), 128; (Nov and Dec.1888), 209–10; Sturge, "letter" (1888), 180.

[86] Rostvig to Stanwood, Tullear [Dec.1886], NMS Copibok 812B (Tulear, 1882–92), 183–4, *FLM/NMS*; *CdM* 138 (10 April 1894); encl. (1 Dec. 1885) in George to Robinson, Andakabe, 10 Feb. 1886; Stanwood to Campbell, 31 Jan. and 27 May 1888 – *US5*; *ASR* (Jul. and Aug. 1888), 128 and (Nov. and Dec. 1888), 209–10; E.Sturge, "letter" Oxon, 13 Sept. 1888 *ASR* (Sept. and Oct. 1888), 180.

Portuguese authorities exercised little control over illicit traffic. Indeed, from at least the late 1870s, Mozambique was the chief distributive center for slaves and arms to Madagascar, and for some foreign firms it was also the chief collection point for Malagasy exports. For instance, Ropes, who established an agency in Mozambique in the late 1870s, thereafter shipped his Malagasy produce there from Maintirano and other west coast ports, for transhipment onto Union steamers. However, such traders quickly discovered that Indians would not relinquish the quasi-monopoly of foreign trade they had long held in Mozambique.[87] Most Mascarene traders, restricted by a relative paucity of capital,[88] moved to the offshore island of Nosy Ve, where by 1890 they were joined by the larger firms deterred from Mozambique by Indian middlemen and growing British naval interest. Unlike European traders, Indians both developed strong trading links with the Swahili coast, Mozambique, Cape Colony, and Natal[89] and expanded into mainland Madagascar, where, by 1894, their commercial triumph was virtually complete, it being noted that "the hinterland is completely closed to Europeans."[90] As a result, other foreign traders, led by Mascarene Creoles, established a persistent call for a French takeover of Madagascar, following which they transferred their agencies from Nosy Ve to Toliara.[91]

To conclude, there existed two major trading structures in nineteenth-century Madagascar. Within the Merina empire, foreign trade was largely monopolized by members of the imperial court through the *deka* system and through a limited number of royal trade contracts with selected foreigners. The system was relaxed slightly from 1861, permitting greater foreign participation and the emergence of a civilian middleman group, although foreign trade was still highly supervised by the imperial court. In the independent regions of the island, foreign trade was dominated by Indian and Swahili traders whose middleman

[87] Hathorne to Arnold, Hines & Co, Zanzibar, 26 July 1878; *idem* to Bertram, Zanzibar, 26 July 1878; *idem* to Thompson, Zanzibar, 10 Dec. 1878 – "Letters of H.Hathorne, agent of Arnold, Hines & Co, New York and john Bertram, Salem, and US consul at Zanzibar, 1878–1880," *PM*.

[88] Memos, 31 March and 7 May 1873 (incl. 1, no. 52), CFM; Hafkin, "Trade, Society and Politics," 232–52; Kirk to Granville, 25 Jan. and 5 March 1872, "Correspondence Respecting the Slave Trade" c.867, *HCPP* LXI (1873); Jackson, *European Powers*, Chs. 3, 6; L. Rostvig, *Sakalaverne og deres land* (Stavanger, 1886), 244; Pickersgill, "North Sakalava-land"; Stanwood to Robinson, incl. in Stanwood to Bayard, 31 Oct. 1886, *US4*; Manassé Esoavelomandroso, "La region du Fiheregna à la veille de la conquête française," *Colloque d'histoire* (Université de Madagascar, 1979); Prud'homme, "Considérations," 29; Campbell, "Madagascar and the Slave Trade," 223–4; *GH* (1928), 39, 249, 299, 304, 317; Samat, "Notes" (1852), 57–8, 61–2.

[89] S. Procter to Dilke, London, 15 Nov. 1882, "Correspondence Respecting Madagascar Relating to the Mission of Hova Envoys to Europe in 1882–83," *Africa* 1 (London, 1883), no. 17; Stanwood, "Commercial Situation," Andakabe, 31 Dec. 1886, *US*.

[90] *CdM* 134 (13 mars 1894). The only region they did not completely dominate by 1895 was the extreme south of the island.

[91] Nèple, *Guide de l'Immigrant*, 270.

services most Mascarene, European, and U.S. firms were obliged to use. The Indians, in particular, seized the commercial opportunities offered by an expanding international economy and incorporated Madagascar into a trading empire that embraced the entire western Indian Ocean, from Bombay to Zanzibar to Natal. The depression from the late 1870s, the French takeover, and the end of the Malagasy slave trade profoundly affected many Swahili, Mascarene, and Merina traders whose capital was tied up in slaves and larger non-French firms against whom the French colonial regime discriminated. However, the financial and organizational resources of the Indians enabled them to make a successful transition to post–slave trade commerce. For this they earned the wrath of the Mascarene community, which had hoped to reap the benefits of the French intervention.[92]

---

[92] Walter Marcuse, *Through Western Madagascar in Search of the Golden Bean* (London, 1914), 45–62, 278–81, 341.

8   Foreign Trade, 1820–1895

Introduction

This chapter examines the nature and value of Malagasy foreign trade excluding slaves (analyzed in Chapter 9). At the start of the nineteenth century, slave exports to the Mascarenes formed the basis of Merina foreign trade and the Merina crown's economic and political power. Industrialization in Europe and the United States and the rise of the international economy presented enhanced possibilities for foreign trade. The prohibition of slave exports in 1820 was based on the supposition that Imerina could rapidly gain monopoly control over the island's other traditional export staples and develop new exports associated with cash crop plantations and craft manufacture. State monopolies were established over staple exports, although following the failure of the attempted industrial revolution, the Merina crown from 1861 looked increasingly to foreign trade to finance government and in consequence relaxed some trading restrictions. Critically, however, the Merina court failed either to curb smuggling within the empire or to gain control of foreign trade in most of south and west Madagascar where an independent trading network developed.

Exports

Serving a brisk maritime traffic, provisions flowed from the west coast to India-bound ships, U.S. whalers, and Muslim markets to the north. From the east coast, they flowed predominantly to the Mascarenes, where the population increased almost fourfold (from approximately 140,000 to over 500,000) from

1810 to 1900 and subsistence cultivation was sacrificed for plantation crops. The Mascarene trade thus increased exponentially.[1] On the Malagasy east coast, bullocks for slaughter cost from $7 to $8 each, Malagasy beef being sold on the Mascarenes for $10 (dried) and $12 (salted) a ton. From 1821 to 1845, 1,410 tons ($16,920) of salted and 80 tons ($800) of dried beef was shipped to Réunion, while in 1835 alone, $15,840 worth of beef was shipped to Mauritius.[2] From 1828 to 1846, American traders on the west coast, notably at Mahajanga, exported dried beef, destined for slaves on Cuba, and salted meat, possibly for sale in Zanzibar.[3] After the 1883–5 war, the Merina ceded Antseranana to the French, who established a slaughterhouse and meat factory serving primarily Réunion[4].

Rice was exported from the west coast, principally to the Mozambique and Swahili coasts, although in the early 1800s about 500 tons was also annually shipped to the Mascarenes,[5] supplementing supplies of east coast rice (2,000 to 2,500 tons from Mahavelona alone). From 1821 to 1845, an annual average of $52,083 worth of rice flowed to Réunion, and in 1835, $7,120 of rice was exported to Mauritius, mainly from the rice ports of Mahanoro, Mananjary, Mahela, and Fenoarivo: Mascarene traders preferred Angontsy rice, from the northeast. On Mauritius in 1862, Angontsy and Toamasina rice was valued at $3.25 and $3.00 per 100 pounds respectively.[6] Rontaunay also exported $2,667

[1] Auguste Toussaint, *Histoire de l'île Maurice* (Paris: Presses Universitaires de France, 1971), 74, 93, 106, 109.

[2] Raombana, "Manuscrit," 10–11; *GH* (1928), 111, 127–8, 136, 297–9; "Foreign Trade – Mauritius (1835)," *HCPP* 47 (1837–8), 567; Campbell, "Role of the London Missionary Society" vol. II, 297.

[3] Razi, "Sources d'histoire," 14, 22; Bennett and Brooks (eds.), *New England Merchants*, xxvi; Log book of the Brig *Susan* from Salem, captain Thomas D.Brace, 24 March 1828–26 Jan. 1829, *EI* (hereafter Log book (1828–9)); see also Hathorne to Arnold, Hines & Co, Zanzibar, 4 May 1877 – Hathorne, "Letterbook" (1878–80); Ephraim Emerton to C. & Howard, Salem, 5 Dec. 1823; Brookhouse and Lovett to Emerton, Salem, 22 July 1826; "Invoice of Merchandise Shipped by William Hunt on Board the Brig *Shaumut* – James Emerton Master," Invoices, Bills of Lading, Bills, 1816–1835, James and Ephraim Emerton, File 2 – mss.733 (1816–1835) E.63 v.6, E. & J. Emerton Shipping, *BLHU* (hereafter Invoice Hunt – *BLHU*).

[4] Foucart, "L'Etat du commerce à Madagascar," 89.

[5] Mayeur, "Voyage au pays de Séclaves" (1774), 123; *idem*, "Voyage dans le nord" (1775), 62; Grégoire Avine, "Notes de voyage à Fort Dauphin" (1804) in Raymond Decary, "Le voyage d'un chirurgien philosphe à Madagascar," *BAM* 36 (1958), 326; Rondeaux, "Mémoire" (1809), 91–108; *GH* (1908), 171 and (1928), 38–9, 297; Rantoandro, "communauté mercantile," 9–10; Hines to Seward, Zanzibar, 25 Oct. 1864, in Bennett and Brooks (eds.), *New England Merchants*, 528.

[6] M.Coignet, "Madagascar. Its Trade and Resources" (1862), *MT* II.41 (15 Oct. 1884), 376; see also Dwyer to Seward, Boston, 9 Dec. 1861; Robinson to Hunter, 1 Oct. 1877 and 1 Oct. 1878 – *US*; *GH* (1928), 136, 297–8; "Foreign Trade – Mauritius (1835)," *HCPP* 47 (1837–8), 567; Campbell, "Role of the London Missionary Society" vol. II, 297.

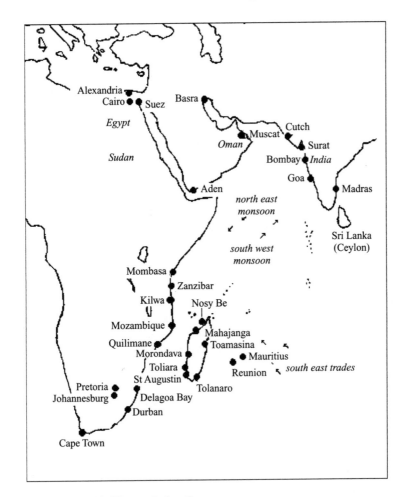

Map 9. *The Western Indian Ocean*

worth of rice to France from 1821 to 1845.[7] On the east coast by 1884, rice, destined for regional markets, was still the second most valuable legitimate export, behind hides.[8]

Other food exports were of minor importance until the late 1870s, when a combination of cattle disease, drought, and locust plague induced sharp periodic declines in crop production in southern Africa. From 1877 to 1886 and 1890 to 1899, independent western Madagascar was an important supplier of

[7] Dwyer to Seward, Boston, 9 Dec.1861; Robinson to Hunter, 1 Oct.1877 and 1 Oct.1878 – *US*; Campbell, "Role of the London Missionary Society" vol. II, 295–7.
[8] *MT* II.22 (4 June 1884), 206.

both maize and beans to South Africa, where vigorous demand developed for imported wheat, maize, vegetables, and dairy produce due to harvest shortfalls, accentuated from the 1880s by the rapid growth in urban mining centers.[9]

Madagascar's large cattle stock also provided the basis for a major export industry in live cattle, notably to the Mascarenes where draft animals were in great demand on the plantations. At the start of the nineteenth century, large numbers of cattle were trekked from northwest to northeast Madagascar and sold to Mascarene traders in the Antongil Bay region by Indian and Swahili agents.[10] With the rise of the Merina empire, cattle for export from imperial territory became a court monopoly. Investment was minimal. Cattle were obtained as battle booty or purchased on domestic markets at an average cost of from $3 to $5 each, vast grazing lands were seized, and slave or forced labor supplied herders. Profits from the cattle trade were so large that the Merina court banned live cow exports lest the Mascarenes expand their own stocks to the point of self-sufficiency. Weight lost on the arduous trek from the plateau necessitated a considerable delay to enable the cattle to be fattened up prior to embarkation; *deka* and other Merina agents used this period to supplement herd numbers through local purchases.[11] Their monopoly of cattle exports enabled the Merina court to dictate a local sale price of $0.071 per bullock, which it resold to foreign merchants on the coast for an average of $11 until 1853 when the price was raised to $15. An export duty of $1.50 per bullock was also imposed.[12] Following the French conquest, the price dropped to between $5 and $6 per bullock on the domestic market and between $8 and $9 in east coast ports.[13]

In the 1830s and 1840s, Rontaunay controlled an estimated 40 percent of the cattle and meat trade to the Mascarenes where live cattle fetched an average of $30 each.[14] An estimated 20 percent of cattle died on the three- to five-day sea voyage to the Mascarenes (in adverse weather, it could take a week).[15] In the

---

[9] Campbell, "Disease, Cattle and Slaves," 123.

[10] Mayeur, "Voyage au pays de Séclaves" (1774), 123; *idem*, "Voyage dans le nord" (1775), 62; Grégoire Avine, "Notes de voyage à Fort Dauphin" (1804) in Raymond Decary, "Le voyage d'un chirurgien philosphe à Madagascar," *BAM* 36 (1958), 326; Rondeaux, "Mémoire" (1809), 91–108; *GH* (1908), 171 and (1928), 38–9, 297; P. D.Curtin, *The Atlantic Slave Trade* (Madison, 1970), 229; Rantoandro, "communauté mercantile," 9–10.

[11] Campbell, "Role of the London Missionary Society" vol. II, 297–9.

[12] Raombana, "Manuscrit," 10–11; *GH* (1928), 111, 127–8, 298–9; Oliver, *Madagascar* vol. II, 196.

[13] Foucart, "L'Etat du commerce à Madagascar," 87.

[14] Campbell, "Role of the London Missionary Society" vol. II, 301.

[15] Mayeur, "Voyage au pays d'ancove" (1777), 153; *idem*, "Voyage au pays d'ancove" (1785), 205; Copland, *History of Madagascar*, 15; Bergsten, "Mémoire" (1825), 16; Oliver, *Madagascar* vol. I, 265, 412, 414; Anon, "Betsimisaraka folk-tales," 217; Sibree, *A Naturalist*, 20, 22–3,

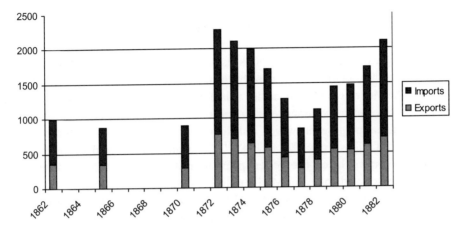

Figure 8. *Toamasina: Trade in British Vessels with Mauritius, 1862–82* ($000s Malagasy).
Source: Oliver, *Madagascar. An Historical and Descriptive Account*, vol. II, 186.

early 1800s, the Mascarenes imported about 1,350 Malagasy cattle annually; from 1821 to 1845, a minimum of 12,178 cattle (507 per annum) worth about $365,340 were exported to Réunion; and in 1835 alone, 11,261 live bullocks worth $123,875 were shipped to Mauritius. By the 1850s, from 10,000 to 12,000 cattle were exported annually to the Mascarenes (between 3,000 and 4,000 to Réunion and from 7,000 to 8,000 to Mauritius), rising to 15,000 by the early 1860s[16] (see Figure 8).

From the late 1870s, the pastoral Bara and Sakalava also drove cattle to southwestern ports of Toliara, St. Augustin, Belo, and Soalara for shipment to South Africa to replace stock depleted by disease and natural blights.[17] The first Malagasy cattle imports reached Natal in 1875 and, although the trade was halted in 1876/7, 1879, and 1892, due to the fear of infection,[18] Madagascar rarely accounted for less than 80 percent of Natal's cattle imports from 1875

35; GH (1928), 297; Robequain, "capitale montagnarde," 287; Valette, "Nouvelle note," 33–6; *Ny Gazety Malagasy* I.8 (1 Dec. 1875); Robinson to Hankey, 21 July 1879; *idem* to Hunter, 22 Sept. 1879; Campbell to Wharton, 2 Sept. 1889 – *US*; *CdM* (16 fév. 1892)(2 jan. 1894); (6 mars 1894); (15 mai 1894); (5 juin 1894).

[16] *GH* (1928), 136, 297–8; "Foreign Trade – Mauritius (1835)," *HCPP* 47 (1837–8), 567; Campbell, "Role of the London Missionary Society" vol. II, 297.

[17] Although some oxen were also purchased from Toamasina: Natal Archives: ms.722/4521 (1879); 723/4636 (1879); 723/4679 (1879); 724/4750 (1879); 726/4955 (1879); 733/5626 (1879); Natal Blue Books.

[18] Natal Archives: ms.614/3825 (1877); ms.718/4170 (1878); 719/4258 (1879); 732/5586 (1879); 733/5746 (1879); 736/145 (1880).

to 1909. Indeed, it was the sole source of Natal imports of oxen in 1878–80, 1884, 1890/1–1891/2, and 1904. Cattle mortality on the 10-day return trip was 9 percent in the period 1878–81.[19]

A brisk export trade in cattle products developed, initially as a by-product of the meat export trade, augmented by the industrial phase from 1828 to 1850 when the Merina crown commanded that all by-products of cattle slaughtered for ritual occasions be surrendered to imperial workshops.[20] Not all was used for industrial purposes, however, and Rontaunay exported to Réunion about 150 tons of tallow from 1821 to 1845.[21] The main cattle by-product and the staple export was hides. The western plains formed the largest grazing grounds in Madagascar and, following Merina military expansion into Iboina in the early 1820s, a large industry developed in Mahajanga and Marovoay producing raw and salted hides for export.[22] East coast hide exports, possibly triggered by the industrial experiment in Imerina, developed later.[23] In 1837, a monopoly over east coast exports of hides was granted to Lastelle, an associate of Rontaunay.[24] From 1821 to 1845, he exported 14,719 hides to Réunion; in 1835, 92,442 hides valued at $3,015 were also exported to Mauritius.[25]

However, the major expansion of hide exports occurred from the early 1870s when international demand proved so great that the indigenous practice, until then common, of eating beef with the hide attached, died out.[26] The years 1873–4 witnessed a 300 percent increase in east coast hide exports.[27] European and

[19] Cattle mortality would have been far higher for cattle exported from the east coast of Madagascar, which was between 23 and 30 direct sailing days from Natal and Cape Colony – Natal Archives: ms.722/4521 (1879); 723/4636 (1879); 723/4679 (1879); 724/4750 (1879); 726/4955 (1879); 733/5626 (1879); *Natal Blue Books*.

[20] See Chapter 4.

[21] *GH* (1928), 136, 297–8; "Foreign Trade – Mauritius (1835)," *HCPP* 47 (1837–8), 567; Campbell, "Role of the London Missionary Society" vol. II, 297. During approximately the same period Americans exported tallow and ox horns from Mahajanga – see note 26.

[22] Razi, "Sources d'histoire," 14, 22; Bennett and Brooks (eds.), *New England Merchants*, xxvi; Log book (1828–9); see also Hathorne to Arnold, Hines & Co, Zanzibar, 4 May 1877 Hathorne, "Letterbook" (1878–80); Ephraim Emerton to C. & Howard, Salem, 5 Dec. 1823; Brookhouse and Lovett to Emerton, Salem, 22 July 1826; Invoice Hunt – *BLHU*.

[23] See Chapter 4.

[24] Rontaunay had in 1826 tried and failed to secure a monopoly over the foreign trade of Mahela and Mananjary. Chapus & Mondain, "Un chapitre inconnu," 118; Campbell, "Role of the London Missionary Society" vol. II, 294, 301.

[25] *GH* (1928), 136, 297–8; "Foreign Trade – Mauritius (1835)," *HCPP* 47 (1837–8), 567; Campbell, "Role of the London Missionary Society" vol. II, 297.

[26] Dawson to Ropes, Emmerton & Co, and Arnold, Hines & Co, Port Louis, Mauritius, 29 Jan. 1884, *REC/CR-MZL*; Robinson to Hunter, 30 Dec. 1874 and 1 Oct. 1877; *idem* to Hankey, 29 Oct. 1877 – *US2*; Oliver, *Madagascar* vol. II, 175, 188–9.

[27] Ropes, Emmerton & Co, to Dawson, Salem, 13 Nov. 1884, *REC/CR-MZL*; *MT* II.41 (15 Oct. 1884), 376.

U.S. traders competed particularly fiercely, stimulating exports from all cattle regions.[28] By the late 1870s, the coast below Cape St. André had become an important source: Maintirano hides, described in 1878 as "the very best equal to the best Tamatave,"[29] were exported to Nosy Be and Mozambique;[30] and from the 1880s hides were shipped from the southwest to Natal – where cattle disease also caused acute shortages of hides.[31] Nevertheless, the east developed as the center of the trade, hides there becoming the most valuable export.[32] By 1883, an estimated 8,000 salted, dried, and folded bullock hides were being dispatched each month from Antananarivo to the coast. Exports fell from the mid-1880s as foreign hide purchasers cooperated to force purchase prices down[33] and, although competition from both foreigners and Merina dealers was too great for agreements to last,[34] prices had fallen dramatically by 1892:

Hides. The trouble with this produce is at your end [i.e., the United States and Europe]. The low price here is causing the supply to fall off, as the people cannot afford to sell at $250 (our present price) per 100 lbs. at Antananarivo. Salt costs $4.50 to $5.00 for 100 lbs and it takes about 25 lbs to properly cure 100 lbs of Hides the way it is done here, hence all the hides we are now getting are inferior.[35]

Despite poor quality and low prices, hide exports continued to grow in volume. Thus, one late 1890s French source claimed that annual west coast exports

---

[28] In 1877 *Arnold Hines*, chief American rival of *Ropes*, exported 600,000 pounds of Malagasy hides, worth approximately $60,000; Hathorne to Arnold, Hines & Co, Zanzibar, 13 Sept. 1878 – Hathorne, "Letterbook" (1878–80). The following year, the major Merina west coast entrepôt of Marovoay was said to produce only hides – see Thompson to Hathorne, Majunga, 27 Nov. 1878, encl.1 in Hathorne to Bertram, Zanzibar, 11 Dec. 1878 – Hathorne, "Letterbook" (1878–80).

[29] Thompson to Hathorne, Majunga, 27 Nov. 1878, encl.1 in Hathorne to Bertram, Zanzibar, 11 Dec. 1878 – Hathorne, "Letterbook" (1878–80).

[30] Hathorne to Arnold, Hines & Co, Zanzibar, 26 July 1878; *idem* to Bertram, Zanzibar, 26 July 1878; *idem* to Thompson, Zanzibar, 10 Dec. 1878 – Hathorne, "Letterbook" (1878–80); Ryder to Ropes, Emmerton & Co, and Arnold, Hines & Co, Nossi Bé, 15 April 1884, *REC/CR-MZL*; Hathorne to Arnold, Hines & Co, Zanzibar, 18 Sept. 1878; *idem* to Geo. Thompson, Zanzibar, 14 Nov. 1878 – Hathorne, "Letterbook" (1878–80).

[31] Campbell, "Disease, Cattle and Slaves."

[32] Ropes, Emmerton & Co, to Dawson, Salem, 13 Nov. 1884, *REC/CR-MZL*; *MT* II.41 (15 Oct. 1884), 376.

[33] Ropes, Emmerton & Co, to Whitney, Salem, 3 May 1883, *REC/CR-MZL*.

[34] Ryder commented in January 1893: "When the writer was in charge of this Agency years ago, scores of Hovas [Merina] came down from Antø to buy your goods, now the trade is in the hands of only four or five parties, and to move goods we must let them have pretty well their own way" – Ryder to Ropes, Emmerton & Co, Tamatave, 6 Jan. 1893, *REC/CR-MZL;* see also Whitney to Ropes, Emmerton & Co, and Arnold, Hines & Co, Tamatave, 14 March 1884, *REC/CR-MZL*.

[35] Duder to Ropes, Emmerton & Co, Antananarivo, 20 March 1893, *REC/CR-MZL*.

totaled about 33,600,[36] while another estimated total annual Malagasy hide exports at 200,000.[37]

Under autarchy, royal contracts led to the development of cash crops on the east coast.[38] Relaxation of the foreign trade regime from the early 1860s, followed by a rise in the world price of tropical produce in the late 1860s and the 1870s, resulted in renewed foreign investment, mainly in the Toamasina region, in coffee, tobacco, and sugar cane, and to a lesser extent cloves, raffia, and Fijian cotton. In the 1860s, as the American Civil War cut off traditional cotton supplies, Britain imported chiefly cotton from Madagascar and secondarily rice; thereafter, imports of Malagasy sugar, tea, and coffee became steadily more important.[39] Initially dominated by Réunionnais merchants, coffee exports were at first limited: by mid-century, approximately 500 kg (worth from $40 to $50) was being shipped annually to France.[40] From 1861, British merchants dominated the coffee trade, although U.S. houses shipped some to the United States, where in 1883 Malagasy coffee fetched $0.15 per lb.[41] However, following the ravages of *Hemileia vastatrix*, exports declined, remaining below their 1883 levels until the twentieth century.[42]

From the mid-1820s, Rontaunay established sugar plantations and distilleries on the east coast.[43] Between 1834 and 1845, he exported about 1,555 tons of sugar to France but faced severe competition on the world market from other regional cane sugar producers such as Réunion and Mauritius and from

[36] Nèple, *Guide de l'Immigrant*, 308.

[37] In early 1884, one U.S. commercial house alone was collecting 1,000 hides a month in Antananarivo for export via Toamasina. See Dawson to Ropes, Emmerton & Co, and Arnold, Hines & Co, Port Louis, Mauritius, 29 Jan. 1884, *REC/CR-MZL*; Robinson to Hunter, 30 Dec. 1874 and 1 Oct. 1877; *idem* to Hankey, 29 Oct. 1877 – *US2*; Oliver, *Madagascar* vol. II, 175, 188–9; see also Foucart, "L'Etat du commerce à Madagascar," 89; "Foreign Trade" in *Parliamentary Papers* (1876–1900).

[38] These included a short-lived experiment in the cultivation of black currants, some 200,000 of which were shipped to France by Rontaunay from 1834–45 – Campbell, "Role of the London Missionary Society" vol. II, 295–7; see also Dwyer to Seward, Boston, 9 Dec. 1861; Robinson to Hunter, 1 Oct. 1877 and 1 Oct. 1878 – *US*.

[39] Oliver, *Madagascar* vol. II, 200–3; Finkelmeier to Secretary of the US Treasury, Tamatave, 5 Jan. 1870; *idem* to Davis, 5 Oct. 1870; "7th Annual Report on Commercial Relations with Madagascar" (Oct. 1872); "8th Annual Report" (24 Oct. 1873); Finkelmeier to Hunter, 30 Dec. 1874; Robinson to Hunter, 1 Oct. 1877 – *US*.

[40] Dwyer to Seward, Boston, 9 Dec. 1861; Robinson to Hunter, 1 Oct. 1877 and 1 Oct. 1878 – *US*; Campbell, "Role of the London Missionary Society" vol. II, 295–7; see also Chapter 4.

[41] "Foreign Trade" in *Parliamentary Papers* (1876–1900); Ropes, Emmerton & Co, to Whitney, Salem, 14 Sept. and 30 Nov. 1883, *REC/CR-MZL*.

[42] Thorel, *La mise en valeur*, 17–18.

[43] Esoavelomandroso, *La province maritime orientale*, 87.

European beet sugar producers.[44] Sugar nevertheless comprised the second most significant export to Britain, sugar plantations benefiting from renewed foreign investment from the 1870s.[45] West coast tobacco was exported to the United States in the early nineteenth century;[46] the main tobacco plantations were established in mid-century on the east coast, where, by the 1860s, British merchants dominated tobacco exports.[47]

Spice and raffia plantations were also established. Cloves, introduced from Mauritius in 1803, were from 1835 cultivated extensively by Laborde at Rianambo near Mahela: Within a decade, 6,610 kg of cloves worth $1,983 had been exported to France.[48] However, they remained relatively unimportant. Raffia palms were also cultivated for raffia, exported primarily by British merchants, to be used as twine. In November 1884, Malagasy raffia was quoted at $0.0925 a pound on the New York market.[49] It was the only Malagasy export that rose in both volume and value in the 1880s, although the value exported was insufficient to compensate for heavy losses sustained by other staples.[50]

Products of Hunting and Gathering

Unlike continental Africa, Madagascar possessed no large game animals, so was a limited source of exotic animal products. An exception was turtle shell, a

[44] Beet sugar was produced on a large scale initially in France and subsequently in Belgium, the German states, the Austro-Hungarian Empire, and Russia – *GH* (1928), 70, 228; Scherer, *Histoire de la Réunion*, 59; Galloway, *The Sugar Cane Industry*, 130–1.

[45] Dawson to Ropes, Emmerton & Co, and Arnold, Hines & Co, Port Louis, Mauritius, 29 Jan. 1884, *REC/CR-MZL*.

[46] "Invoice of Merchandize shipped by Robert Brookhouse onboard the Brig *Shaumut*, James Emerton Master, for Madagascar," "Invoice of Merchandise shipped by William Hunt onboard the Brig *Shaumut*, James Emerton, for Madagascar, 2 January 1829," Invoices, Bills of Lading, Bills, 1816–1835, James and Ephraim Emerton, File 2, mss.1816–1835 E63 v.6 E & J.Emerton, Shipping, *BLHU* (hereafter Invoice Brookhouse *BLHU*).

[47] Ropes, Emmerton & Co, to Whitney, Salem, 14 Sept. and 30 Nov. 1883, *REC/CR-MZL*. Tobacco was one of the few plantation crops that also found a niche on the domestic market. Traditionally, local tobacco was ground to powder and chewed like snuff, but Laborde manufactured cigars which quickly captured a large domestic market and by the 1880s, J. Andrianisa, a Merina entrepreneur, was selling locally cut cigars in Antananarivo at $0.75 per 1,000 – *MT* II.39 (1 Oct. 1884), 364 and I.6 (27 May 1882), 5.

[48] The crown donated the land and 30 laborers to Nicol, who paid a European artisan to maintain his "machine." The produce was to be divided equally between Nicol and the court – "contract," Antananarivo, 25 and 26 Alakarabo, in Ayache, *Raombana l'historien*, 321, 323.

[49] Ropes, Emmerton & Co, to Dawson, Salem, 13 Nov. 1884, *REC/CR-MZL*.

[50] Robinson to Payson, 7 Aug. 1880; *idem* to Third Assistant Secratary of State, 3 July 1885; Campbell to Porter, 6 Oct. 1888; *idem* to Wharton, 23 Dec. 1889; Wetter to Uhl, 8 Oct. 1894 – *US*; Oliver, *Madagascar* vol. II, 200–03; Woodruff, *British Rubber Industry*, 39–40, 63–7.

long-standing export, turtles being hunted on land and at sea.[51] In the imperial era, India was a major market, although tortoise shell also formed a staple of early U.S. trade from Mahajanga and Nosy Be.[52]

Most of Madagascar's exotic exports were products of the forests, which in the nineteenth century formed an almost unbroken belt running along the escarpment and lowlands surrounding the central plateau. Forests on the Merina-controlled east coast were declared a crown monopoly and the right to exploit them granted first to Lastelle in 1837 and, from the 1860s, to a variety of foreign concerns.[53] On the independent west coast, forest products formed staples of traditional Indian and Swahili trade, were also exported by Americans from the 1820s, and, from mid-century, by a small number of European firms.[54] Beeswax remained a relatively minor west coast export until the 1880s, when U.S. and British traders competed fiercely for beeswax from the east, especially from the Angontsy forest of northeast Madagascar.[55]

A similar trend marked the exploitation of hard woods. Ebony, rosewood (used in cabinet making), and sandalwood (for perfumes and pharmaceutical products)[56] were initially exported, by Indian, Swahili, and U.S. merchants, mainly from the independent west coast.[57] From 1861, due to lower duties and closer access to transhipment centers such as Nosy Be, Mozambique, and Zanzibar, precious woods also attracted large foreign firms such as O'Swald, Ropes, Hines, and Fraissinet as well as Cape Town merchants

---

[51] See Chapter 1.

[52] Razi, "Sources d'histoire," 14, 22; Bennett and Brooks (eds.), *New England Merchants*, xxvi; Log book (1828–9); see also Hathorne to Arnold, Hines & Co, Zanzibar, 4 May 1877 – Hathorne, "Letterbook" (1878–80); Ephraim Emerton to C. & Howard, Salem, 5 Dec. 1823; Brookhouse and Lovett to Emerton, Salem, 22 July 1826; Invoice Hunt – *BLHU*; Putnam, "A Cruise" (1848–50); McFarland, "List of goods suitable for Nos Beh, Mayotta, &c," in Bennett and Brooks (eds.), *New England Merchants*, 439; Staatsarchiv Hamburg, Firma Wm. O'Swald & Co. 33 (1873–1896); Nèple, *Guide de l'Immigrant*, 309.

[53] Rontaunay in 1826 failed to secure a monopoly over the foreign trade of Mahela and Mananjary. Chapus & Mondain, "Un chapitre inconnu," 118; Campbell, "Role of the London Missionary Society" vol. II, 294, 301.

[54] Razi, "Sources d'histoire," 14, 22; Bennett and Brooks (eds.), *New England Merchants*, xxvi; Log book (1828–9); see also Hathorne to Arnold, Hines & Co, Zanzibar, 4 May 1877 – Hathorne, "Letterbook" (1878–80); Ephraim Emerton to C. & Howard, Salem, 5 Dec. 1823; Brookhouse and Lovett to Emerton, Salem, 22 July 1826; Invoice Hunt – *BLHU*.

[55] Ropes, Emmerton & Co, to Dawson, Salem, 13 Nov. 1884, *REC/CR-MZL*; *MT* II.41 (15 Oct. 1884), 376; Razi, "Sources d'histoire," 16; *MT* II.41 (15 Oct. 1884), 377.

[56] Raminosoa, "La Maison 'Wm. O'Swald & Co.,'" 73.

[57] Razi, "Sources d'histoire," 14, 22; Bennett and Brooks (eds.), *New England Merchants*, xxvi; Log book (1828–9); see also Hathorne to Arnold, Hines & Co, Zanzibar, 4 May 1877 – Hathorne, "Letterbook" (1878–80); Ephraim Emerton to C. & Howard, Salem, 5 Dec. 1823; Brookhouse and Lovett to Emerton, Salem, 22 July 1826; Invoice Hunt – *BLHU*.

and agents of the main steamer lines servicing East Africa, although initially these also worked through Indian agents.[58] From mid-century, Western traders purchased west coast ebony in exchange for cottons, arms, and, by the mid-1880s, kerosene.[59] Maintirano, long an important slave and arms entrepôt, emerged in the 1870s as a major ebony market.[60] In 1877, Malagasy ebony fetched $15 a candy (3.33 candy = 1 ton) in Zanzibar, rising to over $16 by 1878.[61] In 1899, a monthly average of 20 tons of ebony was exported via Mahajanga.[62] From the 1880s, the imperial court also granted major forest concessions permitting foreigners to fell and export, on a considerable scale, Angontsy hardwoods.[63]

Gum copal, a generic term for a resin exuded from various tropical trees, was in high demand in Europe and the United States, where it was processed and used as a varnish.[64] The resin was tapped directly from trees (congealing in irregularly shaped yellowish or colorless pieces) rather than, as commonly on the east African coast, dug up as a fossil.[65] Americans exported it from the west coast from the mid-1820s,[66] and by the late 1830s, Swahili traders were

58 American traders loaded Malagasy produce onto Union Company steamers in Mozambique; Hathorne to Arnold, Hines & Co, Zanzibar, 19 Sept. 1877, 24 and 29 Aug., 17 Oct., and 14 Nov. 1877, 26 July, 18 Sept. and 16 Oct. 1878; *idem* to Bertram, Zanzibar, 26 July 1878; *idem* to Thompson, Zanzibar, 14 Nov. and 10 Dec. 1878 – Hathorne, "Letterbook" (1878–80); Ryder to Ropes, Emmerton & Co, and Arnold, Hines & Co, Nossi B., 15 April 1884, *REC/CR-MZL*; Bennett and Brooks (eds.), *New England Merchants*, 532; Hermann Kellenbenz, "Zanzibar et Madagascar dans le commerce allemand, 1840–1880," *Colloque d' histoire de Madagascar* (Université de Madagascar, Mahajanga, 1981).
59 Ryder to Ropes, Emmerton & Co, and Arnold, Hines & Co, Nossi Bé, 15 April 1884 and Zanzibar, 15 Nov. 1886, *REC/CR-MZL*; Hathorne to Arnold, Hines & Co, Zanzibar, 19 Sep. 1877 – Hathorne, "Letterbook" (1878–80); Hines to Seward, Zanzibar, 25 Oct. 1864, in Bennett and Brooks (eds.), *New England Merchants*, 532; Hermann Kellenbenz, "Zanzibar et Madagascar dans le commerce allemand, 1840–1880," *Colloque d' histoire de Madagascar* (Université de Madagascar, Mahajanga, 1981).
60 Thompson to Hathorne, Majunga, 27 Nov. 1878, encl.1 in Hathorne to Bertram, Zanzibar, 11 Dec. 1878 – Hathorne, "Letterbook" (1878–80).
61 Hathorne to Arnold, Hines & Co, Zanzibar, 24 and 29 Aug. 1877 – Hathorne, "Letterbook" (1877–79); and 6 Mar. 1878 – Hathorne, "Letterbook" (1878–80); *MT* II.37 (17 Sept. 1884); *MT* II.41 (15 Oct. 1884), 376.
62 Nèple, *Guide de l' Immigrant*, 308.
63 Dawson to Ropes, Emmerton & Co, and Arnold, Hines & Co, Port Louis, Mauritius, 29 Jan. 1884, *REC/CR-MZL*; Razi, "Sources d'histoire," 16; *MT* II.41 (15 Oct. 1884), 377.
64 Ropes, Emmerton & Co, to Dawson, Salem, 13 Nov. 1884, *REC/CR-MZL*; *MT* II.41 (15 Oct. 1884), 376; Webster's *New International Dictionary*.
65 Most copal at Zanzibar was collected on the littoral between Mombasa and Ibo. See Hathorne to Arnold, Hines & Co, Zanzibar, 5 April 1878 – Hathorne, "Letterbook" (1878–80); Webster's *New International Dictionary* (1928).
66 Razi, "Sources d'histoire," 14, 22; Bennett and Brooks (eds.), *New England Merchants*, xxvi; Log book (1828–9); see also Hathorne to Arnold, Hines & Co, Zanzibar, 4 May 1877 – Hathorne,

shipping large quantities from Mahavelona and Vohimara.[67] Declared a crown monopoly in 1837, gum copal was exported by Lastelle, under contract, from northeast Madagascar in the 1840s.[68] In 1862, it was commented:

> Nearly all the gum produced in Madagascar passes through Zanzibar, and for a long time it was thought that it came from there. The Hova [Merina] authorities who know the value of it monopolise the trade.... This gum used to be sold to the Arabs who transported it in dhows to the coast of Africa, where Europeans bought it up. It is only very recently that any cargoes have gone to Mauritius or Réunion.[69]

In the mid-1880s, the court exploited a virgin forest of copal fruit in the Maroantsetra region of northeast Madagascar. U.S. traders described the product as clear and bright, far superior to the "*Gum Copal* of the worthless quality and cindery character such as has been sent us here-to-fore."[70] The American Civil War ended traditional U.S. dominance of the copal trade; subsequently, Europeans shipped most directly to Hamburg and London.[71]

Rubber was another major export. The varieties most valued were *pinky* (from the northeastern forests) and *harangy* (Mahajanga) – described as "large, round, solid pieces quite white and clear inside"[72] that (in 1884) "on a quick market will sometimes pass for Tamatave although not equal in quality to best 'pinky'."[73] Traditionally exported to Zanzibar by Swahili traders, west coast rubber was from the 1820s also purchased by U.S. traders[74] and for a brief

---

"Letterbook" (1878–80); Ephraim Emerton to C. & Howard, Salem, 5 Dec. 1823; Brookhouse and Lovett to Emerton, Salem, 22 July 1826; Invoice Hunt – *BLHU*.

[67] Dwyer to Seward, Boston, 9 Dec. 1861; Robinson to Hunter, 1 Oct. 1877 and 1 Oct. 1878 – *US*; Campbell, "Role of the London Missionary Society" vol. II, 295–7.

[68] Dwyer to Seward, Boston, 9 Dec. 1861; Robinson to Hunter, 1 Oct. 1877 and 1 Oct. 1878 – *US*; Campbell, "Role of the London Missionary Society" vol. II, 295–7.

[69] M. Coignet, "Madagascar," 376 – An increase in the U.S. tariff on gum copal imports in 1861 led to the cleaning of gum copal – with soda ash – being done in Africa – Mansfield to Marcy, Zanzibar, 31 March 1857, in Bennett and Brooks (eds.), *New England Merchants*, 500–1; see also *ibid*, xxxii–xxxiii; Hathorne to Arnold, Hines & Co, Zanzibar, 5 April 1878 – Hathorne, "Letterbook" (1878–80); Webster's *New International Dictionary*.

[70] Ropes, Emmerton & Co, to Dawson, Salem, 13 Nov. 1884, *REC/CR-MZL*; see also *MT* II.41 (15 Oct. 1884), 376.

[71] The American copal trade fell 50 percent by 1864, forcing the closure of a number of Salem turpentine factories – Razi, "Sources d'histoire," 25; Fairburn, *Merchant Sail* V, 3014; see also Hines to Seward, Zanzibar, 25 Oct.1864, in Bennett and Brooks (eds.), *New England Merchants*, 530–1; Kessler Crocker to John Bertram, Tamatave, 11 July 1867, John Bertram Papers B2.F5, Agency Records – Tamatave. Correspondence and Accounts, 1867–1870, *EI*.

[72] Thompson to Hathorne, Majunga, 27 Nov. 1878, encl.1 in Hathorne to Bertram, Zanzibar, 11 Dec. 1878 – Hathorne, "Letterbook" (1878–80).

[73] Ropes, Emmerton & Co, to J.Orme Ryder, Salem, 25 Jan. 1884, *REC/CR-MZL*.

[74] Razi, "Sources d'histoire," 14, 22; Bennett and Brooks (eds.), *New England Merchants*, xxvi; Log book (1828–9); see also Hathorne to Arnold, Hines & Co, Zanzibar, 4 May 1877 – Hathorne,

TABLE 8.1. *Malagasy Rubber Exports to Britain, 1875–99*
(Includes Exports via Mauritius; Value in $ Malagasy)

Year	Quantity (cwt)	Value ($000s)	Price per cwt on London Market	Average Price per cwt of all Rubber on London Market
1875	2,002	82	41	51
1876	32	1	39	48
1877	83	5	58	46
1878	n.a.	n.a.	n.a.	44
1879	110	8	75	54
1880	501	31	61	70
1881	2,908	180	62	66
1882	1,570	87	56	76
1883	3,982	326	82	80
1884	1,100	61	56	57
1885	41	2	44	55
1886	658	35	53	57
1887	1,456	74	52	57
1888	2,502	138	55	58
1889	3,709	184	50	55
1890	5,579	290	52	62
1891	6,511	337	52	60
1892	9,569	399	42	55
1893	10,517	455	43	57
1894	10,294	395	38	54
1895	7,038	291	41	55
1896	4,627	221	48	58
1897	1,601	72	45	57
1898	885	52	58	63
1899	820	60	73	66

Source: Campbell, "Role of the Merina State," 12.

period after 1839, shipped from northeast Madagascar to the Mascarenes by Lastelle (whose concession was subsequently declared a crown monopoly). By 1862, between 20 and 25 tons of rubber (valued at between $2,400 and $4,000) were being exported annually from a forest exploitation of some 466 km², south of Vohimara[75] (see Table 8.1).

During the 1880s depression, Malagasy rubber remained competitive on the world market due to the *pinky* variety which, in the early 1880s, fetched a price

"Letterbook" (1878–80); Ephraim Emerton to C. & Howard, Salem, 5 Dec. 1823; Brookhouse and Lovett to Emerton, Salem, 22 July 1826; Invoice Hunt – *BLHU*.

[75] Campbell, "Role of the London Missionary Society" vol. II, 295–7.

second only to Brazilian *para*.[76] However, only small quantities were required, so that the unloading in New York of 60,000 pounds in February 1884 ruined the market there not only for *pinky*, but also for all Malagasy rubbers.[77] Two months later, it was noted that "the collapse of the great speculation in Rubber caused by the failure of its originators, *Vienna Freres & Cie*, has completely demoralized the market"[78] – although prices were buoyed by the bad winter of 1884–5, which boosted demand for rubber clothing and boots.[79] Malagasy rubber fared less well in Britain where, despite a tenfold increase in African rubber imports from 1870 to 1900, its market share fell between 1870 and 1890 from around 6.5 percent to less than 1 percent.[80]

The decline in the value of Malagasy rubber was largely due to poor production techniques. Adulteration, current in Mozambique by the late 1870s, spread to Madagascar where, in May 1878, the U.S. agent of Hines at Zanzibar received instructions to stop purchasing.[81] By May 1883, west coast rubber was described as "of a black, spongy, watery character,"[82] and in January 1884 it was remarked in the United States that

All Nossi Bé Rubber appears to be in great disfavor with Manufacturers just now, and especially that of the spongy character ... treated with lime juice instead of sulpheric acid! The Haranga sort appears to be the best liked of any from the West Coast, but even this comes far short of Tamatave pinky.[83]

On the east coast, where a royal monopoly of rubber was maintained from 1871, court officials permitted the indiscriminate mixture of the juices of initially non-*pinky* rubbers and subsequently of *pinky* – which was also being

---

[76] Finkelmeier to Seward, 10 Jan.1868, *US*; *CdM* 34 (23 août 1892); Woodruff, *British Rubber Industry*, 63–7; Ropes, Emmerton & Co, to Dawson, Salem, 17 July 1884, *REC/CR-MZL*; Campbell, "Toamasina," table XVI.2.

[77] Ropes, Emmerton & Co, to Dawson, Salem, 16 Jan. 1885 and 13 Feb. 1885, *REC/CR-MZL*.

[78] Ropes, Emmerton & Co, to Whitney, Salem, 8 April 1884, *REC/CR-MZL*.

[79] Ropes, Emmerton & Co, to Tharia Topan, Salem, 10 Jan. 1885, *REC/CR-MZL*. The greatest demand for hides in the United States was also in the winter months – see Ropes, Emmerton & Co, to Dawson, Salem, 17 July 1884, *REC/CR-MZL*.

[80] Robinson to Payson, 7 Aug. 1880; *idem* to Third Assistant Secretary of State, 3 July 1885; Campbell to Porter, 6 Oct. 1888; *idem* to Wharton, 23 Dec. 1889; Wetter to Uhl, 8 Oct. 1894 – *US*; Oliver, *Madagascar* vol. II, 200–3; Woodruff, *British Rubber Industry*, 39–40, 63–7.

[81] Hathorne to Arnold, Hines & Co, Zanzibar, 3 & 31 May 1878 – Hathorne, "Letterbook" (1878–80).

[82] Ropes, Emmerton & Co, to J. Orme Ryder, Salem, 3 May 1883, *REC/CR-MZL*.

[83] Ropes, Emmerton & Co, to J.Orme Ryder, Salem, 11 Jan. 1884, *REC/CR-MZL*; see also Ropes, Emmerton & Co, to Whitney, Salem, 3 May 1883, *REC/CR-MZL*; Ropes, Emmerton & Co, to J.Orme Ryder, Salem, 26 Feb. 1884, *REC/CR-MZL*; *MT* II.41 (15 Oct. 1884), 377.

"exhausted" by harmful methods of "bleeding."[84] This largely explains the great variability in the quality and price of Malagasy rubber:[85] In 1875–9, the average price in London was $52.9 per cwt–$4.2 higher than the average for all rubbers. However, whereas from 1879 to 1893 the total value of Malagasy rubber entering Britain rose from $8,195 to $454,920, its price fell from $74.5 to $43.26 per cwt.[86] *Pinky* was also affected. In July 1891, O'Swald's London brokers rejected a consignment labeled "best *pinky*" for being "very mixed, part fair pinky but large proportion common and ordinary black, part very spongy and weak," and sent it to O'Swald's home port of Hamburg for sale.[87] In 1894, an absolute decline set in, both in the quantity and in the value of rubber exported.[88]

Another natural product of commercial significance was orchil weed, collected in large quantities from Brava, Mogadishu, and Mocha and, from the 1860s, southwest Madagascar. It was generally exported through Zanzibar to Britain, France, and Germany where it was processed to make a purple and crimson dye used for coloring silks[89] (see Tables 8.2–8.4 and Figure 9).

Export of gold, the only mineral export of value in the imperial era, started to be significant from the 1883–5 Franco–Merina War.[90] Despite a crown monopoly, gold was chiefly produced illicitly. On the west coast, Indian buyers circumvented imperial Merina regulations by establishing direct contact with sellers in the countryside. On the east coast, clandestine gold flowed chiefly to British and U.S. traders. In 1890, even missionaries were approached as prospective purchasers; in mid-1894, it was commented that all foreigners

---

[84] Finkelmeier to Seward, 10 Jan. 1868, *US*; *CdM* 34 (23 août 1892); *GH* (1928), 106; Razi, "Sources d'histoire," 39.

[85] Pinky was extracted from the barabanja tree (*siphonia* family?), which grew in the moist habitat of the northeastern forest. Nonpinky varieties of rubber were extracted from the *vahihena* (family *aposyneae*), common in the Angontsy forest. The best derived from the *vahiheana talandoa* fruit, two varieties of the *vahihena ranisto*, which produced a soft gluey juice more difficult to congeal than the *talandoa* and a second variety of rubber obtained from the *barabanja* tree. Although the white and highly elastic juice of the latter produced a quality rubber that initially compared well with the best specimens on the European market, by 1884 Malagasy collectors were indiscriminately mixing the juices of the last two varieties of rubber.

[86] Robinson to Payson, 7 Aug. 1880; *idem* to Third Assistant Secretary of State, 3 July 1885; Camp-bell to Porter, 6 Oct. 1888; *idem* to Wharton, 23 Dec. 1889; Wetter to Uhl, 8 Oct. 1894 – US; Oliver, *Madagascar* vol. II, 200–3; Woodruff, *British Rubber Industry*, 39–40, 63–7.

[87] Tappenback to Whitney, Tamatave, 1 July 1891, *REC/CR-MZL*.

[88] See Campbell, "Toamasina," table XVI.2.

[89] Hines to Seward, Zanzibar, 25 Oct. 1864, in Bennett and Brooks (eds.), *New England Merchants*, 531; see also *idem*, 518, 539.

[90] See Chapter 4.

TABLE 8.2. *Purchase of Black Market Gold by Ropes Emmerton & Co., Antananarivo, February 1893–June 1894* (Weight in Malagasy Ounces and Price in Malagasy $)

Date	Bamboo Stems (no.)	Weight (ozs.)	Purchase Price ($)	Price per oz.
1893 (Feb)	15	515.75	8,194.97	15.89
(Mar)	[33]	1,211.50	19,058.43	15.73
(Aug)	11	246.50	[3,917.39]	[15.89]
(Oct)	8	190.00	3,028.55	15.94
(Nov)	15	347.50	5,548.61	15.97
(Dec)	8	270.64	4,318.92	15.96
1894 (Jan)	6	239.53	3,852.39	16.08
(Feb)	5	369.00	5,915.85	16.03
(Mar)	6	411.25	6,593.29	16.03
(Apr)	4	254.46	4,071.36	16.00
(May)	4	236.38	3,782.00	16.00
(Jun)	7	321.87	5,150.00	16.00

Source: "Invoices of Gold Dust" sent by Edward S. [Duder], in "Antananarivo Accounts" (1884–95), Bx.47.F1; "Invoice of Gold Dust" (7 Oct. 1893), in "Tamatave Accounts" (May–Oct. 1893), Bx.52.F2; Duder to Ropes Emmerton & Co, Antananarivo, 20 Mar. 1893 and Ryder to Ropes Emmerton & Co, Tamatave, 8 May 1893 – Bx.46.F1 (Jan.–July 1893); Ryder to Ropes Emmerton & Co, Tamatave, 28 July and 27 Sept. 1893 – Bx.45.F7 (May 1893–May 1894), *REC/CR-MZL.*

TABLE 8.3. *Madagascar: Exports to British India, 1897 (in Dollars)*

Commodity	Value	% of Total	Commodity	Value	% of Total
Raw sugar	2,326.0	20.37	Rice	594.8	5.20
Precious woods	2,047.4	17.93	Gold powder	457.2	4.00
Salt	2,030.0	17.78	Wooden beams	203.0	1.78
Gold and silver coins	1,430.0	12.53	Fats	103.0	0.90
Shells	1,318.0	11.54	Dried and smoked fish	334.0	0.30
Cattle	863.0	7.56	Gum	10.0	0.09
TOTAL:				11,416.4	

Source: Nèple, *Guide de l'Immigrant*, 328–9.

TABLE 8.4. *Toamasina: Import and Export Figures, 1890 ($ Malagasy)*

Flag	Imports	(% Total)	Exports	(% Total)	Total Foreign Trade	(% Total)
France	318,272	38.62	143,751	30.53	462,022	35.68
USA	309,084	37.50	118,686	25.21	427,754	33.03
Britain	144,145	17.49	168,319	35.75	312,465	24.13
Germany	37,675	4.57	36,279	7.71	73,465	5.71
Madagascar	9,447	1.15	3,770	0.80	13,217	1.02
Italy	3,626	0.44	–	–	3,626	0.44
Austro-Hungary	1,967	0.24	–	–	1,965	0.15
Total	824,214	100.00	470,790	100.00	1,295,003	100.00

Source: Campbell, "Toamasina," 545.

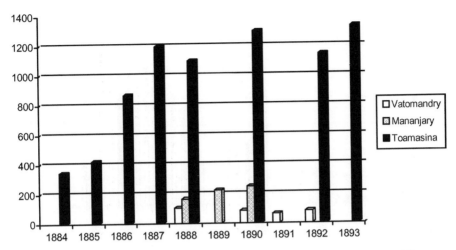

Figure 9. *Official Foreign Trade of Selected Merina Ports in Selected Years* (in $000s Malagasy).

Source: Manassé Esoavelomadroso, *La province maritime orientale du "Royaume de Madagascar" à la fin du XIXe siècle 1882–1895* (Antananarivo, 1979), 397–9.

dealt in black market gold "as there is so much to be bought."[91] Even when illicit gold was confiscated, it was frequently redeposited on the black market by Merina officials. Thus, it was commented in March 1893 that "[Black market] Gold is now getting to be very plentiful, notwithstanding the strict Malagasy laws against the working of it by natives.... No laws that the Government can promulgate will stop the people from getting gold where it is to be had."[92] As early as 1890, an estimated 18,200 ounces of illicit gold were exported annually from Antananarivo via Toamasina and a further 10,000 ounces illegally exported from the west coast. Only 10,000 ounces were retained in Imerina.[93]

[91] Ashwell to Wardlaw Thompson, [Antananarivo] 19 July and 28 Sept. 1894, and 22 March 1895, IDC Letterbook (1875–97), 670–6. Initially black market gold was purchased with little scrutiny, but because so much was adulterated with base metals, buyers quickly learned to apply the nitric acid test – see Duder to Ryder [Antananarivo], 27 Jan. 1894, B45.F7 (May 1893–May 1894), *REC/CR-MZL*.

[92] Duder to Ropes Emmerton & Co, Antananarivo, 20 March 1893, B46.F1 (Jan.–July 1893); see also Ryder to Ropes Emmerton & Co, Tamatave, 6 Jan. 1893, B46.F1 (Jan.–July 1893) and Tamatave, 27 Aug. 1893 and 7 Jan. 1894 – B45.F7 (May 1893–May 1894) – *REC/CR-MZL*; Anon, "Gold in Madagascar"; Francis Maude, *Five Years in Madagascar* (London, 1895), 100–10; "letter," Tamatave, 9 Dec. 1888, in *ASR* (Jan. & Feb., 1889), 46; Alfred Horn, *Trader Horn in Madagascar* (London, 1928), 82, 106, 112, 116.

[93] Lord to Wardlaw Thompson, Antananarivo, 20 Jan. 1892, IDC Letterbook (1875–97), 650–4; Decary, "L'ancien régime," 92; F. Knight, *Madagascar in war time* (London, 1896), 158–60; Owen Letcher, *The Gold Mines of Southern Africa* (Johannesburg, 1936), 273.

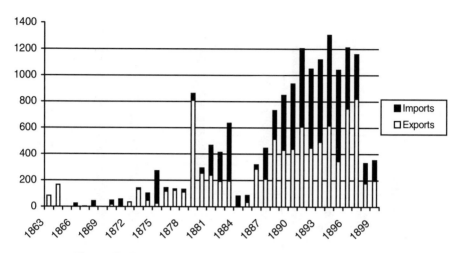

Figure 10. *Britain: Direct Visible Trade with Madagascar, 1863–99* ($000s Malagasy).
Source: Oliver, *Madagascar. An Historical and Descriptive Account* II, 200–3; *Parliamentary Papers* (1876–1900).

From 1890 to 1894, the official buying price of gold fell from $10 to $7.22 to $8.25 an ounce. This was about half its value on the black market, where it was purchased at well below, and resold for just below, its open market value of between $17 and $17.50 an ounce (see Table 8.2).[94] Even in 1893–4, at a time of great economic and social dislocation, the open market gold price remained remarkably stable at between $15.32 and $16.16 per ounce. As a result of the black market, the Merina court found such difficulty selling its own gold that, in 1893, it granted a purchasing monopoly of official gold at below black market rates to Shervington, a British colonel serving in the imperial forces, who resold it to privileged foreigners.[95]

---

[94] Knight, *Madagascar in war time*, 158–9; London Missionary Society (LMS), *Ten Years' Review of Mission Work in Madagascar 1880–1890* (Antananarivo, 1890), 12; *CdM* 144 (22 mai 1894); Whitney to Ropes Emmerton & Co, Tamatave, 13 Aug. 1892, B46.F2 (May–Dec. 1892); Ryder to Ropes Emmerton & Co, Tamatave, 10 March 1892, B46.F1 (Jan.–July 1893), *REC/CR-MZL*; see also L. H. Ransome, "The River Antanambalana" *AAMM* 14 (1890), 230.

[95] In May 1893, Shervington offered Ropes Emmerton & Co., $1,000 worth of gold a month at $16 per ounce – Duder to Ropes Emmerton & Co, Antananarivo, 20 March 1893, B46.F1 (Jan.–July 1893); Whitney to Ropes Emmerton & Co, Tamatave, 26 July 1892, B46.F2 (May–Dec 1892); Shervington to Ryder [Antananarivo] May 1893, B45.F7 (May 1893–May 1894) – *REC/CR-MZL*.

TABLE 8.5. *Toamasina: Imports from British and French Territories and the United States, 1864–90* (in $ Malagasy)

Year	Britain	(%)	France	(%)	United States	(%)	Total
1864–5	47,354	9.3	460,000	90.7	–	–	507,354
1866	114,948	40.0	95,800	33.3	76,815	26.7	287,563
1867	117,092	57.0	3,664	1.8	85,000	41.3	205,756
1868	180,920	52.5	38,400	11.1	125,200	36.3	344,520
1869–70	105,100	39.5	25,000	9.4	135,900	51.1	266,000
1877–8	573,183	25.8	536,593	24.2	1,109,776	50.0	2,219,552
1878–9	n.a.	n.a.	n.a.	n.a.	542,127	n.a.	n.a.
1879–80	n.a.	n.a.	n.a.	n.a.	500,401	n.a.	n.a.
1881–2	n.a.	n.a.	n.a.	n.a.	310,180	n.a.	n.a.
1883	n.a.	n.a.	n.a.	n.a.	299,754	n.a.	n.a.
1885–6	683,813	30.0	452,811	19.9	1,139,688	50.1	2,276,312
1886–7	1,116,624	38.0	351,866	12.0	1,468,498	50.0	2,936,988
1890	144,145	18.7	318,271	41.3	309,084	40.1	771,500

Source: Campbell, "Toamasina," 546.

TABLE 8.6. *Toamasina: Exports to British and French Territories and the United States, 1864–90* (in $ Malagasy)

Year	Britain	(%)	France	(%)	United States	(%)	Total
1864–5	166,299	49.3	170,950	50.7	–	–	337,249
1865	336,370	78.7	91,140	21.3	–	–	427,510
1867	346,260	82.7	72,200	17.2	495	0.1	418,955
1868	378,150	87.1	54,600	12.6	1,175	0.3	433,925
1869–70	236,500	72.8	67,000	20.6	21,475	6.6	324,975
1877–8	n.a.	n.a.	129,124	n.a.	110,150	n.a.	n.a.
1878–9	n.a.	n.a.	n.a.	n.a.	181,192	n.a.	n.a.
1879–80	337,207	56.6	17,828	0.3	240,625	40.4	595,659
1881–2	n.a.	n.a.	n.a.	n.a.	242,332	n.a.	n.a.
1883	n.a.	n.a.	n.a.	n.a.	165,694	n.a.	n.a.
1884	n.a.	n.a.	n.a.	n.a.	182,788	n.a.	n.a.
1885–6	n.a.	n.a.	n.a.	n.a.	171,723	n.a.	n.a.
1886–7	n.a.	n.a.	n.a.	n.a.	200,722	36.7	546,494
1890	164,319	35.8	143,751	30.5	118,670	25.2	470,790

Source: Campbell, "Toamasina," 541.

TABLE 8.7. *Morondava: Imports and Exports, Oct. 1879–Oct. 1880 and 1882*
($ Malagasy)

A. Imports (1882)	Value	(% total)		
Cottons	205,720	34.5		
Crockery & glassware	15,000	2.6		
Arms, slaves, & specie	346,780	57.5		
Miscellaneous	7,500	1.2		
B. Exports	**1879–80**	**(% total)**	**1882**	**(% total)**
Hides	170,000	32.5	138,000	22.9
Beef	15,400	2.9	–	–
Live cattle	1,500	0.3	–	–
Rice	87,500	16.7	–	–
Ebony	78,000	14.9	2,000	0.3
India rubber	46,000	0.8	100,000	16.6
Beans	36,000	6.9	–	–
Beeswax	31,000	5.9	15,000	n.a.
Timber	14,000	2.7	–	–
Maize	14,000	2.7	–	–
Orchil	–	–	48,000	8.0
Miscellaneous	30,000	5.7	–	–
Total	523,400		603,000	

Source: Campbell, "Toamasina," 551.

Imports

Slaves excepted, the staple imports of imperial Madagascar were cloth, arms, and alcohol, followed by hardware and luxury items. Slave exports from Merina-controlled areas had generally been paid for in cash but, following the slave export ban in 1820, exports were largely paid for with staple imports, notably cloth, the major legitimate import (see Tables 8.8 and 8.9). Until the 1820s on the west coast and the 1860s on the east coast, most imported cloth was of Indian or British manufacture, accounting for 62.83 percent of Mauritian exports to Madagascar in 1835.[96] U.S. traders first tested the market for their cloth on the west coast, one consignment in 1826 comprising red flannel, green gauze, light cottons, shirting, Irish linen, white flannel, duck (cloth), and striped, as well as raw

---

[96] Although a foreign observer noted one instance in 1857 when bullockers paid for cattle in silver dollars – Charles Nordhoff, *Stories of the Island World* (New York, 1857), 58; also see Campbell, "Toamasina," 549.

and sewing cotton.[97] Demand proved greatest for cotton piece goods, used for clothing and as the main form of currency outside the chief commercial centers. Annual imports of U.S. cloth included for Mahajanga in the 1830s from 200 to 250 bales of U.S. cottons and 20 to 30 cases of other cloth,[98] and for Nosy Be from 1845 to 1849, 250 bales of cotton sheeting and between 10 and 12 bales of brown drill.[99] Only from the 1860s did U.S. cotton cloth, described by Lugard as "the very best cloth in the market and almost as strong as canvas,"[100] start to dominate east coast imports.[101] In 1884, the *Madagascar Times* announced:

The American import trade is a wholesale business, and consists entirely of grey sheetings and shirtings, and kerosene or paraffin oil. These cotton sheetings and shirtings are a class of goods manufactured specially for the Madagascar market, and up to the present no other goods of the kind have been able to compete with them. English mills have attempted to imitate these goods for the last ten years, but for the same price they cannot produce the same article.... it is not preferred by the Malagasy, even if it could be sold cheaper.[102]

Sophisticated local tastes led U.S. merchants to order cloths designed specifically for the imperial Merina market from U.S.-based factories. Unbleached cotton sheeting, chiefly in six-yard [5.5-meter] pieces and seldom retailed in less than one-yard [0.9 meter] lengths, found ready sale – notably in April and May, when the plateau population lined their *lamba* (made from indigenous fibers) with cotton for protection against the cold.[103] Also popular were brown and white shirting and printed cotton pieces, to make clothes for both sexes. Contrary to the view of some historians of the Nationalist school,[104] imports initially augmented rather than undermined indigenous production of cloth from

---

[97] A.Peabody to James Emerton, Salem, 9 July 1826 – consignment,' Invoices, Bills of Lading, Bills, 1816–1835, James and Ephraim Emerton, File 2, mss. 1816–1835 E63 v.6 E & J.Emerton, Shipping, *BLHU*.

[98] Razi, "Sources d'histoire," 15; see also "Papers of Richard P.Waters," 1831–87, mss. MH-14, *PM*.

[99] Putnam, "A Cruise" (1848–50); McFarland, "List of goods suitable for Nos Beh, Mayotta, &c," in Bennett and Brooks (eds.), *New England Merchants*, 439.

[100] Quoted in Bennett, "Americans in Zanzibar," 37.

[101] Bennett, "Americans in Zanzibar," 36–7; Kessler Vrocker to John Bertram, Tamatave, 11 July 1867, John Bertram Papers B2.F5, Agency Records – Tamatave. Correspondence and Accounts, 1867–1870, *EI*; Finkelmeier to Seward, 1 Oct. 1866 and 11 April 1867; "8th Annual Commercial Report" (24 Oct. 1873); Robinson to Hunter, 1 Oct. 1877; Robinson to Payson, 7 Aug. 1880 – *US*; Catat, *Voyage à Madagascar*, 62.

[102] *MT* 2.9 (5 March 1884), 68.

[103] *MT* 2.16 (23 April 1884), 146.

[104] Jacob, "Influences occidentales," 227, 231; Larson, *History and Memory*, 126–7; Bernard Schlemmer, *Le Menabe, histoire d'une colonisation* (Paris: ORSTOM, 1983), 35.

silk, vegetable fiber, and cotton. Only from the late 1880s did imported cottons begin to adversely affect Malagasy producers in the local market. They did not impact on Malagasy exports: Locally produced coarse cloth, made of cotton mixed most often with other fibers, was cheap and durable, making it valued material for plantation workers on the Mascarenes.[105]

The depression heralded renewed competition for U.S. merchants. Their near monopoly of cotton imports into east Madagascar was broken in 1879–80, when German and British firms captured half of the $4,000 to $5,000 worth of printed calico trade. This challenge was consolidated by a dramatic increase in the import of European cloth fraudulently carrying U.S. trademarks.[106] Similarly, American domination of cotton cloth imports into western Madagascar ended about 1880, when Indians by marketing as "standard" (i.e., 30 yards [27.4 meters]) cloths of only between 25 and 26 yards [22.9 to 24.0 meters] long captured most of the cotton import trade.[107] In the late nineteenth century, European and U.S. cloth importers also faced competition from the Merina crown. Royal agents taxed exports in dollars, but levied duties on imports in cotton piece goods, which were quickly distributed to inland markets courtesy of forced labor and slave porters. Meanwhile, lengthy customs procedures and the subsequent paucity of porters inevitably delayed the distribution foreign traders' consignments:

If a merchant lands 1000 bales of cottons, the Governor with a hundred of them can hold the market to the detriment of the merchant and without any compensating advantage to the Queen's revenues or to the consumers.[108]

Now to such a bigoted, stupid, one-horse government as this, it seems pretty tough to have to pay a duty of 10%, and still harder to pay it in goods. As those goods cost them nothing they can afford to undersell the importers who can do nothing till the Hovas [Merina] sell out.[109]

Competition was accentuated from November 1884, when a poor U.S. cotton harvest, combined with increased South American and Chinese demand and the withholding of stocks by U.S. manufacturers, forced up the price of cotton piece goods.[110] The price remained high despite the bumper cotton crop of 1885, so

[105] GH (1928), 3, 174–5; John Mack, *Malagasy Textiles* (Aylesbury: Shire Ethnography, 1989); Nordhoff, *Stories*, 56.

[106] Campbell, "Toamasina," 532.

[107] Ropes, Emmerton & Co, to Cheney, Salem, 25 Sept. 1883, *REC/CR-MZL*.

[108] A U.S. merchant in Vatomandry, quoted in *MT* II. 46 (19 Nov. 1884), 416.

[109] Edward D. Ropes to [parents, Tamatave, 24 March 1882, B1 (1882–1886) Zanzibar Acc.11840 and 11884: Letters 1882, Papers of Edward D. Ropes Jr, *PM*.

[110] Ropes, Emmerton & Co, to Whitney, Salem, 21 April 1884 and *idem* to Tharia Topan, Salem, 6 May 1884 and 4 Jan. 1885; *idem* to Cheney, Salem, 19 Nov. 1884 – *REC/CR-MZL*.

that when hide exports fell, so did Malagasy demand for cotton imports.[111] The plight of U.S. traders was also affected by the impoverishment of ordinary Merina. In April 1886, an agent for U.S. cotton importers in Vatomandry announced:

> There is a regular stagnancy at the Capital in the cotton market. The war has been the cause of this. Generally in April when winter is near at hand buyers are plentifull and double the quantity of American cottons is disposed of in the market, but this year, deception. The market seems dull and deserted, the people discouraged. . . . Here there is not a single buyer at present and not a five franc piece to be had.[112]

By October 1886, ordinary highland people had become so impoverished that demand for the more valued but expensive U.S. cottons dropped in favor of Indian and Manchester imitations, which sold at "about $3 per thousand yards [914 meters] less than American goods."[113]

Although the Merina market for imported cottons collapsed totally in 1892,[114] the cloth trade from South Africa to southwest Madagascar boomed through the depression years. Cotton piece goods and clothing, mostly reexports from Britain, constituted the two major exports to Madagascar from Natal in the period 1877–94. Indeed, Madagascar never consumed less than 23 percent of Natal's exports of cotton manufactures from 1877 to 1889, taking over 60 percent from 1885 to 1888. A particularly important market for plain, and printed and dyed, piece goods, Madagascar consumed over 75 percent of Natal's exports of plain cottons in 1878, 1883, and 1885–8 and printed and dyed piece goods in 1882 and 1885–9. Exports to Madagascar of ready-made clothing almost rivaled cottons in value in 1888–9, although they represented a far lower share of Natal's total clothing exports, rising above 10 percent only in 1878 and 1879 (16 and 19 percent respectively)[115].

Arms constituted probably the most valuable import behind slaves and cloth. The imperial court's continued dependence upon imported muskets, cannon, and powder was reflected in the 1832 stipulation that exports be paid for only in arms, gunpowder, or dollars. The following year, in response to a dual request from governor Nicolay of Mauritius and the British Secretary of State for Foreign Affairs, these restrictions were lifted, but were reimposed in 1834

111 Ropes, Emmerton & Co, to Cheney, Salem, 22 Sept. and 21 Oct. 1885; Dawson to Ropes, Emmerton & Co, Tamatave, 6 Nov. 1890 – *REC/CR-MZL.*
112 Laborde to Whitney, Vatomandry, 20 April 1886, REC/CR-MZL.
113 Whitney to Ropes, Emmerton & Co, Tamatave, 27 May and 8 Oct. 1891, *REC/CR-MZL.*
114 Duder to Ropes, Emmerton & Co, Antananarivo, 20 March 1893, *REC/CR-MZL.*
115 Campbell, "Disease, Cattle and Slaves," 128.

TABLE 8.8. *Toamasina: Origin of Cotton Cloth Imports, 1864–90* ($ Malagasy)

Year	Britain	(%)	France	(%)	United States	(%)	Total
1864–5	23,648	n.a.	n.a.	n.a.	–	–	n.a.
1866	28,355	n.a.	n.a.	n.a.	75,045	n.a.	n.a.
1867	49,428	n.a.	n.a.	n.a.	82,015	n.a.	n.a.
1868	120,200	48.4	13,000	5.2	115,000	46.3	248,200
1869–70	67,200	32.9	7,000	0.3	130,000	63.7	204,200
1877–8	99,800	19.9*			528,606	84.1	628,406
1879–80	n.a.	n.a.	n.a.	n.a.	489,652	n.a.	n.a.
1883	n.a.	n.a.	n.a.	n.a.	542,465	n.a.	n.a.
1886	120,735	n.a.	n.a.	n.a.	126,000	n.a.	n.a.
1890	n.a.	n.a.	n.a.	n.a.	n.a.	n.a.	511,939

(*Britain & France)
Source: Campbell, "Toamasina," 546.

for the staple exports of rice and cattle.[116] Arms and ammunition comprised 2.79 percent by value of Mauritian exports to Madagascar in 1835,[117] and in 1837 Ranavalona I raised $31,800 in taxes in order to pay Lastelle for imported European arms.[118] Merina demand for arms, which dropped between the 1850s and the late 1870s, grew thereafter as Franco–Merina relations deteriorated.[119] The renewed demand for arms proved a particular boon to U.S. traders, who, from the 1840s, became almost totally dependent upon cotton piece goods to pay for their staple exports and thus were obliged to import specie whenever demand for cottons slackened.[120] Ropes sold $25,000 worth of U.S. arms to the Merina government in 1882, and it was claimed the following year that Robinson, the U.S. consul in Toamasina, was directly associated with arms imports.[121] The British were also involved; thus, in September 1884 the steamer *Normandy*

---

[116] *RA*, 314–5; Baker to Stanley, "Memorial concerning Madagascar" (1852), *SOAS/LMS-MIL* B3.F4.JC; *HR* vol. V, 1156–7; Rasoamiaramana, "Aspects économiques" (1973), 59; G. M. Razi, "Sources d'histoire malgache aux Etats-Unis, 1792–1882," *Colloque des historiens et juristes* (6 Sept. 1977), 59 – *ANM*.

[117] Campbell, "Toamasina," 549.

[118] Oliver, *Madagascar* vol. II, 196.

[119] [Gottel] to Dawson, St Denis, 20 Feb. 1884, *REC/CR-MZL*.

[120] Again, in the late 1870s the failure of the Mahajanga market to move more than 600 bales a year led to the import there of large quantities of French 5-franc pieces – Hathorne to Arnold, Hines & Co, Zanzibar, 16 Nov. 1878 – Hathorne, "Letterbook" (1877–79); Taria Topan to Maclean, Morris & Co, Zanzibar, 5 March 1879 – Hathorne, "Letterbook" (1878–80); see also Bennett, "Americans in Zanzibar," 37; Razi, "Sources d'histoire," 13.

[121] Former Resident, *Madagascar and the United States*, (New York, 1883), 8, 11; see also Edward D. Ropes to [parents, Tamatave, 24 March 1882, B1 (1882–1886) Zanzibar Acc.11840 and 11884: Letters 1882, Papers of Edward D.Ropes Jr, *PM*.

TABLE 8.9. *Imerina: Imports, 1884* ($ Malagasy)

Imports	Bales	Value	(% total)	Exports	Quantity	Value	(% total)
Cotton sheeting	2,800	322,000	52.61	Hides	230,000	861,000	98.42
White shirting	1,500	150,000	24.51	Beeswax	80,000 lbs.	6,400	0.73
Prints, etc.	–	100,000	16.34	Coffee	60,000 lbs.	2,400	0.05
Miscellaneous	–	40,000	6.54	Miscellaneous	–	5,000	0.57
Total		612,000				875,300	

Source: Campbell, "Toamasina," 552.

reportedly landed a vast quantity of British arms for the Merina government at Morondava[122].

Arms also formed a major import into independent west Madagascar, for which – by mid-century – Zanzibar, Nosy Be, and especially Mozambique had developed as the main distributive centers.[123] From the 1820s, U.S. traders shipped muskets (1,000 per annum into Mahajanga alone in the 1830s[124]), ammunition, and other military goods to western Madagascar. They sold indiscriminately to Merina and Swahili agents in exchange for hides and other exports.[125] In 1878, it was estimated that the market in independent Madagascar would absorb 25,000 pounds of gunpowder, retailing at $0.14 a pound – $0.2 cheaper than on the Mozambique coast.[126]

Until the 1870s, Indians were the chief arms suppliers to the Sakalava.[127] However, Merina garrison officers in western Madagascar also collaborated with local chiefs in clandestine commercial ventures, including the importation of arms destined for groups hostile to the Merina court.[128] In addition, from the 1870s, notably from the outbreak of the 1883–5 war, the Sakalava exchanged gold for American guns and ammunition used in their fight against the Merina.[129] From 1882, continued high demand also stimulated imports from

[122] *MT* II.50 (17 Dec. 1884), 451.
[123] Hathorne to Thompson, Zanzibar, 10 Dec. 1878; Thompson to Hathorn, Majunga, 27 Nov. 1878, encl.1 in Hathorne to Bertram, Zanzibar, 11 Dec. 1878 – Hathorne, "Letterbook" (1878–80).
[124] Razi, "Sources d'histoire," 15; see also "Papers of Richard P. Waters," 1831–87, mss. MH-14, *PM*.
[125] Invoice Brookhouse *BLHU*; Log book (1828–9).
[126] Hathorne to Arnold, Hines & Co, Zanzibar, 6 and 13 Mar. 1878 – Hathorne, "Letterbook" (1877–79).
[127] Hathorne to Arnold, Hines & Co, Zanzibar, 17 Oct. and 14 Nov. 1877 – Hathorne, "Letterbook" (1878–80).
[128] Rasoamiaramanana, "Aspects économiques" (1973), 48; Ravelomanana, "La vie religieuse à Ambositra," 43.
[129] "Letter," Tamatave, 9 Dec. 1888, in *ASR* (Jan. & Feb., 1889), 46; Horn, *Trader Horn*, 82, 106, 112, 116.

TABLE 8.10. *Mauritius: Trade with Madagascar, 1835* (B = British; I = Indian; Value in $)

	Imports				Exports			
Item	Unit	Quantity	Value	Item	Unit	Quantity	Value
Live cattle	bullock	6,172	123,875	Cotton goods (B)	yard	123,495	16,350
Beef (salted and dried)	barrel	2,637	15,840	Haberdashery (B)	n.a.	n.a.	3,645
Hides	unit	92,442	3,015	Cotton goods (I)	yard	110,402	16,380
Rice	lb.	417,540	7,120	Silk (foreign)	n.a.	n.a.	345
Tortoise shell	lb.	194	1,535	Muskets	unit	215	825
Grain	bushel	250	450	Lead & shot	lb.	1,920	70
Tobacco	lb.	3,164	190	Gunpowder	lb.	3,200	560
Cotton cloth	yard	1,040	155	Hardware (B)	n.a.	n.a.	130
Linen	yard	36	15	Wrought iron (B)	n.a.	n.a.	220
Glass	n.a.	n.a.	95	Rum	gallon	10,861	3,300
Lead	lb.	900	85	Brandy	gallon	37	60
Fruit	unit	n.a.	60	Cordials	gallon	45	55
Miscellaneous	n.a.	n.a.	14,410	Wine	gallon	1,132	345
				Beer and ale	gallon	26	35
				Horses	unit	12	1,000
				Hay	bale	3,605	2,970
				Beef and pork (B)	barrel	1	20
				Salt	bushel	2,479	1,790
				Coconut oil	gallon	14	10
				Sugar (raw)	lb.	1,322	45
				Rice	lb.	46,980	745
				Miscellaneous	n.a.	n.a.	6,700
Total Value			166,845	Total Value			52,080

Source: Foreign Trade – Mauritius (1835), 567.

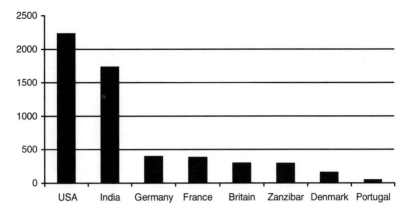

Figure 11. *Nosy Be: Value of Freight Trade, January–May 1887 by National Flag* (in $000s Malagasy).
Source: MT (11 June 1887).

Natal: A. C. Sears, captain of the U.S. sailing ship the *Sicilian* shipped guns to western Madagascar, as did the steamship *Normandy* in 1884; it was claimed in June that year that "Liverpool merchants are doing a large trade between the west Coast and Natal, and the Americans do not intend to be left behind."[130] A decree of October 1894 barred the import of firearms into and transference from French-controlled Nosy Be, Antseranana, and Nosy Boraha, but foreign firms established there, such as O'Swald, continued to run arms to the independent west coast[131].

Another staple import was rum. On the west coast, Mascarene traders traditionally supplied rum, but competition was provided by Americans from the 1820s[132] and South Africans from the 1870s.[133] The rum produced on Rontaunay's east coast plantations in the 1830s and 1840s, which sold locally at $26.40 a barrel, failed to meet demand and was supplemented by large quantities of Mascarene imports.[134] Alcohol was the third most important Mauritian export by value to Madagascar in 1835 (7.29 percent)[135] and continued to constitute a staple Mascarene import, often used in payment for bullocks and rice. Although in the late 1800s, as a result of missionary pressure, Mascarene rum was

[130] *MT* II.24 (18 June 1884), 229; see also Campbell, "Disease, Cattle and Slaves," 128–9.
[131] Raminosoa, "La Maison 'Wm. O'Swald & Co.,'" 87–8.
[132] Invoice Brookhouse *BLHU*.
[133] Campbell, "Disease, Cattle and Slaves," 127.
[134] *GH* (1928), 70, 228; Scherer, *Histoire de la Réunion*, 59; Galloway, *The Sugar Cane Industry*, 130–1.
[135] Campbell, "Toamasina," 549.

banned in Imerina, the cheap *toaka gasy* variety continued to be produced and consumed locally.[136] Mascarene rum was permitted to enter other regions of the Merina empire, where its price fluctuated widely: In the early 1880s, 9,500 barrels of imported rum retailed on the east coast at $0.125 a pint, while the 698,469 liters (3,152 casks) valued at $63,050 imported between 1 July and 31 December 1881 sold for $5 a pint.[137]

As an integral part of most Malagasy rituals, rum may be excluded from the category of imported luxury goods that served more the refined tastes of foreign settlers and of the Merina elite whose demand for items of conspicuous consumption occasionally reached considerable heights. For instance, in 1835, horses and hay constituted the second most valuable Mauritian import into Madagascar (7.62 percent of total imports).[138]

Other imports included an array of hardware, crockery, and beads.[139] Of special note is soap, shipped to west Madagascar by U.S. traders from the 1820s[140] and to the east coast. Nevertheless, locally manufactured soap (it was one of the few foreign industrial techniques successfully introduced onto the plateau) spread steadily from the mid-1830s, meeting a large domestic demand.[141]

Total Value

Lack of statistical evidence renders difficult any assessment of the value of the foreign trade of imperial Madagascar. Moreover, natural factors, such as cyclones and the smallpox epidemics that in 1877 and 1878 devastated the Toamasina region and brought commerce to a standstill, caused considerable year-to-year variations in the total value of trade.[142] Nevertheless, a general

---

[136] *MT* I.6 (27 May 1882), 7.

[137] Former Resident, *Madagascar and the United States*, 14; *MT* I.6 (27 May 1882), 7.

[138] Charles Nordhoff, *Stories of the Island World* (New York, 1857), 58; also see Campbell, "Toamasina," 549.

[139] E.g., imports from the United States in the early nineteenth century included bowls, mugs and dishes, slats, sperm candles, cut glass beads, Spanish dollars, and iron bars – Invoice Brookhouse *BLHU*.

[140] Invoice Brookhouse *BLHU*.

[141] Raombana, B2 Livre 13, 29; [Finaz], "Tananarive, Capitale de Madagascar. Séjour d'un missionnaire Catholique en 1855, 56 et 57," p. 109, sect.II Diaires no.20, *AHVP*.

[142] Robinson to Hunter, 2 April 1877, *US*; Pakenham to Derby, Tamatave, 1 Feb. 1878, *PRO.CO*.84/1509 ERD/2270; *CdM* (5 juillet 1894); Wetter to Uhl, 25 April 1895, *US9*; for a full discussion of problems caused by the imperial transport policy see Chapter 10, and for an analysis of the impact of disease see Gwyn Campbell, "Crisis of Faith and Colonial Conquest: The Impact of Famine and Disease in late nineteenth-century Madagascar," *Cahiers d'Études Africaines* 32 (3) 127 (1992).

idea of the value of trade may be formed. Merina export earnings fell during the 1810s and 1820s. Franco–British conflict in the area caused revenue from foreign trade to drop from approximately $200,000 a year in 1810 and $22,500 in 1817 to a low of $1,500 by 1820, and they were further undermined by the 1820 slave export ban.[143] By 1835, imperial Madagascar had regained a positive balance of trade, but its foreign trade during the era 1825–61 was restricted by the autarkic policies of the court. First, the imperial system of forced labor restricted purchasing power and thus demand for imports. Second, Merina export duties varied according to the commodity and over time, but were always higher than duties in independent ports.[144] Such measures, combined with court monopolies, the expulsion of foreigners in 1835 and 1857, and the closure of imperial ports from 1845 to 1854, led foreign traders to transfer increasingly from imperial to independent west coast ports. On the west coast, competition with the Indians and Swahili drove prices up, by a multiple of 10 for some export commodities between the late 1840s and the early 1860s.[145]

Some indication of early U.S. trade with western Madagascar may be gauged from estimates that the annual value of U.S. imports into Mahajanga in the 1830s averaged $16,000.[146] As total U.S.–east African trade amounted to $1,000,000 in 1850 and the northern network above Zanzibar took only $120,000 (12 percent of the 1850 figure), a considerable proportion of the remaining 88 percent was undoubtedly shipped to western Madagascar by the Indian and Arab traders based at Zanzibar.[147]

The buoyant international economy of the 1860s and early 1870s boosted trade and obscured the negative commercial features of autarky. However, the

---

[143] Chapelier, "Lettres en mission à Madagascar de décembre 1803 en mai 1805" (ed. M. Jully), *BAM* (1904), 34; Chazal, "notes" (1816), 24; Chardenoux, "Journal" (1816), 163; N. Leminier, "Notes sur une excursion faite dans l'intérieur de l'Île de Madagascar en 1825," *BdM* 292 (1970), 797; Hastie, "Diary" (1817), 137, 147, 157, 164, 170, 177, 188–9, 197, 211; *idem*, "Diary" (1820), 489; *RH*, 21, 67, 82, 93–4; Raombana, "texts," 13; Ellis, *History of Madagascar* vol. II, 16, 198; Chapus & Mondain, "Un chapitre inconnu," 117; *HR* vol. I, 441–2; vol. II, 658; vol. III, 120; Prud'homme, "Contribution à l'histoire de l'Imerina" in "Notes d'histoire malgache," *BAM* 14 (1931); Chapus, "Le soin du bien être," 1; Jean Valette, *Études*, 19; Oliver, *Madagascar* vol. I, 221–2, 227–9, 252–3; *idem*, "General Hall," 678; *GH* (1908), 113, 233, 235, 249–52, 268 and (1928), 113, 235, 268, 297, 335; Campbell, "Madagascar and the Slave Trade," 206, 208.

[144] Campbell, "Role of the London Missionary Society" vol. I, 189–91, vol. II, 319; Razi, "Sources d'histoire," 13.

[145] Oliver, *Madagascar* vol. II, 196.

[146] Razi, "Sources d'histoire," 15; see also "Papers of Richard P. Waters," 1831–87, mss. MH-14, *PM*.

[147] Ward to Clayton, Zanzibar, 20 July 1850, in Bennett and Brooks (eds.), *New England Merchants*, 466.

world depression from the late 1870s exposed the imperial regime's failure to have either developed import substitution or widened its export base.[148] From around 1870, reasonably complete figures are available for direct trade with Britain, nominally Madagascar's major trading partner in the late nineteenth century, but these probably constitute a small percentage of total Malagasy–British trade, most of which passed in an undifferentiated manner via India or Mauritius. Some indication of foreign trade is given by the U.S. consular returns, but these are speculative for all save U.S. firms and concern only Toamasina or, more rarely, Morondava.

Available statistics reveal that, by 1882, the British had drawn level with the Americans with a total annual Malagasy trade valued at approximately $500,000.[149] Americans were possibly hardest hit by the 1883–5 Franco–Merina War, during which their trade with imperial Madagascar fell by 40 percent. Unlike European traders, whose commercial interests were diverse, Americans concentrated on hides and cottons, which were affected by French naval blockades, notably of Toamasina and Mahajanga. Also, they were less willing than other Westerners to take risks.[150] By 1890, when an annual average of 40 steamers, between 20 and 30 sailing ships, and 150 coastal vessels visited Toamasina,[151] Americans were responsible for only 40.1 percent of imports and 25.2 percent of exports through that port.[152]

Official statistics also fail to indicate the growth of clandestine trade in imperial Madagascar. First, in return for bribes, unsalaried Merina customs officers commonly permitted up to 50 percent of declared goods to pass unregistered through customs. In addition, although the value of imported arms and specie is unknown, narrative sources indicate it was considerable. For instance, in 1868, the imperial court imported arms valued at $21,650 from one foreign source and in 1880, an estimated $1 million in specie.[153] Smuggling increased

---

[148] Robinson to Hankey, 1 Oct. 1878, *US*; *CdM* (23 août 1892).

[149] Oliver, *Madagascar* vol. II, 173–4; Robinson to Hankey, Tamatave, 1 Oct. 1878, *US*.

[150] Robinson to Third Assistant Secretary of State, 4 and 29 June 1882; *idem* to Payson, 14 July 1880; Stanwood to E.Whitnee, Andakabe, 30 Sept. 1883; *idem* to Adee, 17 Dec. 1884; *idem* to Third Assistant Secretary of State, 2 June 1885; Stanwood to Bayard, Andakabe, 31 Oct. 1886; Campbell to Porter, 12 Dec. 1887; Taylor to Whitnee, 16 Feb. 1885 – in "US Consular Correspondence from Majunga," *US*; *MT* III.2 (14 Jan. 1885).

[151] Foucart, "L'Etat du commerce à Madagascar," 71.

[152] Campbell, "Toamasina," 541, 546.

[153] Robinson to Payson, Antananarivo, 28 April 1881; *idem* to Third Assistant Secretary of State, 22 May, 29 June and 28 July 1882; Campbell to Wharton, 24 May and 6 Dec. 1890; Waller to Wharton, 25 April 1893 – *US*; Cameron, "Newspaper Cuttings"; Rainilaiarivony à Dr. Davidson, Antananarivo, 5 Alahasaty 1868, in "Lettres du gouvernement et de la Reine, 1852–1859," Carton section II c.12, *AHVP*.

markedly from the 1883–5 war, when Toamasina and other main imperial ports were first blockaded and subsequently occupied. In December 1885, when French officials were posted to supervise customs at Toamasina, Fenoarivo, Vohimara, Vatomandry, Mananjary, and Mahajanga, large numbers of foreign traders began smuggling through alternative ports such as Mahanoro.[154] Officially prohibited exports, such as gold and valuable timbers, were smuggled through a myriad of unsupervised landing places along the east coast, as well as from the independent west coast. Indeed, an estimated 50 percent of all gold produced in the Merina empire was clandestinely exported.[155]

Traders also turned to the independent coast where the contraband flow of arms, slaves, and specie could have amounted to 57.5 percent of total imports, and by the 1880s, foreign trade in general probably rivaled that of the east coast.[156] However, the only reliable statistics concern South African trade with southwest Madagascar. These reveal that Madagascar generally accounted for less than 10 percent of Natal's exports to Africa (excluding South African territories), except in 1878–83, 1885, and 1888, when it accounted for 35 percent of Natal's imports in 1878 and from 22 to 29 percent in the years 1881–3.[157] Foreign trade in the southwest declined dramatically after the January 1888 Sakalava attack on the major European entrepôt of Nosy Ve.[158]

Madagascar's foreign trade during the imperial Merina era has hitherto been underestimated due to three main factors: the extent of smuggling, a vast unrecorded trade from areas independent of Merina rule, and the fact that many imports into Europe and America marked as coming from Mauritius, Réunion, and

[154] Robinson to Payson, 2 Oct. 1880; *idem* to Third Assistant Secretary of State, 7 May 1885 – *US*; Esoavelomandroso, *La province maritime orientale*, 237–82; for bribes see Finkelmeier to Hunter, 30 Dec. 1874, *US*; for the French blockade and its consequences, see Robinson to Hunter, 11 Aug. 1876 and 1 Oct. 1878, *US2*; *idem* to Payson, Antananarivo, 15 Jan.1881, *US3*; Whitney to Adee, 28 Nov. and 26 Dec. 1883 and 4 April 1884; Stanwood to Whitney, Andakabe, 30 Sep. 1883; Robinson to Adee, 27 May, 7 Oct.1884 and 8 Jan. 1885; *idem* to Porter, 21 July 1886 – *US4*; Campbell to Porter, 12 Dec.1887, *US5*; Waller to Wharton, 4 May 1893; *idem* to Quincy, 8 May 1893; Wetter to Strobel, 26 Jan. 1894 – *US8*; Wetter to Uhl, 26 Jan. 1895, *US9*; *MT* 2.24 (18 June 1884); 3.13 (1 April 1885); 5.2 (10 July 1886); (5.5 (31 July 1886); 5.7 (14 Aug. 1886); *CdM* (29 mai 1894); for the development of Mahanoro see *MT* (21 June 1886); (14 Aug. 1886); (28 Aug.1886); (27 Nov. 1886); (11 Dec.1886); (17 Dec.1887); (7 April 1888).

[155] See also Chapter 7.

[156] Stanwood to Robinson, Morondava, 1 Dec. 1880; *idem* to Whitney and Robinson, Morondava, 1 Aug.1883; *idem* to Robinson, Morondava, 13 July 1884; *idem*, "Commercial Situation," Andakabe, 31 Dec. 1886 – *US*; see also Chapter 9.

[157] See Figures 12–15.

[158] Rostvig to Stanwood, Tullear [Dec. 1886], NMS Copibok 812B (Tulear, 1882–92), 183–4, *FLM/NMS*; Stanwood to Campbell, 31 Jan. and 27 May 1888; encl. (1 Dec. 1885) in George to Robinson, Andakabe, 10 Feb. 1886 – *US*; *CdM* 138 (10 April 1894).

Zanzibar were in fact reexports from Madagascar. Nevertheless, the commerce of Madagascar never reached its full potential. This was due partly to external factors, namely foreign aggression, but mainly to the restrictive autarkic policies of the imperial Merina regime – chief of which were commercial monopolies and forced labor. A combination of the above factors led the foreign trade of Madagascar from the early 1890s into a deep depression that lasted until well after the French takeover.

9   The Slave Trade, 1820–1895

Introduction

IOA domestic slavery and slave exports grew throughout the nineteenth century, in contrast to West Africa, where in the 1860s slave exports ended and domestic slavery started to expand.[1] The role of Madagascar in the IOW, and notably the IOA, slave trade, has only recently come to light, as has its unique role as both importer and exporter of slaves.

Despite the 1820 ban on slave exports from Merina-controlled territory and radically enlarged *fanompoana* for free subjects, the Malagasy slave trade increased dramatically during the nineteenth century. The British government became aware of the vibrancy of the IOA slave trade only from mid-century, but never realized the extent of the trans-Mozambique Channel trade. Historians to date have not adequately filled this gap.[2] According to traditional assumptions, Swahili coast exports were channeled almost exclusively to Arabia and the plantation islands of Zanzibar, Pemba, and the Mascarenes, while the Mozambique export trade was generated predominantly by Brazilian and Cuban demand, with the French sugar islands constituting a secondary market. Following the closure of the Brazilian and Cuban markets in the 1860s, the Mozambique slave export trade to non-Muslim countries largely

---

[1] Manning, "Contours of Slavery," 841–3; Sheriff, *Slaves, Spices and Ivory*; Lovejoy, *Transformations in Slavery*, 150–3.
[2] Exceptions include Allen, "Licentious and Unbridled Proceedings"; Campbell, "Madagascar and Mozambique," 166–93; *idem*, "East African Slave Trade," 1–27; *idem*, "Madagascar and the Slave Trade," 203–27.

evaporated. Thus, Austen considers that continued slave exports from south-east Africa must have been occasioned by heightened demand in the northern Muslim markets:

French labour demands were too small to account for the scale of the Muslim slave trade from East Africa in the nineteenth century, especially when the traffic from Mozambique to Brazil is taken into account. Instead we must keep in mind the substantial slave trade which existed before the French arrival and also its destination – a Persian Gulf region which was already incorporating servile African immigrants into commercial date planting and pearl fishing.[3]

By contrast, it is here argued that the southern sector of the IOA slave network, from Kilwa to the area immediately south of the Zambezi, cannot be considered without reference to the growing influence both of the French islands and of Madagascar. Indeed, in this as in many other aspects of commerce, Madagascar constitutes the missing link in the economic history of eastern and southern Africa.

Autarky, Emancipation, and the Slave Trade

Central to the 1820 Britanno–Merina treaty was a ban on Malagasy slave exports. Mauritian authorities envisaged this would cripple French planters on Réunion, while Mauritian planters would enjoy access to migrant wage labor from Madagascar – the closest and cheapest source of labor. Réunionnais animosity grew toward both the Merina and the British as the ban proved effective in Merina-controlled regions. Merina forces had by 1825 conquered most of the eastern seaboard, while the British Admiralty maintained strict surveillance over the east coast waters of Madagascar. Hence, while slaves continued to be imported clandestinely into the Mascarenes in the early 1820s, they were predominantly of west coast and Mozambique origin. In 1825, the LMS reported that a French agent transported east African slaves aboard his two ships to his base at Fort Dauphin (Tolanaro), in southeast Madagascar, from where they were shipped in smaller vessels to Réunion.[4] However, Fort Dauphin was that year captured by the Merina, after which the only tangible evidence of slave exports from the Malagasy east coast was of Merina-owned slaves being transferred by boat from one region of the Merina empire to another. Indeed, slavers smuggled their cargoes into Mauritius, falsely claiming Toamasina as their port

---

[3] Ralph Austen, *African Economic History* (London, 1987), 72; see also *ibid*, 67–8, 71–3.
[4] *The Missionary Register* (1826), 50; Allen, "Licentious and Unbridled Proceedings" 110–11.

of origin, in order to allay any suspicions British port officials might entertain. However, British hopes of accessing Malagasy migrant labor were dashed in 1825–6, when Radama I adopted autarkic policies, essential components of which were a state monopoly of labor and a ban on Malagasy emigration, even of a temporary contractual nature.[5]

Mascarene planters characterized Malagasy slaves as more rebellious and unprincipled than others, so from 1820 to 1840, East Africa became their major source of slaves. Nevertheless, supply proved insufficient when, following the emancipation of 76,774 slaves on Mauritius in 1835 and 60,800 slaves on Réunion in 1848, the newly liberated slaves refused to remain on the plantations. The manpower crisis was accentuated by the decline from 1840 of both local sugar production and the price of raw sugar. These factors motivated large planters to mechanize, but rendered small planters, with limited capital resources, more reliant than ever on cheap labor.[6] Mascarene frustration at the Merina rejection of Mauritian and Réunionnais government requests for contract workers from Madagascar culminated in a combined Franco–Britannic naval attack on Toamasina in 1845.[7] However, the invasion force was repulsed, and the Merina court retaliated by closing all imperial ports to foreign trade. Thereafter, until the 1870s, the French and British governments proved reluctant to confront the Merina militarily, focusing instead on alternative labor sources. Mauritius gained access both to Indian labor and to "Prize Negroes" liberated by the British navy from slavers captured in regional waters and immediately snapped up as apprentices by planters.[8] The planters of Réunion were less fortunate. Deprived during the Napoleonic Wars of their base in India and denied access to Indian labor by the British until 1861, they were increasingly tempted into the traffic in slaves, disguised as *engagés* (contract workers) from

---

[5] See Wanquet, *Économies et sociétés*, Chapters four and six.

[6] Scherer, *Histoire de la Réunion*, 62–3; Pietro Profita, "Présence des originaires malgaches dans la population générale de Maurice," *BAM* 53, 1–2 (1975), 23–7; Deerr, *History of Sugar* vol. I, 28–31, 185, 203–4, 242, and vol. II (London, 1950), 521, 530–1; *idem* and Alexander Brooks, *Early Use of Steam Power in the Sugar Cane Industry* (London, 1940), 7–8; Griffiths, *Hanes Madagascar*, 15, 34; Durand, *L'Île Maurice*, 40–1; Antoine Chelin, *Une Île et son passé: Ile Maurice, 1507–1947* (Mauritius, 1973), 150–76; Suresh Mourba, *Misère noire: ou réflexions sur l'histoire de l'Île Maurice* (n.d.), 23–88.

[7] AHVP 36b, C28f; Grandidier, "Souvenirs," 10; A Resident, *Madagascar*, 231–2; Prud'homme, "Considérations sur les Sakalaves," *Notes reconnaissances et explorations* VI (1900), 271; Peter Burroughs, "The Mauritius Rebellion of 1832 and the Abolition of British Colonial Slavery," *Journal of Imperial and Commonwealth History* IV.3 (1976).

[8] James Dacres to W. Gomm, Tamatave, 5 Aug. 1848, in "papers Relative to the Condition of the Colonies" (1849), 729; P.Colomb, *Slave Catching in the Indian Ocean* (London, 1873 – reprint 1968), 343, 348; Chelin, *Une Île*, 166, 169, 171–3, 176; Mourba, *Misère noire*, 34–9, 64, 71; Campbell, "Madagascar and the Slave Trade," 212.

East Africa and independent regions of Madagascar; from 1848 to 1859, they imported an estimated annual average of 7,500 Malagasy engagés.[9]

Despite the reopening of the Merina empire to outside investment following the death of Ranavalona I in 1861, the Merina regime maintained a monopoly of its labor resources. Moreover, the French islands suffered a succession of mishaps: a series of human and plant diseases, cyclone damage, falling international maritime traffic after the Suez Canal opened in 1869, and a decline in world sugar prices from the 1870s. Planters became desperate for cheap labor to compensate for reduced profits. In 1860, the British permitted Réunion access to 6,000 Bengali laborers. However, these proved insufficient given an annual plantation workforce mortality rate of up to 20 percent. Moreover, the remark made in 1860 on Mauritius, that "the Indian is . . . a slave with a limit to his slavery,"[10] was as applicable to Réunion. In response to outcries against labor abuses, the British in November 1882 halted supplies of Indian workers to Réunion; within 18 months, at least 163 Indians had migrated to Mauritius and a further 962 had returned to India. In 1883, despite British opposition, a Franco–Portuguese agreement was reached for the shipment to Réunion of Mozambique *engagés*. However, the scheme faltered due to the inability of French agents to secure ready supplies of labor to meet steamer schedules. Subsequently, Réunionnais planters became dependent upon slaves supplied directly from East Africa by Swahili/Arab traders or, increasingly, on east African and Malagasy slaves channeled via the entrepôts of independent west Madagascar.[11] As was commented in 1886, "Planters in Réunion are becoming utterly ruined; labour they must obtain, or become bankrupt."[12] For the same reasons, after declaring a protectorate over the entire Comoro group in 1886,

---

[9] Lefevre, *Saint-Pierre*, 22, 24–6, 31, 34; "Report," Cape Town, 25 April 1844, *PRO.CO*.84/515 ERD/1144 no. 29; Beachey, *Slave Trade*, 30; Guillain, *Documents* II, 273–82; Allen Isaacman, *Mozambique. The Africanisation of a European Institution. The Zambesi Prazas, 1750–1902* (University of Wisconsin, 1972), 93–4, 98–102; Gerhard Liesegang, "A First Look at the Import and Export Trade of Mozambique, 1800–1914" in *idem*, H. Pasch and A. Jones (eds.), *Figuring African Trade* (Berlin, 1986), 466; Christopher Lloyd, *The Navy and the Slave Trade* (London, 1968), 240.

[10] Colomb, *Slave Catching*, 100; see also Crémazy, *L'Île de la Réunion et Madagascar* (London, 1822), 16.

[11] A slave revolt erupted on Johanna in February 1891. See *ASR* (May and June 1889), 146; *ASR* (May and June 1891), 99; see also Pakenham to Derby, Tamatave, 21 Feb. 1876, *PRO.CO*.84/1369 ERD/1142; Robinson to Third Assistant Secretary of State, Tamatave, 22 May 1882, *US*; Samat, "Notes" (1852); Guerret, *Trois mois autour de Madagascar* edited by E.Genin (Douai, 1883), 37–54; Auguste Toussaint, *Histoire des Îles Mascareignes* (Paris, 1972), Chs. 4 and 5.

[12] Haggarad, Tamatave, 18 Nov. 1886 in *ASR* (July and Aug. 1883), 135.

the French maintained the institution of slavery in defiance of the British treaty of 1883 stipulating emancipation by August 1889.[13]

While recognizing Réunion's role, historians have generally missed the critical importance of the Malagasy market for east African slaves. This in turn can only be fully appreciated in the context of the rise of the Merina empire in which unfree labor played a pivotal role. Despite the 1820 ban on slave exports, demand for such labor so outstripped domestic supply that, by the mid–1820s, Imerina was importing growing numbers of African slaves. As Hastie commented, following Radama I's refusal in 1824 to ban slave imports (as he had slave exports):

I asked him [Abdalla – a prominent Mahajanga slave trader] if Radama had not given my orders about the importation trade. he replied, "No," but the orders against exportation were repeated previous to his [Radama I's] departure from Majunga, and he [Radama I] had laid a duty of five per cent on the exports and two per cent on all importation commerce; and of course, said Abdalla, slaves are included as he [Radama I] knew that to be our [i.e., Swahili traders'] principal commerce.[14]

The high death toll in imperial campaigns and intensification of *fanompoana* for the industrial experiment led simultaneously to further *fanompoana* and a heightened domestic and import slave trade; the estimated number of slave imports into Imerina quadrupled from 1828 to 1861.[15]

Economic prosperity in the 1860s and early 1870s coupled with a less repressive domestic policy led to a temporary expansion in wealth and therefore of slave ownership in Imerina.[16] Simultaneously, the Merina bureaucracy, which expanded rapidly following the creation of a state church in 1868–9, generated a heavy demand for servile labor to maintain them in a life of luxury. The 1868 Britanno–Merina treaty reaffirmed the prohibition on slave exports. It also proclaimed a slave import ban, although this remained largely nominal. More effective was the 1877 liberation of an estimated 150,000 *Masombika* into state work camps. Combined with growing flight from *fanompoana*, this boosted

[13] *ASR* (Jan. 1883), 4–5; (Oct. 1885), 465; Lyons to Duclerc, Paris, 12 Aug. 1882 in *ASR* (May, 1883), 121; O'Neill to Granville, British Consulate, Mozambique, 14 Aug. 1882, in *ASR* (May, 1883), 125.

[14] Hastie, "Diary" (1824–25); *idem*, "Diary" (1817), 158, 164–5; Commodore Nourse to Croker, HMS "Andromarche," 26 Sept. 1823, and Moorson to Commodore Christian, HMS "Andromarche," 24 May 1825 in Theal, *Records* IX, 32, 51–2; Campbell, "Madagascar and the Slave Trade."

[15] Colomb, *Slave Catching*, 309.

[16] Campbell, "Slavery and Fanompoana."

the demand for servile labor, ensuring a sometimes vigorous slave import trade up to the French takeover of 1895.[17]

Africa as a Source of Slaves

Africa was a major source of slaves shipped to the French islands and to West Madagascar from where they were distributed either to the markets of the interior or to the sugar islands. This supply network centered on Portuguese Mozambique. Ibo was practically a French reserve from 1820 to 1829, in which year the number of French slave traders visiting the port was described as "fantastic."[18] Angoche, ruled by a sultan practically independent of both Omani and Portuguese rule, also became a major supplier of slaves to the French islands and Madagascar; by the mid–1840s it surpassed Mozambique Island, Quelimane, and Ibo Sancul, Sangaye, and Quintangonhe, similarly independent sultanates, also supplied slaves to the western Indian Ocean islands. Edward Alpers considers that from mid-century Quintangonhe and Angoche were the chief centers of slave exports to Madagascar. By the late 1830s, Réunionnais merchants were visiting Angoche over which, in 1846, a combined Britanno–Portuguese expedition imposed nominal Portuguese sovereignty. Nevertheless, Swahili traders dominated foreign commerce in the sultanates, including Angoche, which remained largely independent and maintained its slave network into the second half of the nineteenth century.

Further north, Omani-dominated Kilwa was the largest east African supplier of slaves to the Mascarenes from the late 1700s to c.1822. Approximately 20 percent of its slave exports were channeled into the southern trading network in the nineteenth century, initially for shipment to the Americas, but increasingly to the French islands and Madagascar. To the south, Inhambane was also frequented by French slavers from the 1820s. However, by mid-century British antislave trade patrols had obliged slavers to decentralize the trade and the phenomenon of a few large slaving ports gave way to a multitude of small slave ports. This further stimulated Swahili/Arab dominated slave networks, as Portuguese influence was limited to a few main ports.[19]

---

[17] L.Street, "letter" in *The English Independent* (15 and 22 Nov. 1877); W. E. Cousins, "The Abolition of Slavery in Madagascar," *AAMM* 20 (1896), 446–50; Campbell, "Missionaries, Fanompoana and the Menalamba Revolt"; *idem*, "Madagascar and the Slave Trade."

[18] E. A. Alpers, *Ivory and Slaves in East and Central Africa to the Later Nineteenth Century* (London, 1975), 217.

[19] Barnard, *Three Years' Cruise*, 258–9; Alpers, *Ivory and Slaves*, 210–11, 214–15, 218, 236–8; Shepherd, "The Comorians," 76–9; Wolf, "Analysis"; Frere to Granville, 29 May 1873 – *CFM*;

Thus, although the antislave trade campaign achieved considerable success in the Zanzibar region by 1888, the southern network maintained a vigorous slave traffic through a multitude of small ports along the coast between Kilwa and Sofala, as well as from established entrepôts such as Ibo, Quelimane, Moçimboa, Angoche, and Mozambique Island – from which, as late as 1875, some 2,000 to 4,000 slaves were exported annually.[20] According to one estimate, the coast between Cape Delgado and Angoche was responsible for between 12 and 18 percent of slave exports to Madagascar by the start of the 1880s – although the coasts south to the Zambezi delta and north of Cape Delgado, notably around Lindi, Kilwa, and the Rovuma River, were also important.[21] In 1882, Lindi, which possessed a stockade that could house 800 captives, exported 5,000 slaves to the Comoros and Madagascar in Malagasy dhows flying French flags.[22] In the late 1880s, British pressure caused slavers to move from the Swahili coast back to Mozambique, notably to the ports of Tunghi and Angoche (see Map 10).[23]

Two main trading complexes operated in the Mozambique interior in the first half of the nineteenth century. The first, linking Mozambique Island with the Yao and Makua homelands, stretched as far as the southern Lunda and southern Tanzania.[24] The second, connecting Quelimane with its hinterland, extended as far as the southern Lunda kingdom of Kazembe and the Changamira kingdom in Zimbabwe. The main supply areas were Nsenga, Manganja, and especially the Southern Chewa chieftaincies, in the highlands north of the Zambezi[25] (see Table 9.1).

By the 1870s and 1880s, a voracious demand for slaves on the Indian Ocean islands and the Zambesia *prazos* resulted in the depopulation of certain regions of Zambesia and Malawi and to the disintegration of the Makua

---

Auguste Toussaint, *La route des Îles – contribution à l'histoire maritime des Mascareignes* (Paris, 1967), 133–4; Isaacman, *Mozambique*, 93–4, 98–102; M. D. D. Newitt, *Portuguese Settlement on the Zambesi* (London, 1973), 222; Duffy, *Question of Slavery*, 42, 46; René Pélissier, *Naissance de Mozambique* I (Orgeval, 1984), 37.

[20] O'Neill to Granville, Mozambique, 30 April 1883, *ASR* (March 1884), 47; *ASR* (Dec. 1884), 225; (Jan. 1885), 262; (Oct. and Nov. 1886), 113; (Dec. 1886), 156; (Nov. and Dec. 1888), 207–8; Rear Admiral Richards to Macgregor, Mauritius, 30 Aug.1886, *ASR* (Sept. and Oct. 1887); Lindsay, "How to Fight the Slave Trade in East Africa," *ASR* (July and Aug. 1888), 123; see also Cameron, "Cardinal Lavigerie and the Anti-Slavery Crusade," *ASR* (Sept. and Oct. 1888), 190–1; Marquis of Salisbury to Egerton, Foreign Office, 14 Sept. 1888, *ASR* (Nov. and Dec. 1888), 205.

[21] *ASR* (April 1882), 100–1.

[22] *ASR* (Jan. 1883), 4–5; (June 1883), 165.

[23] *ASR* (March and April 1887), 62; (Jan. and Feb. 1888), 21.

[24] In West Madagascar, most *Masombika* were known as *Makoa*.

[25] Isaacman, *Mozambique*, 72, 200–1.

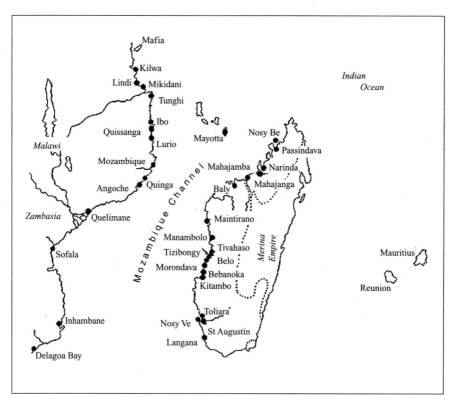

Map 10. *Indian Ocean Africa: The Southern Slave Network*

polity.[26] This prompted intensified slaving in regions east and west of Lake Malawi, notably around Lakes Chilwa, Chiuta, and Amaramba. This slave traffic was supplemented by others, including the diversion to the Mozambique coast of slaves traditionally sent via Kota Kota to outlets near Zanzibar, slaves produced by wars in the interior, and a general crop failure in 1885 that led many famine stricken families to sell their children into slavery.[27] Certainly the supply area

[26] Frere to Granville, 10 and 12 March 1873; Elton, "Report," encl.2 in Frere to Granville, 3 April 1873 – *CFM*; Kirk to Granville, Zanzibar, 3 April 1872, no. 8, "Correspondence Respecting the Slave Trade" (1873); Salisbury to Adams, 9 Sept. 1879, and 29 Sept. 1879, no. 67; Pakenham to Salisbury, 3 Oct. 1879, no. 77; O'Neill to Salisbury, Mozambique, 6, 7, and 9 Sept. 1879, nos. 117 and 120, "The Slave Trade, 1879–80," *Foreign Office Correspondence Relating to the Slave Trade* (London, 1873 and 1880); Alpers, *Ivory and Slaves*, 218–19, 227–8, 239, 257; Landmark, *Det Norske missionsselskab*, 169; Duffy, *Question of Slavery*, Ch. 3; Etienne Berlioux, *The Slave Trade in Africa in 1872* (London, 1871), 53–4.

[27] *ASR* (April 1882), 100; (Dec. 1884), 233; (Jan. 1885), 262–3; (May 1885), 383; (Jan. and Feb. 1888), 21; (Nov. and Dec. 1888), 218; (July and Aug. 1889), 176; O'Neil to Salisbury, Mozambique, 30 May 1888, *ASR* (Nov. and Dec. 1888), 217; Eric Axelson, *Portugal and the Scramble for Africa* (Johannesburg, 1967), 137, 141, 143–4, 163–4, 167–8.

TABLE 9.1. *Ports Involved in the Trans-Mozambique Channel Slave Trade, 1800–95*

East Africa (exports)			East Madagascar (exports)			West Madagascar (imports & exports)		
Port	Position	Dates	Port	Position	Dates	Port	Position	Dates
Kilwa Kivinje	8°45'S	1810–91	Antongil Bay	15°23'S	1800–25	Nosy Be	13°20'S	1840–95?
Lindi	10°00'S	1800–90s	Nosy Boraha	16°50'S	1800–30	Passandava	13°48'S	1840–95
Mikindani	10°16'S	1880–90s	Fenoarivo	17°21'S	1800–20	Narinda	14°38'S	1840–95
Rovuma River	10°30'S	1860–94	Mahavelona	17°40'S	1800–20	Mahajamba	15°27'S	1800–95
Tunghi Bay	10°46'S	1840–90s	Toamasina	18°10'S	1800–20	Mahajanga	15°40'S	1800–95
Moçimboa	11°19'S	1880s	Ste Luce	24°46'S	1800–25	Baly Bay	16°05'S	1830–95
Ibo	12°21'S	1800–95?	Mananivo River	24°58'S	1800–25	Maintirano	18°01'S	1850–95
Quissanga	12°24'S	1820–80s	Tolanaro	25°01'S	1800–25	Manambolo River	19°00'S	1850–95
Lurio	13°32'S	1870–90s?				Morondava	20°19'S	?–95
Mozambique Island	15°00'S	1800–80s				St Augustin	23°31'S	1800–95?
Condúnçia Bay	15°15'S	1840–70s						
Quinga	15°50'S	1840–80s						
Angoche	16°11'S	1840–80s						
Moma	16°46'S	1840–90s?						
Sena	17°30'S	1820s						
Quelimane	17°53'S	1806–90s						
Inhambane	23°51'S	1824–[80s?]						
Delagoa Bay	25°58'S	1880s?						

Source: Campbell, "Madagascar and Mozambique in the Slave Trade of the Western Indian Ocean, 1800–1861" in *The Economics of the Indian Ocean Slave Trade in the Nineteenth Century* edited by W. G. Clarence-Smith, (London, 1989), 166–93; *idem*, The East African Slave Trade, 1861–1895: The "Southern" Complex, *International Journal of African Historical Studies* 22.1 (1989), 1–27.

affected by the slave trade to the western Indian Ocean islands was vast: "Slaves are brought down from the whole country between the lakes and the coast, a district measuring from west to east 200 to 500 miles [322 to 805 km], and from north to south about 700 miles [1,126 km]."[28]

Effective Portuguese administration in Mozambique was limited on the coast and petered out about 100 km above the confluence of the Zambezi and Shire. In 1888, the British government, frustrated by the inability of the Portuguese to stem the slave trade, proposed an international blockade of the northern Mozambique coast. The Portuguese countered by imposing their own blockade. However, it proved ineffective, prompting the Anti-Slavery Society to demand the appointment of British consular representatives at Lake Malawi and at Ibo.[29] Because of mounting international and notably British attention from the 1880s, slaves were increasingly diverted from the northern routes running to the Swahili coast to the less closely supervised German and Portuguese territories of East Africa. In 1892, Mackenzie, managing director of the Imperial British East Africa Company, claimed the existence of nine main slave routes from interior East Africa to the coast: Four crossed German Tanganyika; three linked Lake Malawi to Lindi, Kilwa, and Mikindani; while the remaining two cut across Portuguese territory to the Ibo and Quelimane regions.[30]

African slaves were purchased mainly with arms, gunpowder, and cloth – both foreign cloth imported from Zanzibar and Madagascar and locally manufactured manchilla, which formed a staple of internal trade and a local commodity money.[31] On the Mozambique coast, slaves were washed and oiled. Those destined for Indian Ocean islands and Swahili coast markets were split into three main groups: The *pesca*, comprising healthy men and women aged from 18 to 25, commanded the highest price; followed by the *pote d'agua*, healthy slaves aged 14 to 18; and finally other, less desirable slaves. Strong young men were at a premium for the plantation islands; Malagasy demand was greatest for

[28] *ASR* (Feb. 1882), 38; see also *ASR* (March 1882), 69; Colomb, Slave *Catching*, 106, 298, 308–9, 315–17; John Kirk, "Notes on Two Expeditions up the River Rovuma, East Africa," *Journal of the Royal Geographical Society* 35 (1865).

[29] Smith to River, Mozambique, 18 Dec. 1888; *idem* to Assistant Secretary of State, Mozambique, 20 and 21 Feb., 10 April, 10 May and 1 June 1889, US-Moz; Buchanan to Salisbury, Zomba, 29 Jan. 1889 in *ASR* (Nov. and Dec. 1889), 257; Axelson, *Portugal and the Scramble*, 7, 22–3, 62–3, 171–3; Von Wissmann, "From the Congo to the Zambesi," *ASR* (Nov. & Dec. 1891), 292.

[30] O'Neill to Granville, Mozambique, 30 April 1883, *ASR* (March 1884), 47; *ASR* (Dec. 1884), 225; (Jan. 1885), 262; (March and April 1892), 79; Lindsay, "How to Fight the Slave Trade in East Africa," *ASR* (July and Aug. 1888), 123.

[31] Curtin, *Atlantic Slave Trade*, 269, 273–6; Duffy, *Question of Slavery*, 91–3; Axelson, *Portugal and the Scramble*, 41; Alpers, *Ivory and Slaves*, 242.

young men (for reexport) and young women and children (for the domestic market).[32]

The Sea Crossing

Madagascar was not subject to the regular half yearly alternation of the monsoons that characterized the waters of the equatorial and northeast African coast.[33] Mascarene slavers to Madagascar sailed between March and December; seas were calm and there was a regular supply of slaves from the interior of the island where the slaving/trading season coincided with the dry winter months. While the Mascarenes–Madagascar voyage might take only 7 to 10 days, the average length of a return trip was between three and four months – due to the vagaries of the weather and the long preliminary negotiations that traditionally accompanied commercial transactions in Madagascar. Whereas the general pattern of winds and currents was dependable, the advent of cyclones in the rainy season (November to April) was unpredictable. As the southwestern Indian Ocean experienced an average of five to six cyclones a year during the summer, shipping was generally restricted to the months of April to October. Permanent southeast trade winds propelled ships to Madagascar's east coast, but the wind split at approximately latitude 18°S, some 113 km offshore. North of this point, south-southwest winds and a current traveling at about three knots took ships toward Toamasina, Mahavelona, and Antongil Bay; they were obliged to return by sailing in a wide arc, passing close to Tromelin Island. South of latitude 18°S, north-northeast winds and currents of less than three knots pushed ships down the east coast as far as Tolanaro; the return trip involved sailing in a large arc south, then east, and finally northwest. From November to December, coastal winds blew uniformly from the north, so slavers headed for Antongil Bay before turning south.[34]

Conditions differed in the Mozambique Channel. Off the east African coast, a trade current (reaching almost 65 km in 24 hours during the northeast monsoon

[32] Isaacman, *Mozambique*, 88; Leroy Vail and Landeg White, *Capitalism and Colonialism in Mozambique* (London, 1980), 19.

[33] Michel Mollet, "Les relations de l'Afrique de l'est avec l'Asie: essaie de position de quelques problèmes historiques" *Cahiers d'historique mondiale* 13.2 (1971), 294; Colomb, *Slave Catching*, 24, 26–7; Moorson to Commodore Christian, HMS Andromarche, 24 May 1825, in Theal, *Records* IX, 53.

[34] Moorson to Commodore Christian, HMS Andromarche, 24 May 1825 in Theal, *Records* IX, 53; Filliot, *La traite des esclaves*, 13–14, 104–5, 222; Auguste Toussaint, "Le trafic commercial entre les Mascareignes et Madagascar de 1773 à 1810," *Annales de l'Université de Madagascar* (1966), 95–6.

from April to November) ran past Cape Amber and divided at Cape Delgado. A perennial southern current (attaining a velocity of almost 100 km in 24 hours during the southwest monsoon) affected the Mozambique coast. From October to April, the northeast monsoon affected northwest Madagascar, while for the rest of the year winds varied from south to west between noon and nightfall, after which they varied between south and east.

Nevertheless, trans-Mozambique Channel traffic was generally determined by the monsoons. As was noted in 1859,

The slaves are first taken to depots in St. Augustine's Bay and Bojanna [Boina] bay on the west coast of Madagascar from all parts of the east coast of Africa, but principally from Quiloa [Kilwa] and Ibo during the northeast monsoon and from St.António [Angoche] and Quizungo [Quissanga] during the southwest monsoon.[35]

In the early nineteenth century, trade expeditions into interior Mozambique aligned themselves with this pattern, leaving the coast from late January, after the first ships with foreign trade goods started to reach the coast on the northeast monsoon. From May or June, expeditions that commonly remained for two years in the interior began to return to the coast by August in time for the start of the southwest monsoon. However, the system of winds and currents in the Mozambique Channel differed from the more regular pattern in the equatorial region further north. This had two major effects on the slave export trade. First, slave dhows plying the trans-Channel trade from Mozambique were able to ship slaves to Madagascar all year round. This contrasted with trade between Madagascar and both the Swahili coast and the Mascarenes, which was seasonal. Second, in contrast to Madagascar, slaving in hinterland Mozambique, notably in the region of Lake Malawi, continued throughout the year, ensuring a ready supply of slaves in coastal embarkation points and keeping slave prices low on the Mozambique coast.[36] The trans-Mozambique Channel run, which generally peaked from December to January (when Mascarene–Malagasy trade was at a standstill), kept the Sakalava and Bara well-supplied with trade goods, notably

---

[35] Cape Commissioners (June, 1859), quoted in Duffy, *Question of Slavery*, 46; see also Moorson to Commodore Christian, HMS Andromarche, 24 May 1825 in Theal, *Records* IX, 53; Lloyd, "Memoir" (1851), 54.

[36] Colomb, *Slave Catching*, 32–3, 457–8; Frere to Granville, 3 April 1873, *CFM*; Kirk to Granville, Zanzibar, 3 April 1872, no. 8 in "East Coast of Africa: Correspondence Respecting the Slave Trade" (1 Jan.– 31 Dec. 1872); Salisbury to Adams, 9 Sept. 1879, no. 65; *idem*, 29 Sept. 1879, no. 67; Pakenham to Salisbury, 3 Oct. 1879, no. 77; O'Neill to Salisbury, Mozambique, 6, 7, and 9 Sept. 1879, nos. 117 and 120 – in "The Slave Trade, 1879–80" – *Correspondence Relating to the Slave Trade*; M.A. Cutfield, "letter," Mozambique Channel, 16 July 1883, in *ASR* (Sept. 1883), 228; see also O'Neil, "Journey in the District West of Cape Delgado Bay, September–October 1882," in *ASR* (July, 1883), 180–1; *ASR* (Aug. 1883), 194; Isaacman, *Mozambique*, 75, 82.

arms, throughout the year. It thus played a critical role in enabling them to resist the Merina imperial advance. Slave cargoes destined for the French sugar islands were often shipped around July, at harvest time, when demand for field hands was at its height. A slave dhow generally took from three to nine days to cross the Channel, depending on the currents, weather, and destination.[37]

From 1806 to 1816, during the Napoleonic Wars, the British Navy liberated at Cape Town over 2,000 slaves captured aboard French ships in the southwest Indian Ocean.[38] However, with the conclusion of peace, the British were forbidden from searching foreign vessels. Subsequently, the British concentrated their antislave patrols almost exclusively off West Africa and the trans-Mozambique Channel slave trade was conducted openly. Indeed, until Owen's 1823 survey, the British were more familiar with the coastal geography of Australia and China than of the 2,100-km coastline of Portuguese East Africa or the 9,935-km coastline of Madagascar. The 1815 Britanno–Portuguese Treaty prohibited Portuguese subjects from the slave trade north of the equator, but left them free south of the line. The first measure affecting the slave trade of the region was the 1820 Britanno–Merina treaty banning slave exports from Merina territory. This was given teeth in a revised treaty of 1823 empowering the British navy

to seize and detain all ships and other vessels, whether of or belonging to the subjects of Madagascar, or of any other nation or people whatever, which shall be found in any harbour, port, roadstead, creek or river, or on or near the shores and coasts of Madagascar, carrying on the traffic in slaves, or aiding and abetting in carrying on such traffic.[39]

Nevertheless, the British antislave trade squadron largely ignored the region until the 1840s. Not until 1839 did Britain proclaim the right to search suspect Portuguese ships, and only in 1842 was a naval patrol established in the Mozambique Channel. This resulted in some 4,000 prize Negroes being landed at Cape Town between 1839 and 1846 and a further 2,532 being shipped to the Seychelles from 1861 to 1872.[40] However, rarely as many as three cruisers were employed, and captains of slaving ships quickly became adept at avoiding them, cooperating to establish an effective system of warning signals.[41]

Slaves were shipped on vessels of varying sizes. Although rarely directly involved in slave shipments, Indian merchants provided old India-built ships

---

[37] Moorson to Commodore Christian, HMS Andromarche, 24 May 1825 in Theal, *Records* IX, 53; Lloyd, "Memoir" (1851), 54.

[38] Patrick Harries, "Culture and Classification: A History of the Mozbieker Community at the Cape," *Social Dynamics* 26.2 (2000), 32.

[39] Quoted in Colomb, *Slave Catching*, 313; see also *ibid*, 314; Lloyd *The Navy*, 198–9, 227.

[40] Harries, "Culture and Classification," 32–3.

[41] Beachey, *Slave Trade*, 19–20; Vail and White, *Capitalism*, 17–18, 21–2.

that had made their last respectable voyage with the annual flotilla from western India to Madagascar and Mozambique. It was noted that "cheap and old vessels are preferred; they have an almost equal chance of making the voyage before a regular trade wind and, if captured, are a smaller loss."[42] However, the most commonly used vessel for the trans-Mozambique Channel run was the Swahili or Arab captained *betela* dhow, possessing an average crew of five or six men. The *betela* could match most British naval vessels for speed until the development of steam from the 1840s. Even then, capture was rare, as sighted dhows would run for coastal waters where they were generally safe because of their shallow draft. Not until 1883 did the British Navy order special light draft steam launches that could follow dhows into the innumerable small coastal creeks and channels that characterized both the Malagasy and African sides of the Mozambique Channel. Again, however, a combination of speed and an intimate knowledge of local coastlines, winds, and currents frequently enabled dhow pilots to outmaneuver British patrols.[43]

Swahili and Mascarene traders also devised devious slave trade routes. For example, many Mozambique slaves, destined for Réunion, were shipped first to coastal barracoons in West Madagascar. There, they were joined by Malagasy captives from the interior and then dispatched to the Seychelles, where they could be detained for several months awaiting the opportune moment to be sent to the Mascarenes.[44] The 1833 British extension of the Franco–British naval accord on the mutual right of inspection in all waters within 20 leagues (111 km) of Madagascar encouraged slavers to run up flags of other nations, until the French withdrew from the agreement in 1841. In 1844, the British insisted that ships' flags be verified, but their patrols could not enforce this measure on ships carrying French colors, unless within Malagasy waters as defined by the 1833 accord. Slavers minimized risks by sailing under cover of dark and carrying false papers in which Nantes forgers specialized, and which the French readily made available to regional slave runners.[45] From the 1840s, slavers also flew

---

[42] Frere to Granville, 29 May 1873, *CFM*.

[43] *ASR* (Feb. 1882), 39 and (Sept. 1883), 230; Colomb, *Slave Catching*, 38, 457; Daniel P. Mannix, *Black Cargoes. A History of the Atlantic Slave Trade, 1518–1865* (New York, 1962), 259.

[44] Darling to King, Mauritius, 18 May 1820, *PRO.CO*.167/50, 115; De Polignac, "The Slave Ship Success" (4 Oct. 1821), *PRO.CO*.167/77; Farquhar to Iman of Muscat, Port Louis, 10 July 1822; Moresby to Farquhar, 12 and 13 Aug. 1822; Hay to Moresby, Port Louis, 15 Oct.1822; Moresby to Farish, Bombay, 25 Sept. 1822 – *PRO.CO*.167/63; *La feuille hebdomadaire* (1819–32); "Further Returns Relating to Slaves in the Colonies: no. 2, Mauritius," *HCPP* 15 (1828); Lowry Cole to Horton, Mauritius, 22 June 1825, *PRO.CO*.167/77; Owen to Lowry Cole, 4 Aug. 1825, *PRO.CO*.167/78 pt.II.

[45] Owen to Lowry Cole, 4 Aug. 1825, *PRO.CO*.167/78 pt. II; Louis Lacroix, *Les derniers négriers* (Paris,[1939]), 35–6, 38, 40–1, 43–4, 67–8, 86, 184; Lovejoy, *Transformations in Slavery*, 145–7; Campbell, "Madagascar and the Slave Trade," 210–12; Barnard, *Three Years' Cruise*,

U.S. colors. However, the United States admitted the right of search in 1863, and it was noted in 1878 that flying the American flag 'would not afford the protection it would were the craft American built.'[46]

British recognition of French dominance in Madagascar, following the 1883–5 Franco–Merina War, led to increased use of the French flag. In 1890, when the British formally acknowledged a French protectorate in Madagascar, they relinquished their right to stop vessels in Malagasy waters. Indeed, when H.M.S. *Redbreast* searched a dhow carrying French colors off Madagascar, French authorities successfully claimed an indemnity from the British government, on the grounds that the search violated the Brussels Convention.[47] The consequence, it was claimed, was a resurgence in the slave trade:

The Africa-Malagasy Slave-trade has received a great impetus by British cruisers having been withdrawn from Malagasy waters. The Slave-traders, who are mostly Arabs flying the French flag on their dhows, now carry on their horrible calling with impunity, a French cruiser not having for a long while come south of Mojanga – to the southward of which the Slave-trade is conducted.[48]

French flags dominated on slavers catering for the French plantation islands, although from the 1883–5 war, due to a decreased British naval presence, Zanzibari/Arab colors flourished on the Madagascar run, it being noted that "the [slave] traffic is principally carried on in vessels under Arab colours, though dhows under French colours are reported to have landed Slaves at some Sakalava ports."[49] Alidy, a prominent Muslim Sakalava and Abd-er-Rhamen, a Swahili trader, were among those who flew the red flag of Zanzibar on their boats.[50] American colors also proved popular, especially on the southwest coast, and their use increased from the outbreak of the 1883–5 war, as non-French slavers sought to escape possible harassment by the French fleet.[51]

218; Hafkin, "Trade, Society and Politics," 233–54; Frere, to Granville, 27 Feb. 1873, *CFM*; Curtin, *Atlantic Slave Trade*, 79, 269, 273–6; Samat, "Notes" (1852), 67; Beachey, *Slave Trade*, 23; see also Norman R. Bennett, "Americans in Zanzibar: 1865–1915" in *idem, Studies in East African History* (Boston, 1963), 33–4; Colomb, *Slave Catching*, 59; Duffy, *Question of Slavery*, 91–3; Axelson, *Portugal and the Scramble*, 41.

46 Hathorne to Arnold, Hines & Co, Zanzibar, 3 May 1878 – Hathorne, "Letterbook" (1878–80).
47 Rear Admiral Richards to Macgregor, Mauritius, 30 Aug. 1886, *ASR* (Sept. and Oct. 1887), 149; *ASR* (March and April 1893), 79, 84, 87; Smith to Assistant Secretary of State, Mozambique, 20 Feb. 1889, *US-Moz.*
48 Anon, "letter," Madagascar, 21 March 1893, *ASR* (March and April 1893), 86.
49 Commander Forsyth, "Despatch" to Rear Admiral Fremantle, 30 Oct. 1888, *ASR* (Oct. 1888) 257; see also Bennett, "Americans in Zanzibar," 33–4; Colomb, *Slave Catching*, 59.
50 McMahon, "The Sakalava"; Bousserand, "Notice sur les tribus," 130; *CdM*, 134 (13 March 1894).
51 Stanwood to Whitney, 30 June 1883, *idem* to Whitney and Robinson, Morondava, 1 Aug. 1883; "Memo" no. 1 in Stanwood to Robinson, 13 July 1884 – *US*.

Slaves crossed the Mozambique Channel either as a specific cargo, of on average 150 to 200 slaves, or as part of a general cargo, of which they constituted a profitable sideline. Slave dhows could be up to 350 tons. Those of between 80 and 100 tons could carry up to 150 slaves and specially adapted dhows as many as 250 slaves – in August and September 1867, two cargoes, totaling 500 slaves, were landed in Passandava Bay.[52] Occasionally, specialist long distance slaving dhows from the northern network were diverted into the southern Mozambique Channel trade. They could carry up to 400 slaves, although this was still 50 percent of the slave-carrying capacity of the large European slavers used for the Atlantic run during the first half of the nineteenth century.[53] Most European and American slavers were specially adapted for the purpose, while Arab dhows would normally carry a mixed cargo. This entailed far less risk as the 5 to 20 slaves aboard could generally be passed off as crewmembers. In 1865, it was even noted of the northeast coast of Madagascar, an area relatively unfrequented by slavers from the 1820s, that "notwithstanding the efforts of the British against the slave trade, several slaves are brought to Vohimare under the pretence of being sailors and servants of the owners of the Arab dhows, and then sold to the Hova [Merina] officials."[54] As Frere commented generally of the slave trade to Madagascar in the early 1870s:

After landing their Indian supercargo with the import cargo of cloth etc., at Madagascar, they [the Arabs – i.e., Swahili] stand over to the opposite Portuguese coast, pick up a small cargo of slaves at the outposts with which they return to Madagascar, making sometimes more than one trip of this kind before it is time to return northwards. These dhows are said frequently to put into the Comoro islands for water and provisions, and sometimes clandestinely part with some of their slaves there; but they generally put into the Sakalava ports or unfrequented harbours which abound on the Madagascar coast.[55]

Mounting demand for slaves in the Merina empire in the 1880s led to higher profits and continued involvement despite the risks. To minimize the latter, dhows carried arms, often modern pieces obtained from American and European traders. In one case, in October 1888, the armed crews of three slave dhows off

[52] Colomb, *Slave Catching*, 311; Duffy, *Question of Slavery*, 46.

[53] Hafkin, "Trade, Society and Politics," 233–54; Colomb, *Slave Catching*, 35, 48; *CFM* (27 Feb. 1873); Curtin, *Atlantic Slave Trade*, 79; Samat, "Notes" (1852), 67; Beachey, *Slave Trade*, 23; Barnard, *Three Years' Cruise*, 76, 137–8; Kirk to Granville, Zanzibar, 3 April 1872 no. 8 in "East Coast of Africa: Correspondence Respecting the Slave Trade" (1 Jan.–31 Dec. 1872); Earl to Corbett, Zanzibar, 30 June 1879, no. 407, "The Slave Trade, 1879–80" – *Correspondence Relating to the Slave Trade*.

[54] H.Maundrell, "A Visit to the North-East Province of Madagascar," *Journal of the Royal Geographical Society* 37 (1867), 115–16.

[55] Report, 12 March 1873; see also "Report" (1844); Granville's correspondence, 31 Oct.–9 Nov. 1872 – *CFM*; Colomb, *Slave Catching*, 41; Alpers, *Ivory and Slaves*, 211; Liesegang, "First Look," 491–2.

Maintirano took on a British patrol, killing one British seaman before landing 142 slaves.[56]

The Slaving Frontier in West Madagascar

Following the 1820 Britanno–Merina treaty, the Malagasy slave trade was concentrated in the west of the island. A unique feature of this trade was that it involved both the import and the export of slaves: Most ports north of the Manambolo River imported east African slaves for the domestic market and for reexport to the French plantation islands; those to the south exported Malagasy slaves, chiefly of plateau origin, to the French islands, notably Réunion, via the Seychelles.[57] A number of west coast ports received east African slaves: By the early 1870s, an estimated 13 percent (rising to over 30 percent in the 1880s) were landed at Maintirano, 35 percent (4,000 slaves annually) to ports to its north, and 35 percent to ports to its south.[58]

Most African slave imports destined for imperial Merina markets were subsequently transhipped to Mahajanga, the main west coast port under Merina rule. Possessing good anchorage, Mahajanga lay at the mouth of the Betsiboka river, navigable for 80 km, which provided a clear route to the plateau. The route passed through the major upriver collection center of Marovoay, where Frere (1873) noted "the enormous numbers of African negroes everywhere seen."[59]

The independent northwest coast was also the initial center for the export of Malagasy and reexport of African slaves to the French plantation islands. From the early 1830s, a significant role was played by the port of Baly, of which it was commented in 1859:

This trade, infamous in the way it is generally carried on, brings to every beach numerous boats lured by the prospect of a fabulous profit (the engagé who may be purchased for 20 to 29 piastres can be sold on Réunion for up to 200 or 240 piastres).[60]

---

[56] Colomb, *Slave Catching*, 39–40; "Letter," Majanga, 10 Nov. 1888, *ASR* (March and April 1889), 104.

[57] Grandidier, "Souvenirs," 26–8; Beachey, *Slave Trade*, 28–9; Campbell, "Madagascar and the Slave Trade."

[58] Frere to Granville, Mozambique, 27 Feb. 1873 and 29 May 1873, *CFM*; see also Colomb, *Slave Catching*, 309–11; Stanwood, "memo" 2 (21 Aug. 1883); "Memo" no. 2 in Stanwood to Robinson, 13 July 1884, *US*; R.Coupland, *Exploitation of East Africa* (London, 1939), 53–6; Freemantle, despatch, Zanzibar, 8 Sept. 1888, and Michahelles to Lacau, Zanzibar, 12 Sept. 1888, *ASR* (Nov. and Dec. 1888), 206–8.

[59] Frere to Granville, 29 May 1873, *CFM*; see also Colomb, *Slave Catching*, 309–11; see also Jean Valette, "Quelques renseignements sur Madagascar en 1843," *BdM* 183 (1961), 688.

[60] P. Jouen aux supérieurs en France (1859), *AHVP* C28i; Grandidier, "Souvenirs," 10; *Annales maritimes et coloniales* II.46 (1831), 91–108; see also Johns to [LMS], Antananarivo, 8 Nov. 1826, *SOAS/LMS-MIL*, B2.F3.JC.

One source claims that from 1835, Arab and Indian slavers conducted "veritable round-ups of population" in western Madagascar for new markets in the Americas and in India.[61] If it existed, such demand was a temporary phenomenon for, from the 1830s, virtually the sole market for Malagasy slaves was the French plantation islands. It is more likely that the slave trade, including the clandestine traffic in *engagés*, expanded in mid-century because of higher demand on Réunion (where slavery was abolished in 1848) and increased supply both from Mozambique and from West Madagascar as the Mascarene trading frontier moved south of Cape St. André.[62]

Samat, a Creole trader, boasted that, at a moment's notice, he could supply between 6,000 and 8,000 *engagés* from Baly Bay. However, Mascarene traders found their activity on the northwest coast hindered by imperial Merina hostility to the export of potential manpower and by the entrenched position of the Swahili, described by Samat as a "a damnable caste who greatly obstruct the Europeans who visit this coast."[63] Consequently, Mascarene traders moved steadily southward down the west coast, establishing direct commercial contact with Sakalava chiefs. However, they were followed immediately by Indian and Swahili traders who, because they possessed more resources and forged political alliances with the Sakalava, quickly established control over the slave traffic. Thus Maintirano, the major slave entrepôt in the late 1800s, was ruled in the name of Queen Bibiasa of southern Menabe by Alidy, who, in conjunction with Abd-er-Rhamen, dominated the slave trade of the mid-west coast. With Indian backing, the Swahili in Madagascar managed a two-way slave traffic, buying from the Sakalava for export to the French plantation islands and importing from the Mozambique and Swahili coasts to supplement the regional French trade and supply the internal Malagasy market. Their middlemen position was so dominant that they could demand higher prices from Mascarene and Western slave traders than could Sakalava chiefs and insist on payment in dollars.[64]

The arms received in return for slaves helped to fuel Sakalava and Bara slaving forays, which, following the halt to Merina military expansion in mid-century, became increasingly daring, penetrating both Betsileo and Imerina. These raids exacerbated the manpower shortage in the imperial Merina heartland,

---

[61] Chapus, *Quatre-vingts années*, 280.

[62] Campbell, "Madagascar and the Slave Trade."

[63] Samat, "Notes" (1852), 62; see also Rasoamiaramanana, "Aspects économiques" (1973), 10–11, 35, 54; Noel, "Ile de Madagascar" (1843), 19, 27–38, 93, 99; Grandidier, "Souvenirs," 28.

[64] W. H. Hall, *Narratives of the Voyages and Services on the Nemesis* (London, 1844); Noel, "Ile de Madagascar" (1843); "Report" (1844); N.Landmark, *Det Norske missionsselskab* (Kristiania, 1899), 169; J. Duffy, *A Question of Slavery* (Oxford, 1967), Ch. 3.

intensifying demand there for imported African slaves.[65] Merina officials in provincial garrisons proved powerless to stop the raids. Indeed, some colluded with them. When Ramboamadio, an officer at Mahabo garrison (near Morondava), was summoned to Antananarivo in 1874 to answer charges of collusion with Tovenkery, the local Sakalava king, in slave raiding in the area, he secured his acquittal by bribing Rainimaharavo, the Merina secretary of state, with a gift and $2,000 in cash.[66]

The Sakalava retained some female plateau captives, but as the numbers seized were always surplus to requirements in a predominantly pastoral economy, most were sold for export to Mascarene and other slavers on the coast. The price differential meant that the Sakalava could work a slave during his or her prime years, usually in agriculture, and subsequently still sell the slave at a high price to the Merina or the French.[67]

Attempting to bypass the Indians and Swahili, Mascarene traders moved south from Maintirano to the ports of Morondava, Morombe, and Toliara.[68] However, the absence on the coast south of Maintirano of an organized body of middlemen frequently obstructed trade as, due to a lack of capital and credit, suppliers were almost totally dependent upon fluctuations in demand. Thus, slave raids were launched into the Malagasy interior only after the arrival of the first Mascarene slaving ships of the season in June. Chiefs were rarely able to guarantee sufficient slaves even for later arrivals, and frustrated buyers frequently either tried to enslave local people, particularly if they had already expended considerable sums on trade preliminaries, or sailed north to the more stable markets of Iboina.[69] Some firms established agents on the west coast to

[65] Barnard, *A Three Years' Cruise in the Mozambique Channel for the Suppression of the Slave Trade* (London, 1848), 133; Lloyd, "Memoir" (1851), 62; E. O. McMahon, "The Sakalava and their Customs," *AAMM* 4 (1890); FJOD, "South West Coast," *The Madagascar Times* (27 Nov. 1886); Stanwood, "letter," Andakabe, 12 Oct. 1882, *US*.

[66] Pakenham to Granville, Tamatave, 3 Jan. 1874, *PRO.CO*.84/1397, and 19 Oct. 1876, *PRO.CO*.84/1474 ERD/2270; *idem* to Derby, Tamatave, 30 Jan. 1877, *PRO.CO*.84/1474 ERD/2270; Kestell-Cornish to Pakenham, "Tsoavanandriana," 26 Sept. 1876, *PRO.CO*.84/1474 ERD/2270; Rasoamiaramanana, "Aspects économiques" (1973), 40–54; *ASR* (Jan. and Feb. 1887), 10; Knott to Aitken, Mojanga, 21 March 1888, *ASR* (Nov. and Dec. 1888), 217; Mullens, *Twelve Months in Madagascar*, 326–7; Anon, "Report," Tamatave, 9 Dec. 1888, *ASR* (Jan. and Feb. 1889), 46; Campbell, "Madagascar and the Slave Trade."

[67] Alpers, *Ivory and Slaves*, 214–15; *ASR* (June, 1883), 170; Lloyd, "Memoir" (1851), 55, 63.

[68] Campbell, "Madagascar and the Slave Trade."

[69] Hathorne to Arnold, Hines & Co, Zanzibar, 26 July 1878; *idem* to Bertram, Zanzibar, 26 July 1878 – "Letters of H.Hathorne, agent of Arnold, Hines & Co, New York and John Bertram, Salem, and US consul at Zanzibar, 1878–1880" – *PM*; Ryder to Ropes, Emmerton & Co, and Arnold, Hines & Co, Nossi Bé, 15 April 1884 – Partner and Agency Records. Madagascar Agencies. Correspondence Sent (Letterbook, 1884–7), Feb.–May 1884, B44.F6, *EI*.

stockpile slaves for regular shipment. However, they were subject to frequent and arbitrary demands by local chiefs and their retinue for gifts which, if not forthcoming, would be seized by force.[70]

The Franco–Merina War, in which the labor issue was prominent, undermined what little authority the Merina possessed on the west coast. This resulted in a dramatic increase in the slave trade and fueled Sakalava resistance to the Merina, as French merchants imported large quantities of arms in return for slaves.[71] Subsequently, most foreign traders on the west coast became involved directly or indirectly in the slave trade. Large, supposedly respectable concerns such as Roux de Fraissinet and Vidal et Roger were quickly drawn into the dubious *engagé* trade, while most foreign firms imported arms from the United States, South Africa, and Mozambique. These constituted the chief payment for slaves and were an essential component in slave raiding.[72]

However, Franco–Sakalava relations deteriorated once it became apparent that the French protectorate imposed in 1885 was a sham. Consequently, in 1886, Mascarene traders at Toliara for the first time started mounting their own slave raids, causing severe disruption in the hinterland.[73] The Sakalava countered by attacking European trading posts, forcing the abandonment of agencies on the Malagasy mainland.[74] This served to profit Indian and Swahili traders who, by the late 1880s, comprised an estimated 90 percent of arms and slave dealers on the west coast.[75]

---

[70] Grandidier, "Souvenirs," 24–5; Stanwood to Robinson, Morondava, 1 Dec. 1880, *US* ; *GH* (1928), 272; Campbell, "Madagascar and the Slave Trade," 220–4; see also Sundström, *Exchange Economy*, 17; Beachey, *Slave Trade*, 60; Pankhurst, *Economic History of Ethiopia*, 884–9.

[71] *ASR* (Feb. 1883), 43; (Sept. 1883), 302; Waller, "letter" to the Times, *ASR* (June 1883), 164); Haggard, "letter," Tamatave, 18 Nov. 1886 in *ASR* (July and Aug. 1888), 135; Lawrence C. Goodrich, "France and the Slave Trade in Madagascar," *The Nineteenth Century* (Aug. 1883); Robinson to Third Assistant Secretary of State, 15 Oct. 1881; Stanwood to Robinson, Andakabe, 28 Aug. 1884 – *US*.

[72] The 1888 East African arms embargo did not apply to Madagascar – see Smith to Rives, Mozambique, 18 Dec. 1888; Smith to Assistant Secretary of State, Mozambique, 21 and 26 Feb. 1889, *US-Moz*; Stanwood to Ravoninahitriniarivo, Andakabe, 31 Aug. 1886; Stanwood to Robinson, Andakabe, 23 Sept. 1886 – *US*; Campbell, "East African Slave Trade," 11.

[73] Stanwood, "Commercial Situation," Andakabe, 31 Dec. 1886; Stanwood's correspondence, 20 Aug. to 27 Dec. 1887, *US*; Dahle to PM, Antananarivo, 1 Dec. 1883, HH6, 489–90, *ANM*.

[74] See Chapter 8.

[75] McMahon, "The Sakalava"; Bousserand, "Notice sur les tribus," 130; *CdM* 134 (13 March 1894); Kirk to Granville, Zanzibar, 3 April 1872, no. 8 in "Correspondence Respecting the Slave Trade" (1873); Frere to Granville, Mozambique Channel, 27 Feb. and 12 March 1873 – *CFM*; Graves to Granville, 22 March 1884, no. 26, *English Blue Book*; Rostvig, *Sakalaverne*, 244; Pickersgill, "North Sakalava-land," 29–43; Robinson to Adee, 29 Oct. 1884; Stanwood to Robinson (incl. in Stanwood to Bayard), Andakabe, 31 Oct. 1886; Stanwood to Campbell, Andakabe,

Prices and Profits

In Imerina, as on the Mascarenes, *Masombika* were reputed to be strong, hard-working, and less truculent than Malagasy slaves. This was reflected in slave prices; as Abdalla commented in Mahajanga, in 1824: "Mozambiques are in demand in the interior and bring from 40 to 50 head of cattle, though Ova [i.e., Merina] slaves are not worth more than 8 to 10 bullocks in their own country."[76] A slave trader needed to lubricate transactions through numerous small gifts to the local sovereign and court entourage, while the contract was frequently sealed by a *fatidra* (blood brotherhood ceremony).[77] Until 1820, Mascarene traders bought slaves for cash, arms, or cloth. Subsequently, cloth and arms were the dominant forms of payment, although the Swahili on the northwest coast – while buying nonslave staples with imported cotton cloth and slaves – insisted that Mascarene traders pay dollars for slaves.[78] By contrast, on the west coast south of the Manambolo River, arms were by far the chief form of payment for Malagasy slaves. For instance, 81 percent of the price paid for slaves in Toliara in the mid–1880s comprised gunpowder and arms; and approximately $50,000 in arms and $7,000 in cotton piece goods were imported annually into St. Augustin Bay to pay for slave exports. European, South African, and U.S. traders dominated the arms import trade.[79] On the Mascarenes, most slaves were purchased in cash. Those exported from Madagascar after 1820 were generally landed on Réunion; surveillance there was slacker than on Mauritius and, as noted in 1825, "slaves are sold for much higher prices at Bourbon [Réunion] than here [Mauritius]" (see Table 9.2 and Illustration 9).[80]

Slave trading profits could be high. In 1860, Richard Burton considered that in East Africa, slave traders buying in the interior gained a 500 percent profit when selling in coastal markets where slave prices more than trebled

---

25 Aug., 19 Sept., and 21 Dec. 1887; Campbell to Razafindrazaka, 26 May 1890 – *US*; Knott to British Foreign Secretary, Mahajanga, 29 March 1895, "Correspondence of the British Vice Consulate in Majunga" (1894–7), *AM*; Esoavelomandroso, "La region du Fiheregna"; Prud'homme, "Considérations," 29; Liesegang, "First Look," 451–523; Jose Capela, "The Mujojos Slave Trade in Moçambique, 1830–1902" paper presented at the *Workshop on the Long-Distance Trade in Slaves*, SOAS (December, 1987), 4–5.

[76] Quoted in Hastie, "Diary" (1824–5); see also Hastie, "Diary" (1817), 158, 164–5.

[77] Filliot, *La traite des esclaves*, 192–5.

[78] Maundrell, "A Visit," 115–16; *GH* (1928), 39, 304; Samat, "Notes" (1852), 57.

[79] *ASR* (Jan. and Feb. 1887), 11; Stanwood to Whitney, 30 June 1883; *idem* to Whitney and Robinson, Morondava, 1 Aug. 1883; "Memo" no. 1 in Stanwood to Robinson, 13 July 1884 – *US*.

[80] Lowry Cole to Bathurst, Mauritius, 21 June 1825, *PRO.CO*.167/50, 193–203, 320–3; see also Lacroix, *Les derniers négriers*, 69–81, 215.

TABLE 9.2. *The Slave Trade of the Western Indian Ocean Islands: Estimated Annual Value, 1800–95 (in $000s at Point of Import/Export)*

| | Exports | Imports | |
Period	Madagascar	French Islands	Imerina
1801–10	135	n.a.	—
1811–15	33	n.a.	—
1816–20	160	244	—
1821–25	n.a.	198	n.a.
1826–30	n.a.	n.a.	n.a.
1831–40	15	n.a.	43
1841–50	73	n.a.	n.a.
1851–60	150	1,085	n.a.
1861–70	138	n.a.	207
1871–80	94	n.a.	229
1881–90	104	744	191
1891–95	102	744?	n.a.

Source: Campbell, "Madagascar and Mozambique," 177; *idem*, "East African Slave Trade," 18.

9. Public Slave Market, Antananarivo circa 1865

between 1847 and 1856. However, Burton grossly underestimated the capital costs and risks of slaving ventures into the African interior.[81] On regional routes, slave trade profits were as high as 1,000 percent by the second half of the nineteenth century, similar to those made until 1853 on the Mozambique to Rio de Janeiro run. High profits reflected growing demand. In Imerina, for example, the average price of a slave doubled between 1860 and the early 1870s, from around $30 to $62. However, the price then plummeted as a result of the insecurity that followed the 1877 emancipation measure and the deterioration of relations with the French that led to the 1883–5 War. Thereafter, the acute shortage of labor and competition from the French islands drove the price of slaves to $60 by 1895. Such demand induced many former coastal dhows to enter the trans-Mozambique Channel slave trade, making multiple crossings in a single season.[82]

The export price for slaves from Madagascar dropped sharply from 1860 to 1880. On the northwest coast, the average slave price roughly halved, from around $40 to just above $20 between the mid-1860s and mid-1870s. Slaves were even cheaper on the southwest coast due to the lack of middleman charges. At Toliara, the average slave price, only $14 in 1880, rose rapidly during the 1883–5 War: In 1883 *Masombika* at St. Augustin Bay fetched up to $60 for shipment to Réunion – where they sold for an average price of $175. With the resumption of supplies after the war, the price fell to between $25 and $30, although never below the prewar level, due to restricted supply, middleman charges, and sustained demand from the French islands following the 1882 ban on Indian labor.[83] The price varied geographically as, unlike the more stable northwest, each port on the independent mid- and southwest coast charged different rates of duty; in 1880, Toliara taxed most and Maintirano the least.[84]

[81] Colomb, *Slave Catching*, 58; A. G. E. and H. J. Fisher, *Slavery and Muslim Society in Africa* (London, 1970), 61; Cyrus T.Brady Jr, *Commerce and Conquest in East Africa with particular reference to the Salem Trade with Zanzibar* (Salem, 1959), 157.

[82] Curtin, *Atlantic Slave Trade*, 269, 273–6; Duffy, *Question of Slavery*, 91–3; Axelson, *Portugal and the Scramble*, 41; Lloyd, *The Navy*, 189; Campbell, "Madagascar and the Slave Trade."

[83] *ASR* (April 1882), 100; (Feb. 1883), 43; (Sept. 1883), 302; (Jan. and Feb. 1888), 21; (July and Aug. 1889), 176; Campbell, "Madagascar and the Slave Trade," 206–7; Goodrich, "France and the Slave Trade"; Waller, "letter" to the Times, *ASR* (June 1883), 164; Haggard, "letter," Tamatave, 18 Nov. 1886, *ASR* (July and Aug. 1888), 135.

[84] Rostvig to Roll, Tullear, 2 Sept. 1881, and *idem* to Larsen, Toliara, 22 Nov. 1881 – "Toliara Copibok," 458, 480–1, *FLM/NMS*; Stanwood to Robinson, Morondava, 1 Dec. 1880, *US*.

Slave Numbers

An evaluation of the volume of the slave trade needs to take into account slave mortality en route. Treatment of slaves aboard dhows engaged in the northern slave trade, supplying the Muslim markets of Arabia, was generally considered reasonable by British naval officers. Indeed, slave mortality was higher prior to embarkation. Possibly as high as 25 percent of east African slaves died in transit to the coast and in barracoons, while on the Mozambique coast there were instances of almost 30 percent slave mortality.[85] A major influence on slave mortality aboard ship was the weather, dhows generally embarking slaves only in fine weather and with a strong backing wind to ensure a speedy journey. For the East Africa–Mascarene voyage in the early 1800s, J. M. Filliot estimated a 21 percent slave mortality. Estimates for the shorter Mozambique–West Madagascar and East Madagascar–Mascarene runs are of a 12 percent slave mortality – roughly similar to that on Atlantic slave ships during the first half of the nineteenth century.[86] It is highly unlikely that slave mortality at sea declined in succeeding decades; boat speeds remained unaltered and harassment from British naval patrols and overcrowding increased – both of which would have contributed to slower crossings and a greater number of deaths, especially from disease. Specialist slave dhows to the islands of the western Indian Ocean were frequently packed to overcapacity, some boats capsizing as a result; in one such instance a cargo of 120 Makua slaves drowned off the Malagasy coast. In addition to natural hazards, smallpox and dysentery took a heavy toll.[87]

Estimates of the number of slaves involved in the regional slave trade vary considerably. Higher estimates consider over two million slaves were exported from East Africa between 1830 and 1873, when slave shipments from Zanzibar were banned. If mortality through slave raiding and losses en route to the coast are taken into account, the total loss of east African manpower in the nineteenth century could have been over 20 million[88] (see Figure 12 and Table 9.3).

---

[85] Colomb, *Slave Catching*, 41; Alpers, *Ivory and Slaves*, 211; Liesegang, "First Look," 491–2; Mullens, *Twelve Months in Madagascar*, 328.

[86] However, two estimates from the 1820s give 28 percent mortality for slaves in transit between Mozambique and Brazil. See Duffy, *Question of Slavery*, 46; Filliot, *La traite des esclaves*, 227–8; Peter Duignan and Clarence Clendenen, *The United States and the African Slave Trade, 1619–1862* (Stanford University, 1963), 56; Colomb, *Slave Catching*, 43–4; Alpers, *Ivory and Slaves*, 211.

[87] *ASR* (March and April 1893), 86; Mullens, *Twelve Months in Madagascar*, 328; Duignan and Clendenen, *The United States*, 56; Colomb, *Slave Catching*, 41, 43–4.

[88] Helge Kjekshus, *Ecology Control and Economic Development in East African History* (London: Heinemann, 1977), 14–16; Gwyn Campbell, "Introduction" to *idem* (ed), *The Structure of Slavery*.

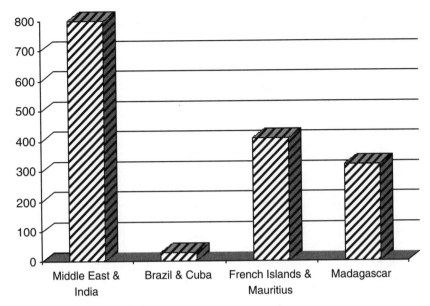

Figure 12. *Estimated Maritime Traffic in East African Slaves in the Nineteenth Century by Final Destination* (Thousands).

Source: Clarence-Smith, *Economics of the Indian Ocean Slave Trade*, 5, 10; Campbell, "Madagascar and Mozambique"; *idem*, "East African Slave Trade"; Pedro Machado, "A Forgotten Corner of the Indian Ocean: Gujarati Merchants, Portuguese India and the Mozambique Slave Trade, c. 1730–1830," in Gwyn Campbell (ed.), *The Structure of Slavery in Indian Ocean Africa and Asia* (London, 2004), Ch. 2.

Austen's revised estimates indicate 800,000 slaves exported from East Africa to Islamic countries to the north in the nineteenth century, 300,000 across the Red Sea and Gulf of Aden, and the rest from the Swahili coast.[89] However, Sheriff emphasizes that nineteenth-century demand for African slaves in the Middle East was generally low as few sectors there experienced economic development. This was reflected by the relocation of the Omani ruling elite to East Africa where the slave trade fed its Zanzibar and Pemba plantations and only in part Persian Gulf markets.[90] Indeed, demand from the French islands and

---

[89] Ralph Austen, "The 19th Century Islamic Slave Trade from East Africa (Swahili and Red Sea Coasts): A Tentative Census" in William Gervase Clarence-Smith (ed.), *The Economics of the Indian Ocean Slave Trade* (London: Frank Cass, 1989), 21–44.

[90] Behnaz Mirzai, "The, 1848 Abolitionist *Farman*: a Step Towards Ending the Slave Trade in Iran" in Campbell (ed.) *Abolition and its Aftermath*; Abdul Sheriff, "The Slave Trade and its Fallout in the Persian Gulf" in Campbell (ed.), *Abolition and its Aftermath*; see also *idem, Slaves, Spices and Ivory*.

TABLE 9.3. *The Slave Trade in the Southwest Indian Ocean: Estimated Annual Traffic, 1801–95*

Traffic Period	Exports			Imports	
	Portuguese East Africa	Swahili Coast	Madagascar	French Islands	Madagascar
1801–10	5,000	3,000	1,500	2,000	n.a.
1811–15	10,000	8,000	600	3,720	n.a.
1816–20	14,000	20,000	3,560	6,975	n.a.
1821–25	20,000	20,000	n.a.	6,588	2,500
1826–30	20,000	20,000	n.a.	7,823	4,906
1831–40	20,000	30,000	3,000	n.a.	8,536
1841–50	15,000	20,000	3,500	n.a.	n.a.
1851–60	20,000	20,000	4,000	10,338	n.a.
1861–70	n.a.	18,691+	4,000	4,250+	5,000
1871–80	8,000	20,000+	4,000+	4,250+	6,750
1881–90	20,000	10,000	4,000+	4,250+	5,500
1891–95	n.a.	9,000	4,250	4,250	n.a.

Source: ASR (April 1882), 100–1; (June 1883), 164–5; (July 1883), 176; (Aug. 1883), 197; (Jan. and Feb. 1887), 11; (Mar. and Apr. 1889), 106; (Nov. and Dec. 1889), 278; (Sept. and Oct. 1893), 257; Berlioux, *Slave Trade in Africa*, 1–2; Colomb, *Slave Catching*, 46; Fisher, *Slavery and Muslim Society*, 61; Mannix, *Black Cargoes*, 246, 250; Alpers, *Ivory and Slaves*, 215, 217; *Les Missions Catholiques* 435 (1877); Norman R. Bennett, "France and Zanzibar" in *idem* et al. (eds.), *Eastern African History* (New York, 1969), 148–75; Filliot, *La traite des esclaves*, 67–9, 126–8; Horace Waller, "letter" to *The Times* in ASR (May, 1881), 78–9; Frere to Granville, 27 Feb. & 29 May 1873 – *CFM*; Stanwood, "memo" 2 (21 Aug. 1883); Memo no. 2 in Stanwood to Robinson, 13 July 1884 – *US*; Lowry Cole to Bathurst, Mauritius, 21 June 1825, PRO.CO 167/50, 193, 203, 320–3; Lacroix, *Les derniers négriers*, 69–81, 215; Hastie, "Diary" (1824–5); Campbell, "Madagascar and the Slave Trade," 208; Coupland, *Exploitation of East Africa*, 53–6; Hafkin, "Trade, Society and Politics," 233–54; M. D. D. Newitt, "Angoche, the Slave Trade and the Portuguese, c. 1844–1912," *JAH* 13.4 (1972), 659–72; Kirk to Granville, 5 March and 3 April 1872, "Correspondence Respecting the Slave Trade" (1873); Pakenham to Lord Tenterden, Tamatave, 3 April 1876, *PRO.CO* 84 1449/ERD/2270; Duffy, *Question of Slavery*, 46, 51–2, 65–8; Borchgrevink, "letter," Morondava, 27 Sept. 1870 in *Norsk Missionsytilande* (1871), 224; Vail and White, *Capitalism*, 12–24; Beachey, *Slave Trade*, 14, 17, 24–5; Alpers, *Ivory and Slaves*, 187, 192–3, 213, 215–16; Liesegang, "First Look," 460, 466, 563; Allen Isaacman, *The Tradition of Resistance in Mozambique* (London, 1976), 6; Sheriff, *Slaves, Spices and Ivory*, 226; Newitt, *Portuguese Settlement*, 22.

Madagascar may have promoted east African slave exports more than Middle Eastern markets.[91]

---

[91] Gwyn Campbell, "Unfree Labour and the Significance of Abolition in Madagascar, circa 1825–1897" in *idem* (ed.) *Abolition and its Aftermath*; Richard Allen, "The Mascarene Slave Trade and Labour Migration in the Indian Ocean during the Eighteenth and Nineteenth Centuries" in Campbell (ed.), *The Structure of Slavery*, 33–50; see also Richard Allen, "Licentious and Unbridled Proceedings: The Illegal Slave Trade to Mauritius and the Seychelles during the early nineteenth century," *Journal of African History* 42 (2001), 91–116; Campbell, "The East African Slave Trade,"1–27.

Conventional assumptions that the 1820 Britanno–Merina Treaty and the Moresby Treaty of 1822 ended the slave trade in waters south of Cape Delgado have long been discredited. Slaves were exported from the Swahili and Mozambique coasts to the Mascarenes, neighboring French islands, and, increasingly from the 1820s, Madagascar. Indeed, there is evidence that from 1873 a considerable portion of the slave traffic formerly channeled through Zanzibar to Muslim markets in the north was diverted into this southern trade.[92]

Possibly over 12,000 slaves per annum were shipped from Mozambique Island (during the 1810s) and Quelimane (from 1814). Figures rose to over 20,000 a year in the 1820s, when many slaves were also exported from Zanzibar. The Americas were the initial destination of 60 percent of Mozambique exports. Most of the remainder – an estimated 4,800 a year in the 1810s, rising to over 8,000 during the 1820s – were shipped to the Indian Ocean islands. Figures for the Mascarenes are unclear. From 1811 to 1822, possibly 30,000 to 50,000 slaves reached Mauritius, an annual average of between 2,700 and 4,500. This represented between 45 and 75 percent of all slaves entering the Mascarenes. An estimated 77 percent were of east African origin, a significant contrast to the pre-1810 situation, in which East Africa was the source of origin of 40 percent of Mascarene slave imports and Madagascar of 45 percent. From 1820, Mascarene demand for east African slaves increased significantly due to the widespread adoption of sugarcane cultivation and the 1819–20 cholera epidemic in which many slaves died. From 1817 to 1825, between 8,700 and 12,200 slaves were shipped annually to the Mascarenes, rising to between 13,300 and 16,800 by the early 1830s.[93] From 1824 to 1826, the French exported approximately 3,500 slaves a year from Inhambane alone. Indeed, the demand for east African slaves grew to such an extent that, contrary to traditional assumptions, the French islands were rivaling and might even have replaced Brazil as the major export market for Mozambique slaves by 1830.[94]

Simultaneously, a market for east African slaves emerged in imperial Madagascar. By 1824, Imerina was importing (via Mahajanga) some 2,000 to 3,000

[92] Campbell, "The East African Slave Trade."

[93] Lowry Cole to Bathurst, Mauritius, 21 June 1825, *PRO.CO*.167/50, 193–203, 320–3; Lacroix, *Les derniers négriers*, 69–81, 215; Beachey, *Slave Trade*, 29; Allen, "Licentious and Unbridled Proceedings," 94, 100–1; see also note 80.

[94] *RA*, 269; Ellis, *History of Madagascar* vol. II, 464; "Madagascar" in Anon, *Notices statistiques sur les colonies françaises*. IV (Paris, 1840), *AHVP*.M.71126, 8; Fontoynont et Nicol, *Les traitants français*, 24; Andriamarintsoa, "Le gouvernement de Tamatave de 1845 à 1865; développement économique" thèse, Université de Madagascar, (1973), 111–12; Burroughs, "The Mauritius Rebellion," 243–65; Campbell, "Role of the London Missionary Society" vol. I, Chs. 3 and 5; Liesegang, "First Look," 456; Alpers, *Ivory and Slaves*, 211–13; C. Duncan Rice, *The Rise and Fall of Black Slavery* (London, 1975), 124.

slaves annually. These represented possibly 10 percent of Mozambique slave exports, depending on the numbers exported to Madagascar from the coast north of Cape Delgado. As Antananarivo's slave population probably quadrupled in the 13 years from 1820, it is likely that east African slave imports increased at a similar rate. This would indicate an annual influx into Imerina of 10,000 east African slaves by 1833 – an increase in the slave import trade of Madagascar of between 10 and 40 percent of Mozambique slave exports in a decade. This would in turn signify the emergence of Madagascar as a major factor in the east African slave trade network.[95]

Slave exports from Mozambique declined in the 1840s, reflecting, on the demand side, a decline in the world sugar price (which diminished demand for slave labor on the Mascarenes), the transference of French slaving activity to western Madagascar, and a slowing in the growth of demand in the Merina empire for slave imports. Moreover, slave supplies were disrupted by the decline of the *prazos* from the mid-1830s and by the Nguni invasions of Zambesia. However, stability returned to Zambesia from mid-century with the rise of "supra-*prazo*" polities like Massingire. Also, buoyant sugar prices from 1845 to 1860, the 1848 emancipation measure, and a 20 percent mortality rate among plantation workers provoked a labor crisis on Réunion, Mayotta, and Nosy Be. Possibly more important was the demand for slaves in the Merina empire. Thus, despite the closure of the Brazilian market in the 1850s, regional demand pushed the slaving frontier in West Madagascar south of Maintirano and sustained the east African slave export trade: The French islands imported possibly 11,000 slaves a year from Mozambique in the 1850s. Slave imports into Madagascar fluctuated considerably so overall figures are difficult to gauge. Shipments to the island rose after a lull in the 1840s and 1850s and, despite a temporary slump due to the cholera epidemic of 1869–70, reached possibly 11,000 in peak years during the 1870s, which would indicate that Madagascar was then absorbing possibly 66 to 75 percent of all east African slave exports to the western Indian Ocean islands.[96] With the buildup of demand during the 1883–5 conflict and a lessening of British naval supervision, it is possible that up to 18,000 slaves

---

[95] Hastie, "Diary" (1824–5); Campbell, "Madagascar and the Slave Trade"; Mannix, *Black Cargoes*, 246, 250.

[96] *ASR* (May 1881), 78–9; (April 1882), 100–1; (June 1883), 164–5; (July 1883), 176; (Aug. 1883), 197; (Jan. 1888), 21; (March and April 1888), 33; Alpers, *Ivory and Slaves*, 215, 217; Hafkin, "Trade Society and Politics," 233–54; Frere to Granville, 27 Feb. 1873 – *CFM*; Newitt, "Angoche," 659–72; Beachey, *Slave Trade*, 24–5; Kirk to Granville, 5 March and 3 April 1872, "Correspondence Respecting the Slave Trade," *Parliamentary Papers* LXI (1873), c.867; Pakenham to Lord Tenterden, Tamatave, 3 April 1876, *PRO.CO*.84 1449 ERD/2270; Duffy, *Question of Slavery*, 65–8; Isaacman, *Mozambique*, 115–23; Lloyd, *The Navy*, 240; Vail and White, *Capitalism*, 21, 23, 32.

were shipped to western Madagascar in 1886–7, immediately following the end of hostilities. Significant numbers of these were subsequently transhipped to the French islands, but possibly 11,000 slaves entered the Merina market.[97]

It is unlikely that export of Malagasy slaves to the Mascarenes exceeded 5,000 a year from 1800–20, and were often as low as 600. After the 1820 slave export ban and the initial phase of Merina imperial expansion, slave exports dropped sharply. They picked up from the mid-1830s in areas of the island independent of Merina rule, notably the west and isolated pockets in the southeast, from where some 5,000 slaves/*engagés* were exported annually by the 1850s.[98]

In sum, total slave imports into Madagascar from East Africa, for the Malagasy market and for reexport, are estimated at approximately 400,000 from 1821–95, of whom some 320,000 remained in the island, while some 35,800 Malagasy were exported as slaves to the Mascarenes from 1801–20.[99] Over 400,000 East Africans are estimated to have entered the French islands, many via Madagascar, from 1801–95, most under the guise of contract labor (some 145,500 were landed in the period 1801–30). Richard Allen considers that some 165,000 to 173,000 slaves, mostly east African and Malagasy, were imported into the Mascarenes alone from 1800–48.[100] Combined "Southern" and "Northern" western Indian Ocean sector estimates indicate that total east African slave exports in the nineteenth century may have reached 1.5 million.

The End of the Malagasy Slave Trade

Madagascar played an integral – in the later nineteenth century, possibly the pivotal – role in the southern network of the east African slave trade. Both a source and a market for slaves, Madagascar was also a slave entrepôt serving the French plantation islands. Domestic demand for slaves intensified from the 1883–5 Franco–Merina War. However, despite continued slave exports from

[97] This would indicate a peak and not a constant trend as I have before argued, due to the deterioration of the imperial Merina economy. For previous estimates, see Campbell, "East African Slave Trade," 23–4; see also Stanwood, "memo" 2 (21 Aug. 1883); "Memo" no. 2 in Stanwood to Robinson, 13 July 1884 – *US*; Frere to Granville, Mozambique, 27 Feb. 1873, *CFM*; Coupland, *Exploitation of East Africa*, 53–6; Freemantle, "despatch," Zanzibar, 8 Sept. 1888, and Michahelles to Lacau, Zanzibar, 12 Sept. 1888, *ASR* (Nov. and Dec. 1888), 206–8.
[98] Campbell, "Madagascar and the Slave Trade."
[99] Campbell, "Introduction" to *ibid* (ed.), *Abolition and its Aftermath*.
[100] Gwyn Campbell, "Madagascar and Mozambique in the Slave Trade of the Western Indian Ocean, 1800–1861" *Slavery and Abolition* 9, 3 (1988), 165–192; *idem*, "The East African Slave Trade"; Allen, "The Mascarene Slave Trade."

southeast Africa, the obstacles to the east African slave export trade grew steadily from the mid-1880s. This stemmed mainly from increasing European intervention and control in the region. The growing presence of British settlers and missionaries in Malawi from the late 1870s, the establishment of a German administration in Tanganyika in the mid-1880s, and the extension of Portuguese control in the interior of Zambesia, all led to military clashes with Arab/Swahilis and Africans – which in turn disrupted the slave export trade. In addition, the 1884 Britanno–Portuguese Treaty gave foreigners access to the Zambezi. This permitted the more effective application of anti–slave trade measures, which greatly constricted the supply side of the trade by the late 1890s.[101] On the demand side, the main Malagasy market for east African slaves declined precipitously following the French takeover of 1895, as the French proclamation, abolishing slavery in 1896, was backed by the effective military occupation of the island by 1904.[102]

---

[101] *ASR* (Nov. and Dec. 1888), 156; *ASR* (Jan. and Feb. 1889), 4–6; Bennett, "Americans in Zanzibar," 47–8; Owen Kalinga, "The Karonga War: Commercial Rivalry and the Politics of Survival," *JAH* 21 (1980), 209–18; Axelson, *Portugal and the Scramble*, 23, 62–3, 137, 141, 143–4, 157–8, 163–4, 167–8, 171–3.

[102] Campbell, *Unfree Labour*.

10 Transport and Communications, 1820–1895

Introduction

An efficient transport and communications network was central to the integration of the IOW into the international economy, notably with the expansion of steam transport in the later nineteenth century.[1] However, this key element in economic development was singularly lacking in imperial Madagascar, due to both natural and manmade factors.

Madagascar's size and geography present considerable obstacles to communication. With a total land surface of 587,041 km², the world's fourth largest island has been described as "a veritable continent."[2] Trans-island communication was difficult due to the high central plateau that runs on a north–south axis almost the entire 1,592-km length of the island. An often-precipitous eastern escarpment, mostly forested in the nineteenth century, dropped to a narrow coastal plain largely devoid of natural harbors. Coastal–interior communications were better in western Madagascar, which possesses a number of fine natural harbors and substantial rivers, such the Onilahy (400 km) and Ikopa (300 km). Communication along the island's 9,935 km of coastline was generally easier,[3] but the cyclone season from January to March halted east coast maritime traffic. Indeed, most overland transport was restricted to the dry winter season between April and late October.

Natural factors were complicated by imperial Merina policies under autarky. Following the 1820 Britanno–Merina treaty, Farquhar informed Radama I that

---

[1] See Chapter 12.
[2] P. Samat, "lettre" (1848).
[3] See Chapter 1.

the economic development of Madagascar depended upon

the formation of a good road from your capital to Tamatave . . . [which] would facilitate the intercourse between us, very much, and contribute to enrich your country, by the interchange of our productions; were this road so constructed by winding around the bottom of hills, as to enable carts, and carriages, drawn by bullocks, to ascend and descend without difficulty, from and to the coast, greater numbers of ingenious men would also thus be induced to visit you, who are deterred by the nature, almost impracticable, of your present roads.[4]

Radama I responded with a number of transport improvements. Bridges were built over the river Ivondrona (near Toamasina) in 1817 and Ikopa (at Ampitantafika, Antanjombato, and Ambaniala in central Imerina–see Illustration 10) from 1823; the ban on non-*Andriana* use of palanquins was lifted; an "excellent road fit for a carriage" was constructed in Antananarivo and similar roads in Mahavelona in 1822–3; and in 1827, an 800-man-strong *fanompoana*,[5] supervised by imperial dignitaries Philibert and Prince Ratefy, built canals to link a natural series of east coast lagoons.[6] Europeans also introduced transport innovations: In the 1820s, Lambros manufactured wheeled carts (hitherto unknown) to transport sugarcane on the banks of the Mananjary. Their use spread to other European and Creole-managed east coast plantations and, by 1822, the first wheeled horse-drawn carts appeared in Imerina[7].

However, mounting concern that such improvements might facilitate an influx of European colonists, and even a foreign invasion – reinforced by the 1829 French occupation of the Pointe-à-Larée, opposite Nosy Boraha – resulted in a ban on transport improvements. Except for the brief reign of Radama II (1861–3), when some stone bridges were built in Imerina, and desultory interest

---

[4] Farquhar to Radama I, Port Louis, 29 Sept. 1821, in *RH*, 15.

[5] For a full explanation of *fanompoana*, see Chapter 6.

[6] *RA*, 263.

[7] The island possessed few species of animal that could be used as beasts of burden. Zebu were abundant and used to prepare paddy fields, but were rarely utilized for transport. Farquhar reported of the Merina colony started in 1823 at Mahavelona that they "have succeeded in disciplining their oxen to draught work and carrying" (Farquhar quoted in *RH*, 14–15), but the colony had failed by 1825. Although the concept of the wheel had long existed, its application was limited: In Imerina wheels were fitted to sledges that, dragged by gangs of men, were used to transport slabs of rock for the construction of tombs. Again, in 1845, 300 bullocks, many of them shackled to carts, formed part of the royal procession to Manerinerina. These remained, however, isolated incidents. See *RH*, 161, 178, 403, 406, 456; *HR* vol. I, 281; vol. II, 693–4; Griffiths, *Hanes Madagascar*, 38; "Commercial Reports," *US*; *GH* (1928), 355–6; Fontoynont et Nicol, *Les traitants français*, 27.

10. Ambaniala Bridge

in developing a fleet,[8] this ban was maintained for the entire imperial era. It formed, alongside "generals" *hazo* and *tazo*, the cornerstone of the imperial Merina defense policy. *Tazo* is Malagasy for malarial fever, which had foiled all previous European attempts at colonization – and almost succeeded in blocking the final French advance of 1895.[9] *Hazo* was a reference to the dense tropical rainforest of the eastern escarpment up which any European military advance was expected to come. The policy was completed by the 1824 Merina capture of the main riverine access to the interior from the west coast port of Mahajanga. As an American trader noted in 1877, "the only reason that Majunga route is not opened is because the Hovas [Merina] are afraid (the road being so very much easier than that from Tamatave) that foreigners will march to, and take the Capitol from them."[10]

---

[8] For example, in 1828, Radama I was offered the American brig, *Spy*, by Andrew Ward. However, the king took such a long time to reply to the offer, delivered in Mahajanga, that the *Spy* sailed without awaiting the response. Even had the captain received Radama I's letter, he would probably have refused the sale because of the multiple conditions the Merina sovereign wished to impose. See Razi, "Sources d'histoire," 10–11.

[9] For malaria, see Campbell, "Crisis of Faith."

[10] Hathorne to Arnold, Hines & Co, Zanzibar, 14 Nov. 1877 – Hathorne, "Letterbook" (1877–9).

This policy meant that, until the French conquest, the transport of mail, freight, and people relied almost exclusively upon human labor.[11] Indeed, dependence on human porterage intensified rather than diminished during the imperial Merina era, despite the regime's avowed aim of thoroughly modernizing the island's economy. This chapter investigates the development of dependence upon human labor in transport and analyzes its wider economic impact.

The Domestic Transport System: Porterage

Traditionally, foreign traders hired coastal porters on a seasonal basis.[12] However, following the adoption of autarky in the 1820s, two distinct porterage systems developed in imperial Madagascar. The first, using *fanompoana* labor, expanded phenomenally during the industrial experiment of the early nineteenth century.[13] The collection and carriage of nitre and other raw materials for the armaments and soap factories involved some localized, specialist porter teams. For instance, each day villagers from Namehana, near Antananarivo, collected urine from the capital and transported it to the Ilafy powder-works, while a female unit in Antananarivo collected and carried offal to the Analakely gunpowder factory.[14]

More general porter units collected furnace fuel and wormwood and lard for soap manufacture. The traditional *fanompoana* of the Sihanaka – collecting and transporting firewood for the royal household[15] – expanded to include supplying firewood to the Antananarivo factory boilers and *boribory* wood (from which potash was extracted) to gunpowder and soap factories. Also, in June 1857, Ida Pfieffer witnessed 1,500 (probably Sihanaka) men carrying fuel to state forges. Industrial demand for fuel was such that the Bezanozano – numbered at 3,060 for *fanompoana* under Radama I – were also enlisted. Thereafter, every one to two months, convoys of up to 1,000 porters transported fuel from both

---

[11] There were short-lived experiments with other forms of transport. In 1877, for example, Roux de Fraissinet imported 12 camels to convey goods from Mahajanga to Antananarivo, but it would appear from the lack of any subsequent reference to them that they perished within a short period – Campbell, "Labour and the Transport Problem"; see also Hathorne to J. Orme Ryder, Zanzibar, 12 May 1877 – Hathorne, "Letterbook" (1877–79).

[12] See Mayeur, "Voyages, 1774–1776" *BAM* 10 (1912), 93–156.

[13] Oliver, *Madagascar* vol. I, 492, 494; Chapus, *Quatre-vingts années*, 206.

[14] Freeman and Johns, *A Narrative*, 45; *RA*, 357; Raombana, B2 Livre 13, 29; J. Chauvin, "Jean Laborde, 1805–1878," *Mémoires de l'Académie Malgache* 29 (Tananarive, 1939), 8.

[15] Campbell, "Labour and the Transport Problem," 346.

Antsihanaka and Bezanozano to Antananarivo.[16] For the tanning industry, bark (collected from the eastern forest) was by the late 1820s replaced by lime, which, like sulfur, was carried from the Sirabe plain in Betsileo, six to seven days (70 km) south of Antananarivo.[17]

Construction work also involved large numbers of porters. Imerina lacked forests and even at Mantasoa, on the periphery of the great eastern forest, workers had to travel from 11 to 13 km to locate suitable construction timber.[18] Both civilian and army units were employed to fell and transport timber, although there was a general division of labor: Workers from Antsihanaka and Betsileo were assigned respectively the northeast and southeast forest, while Bezanozano were summoned to select and carry specially rounded timber and *hafotra* – small trees and shrubs, the fiber of which was used to manufacture rope. As 75 men were required to drag an average tree trunk the 60 km from the eastern forest to Antananarivo, huge numbers were involved. For example, in 1869, Grandidier witnessed a 1,000-strong Sihanaka *fanompoana* transporting construction timber for a royal palace. Exceptionally large pieces required more men: A 5,000-strong *fanompoana* was drafted to carry a 39-meter-high trunk to the Manjakamiadana palace construction site to which, in 1861, a further timber transport unit of 15,000 was summoned.[19]

The carriage of other construction material and capital equipment was as arduous. For example, a 6,000-man *fanompoana* took four months to convey sugarcane-crushing machinery from the coast to Laborde's Lohasoa distillery.[20] Slates could only be carried singly from the Manandriana quarries in Betsileo to Antananarivo – the round trip averaging 13 days. By contrast, a porter-load of Sirabe lime took on average 10 days to reach Mantasoa. The lime continued to be exploited after the Mantasoa complex closed in the 1850s – in 1872, Roman Catholic missionary Finaz witnessed a 4,000-strong Betsileo unit transporting lime to Imerina.[21]

---

[16] *RA*, 357–60; Raombana, B2 Livre 13, 29; Pfieffer, *Last Travels*, 267; Grandidier, "Souvenirs," 39–40; Chauvin, "Jean Laborde," 8–9; F. Raminadrasoa and Gilbert Ratsivalaka, "De l'usage du concept 'ethnie' dans l'historiographie de Madagascar. L'exemple des Bezanozano au XVIIIe siècle" *Colloque d'histoire*, Université de Madagascar (Toliara, 1979), 9.

[17] Campbell, "Slavery and Fanompoana."

[18] Raombana, B2 Livre 13, 18.

[19] *HR* vol. I, 57; Hewlett, "Mantasoa," 378; Chapus, *Quatre-vingts années*, 206; Freeman and Johns, *A Narrative*, 44; Grandidier, "Souvenirs," 29–40; Jouen au Pie IX, Tananarive, 8 nov 1861, "Correspondance du P. Jouen, 1859–69," C52, *AHVP*.

[20] Campbell, "Slavery and fanompoana."

[21] Oliver, *Madagascar* vol. I, 503; Chapus, *Quatre-vingts années*, 197, 206; *Les Missions Catholiques* 153 (1872), 334.

Again, in 1833–4, Merina soldiers and local Betsimisaraka were summoned to quarry stones and red earth and fell the timber required to burn mortar – and transport all to fort construction sites at Toamasina and Mahavelona.[22] As LMS printer Edward Baker commented, "The difficulty of travelling is now exceedingly great, in consequence of almost all the people being occupied in building batteries on different parts of the coast."[23] Consequently, cultivation was neglected around Toamasina and Mahavelona, and famine ensued.[24] Following the 1845 Britanno–French naval assault, massive *fanompoana* was employed to reinforce imperial defenses. For instance, in 1846, 30,000 small farmers were drafted for two weeks to carry Sirabe stone and chalk needed to fortify Ambohimanga.[25]

General *fanompoana* was also used to carry government freight. State property was carried, from Morondava and Ampasinafindra by Betsileo *fanompoana*,[26] and along the Antananarivo–Toamasina route by the Bezanozano and Betsimisaraka.[27] In 1835, Nicolay, governor of Mauritius, sent Ranavalona I a pleasure boat: 100 Betsimisaraka were needed to carry it (implying, with changeovers, at least 200 men) and more to clear a sufficiently wide (but temporary) path through the eastern forest.[28]

From 1820–5 and 1829–36, LMS freight was carried free of charge by Betsimisaraka and Bezanozano *fanompoana*.[29] This clearly indicated the status of early nineteenth-century missionaries as imperial agents. The volume of such freight is reflected in the missionary statement that the cost of porterage in 1826 came to "an enormous sum."[30] In 1834, for example, 300 imperial porters were summoned to transport, from Toamasina to Antananarivo, an LMS press and type, plus over 5,000 books.[31] The missionaries were exiled from Madagascar from 1836 to 1862, but in 1864, leading LMS missionary William

[22] Freeman to Baker, Port Louis, 29 Aug. 1833, *SOAS/LMS-MIL* B4.F4.JB; *RA*, 322.
[23] Baker to Ellis, Ivohitsara, 30 July 1834, *SOAS/LMS-MIL* B5.F1.JC; see also Baker to Ellis, Tamatave, 15 July 1834, *SOAS/LMS-MIL* B5.F1.JC; Ellis, *History of Madagascar* vol. II, 479–80.
[24] Campbell, *Unfree Labour* Ch. 4.
[25] Raombana, B2 Livre 13, 2.
[26] Dubois, *Monographie des Betsileo*, 426.
[27] Campbell, "Labour and the Transport Problem," 346.
[28] *RA*, 358–60.
[29] Extract of letter from Jones and Griffiths, Antananarivo, 16 Dec. 1825, in *Minutes of the Southern Committee* (20 Oct. 1826), *Committee Minutes: Africa and Madagascar Book 1 (1826–1837)*, *SOAS/LMS*.
[30] Extract of letter from Jones and Griffiths, Antananarivo, 9 Nov. 1826, in *Minutes of the Southern Committee (1826–1837)*.
[31] Johns & Freeman to Ellis, Antananarivo, 6 Nov. 1834, *SOAS/LMS-MIL* B5.F1.JD; Munthe, *La bible à Madagascar*, 84, 112–13.

Ellis successfully negotiated with Rainilaiarivony to have LMS goods imported free of duty,[32] and from the creation of the state church in 1868–9, missionaries outside central Imerina summoned at will imperial *fanompoana* for their own porterage needs.[33]

Finally, *fanompoana* porterage was conscripted to serve the commercial needs of the imperial court. For instance, garrison commanders on the northeast coast summoned local people to collect and transport ebony, timber, gum copal, and beeswax for the Garnot monopoly.[34] The closure of imperial ports from 1845 to 1853 led to a dramatic decline in trade and thus to a decrease in demand for porters. An immediate increase in porterage *fanompoana* followed their reopening, particularly for the Betsimisaraka, 1,600 of whom had been summoned by December 1853 to carry royal imports from Toamasina to the imperial capital.[35] However, with the 1860s foreign trade boom, transport of merchandise passed almost exclusively to a class of porters belonging to a powerful Antananarivo slave syndicate.

The Private System

In addition to state-organized porterage, private porterage systems emerged. First, certain ethnic groups, such as the pastoral Tankary (of the Mangoro Valley), Antaimoro (southeast coast), and Antanosy (from the hinterland of Tolanaro), became involved, much as contemporaneously the Sukuma and Nyamwezi entered porterage in East Africa. They hired their services for lengthy, long distance transport. In the dry season, for instance, the Tankary carried hides and calico between the Ankay and Antananarivo. Such porters always returned home with their earnings. Unlike their east African counterparts, they also contracted for nonporterage work. Thus, the only truly specialized transport workers in imperial Madagascar developed within the ranks of certain *fanompoana* groups and within a private slave porterage syndicate. This contrasted with East Africa, where most porters were freemen, voluntarily hiring out their services, and where slaves were reserved mainly for domestic and agricultural labor on the coast.[36]

---

[32] Ellis, *Madagascar Revisited*, 424–5.

[33] Finaz, "Mémoires sur le commencement de la mission dans la province du Betsileo" (1876), Diaires II no. 24, 16–18 – *AHVP*.

[34] Guillain, *Documents* II, 214; Rasoamiaramanana "Aspects économiques," 31, 70.

[35] Raombana, "Manuscrit," 4, 16.

[36] Cousins, *Madagascar of Today*, 40–1; Grandidier, "Souvenirs," 14–20; L. Besson, *Voyage au pays des Tanala Indépendants de la région d'Ikongo* (Paris, 1894). For the East African

11. Hide Carrier, Maharidaza circa 1880

The private slave porterage syndicate, which first developed by the early 1830s in response to the disruption in freight traffic between Imerina and the east coast caused by the Betsimisaraka and Bezanozano, expanded rapidly with the growth of foreign trade in the 1860s.[37] The syndicate was organized by members of the court elite – headed by Rainimaharavo, the chief secretary of state – each of whom owned thousands of slaves. Those assigned to be slave porters were

comparisons, see V. Harlow and E. M. Chilver (eds.), *History of East Africa* (Oxford, 1965), 168; R. Gray and David Birmingham (eds.), *Pre-Colonial African Trade* (Oxford, 1970), 61.
[37] See Chapter 8.

12. Palanquin Carriers circa 1880

registered with the government and split into gangs, each under the supervision of a commander or captain, himself a slave. The porters, generally known as *maromita* or *borizano*, fell into two main categories: the *mpaka* or *mpitondra entana*, who carried freight, and the *mpilanjana* who transported travelers. The *mpaka entana* (lit. "taker or fetcher of baggage") generally traveled in groups:

> The usual convoys consist from ten to forty carriers, according to the amount of the invoice, with one man in charge called the captain, who carries no load. They are all natives, including the captain, and generally all slaves. Many, perhaps most of them belonging to the high officers of the Government – some to the Prime Minister.[38]

Porterage imposed severe problems in terms of the bulk of goods transported (see Illustrations 11 and 12). Thus, in May 1886, an agent for importers of American cloth stated:

> Owners should be informed of the important fact that the Augusta Sheetings ex "Essex" 17th Voyage contained 29 to 30 pieces per bale, of different lengths, some having only 24 yards [21.9 meters]; this makes it difficult for buyers to arrange pieces of transportation with "bearers," and it is likely to bring the mark into bad repute.[39]

The preferred length was 40 yards [36.6 meters].[40] Most accounts indicate that *mpaka entana* generally carried 60-pound [27.24 kg] loads, except for

---

[38] Robinson to Hunter, US Consul, Tamatave, 21 July 1879, *US*.

[39] Dawson in Whitney to Ropes, Emmerton & Co, and Arnold, Hines & Co, *REC/CR-MZL*.

[40] Dawson to Ropes, Emmerton & Co, and Arnold, Hines & Co, Tamatave, 11 March 1886, *REC/CR-MZL*.

hides – transported in 100-pound [45.5-kg] consignments.[41] Unlike their east African, but like their Far Eastern counterparts, *mpaka entana* carried loads, not on their heads, but on their shoulders, where they frequently developed a characteristic tumescent lump called a *sangongo*. Packs were suspended from the ends of a bamboo pole, from 1.5 to 1.8 meters long, which, like that used in China, was rigid rather than flexible. Heavier loads were hung from the center of a pole shouldered by two men. Before the start of a journey, the consignment was unpacked, sorted, and repackaged in waterproof ravanna leaves, to the bearer's convenience. Some substances, such as gold dust, were carried in the hollow of a bamboo, which, after packing, was sealed.[42]

The *mpilanjana* (lit. "carrier on the shoulder") transported palanquins, which in Imerina were traditionally confined to court members until 1821, when Radama I abolished all prohibitions on their use. The usual model, similar to a Chinese palanquin, comprised a seat made of hide stretched between two poles of from 1.5 to 2.0 meters in length. Arm-chairs or baskets were also commonly used by both sexes until the 1860s, when they became an almost exclusively female mode of conveyance. Eight *mpilanja* were normally allotted to each palanquin: Four carried the burden (generally weighing between 80 and 100 kg, including the passenger), while a relief team ran alongside. However, the precise number of carriers depended upon the weight and importance of the passenger. Children rarely required more than four bearers, although 20 were needed to carry Thomas Pakenham, the 127-kg British consul. Most *mpilanja*, unlike the *mpaka entana*, were based in Antananarivo, where carriers enjoyed the best reputation for speed and safety. Whereas a *mpaka entana*, carrying from 40 to 50 kg of hides, covered the 350-km Toamasina–Antananarivo trip in an average of between 15 and 30 days, those carrying 20 to 25 kg could travel the distance in seven days, about the same time (five to eight days) that it took the laden *mpilanjana*.[43]

---

[41] Although Ellis in the early 1860s considered that the average porter load in Antananarivo was 20 kg – see Ellis, *Madagascar Revisited*, 490; G. Foucart, "L'Etat du commerce à Madagascar" in E. Caustier, A. Milne-Edwards, De Faymoreau, L. Suberbie, G. Foucart, Lacaze and L. Olivier (eds.), *Ce qu'il faut connaitre de Madagascar* (Paris: Paul Ollendorf, [1897?]), 74; Bachelder to Dawson, Antananarivo, 20 June and 10 July 1885, *REC/CR-MZL*.

[42] *GH* (1928), 351–3; Campbell, "Gold Mining and the French Takeover."

[43] The *filanjana*, also known in coastal regions as *fitakonana* and *ankolanjy*, was possibly introduced into the island by the Zafindraminia, a dynasty of Arabic origin who settled in Anosy, a province on the southeast coast. – W. E. Cousins, *Madagascar of Today* (London, 1886), 471; *idem*, "Abolition of Slavery," 371; Catat, *Voyage à Madagascar*, 21; Wilkinson to IDC, Antananarivo, 12 Feb. 1867, File "Local, Commecial, Transport," *FJKM*; Grandidier, "Souvenirs," 44; Henry W. Little, *Madagascar, Its History and People* (London, 1884), 131; *Juvenile Missionary Magazine* (June, 1886), 63; E. F. Knight, "From Fort Dauphin to

Weather was a critical factor. The heaviest rain fell on the eastern littoral from January to March, when porterage proved virtually impossible.[44] Even when roads were passable, the rough terrain proved difficult for the bearers, as Ellis noted when carried through the eastern forest in the 1850s:

The road here was frightful, – the soil stiff clay, with deep holes of mud and water. Our way was sometimes covered with water, but more frequently up and down steep slippery ravines, requiring detours on account of the gigantic trees which had fallen across the track. The clayey sides and rocky portions of the ravines were sometimes so steep that my position was almost upright, and it frequently required ten or twelve men to get the palanquin up and down. . . . I certainly felt, while the men were toiling up the rugged ascent, that there was some ground for the late Radama's remark, that he had two generals, viz. General Hazo, *forest*, and General Tazo, *fever*, in whose hands he would leave any invading army. . . . I could also readily imagine why, in 1816, some of Captain Le Sage's men should have thrown themselves on the ground, declaring they would die rather than attempt to proceed farther.[45]

The total number of porters was considerable. For example, from 1st to 20th June 1885, approximately 1,305 men were involved carrying hides from Antananarivo to the coast (and presumably the return traffic in cottons).[46] The organized porterage system comprised possibly 60,000 carriers by the late 1800s. All were slaves and formed from 19 to 23 percent of the entire slave population, and some 57 to 60 percent of male slave population, of Imerina. The absolute number of *maromita* and their percentage relative to the slave and free population probably stayed constant from the 1860s.[47]

As a body, porters were one of the island's most important recipients of foreign exchange. They were a source of great profit to the slave syndicate, which strengthened its control over porterage through labor legislation, two aspects of which had particular relevance. The first, inserted as a clause into all foreign treaties, was the right of the imperial government to withdraw manpower from foreign employers without warning. This enabled syndicate members to remove "free" hired labor from foreign planters and traders who, in consequence, were

Fianarantsoa," *AAMM* 19 (1895), 363; W. Gore-Jones, *Report* (London, 1881), 9; S. P. Oliver, *Madagascar and the Malagasy* (London, 1866), 4, 12; Foucart, "L'Etat du commerce à Madagascar," 74, 78.

[44] Whitney to Ropes, Emmerton & Co, and Arnold, Hines & Co, Tamatave, 21 Oct. 1886 and 27 March 1891; Ryder to Ropes, Emmerton & Co, and Arnold, Hines & Co, Zanzibar, 15 Nov. 1886 – *REC/CR-MZL*.

[45] Ellis, *Three Visits*, 319. British admiral Gore-Jones commented of the same route in 1881 that, "had honest John Bunyan tried the road to Antananarivo, he could have improved his description of Christian's Slough of Despond" – Gore-Jones, *Report* (1881), 11.

[46] Bacheler to Dawson, Antananarivo, 20 June and 10 July 1885, *REC/CR-MZL*.

[47] *GH* (1928), 354; Oliver, *Madagascar* vol. II, 75–8; *AAMM* 22 (1898), 247.

obliged to hire syndicate slaves.[48] To hire the latter, the written consent of owners had to be obtained and government passports issued that were checked at all garrisons en route. Porters found without passes were liable to arrest and punishment. To obtain the requisite permits, porter captains had to be informed of long trips several days in advance.[49] Even armed with passes, the *maromita* were frequently obliged to bribe Merina officials with *vola kely* (lit. "a little money").[50]

As Grandidier observed, the owner–slave porter relationship remained distant:

There are many slaves who are neither fed nor clothed by their masters.... [T]hey are at liberty to do as they seem fit provided that each year, at the time of the *Fandroana* [Merina New Year] festival, they bring their masters either a bundle of firewood or a small amount of money.[51]

Porters forged strong bonds of solidarity, as was reflected in the development of a *maromita* culture, which included songs emphasizing porter comradeship and a pride in their arduous occupation:

> We are people going back home
> And see how we go!
> Hey there! have us brought a glass of rum, good sirs!
> But is there any? – No.
> Oh, then let us hurry!
> And beef, pork – shall we have any?
> And good fatted birds?
> And good rice?
> But is there any? – No.
> Then what's the use of talking so much and of making so much noise.
> Because there is none,
> We must work hard, my gay companions,
> Until we arrive!
> For we shall have a good meal,
> When we are at the end of our journey.[52]

Shared work experience helped forge a sense of occupational identity. The *mpilanjana* were especially well-organized, as their work necessitated "some coaching and special training." They were younger (rarely older than 24 years) and more skilled than the *mpaka entana* (some of whom worked until aged 55). Moreover, whereas *mpaka entana* were notoriously pagan, *mpilanjana* were

---

[48] See, e.g., Charles Finkelmeier, U.S. deputy consul, to Hunter, Tamatave, 30 December 1874, *US*.
[49] H. E. Clark, "How We Travel in Madagascar" *AAMM* 8 (1884), 342.
[50] Ibid.
[51] Grandidier, "Souvenirs," 32.
[52] *GH* (1928), 352.

13. Roadside Restaurant circa 1880

mostly Christian and Protestant. *Maromita* developed a mutual-aid system, often forcing a halt if a fellow worker fell ill or, for a slight monetary consideration, securing a replacement. As L. Catat remarked, "It is their occupation far more than their origin that makes of them a body with its own habits and customs."[53] Porter solidarity and demands for better conditions in part reflected the dangers of their occupation. The terrain was often difficult, malaria was a risk in nonplateau regions, and porters were vulnerable to brigand attacks, even on the main commercial routes. As they were paid at the conclusion of each trip, robbery or the forced abandonment of goods resulted in wages being forfeited. In some cases, hirers evaded payment or, when porters reached their destination, sold them as slaves.[54]

---

[53] Catat, *Voyage à Madagascar*, 20, 21; see also Mayeur, "Voyages" (1777) *BAM* 12.I (1913), 145; Little, *Madagascar*, 131; Ellis, *History of Madagascar* vol. I, 193; Ransome, "The River Antanambalana," 231; Foucart, "L'Etat du commerce à Madagascar," 78.

[54] Larsen, *Livet for Doden*; McMahon, "First Visit," 280; Ellis, *History of Madagascar* vol. I, 10–13, 35, and II, 387–8; Grandidier, "Souvenirs," 30; Knight, "From Fort Dauphin," 399.

Unlike other forms of forced labor, porterage led to few violent protests. This was due largely to a remarkable degree of organization and unity among carriers, who considered their economic opponent to be the hirer of their labor, rather than their owner. If well-treated by their employers, *maromita* took good care of both the traveler and his goods. The captain imposed a rigorous work discipline even in the most perilous circumstances: When transporting freight or passengers, porters marched, with a small 10- to 15-minute break around 8 A.M., from sunrise until about 11 A.M., when they would attempt to locate a village where they might obtain a meal. At 12.30 P.M., the caravan would restart, continuing until sundown, when overnight accommodation was sought.[55] Bearers received *vatsy* (regular food money) from their employers and extorted forced hospitality from villagers.[56] Within the empire, exactions were greater if a state dignitary accompanied the caravan. In Imerina, cheap wayside restaurants sprang into existence from the 1860s, where travelers could purchase a basic meal of cooked rice or manioc, usually served by women, for a *varifitoventy* ($0.02) (see Illustration 10).[57]

Despite their slave status, porters were the only large wage-earning body of workers in imperial Madagascar, lived a more independent lifestyle than free subjects, and behaved in many respects more like wage earners in Europe than did other Malagasy workers – most of whom were, under the imperial regime, subject to *fanompoana*. Such was the growing organizational strength of the porters in the context of vulnerability to market forces, that they came nearer than any other body of Malagasy labor to forming an embryonic labor union. Their unity was cemented by the *fatidra*. Also common among other categories of slaves, and among brigands, the *fatidra* was the most commonly utilized form of forging a relationship of trust between two parties that possessed no structural cohesion and linked the slaves very much as common ancestral ties linked ordinary Malagasy.[58] It ensured cooperation whenever work grievances arose and assisted in the development of a proto-trade union – of which each porter gang formed a branch.[59]

The 1860s export boom stimulated demand for porters. This placed them in a strong bargaining position, and there emerged a familiar pattern of trade-union tactics, including strikes, to obtain better wages and work conditions. By the early 1870s, the *maromita* were considered extremely independent, a

[55] Colin et Suau, "Album Malgache – Les borizanos," *Les missions catholiques* (1896), 11.

[56] Laborde to Whitney, Vatomandry, 29 Nov. 1886, *REC/CR-MZL*.

[57] Colin et Suau, "Album Malgache," 11; *GH* (1928), 354.

[58] For the *fatidra*, see Chapter 2; see also Dubois, *Monographie des Betsileo*, 364; Dalmond, "Mission Apostolique" (1837–47), 86.

[59] Ellis, *History of Madagascar* vol. I, 189–90, 192.

characteristic further enhanced by the labor shortage experienced during the Franco–Merina dispute of 1883–5, as well as by the trade boom that followed its settlement.[60] Of particular importance was the role of the porter captain. He did no carrying, but chose the routes, arranged accommodation en route for his men and for any passengers, and, where necessary to secure passage, bribed Merina officials and paid informal road taxes to brigands and chiefs hostile to Merina rule. He further represented his porters' interests in bargaining with the employer.[61]

Porters accentuated any natural short-term manpower shortages in order to demand a temporary rise in pay rates. This happened frequently during the *Fandroana*, which the *maromita* claimed as a trade holiday; as reflected in the December 1886 protest against the LMS agent at Mahanoro by Captain Rainiketramanga and his gang of 50 *maromita*.[62] From 1883, when the *Fandroana* was fixed on 22 November, foreign trade ground to a virtual halt in November. Higher wages were also demanded on special occasions, such as the Merina royal visit to Betsileo in 1873. The queen's retinue absorbed almost the entire body of *maromita*, which greatly impeded commercial activity for several months. Consequently, the few available porters were at a premium among foreign traders and travelers and, once hired, used their enhanced bargaining position to effect; the porters secured that year by LMS director Joseph Mullens mutinied three times between Antananarivo and Ambositra.[63]

Short-term wage rates were also heavily influenced by the slave syndicate's control over access to *maromita*, who became unavailable to others when summoned to work for their masters, as occurred during rice planting and harvesting.[64] Thus, in January 1890, when the *vary aloha* rice harvest retained many porters in Imerina, *maromita* captains in Toamasina demanded wages of $0.75 per bale of imported cotton, dropping to $0.625 by May when porter

[60] Procter to Briggs, Tamatave, 13 Aug. 1873, file, "Commercial Correspondence from Procter"; James Levy to LMS, Tamatave, 17 Nov. 1886, file M, "Local, Commercial, Transport" – *FJKM*; Taix, "Tamatave: notes historiques."

[61] Procter to Pearse and Parret, Tamatave, 9 April 1872, file, "Commercial Correspondence from Procter"; Thorne to Whitehouse, 4 Dec. 1879, and Lord to Pearse, 30 March 1882, IDC Letterbook 2 – *FJKM*; Mullens, *Twelve Months in Madagascar*, 134; Knight, "From Fort Dauphin."

[62] J. G. to Houlder, Mahanoro, 11 Dec. 1886, file M, "Local, Commercial, Transport"; Procter to Pearse and Parrett, Tamatave, 9 April 1872, file, "Commercial Correspondence from Procter"; Thorne to Whitehouse, 4 Dec. 1879, and Lord to Pearse, 30 March 1882, IDC Letterbook 2 – *FJKM*; Mullens, *Twelve Months in Madagascar*, 134; Knight, "From Fort Dauphin."

[63] J. Mullens to Briggs, Ambositra, 22 Sept. 1873, file, "LMS, Local, T & F, D & E"; Procter Bros to Briggs, Antananarivo, 13 Aug. 1873, and Procter to Houlder, Antananarivo, 27 Nov. 1886, file, "Commercial Correspondence from Procter"; Porter to Baron, Analakely, 7 Jan. 1887, file M, "Local, Commercial, Transport" – *FJKM*; Colin et Suau, "Album Malgache," 10–12.

[64] Bachelder to Ropes, Emmerton & Co, Antananarivo, 14 Aug. 1885, *REC/CR-MZL*.

shortages eased.[65] Such short-term variations in porter wage rates were accentuated by fluctuations in the money supply. Thus in 1872, a temporary flood of specie imports forced up prices and wages, which remained high for some time after inflation slowed.[66]

The initial wages demanded by porter captains were often so high that hiring agents would request of their clients a delay of up to one month in an attempt to force down *maromita* claims. Higher rates were always asked from Westerners or for unusually bulky freight.[67] A premium was also imposed for deviations from the main routes. Thus, LMS missionary Richardson, traveling in South Betsileo in the 1870s, found that

> The people, encouraged by the chief men of the place, refused to have anything whatever to do with them [i.e., the baggage] because they had been brought to the town direct from Ambohimandroso, instead of having been taken first to a town (the name of which I now forget) some miles out of the street road. There was nothing to be done but to have the boxes taken back.... [W]e never saw those boxes again until the Sunday following, when they arrived carried by the very men who had refused to have anything to do with them on their first arrival at Ambalavao.[68]

Only very high incentives could induce porters to cross the *efitra* or no-man's land between areas under firm imperial rule and those vaster reaches of the island that were semi- or fully independent. This was due to the danger from brigands and chiefs hostile to the Merina.

Porter shortages became permanent from the mid-1880s when, in a desperate effort to shore up the economy, the imperial court intensified its demands for forced labor. *Fanompoana* was traditionally imposed only on free subjects. However, faced with the threat of economic and political collapse, the court could not ignore the labor potential of up to 60,000 healthy, strong men who, because of their organizational structure, could be easily manipulated. Thus in January 1885, the prime minister turned to the slave syndicate for porters to transport guns from the west coast imported to use against the French.[69]

---

[65] Within four months, however, the rice planting season led to renewed shortages and *maromita* wages again rose to a new height of $0.66 per bale of cotton – Dawson to Ropes, Emmerton & Co, Tamatave, 27 Aug. 1890, Ropes, Emmerton & Co, *REC/CR-MZL*. See also Dawson to Ropes, Emmerton & Co, Tamatave, 26 Jan., 8 May, 8 June 1890, *REC/CR-MZL*.

[66] "Report of the Buildings Sub-Committee on LMS Houses at Ambohibeloma and Isoavina" in Imerina District Committee (IDC), Letterbook 2, *FJKM*.

[67] Procter to Pearse and Parret, 9 April 1872, file, "Commercial correspondence from Procter," *FJKM*.

[68] Richardson, *Lights and Shadows*, 6–7; see also Procter to Briggs, Antananarivo, 16 April 1874, file, "Correspondence from Procter," *FJKM*.

[69] Pakenham to Lord Russell, Tamatave, 30 July 1863, *PRO.CO*.84/1205; *idem* to Granville, Tamatave, 3 Jan. 1874, *PRO.CO*.84/1397; Richardson to Mullens, 21 June 1877 – ext. *BAM* 18 (1935), 12–15; Wills to Thompson, Antananarivo, 29 Jan. 1885, IDC Letterbook 2, *FJKM*.

The result was evident: By July that year, a major foreign firm noted, "Bearers are getting scarcer and we may have to ease buying hides for this reason ere long."[70] The demands of the Merina elite ensured that porterage shortages continued after the end of the conflict. Thus, in July 1886 it was commented that "transportation from that port [Vatomandry] to the capital has been high for the reason that the Government have taken many men to transport its cottons (customs duties) to the Capital."[71]

Government pressure on porters intensified from 1889 in preparation for the final showdown with France. It was announced in May that year:

Men are scarce at the Capital on account of Government enrolling for the army which upsets business in every way. Men now at Tamatave cannot get permits to leave the town on account of the conscription which is to take place here within the next ten days.[72]

Conscription coincided with the start of the commercial season. Consequently, porter wages, and therefore transport costs, rose. For instance, hides in August 1889 cost \$4.60 per 100 pounds in Antananarivo, but transport to Toamasina added \$3.25, or 41.4 percent, to the cost.[73] The dearth of porters continued into 1891. The low buying price for hides led in early 1892 to fewer hides being produced in the interior. As a result, fewer porters were despatched to Toamasina where the lack of carriers aggravated costs, further undermined commercial confidence, and accelerated the slide into economic depression.[74] A second military draft in June 1893 accentuated the crisis. A U.S. firm commented,

During this month some twelve or fifteen of my convoys have been stoped on the road between here and Andovarante [Andevoranto], the goods left in the villages where they happened to be, and the bearers sent back to Tamatave by government officials.[75]

They were released only after the American consul protested to the Merina governor of Toamasina. Thousands of porters were also drafted into munitions factories and the gold fields or requisitioned to transport lead and charcoal required for the war industry. Accustomed to an independent lifestyle, many *maromita* rejected such constraints and fled the empire to join slave republics or brigands in the *efitra*.[76]

---

[70] Bachelder to Dawson, Antananarivo, 17 July 1885, *REC/CR-MZL*.

[71] The same situation occurred in 1887 – Whitney to Ropes, Emmerton & Co, and Arnold, Hines & Co, Tamatave, 31 July 1886 and 20 Sept. 1887, *REC/CR-MZL*.

[72] Whitney to Ropes, Emmerton & Co, Tamatave, 7 May 1889, *REC/CR-MZL*.

[73] Whitney to Ropes, Emmerton & Co, Tamatave, 26 Aug. 1889, Ropes, Emmerton & Co, *REC/CR-MZL*.

[74] Whitney to Ropes, Emmerton & Co, Tamatave, 8 March 1892, *REC/CR-MZL*.

[75] Ryder to Ropes, Emmerton & Co, Tamatave, 27 June 1893, *REC/CR-MZL*.

[76] See Campbell, "Crisis of Faith."

External Transport

Until 1869, Madagascar was served by sailing ships whose itineraries were largely dictated by winds and currents. The advent of steamships and the opening of the Suez Canal in 1869 had a major impact upon trade and communications in the region. First, it inaugurated an era of fast and regular maritime links between Europe and Indian Ocean Africa IOA.[77] Consequently, European steamers carrying small loads of import staples could cater for demand in a much more flexible and competitive manner than the old New England sailing ships, which often sailed with large limited-item cargoes.[78] When the last Salem clipper sailed to East Africa in 1870, U.S. sailing vessels to Madagascar were increasingly specializing in the carriage of low-value high-bulk goods such as hides and cottons[79] and, from the late 1870s, kerosene.[80] Even so, falling steamship rates meant that by 1888 U.S. consignments were increasingly being carried in British ships via the Suez Canal.[81]

By the mid-1870s, three steamship companies serviced the Mascarenes: Messageries Maritimes, from Marseille, and two British lines, the Union and its competitor from 1872, Donald Currie. In 1864, the Union, which from 1857 ran monthly to Cape Town, extended its Natal service to Mauritius, from where a subsidized line ran to Toamasina. In 1879, British concerns in Madagascar failed to persuade Donald Currie to make Madagascar a port of call. Union discontinued its Mauritius service in 1881, but Messageries Maritimes – which ran from Zanzibar via Mayotta to Réunion – opened a French government-subsidized service from Réunion to Toamasina, Nosy Boraha, Vohimara, Antseranana, Mahajanga, and Nosy Be (from where it also ran to Nosy Ve).[82] Further, after

---

[77] Bennett, "Americans in Zanzibar," 44.

[78] Edward D. Ropes to father, Zanzibar, 21 Nov. 1886, B1 (1882–1886) Zanzibar Acc.11840 and 11884: Letters 1886, Papers of Edward D. Ropes Jr, *PM*.

[79] Bennett, "Americans in Zanzibar," 45.

[80] Americans held a virtual monopoly of kerosene sales in the region, despite occasional appearances of Russian oil. The chief regional markets for kerosene were Zanzibar and the Mascarenes – on Réunion, kerosene imports lept from 3,566 cases in 1881 to 34,903 cases in 1883; Malagasy demand for kerosene grew during the 1880s following governor Rainandriamampandry's order that all Toamasina residents maintain a lighted lantern outside their houses in order to promote night-time security – see Hathorne, "statement," Zanzibar, 23 Jan. 1878 – Hathorne, "Letterbook" (1878–80); Razi, "Sources d'histoire," 25, 72; W. H. Beehler, *The Cruise of the Brooklyn* (Philadelphia, 1885), 183.; [Gottel] to Dawson, St. Denis, 20 Feb. 1884, *REC/CR-MZL*.

[81] Bennett, "Americans in Zanzibar," 44; Manuscript Collection Register v. III, *EI*.

[82] By the 1880s, the French government was also subsidizing a steamship line from Réunion to Australia in the hope that the latter would constitute a major market for its flagging sugarcane industry, as the metropolitan French market had become dominated by beet sugar – *MT* II.44 (5 Nov. 1884), 404; Finkelmeier to Seward, Tamatave, 12 Dec. 1867; Robinson to Hunter, Tamatave, 20 Oct. 1875 – *US*; Kestell-Cornish to Principal of St Boniface, 7 Nov. 1881,

the Deutsch Ostafrikanische Gesellschaft (DOAG) opened a Mahajanga agency in 1890, many DOAG ships returning from East Africa to Germany called at Mahajanga, Analava, and Nosy Be.[83]

Steamships operated year-round, independent of the trade winds that made November to January the heaviest shipping season for the dhow trade between north west Madagascar and Zanzibar.[84] They nevertheless strengthened the position of Indian traders, freeing them from dependency on resident foreign agents and enabling them to deal directly with the steamship companies for their European and U.S. business.[85] Moreover, steamship companies could not compete regionally with the rates offered by dhows, which had much smaller overheads: They were largely wind and current driven, often manned by slaves, and paid no insurance premiums (no one in Zanzibar would insure dhows).[86] By contrast, steamship companies had large overheads and applied quasi-monopolistic rates: For example, in 1884, O'Swald took advantage of the bankruptcy of Roux de Fraissinet, its main European rival in Nosy Be, to raise its steamer freight rates – although these remained lower than the rates of Messageries Maritimes, which operated in the region from about 1885.[87]

The Merina regime showed little interest in improving maritime transport facilities.[88] No harbor or breakwater was built even at Toamasina. Most ships on the east coast had to weigh anchor in deep water offshore. They were therefore highly vulnerable to the cyclones that often hit the region between January and April: One in March 1885 destroyed two French steamers and a French brig, as well as a British and an American schooner; another in February 1888 sank every boat off Toamasina; and in 1893 a minor squall was sufficient to wreck the *Joseph A. Ropes* of Boston.[89]

Kestell-Cornish Letterbook (1874–88), *ACM*; Néple, *Guide de l'Immigrant à Madagascar* II (Paris, 1899), 269.

[83] Raminosoa. "La Maison 'Wm. O'Swald & Co.,'" 27, 224, 226, 228–9, 231.

[84] Hathorne to Arnold, Hines & Co, Zanzibar, 6 Mar. 1878, "Letterbook of William H. Hathorne, Zanzibar (1877–1879), acc.11.584, *PM*; Razi, "Sources d'Histoire Malgache," 15.

[85] Bennett, "Americans in Zanzibar," 44.

[86] The trading seasons of dhows, which were generally between 150 and 200 ton and could carry up to 60 men, were governed by trade winds. March, for example, marked the end of the monsoon on which dhows from northwest Madagascar could sail to Zanzibar – Hathorne to Arnold, Hines & Co, Zanzibar, 6 Mar. 1878 and Hathorne to Thompson, Zanzibar, 8 Jan. 1879 – Hathorne, "Letterbooks" (1877–9) and (1878–80); Putnam, "A Cruise" (1848–50).

[87] Ropes, Emmerton & Co, to J. Orme Ryder, Salem, 30 April and 7 May 1883, ms.103, Ropes, Emmerton & Co. Records (1873–1902) B42.F4: Correspondence Received. Madagascar and Zanzibar Letterbook, 1883–5, *EI*; Raminosoa, "La Maison 'Wm. O'Swald & Co,'" 31.

[88] See Grandidier, "Souvenirs," 40; F. Birkeli, "Sur les projets maritimes de l'ancien gouvernement hova," *BAM* 27 (1946), 147–56.

[89] Finkelmeier to Hunter, Tamatave, 3 April 1872; Robinson to Hunter, 29 March 1875; Robinson to Third Assistant Secretary of State, 7 March 1885; Waller to Quincy, 21 July 1893 – *US*; Catat, *Voyage à Madagascar*, 12, 19; *CdM* (2 Feb. 1892).

14. Offloading Lighters, Toamasina circa 1880

Live cattle, an important export, were linked by rope and forced to swim from the shore to waiting Mascarene bullockers,[90] while lighters had to be used to tranship goods to and from the mainland. In 1884, it was noted of Toamasina that "vessels usually take from three weeks to a month discharging 4000 to 5000 cases of oil."[91] During the 1883–5 French naval blockade of Toamasina, some foreign merchants switched to Vatomandry, where transhipment of goods was hindered by a bar over which no more than half-loaded lighters could pass. The diversion of traffic to Vatomandry proved a boon to Pelisier, a resident Creole, who owned initially the only lighter in the port. In addition to imposing exorbitant lighterage fees, he charged 33 percent of the net profits on the sale of any goods landed[92] (Illustrations 14 and 15).

[90] Mayeur, "Voyage au pays d'ancove" (1777), 153; *idem*, "Voyage au pays d'ancove" (1785), 205; Copland, *History of Madagascar*, 15; Bergsten, "Mémoire" (1825), 16; Oliver, *Madagascar* vol. I, 265, 412, 414; Anon, "Betsimisaraka folk-tales," 217; Sibree, *A Naturalist*, 20, 22–3, 35; *GH* (1928), 297; Robequain, "capitale montagnarde," 287; Valette, "Nouvelle note," 33–6; *Ny Gazety Malagasy* I.8 (1 Dec. 1875); Robinson to Hankey, 21 July 1879; *idem* to Hunter, 22 Sept. 1879; Campbell to Wharton, 2 Sept. 1889 – *US*; *CdM* (16 fév. 1892)(2 jan. 1894);(6 mars 1894); (15 mai 1894); (5 juin 1894).

[91] Dawson to Ropes, Emmerton & Co, and Arnold, Hines & Co, Tamatave, 3 March 1884, *REC/ CR-MZL*.

[92] Dawson to Ropes, Emmerton & Co, and Arnold, Hines & Co, Tamatave, 10 Oct. 1884, and St Denis, Réunion, 25 Dec. 1884; Laborde to Whitney, Vatomandry, 15 Nov. 1886 – *REC/ CR-MZL*; see also Fenviligan to Ropes, Emmerton & Co, and Arnold, Hines & Co, Tamatave, 8 Nov. 1886, *REC/CR-MZL*.

15. Toamasina circa 1880

A chronic shortage of port labor also existed, due to manpower being tied up in the state *fanompoana* and private slave porterage systems. For example, in February 1885, an American trader in Vatomandry announced, "We have been detained longer than I expected on account of not being able to get laborers to man the lighters. Since November fully one third of the laborers have left Tamatave for the interior."[93] Moreover, port storage facilities were minimal. Merina authorities refused to ameliorate the situation, it being commented in 1882:

This government is so scared of foreigners that they refused permission to some of the Europeans to build a small boat pier *at their own expense* (I think it was to be 10 × 3 ft [3.04 by 0.91 meters]) to land passengers, giving as reason that troops might be landed there; also a firm had a cast iron store house come over from Europe, and it laid in the sand a whole year before that *blockhead* government could be persuaded that it wasn't a fortification; also they refuse permission for the same reason to parties here to erect an *open shed* to cover their goods at the landing. As it is now, a vessel comes in the rainy season and lands bales, they have to employ double as many hands to hold tarpaulins etc. etc. besides having to wait 'til pleasant weather to ship hides.[94]

---

[93] Savory to Ropes, Emmerton & Co, Tamatave, 8 Feb. 1885, *REC/CR-MZL*. See also Dawson [in Whitney] to Ropes, Emmerton & Co, and Arnold, Hines & Co, Tamatave, 5 May 1886, *REC/CR-MZL*.

[94] Edward D. Ropes to [parents], Tamatave, 24 March 1882, B1 (1882–6) Zanzibar Acc.11840 and 11884: Letters 1882, Papers of Edward D. Ropes Jr., *PM*.

Inadequate storage facilities increased the opportunity for theft, which was common, and added considerably to costs in time and labor.

Post and Communications

Domestic

Traditionally, messages were conveyed verbally by couriers, relays of whom were used over long distances. However, the rapid spread of literacy from the 1820s enabled the Merina administration to replace verbal with written communication within the empire. A special state courier service was established, manned by relays of *Tsimandoa/Tsimandao* [lit. "Will not forsake"], selected from the *Tsiarondahy*, a royal servant caste that originated from Andriambongo. In 1821, a courier service taking as little as two days was inaugurated along the 200-km Antananarivo to Toamasina route.[95] Missionaries had access to this service from 1820–5, 1829–35, and 1862–3[96] and, from the 1868–9 creation of the state church, could, outside central Imerina, freely summon imperial forced labor for their courier needs. In Betsileo, where Roman Catholic missionaries fought for the same rights as those enjoyed by their Protestant counterparts, Finaz noted in 1876,

We also take advantage of the postal service to transport parcels. Stopping points are arranged where the porters change over. Father Abinal, during the porterage of his luggage to his new post at Ambohimandroso, noted that a fire producing a great amount of smoke had been lit in the middle of an extensive plain. It was a signal: the Betsileo liable to *corvée* came down from the surrounding slopes and each assumed his position, to take his burden and carry it to the next changeover stop, for the route did not pass through the villages.[97]

---

[95] The *Tsimandoa* could run up to 60 km a day. See Hastie, "Diary" (1820), 476; *idem*, "Diary" (1822–3); Hastie to Griffiths, Port Louis, 18 Feb. 1821, *SOAS/LMS-MIL* B1.F2.JB; Hilsenburg, "Journal" (ed. Jean Valette) *BdM* (avril-mai 1963), 41; Rabary, *Daty Malaza* vol. I, 23, 26–7; Farquhar to René, Port Louis, 26 April 1821 in *RH*, 101; Finaz, "Journal" (1855–7), 57; *HR* vol. II, 634; vol. V, 1081, 1110; *GH* (1928), 344, 350, 376; Sibree, *Fifty Years*, 46; Oliver, *Madagascar* vol. I, 236, 238; Finkelmeier to Seward, Tamatave, 12 Dec. 1867, *US*; *CdM* 140 (24 avril 1894); Campbell, "Role of the London Missionary Society" vol. I, 147–9, vol. II, 222–4.

[96] Extract of letter from Jones and Griffiths, Antananarivo, 16 Dec. 1825 and 9 Nov. 1826, in *Minutes of the Southern Committee (1826–1837);* Baker to Ellis, Ivohitsara, 30 July 1834, *SOAS/LMS-MIL* B5.F1.JC; see also Baker to Ellis, Tamatave, 15 July 1834, *SOAS/LMS-MIL* B5.F1.JC; Ellis, *History of Madagascar* vol. II, 479–80.

[97] Finaz, "Mémoires sur le commencement de la mission dans la province du Betsileo" (1876), Diaires II no. 24, 16–18 – *AHVP*.

In Antananarivo, site of most mission headquarters and residences, missionaries established their own courier services, generally comprising two sets of runners, one to carry letters and the other to transport cash – both in large (imported), waterproof leather bags. Initially, sums of up to $2,000 or more in cash were entrusted to *maromita* captains, a missionary commenting that "Goods or money intrusted to them are always safe; and a poor native will travel hundreds of miles of trackless country with a parcel of specie or other valuables without any danger of the loss of the property."[98]

Despite this sanguine picture, mounting losses in transit – unlike gold, specie proved particularly vulnerable to theft – had become so great by 1888 that the LMS in Antananarivo sought couriers exclusively for its specific needs.[99] For example, Ratsimiza and Ranamo, trusted slaves of the governor of Fianarantsoa, were hired every quarter to transport $1,600 in 10 sealed bags from the central mission treasury in Antananarivo to Fianarantsoa.[100]

In c.1871, the LMS opened a monthly mail service for public use between Antananarivo and Toamasina. When it was disrupted by a cyclone or an epidemic, as during the 1876 smallpox outbreak, the Merina government granted foreigners emergency access to the *Tsimandoa*.[101] Larger firms, foreign consuls, and other missions also established independent courier services. In November 1872, within two months of their arrival in Imerina, the Society for the Propagation of the Gospel (SPG) started a monthly mail to Toamasina. It attempted to capture LMS postal business by leaving a week earlier. Rivalry was such that in September 1878, when Toloto, the SPG courier from Toamasina, arrived in Antananarivo later than the LMS runner, Kestell-Cornish, the SPG Bishop of Madagascar, fined him $0.50 – representing one-quarter of his wages for the trip.[102]

---

[98] Little, *Madagascar*, 100.

[99] Robinson to Hunter, Tamatave, 21 July 1879, *US*; Wills to Aitken, Antananarivo, 24 March 1888, IDC Letterbook. 2, *FJKM*; Ryder to Ropes Emmerton & Co, Tamatave, 27 March 1893, *REC/CR-MZL*.

[100] Briggs to Mullens, Antananarivo, 29 April 1875, LMS Letterbook (1868–75), *FJKM*; Wills to Aitken, Antananarivo, 6 Jan. 1876; Lord to Pearse, 30 March, 19 June, and 20 Sept. 1882, IDC Letterbook (1875–97), *FJKM*; Chiswell to Aitken, Antananarivo, 13 Oct. 1876, SPG Letterbook (1876–84) – *ACM*.

[101] See, e.g., Cousins to Mullens, Antananarivo, 31 July 1871, LMS Letterbook (1868–75), *FJKM*; Wills to Procter, Antananarivo, 9 Dec. 1875; *idem* to Mullens, 7 Dec. 1876 – IDC Letterbook (1875–97), *FJKM*; Chiswell to Aitken, Antananarivo, 3 Oct. 1876, SPG Letterbook (1876–84), *ACM*; Chapus & Mondain, *Rainilaiarivony*, 101.

[102] Chiswell to Cousins, Antananarivo, 11 Nov. 1872, "LMS Correspondence with the SPG (1870–1926)," *FJKM*; Cousins to Chiswell, Antananarivo, 13 Nov. 1872, LMS Letterbook (1868–75), *FJKM*; Wills to Procter, Antananarivo, 9 Dec. 1875, IDC Letterbook (1875–97), *FJKM*; Kestell-Cornish to Chiswell, Antananarivo, 6 Sept. 1878, Kestell-Cornish Letterbook (1874–88).

Smaller traders cooperated to establish commercial courier services. In 1875, foreign merchant residents of Antananarivo started a weekly service to Toamasina where their counterparts in 1879 founded a parallel service to the imperial capital – thus creating a twice-weekly mail between the coast and the interior. By 1881, at least six courier organizations linked Antananarivo to Toamasina, prompting British missionaries in Antananarivo to cooperate with their merchant compatriots in the appointment of a postmaster to collect, charge for, and dispatch all British mail. Arrangements were made with the French Post Office to debit the cost of mail to Europe to the British consulate in Toamasina, which established a British Consular Mail Service charging a standard rate of $0.0417 per 15 grams, issued a local frank, and dispatched runners to the interior three times a week. By early 1884, the British vice-consul in Antananarivo was also issuing special $0.125 stamps to cover postage both to the coast and to Britain. British consular agents in Toamasina, Port Louis, or Durban replaced local consular stamps, not recognized by the Postal Union, with authorized stamps.[103] Incoming mail continued to experience considerable delays until 1888, when the Mauritius Postmaster agreed to expedite mail delivery to Madagascar provided the British consul in Toamasina guaranteed postage.[104]

The missions were also the first foreign organizations to forge nongovernmental interregional courier services. In 1875, the Norwegian Missionary Society (NMS) and LMS linked Antananarivo to Antsirabe and Fianarantsoa respectively. The latter service, which took five to six days, became so overburdened that the LMS restricted its Betsileo-based agents to an annual postage allowance of $6. In 1878, the LMS opened an Antananarivo to Ambatondrazaka service. Other organizations followed suit; thus, in May 1882 the U.S. consulate extended its courier network to link Antananarivo with Mahajanga (see Table 10.1).[105]

The 1883–5 war considerably disrupted the postal service. First, all bar imperial government correspondence was excluded from the *Tsimandoa* courier

[103] Briggs to Pakenham, Antananarivo, 29 April 1875, LMS, Letterbook (1868–75), *FJKM*; Wills to Aitken, Antananarivo, 6 Jan. 1876; Lord to Pearse, 30 March, 19 June and 20 Sept. 1882 – IDC Letterbook (1875–97), *FJKM*; Chiswell to Aitken, 13 Oct. 1876, SPG Letterbook (1876–84), *ACM*; Norby, "Norwegian 'local' stamps – on Madagascar," *The Posthorn* 24.3 (July, 1967), 42; Samuel Graveson, "British Inland Mail Stamps of Madagascar," *The Raconteur and Philatelist* (Oct. 1935), 7–9.

[104] Kestell-Cornish to Porter Aitken, Antananarivo, 19 Nov. 1881 and 23 June 1882, Kestell-Cornish Letterbook (1874–88), *ACM*; "letter" [1883], SPG Letterbook (1882–95), *ACM*; Baron to Postmaster General, Antananarivo, 23 July 1886, IDC Letterbook (1875–91), *FJKM*; Ireland, Fraser & Co, to IDC Treasurer, Mauritius, 10 May 1887, "Local, Commercial and Transport," File M, *FJKM*; Thorne to IDC, 2 Feb. 1888, Folder, "Correspondence from the Secretary to Missionaries and Committees (1888–99)," *FJKM*.

[105] Price to BDC, Faravohitra, 10 June 1875, IDC Letters (1874–96), B10, *FJKM*; Riordan to Brockway, Fianarantsoa, 29 Nov. 1877, BDC Letterbook 1, *FJKM*; "Estimates for 1879"

TABLE 10.1. *Madagascar – Courier Distances*

Route	Distance (km)	Length of Journey (days) Courier	Mpaka entana (freight porter)
Antananarivo to:			
Toamasina	322	2–7	11–23
Mahajanga	483	3.5–8	15–18
Tsimanandrafozana	510	4	13
Fianarantsoa	465	3–7	10
Ambatondrazaka	193	6	28
Mahanoro	254	3–8	11–24
Fianarantsoa to:			
Ambositra	150	2.5	8
Antananarivo	465	3–7	10
St.Augustin	541	5–8.5	22–34
Toamasina to:			
Antananarivo	322	2–7	11–23
Ambatondrazaka	409	2	8

Source: Price to Wardlaw Thompson, Fianarantsoa, 20 April 1881, BDC Letter Book 1, *FJKM*; Rabeony to Andriamifidy, Ambatondrazaka, 12 Nov. 1887, HH1, 705, *ANM*; Oliver, *Madagascar* vol. 1, 319, 334–5, 348, 355, 384–8, 392–3; *Le courrier de Madagascar* 128 (30 Jan. 1894); Deschamps, *histoire*, 212.

system. Also, the French occupation of Toamasina and coastal blockade forced foreign agencies to follow the example of the Merina court and establish alternative routes for overseas mail. The first was a fortnightly service to the east coast port of Mahanoro to catch a connection to Zanzibar; the second, a monthly mail to Morondava on the midwest coast. However, private runners were frequently confiscated by Merina officials in order to carry government correspondence.[106] Moreover, the mobile French blockade resulted in the mail being continually switched to nonblockaded ports of the east coast. For instance, when the French navy appeared off Mahanoro in October 1883, mail was redirected to Mananjary, although by early 1884, Mahanoro was again open. An attempt in 1884 by ex-FFMA (Friends Foreign Mission Association) printer Kingdon to launch a direct Madagascar-to-Britain mail boat service failed[107].

in IDC Letterbook (1875–91), 313–19, *FJKM*; Rabeony to Andriamifidy, Ambatondrazaka, 12 Nov. 1887, HH1, 705, *ANM*; Norby, "Norwegian 'local' stamps," 42.

[106] Robinson to Third Assistant Secretary of State, Tamatave, 5 May 1885, *US*.

[107] Taylor to Whitnee, Majunga, 27 June 1883, "US Consular Agency Correspondence from Majunga (1881–5)"; Whitnee to Adee, Tamatave, 30 Aug, 4 Sept., 28 Nov., and 20 Dec. 1883; Robinson to Adee, Tamatave, 27 May 1884; Stanwood to Campbell, Andakabe, 30 May 1887 – *US*; Briggs to Wardlaw Thompson, Antananarivo, 1 Aug. 1883, IDC Letterbook

The war led to a suspension of the Antananarivo–Ambatondrazaka service from 1883 to 1887 and the plateau to Morondava service from 1884 to 1886, by which time a dramatic growth in brigandry threatened the security of mail services throughout the Merina empire.[108] Governors of isolated Merina garrisons would often confiscate passing mail and even seize couriers for nonpostal *fanompoana*. For example, by 1887, the Merina governor of Mahabo was stopping all plateau-bound mail and destroying letters alluding to official Merina corruption in Sakalava land. Remaining mail was allowed to continue after the payment of a heavy duty. On rare occasions, the courier himself would abscond with the mail.[109] As a result, foreign agents on the west coast generally dispatched Antananarivo-bound mail by sea to Mahajanga, Zanzibar, or Natal, where it was transferred onto European mail steamers. In 1887, it cost $1.00 to ship mail from Morondava to Mahajanga; from there, the courier service to Antananarivo cost $0.50.[110] In 1888, a plan by the French customs and the U.S. consul at Morondava for a monthly service to connect at Mahajanga with Messageries Maritimes collapsed when the latter eliminated Mahajanga as a port of call.[111] Foreign residents south of Morondava generally shipped their mail to Natal. Thus agents of the Natal firm of *Oman* were paid by Lars Røstvig, an NMS missionary in Toliara, to carry his mail to Durban, where they placed the correct stamps on it for postage to Europe or to Antananarivo (on the *Castle Mail* via Mauritius).[112]

In 1886, Rainilaiarivony failed to raise a $4 million European loan partly earmarked to construct railway and telegraph lines between Antananarivo and Toamasina. However, in 1887, the French, who continued to occupy Toamasina after the end of the war in 1885, established an Antananarivo–Toamasina telegraph link. In 1888, the inauguration of a free public empire-wide postal service by the NMS precipitated the collapse of the fee-charging British consular mail. However, despite the establishment in 1892 of a twice-weekly

(1875–91), *FJKM*; "letter" [1883]; Kestell-Cornish to James, Antananarivo, 22 May, 17 July, 17 Aug. 1883 and 3 March 1884 – SPG Letterbook (1882–95), *ACM*.

[108] Robinson to Payson, Tamatave, 9 June 1881; "enclosure 2" in Stanwood to Third Assistant Secretary of State, Andakabe, 11 Feb. 1884; Stanwood to Robinson, 28 Aug. 1884; *idem* to Batard, 31 Oct. 1886; *idem* to Porter, Andakabe, 1 Jan. 1887 – *US*.

[109] Briggs to Mullens, Antananarivo, 17 Oct. 1875, IDC Letterbook (1875–91), *FJKM*; Robinson to Hunter, Tamatave, 1 Oct. 1878 – *US*; Price to Whitehouse, Fanjakana, 7 Oct. 1880, BDC Letterbook 1, *FJKM*. For official tampering with mail see Stanwood to Robinson, Morondava, 1 Dec. 1880; *idem* to Porter, Andakabe, 1 Jan. 1887; *idem* to Campbell, 20 Aug. 1887 – US. For Brigandry, see Campbell, *Unfree Labour*.

[110] Stanwood to Campbell, Andakabe, 30 May and 30 Sept. 1887, *US*.

[111] Stanwood to Campbell, 10, 11 Oct. and 12 Dec. 1887, 9 March 1888; Campbell to Stanwood, Tamatave, 30 Aug. 1888 – *US*.

[112] Røstvig to Oman, Tullear, 28 Feb. 1888, NMS Kopibok (1882–92), 812B, *FLM/NMS*.

Toamasina–Antananarivo commercial mail by the French, the strain on postal services that followed the dramatic influx of foreigners into Madagascar from the mid-1880s led the NMS in 1894 to impose a charge of approximately $0.007 for letters and $0.021 for parcels. Stamps were printed on the mission press in Antananarivo using a design based on the earlier British consular stamps, representing the values of $0.0014 (*vari*), $0.007 (*varidimiventy*), $0.014 (*efa*), and $0.021 (*ilavoamena*).[113]

The renewal of Franco–Merina hostilities in 1894–5 again disrupted the postal network. The British community, favored by the Merina court, was granted access to the *Tsimandoa*,[114] but this service collapsed within a few months when the Merina capital fell to the French. Nevertheless, not until 1904 did a road capable of carrying motor vehicles connect Antananarivo to Toamasina, and even then the journey took a minimum of two days.[115]

Overseas

From the 1870s, steamship companies secured most overseas mail connections. Mail chartered for Madagascar from countries other than France was first shipped to Réunion or Mauritius. As Madagascar was not in the Postal Union, non-French foreign residents were obliged to hire agents or maintain deposits with the relevant postmaster to ensure that mail was forwarded.[116] British steamers serving Mauritius from South Africa generally arrived a month sooner than Marseille steamers to Réunion via the Suez Canal.[117] However, mail for Madagascar suffered heavy delays due to transhipment, surcharges imposed by Mauritian officials, and the use of "bullockers" – old sailing cattle-boats that in the December to March cyclone season ceased to run.[118] Even using the

---

[113] Wetter to Uhl, 7 Aug. 1894, US; Norby, "Norwegian 'local' stamps," 43, 49; *CdM* 6 (12 jan. 1892) and 15 (15 mars 1892).

[114] For mail to Britain, special stamps were printed on the LMS press, and other stamps were printed by John Haddon of London and dispatched to Madagascar. At the coast, mail was transferred onto Donald Currie steamers to Natal. See Graveson, "British Inland Mail," 42.

[115] Robequain, *Madagascar*, 302.

[116] Finkelmeier to Seward, Tamatave, 11 July 1867; Robinson to Hunter, Tamatave, 1 July 1876 – *US*; Wills to Wardlaw Thompson, Antananarivo, 28 Jan. 1886, IDC Letterbook (1875–97), 467–9, *FJKM*; R. F. M. Immelman, *Men of Good Hope, 1804–1954: The Romantic Story of the Cape Town Chamber of Commerce* (Cape Town, 1955), 99, 211; Archibald Hurt, *The Sea Traders* (London, 1921), 184, 188–9.

[117] Briggs to Wardlaw Thompson, Antananarivo, 22 Aug. 1882; Baron to Ireland, Fraser & Co, 27 Jan. 1885; *idem* to Wardlaw Thompson, 15 Oct. 1886 – IDC Letterbook (1875–91), *FJKM*.

[118] Finkelmeier to Seward, Tamatave, 1 Oct. 1866; Robinson to Hunter, Tamatave, 18 June 1879 – *US*; Thorne to Whitehouse, 22 April and 20 May 1880, IDC Letterbook (1875–91).

TABLE 10.2. *Mail Boat Services between Europe and Madagascar*
(Distance in Nautical Miles)

Messageries Maritimes (total distance Marseille–Toamasina = 5,760)
1. Main Marseille–Australia route via Mascarenes

Marseille to:	Port Said	Suez	Aden	Mahé	Réunion	Mauritius
	1,548	1,635	2,043	4,338	5,310	5,432

2. Branch line from Réunion to Madagascar and East Africa

Réunion to:	Toamasina	Nosy Boraha	Vohimara	Antomboka	Nosy Be
	450	540	790	880	1,035
	Mayotta	Mahajanga	Mozambique	Zanzibar	
	1,215	1,400	1,750	2,230	

Donald Currie "*Castle Mail*" (total distance London–Toamasina = 9,046)
1. Main London–Cape Town route

London to:	Dartmouth	Madeira	St Helena	Cape Town
	280	1,490	4,436	6,131

2. Branch line from Cape Town to Mauritius and Toamasina

Cape Town to:	Port Elizabeth	Natal	Mauritius	Toamasina
	450	845	2,445	6,600

Source: Oliver, *Madagascar* vol. 1, 446.

Réunion route, U.S. consular mail from New York to Toamasina took at least five months[119] (see Table 10.2).

Consequently, some foreign residents shipped mail via Mahajanga to Zanzibar, the major port of call on the east African coast for European mail steamers. However, as overland courier costs from Antananarivo to Mahajanga were twice those to Toamasina, and mail to Europe via Mahajanga took on average 67 days – 16 days longer than via the more erratic Toamasina route – its popularity soon waned.[120] During the 1883–5 war, non-French residents switched back to sailing vessels such as the NMS-owned *Elieser* and *Paulus* that from the 1880s voyaged between Norway and Madagascar[121] or the vessels of John Bertram and Arnold Hines that plied regularly between New York and Madagascar.[122]

---

[119] Finkelmeier to Hunter, 1 April 1875; Robinson to Payson, Tamatave, 2 Sept. 1881 – *US*.

[120] Kestell-Cornish to James, Antananarivo, 28 March 1876; *idem* to Tucker, 18 July 1877 and 15 May 1878 – Kestell-Cornish Letterbook (1874–88), *ACM*; Briggs to Mullens, Antananarivo, 14 May and 2 Dec. 1878; 24 April 1879 – IDC Letterbook (1875–91).

[121] "Sombintsombin'ny Tantaran'ny Sosieten'ny Misiona Norveziana Tanatin'ny 100 Taona, 8 août 1842 – 8 août 1942," ms. Boks.56f, 1–11, *FLM/NMS*.

[122] Finkelmeier to Hunter, Tamatave, 1 April 1875; Robinson to Hunter, Tamatave, 11 March 1879 – *US*.

In 1886, a British government subsidy induced Donald Currie to reestablish its Cape Town to Mauritius mail service. As Donald Currie and Messageries Maritimes offered alternate monthly mails, this in theory created a fortnightly service between Europe and the islands of the Western Indian Ocean. In reality, such services proved irregular, it being noted of the Donald Currie line in May 1888:

We find by the timetables that steamers leave Durban, Port Natal, every six weeks.... These steamers however, are very irregular in their arrivals and departures at all points. Sometimes they make Tamatave first, and sometimes Mauritius, and they are almost always ten days behind time at Tamatave.[123]

The British Post Office campaigned successfully for the removal of the subsidized Donald Currie line to Toamasina.[124] Nevertheless, some British concerns in Madagascar hostile to the French, such as the LMS, continued to use Donald Currie via Mauritius, although it was more expensive and took a month longer than shipping directly with Messageries Maritimes.[125]

Transport Costs and Economic Development

A deficient transport and communications infrastructure formed a major barrier to any foreign invasion. However, it was also a major contributory factor to the decline of the imperial Merina economy. Poor roads and human porterage limited the volume and added substantially to the time and cost of transport.[126] *Maromita* daily wages, stable at two *voamena* or $0.17 from the end of the eighteenth century to the mid-nineteenth century, rose to $0.25 by 1884. This compared badly to the wages of skilled workers, who received one dollar a day from foreign hirers in 1888, but compared well with the daily wage of an ordinary laborer, estimated at $0.028 in 1884 (see Table 10.3). There was considerable variety in wage rates for specific tasks. Thus *mpilanjana* in the Antananarivo area in 1882 would not accept less than "3 pence [$0.0625] a

---

[123] Whitney to Ropes, Emmerton & Co, Tamatave, 1 May 1888, *REC/CR-MZL*.

[124] Robinson to Hunter, Tamatave, 22 Sept. 1879; Campbell to Porter, Tamatave, 20 Sept. 1887 – *US*; Kestell-Cornish to Principal of St Boniface, Antananarivo, 7 Nov. 1881, Kestell-Cornish Letterbook (1874–88), *ACM*; Oliver, *Madagascar* vol. 1, 443–6; Graveson, "British Inland Mails," 8.

[125] Houlder to Ireland, Fraser & Co, Antananarivo, 15 Oct. 1886 and 13 April 1887; *idem* to Wardlaw Thompson, 2 March 1887; *idem* to Porter Aitken, 20 July and 2 Sept. 1887, IDC Letterbook (1875–91), *FJKM*; Ireland, Fraser & Co. to Houldr, Mauritius, 3 Nov. 1886, "Local, Commercial and Transport," File M, *FJKM*.

[126] Grandidier, "Souvenirs," 32.

TABLE 10.3. *Comparative Wage Rates in Nineteenth-Century Madagascar ($) –*
Selected Years

| Year | Antananarivo–Toamasina | | Daily wage rates in Antananarivo ($) | | |
	Mpaka Entana	Courier	Maromita	Skilled	Unskilled
c.1800–61	n.a.	n.a.	n.a.	0.170	n.a.
c.1865	3.00	n.a.	0.125	0.125	0.083
1866	2.00	n.a.	n.a.	n.a.	n.a.
1871	3.00	n.a.	n.a.	n.a.	n.a.
1872	2.43	n.a.	n.a.	n.a.	n.a.
1873	2.79	n.a.	n.a.	n.a.	n.a.
1874	3.00	n.a.	n.a.	n.a.	n.a.
1875	2.29	n.a.	n.a.	n.a.	n.a.
1876	2.54	2.00	n.a.	n.a.	n.a.
1878	n.a.	2.00	n.a.	n.a.	n.a.
1880	n.a.	2.00	n.a.	n.a.	n.a.
1882	n.a.	n.a.	0.063	n.a.	n.a.
1884	3.29	n.a.	0.250	0.028	n.a.
1885	n.a.	2.00	n.a.	n.a.	n.a.
1887	3.13	n.a.	n.a.	n.a.	n.a.
1888	5.00	n.a.	n.a.	n.a.	n.a.
1893	3.50	n.a.	n.a.	1.000	n.a.
1894	8.00	n.a.	n.a.	n.a.	n.a.
1897	9.00	5.00	n.a.	n.a.	n.a.

Source: Ellis, *Madagascar Revisited*, 490; Richardson to Cousins, Fianarantsoa, 1 May 1871, BDC Correspondence (1870–80), Folder, *FJKM*; Briggs to Procter, 15 and 16 April 1874, LMS Letter Book (1868–75), *FJKM*; Procter to Pearse and Parrett, Tamatave, 9 April 1872; *idem* to Briggs, Tamatave, 11 April 1874 and 2 April 1875 – "Commercial Correspondence from Procter," *FJKM*; Briggs to Procter, Antananarivo, 24 April 1878; *idem* to Shaw, 14 Dec. 1880; "Estimates for 1879" – IDC Letter Book (1875–91), *FJKM; Ny Gazety Malagasy* (1 Sept. 1875) and (1 Jan. 1876); Price to LMS, [Fianarantsoa], March 1881, BDC Letter Book (1876–95), *FJKM*; Robinson to Payson, Tamatave, 9 June 1881; Andrew to Robinson, Majunga, 26 Jan. 1882, "US Consular Agency Correspondence from Majunga," 81–5; Stanwood to Robinson, Andakabe, 16 Aug. 1885; Wetter to Uhl, Tamatave, 7 Aug. 1894 and 18 Feb. 1896 – *US*; Lord to Foxhall, 12 Jan. 1892, IDC Letter Book (1875–86), *FJKM*; SPG Accounts Book (1877–1903), *ACM*; Campbell, "Labour and the Transport Problem," 355; Bachelder to Dawson, Antananarivo, 11 Sept. 1884; Dawson to Ropes, Emmerton & Co, and Arnold, Hines & Co, St. Denis, Réunion, 25 Dec. 1884; Whitney to Ropes, Emmerton & Co, and Arnold, Hines & Co, Tamatave, 6 Feb. 1887 – *REC/CR-MZL*.

voyage and refuse to touch a spade."[127] Nevertheless, on the main long distance routes, notably between Antananarivo and Toamasina, *mpilanjana* continued to receive the same wages as *mpaka entana* – although the captain earned more than

[127] Quoted in *MT* I.14 (22 July 1882), 92.

his men for assuming responsibility for the fulfillment of hiring contracts.[128] The rate for the Toamasina–Antananarivo route, while fluctuating according to local exigencies, rose steadily between 1866 and 1888 from two to six dollars a man and then fell in 1893 before reaching eight dollars by 1894.[129] Additional payments for the hirer included *maromita* passports (in 1884, they cost $0.24 each);[130] *vatsy* (food money), the amount of which (generally from $9 to $26) varied according to the size of the convoy's[131] lighterage fees (generally $1 a load); and port labor wages.[132]

A further cost was the loss of merchandise, especially cloth. Merchant anger was aroused from the early 1870s by the seizure of goods by porters on the Toamasina to Antananarivo route. Austen asserts that slaves were much more likely to be involved in criminality than free groups structured, as were the Malagasy, into caste.[133] However, given the strict regulation of slaves, robbery by slave porters was only possible with the cooperation, and probably at the instigation, of the slave syndicate at court. The slaves stole notably cotton pieces, which they stored in isolated depots until stocks could be safely distributed, often through Indian wholesalers. The culpable slaves were then "made to vanish" until the hue and cry had passed. Obstructed at every turn by the court elite responsible for the robberies, European merchants rarely succeeded in tracing or recovering their goods.[134] Export staples were not so vulnerable. Although foreign exporters counted on some hides going missing en route to the coast, most were later recovered.[135]

Total domestic transport costs for foreign traders were therefore considerable. For instance, the $1.5 million import and export trade of Imerina in 1884 is estimated to have borne an additional $55,000 in transport costs on the

[128] Procter to Pearse and Parret, Tamatave, 9 April 1872, file, "Commercial Correspondence from Procter"; Thorne to Whitehouse, 4 Dec. 1879, and Lord to Pearse, 30 March 1882, IDC Letterbook 2 – *FJKM*; Mullens, *Twelve Months in Madagascar*, 134; Knight, "From Fort Dauphin."
[129] *MT* I.14 (22 July 1882), 92.
[130] H. E. Clark, "How We Travel in Madagascar" *AAMM* 8 (1884), 342.
[131] Laborde to Whitney, Vatomandry, 29 Nov. 1886, *REC/CR-MZL*.
[132] Dawson to Ropes, Emmerton & Co, and Arnold, Hines & Co, Tamatave, 10 Oct. 1884, and St Denis, Réunion, 25 Dec. 1884; Laborde to Whitney, Vatomandry, 15 Nov. 1886 – *REC/CR-MZL*; see also Fenviligan to Ropes, Emmerton & Co, and Arnold, Hines & Co, Tamatave, 8 Nov. 1886, *REC/CR-MZL*.
[133] Ralph A. Austen, "Social bandits and other heroic criminals. Western models of resistance and their relevance for Africa," in Crummey (ed), *Banditry*, 95.
[134] Robinson to Hunter, Tamatave, 21 July 1879, *US*; Wills to Aitken, Antananarivo, 24 March 1888, IDC Letterbook. 2, *FJKM*; Ryder to Ropes Emmerton & Co, Tamatave, 27 March 1893, *REC/CR-MZL*.
[135] Whitney to Ropes, Emmerton & Co, and Arnold, Hines & Co, Tamatave, 17 Dec. 1886; Whitney to Ropes, Emmerton & Co, Tamatave, 26 July 1887 – *REC/CR-MZL*.

Antananarivo to Toamasina route. As William Pickersgill, the British vice-consul, remarked that year,

> Every article of merchandise offered for sale in the interior of Madagascar has to be carried hither from the coast on human shoulders. Packages which cannot be broken or rearranged at the port of landing should therefore be made up in certain weights. One man will carry two packages of from 40 to 45 lb. each, but the same weight in a single bale will require two men, and the expense of the transit will be doubled. Large packages and heavy packing materials often increase the cost of imported goods enormously. It is impossible to pay too much attention to this matter.[136]

Poor routes, porterage costs, and rising international competition also debarred from external markets all but the most valuable and low-bulk exports. Transport costs constituted roughly 50 percent of the price of plateau hides at Toamasina.[137] Although coffee grown above 270 meters was both disease-free and potentially a significant export crop, it proved too expensive to transport to the coast. The same problem faced European forest and mining concessionaires in the 1890s.[138] Indeed, the cost of shipping a unit of goods from France to Toamasina was less than that of transporting the same unit from Toamasina to Antananarivo, on which route porterage costs rose from $230 to $400 a ton between 1890 and 1896.[139]

In sum, although the porterage system was a cornerstone of imperial Merina defense policy, it proved a major obstacle to economic development. It maintained excessive costs at a time when radical improvements in transport and communications, notably through the expansion of steam transport, were causing costs elsewhere in the world to fall. Moreover, the human porterage system was doomed to failure. The *maromita*, emancipated in 1896, initially gained substantially from the transport demands of the French colonial regime: By 1897 porters' wage rates were so inflated that Gallieni, the French governor general, attempted to impose a maximum tariff of $9.[140] Nevertheless,

---

[136] Quoted in Oliver, *Madagascar* vol. II, 184.

[137] E.g., transport costs from the interior constituted at Toamasina 52.8 percent of the price of hides in September 1884 and 41.8 percent in February 1887 – see Bachelder to Dawson, Antananarivo, 11 Sept. 1884; Dawson to Ropes, Emmerton & Co, and Arnold, Hines & Co, St. Denis, Réunion, 25 Dec. 1884; Whitney to Ropes, Emmerton & Co, and Arnold, Hines & Co, Tamatave, 6 Feb. 1887 – *REC/CR–MZL*.

[138] Robequain, *Madagascar*, 216–220; Louis Cros, *Madagascar pour tous* (Paris [1922]), 385, 410; de Coppet (ed.), *Madagascar* vol. II, 328; *MT* II.41 (15 Oct. 1884), 376; Campbell, "Toamasina," 537.

[139] *MT* I.9 (17 June 1882), 56; Campbell, "Toamasina," 537.

[140] Grandidier, "Souvenirs," 14, 20; *GH* (1928), 351, 353–7; Colin et Suau, "Album malgache," 10–12; Catat, *Voyage à Madagascar*, 22–3; Clark, "How We Travel," 342; Campbell, "Labour and the Transport Problem," 355.

the porterage system came under increasing pressure as the French authorities invested in an island-wide road network and a skeletal railway system. Such improvements were opposed by the *maromita*, who even before the French conquest had protested against the increasing European use of horses by stoning riders. *Maromita* protest climaxed in 1901 in opposition to the introduction of the rickshaw. Although such demonstrations again illustrated the organizational strength of the porters, they were unsuccessful; the rickshaw cut passenger rates by half, and when the main road from the east coast to Imerina was completed, the cost of freight between Toamasina and Antananarivo dropped to $30 per ton. Ultimately *maromita* strength could not outlast the Merina empire, and the traditional porterage system had effectively disintegrated by the first years of the twentieth century.[141]

[141] *GH* (1928), 353–7; Campbell, "Labour and the Transport Problem," 355–6.

11 Currency and Finance, 1820–1895

Introduction

As imperial Madagascar lacked domestic capital formation and autarkic policies precluded the raising of foreign loans, economic growth largely depended upon human capital. Nevertheless, growing defense expenditure, increasing involvement in the international economy, and from the 1860s a relaxation in autarkic principles ensured that currency and finance remained issues of central importance.

Taxation

Taxes traditionally collected in kind proved sufficient to build up considerable grain stocks and grant the Merina aristocracy a life of leisure.[1] After a standing army and the *deka* system were created, the elite used such stocks to speculate during army expeditions, selling rice to conscripts at extortionate prices. This resulted in a considerable flow of cash from ordinary soldiers to the crown and court elite. However, as the cultivator became increasingly impoverished, this system led to diminishing returns, lasting only until about 1840.[2] The court also let army officers take much of the one-third of campaign booty, in the form of

---

[1] See Chapter 3.
[2] Gabriel Rantoandro, "Le gouvernement de Tamatave de 1845 à 1865; développement économique," thèse (Université de Madagascar, 1973), 83–6; Campbell, "Slavery and Fanompoana," 472–4.

cattle and slaves, normally reserved for the crown,[3] and permitted European traders and artisans to ignore an 1822 injunction to surrender 20 percent of their profits.[4] Another traditional, if irregular, revenue source was *hasina*, a tribute, originally in kind, paid to the sovereign on ritual occasions. It became a substantial and regular source of cash revenue when extended to the private porterage system as each *maromita*, upon entering the imperial capital, paid a $1 *hasina*. From the late 1860s, this raised an estimated annual minimum of $120,000 for the royal treasury.[5]

However, traditional tax revenue proved insufficient to pay for imported arms and machinery and the wages of Europeans involved in the industrial experiment. Consequently, extraordinary levies were imposed. In 1835, a minimum of $23,500 was thus raised to pay the salaries of Chick, Canham, Droit, Laborde, and Cameron,[6] and from 1837 to 1839, a minimum of $201,800 was raised to finance arms imports and the construction of the Mantasoa cannon foundry.[7] Again, in 1880, Rainilaiarivony offset through taxes the estimated $1 million in specie imported to pay for arms,[8] and in 1891–2, a new poll tax was imposed in an attempt to meet interest payments on the 1886 French loan.[9] To meet extraordinary taxes, many people had to borrow at exorbitant rates of interest from, or sell cattle to, members of the court elite whose monopoly of cattle exports allowed them to dictate the sale price.[10]

Nevertheless, the major form of taxation during the imperial era was *fanompoana*, which constituted a tax on both labor and commerce. Thus, of the

---

[3] Gabriel Rantoandro, "Le gouvernement de Tamatave de 1845 à 1865; développement économique," thèse (Université de Madagascar, 1973), 83–6; Campbell, "Slavery and Fanompoana," 472–4.

[4] Munthe et al., "Radama I et les Anglais," 56; Leminier, "Notes" (1825), 797; Canham to Burder, Ifenoarivo, 3 Oct. 1827, *SOAS/LMS-MIL* B2.F4.JC; Lyall, "Journal," 11–13, 33; Jones and Griffiths to LMS, Antananarivo, 9 Nov. 1826, *SOAS/LMS-MIL* B2.F3.JD.

[5] See *GH* (1928), 354; Oliver, *Madagascar* vol. II, 75–8; *AAMM* 22 (1898), 247; Campbell, "Role of the London Missionary Society" vol. II, 244.

[6] Griffiths, *Hanes Madagascar*, 52–3.

[7] Oliver, *Madagascar* vol. II, 196.

[8] Robinson to Payson, Antananarivo, 28 April 1881; *idem* to Third Assistant Secretary of State, 22 May, 29 June, and 28 July 1882; Campbell to Wharton, 24 May and 6 Dec. 1890; Waller to Wharton, 25 April 1893 – *US*; Cameron, "Newspaper Cuttings"; Rainilaiarivony à Dr. Davidson, Antananarivo, 5 Alahasaty 1868, in "Lettres du gouvernement et de la Reine, 1852–1859," Carton section II c.12, *AHVP*.

[9] Whitney to Ropes, Emmerton & Co, Tamatave, 1 May 1888, *REC/CR-MZL*; Gregory to Andriamfidy, Ambatobe, 23 Sept. and 27 Dec. 1889, 23 Dec. 1890, 22 Jan., 16 March, and 1 June 1891 – HH3, 697–717, *ANM*; *The Madagascar Mail* 3 (23 Aug. 1892) and 38 (13 Sept. 1892); *CdM* 14 (22 March 1894).

[10] Oliver, *Madagascar* vol. II, 196.

collection of gum copal – a royal monopoly – it was commented in 1884:

This resin is a rapid source of profit for the Hovas [Merina]. Suppose the Prime Minister wants money: he sends an aide-de-camp [*deka*] to the Governor of the province where the quantity is to be levied. The Governor calls the native chiefs and tells them that the Prime Minister counts upon them for the accomplishment of the orders. . . . A system of forced labour is immediately organised and the natives go out into the forest and collect the quantity assigned to each man. At the appointed day every one is to bring in the quantity collected under penalty of punishment if any part is withheld.

In the time of Radama II the results of the sale were divided as follows: One half for the Prime Minister, one quarter for the chiefs directing the work, and the rest for the people who fetch the gum; but out of these latter shares the Governor claimed such a high percent that the sums received by the natives was reduced to nothing. Since the death of Radama II the Governors dispose of the shares which belong to the native workmen and chiefs and use them to fill their own purses.[11]

Extraordinary taxation was increasingly resisted by the small farmers it impoverished and who resented those who most benefited from the system, such as the foreigners under royal contract and members of the court elite.[12]

Customs

The main source of cash revenue for the Merina court was foreign trade. In the early 1800s, Merina demand for piastres from Mascarene traders was generally satisfied,[13] but an estimated $96,000, or 80 percent of annual earnings from east coast exports, flowed to Indian and Swahili traders in payment for west coast imports.[14] Moreover, trade slumped during the Napoleonic Wars. The Britanno–Merina treaties of 1817, revised in 1820, envisaged minimal duties and therefore a growth in trade. However, royal revenues fell rapidly following the 1820 ban on slave exports, leading Radama I to reject free trade and increase customs

---

[11] *MT* II.41 (15 Oct. 1884), 376.

[12] Shipton to LMS, Tamatave, 10 Aug. 1834, *SOAS/LMS-MIL* B5.F1.JC; Campbell, "The History of Nineteenth Century Madagascar: "le royaume" or "l'empire"?" *Omaly sy Anio* 33–36 (1994), 331–79; *idem, Brigandry and Revolt in Pre-Colonial Africa: Imperial Madagascar, 1750–1900* – forthcoming.

[13] Mayeur, "Voyage dans le nord" (1775), 60–3; *idem*, "Voyage au pays d'ancove" (1777), 22; *idem*, "Réflexions" (1802); Morice, "Mémoire" (1777), 107–13; [Jouette], "Mémoire sur Madagascar" (1 juin 1806), *BL*.Add.18135; Hugon, "Aperçu" (1808), 15, 17, 22; GH (1928), 336; Delivré, *L'histoire des rois*, 224.

[14] Hastie, "Diary" (1817), 157, 188; *idem*, "Diary" (1824–5); Copland, *History of Madagascar*, 12–18; Oliver, *Madagascar* vol. II, 16–17; *GH* (1908), 106, 160, 162, 171 and (1928), 260, 302–3, 322–3, 327, 332; Horn, *Waters of Africa*, 97; Mayeur, "Voyage dans le nord" (1775), 86; *idem*, "Voyage au pays d'ancove" (1785), 227; Anon, "Mémoire historique" [1790], 55; Dumaine, "Voyage à la côte de l'ouest" (1793), 294–7; Chapelier, "Lettres adressées," 34.

duties. In 1825, he banned the import of French arms and obliged all non-British merchants, most of whom were French subjects, to pay export duties in cash – except on bullocks, which were taxed in cotton cloth. In 1826, he raised custom duties, generally to 25 percent ad valorem, and on cattle exports to 100 percent. In 1827, duties were regularized, imports at 20 percent and exports at 25 percent, except for rice (5 percent), live cattle ($5 a head), and salted carcasses ($6 each). To ensure compliance, foreign merchants were restricted to 12 imperial ports, the seas within four leagues (approximately 22 km) of the coast were declared imperial waters, and any irregular vessels within that limit were threatened with confiscation. As the Merina possessed no navy, such threats were a signal to the British that Radama I intended to break free of their tutelage.[15]

Repeated Mauritian and Réunionnais protests and the tendency of European merchants to seek non-Merina ports on the west coast, where duties were far lower than in imperial ports, led to east coast export duties being dropped to 10 percent ad valorem to recapture foreign traders. In the few Merina-controlled west coast ports, export duties were initially lowered to 5 percent ad valorem but in September 1842 were raised to equal east coast rates.[16] By April 1843, new duties had been imposed at Mahajanga; soap, crockery, and textiles were taxed at 10 percent ad valorem, muskets and specie at 5 percent, and the staple exports of hides and tallow at 10 percent.[17]

The closure of imperial ports in 1845, in protest against the Franco–British naval attack on Toamasina, led to a decline in foreign trade and thus in customs revenue although imported arms and luxury goods for the Merina elite contributed to a continued seepage of specie.[18] Imperial ports reopened in November 1853, after Mauritian merchants and planters paid an indemnity to Ranavalona I, but foreign commerce did not recover until Radama II's reign (1861–3)[19]

From 1861 to 1875, relative commercial prosperity, due to the liberalization of foreign trade, a dramatic growth of exports, and the absence of war, resulted in a marked influx of foreign currency: In Toamasina, in 1866 it was noted that "all trading is done exclusively in cash"[20] while on the plateau the

---

[15] Munthe et al., "Radama I et les Anglais," 56; Leminier, "Notes" (1825), 797; Canham to Burder, Ifenoarivo, 3 Oct. 1827, *SOAS/LMS-MIL* B2.F4.JC; Lyall, "Journal," 11–13, 33; Jones and Griffiths to LMS, Antananarivo, 9 Nov. 1826, *SOAS/LMS-MIL* B2.F3.JD.

[16] Campbell, "Role of the London Missionary Society" vol. I, 189–91, vol. II, 319.

[17] Razi, "Sources d'histoire," 13.

[18] This reversed the previous trend whereby American traders were obliged to ship specie to Madagascar to pay for their exports – Razi, "Sources d'histoire," 13, 17–18.

[19] Raombana, "Manuscrit," 4, 16; see also Tables 11.2 and 11.3.

[20] Finkelmeier to Seward, Tamatave, 1 Oct. 1866, US.

TABLE 11.1. *Total Value of Imerina–Réunion Trade, 1840–7 ($)*
(% = Percentage Change from Previous Year)

Year	Value	%	Year	Value	%
1840	176,082	n.a.	1844	330,145	+10.17
1841	223,878	+27.14	1845	221,399	−32.94
1842	306,532	+36.92	1846	196,577	−11.21
1843	299,679	−2.24	1847	62,277	−68.32

Source: Samat, "lettre" (1848).

surge in foreign trade from 1870 to 1875 induced a "great influx of coins."[21] Available commercial statistics, backed by narrative sources, indicate that the Merina empire maintained a positive balance of trade for almost a decade from 1865. A particularly large influx of specie in 1872 raised commodity prices and wages. Moreover, increased trade augmented the number of porters – the only significant group of salaried workers – who considerably boosted specie circulation and widened the concept of a cash economy within Madagascar.[22]

However, the surplus on visible commodity trade steadily diminished from 1870 and, by 1876, had evaporated. As Finkelmeier, the U.S. consul to Madagascar, stated,

Already our Commercial dealers here complain of being obliged to ship money from here for a large portion of their cargoes brought in – sending their ships to other ports to seek the larger part of homeward cargoes, when they would much prefer to receive the whole value of their goods in the products of the island.[23]

Moreover, the increase in the money supply was not immediate or comprehensive in its geographical impact. For example, in the 1860s, the LMS imported goods rather than dollars to barter for their local requirements because of the expense and risk of transporting large amounts of silver coinage by human porterage.[24]

A major reason for restricted domestic circulation of coinage was that, despite the court's nominal avowal of free trade from 1861, foreign commerce, and hence export earnings, continued to be largely monopolized by the Merina elite. Imported coins were thus generally sent to Imerina where, in a pattern reminiscent of currency flows prior to 1810, they were either hoarded or passed

[21] Report of the Building Sub-Committee,' IDC Letterbook (1875–97), 38–49, *FJKM*

[22] Campbell, "Labour and the Transport Problem," 355.

[23] Finkelmeier to Hunter, 11 Aug. 1876, US; see also Wills to Procter, Antananarivo, 16 Oct. 1875, IDC Letterbook (1875–97), 51–2; "Report" of the Buildings Sub-Committee on LMS houses at Ambohibeloma and Isoavana, IDC Letterbook 2 – *FJKM*.

[24] Ellis, *Madagascar Revisited*, 406.

to Indian and Swahili merchants in payment for luxury imports. For example, the trade dollar, which Merina traders considered inferior to the French 5-franc piece, was transferred to Indian merchants who remitted it to Bombay.[25] Also, while export duties were payable in cash, import duties continued to be levied in kind – a policy that both angered foreign merchants and accentuated the lack of coinage.[26] As Finkelmeier remarked in 1877, "There is not a cent of money except what is imported in exchange for live cattle or for the current expenses of Missionaries, foreign Officials, and a few travelers."[27]

From late 1876, the imperial economy slid into a prolonged and terminal financial crisis. In part, this was due to natural causes, such as the smallpox outbreak on the east coast in December 1876 that severely disrupted commerce.[28] However, the plight of foreign merchants was aggravated by the Merina merchants' insistence on payment in French 5-franc pieces – a demand impossible to meet. Following the April 1876 slump in foreign trade, the dollar leaped to 26 percent above par against sterling, compared to a previous 1873 peak of 15 percent. The 5-franc piece and other coins normally accepted as *ariary* or "dollars" were in such short supply by November 1878 that rupees were introduced into Toamasina at a discount – although it was correctly observed that "a long time must elapse ere it will take any place in the currency of the country."[29]

By April 1879, a slight trade upturn brought in a plethora of dollars. However, worsening Franco–Merina relations resulted in both commercial stagnation and a rise in Merina military expenditure from possibly $21,650 in 1868 to over $1 million in 1880.[30] These so accentuated the shortage of dollars that trade ground to a virtual halt. By February 1882, the dollar carried a premium as

[25] Stanwood, Andakabe, 31 Dec. 1886; Stanwood, "Enclosure no.5," 5 Jan. 1886 in Whitney to Porter, 2 Feb. 1887 – US; Rantoandro, "gouvernement de Tamatave."

[26] Finkelmeier to Hunter, 1 Oct. 1878, US; Wills to Mullens, Antananarivo, 7 Nov. 1878, IDC Letterbook (1875–97), 174, *FJKM*.

[27] Finkelmeier to Hunter, 1 Oct. 1877, US.

[28] Wills to Mullens, Antananarivo, 7 Dec. 1876 and 13 April 1877, IDC Letterbook (1875–97), 103, 123, *FJKM*.

[29] Wills to Mullens, 25 April and 5 Dec. 1878, IDC Letterbook (1875–97), 177–8, *FJKM*; see also Wills to Mullens, & Nov. 1878, IDC Letterbook (1875–97), 174, *FJKM*; Finkelmeier, "8th Annual Commercial Report on Madagascar," Oct. 1873; Robinson to Hunter, 1 April, 3 and 21 July, and 22 Sept. 1879 – *US*.

[30] Wills to Procter, 24 April 1879; Thorne to Whitehouse, 29 Jan. 1880 – IDC Letterbook (1875–97), 191, *FJKM*; Robinson to Payson, Antananarivo, 28 April 1881; *idem* to Third Assistant Secretary of State, 22 May, 29 June, and 28 July 1882; Campbell to Wharton, 24 May and 6 Dec. 1890; Waller to Wharton, 25 April 1893 – *US*; Cameron, "Newspaper Cuttings"; Rainilaiarivony à Dr. Davidson, Antananarivo, 5 Alahasaty 1868, in "Lettres du gouvernement et de la Reine, 1852–1859," Carton section II c.12, *AHVP*; Campbell, "Toamasina," 525–55; *idem*, "Role of the Merina State," 2–23.

high as 30 percent[31] and late that year, immediately prior to the outbreak of the 1883–5 war, the U.S. consul in Toamasina noted,

The Hova [i.e., Merina] wholesale traders who come to this port and purchase of the foreign importers are frightened for the safety of their capital, at the least noise about political difficulties: and prefer to bury their money to risking it in goods at such times.[32]

Given the lack of money supply, much domestic commerce, especially outside the main commercial centers, continued to be lubricated by commodity monies – notably blue cotton cloth, probably the dominant form of payment and credit. Thus, it was noted in the mid-1880s that "money is never used in purchase of food, [and] payment of labour etc." in most regions of the island.[33] Most cloth was imported by Indian or U.S. traders, although by the late nineteenth century NMS agents in Sakalava land were placing direct orders for "currency cloth" from Procter Brothers of London.[34]

The peace treaty of December 1885 imposed a $2 million indemnity on the Merina court, which it attempted to raise in part through a CNEP (Comptoir national d'Escompte de Paris – National Discount Bank of Paris) loan, the interest on which was to be met by customs receipts. Theoretically sufficient to both service the loan and finance government, customs levies failed to do either. On revised estimates, the total value of the foreign trade of the major imperial port of Toamasina for 1877–8, 1886–7, and 1890 amounted to $4,047,146, $6,044,978, and $3,885,011, respectively. There are few extant returns from other ports, but given the estimate that the annual foreign trade of the relatively minor west coast port of Morondava was worth $1.5 million, it is reasonable to assume that an island empire possessing several similarly sized or larger ports – such as Mahajanga, Tolanaro, Mananjary, Manakara, Mahanoro, Vatomandry, Fenoarivo, Mananara, Maroantsetra, Sambava, and Vohimara – would potentially have enjoyed a minimum annual customs revenue of $2 million – a sum that could have easily secured interest payments on the French loan.

---

[31] Gregory to Aitken, Ambatoharanana, 22 March 1880, SPG Letterbook (1876–84), 321, *ACM*; Robinson to Payson, 20 May 1880, *idem* to 3rd Assistant Secretary of State, 13 Feb. 1882 – *US*.

[32] Robinson to Third Assistant Secretary of State, Tamatave, 22 May 1882, *US*.

[33] Pickersgill to Briggs, Nosibe, 30 May 1882, "T & F, LMS Local, D & E," *FJKM*; see also Chapter 2.

[34] Campbell, "Role of the London Missionary Society" vol. I, 66–7; *idem*, "East African Slave Trade," 20; Stanwood to Robinson, Morondava, 1 Dec. 1880; Stanwood, "Commercial Situation," Andakabe, 31 Dec. 1886; "enclosure 5" (Jan. 1886) in Whitney to Porter, 2 Feb. 1887; Campbell to Wharton, 26 April 1890 – US; Rostvig to Procter Bros, Tulear, 16 Dec. 1892, NMS Kopibok (1882–1892), *FLM/NMS*; *MT* II.11 (19 March 1884), 72.

TABLE 11.2. *Estimated Export Duty Revenue: Mahajanga, 1862–81 ($)*

Year	Actual Revenue	Estimated Potential Revenue	Year	Actual Revenue	Estimated Potential Revenue
1865	126.00	504.00	1874	5,250.50	21,002.00
1866	n.a.	n.a.	1875	n.a.	n.a.
1867	710.93	2,843.72	1876	1,577.38	6,309.52
1868	753.92	3,015.68	1877	1,679.27	6,717.08
1869	1,740.67	6,962.68	1878	3,646.13	14,584.52
1870	2,678.25	10,713.00	1879	3,397.13	13,588.52
1871	4,537.50	18,150.00	1880	5,387.75	21,551.00
1872	3,387.85	13,551.40	1881	9,317.63	
1873	3,480.75	13,923.00			

Source: Based on Rasomairanana, "Aspects économiques," 65–6.

It is unlikely that more than a third of foreign trade was ever taxed.[35] By September 1887, it was apparent that Merina officials were failing to fully collect customs dues and, that December, the French insisted that all main imperial customs be transferred to their jurisdiction.[36] However, French officials merely supervised the existing Merina customs structure and the realization of potential customs revenue was frustrated by continued mismanagement. First, while import and export duties were nominally 10 percent ad valorem, payable in cash, import duties were usually less than export duties and continued to be levied mostly in kind.[37] Second, although a harbor duty, based on a ship's tonnage, was in theory levied on all boats visiting imperial ports, it was not universally applied. Thus, the U.S. consul negotiated an exemption for vessels flying U.S. colors, while in 1889 tonnage fees were payable in Mananjary and Vatomandry, but not in Toamasina and Mahajanga, the two main imperial ports.[38]

However, the failure to realize potential customs revenue was mainly due to massive corruption by customs officials, which stemmed from the fact that they were unsalaried (Tables 11.2 and 11.3). The Merina court farmed out imperial posts to the highest bidder, who was expected to remit to the crown a proportion of the profit gleaned from the sale of goods seized in levies on

---

[35] *MT* II.50 (17 Dec. 1884), 451.

[36] Campbell to Porter, 20 Sept. and 12 Dec. 1887, *US.*

[37] Robinson to Hunter, Tamatave, 11 Aug. 1876; Campbell to Rives, Tamatave, 24 Jan. 1889 – US; Whitney to Ropes, Emmerton & Co, and Arnold, Hines & Co, Tamatave, 31 May 1884, *REC/CR-MZL.*

[38] Finkelmeier to Hunter, Tamatave, 30 Dec. 1874; Campbell to Wharton, Tamatave, 26 Oct. 1889 – *US.*

TABLE 11.3. *Estimated Customs Revenue: Six Main Imperial Merina Ports,*
1888–92 ($)

Year	Total Estimated Foreign Trade	Actual Revenue (at 10% Ad Valorem)	Estimated Minimum Potential Revenue
1888	1,448,000	144,800	289,600
1889	1,450,000	145,000	290,000
1890	1,632,000	163,200	326,400
1891	1,646,000	164,600	329,200
1892	1,480,000	148,000	296,000
1893	n.a.	n.a.	n.a.
1894	1,500,000	150,000	300,000

Source: Le courrier de Madagascar 145 (29 mai 1894), 147 (12 juin 1894). The ports were
Fenoarivo, Vohimara, Toamasina, Vatomandry, Mananjary, and Mahajanga.

imports."[39] Consequently, the governorship and customs controller of imperial ports were coveted positions, often reserved by the Prime Minister, Rainilaiarivony, for family members. Merina officials easily evaded detection by
the French customs supervisors, who were few in number and ignorant of
the local language and commercial practices. It was traditional for Merina
customs officers and port governors to permit through customs two-thirds
or more of imported commodities, free of official duty, upon payment of
a considerable bribe – generally 25 percent of potential tax revenue. They
also fabricated false customs passes, which they sold to foreign merchants –
Muslim, Creole, and Western; such a pass sold for $0.50 in Toamasina in 1882.
A British firm even allegedly possessed a counterfeit of a port governor's seal.[40]
Smuggling was widespread; commonly only 50 percent of merchandise was
openly declared. Indeed, in Toamasina, allegedly both quinine and gunpowder,
over which the government claimed a monopoly, could be purchased on the
open market. Of such practices, the U.S. consul noted in 1880,

I state only facts ... which I think I can now substantiate by legal proof ... that the
practice prevails very generally of swindling the Government, not only by common
smuggling, but by forgery. . . . [T]hese practices have continued so long with impunity,
that a large part of the traders have actually arrived to the belief that such manner of
dealing is only shrewd mercantile honesty.[41]

[39] *MT* II.46 (19 Nov. 1884), 416.
[40] Robinson to Payson, Tamatave, 2 Oct. 1880, *US*; Campbell, "Role of the Merina State"; *idem*,
"Toamasina."
[41] Finkelmeier to Hunter, Tamatave, 30 Dec. 1874, *US*.

Attempts by the French or Merina authorities to crack down on tax evasion merely resulted in the transference of business to largely unsupervised ports and inlets. Smuggling, notably of arms and ammunition, was especially prevalent along the west coast and, after 1885, through French-controlled Diego Suarez.[42] Direct clandestine trade links between minor Malagasy ports and foreign markets on the Mascarenes, the Swahili and Mozambique coasts, and in Natal were facilitated from the 1880s by the widespread application of steam power to regional shipping.[43] U.S. consular official Stanwood's allegation that, even in Merina-controlled ports of the west coast, 75 percent of goods were contraband is corroborated by missionary and other local reports.[44]

Currency

From the 1820s (with the exception of the 1861–75 trade boom), Madagascar suffered from a chronically deficient money supply – a problem accentuated by inadequate currency regulation. Although coins were, by 1810, firmly established as a major form of currency in both the domestic and the external long-distance trade networks of imperial Madagascar, the deficient money supply had a number of serious repercussions. First, the traditional system of subdividing coins continued. In the interior, where coins were less common than on the coast, there emerged as early as 1785 five basic divisions of coin, equivalent to $1.00, $0.50, $0.25, $0.125, and $0.0625. The coin was chipped into fractions with a cold chisel by a *mpanakalo-vola*, or moneychanger, who retailed cut coinage (termed *vakim-bola* or *torotorombola*) in local markets. He gained a commission (*sandamparantsa*) of between $0.042 and $0.125 per dollar changed, depending on the supply of whole to cut dollars – a ratio that could change daily.[45]

As whole and cut coins were weighed to determine their value, both parties to a transaction possessed a pair of iron or brass scales (*mizana*). These posed two major problems. First, the small standard scale used to evaluate the value of coins was incapable of weighing anything over 54 grams with any

---

[42] Finkelmeier to Hunter, Tamatave, 30 Dec. 1874; Robinson to Payson, Antananarivo, 15 Jan. 1881 – *US*; Shaw to PM, Toamasina, II May 1882, HH2, 19, *ANM*; Esoavelomandroso, *Problèmes de police*, 30.

[43] Robinson to Hunter, Tamatave, 22 Sept. 1879, *US*.

[44] Robinson to Payson, 7 Aug. and 2 Oct. 1880; Stanwood to Robinson, 1 Dec. 1880 – *US*.

[45] Oliver, *Madagascar* vol. II, 206; *HR* vols. III–IV, 919; *MT* (7 April 1888); Campbell, "Role of the London Missionary Society" vol. I, 69.

TABLE 11.4. *Malagasy Dollar Subdivisions and Rice Equivalents*

Dollar Subdivisions	Equivalence in Rice Grains
1.0000	720
0.5000	360
0.2500	180
0.1250	90
0.0625	45

Source: HR vols. III–IV, 918; Baron, "Malagasy Terms," 191–2.

accuracy, although under that limit they proved highly accurate.[46] By 1810, the Merina administration enforced five iron weights possessing fixed equivalent weights in dollars and in fractions thereof: 27 grams, 13.5 grams, 6.75 grams, 3.375 grams, and 2.25 grams. The *loso*, the standard 13.5-gram weight, was equivalent to $0.50. The system derived from that used by Arab merchants, which was in turn based upon the basic monetary weights used in Europe: The *ariary*, the Malagasy unit of account, which was based on the Spanish silver dollar, theoretically weighed 27 grams, but the use of false weights and loaded scales was widespread.[47]

Moreover, the traditional system of using grains or beans as a supplement to, and occasionally replacement for, standard weights was often inaccurate. There existed three systems of weights, in addition to that founded upon the silver dollar. The first was based upon the *voamena* (1.125 grams – equivalent to $0.0417), a bean or seed of the *Abrus precatorius*; and the second on the *eranambatry* (0.375 grams – equivalent to $0.0139), named after another seed (again a bean) of the *ambatry* or pigeon pea shrub (*Cajanus indicus spreng*).[48] The third and lowest system of monetary weights was founded on the *vary*, or

---

[46] The use of scales, which were probably introduced by the Arabs, spread at the same rate as the use of money – gunpowder and piastres were generally the only commodities to be measured on scales – see *HR* vol. I, 71; Dahle, "influence of Arabs," 85; Oliver, *Madagascar* vol. II, 210.

[47] The term *ariary* or Malagasy dollar, used for the piastre, imported dollars and the French five franc piece, derives from the Arabic *ar-riyal* or *ar-rial*, which in turn comes from the Spanish *real* – 27 grams was also the weight of the Venetian ounce, which constituted the basis of the Venetian *denier* – Dahle, "influence of Arabs," 84–5; R. Baron, "Malagasy Terms of Monetary Values," *AAMM* 14 (1890), 192; Campbell, "Role of the London Missionary Society" vol. I, 65.

[48] The *abrus precatorius*, which probably originated in Austronesia where it was used to weigh gold, is closely related to the *Erythrina abyssinia* or Abyssinian coral flower, the seeds of which are the *carat* used as the standard weight for gold. The system of using grain weights was common throughout Asia, while wheat and barley grains were common standards of monetary weight in medieval Europe – Baron, "Malagasy Terms," 190–1; P. Nightingale, "The Evolution of Weight Standards and the Creation of New Monetary and Commercial Links in Northern Europe from the Tenth to the Twelfth Century," *Economic History Review* 38 (1985), 192–209.

TABLE 11.5. *Malagasy Monetary Weights Expressed in Rice Grains*

Name	Value ($)	Equivalent in Moist Grains	Equivalent in Dry Grains
Voamena	0.0416666	30	40
Ilavoamena	0.0208333	15	20
Eranambatry	0.0138888	10	13
Varifitoventy	0.0097216	7	10
Varienimbenty	0.0083328	6	8
Varidimiventy	0.0069440	5	7
Variefabenty	0.0555555	4	5
Variteloventy	0.0041664	3	4
Variroaventy	0.0027776	2	3
Variraiventy	0.0013888	1	1.5

Source: HR vols. III–IV, 918; Baron, "Malagasy Terms," 191–2.

rice grain, and accounted for the nine units of weight below the *eranambatry* (1 *eranambatry* = 10 grains of rice). The four weight systems worked in tandem so that in theory a dollar's weight in silver (*ariary*) equaled 720 grains of rice, and a dollar could be subdivided into fractions as small as 1/720th (see Tables 11.4 and 11.5). From 1861 to 1875 (as from 1750 to 1810), the use of rice grain weights largely lapsed, as the circulating volume of whole dollars was sufficient to prevent a significant morseling of coins. However, from 1810 to 1861, and from 1875, sharp reductions in the money supply resulted in increased circulation of cut money and the use of rice grain weights. The traditional system had been based upon the weight of moist grains of dehusked rice, but problems were caused from the 1820s by the adoption of a dual rice grain weight system that used both moist and dry rice grains. To enhance his profits, a moneychanger would, when purchasing, employ the heavier moist grains and, when selling, use the lighter dry grains. This enabled him to represent $0.749 in cut money as the equivalent of a dollar. With his commission added, he could expect to make, at a time of rising demand for cut money, approximately $0.375 on every dollar changed.[49] Finally, the weighing of money inevitably delayed commercial exchange. As both parties carefully weighed the money on their respective scales, transactions involving money could well take longer than barter exchange. For example, in the early 1890s, Catat estimated that it could take up to 30 minutes in the marketplace to conclude the purchase of a single chicken[50] (see Tables 11.6 and 11.7).

[49] *HR* vols. III–IV, 918; Baron, "Malagasy Terms," 191–2.
[50] Catat, *Voyage à Madagascar*, 14.

TABLE 11.6. *Malagasy Terms for Dollars*

	Term	Meaning
Pre-1800	Behatoka	Large neck
	Amparitra	Stretched out like a corpse
	Ampanga	Crown of fern leaves (i.e., Austrian dollar)
	Helatra	Lightening
	Tokazo	A solitary tree
	Adohalambo	An arch
From c.1820	Tombotsisina	"Growth on the edge" (= indentation on edge of French 5-franc coin)
	Malamakely	"Small smooth one" (Mexican dollar with effigy of Napoleon 1 introduced in 1880s)
	Ngita	Well-twisted cord/woolly hair
	Tanomasoandro	The sun and its rays
	Kelihandrina	Small forehead (a coin depicting man with large head and small face)
	Tsanganolona	"Shape of a person" (a 5-franc coin with 3 standing allegorical figures on its obverse)
	Belaka	"Full faced" (type of dollar)
	Tranompitaratra	A window frame (refers to coin with outline relief of mirror frame in reverse)

A second major consequence of diminished money supply was adulteration of coinage. The different coins in circulation in Madagascar were calculated in terms of the *ariary*. From the outset, this posed problems because of the different silver content of the various coins. In the early 1800s, most coins in circulation were the Spanish and Mexican piastres of the Hispanic Union. These were joined, from the 1820s, by Mexican dollars shipped in quantity to Africa from European financial centers (notably London, Amsterdam, and the Iberian and Italian ports),[51] U.S. dollars, and the French 5-franc piece – which became the dominant coin from mid-century. The rupee, a standard currency on Mauritius

---

[51] The main coins in circulation were the Spanish *colonne* piastre, and silver dollars; some of the latter bore the images of Charles II and IV and Ferdinand VII – introduced from 1732 and 1772, respectively (and equivalent in 1780 to 5.6 French francs) – but most common was the Maria Theresa dollar which was first minted in 1751, the year of Maria Theresa's coronation as empress of Austria. The Maria Theresa dollar gained such popularity in the East, where European silver and gold commanded a significant premium, that annual production of the coin rose from 583,750 in 1751 to 5,091,055 in 1765. When the empress died in 1780, the Austrian government continued to mint coins carrying her effigy, and these soon constituted the standard currency of the western Indian Ocean. Thus, on the east African coast the imperial Austrian dollar circulated from as early as 1754. The Venetian sequin was also accepted there, but was less important – Freeman Grenville, *French at Kilwa Island*, 25, 52, 118; Pankhurst, *Economic History of Ethiopia*, 468; Campbell, "Role of the London Missionary Society" vol. I, 67–8.

TABLE 11.7. *Premium on the Ariary (dollar) Antananarivo, 1866 and 1872–93*

	Premium (%)			Premium (%)	
Year	Minimum (Privileged Rates)	Maximum (Open Market Rates)	Year	Minimum (Privileged Rates)	Maximum (Open Market Rates)
1866	n.a.	5.5	1882	4.0	25.0
1872	7.0	11.0	1883	4.0	17.5
1873	12.0	15.0	1884	4.0	n.a.
1874	7.7	n.a.	1885	3.0	4.0
1875	5.0	15.0	1886	par	n.a.
1876	4.0	n.a.	1887	3.625	16.0
1877	4.0	n.a.	1888	1.5	n.a.
1878	2.0	n.a.	1889	n.a.	n.a.
1879	2.333	23.0	1890	0.125	n.a.
1880	4.0	n.a.	1891	n.a.	n.a.
1881	2.0	n.a.	1892	1.0	n.a.

Source: Campbell, "Currency Crisis," 280.

from 1876, also entered east and northwest Madagascar and by 1890 had gained widespread acceptance on the west coast south of Mahajanga.[52]

Malagasy authorities initially made no attempt to stipulate what coin might constitute legal tender. As Mayeur noted of Imerina in the late eighteenth century, "Provided it is made of silver, each and every minted coin is acceptable to them."[53] The circulation of coins of different nationalities opened the monetary system to abuse both because of the use of cut coins and because of their different silver content. Moreover, the silver was frequently adulterated with iron, tin, and copper by Malagasy silversmiths, leading Mayeur to observe of the Merina that although they "accept cut or worked money [silver coins] ... [they] prefer that which has been minted."[54] Adulteration of coinage, a minor problem from 1750 to 1810 due to the volume of imported coinage and the velocity of its circulation, became a source of growing concern when the money supply slumped from 1810. Little was done during the years of rigid autarky or from 1861 to 1875, when a recovery of trade led to a large increase in the money supply. However, the 1883–5 war dramatically increased the Merina need for

---

[52] Campbell, "Role of the London Missionary Society" vol. I, 68.

[53] Mayeur, "Voyage au pays d'ancove" (1777), 176–7.

[54] Mayeur, "Voyage au pays d'ancove" (1777), 176–7; Milices, "Mémoire" (1780), 20; Legentil, "Voyage à Madagascar" (1781), *BL*.Add.18126, 557; Jacques Dez, "Considérations sur les prix pratiqués à Tananarive en 1870," *BAM* 40 (1962); Raymond Decary, "Moeurs maritimes au XVII siècle," *BAM* 18 (1935), 37–8; Alpers, "French Slave Trade," 87, 101–4; Dubois, *Monographie des Betsileo*, 601.

foreign exchange as firms from which it wished to purchase arms were reluctant to accept cut coins and wary of the silver content of uncut coins. In addition, wartime inflation and insecurity encouraged foreign traders to export specie. For instance, Ropes, Emmerton, and O'Swald shipped from Toamasina in mid-1883 and from June to August 1884 respectively, 20,000 5-franc pieces and 25,000 rupees (a total value of $10,750), and 80,000 5-franc coins.[55]

Currency speculation accentuated the situation. Speculation started in the 1860s trade boom when it became apparent that the various coins in circulation, traditionally all accepted at par, possessed different silver contents: The Maria Theresa dollar contained less silver than the Spanish piastre, while a new Mexican dollar, issued in the 1880s and bearing the image of Napoleon I, contained 8 percent less silver than the dominant 5-franc piece. Also, when gold was worked into the piastre, the latter was considered 12 times more valuable than its silver counterpart, despite the fact that, internationally, gold was normally accepted as being only eight times the value of silver.[56] In the 1880s, speculators such as George Ropes flooded the island with the new Mexican coin that they purchased in bulk in the United States and used to meet customs duties and other financial obligations in Madagascar. However, from 1886 the French refused indemnity payments from the imperial court in coins with a silver content less than that of an unsullied 5-franc piece.[57]

In similar circumstances, in Merina-controlled regions of the west coast in 1879, the imperial government had attempted in vain to ban the rupee, the circulation of which permitted considerable exploitation of exchange rates. Thus, an American trader complained of his Swahili agent on Nosy Be in 1889:

I am thinking seriously of returning to the old custom of giving Sheik Adam our limits in dollars instead of, as at present, in Rs [rupees] as he buys nearly all our produce in dollars and it creates thus an exchange a/c between ourselves and him in which we are always I believe the losers. On a recent shipment of five francs from Nossi-be of 14000 bought there at 280 per 100 Sheik would only allow 270 making a loss to us of $35 or $2\frac{1}{2}\%$.[58]

---

[55] Ropes, Emmerton & Co, to Whitney, Salem, 14 July 1883, ms.103, Ropes, Emmerton & Co. Records (1873–1902), B42.F4; Ropes, Emmerton & Co, to J. Orme Ryder, Salem, 17 July 1884; Dawson to Ropes, Emmerton & Co, and Arnold, Hines & Co, Tamatave, 18 July and 14 Aug. 1884 – REC/CR-MZL.

[56] Mayeur, "Voyage au pays d'ancove" (1777), 176–7; Milices, "Mémoire" (1780), 20; Legentil, "Voyage à Madagascar" (1781), BL, Add.18126, 557; Jacques Dez, "Considérations sur les prix pratiqués à Tananarive en 1870," BAM 40 (1962); Raymond Decary, "Moeurs maritimes au XVII siècle," BAM 18 (1935), 37–8; Alpers, "French Slave Trade," 87, 101–4; Dubois, Monographie des Betsileo, 601.

[57] Campbell, "Role of the London Missionary Society" vol. I, 68.

[58] Bachelder to Ropes, Emmerton & Co, Mojanga, 23 Jan. 1889, REC/CR-MZL.

The Merina court broached the question of currency reform several times. Radama I, like some of his predecessors, entertained the idea of minting a Malagasy coinage with the short-term aim of devaluing the currency to relieve state finances. In 1826, several 13-gram silver coins were minted, 36 mm in diameter and embossed with the royal profile. They were intended to pass as *loso*, although 0.5 grams lighter. However, few such coins entered circulation and the venture crumbled, due to a shortage of domestic silver deposits and to autarkic policies that, like state trade monopolies, raised expectations of increased foreign exchange earnings.[59] Thereafter, little was done until the buildup to the Franco–Merina War. Article 160 of the Merina Code of 1881 stipulated that the only coins to be accepted as standard monies at par would be the Mexican and Spanish dollars, the 5-franc piece of Subalpine Gaul and Louis XIII, "and any other dollars that are smooth by usage or that have the inscription on the exerque engraved instead of being in relief."[60] Also, some measures were taken to counter adulteration; for instance, between May and September 1884, government officials seized on Merina markets counterfeit coins nominally valued at $52.[61] However, such measures proved woefully inadequate.

In 1885 and 1888, on the strength of new gold exploitation, the Merina court again considered minting a Malagasy coinage. However, foreign investors, who alone could finance the equipment necessary to fully exploit the gold deposits, were initially deterred by the stringent conditions proposed by the court. Although the court lifted most restrictions by early 1895, domestic insecurity and the renewal of French hostilities reinforced the doubts of potential foreign investors.[62]

Rainilaiarivony's attempt in December 1889 to regulate the currency by imposing a ban on the import of the new Mexican dollar placed Ropes and other American agents who had stockpiled the coin in a financially precarious situation. As he held no fund of 5-franc pieces, Ropes had to pay his duties in cotton cloth. By the early 1890s, the Mexican coin was again being imported, this time by Kingdon, who had repeatedly failed to establish a British bank in the island. He introduced such huge quantities of the coin that it was popularly termed *vola Kingdon* ("Kingdon's money") and started to adversely affect the financial standing of the Merina court, which was a major creditor.[63]

---

[59] Chauvicourt, "premières monnaies," 150; Valette, Études, 45.

[60] *MT* II.30 (30 July 1884), 276.

[61] *MT* (3 Sept. 1884), 330.

[62] Campbell, "Gold Mining and the French Takeover."

[63] Pickersgill to Briggs, Nosibe, 30 May 1882, "T & F, LMS Local, D & E," *FJKM*; Campbell to Wharton, 26 April 1890; Campbell to Procter, 23 Aug. 1887 and *idem* to Razafindrazaka, 26 May 1890 – *US*; Rasoamiaranana, "Aspects économiques," 55; *CdM* 139 (17 avril 1894).

In March 1894, Rainilaiarivony declared the new Mexican dollar illegal tender, and shortly afterward extended his ban to the U.S. dollar and French 5- and 10-cent coins. By 20 March 1894, no business was being transacted in the 5-franc coin of the Latin Union, while the U.S. dollar could only be exchanged at a loss of 3.5 percent. In May 1894, the *Tanomasoandro, Ngita, Tsanganolona*, and *Tokazo* coins were declared illegal, leaving as valid currency only the *Malamakely, Behatoka*, and *Tombotsisina* – thus underlining the dominance of the 5-franc piece in the Merina empire. The effective devaluation of the U.S. dollar hit not only the U.S. but also the Indian mercantile community, which speculated in the different coins, and small Malagasy traders and porters. The prohibition on the use of the relatively abundant Mexican *Tanomasoandro* dollar exacerbated the financial plight of all merchants as they found no outlet for their stocks of the proscribed coin.[64]

Finally, currency problems, notably adulteration, caused traders to react to the increase of "bad money" by withholding their stocks of *vola madio* (i.e., "good money").[65] This further reduced the money supply; as a result, the internal market shriveled, credit was withdrawn, and trade suffered.[66]

The Credit Structure

Indian traders dominated the commercial credit system of the southwest Indian Ocean. Merchant families in northwest India cooperated closely overseas, despite differences in caste. Their IOA headquarters was Zanzibar, where leading Indian merchants acted as financial advisers to the Sultan and farmed his customs.[67] The first bank in Zanzibar accessible to Indians was opened only in 1880, and no credit was extended until 1884.[68] Consequently, most Indian traders in the region turned to their compatriots for credit.[69] The wealthier

---

[64] Kingdon left for Britain immediately following the ban – Wetter to Strobel, 20 March and *idem* to Uhl, 26 May and 7 Sept. 1894 – *US*; *CdM* 139 (17 avril 1894) and 150 (5 juillet 1894).

[65] Mayeur, "Voyage au pays d'ancove" (1785), 227; Anon, "Mémoire historique" [1790], 95–6; Dumaine, "Voyage au pays d'ancaye" (1790), 267; *idem*, "Voyage à la côte de l'ouest" (1793), 308; *RH*, 10; *GH* (1928), 268, 335; Sundström, *Exchange Economy*, 111, 114, 117–18; Ellis, *History of Madagascar* vol. I, 243–7, 254–5; Griffiths, *Hanes Madagascar*, 46; Campbell, "Role of the London Missionary Society" vol. II, 326.

[66] Campbell, "Toamasina," 535.

[67] Browne, *Etchings*, 274; Ward to State Department, Zanzibar, 21 March 1847; Hines to Seward, Zanzibar, 25 Oct. 1864 – in Norman R. Bennett and George E. Brooks (eds.), *New England Merchants in Africa* (Boston, 1965), 387, 532, 539.

[68] Evers, "Das Hamburger Zanzibarhandelshaus Wm. O'Swald," 20; see also *ibid*, 19, 28.

[69] Most Indian traders possessed little capital – in the 1850s those in Zanzibar lived on an estimated $25 per annum compared to the $300 a year of O'Swald's European agents – Karl Evers,

merchants proved amenable for two main reasons: Strong kinship or caste ties acted as a form of collateral, and smaller traders fulfilled an entrepreneurial function in steadily advancing the Indian trading frontier into regions where, if it proved sufficiently lucrative, established companies founded agencies.[70] Access to credit enabled small Indian traders to undermine and dislodge, on both sides of the Mozambique Channel, Swahili and Creole middlemen who were unable to match their capital or organizational resources.[71]

Indian credit also proved critical to the survival of foreign firms, which, in the absence of banks, and far from base, frequently suffered cash flow problems. This was most apparent in Zanzibar – from the 1830s the regional headquarters for big Indian, European, and U.S. firms. In general, cash was dispatched from Europe and North America at the close of the northeast monsoon, enabling European and American agents to purchase hides, orchil, and plantation crops locally. However, their cash reserves were often exhausted by the end of May, when caravans started arriving from the east African interior with ivory, cowries were plentiful, and produce had only just started arriving from Madagascar (where the trading season opened at the end of March, at the start of the dry season). Had they been unable to procure funds from Indian financiers, U.S. and European firms would have lost the trust of the local middlemen who largely controlled regional trade.[72] In 1873, of the £434,000 invested in the east African region by one Indian firm, an estimated £60,000 had been advanced to the Sultan, £200,000 to leading Arab slave dealers, and £140,000 (32.25 percent of the total) to European and U.S. traders.[73] An indication of the importance of Indian financiers was the gradual rise to dominance of the rupee over the Maria Theresa dollar in Zanzibar and its expansion to Madagascar.[74]

European and U.S. firms also advanced credit, sometimes to large Indian firms – Tharia Topan of Zanzibar was the beneficiary of a loan from Ropes, Emmerton in 1883[75] – but in the main, to smaller Indian traders due to their importance as middlemen and reputation for trustworthiness. An O'Swald agent in Zanzibar commented,

The Banians here are so honest in their commercial transactions that should someone be seen cheating, it becomes totally impossible for him to do business with anyone. The

---

"Das Hamburger Zanzibarhandelshaus Wm. O'Swald & Co. 1847–1890 zue Geschichte des Hamburger Handels mit Ostafrika," Ph.D., Universität Hamburg, 1986, 16.

[70] Frere no. 51 inclosure 1 and no. 56.

[71] See, e.g., Frere no.51 inclosure 1.

[72] Evers, "Das Hamburger Zanzibarhandelshaus Wm. O'Swald," 225–6, 28.

[73] Frere no. 36, no. 37 inclosure 1, and no. 51 inclosure 1; Jackson, *European Powers*, 31.

[74] Evers, "Das Hamburger Zanzibarhandelshaus Wm. O'Swald," 24.

[75] Ropes, Emmerton & Co, to Cheney Salem, 2 Aug. 1883, *REC/CR-MZL*.

honesty of this people is so profound that it is scarcely necessary to stipulate anything with them in writing.[76]

The monthly interest on loans charged by Indian financiers stood in 1851 at 12.1 percent, and was reduced in 1853 to 0.75 percent at which level it hovered, never falling below 0.625 percent until 1890.[77] By contrast, to ensure the regular flow of export goods from the interior, foreign firms extended six months' interest-free credit to Indian middlemen in East Africa.[78]

In their turn, smaller Indian traders extended credit to Swahili, Sakalava, Merina, and even Mascarene traders, arranging "loans, advances and mortgages, on every kind of property, real and personal, and on various kinds of security; by advances of goods for trade etc."[79] Their credit was especially important for Malagasy west coast trade. Thus, in the 1820s, Hastie noted of the Indians that "usurious transactions, particularly in the advancing of money for the purchase of slaves, were carried on to a great extent at Majanga [Mahajanga],"[80] and trade south of Maintirano was severely hindered by a lack of capital and credit until the Indians moved there from mid-century. In general, however, Creole traders were financed by larger Mascarene houses: Most boats sailing between the Mascarenes and Madagascar were owned by large Mascarene firms to whom mainly Creole traders in Madagascar sold their produce, although Creoles sometimes hired small (50–150 ton) brigs or schooners to speculate in regional trade on their own account.[81]

[76] Quoted in Evers, "Das Hamburger Zanzibarhandelshaus Wm. O'Swald," 20; see also *ibid*, 19, 28. The same picture of Indian credit worthiness emerges elsewhere in the region: For Mozambique, see Sebastio Xavier Botelho, "Memória Estatística sobre os Domínios Portugueses na Africa Oriental" (Lisboa, 1835) quoted in Valentim Alexandre, *Origens do Colonialismo Portugues moderno (1822–1891)* II (Lisboa, 1979), 3–4; for Madagascar, see Staatsarchiv Hamburg – Firma Wm. O'Swald & Co. 33: Briefe von Wm. O'Swald & Co, Loucoube, 1873–1896.

[77] Evers, "Das Hamburger Zanzibarhandelshaus Wm. O'Swald," 16.

[78] Evers, "Das Hamburger Zanzibarhandelshaus Wm. O'Swald," 16; Hieke, *Zur Geschichte des deutschen Handels*, 70.

[79] "Memos," 31 Mar and 7 May 1873, incl.1 no. 52, *CFM*; East African trade was largely the monopoly of the British Indians, up to 2,000 of whom were active on the littoral in 1847. See "Report" (1844); Hafkin, "Trade Society and Politics," 232–52; Kirk to Granville, 25 Jan. and 5 Mar. 1872, "Correspondence Respecting the Slave Trade" (1873); Jackson, *European Powers*, Chs. 3, 6.

[80] Hastie, "Diary" (1824–25).

[81] Mayeur, "Voyage au pays d'ancove" (1777), 153; *idem*, "Voyage au pays d'ancove" (1785), 205; Copland, *History of Madagascar*, 15; Nils Bergsten, "Mémoire sur les moyens d'augmenter à Madagascar les revenus du gouvernement" (1825), (Jean Valette ed.), *BAM* 44 (1966), 16; Oliver, *Madagascar* vol. I, 265, 412, 414; Anon, "Some Betsimisaraka folk-tales and superstitions" (trans. J. Sibree), *AAMM* 22 (1898), 217; Sibree, *A Naturalist*, 20, 22–3, 35; *GH* (1928), 297;

The Indian credit structure scarcely penetrated the Merina empire, which suffered from a chronic lack of money supply. Traditionally, Malagasy with stocks of gold, silver, and other valuable objects stored them in caches. Toward the close of the eighteenth century, the Merina annually hoarded coins worth an estimated $24,000, approximately equivalent to 20 percent of east coast foreign exchange earnings. Such funds were concentrated in the hands of the court elite,[82] whose favorite depository was the family tomb – popularly believed to be guarded by ancestral spirits. Thus, when Radama I died in 1828, $10,300 in cash, besides jewelry and silks, were entombed with his corpse. It is an indication of the success of autarky for the elite that 22 years later, $50,000 was buried alongside Rainiharo, Ranavalona I's chief minister.[83] From the mid-1820s, the widening gap between rich and poor and the dwindling money supply resulted in an increasing transgression of the taboo against robbing tombs. This probably explains why Ranavalona I started instead to store funds in earthenware jars, buried in secret locations.[84]

From the start of the imperial era, an inadequate money supply resulted in high interest rates that enticed those with stocks of money into usury. By at least 1810, a group of professional moneylenders, called *mpanana* (i.e., "rich"), had emerged in Imerina. Hastie noted in 1817 that "money is lent at interest and the interest calculated with a scrupulous nicety."[85] They were joined from the

Robequain, "capitale montagnarde," 287; Jean Valette, "Nouvelle note pour servir à l'étude des exportations de boeufs de Fort-Dauphin à Bourbon (1820)," *BAM* 50 II (1972), 33–6.

[82] Mayeur, "Voyage au pays d'ancove" (1785), 227; Anon, "Mémoire historique" [1790], 95–6; Dumaine, "Voyage au pays d'ancaye" (1790), 267; *idem*, "Voyage à la côte de l'ouest" (1793), 308; *RH*, 10; *GH* (1928), 268, 335; Sundström, *Exchange Economy*, 111, 114, 117–18; Ellis, *History of Madagascar* vol. I, 243–7, 254–5; Griffiths, *Hanes Madagascar*, 46; Campbell, "Role of the London Missionary Society" vol. II, 326.

[83] Mayeur, "Voyage au pays d'ancove" (1785), 227; Anon, "Mémoire historique" [1790], 95–6; Dumaine, "Voyage au pays d'ancaye" (1790), 267; *idem*, "Voyage à la côte de l'ouest" (1793), 308; *RH*, 10; *GH* (1928), 268, 335; Sundström, *Exchange Economy*, 111, 114, 117–18; Ellis, *History of Madagascar* vol. I, 243–7, 254–5; Griffiths, *Hanes Madagascar*, 46; Campbell, "Role of the London Missionary Society" vol. II, 326. For tomb theft of coins placed in corpses' mouths and other valuables, see Campbell, *Brigandry and Revolt*.

[84] Milius (8 June 1820), in *GH* (1928), 278; Hastie, "Diary" (1822–3); Griffiths to Arundel, Antananarivo, 20 Dec. 1825, *SOAS/LMS-MIL* B2.F2.JC; Louis Molet, "Les monnaies à Madagascar," *Cahiers de l'institut de science économique appliquée* supplt.129.V (1962), 4, 9–12, 26–7, 30, 33–4; Bloch, *Placing the Dead*, 114–21; Jacques Dez, "Monnaie et structure traditionnelle à Madagascar," *Cahiers Vilfredo Pareto – Revue européene des sciences sociales* (1970), 175–202; Campbell, "Madagascar and the Slave Trade"; *idem*, "Role of the London Missionary Society" vol. I, 176, vol. II, 293; *idem, Brigandry and Revolt*; Oliver, *Madagascar* vol. II, 206–7, 217; Grandidier, "Property among the Malagasy," 226; *GH* (1928), 269; see also Sundström, *Exchange Economy*, 34–5, 37.

[85] Hastie, "Diary" (1817), 186; *HR* vols. III–IV, 919.

onset of autarky by members of the Merina elite who accumulated large cash reserves from the sale of campaign booty and from commercial monopolies.[86] Through their *deka* and via the Ambohimalaza cartel, they even extended credit to Mascarene Creole traders for regional trade.[87]

Merina moneylenders made their capital available as "usurious consumption credit" rather than for commercial or industrial investment. Extortionate interest rates were intended to push creditors further into debt. Small farmers, who required cash primarily to meet taxes, competed fiercely to be the first to market their crop while the money supply was, at the commencement of the harvest and trading season, still relatively plentiful. As Bojer noted, this practice had disastrous consequences for the quality of produce for

[the cultivator] rarely waits until the products of the soil have reached maturity; they pick their vegetables and their fruit well before the proper harvest time and carry them to market, in order to secure a few petty pieces of silver.[88]

Those with insufficient cash were forced to borrow in order to pay taxes, which increased steadily during the autarkic era, and to meet other financial commitments, notably the construction of the family tomb and other funeral costs. As a result, large numbers of small farmers found themselves mortgaging their crop before it had even been sown.[89] A debtor failing to clear his debt within the stipulated period was obliged to pay double the capital or, in exceptional cases where the loan carried no interest, to pay his creditor double, plus an additional one-third of the capital. However, there was no law stipulating the terms upon which capital might be borrowed. All loan agreements were in essence private agreements, although once signed by the contracting parties they carried the force of law.[90]

The Merina elite was backed by the domestic judicial system. Almost inevitably the debtor failed to meet repayment conditions, his property was seized, and he and his family could be sold into slavery to pay off the debt. As Hastie commented in 1824,

if the money lender risques a portion of his treasure it must be under the expectation of receiving exorbitant interest, and when the usurious covenant is not fulfilled, he does not hesitate to sell the person of his debtor.[91]

---

[86] See R. S. Lopez, *The Commercial Revolution of the Middle Ages, 950–1350* (New Jersey, 1971), 72.

[87] *MT* II.22 (4 June 1884), 206; Laborde to Dawson, Vatomandry, 20 June 1885, *REC/CR MEL*; Duder to Dawson, Antananarivo, 21 & 27 December 1889, *REC/CR-MZL*.

[88] Bojer, "Journal," 14.

[89] Oliver, *Madagascar* vol. II, 196.

[90] *HR* vols. III–IV, 919.

[91] Hastie, "Report" (April 1824).

An estimated 50 percent of the slave population of Imerina (possibly totaling 300,000 by 1830) comprised Merina bankruptcies and members of their families. Moreover, this figure excludes Betsileo kidnapped by Merina debtors and brought illegally into Imerina to be sold as slaves in order that the kidnapper might pay off his debts. Radama I attempted to ameliorate the effects of indebtedness by halving officially prescribed interest rates from 66 to 33 percent in the early 1820s and, in 1823, declaring void all debts contracted to pay for funerals or tombs. However, these and subsequent rulings by Merina authorities proved largely unenforceable.[92]

In the early nineteenth century, foreign merchants in Madagascar adopted various credit policies. Frequent dollar shortages on Mauritius and Réunion obliged Creole traders to use rum, rather than cash, as the usual form of advance to Malagasy suppliers of cattle, the staple export to the Mascarenes.[93] U.S. traders on the west coast generally advanced cottons to obtain their staple export of hides.[94] For instance, in 1849 Horace Putnam left with Calfaun bin Alhi, his Zanzibari agent on Nosy Be, $7,000 worth of trade goods, mostly cotton pieces.[95]

The 1860s trade boom, when funds and credit proved plentiful, was followed by a deterioration in Franco–Merina relations. This climaxed in the 1883–5 war during which the Oriental Bank of Mauritius failed. Many of its Madagascar-based foreign clients turned elsewhere for help: By late 1884, $25,000 worth of money and valuables had been secured in the U.S. consular safe in Toamasina, while NMS agent Røstvig, based at Toliara in southwest Madagascar in the 1880s, opened an account with the Natal Bank in Durban, South Africa.[96]

In difficult economic circumstances, foreign traders nevertheless proved flexible in order to encourage trade. O'Swald established an extensive credit network on the northwest coast involving Creoles, chiefly Réunionnais planters and shopkeepers, and Indian traders. To the former, individual credit mainly

---

[92] Chauvicourt, "premières monnaies," 150; Valette, *Études*, 45.

[93] Finkelmeier to Tucker, Antananarivo, 14 Dec. 1877, Kestell-Cornish Letterbook (1874–88), 310, *ACM*.

[94] Thompson to Hathorne, Majunga, 27 Nov. 1878, encl.1 in Hathorne to Bertram, Zanzibar, 11 Dec. 1878 – Hathorne, "Letterbook" (1878–80).

[95] Razi, "Sources d'histoire," 66; see also Bennett and Brooks (eds.), *New England Merchants*, xxvi.

[96] S. Procter to PM, Consulate of Madagascar [London], 13 April 1883, *AN*.DD21, 131–4; Lord to Wardlaw Thompson, 20 April 1889, IDC Letterbook (1975–97), 569, *FJKM*; Rostvig to Manager of the Natal Bank, 28 Feb. 1888, NMS Kopibok, 812B Tulear (1882–92), 299, *FLM/NMS*; Robinson to Adee, 20 Nov. 1884; Robinson to Porter, Tamatave, 20 July 1886; Geldart to Campbell, 28 Dec. 1889, "enclosure no.8" in Campbell to Wharton, 26 April 1890 – US; F. A. Gregory, "Annals of St. Paul's College, Ambatoharanana," 61–8, ms. *ACM*.

took the form of provisions and building material to the value of from $2,000 to $3,000 – repayable in cash or kind within a stipulated period varying between two and six months. Credit extended to an Indian generally totaled less than $1,000 unless that individual represented O'Swald's business – when up to $20,000 was granted. As in East Africa, Indians in northwest Madagascar normally received six months' credit, although in periods of general economic difficulty, as in 1884, it was sometimes extended to nine months. In all cases, interest was charged at the rate used by Indian financiers in Zanzibar – 0.75 percent a month.[97]

During the 1883–5 conflict, most British firms operating in east and central Madagascar turned for funds to the Protestant missions. The latter's ability to provide internationally acceptable means of finance also proved invaluable to an imperial regime under growing strain: In addition to payments of $24,000 in the mid-1860s to compensate France for the annulment of the Lambert Charter, and of $9,740 in a vain attempt to prevent the French attack of 1883,[98] the Merina court had been forced to unearth $50,000 of Ranavalona I's buried national treasury for the purchase of imported rifles and ammunition to counter the French military threat. Such sums had, by the start of the 1883–5 war, exhausted royal coffers.[99]

The LMS was a particularly important source of funds, as its treasurer remarked, "our consumption of five franc pieces is large and regular, and . . . our drafts are first rate security."[100] No other foreign institution in Madagascar spent such large and regular amounts of dollars locally. From the early 1870s, the LMS possessed headquarters in both Imerina and Betsileo: From 1871 to 1876, the former spent an annual average of $38,663 in missionary salaries and other expenses; and from 1887 to 1894, the latter spent $12,115. Even the SPG, the poorest of the four Protestant missions in the island, spent an annual average of $4,233 throughout the 1880s.[101]

Rather than pay the excessive cost and risk theft by transporting bulk silver coin from Britain, local missions issued bills on London in exchange for dollars supplied locally. Initially, these bills were generally issued to Mauritian banks, such as the Oriental Bank, to respectable British firms operating locally, such

---

[97] Staatsarchiv Hamburg. Firma Wm. O'Swald & Co: 33 (1873–1896). On opening an agency at Mahajanga in 1878, Bertram & Arnold Hines sent the agent there credit comprising 2,000 rupees and 1,945 French 5-franc coins – Hathorne to Thompson, Zanzibar, [December] 1878 – Hathorne, "Letterbook" (1878–80).

[98] Campbell, "Toamasina," 534.

[99] Oliver, *Madagascar* vol. II, 217.

[100] Wills to de Lastelle, Antananarivo, 29 October 1875, IDC Letterbook (1875–97), 53–4, *FJKM*.

[101] Letters to the Treasurer (1886–97), B.7, *FJKM*; SPG Accounts Books (1877–1903), *ACM*.

as Aitken and Procter Brothers or to individuals of impeccable status, such as Pakenham, the British vice consul. The suppliers usually shipped dollars from Mauritius to the Malagasy east coast from where government couriers in mission hire carried them to Antananarivo.[102]

Mission bills were in sterling, which enjoyed a cast-iron reputation as the basic monetary value of the international financial system. No other currency was so sought after, as U.S. merchants offering U.S. dollar bills on New York found to their cost.[103] Moreover, the mission headquarters in Britain felt morally obliged to honor each bill issued. Few foreign firms of comparable standing operated in Madagascar. Also, the Merina government had forged a close relationship with the Protestant missions, notably the LMS, whose members were committed to the imperial Merina cause and advised the court on both foreign and domestic affairs.[104]

In return for yearly agreements to provide monthly sums of dollars, Protestant missions offered the Merina government bills on London. Such bills were in heavy demand among foreign merchants in Madagascar who, with the dollar particularly scarce during the 1883–5 war, offered to exchange dollars for sterling at anything from 10 to 25 percent above par. Because of the initial effectiveness of the French blockade, Rainilaiarivony was initially unable to import large quantities of dollars. However, by September 1883, he had devised a supply route bypassing the French fleet and was able to offer unlimited supplies at 4 percent above par – thereby procuring a near monopoly of missionary bills: In 1883, the LMS were offered $36,000 at 4 percent and, in 1884, $60,000 at 3.5 percent. The SPG alone was offered $50,000, sufficient to meet its cash requirements for an entire decade![105] As the French had blocked alternative dollar supply routes by early 1883, the Protestant missions, who were fully aware that their bills were used to finance arms imports, accepted the terms of exchange offered by Rainilaiarivony.[106]

---

[102] Courier costs proved expensive; e.g., the SPG payed $26 to have one load of silver carried from Mahanoro to the imperial capital in 1884 – SPG Letterbook (1876–84), 1, 11–14; SPG Accounts Book (1877–1903) – *ACM*; IDC Letterbook (1875–97), 10, 13, 60–1, 67, 75–6, 101–2, 106–8, 113–14, 145, *FJKM*.

[103] Finkelmeier to Seward, Tamatave, 1 Oct. 1866, US.

[104] Campbell, "Role of the London Missionary Society"; *idem*, "Missionaries, Fanompoana and the Menalamba Revolt," 54–73.

[105] Lord to PM, 27 Oct. 1882; Lord to Whitehouse, 4 Nov. 1882; Wills to Whitehouse, 8 Sept. 1883; Richardson to Whitehouse, 25 Sept. 1883 – IDC Letterbook (1875–97), 337–40, 381, *FJKM*; Kestell-Cornish to Tucker, Antananarivo, 22 Sept. 1883, and "letter" [1883], SPG Letterbook (1876–84), 104, 467–8; and SPG Accounts Book (1877–1903) – ACM.

[106] [Gottel] to Dawson, St Denis, 20 Feb. 1884, *REC/CR-MZL*; Cousins to Whitehouse, Antananarivo, 24 Aug. 1883, Richardson to Whitehouse, Antananarivo, 25 Sept. 1883; Wills to Whitehouse, 9 Jan. and 24 April 1884, IDC Letterbook (1875–97), 386, 388–9, 408, 656,

From April 1884, with mounting hope of a peace settlement, dollars again began to flow into Madagascar, although not enough to meet demand: Thus, as late as September 1884, Bachelder, the Antananarivo agent for Ropes, Emmerton, had to request $400 from Rainilaiarivony in exchange for a bill at 6 percent.[107] As difficulties with the French continued, the imperial court's import of foreign arms was maintained, as was its financial relationship with the Protestant missions. The regularity and volume of the exchange between the two parties was such that Rainilaiarivony opened a sterling deposit account with the Alliance Bank in London.[108]

However, missionary finance failed to meet imperial needs from the end of the 1883–5 conflict when the French insisted on the payment of a $2 million indemnity,[109] and the United States on $3,000 in damages for a Sakalava attack in 1885 on the U.S. ship *Surprise*.[110] As most locally produced gold was illegally sold to and exported by foreign firms,[111] the Merina court was obliged to seek external finance. In 1883, Procter Brothers, the Merina consul in London from 1880, failed to find backers for a Bank of Madagascar,[112] so in 1886, Rainilaiarivony granted Kingdon a charter to establish a Royal Bank of Madagascar with a capital of $10 million and authority to issue paper money proportional to its deposits. All cut money in circulation was to be withdrawn and a new mixed nickel and copper coinage minted. To meet the French indemnity and to maintain a $2 million public works fund, the court planned to contract a $4 million loan from the bank at 7 percent interest. Customs revenues from the ports of Toamasina, Vatomandry, Fenoarivo, Maroantsetra, Vohimara, Mahajanga, and Andakabe (Morondava) were offered as security. France, which under the peace treaty of 1885 considered Madagascar a French protectorate, declared the Kingdon charter void and insisted on a $2 million loan from the

FJKM; Kestell-Cornish to Tucker, Antananarivo, 15 Aug. 1884, Kestell-Cornish Letterbook (1874–88), 532, *ACM*.
[107] Bachelder to Dawson, Antananarivo, 11 Sept. 1884, Partner and Agency Records: Madagascar Agencies. Correspondence Sent. Letterbook 1884–87 (May–Oct. 1884), B44.F4, *EI*.
[108] Kestell-Cornish to SPG Secretary, Ambatobe, 21 April 1884, Kestell-Cornish Letterbook (1874–88), 528–9, *ACM*.
[109] Campbell, "Toamasina," 534.
[110] Campbell to Wharton, 25 June 1891, US; Campbell, "Role of the Merina State."
[111] See Chapter 4.
[112] S. Procter to PM, Consulate of Madagascar [London], 13 April 1883, *AN*.DD21, 131–4; Lord to Wardlaw Thompson, 20 April 1889, IDC Letterbook (1975–97), 569, *FJKM*; Rostvig to Manager of the Natal Bank, 28 Feb. 1888, NMS Kopibok, 812B Tulear (1882–92), 299, *FLM/NMS*; Robinson to Adee, 20 Nov. 1884; Robinson to Porter, Tamatave, 20 July 1886; Geldart to Campbell, 28 Dec. 1889, "enclosure no.8" in Campbell to Wharton, 26 April 1890 – US; F. A. Gregory, "Annals of St. Paul's College, Ambatoharanana," 61–8, ms. *ACM*.

CNEP at 7 percent interest.[113] In 1888 and 1889, unexpectedly heavy customs receipts covered the interest payment on the loan. However, from 1890, foreign trade slumped and customs duties failed to generate sufficient revenue to either service the loan or help finance the Merina government. Instead, the imperial regime became almost totally reliant on extraordinary domestic taxation and on *fanompoana* impositions.[114]

The CNEP also started to play a considerable role in supplying commercial credit in the form of acceptance credit, whereby large creditworthy foreign firms importing cotton piece goods were offered bills of exchange on Paris. The New Oriental Bank of London, which opened its Madagascar branch in 1888, followed the CNEP's example. However, firms dealing with the Mascarenes continued to export Malagasy goods in payment for their imports.[115]

The Collapse of the Credit Structure, 1891–1895

In 1890, supplies of staple exports to Europe and North America, such as hides, were insufficient to absorb receipts from sales of imports. This resulted in a commercial slump during which some of the larger, notably U.S., firms started to ship out specie, which impacted negatively on the credit structure.[116] In 1891, international overproduction of hides caused prices to plummet in the major markets of Europe and the United States, ruining the Malagasy hide export trade and plunging imperial Madagascar into a business crisis worse than that of the 1883–5 war.[117] Initially, foreign traders competed to extend credit to Malagasy merchants to stimulate purchases, notably of imported cloth.[118] Merina traders on the east coast obtained credit at 90 days for amounts of up to

---

[113] J. Procter to PM, London, 8 Feb. 1886; S. Procter to PM, London, 24 July and 20 Sept. 1886, and 10 Jan. 1887, DD21, 229–36, *ANM*; Robinson to Porter, 20 July 1886; Whitney to Porter, 13 Jan. 1887; Campbell to Porter, 12 Dec. 1887 – US.

[114] Dawson to Ropes, Emmerton & Co, Tamatave, 27 Sept. 1890, REC/CR-MZL.

[115] "It must be remembered that these English houses [Procter Bros, Rogers., etc.] have a Mauritius trade and they can take Rice, Empty bags & Bees Wax in exchange for their goods" – Dawson to Ropes, Emmerton & Co, Tamatave, 27 Sept. 1890, *REC/CR-MZL*.

[116] Dawson to Ropes, Emmerton & Co, Tamatave, 27 Sept. 1890; Whitney to Ropes, Emmerton & Co, Tamatave, 8 July 1892 – *REC/CR-MZL*.

[117] Whitney to Ropes, Emmerton & Co, Tamatave, 1 May 1888; Duder to Ropes, Emmerton & Co, Antananarivo, 20 March 1893 – *REC/CR-MZL*; Gregory to Andriamfidy, Ambatobe, 23 Sept. and 27 Dec. 1889, 23 Dec. 1890, 22 Jan., 16 March and 1 June 1891 – HH3, 697–717, *ANM*; *The Madagascar Mail* 3 (23 Aug. 1892) and 38 (13 Sept. 1892); *CdM* 14 (22 March 1894).

[118] Dawson to Ropes, Emmerton & Co, Tamatave, 27 April 1890, *REC/CR-MZL*.

$200 from O'Swald and $100 from French firms – 80 percent of O'Swald's loans there were repayable in dollars; 20 percent in kind.[119] U.S. firms were more cautious; from February 1891, Ropes, Emmerton restricted credit to between 15 and 28 days and charged 10 percent per annum on all overdue bills from Merina traders in cottons.[120] This was nevertheless much more generous than the officially established maximum interest rate of $0.0208 in the dollar, or $0.50 per month.[121] Overall, relatively easy commercial credit led local dealers to overextend. In 1892 the Malagasy market for imported cottons collapsed due to oversupply, and many Merina traders went bankrupt.[122]

Banks reacted by exporting specie. Between February and June 1891, they dispatched over $500,000, as "Business in general is so poor here that the Banks do not want money, as what they take they must ship to Europe."[123] The change in bank policy caused major problems in commercial exchange. Thus, a U.S. importer of cotton piece goods in Toamasina commented in May 1892,

Buyers have been embarrassed of late by not being able to get much money to Tamatave from the Capital through the Banks. The Banks would receive money at the Capital but they are short of funds at Tamatave and this is because business in general is so bad at this port. I expect buyers will now be more perplexed as regards making payments to me if I refuse to take French bills on London or Boston against dollars they would give the Bank . . . for that reason I have not of late been able to hold them strictly to their agreements as regards making payments.[124]

In June 1892, banks curtailed all credit and called in their debts. Malagasy buyers quickly ran out of funds to either repay the banks or purchase imports. Consequently, foreign traders found themselves overstocked with cottons, which had arrived in large quantity from the start of 1892, and had to sell quickly in order "to meet importers acceptances."[125] As the domestic market for cottons collapsed, the smaller foreign firms slid into bankruptcy.[126] Still

[119] Raminisoa, "La Maison 'Wm. O'Swald & Co.,'" 93.

[120] Whitney to Ropes, Emmerton & Co, Tamatave, 27 Feb., 19 and 27 March 1891, *REC/CR-MZL*.

[121] Dawson to Ropes, Emmerton & Co, Tamatave, 27 April 1890; Ryder to Ropes, Emmerton & Co, Tamatave, 27 Dec. 1892, *REC/CR-MZL*; *MT* II.30 (30 July 1884), 276.

[122] Duder to Ropes, Emmerton & Co, Antananarivo, 20 March 1893, *REC/CR-MZL*. A similar situation arose in 1902 – see André Prunières, *Madagascar et la crise* (Paris, 1934).

[123] Whitney to Ropes, Emmerton & Co, Tamatave, 7 and 26 June 1891, *REC/CR-MZL*.

[124] Whitney to Ropes, Emmerton & Co, Tamatave, 8 and 27 May 1892, *REC/CR-MZL*.

[125] And Duder to Ropes, Emmerton & Co, Antananarivo, 20 March 1893 – *REC/CR-MZL*.

[126] *AAMM* 12 (1888), 755; Gregory to Andriamifidy, Ambatobe, 23 Sept. and 27 Des 1889, 23 Des 1890, 22 Jan, 16 Martsa and 1 Jona 1891, HH3, 697–717 – *ANM*; Ryder to Ropes, Emmerton & Co, Tamatave, 27 Dec. 1892, *REC/CR-MZL*; *The Madagascar Mail* 34 (23 Aug. 1892) and 38 (13 Sept. 1892); Devred, "Les mines," 64; Alan H. Jeeves, *Migrant Labour in South Africa's Mining Economy. The Struggle for the Gold Mines' Labour Supply* (Kingston and Montreal, 1985), 37; Gwyn Campbell, "Missionaries, Fanompoana and the Menalamba Revolt in late

solvent firms deepened the banking crisis by refusing bills of exchange. Some, like O'Swald, continued shipping all specie receipts directly to Europe,[127] but most also started to trade their dollars for black market gold, it being noted that "leading firms here prefer to make remittances home in the form of gold to purchasing drafts."[128] Thus Ropes, Emmerton, who in 1892 shipped out $13,000 in specie to London in April, $20,00 from June to August, and a further $4,000 in December,[129] purchased an estimated average of 5,698 ounces of gold each month for which figures are available in 1893–4.[130]

However, even larger firms found the strain of unpaid debts onerous. From 1875 to 1890, nine Merina and two Creole traders defaulted on loans extended on the Malagasy east coast by O'Swald, while in July 1893, the Toamasina agency of Ropes, Emmerton had $10,000 in outstanding credit, mainly to Merina purchasers of cotton piece goods. Loan recovery was extremely difficult as the Merina judicial system was inefficient and prejudiced in favor of creditor members of the imperial court.[131] Moreover, the business slump deepened as France prepared for another war with the Merina and domestic security collapsed. By early 1894, almost all foreign firms had closed their agencies in Madagascar.[132]

In summary, problems associated with an insufficient money supply were a major factor influencing the Merina court to adopt autarkic economic policies in the mid-1820s. However, these policies, notably regarding commercial practices, taxation, and *fanompoana*, ensured continued shortages of

nineteenth century Madagascar," *Journal of Southern African Studies* 15.1 (1988); Crosfield, *Man in Shining Armour*, 96; LMS *Ten Years' Review* (1880–1890), 12; Decary, "L'ancien régine," 91; for foreign trade see Campbell, "Toamasina" and "Role of the Merina State."

[127] Whitney to Ropes, Emmerton & Co, Tamatave, 8 July 1892, *REC/CR-MZL*.
[128] Mathews to PM, Faravohitra, 8 Oct. 1889, HH1, 762–3, *ANM*.
[129] Whitney to Ropes, Emmerton & Co, Tamatave, 26 June & 26 July 1892; Whitney to Ropes, Emmerton & Co, Tamatave, 20 Aug 1892; Whitney to Ropes, Emmerton & Co, Tamatave, 2 & 26 April 1892; Ryder to Ropes, Emmerton & Co, Tamatave, 10 Dec. 1892 – *REC/CR-MZL*.
[130] Whitney to Ropes Emmerton & Co, Tamatave, 26 July and 7 Sept. 1892, B46.F2 (May–Dec. 1892) Ryder to Ropes Emmerton & Co, Tamatave, 6 Jan. 1893; Duder to Ropes Emmerton & Co, Antananarivo, 20 March 1893 – B46.F1 – *REC/CR-MZL*.
[131] Beby Soa Sahohy Raminosoa, "La Maison 'Wm. O'Swald & Co' dans les relations Germano-Malgaches à la fin du dix-neuvième et au début du vingtième siècle," thèse du doctorat, Université de la Sorbonne Nouvelle, Paris III (1987–88), 126, 153, 155–62; Ryder to Ropes, Emmerton & Co, Tamatave, 8 July 1893, *REC/CR-MZL*. The British and French briefly experimented with consular courts to try cases brought by their respective subjects – but this system disintegrated in October 1877 when Pakenham, the British vice-consul, declared himself unqualified to hear complaints lodged against British subjects by foreigners and, in retaliation, the French consul followed suit – Finkelmeier to Hunter, 29 Oct. 1877, US.
[132] Thus the New Oriental Bank branch dissolved by 1893 and Ropes, Emmerton by February 1894 – Ryder to Ropes, Emmerton & Co, Tamatave, 7 Feb. 1893; Duder to Ropes, Emmerton & Co, Antananarivo, 20 March 1893; Duder, 29 Nov. 1893, in Ryder to Ropes, Emmerton & Co, Tamatave, 27 Dec. 1893 – *REC/CR-MZL*.

revenue and money supply. When foreign trade was buoyant, as in the 1860s, money was comparatively plentiful, but at other times extraordinary taxation was imposed. Consequently, business confidence slumped, credit and the money supply contracted, and fraud increased. It was therefore no surprise that in the two decades following the reopening of Madagascar in 1861, there was no substantial domestic investment in industry or any development of wage labor, as all economic sectors bar transport remained reliant upon unremunerated slave or *fanompoana* labor.[133]

From this shaky economic basis, a currency crisis of major proportions developed from the late 1870s. The crisis was occasioned by the general decline in foreign trade from 1877, the cost of conflict with France, customs mismanagement, and the adulteration of coinage. Recourse to missionary institutions and foreign banks to finance government were temporary palliatives. Imperial taxation became increasingly unbearable; the resultant impoverishment of ordinary cultivators led to diminishing returns on taxation. Also, growing political and economic insecurity resulted in the sharp curtailment of foreign trade and credit. It was a vicious cycle as the lack of credit undermined trade, thus hastening the flight of specie and gold from the country. From the late 1880s, total revenue declined proving one of the factors that helped to precipitate the collapse of the imperial Merina regime.

[133] See Chapters 5 and 10.

12   Madagascar in the Scramble
for Indian Ocean Africa

Introduction

In 1895, France conquered Madagascar and in 1896 declared it a French colony, thus ending the century-old Merina empire. The colonization of Madagascar formed part of a general European scramble for colonies in Africa in the late nineteenth century, the debate over which has centered on the interplay of three factors; developments in Europe, European agents in Africa, and indigenous African forces. Of primary concern has been the way in which, largely in the context of the 1880s depression and rise of new technologies, the relationship between European and indigenous forces on the geographical periphery of the international economy altered so as to favor the former.[1]

India played a central role in the scramble for IOA, including Madagascar. The "jewel of the empire" and the one glaring exception to British free-trade policy, India not only provided the soldiers to defend Britain's overseas interests, but it also sustained the British economy. From 1857 to 1865, India attracted the major part of British capital flows overseas, while in the 1880s, India alone settled more than one-third of British trade deficits with Europe and the United States.[2] Securing the routes to India was a vital concern to Britain and the origin of initial British interest in IOA. The colonization of Mauritius (1810), Aden (1839), and Natal (1843) can be viewed in this light, as can the extension of

---

[1] For useful expositions of this debate, see Martin Wolfe (ed.), *The Economic Causes of Imperialism* (New York, 1972); Roger Owen & Bob Sutcliffe (eds.), *Studies in the Theory of Imperialism* (London, 1972); D. K. Fieldouse, *Economics and Empire 1830–1914* (London, 1973); P. J. Cain & A. G. Hopkins, *British Imperialism. Innovation and Expansion, 1688–1914* (London, 1993).

[2] Michael Barratt Brown, *The Economics of Imperialism* (UK, 1974), 195; Rusi J. Daruwala, *The Bombay Chamber Story* (Bombay, 1986), 35.

British informal influence over Oman, Mozambique, and the Swahili coast.[3] By 1860, British dominance was such that a French priest visiting the region remarked, "one would say that the entire universe belongs not to God but to the British."[4] The British forward movement in IOA from the 1870s has been accredited to the insecurity of the routes to India arising from local disturbances, notably nationalist uprisings in Egypt, and friction with Boers and Zulus in South Africa,[5] although Cain and Hopkins have in addition emphasized the role of well-connected British merchants and administrators – such as Scottish ship owner William Mackinnon and government official Bartle Frere – who had vested interests in the region.[6]

However, this debate has largely excluded Madagascar, the colonization of which has been viewed largely in terms of French imperial ambitions. Initially, historians converged around two main versions of the 1895 French takeover: first, that colonization formed part of a civilizing mission and was the culmination of historic French claims to the island,[7] and second, that it was a violation of the rights of a unified, Christian, and civilized Malagasy kingdom. The former, colonial school dominated until the 1960s. In the postindependence era, the scholarly pendulum swung in favor of a nationalist school bolstered by claims that the 1895–7 *Menalamba* rebellion was possibly the earliest African nationalist revolt against colonial rule. Explanations for the French takeover have generally concentrated on describing French historical claims to Madagascar and the chronology of French military intervention in the island up to the 1895 conquest.[8]

To date, there has been no serious attempt to examine the French conquest of Madagascar within the framework of the general debate over the scramble for Africa or with reference to the post-1815 Franco–British *modus vivendi*. Under the latter, France generally accommodated British foreign policy aims, recognized British dominance in the western Indian Ocean, and, from the start of the scramble, showed little official inclination to include Madagascar in plans for an African empire based on the north and west of the continent. This chapter breaks from traditional historical approaches. Drawing on material presented in

---

[3] Jackson, *European Powers*, 122–45; G. S. P. Freeman-Grenville, "The Coast 1498–1840" in Roland Oliver & Gervase Mathew (eds.), *History of East Africa* I (Oxford, 1963), 156–61.

[4] Guerret, *Trois mois autour de Madagascar*, 25.

[5] Roland Robinson & John Gallagher *Africa and the Victorians* (London, 1965).

[6] Cain & Hopkins, *British Imperialism*, 387–91.

[7] See Appendix A.

[8] Two standard expositions of Franco–British rivalry in the island are Deschamps, *histoire* and Mervyn Brown, *A History of Madagascar* (London, 1995); for the *Menalamba*, see Ellis, *Rising of the Red Shawls*.

previous chapters, it analyzes the colonization of Madagascar within the context of the western IOW and the scramble for Africa debate.

Britain and Madagascar in the Western Indian Ocean

Why did Madagascar not become integrated, along with almost all other areas of the western Indian Ocean, into the formal British imperial sphere? Given British dominance in the IOW from 1815, this question is fundamental. The island straddled the sea lanes from the Cape to India: the inner route passing through the Mozambique Channel and the outer one swinging around the southern Malagasy coast in a wide arc toward the Mascarenes. Madagascar first attracted serious attention from the British government during the Revolutionary and Napoleonic Wars when, in order to secure mastery of the Cape route to India, Britain successively captured Réunion (1809), Mauritius (1810), and the French posts in Madagascar at Toamasina and Mahavelona (1811). Under the Treaty of Paris in 1814, Réunion was returned to France, but the British retained Mauritius, and the 1820 Britanno–Merina treaty incorporated Imerina into the informal British empire.[9] However, in 1825–6, Radama I rejected the British alliance and adopted autarkic policies. In 1835–6, LMS missionaries in Madagascar were expelled – largely because Joseph Freeman, their leader in the 1830s, worked openly for the restoration of British political influence in the island.[10]

From 1836 to 1845, the British and French governments supported calls, such as those made by Freeman, demanding that the Merina adopt open door policies. However, military attacks by a mixed Sakalava–European force (1838), Seyyid Said (1838–9), and a combined Franco–British naval force (1845) failed to influence the Merina court.[11] Subsequently, the British and French governments abandoned the use of force. From 1861 to 1863, the Merina regime experimented with an open door policy, but when it then reimposed many traditional economic restrictions, the British and French signed treaties, in 1865 and 1868 respectively, reiterating their recognition of Merina sovereignty in

---

[9] See Chapter 3 and Appendix B for British imperial interest in Madagascar.
[10] Campbell, "Adoption of Autarky"; *idem*, "Role of the London Missionary Society" vol. II, 269–70; see also Chapter 3.
[11] In 1834, Seyyid had himself unsuccessfully requested the Merina court for 2,000 soldiers to help him conquer Mombasa – Wastell, "British Imperial Policy," 258, 260–1; see also Prud'homme, "Considerations sur les Sakalaves," 26; *RA*, 467–8; Johns to Hankey, Antananarivo, 23 June 1830, *SOAS/LMS-MIL* B3.F3.JB; Aujas, "Notes sur l'histoire des Betsimisaraka," 183–94; Raombana, vol. 8 B.1, 25–31; Sonia Howe, *L'Europe et Madagascar* (Paris, 1936), 205–8, 213.

Madagascar.[12] However, from 1869, after the Merina regime had converted to Christianity and established a state church in which British LMS and FFMA missionaries held pride of place, Madagascar was reabsorbed into Britain's informal empire. British missionaries exerted great influence at the Merina court, and British subjects dominated the island's foreign trade.[13] Thus, by the 1870s, when the scramble for Africa started, Madagascar was, like the rest of Indian Ocean Africa, under the umbrella of British paramountcy.

The Economic Foundations of the British Forward Movement in Indian Ocean Africa

Regional Trade

The growth of international and intraregional trade in the IOA from the mid-nineteenth century has traditionally been underestimated, in large part due to the hidden dimensions of the trade, much of which flowed via indirect channels or bypassed Europe altogether. It is thus missing from official bilateral trade statistics. One example is ivory, the main source of which had long been East Africa. Traditionally, India constituted the chief ivory market, but with the rise of bourgeois demand for ivory products in Europe and the United States from the mid-nineteenth century, ivory was increasingly reexported from India to the West. Only from the mid-1880s did European merchants start shipping ivory directly from East Africa, with the result that the reexport trade from India declined sharply. Rising demand and finite stocks of elephants pushed the ivory frontier rapidly into hinterland Africa, helping to expand commercial links between the east African interior and the coast throughout the second half of the nineteenth century[14] (Figures 13–14).

Another hidden commodity of Indian Ocean Africa was cowries. Traditionally, cowries were shipped from their main source in the Maldive Islands via India or Sri Lanka to Britain for reexport to West Africa, where they formed one of the principal currencies. However, from 1851 to 1870, three German and

---

[12] G. N. Sanderson, "The European Partition of Africa: Coincidence or Conjecture?" *Journal of Imperial and Commonwealth History* 3.1 (1974), 20; Hubert Deschamps, *Méthodes et doctrines coloniales de la France* (Paris, 1953), 109–12; Brown, *History of Madagascar*, 161–3, 198; Thomas F. Power, *Jules Ferry and the Renaissance of French Imperialism* (New York, 1944), 116.

[13] Gow, *Madagascar and the Protestant Impact*; Campbell, "Toamasina."

[14] Abdul Sheriff, "Ivory and Commercial Expansion in East Africa in the Nineteenth Century" in Liesegang et al. (eds.) *Figuring African Trade; idem, Slaves, Spices and Ivory*.

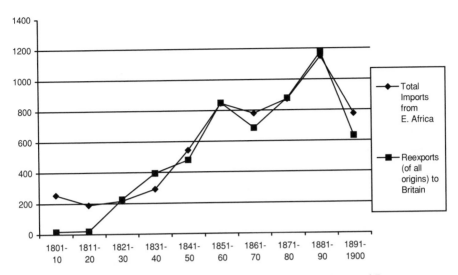

Figure 13. *Bombay Ivory Trade: Imports from East Africa and Reexports to Britain, 1801–1900* (10-Year Averages in Rs. 000s).
Source: Abdul Sheriff, "Ivory and Commercial Expansion in East Africa in the Nineteenth Century" in Liesegang et al. (eds.), *Figuring African Trade*, 423–6.

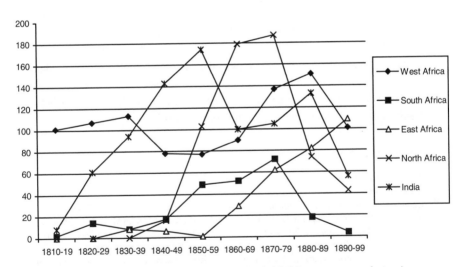

Figure 14. *Britain: Ivory Imports, 1810–99* (10-year averages in tons).
Source: Sheriff, "Ivory and Commercial Expansion in East Africa," 428–32.

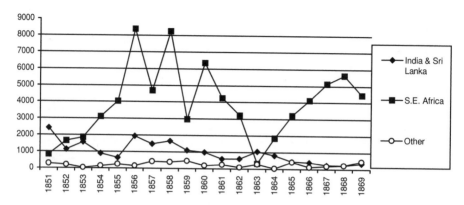

Figure 15. IOA *Cowrie Supplies by Origin, 1851–69* (lbs avoirdupois).
Source: Hogendorn & Johnson, *Shell Money*, 70, 76.

two French firms, led by O'Swald, shifted the center of the trade to east African
waters, shipping cowries directly to West Africa (Figure 15.)[15]

Similarly obscured have been the dimensions of the regional traffic in humans. Traditionally, historians have focused on the slave export trade from the
Swahili coast to offshore plantations and to Muslim countries to the north,
which declined rapidly following the 1873 treaty with Zanzibar.[16] However,
it is now clear that there was also a vibrant slave export trade south of Cape
Delgado (essentially from Mozambique to Madagascar and the Transvaal and
from Mozambique and Madagascar to the French islands) continuing into the
1890s.[17] Moreover, when slave imports were effectively suppressed on the
Mascarenes and in Natal, they were replaced by a vigorous and partially hidden
trade in contract labor, notably from India and Mozambique.[18] Between 1780
and 1880, some 25,000 laborers were brought to South Africa, first as slaves
and subsequently as liberated slaves and contract workers.[19]

[15] Jan Hogendorn & Marion Johnson, *The Shell Money of the Slave Trade* (Cambridge, 1986),
71–7.

[16] Toussaint, *Histoire de l'Ile Maurice*, 85; Beachey, *Slave Trade*, 113.

[17] See Chapter 9.

[18] Campbell, "Madagascar and Mozambique"; *idem*, "The East African Slave Trade"; Peter
Richardson, "The Natal Sugar Industry, 1849–1905," in Bill Guest & John M. Sellers (eds.), *Enterprise and Exploitation in a Victorian Economy. Aspects of the Economic and Social History
of Colonial Natal* (Pietermaritzburg, 1985), 184–5; Allen "Licentious and Unbridled Proceedings," 91–116; Patrick Harries, "Slavery, incorporation and surplus extraction; the nature of
free and unfree labour in South-East Africa" *JAH* 22 (1981), 309–30; Galloway, *Sugar Cane
Industry*, 218–22.

[19] Patrick Harries, "Culture and Classification: A History of the Mozbieker Community at the
Cape," *Social Dynamics* 26.2 (2000), 29; see also *idem, Work, Culture, and Identity. Migrant
Laborers in Mozambique and South Africa, c.1860–1910* (London, 1994), Ch. 2.

The Impact of Steam

This mid-century growth in western IOW trade was assisted by the technological spin-offs of the Industrial Revolution, notably steam transport. The process started in India where, from 1845 to 1875, some £95 million were invested in railways, helping to stimulate linkages with the interior and promote, from 1870 to 1914, a fivefold increase in the value of Indian exports.[20] There was a similar explosion in railway construction in South Africa. The first line established in Durban (1860) was extended to Pietermaritzburg by 1880, and in 1895 to Johannesburg, which had already been linked to Cape Town in 1893.[21]

Rail was considered an auxiliary to steamships, which increasingly replaced sailing vessels, both on the long haul to Europe and in regional waters. India and South Africa were early linked to Europe, and in 1864 the first steamship link between Natal and Mauritius was established. The following year, the Holt Line introduced the first direct steamship service between Liverpool and Mauritius. East Africa was drawn into the steamship network in 1872 when Mackinnon, who in the early 1860s secured the mail steamship contract to India, organized the first regular mail boat service between Britain, India, and Zanzibar. In 1873, he obtained the Aden–Zanzibar British mail contract, as well as a 10-year contract from the French to extend the British and India Steam Navigation Company service from Zanzibar to Mayotta and Nosy Be. Also, in 1875 he obtained a Portuguese contract to establish a regular Zanzibar–Mozambique service.[22] Competition quickly appeared: In 1878, the Clan Line opened a steamship service between Glasgow and Liverpool, and Bombay via Suez; in 1879 – the year Zanzibar was connected to the submarine cable (with lines to South Africa and Mauritius) – Donald Currie recommenced a steamship service linking the Cape, Natal, and Mauritius; and in 1881, Clan also started a direct service to the Cape and from there to Natal, Mauritius, and Bombay, returning via Suez. Competition intensified with the establishment of a number of rival subsidized national lines (British, French, and German) in the 1880s, forcing freight rates down at a time when the terms of trade were generally in favor of African producers.[23]

---

[20] Cain & Hopkins, *British Imperialism*, 333; A. G. Kenwood & A. L. Lougheed, *The Growth of the International Economy 1820–1990* (London, 1992), 30.

[21] Hein Heydenrych, "Railway Development in Natal to 1895" in Guest & Sellers (eds.), *Enterprise and Exploitation.*

[22] Andrew Porter, *Victorian Shipping, Business and Imperial Policy. Donald Currie, the Castle Line and Southern Africa* (Woodbridge & New York, 1986), 83; M. E. Chamberlain, *The Scramble for Africa* (UK, 1984), 64; Cain & Hopkins, British Imperialism, 340.

[23] Porter, *Victorian Shipping*, 85, 103, 121; Archibald Hurd, *The Sea Traders* (London, 1921), 183–4.

Costs were further cut due to the Suez Canal, which opened in 1869 – although as late as 1878, £91 million worth of British trade still flowed to the East via the Cape of Good Hope compared to £65 million via Suez.[24] Indeed, in 1883, when competition from rival shippers and the depression was cutting profit margins, the chairman of the Union Steam Ship Company argued that, given first, the low freights to India from Britain and the high cost of passing through Suez, and second, the sizeable return freights, many in the India trade found it "more economical . . . to go double the distance, round the Cape, and pay the extra cost . . . by taking cargo to the Cape at very small cost."[25]

Steam transport accelerated the growth in regional trade and helped expand interior–coastal links. This was particularly marked in the cases of Zanzibar and Mozambique. Zanzibar witnessed a sevenfold increase in the tonnage of British shipping from 1870 to 1879.[26] Further south, the Witwatersrand gold discoveries and the construction of Transvaal-Lourenço Marques railway from the mid-1880s (completed in 1895) underpinned a more than fivefold increase in the value of Lourenço Marques' foreign trade between 1885 and 1896.[27] Some of this trade was with Portugal, but Mozambique's intraregional trade also rose – notably with South Africa – while a strong clandestine trade in slaves and arms with Madagascar lasted until at least 1890.[28]

In addition, Natal established a brisk trade with Madagascar from the late 1870s. In part, this evolved from the Natal mail steamship service to Mauritius. The latter had a strong trading relationship with imperial Madagascar, the foreign trade of which engaged some 202,000 tons of shipping annually immediately prior to the 1883–5 Franco–Merina War.[29] Further, while the value of Madagascar's direct visible trade with Britain, its main trading partner, only once exceeded $300,000 before 1879, it thereafter rose rapidly, averaging $534,000 a year from 1879 to 1883. It was adversely affected by the Franco–Merina conflict but recovered strongly from 1886, and from 1891 to 1897 averaged over $1 million a year. French colonial protectionist measures then caused it to drop precipitously.[30]

[24] William Ashworth, *A Short History of the International Economy since 1850* (UK, 1981), 70; Robinson & Gallagher, *Africa and the Victorians*, 56–61.

[25] Quoted in Porter, *Victorian Shipping*, 121–2.

[26] J. M. Mackenzie, *The Partition of Africa 1880–1900* (London, 1983), 25; Chamberlain, *Scramble for Africa*, 63.

[27] Heydenrych, "Railway Development in Natal to 1895," 61; Liesegang, "First Look," 472–3.

[28] See Chapter 9.

[29] Of the 196 vessels visiting Toamasina from 31 May 1881 to 30 June 1882, 46 were steamships of which four ran regularly between the Mascarenes and the east coast of Madagascar – Oliver, *Madagascar* vol. II, 188; see also Chapter 8.

[30] See Figure 21 and Chapter 8.

The Role of British Indians

After the defeat of France in the Napoleonic Wars, British global supremacy stimulated a spectacular resurgence of Indian IOA trade. First, the British navy suppressed piracy and established a Pax Britannica – essential safeguards to the British maritime route to India. This occurred by the early 1820s in the coastal waters off north and east Madagascar and the Mascarenes, although piracy was widespread in Arabian and Persian waters until the 1830s. British promotion of Omani power also secured east African waters. With both the Omani and Portuguese authorities under an informal British protectorate, backed by the British and Indian navies, piracy in the region experienced an absolute decline.[31] Second, the abolition of the British East India Company monopoly benefited smaller companies and individual traders, including those from Malabar.[32]

Taking full advantage of the new conditions of liberty of commerce and the security emanating from Pax Britannica, Indian traders reestablished their maritime commercial network and trading colonies from the 1820s, expanding across the Persian and Arabian coasts and, under the protection of the Omani power, down the east African coast. In the 1840s, the first Europeans attracted to the commercial rise of Zanzibar found British Indians there playing the dominant role as capitalists, wholesalers, and retailers.[33] Moroever, although the Swahili coast, notably Zanzibar, remained the center of Indian trade and investment, the Indian commercial frontier spread rapidly south of Zanzibar from the 1840s, into Mozambique, to the Comoro islands and northwest Madagascar where it embraced long-standing colonies of Indians.[34] By the 1860s, Indians, whose trading structure covered most of Indian Ocean Africa from the Red Sea to Natal and the islands, dominated regional trade, as middlemen, financiers, and as shippers.[35]

While hurting the imperial Merina economy, the 1883–5 war stimulated foreign trade on the independent west coast of Madagascar, which attracted traders seeking to avoid the French naval embargo on the east coast. As in imperial Madagascar, British subjects, notably Indians, directly or indirectly controlled much of the foreign trade of independent West Madagascar. Throughout the

[31] Graham, *Great Britain*; Jackson, *European Powers*.

[32] C. Northcote Parkinson, *Trade in the Eastern Seas, 1793–1813* (Cambridge, 1937); J. Gallagher & R. E. Robinson, "The Imperialism of Free Trade" *Economic History Review* 6 (1953).

[33] Owen, *Narrative of Voyage*; Hall, *Narrative*; no. 51, inclosure 1, *CFM*.

[34] Jackson, *European Powers*, 22–3.

[35] See Chapter 7. See also *CFM*, esp. Frere to Granville, 27 February, 10 & 12 March 1873; Sheriff, *Slaves, Spices and Ivory;* Gwyn Campbell, "Indians and Commerce in Madagascar, 1869–1896" University of the Witwatersrand *African Studies Seminar Paper* 345 (23 August 1993).

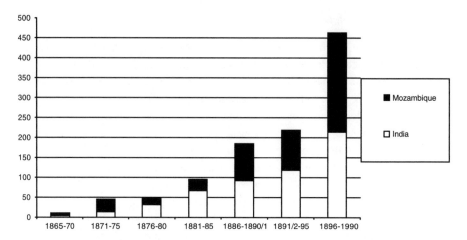

Figure 16. *Natal: Trade with India and Mozambique, 1865–1900* (in £000s) (expressed in five-year averages except for India for which the value of the last year of each five-year grouping is given).
Source: Natal Blue Books; Colony of Natal Statistical Year Book; Surendra Bhana, "Indian Trade and Trader in Colonial Natal" in Guest & Sellers (eds.), *Enterprise and Exploitation,* 254.

1880s, a fleet of Indian-owned dhows, of 60–100 tons each, sailed annually from Bombay and other western India ports directly to Maintirano and Manambolo on the independent west coast of Madagascar before crossing to East Africa.[36] There, these British Indians joined the established Indian community, which, in Delagoa Bay, largely comprised Portuguese Indian merchants from Goa, Diu, and Damão.[37] Although sailing vessels offered low freight rates for intraregional trade, Indian merchants increasingly took advantage of steamship services for their trade to Europe.[38]

After the 1883–5 war, the Indian commercial frontier rapidly moved south. By 1895, Nosy Ve, the main entrepôt on the southwest coast of Madagascar, boasted 27 Indian traders who dominated the foreign trade of West Madagascar. Indians traders there maintained regular commercial contact with their counterparts on the Swahili and Mozambique coasts. Through them, even prior to the 1883–5 conflict, they had forged strong trading links with Cape Colony and with Natal where, from the late 1860s, there emerged a mercantile community of Indians, known locally as Arabs. Some were exindentured laborers from Mauritius, but most were traders representing family firms from Surat and Bombay. As

[36] Stanwood, "Commercial Situation," Andakabe, 31 Dec. 1886 – *US.*
[37] Harries, *Work, Culture, and Identity,* 14, 88.
[38] See Chapter 7.

elsewhere in IOA, they possessed access to capital, making them important sources of credit, and established trading relationships with both petty Indian traders and with larger European concerns – including McCubbin of Natal. In a very real sense, therefore, the Indian mercantile empire in the western IOW formed the basis for British economic influence in IOA.[39]

The Role of South Africans

The considerable role of South Africans in the nineteenth-century trade of Madagascar has been neglected. By the 1880s, most U.S. and European agents on the west coast below Mahajanga either came from South Africa or represented Natal houses. Indeed, most U.S. trade with West Madagascar, less than 5 percent of which was direct, was conducted in vessels chartered from Cape Colony or Natal, which shipped Malagasy exports to Zanzibar for transhipment onto U.S.- or Europe-bound steamers.[40] By mid-1884, four sailing vessels and a 450-ton steamer were running regularly between Natal and the Malagasy west coast. They flew British colors but conveyed generally U.S. goods in a trade of rapidly growing value: By 1886, the U.S. consular agent at Andakabe claimed that U.S. trade with independent West Madagascar had tripled since 1881 to about $1 million annually, equivalent to U.S. direct trade with Toamasina.[41] As he had noted in late 1883:

The whole West coast [of Madagascar] i.e. from Cape St. Andrew to Cape St. Mary must be taken as one port, as nearly all the traders have interests along the coast, some of them as many as 25 different stations, and ships discharge and load wherever required, and boats are constantly passing between this station [Morondava] carrying goods and produce as the demands of the import trade and the conveniences of the export trade require.[42]

Regional British interest in Madagascar was heightened by news of the exploitation of gold fields by the imperial Merina regime during the 1883–5 war. Groups of South African prospectors landed in West Madagascar in 1884 and

[39] Firma Wm. O'Swald & Co, Staatsarchiv Hamburg; Razi, "Sources d'histoire"; Campbell, "Indians and Commerce"; Samuel Procter to Sir Charles Dilke, London, 15 Nov. 1882, *Correspondence Respecting Madagascar relating to the Mission of Hova Envoys to Europe in 1882–93* (London, 1883), no.17; Knott to British Foreign Secretary, Mahajanga, 29 Mar. 1895 in *Correspondence of the British Consulate in Majunga* (1894–7), *AAM*; Bhana, "Indian Trade," 237–46.

[40] Stanwood to Robinson, 1 Dec. 1880; Whitney to Adee, 19 Feb. 1883; encl.2 in Stanwood to 3rd Asst. Secretary of State, Andakabe, 11 Feb 1884; Stanwood to Robinson, Andakabe, 28 Aug. 1884 – *US*.

[41] Stanwood to Bayard, Andakabe, 31 Oct. 1886; Stanwood to Porter, Andakabe, 11 Nov. 1886; Stanwood, "Commercial Situation," Andakabe, 31 Dec. 1886; Campbell to Porter, Tamatave, 12 Dec. 1887 – *US*.

[42] Encl. 30 Sept. 1883 in Stanwood to 3rd Asst. Secretary of State, Andakabe, 11 Feb. 1884 – *US*.

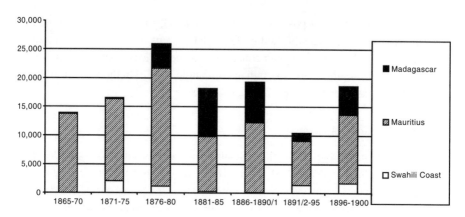

Figure 17. *Natal: Trade with Swahili Coast, Mauritius, and Madagascar,*
1865–1900 (in £ – expressed in five-year averages).
Source: *Natal Blue Books; Colony of Natal Statistical Year Book;* Bhana, "Indian Trade,"
254.

1893, and in 1895–6 there was a major gold rush to the island from South
Africa, Matabeleland, Rhodesia, Mashonaland, and the Mascarenes. Most dig-
gers proved disappointed and had left the island by the close of 1896 but some,
including Zambesi Smith, alias Trader Horn, prospected successfully. Another
gold rush occurred in 1904–5, by which time gold was Madagascar's chief
export and provoked considerable excitement on Johannesburg's open call exchange.[43]

The Mascarenes

The major exception to this commercial expansion was the Mascarenes, for
which Madagascar constituted a critical source of labor, provisions, and, increasingly, land. Rail and steamer investment failed to prevent the monocrop
sugar economy of Réunion and Mauritius from declining sharply. Their predica-
ment was due partly to rising labor costs, international competition from other
sugarcane growers and, after 1863, from beet sugar. It also stemmed from natural
disasters: cyclones, sugarcane borer, cholera (notably in 1858), and malaria –
which killed 50,000 on Mauritius alone from 1866 to 1868 (Figure 18.) By
contrast, favorable tariffs from 1856 and a growing home market assisted the

---

[43] Stanwood to Robinson, Andakabe, 28 Aug. 1884; Robinson to Adee, 29 Oct. 1884; Stanwood
to Campbell, 8 Sept. 1887; Du Verge to Campbell, Belo, 30 Oct. 1888; Du Verge to Rainizafindrazaka, Belo, 8 Nov. 1888; Du Verge to Campbell, Adlanda, 30 Apr. 1889; Campbell to Wharton,
26 July 1889; Wetter to Uhl, 31 Mar. 1896 – *US*; Campbell, "Gold Mining," 117–19.

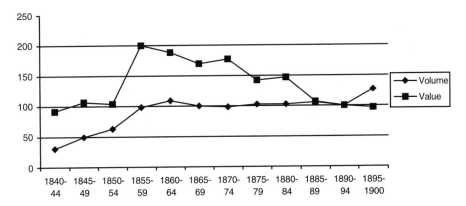

Figure 18. *Mauritius Sugar Export Index by Volume and Value, 1840–1900* (Five-Year Annual Average (1890–94 = 100)).
Source: Constructed from data in Allen, *Slaves, Freedmen and Indentured Laborers*, 23.

Natal sugarcane industry[44]. On the Mascarenes, growing capitalization, which resulted in a decline of small sugar refineries (from 189 to 121 between 1830 and 1860 on Réunion; from 258 to 104 between 1860 and 1892 on Mauritius), accentuated the economic marginalization of small planters whose concerns were critically dependent on cheap labor.[45] Their problems were aggravated by the tendency of Indian indentured laborers, upon the termination of their contract, to either migrate (home to India or to South Africa or Madagascar) or enter petty commerce and (on Mauritius) agriculture, thus competing for land and in trade with local Creoles.[46]

Thus, Creoles were considerably impoverished and many sought to emigrate. In the early nineteenth century, Réunionnais Creoles emigrated to Mauritius, the Seychelles and Rodrigues, or the small French island colonies off Madagascar. However, these destinations quickly became overpopulated and, from mid-century, Réunionnais Creoles turned increasingly to Madagascar.[47] There was similar pressure on Mauritius that, because of a higher birthrate in the second half of the nineteenth century, experienced a greater overpopulation crisis than Réunion (Figure 19). Until French colonization precluded Madagascar as

[44] Toussaint, *Histoire de l'Ile Maurice*, 99, 106; Scherer, *Histoire de la Réunion*, 76; Wanquet, *Fragments pour une histoire*; Richardson, "The Natal Sugar Industry"; Galloway, *Sugar Cane Industry*, 218–28.

[45] Toussaint, *Histoire de l'île Maurice*, 101; Scherer, *Histoire de la Réunion*, 61.

[46] Allen, *Slaves, Freedmen and Indentured Laborers*, Chs. 5 & 6; Bhana, "Indian Trade," 236.

[47] Georges Athenas, "Ethnographie [de la Réunion]" in de Coppet (ed.), *Madagascar* vol. I, 304; Toussaint, *Histoire de l'île Maurice*, 99–104.

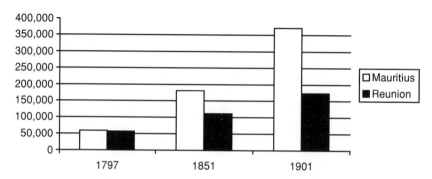

Figure 19. *Mascarenes: Population 1797, 1851, and 1901* (thousands).
Source: From Toussaint, *Histoire de l'île Maurice*, 67, 93, 109.

a destination, the wish to settle Madagascar was almost as prevalent among Mauritians as it was among the Réunionnais.[48] By 1887, some 500 Creoles had settled in Diego Suarez, ceded to France in 1886.[49] Many also migrated to the Malagasy east coast,[50] Grandidier commenting that

each mail steamer brings a crowd of immigrants.... [I]n 1887 and 1888 especially, every mail boat carried from the islands of Réunion and Mauritius a crowd of unfortunate Creoles who believed they would make their fortune there [in Madagascar] although many left on the following steamer, being quickly convinced that gold could not simply be shovelled up.[51]

Most Creole emigrants returned to the Mascarenes disillusioned. However, conditions there worsened, notably on Mauritius, which was hit by two epidemics in 1891 and 1893, a devastating cyclone in 1892, and a fire in 1893 that destroyed the capital Port Louis. As Auguste Toussaint comments, "After having long been 'the jewel and key to the Indian Ocean', Port Louis was by the end of the [nineteenth] century a dilapidated, decayed and impoverished town."[52] These disasters led to renewed emigration. In 1893, 151 Mascarene Creoles landed in Toamasina, of whom 76 were sent back destitute, as were 55 of the 73

[48] Toussaint, *Histoire de l'Ile Maurice*, 108–9.
[49] *GH* (1908), 533; Oliver, *Madagascar* vol. II, 449; Kestell-Cornish, "letter," Antananarivo [May 1875], "Kestell-Cornish Letterbook, 1874–88," *ACM*; Deschamps, *Méthodes et doctrines coloniales*, 107.
[50] Although one volunteer battalion from Réunion participated in the 1895 conquest – Oliver, *Madagascar* vol. II, 355; Reibell, *Le Calvaire de Madagascar. Notes et souvenirs de 1895* (Paris, 1935), xix.
[51] *GH* (1908), 532–3 (incl.533 n.1).
[52] Toussaint, *Histoire de l'île Maurice*, 106; SPG, *SPG Records 1701–1892* (London, 1893), 373.

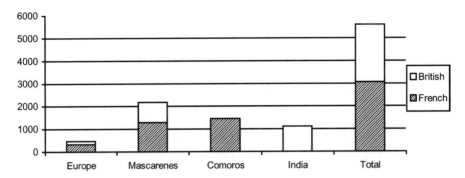

Figure 20. *Madagascar: Estimated Population of British and French Residents by Region of Origin, 1894.*

Source: From GH (1908), 533–5; Pakenham to Granville, Tamatave 3/01/83 in *Correspondence Respecting Madagascar*, 50; Richard Lovett, *History of the London Missionary Society* vol. I (London, 1899), 801–2.

to disembark in the first six months of 1894.[53] By that time, there were about 3,000 French and 2,500 British subjects resident in Madagascar, most of them of Comorian, Mascarene, or Indian, rather than of European, origin (Figure 20.)[54] Thereafter, political insecurity, the French conquest of 1894–5, and suppression of the *Menalamba* revolt largely deterred Mascarene immigrants. However, the return of security triggered a huge influx: From 3 January to 3 October 1898, 963 Creoles (525 from Réunion and 368 from Mauritius) reached Toamasina on Messageries Maritimes steamers alone. Of the Réunionnais Creole immigrants, only 46 were this time repatriated as destitute.[55]

Most Mascarene Creoles in Madagascar entered cash crop production, but performed poorly in comparison with indigenous Malagasy farmers. They rarely entered trade. On the east coast, British merchants held the dominant position in foreign commerce, while petty trade was dominated by the Malagasy and, increasingly, by Indian and Chinese immigrants. On the west coast, Indians dominated both local and foreign trade.[56]

[53] *GH* (1908), 533 n.1.a; see also *CdM* (19 janvier 1892, 9 septembre 1892).

[54] *GH* (1908), 533–5; Pakenham to Granville, Tamatave 3/01/83 in *Correspondence Respecting Madagascar*, 50; Lovett, *History* vol. I, 801–2.

[55] Toussaint, *Histoire de l'île Maurice*, 104; GH (1908), 533 n.1.a. Even later, the French empire, unlike British dominions, attracted few French settlers except for Algeria. By 1947, 50 percent of the French population of Madagascar were from Réunion – see Athenas, "Ethnographie," 304; C. M. Andrew & A. S. Kanya-Forstner, *France Overseas. The Great War and the Climax of French Imperial Expansion* (London, 1981), 18; Cros, *Madagascar pour tous*, 26.

[56] They continued to perform poorly even later under a French colonial regime that discriminated in their favor – Gwyn Campbell, "The Cocoa Frontier in Madagascar, the Comoro Islands and Réunion, c.1820–1970" in William Gervase Clarence-Smith (ed.), *Cocoa Pioneer Fronts since*

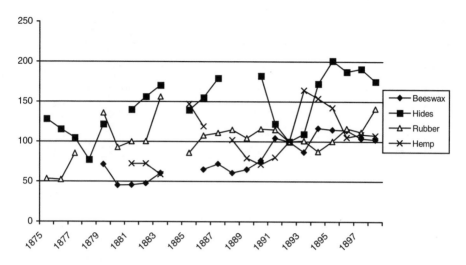

Figure 21. *Madagascar: Terms of Trade of Staple Exports to Britain, 1875–99* (1892 = 100).
Source: Based on overseas trade statistics in *British Parliamentary Papers* (1876–1900).

The Scramble for Indian Ocean Africa

By the 1870s, there was thus a considerable British economic stake in IOA, including Madagascar. However, the unparalleled growth in trade and migration in IOA and the concomitant expansion of coastal–hinterland linkages posed major challenges for British imperial policy in the region. Hitherto, Britain had relied on naval predominance to safeguard the maritime routes to India. However, in British business and political circles a growing conviction emerged of the need for intervention to control political and economic forces, both indigenous (e.g., Egyptian, Boer, Zulu) and European (French and German), which threatened British dominance in the region.

This concern led to increasing British involvement not only in Egypt, but also in southern and eastern Africa. Carnarvon, colonial secretary from 1874 to 1878, sent an army against the Zulus and attempted to pull the Boer Republics into a federal union of South Africa in order to control the forces released by the diamond and gold discoveries and to secure the Cape route to India that he considered was threatened by the Boer and Zulu polities.[57] In 1875, the Egyptian Khedive annexed small portions of the east African coast as part of his campaign to secure the headwaters of the Nile, prompting a warning against interference in Zanzibari territory from the British government. Indeed, Carnarvon, who anticipated informal British influence from Zanzibar would extend inland to link up with similar British interests spreading north from southern Africa, argued in 1876, "We cannot admit rivals in the east or even in the central part of Africa [and] to a considerable extent, if not entirely, we must be prepared to apply a sort of Munro doctrine to much of Africa."[58]

From 1877 to 1879, Britain took a number of steps toward bolstering its influence in East Africa: In 1877–8, the sultan was encouraged to expand his formal – and thus British informal – dominion in East Africa; in 1878 Mackinnon unilaterally extended British influence in hinterland East Africa; and in 1879, Portugal was pressurized into conceding Delagoa Bay to Britain and permitting British influence to expand into hinterland Mozambique.[59]

Mackinnon had business interests in the Suez Canal, India, Zanzibar, Mozambique, Madagascar, and the Mascarenes. He thus maintained close contact with British businessmen with interests in the western IOW, with consular agents John Kirk and Frederick Eton in East Africa and with Bartle Frere. The latter served in India, before conducting an official investigation into the east African slave trade (1872–3) and acting as high commissioner and governor of Cape Colony (1877–80). Although these businessmen and diplomats possessed little statistical evidence of wealth in the region, they were well-aware of the formidable trading structure of Indian traders and of other local British stakes and believed strongly in the economic potential of IOA and the British imperial cause.[60] They clearly viewed the entire western IOW (including IOA) as a region of British domination. As Currie stated in May 1881, when underlying

[57] Robinson & Gallagher, *Africa and the Victorians*, 62; Axelson, *Portugal and the Scramble*, 28; Sanderson, "European Partition of Africa," 22.

[58] Carnarvon quoted in G. N. Sanderson, "British Informal Empire, Imperial Ambitions, Defensive Strategies, and the Anglo-Portuguese Congo Treaty of February 1884" in Stig Förster, Wolfgang J. Mommsen & Ronald Robinson (eds.), *Bismarck, Europe, and Africa. The Berlin Africa Conference 1884–85 and the onset of Partition* (Oxford, 1988), 198; see *ibid*, 7; *idem*, "European Partition of Africa," 21; Cain & Hopkins, *British Imperialism*, 388–9; Chamberlain, *Scramble for Africa*, 64–5.

[59] Axelson, *Portugal and the Scramble*, 7, 22–3, 28, 137; Sanderson, "European Partition of Africa," 26; *idem*, "British Informal Empire," 198–9; Mackenzie, *Partition of Africa*, 25.

[60] In India, Bartle Frere served successively as writer in the Bombay Civil Service, Chief Commissioner of Sind, member of the Viceroy's Council and governor of Bombay (1862–7). Cain & Hopkins, *British Imperialism*, 387–91; M. S. Green, *The Making of South Africa* (Cape Town, 1958), 158–63; Daruwala, *Bombay Chamber Story*, 30, 44.

the need for an imperial subsidy for his Cape to Mauritius service, "Mauritius is a British Colony, and a strategic possession; it ought to be united to our Colonies, and a British line should be subsidized . . . irrespective of the steamers of particular Companies."[61]

This context allowed Britain to augment its informal influence in Madagascar. In 1881, Gore Jones, British naval commander of the East India station, visited Antananarivo. The same year, a British naval ship was sent to the south and west Malagasy coasts to attempt to neutralize French and bolster Merina influence. Gore Jones advised that the British navy offer to transport Merina troops to those regions.[62] His concerns appeared real when, in 1883, the French navy bombarded and occupied Mahajanga and Toamasina. The British Foreign Office, already alarmed at French imperial advance in Tunisia and Indo-China, considered the French action a contravention of existing Franco–Britannic agreements to "recognise the Queen of Madagascar as absolute monarch of the whole island."[63] As a result of British Foreign Office and Admiralty pressure to counter the French advance in Madagascar, the British Treasury in 1883 granted a £12,000 subsidy to Donald Currie to maintain his steamship line from Cape Town to Mauritius via Natal. Once obtained, the subsidy continued due to sustained pressure on the Colonial Office by Mauritian merchants and by British ship owners, bankers, sugar merchants, and other businessmen with interests in the region.[64] In 1884, after an incident between one of his steamships and French naval vessels off Madagascar, Currie even called in the British parliament for "a Naval Force sufficient to contend against any three Powers combined, and double the Navy of France."[65]

The 1883–5 Franco–Merina War confirmed British influence and undermined French influence in Madagascar when French subjects were expelled from Merina-controlled regions. French trade plummeted and France acceded to the British demand that other foreign governments maintain consuls and direct diplomatic relations with the Merina regime. Meanwhile, the latter intensified its use of the state church structure to impose imperial *fanompoana* and other war taxes; by the end of 1884, $25,000 had been raised for the war effort from LMS and FFMA churches in Imerina. British mission funds enabled the Merina regime to import arms, while LMS agents promoted its cause abroad. In

[61] Quoted in Porter, *Victorian Shipping*, 92.
[62] Howe, *L'Europe et Madagascar*, 269–70; Brown, *History of Madagascar*, 205; Sanderson, "British Informal Empire," 190.
[63] Granville to Plunkett, 7 October 1882 in Oliver, *Madagascar* vol. II, 299; see also Power, *Jules Ferry*, 69.
[64] Porter, *Victorian Shipping*, 129–31.
[65] Speech on 2 December 1884, in Porter, *Victorian Shipping*, 138.

1883, one LMS missionary, William Pickersgill, became British vice-consul in Antananarivo, from where he urged the British government to support Merina against French interests. As the LMS secretary in Antananarivo confessed, had the French captured the island, one of their first aims would have been "to break up our compact Educational and Ecclesiastical arrangements which indirectly, no doubt act as a barrier to the success of the Roman Catholic priests and of any outside national influence."[66] A measure of LMS success was British military interest in supporting the Merina. Gore Jones went no further than calling for British Army support. Other British military personnel joined the imperial Merina army. These included Lieutenant-Colonel Digby Willoughby, a Zulu Wars veteran, who in 1884 was appointed an adjutant-general in the Merina army and chief military advisor to the Merina court.[67]

Meanwhile, French forces (2,350 soldiers, 11 ships, and 2,200 sailors by March 1884) grossly underestimated the difficulties of the Madagascar campaign. Far from effecting a rapid conquest, as anticipated, they became bogged down on the coast. Non-Merina Malagasy failed to rally to their cause, malaria ravaged their soldiers, cyclones seriously damaged their ships, and, in possibly the most important military engagement of the war, imperial forces repulsed them from Manjakandrianombana, near Toamasina, in September 1885.[68] Lack of military progress and the cost of the war, estimated at 1 million francs a month, proved increasingly unpopular in France: The parliamentary majority in favor of the Madagascar campaign fell from 279 in July 1884, to 157 in July 1885, to only 4 by December 1884 – when it constituted a major reason for the resignation of the French government.[69]

This was the backdrop to the peace treaty of December 1885 from which the most tangible gain for France was the major harbor of Diego Suarez. Its declared

---

[66] Wills to Wardlaw Thompson, Antananarivo, 19 June 1884, *IDC Letterbook 1875–86* – FJKM.

[67] Colonal C. R. St. Leger Shervington, a veteran of the Zulu campaigns, and Captain du Verge, a Mauritian officer – see Anon, "Brief Summary of Important Events in Madagascar during 1884" *AAMM* 8 (1884), 118; George A Shaw, *Madagascar and France* (London, 1885); Brown, *History of Madagascar*, 209, 225–6; Oliver, *Madagascar* vol. II, 447.

[68] Anon, "Brief Summary of Important Events in Madagascar during 1884," 118; Anon, "Brief Summary of Important Events in Madagascar during 1885" *AAMM* 9 (1885), 161; Brown, *History of Madagascar*, 211; Oliver, *Madagascar* vol. II, 431.

[69] Deschamps, *Méthodes et doctrines coloniales*, 132, 163; Henri Brunschwig, "Anglophobia and French African Policy," in Prosser Gifford & William Roger Louis (eds.) *France and Britain in African Imperial Rivalry and Colonial Rule* (New Haven, 1971), 3; James J. Cooke, *New French Imperialism 1880–1910: The Third Republic and Colonial Expansion* (Newton Abbot, 1973), 12, 14, 23; Jean Stengers, "The Scramble: Effect of French African Activity" in Raymond F. Betts (ed.), *The "Scramble" for Africa. Causes and Dimensions of Empire* (Lexington MA, 1966), 42–3; Robinson & Gallagher, *Africa and the Victorians*, 162–3, 166–7, 170, 174–88; Sanderson, "European Partition of Africa," 24–5; Oliver, *Madagascar* vol. II, 440–1, 468.

protectorate over Madagascar remained illusionary as it was ignored both by the Merina regime and foreign powers. In France, the cost of the Malagasy and Tonkin wars heightened the republican distaste for colonial ventures outside the already well-established areas of French imperial interest in North and West Africa, and from 1886 French government interest in Madagascar waned. For the next two decades, France again prioritized the maintenance of good relations with Britain. Meanwhile, British political influence in Madagascar had been reinforced by the 1883–5 conflict, and British trade with the island reached unparalleled growth from 1886.[70]

The French Conquest of 1895

British Acquiescence

Given this background, the traditional theories of the French colonization of Madagascar in 1895–6 are clearly inadequate. An alternative explanation points to three main contributory factors. The first was the breakdown of the post-1815 status quo whereby Britain had enjoyed global superiority. The 1880s Depression revealed that Germany and the United States were rapidly overtaking Britain as industrial powers. Britain's naval superiority was also challenged. By 1882, the number of French and German first-class ships outnumbered those possessed by the British for the first time. By 1884–5, when the sail-less, mechanized battleship became standard, France drew level with the British navy in terms of number of ships in its fleet and surpassed it in quality. In a similar build up, the U.S. fleet came to surpass that of Britain, ending the latter's pretensions to global maritime predominance. In 1889, Britain declared the "two power standard" whereby its naval power should always exceed that of the nearest two European powers combined. However, by the early 1890s its navy still trailed those of France and Russia.[71]

This formed the wider context for disagreements with France over Egypt and Madagascar. Some historians have argued that the British occupation of Egypt in 1882 ignited the scramble.[72] It certainly provoked anti-British feeling in France,

---

[70] Power, *Jules Ferry*, 196; Kent, "How France acquired Madagascar," 18; Brown, *History of Madagascar*, 212–14.

[71] Bernard Porter, *The Lion's Share. A Short History of British Imperialism 1850–1970* (London, 1975), 123–4; *idem, Britain, Europe and the World 1850–1982: Delusions of Grandeur* (London, 1983), 18–19; Sanderson, "European Partition of Africa," 26; James Williamson, *Great Britain and the Empire* (London, 1946), 128–9; E. J. Hobsbawn, *The Age of Empire 1875–1914* (London, 1987), 317–19; Richard Shannon, *The Crisis of Imperialism 1865–1915* (UK, 1976), 259–62; Brunschwig, "Anglophobia and French African Policy," 24.

[72] Sanderson, "European Partition of Africa," 24; Cain & Hopkins, *British Imperialism*, 367–8.

which assisted the French Marine in its forward movement in Madagascar in 1882–3 and dissuaded the British government from protesting too strongly against French action there. Thus the British Foreign Office in November 1882 informed Procter, the Merina consul in London, that

Important negotiations are proceeding between France and England relative to the reestablishment of authority in Egypt, and England is most anxious, while the Egyptian question is under discussion, not to irritate France by offering any remonstrance on the Malagasy case.[73]

In 1884, France, offended at being omitted by Britain from attempting to settle Egyptian finances and worried that British control in Egypt threatened its route to Indo-China and Madagascar, seized Djibouti, thus countering Aden's control over the Indian Ocean approach to the Red Sea.[74] Egypt provided the context for German proposals to France to form an anti-British front in Africa, which G. N. Sanderson considers to have signaled the real collapse of the post-1815 status quo.[75] The Franco–German entente manifested itself in opposition to the 1884 Congo treaty that proposed placing navigation on the Congo under Britanno–Portuguese control and in the 1884–85 Berlin Conference, which opposed British monopoly access to the Niger.[76] Moreover, from 1883 Germany entertained proposals for a Germano–Boer link from southwest Africa to the Transvaal (and thence to Delagoa Bay); in 1884, Karl Peters' Company for German Colonisation (Gesellschaft für deutsche Kolonisation), which received financial backing from O'Swald, was busy signing treaties in hinterland East Africa, prompting Granville to state,

Its annexation [the Swahili coast] by France or Germany, and the seizure of a port would be ruinous to British . . . influence on the East Coast. The proceedings of the French in Madagascar make it all the more necessary to guard our sea route to India.[77]

[73] Quoted in Mutibwa, *The Malagasy*, 231.
[74] Cain & Hopkins, *British Imperialism*, 356; Förster et al. (eds.), *Bismarck, Europe and Africa*, 4; Deschamps, *Méthodes et doctrines coloniales*, 163; Power, *Jules Ferry*, 152–3.
[75] Power, *Jules Ferry*, 142–52; Sanderson, "British Informal Empire," 195; Chamberlain, *Scramble for Africa*, 69.
[76] Sanderson, "European Partition of Africa," 6; John D. Hargreaves, *Prelude to the Partition of West Africa* (London, 1966), 330–8; Power, *Jules Ferry*, 84–115.
[77] Granville to Kirk, 23 November 1884, quoted in Robinson & Gallagher, *Africa and the Victorians*, 189; see also Sanderson, "European Partition of Africa," 29–31; Georges Hardy, "The Scramble: Preconditions and postconditions in Africa," in Betts (ed.), *The "Scramble" for Africa*, 53; William Louis, "Great Britain and German Expansion in Africa, 1884–1919," in P. Gifford & William Louis (eds.), *Britain and Germany in Africa* (New Haven, 1967), 21, 25; Simon Katzenellenbogen, "British businessmen and German Africa, 1885–1919" in Barrie M. Ratcliffe (ed.), *Great Britain and Her World 1750–1914; Essays in honour of W O Henderson* (Manchester, 1975), 239, 241.

In 1885, Britain declared a protectorate in Bechuanaland (Botswana) and tightened informal control over Portugal in an attempt to neutralize the threat of a link between German East Africa and the Transvaal (although the project remained alive until the Britanno–German treaty of 1898 granted Britain Delagoa Bay and Maputo).[78] Britain also urged the sultan to make good Zanzibari claims to the interior as far as Kilimanjaro. However, hamstrung by confrontation with Russia and by commitments in the Sudan and Egypt, Britain decided, in return for Bismarck's acceptance of British action in Egypt, to acknowledge a legitimate German presence in East Africa. Salisbury, for whom France and Russia were the chief imperial rivals, considered German territory in East Africa to be of little commercial value and of no real threat to Britain's strategic interests in the region. Two Germano–British treaties were signed: The first, in December 1885, recognized a German protectorate over Dar-Es-Salaam and the adjacent portion of coast and the second, in October 1886, defined a frontier running east from Lake Victoria that divided German and British areas of influence and limited the sultan's sovereignty to the island of Zanzibar and a 10-mile corridor on the opposite coast.[79]

Consequently, Bismarck refused to ratify treaties signed with local chiefs as far afield as Somaliland and the Comoro Islands by the D.O.A.G., which subsequently evaluated Madagascar's potential as a colony and in 1892 planned to establish a base in Mahajanga.[80] However, the 1888 east African revolt against the Germans, who had expanded into the Great Lakes region, induced a more aggressive attitude from British officials in the region. Kirk, the British consul at Zanzibar, argued that a concession of mainland Zanzibari territory be granted to Mackinnon – who planned to push British interests west to the Congo and south to South Africa.[81]

Unable to constrain rivals on all fronts, the Foreign Office preferred to negotiate a series of treaties designed to establish a new status quo in IOA that would preserve British dominance in areas deemed of vital strategic and economic

---

[78] A provision was also made in 1898 for the independence of the British settlement in Nyasa: Axelson, *Portugal and the Scramble*, 62–3; Katzenellenbogen, "British businessmen and German Africa," 254–5; Robinson & Gallagher, *Africa and the Victorians*, 161, 202–8; Mackenzie, *Partition of Africa*, 22.

[79] Brunschwig, "Anglophobia and French African Policy," 25–9; Sanderson, "European Partition of Africa," 16, 31–40; Robinson & Gallagher, *Africa and the Victorians*, 189, 191–8; Louis, "Great Britain and German Expansion," 1–12.

[80] The *DOAG* grew out of Peter's *Gesellschaft für deutsche Kolonisation* – Katzenellenbogen, "British businessmen and German Africa," 239; see also Evers, "Das Hamburger Zanzibarhandelshaus Wm. O'Swald," 308–9; *CdM* (27 décembre 1892).

[81] Louis, "Great Britain and German Expansion," 14; Sanderson, "European Partition of Africa," 21.

importance. Treaties with Portugal in 1890 and 1891 defined respective frontiers and reiterated the rights to free trade, navigation, and settlement in Mozambique, as well as negating Portugal's claim to the gold-producing hinterland.[82] Also, in return for German and French recognition of British predominance in Zanzibar, Britain ceded Heligoland, in the North Sea, to Germany, agreed to partition German and British spheres of influence in Africa, and recognized French hegemony in Madagascar. With the 1891 Italian agreement over boundaries between Egyptian Sudan and Ethiopia, international recognition for British paramountcy in East Africa was complete.[83]

Madagascar was a small price to pay. While British subjects were the island's most important foreign trade partners, Britain's trade with continental East Africa was of a far greater magnitude. The British were the greatest external influence on the imperial Merina regime, but Britain already possessed a regional island base in Mauritius. Madagascar, where France controlled the port of Diego Suarez, was thus expendable, notably as British fears of French rivalry in Africa from the late 1880s lay more with the French forward movement to the hinterland of Lagos and the Sudan.[84] When imperial rivalry was renewed from 1892, the British Foreign office refused to reengage France over Madagascar.[85]

Samuel Procter, the Merina consul in London, wrote to Rainilaiarivony following the 1890 treaty: "Here in England, I regret to say the feeling is now prevalent that France has at last obtained definitively the Protectorate over Madagascar which she has so long striven to secure."[86] Many historians have considered that treaty as the critical factor in promoting the French takeover of Madagascar.[87] However, as Kent points out, in 1890 France possessed only one harbor in Madagascar – another five years passed before it enforced its theoretical protectorate.[88] The British decision in 1891 to withdraw consul Pickersgill

[82] Following a revolt in 1885 and civil strife in 1887–8, the Portuguese had tried to assert their authority both in the Zambezi Valley and, by 1889, in the Nyasa region – Axelson, *Portugal and the Scramble*, 143–5, 182–5; 192, 194, 213, 238–9, 297.

[83] Hardy, "The Scramble," 53.

[84] Sanderson, "European Partition of Africa," 7, 9, 36–8; Louis, "Great Britain and German Expansion," 1–12, 14–24.

[85] Some senior officials backed Roseberry, notably Percy Anderson of the Africa Department and assistant under-secretary from 1894–6. Anderson was a Germanophile who considered France, not Germany, to constitute the greatest threat to the British empire, but this did not prevent the ending the *entente* with Germany – Sanderson, "European Partition of Africa," 36–7; Louis, "Great Britain and German Expansion," 1–12.

[86] Samuel Procter to Prime Minister, London, 30 August 1990, *DD21*, 292 – *ANM*.

[87] Brown, *History of Madagascar*, 216; Mutibwa, *Malagasy and the Europeans*, 332.

[88] Kent, "How France Acquired Madagascar," 19.

from the island, while acceding to long-standing demands of the French, in fact served to embarrass the latter, whose lack of real authority led the U.S. consul in 1891 to bypass the French Resident and obtain his *exequatur* directly from the Merina regime. This, in turn, caused Britain to reject French jurisdiction over British subjects in Madagascar until the French proved their ability to enforce judicial decisions.[89] When France finally conquered the island in 1895, the only British dissent came from Henry Loch, High Commissioner for South Africa, who feared that the French expeditionary force might subsequently turn on the Cape. He was overruled by a British government anxious to avoid further aggravating relations over Upper Egypt or provoking German interference in Mozambique and the Transvaal.[90] After Fashoda in 1898, British acceptance of the status quo in Madagascar was confirmed by a warming in relations with France that culminated the Entente Cordiale of 1904.[91]

The French Pro-Colonial Grouping

The second main factor promoting the French takeover was the imperialist movement in France, which by the early 1890s wielded considerable public and political influence. In the case of Madagascar, this comprised three main elements: the French Navy (Marine), Réunionnais deputies, and the pro-colonial grouping. The Marine and Réunionnais deputies deeply regretted the loss to Britain during the Napoleonic Wars of Mauritius, which possessed in Port Louis a port and shipyards of major significance (in contrast to Réunion, the sole remaining French possession on the route to India, an "island without a port").[92] They considered that the seizure of Madagascar would compensate France for that loss.[93]

---

[89] Martin E. Schmidt, "Prelude to Intervention: Madagascar and the Failure of Anglo-French Diplomacy, 1890–1895," *Historical Journal* 15.4 (1972), 718, 719–27; Louis, "Great Britain and German Expansion," 14–21; Hardy, "The Scramble," 53; J. Peill, "Historical sketch in memorial to W. W. Wilson" [1909] in Crosfield, *Man in Shining Armour*, 259; William G. Hynes, *The Economics of Empire. Britain, Africa and the New Imperialism 1870–95* (UK, 1979), 97–8, 100–1.

[90] Anthony Nutting, *Scramble for Africa* (London, 1970), 294; Sanderson, "European Partition of Africa," 36; Louis, "Great Britain and German Expansion," 21, 25.

[91] Henri Brunschwig argues that French imperial sentiments were by the 1890s shaped less by anglophobia than by a more general xenophobia – Brunschwig, "Anglophobia and French African Policy," 28–34; C. M. Andrew & A. S. Kanya-Forstner, "Hanotaux, the Colonial Party & the Fashoda Strategy," *Journal of Imperial & Commonwealth History* 3.1 (1974), 61–4; Sanderson, "European Partition of Africa," 36–7.

[92] Thiriot, *L'Ile Maurice, La Réunion et les productions de l'Inde, 1785* E. Génin (ed.), (Douai, 1882), 41; Deschamps, *Méthodes et doctrines coloniales*, 96–7; P. J. Barnwell & Auguste Toussaint, *A Short History of Mauritius* (London, 1949), 125; Brunschwig, "Anglophobia and French African Policy," 6.

[93] *GH* (1908), 532; Wastell, "British Imperial Policy," 75–6, 126.

It has been argued that the fragmented structure of French colonial administration gave the military great freedom in initiating forward movements in West
and North Africa.[94] However, French Navy initiatives in Madagascar were generally overruled by the Quai d'Orsay, where foreign policy aims were limited
by treasury constraints and the wish, in the post-1815 balance of power, not
to offend Britain. Indeed, in the 1840s, an entente with Britain was reached,
consolidated in the Cobden Treaty of 1860, which laid the basis for free trade
and further mitigated against French expansion overseas. From 1860 to 1867,
even the Ministry of the Marine (under Chasseloup-Lambat) advocated imperial
expansion on free-trade principles. From 1845, France accepted British dominance in the western Indian Ocean region and the assimilation of East Africa
into the sphere of influence of British India.[95]

Within this framework, following the 1861 government of India ruling that
Muscat and Zanzibar be separated, France signed an accord with Britain in
1862 that guaranteed Zanzibari independence. Further, in 1868, France signed
a treaty with Imerina recognizing Merina sovereignty in Madagascar and confirmed acceptance of British domination in East Africa between Somalia and
Mozambique.[96] Britain's industrial, financial, and commercial predominance
ensured that it was the main victor in free trade and open door arrangements,
leading to the argument that the mid-nineteenth century was characterized by
British "free-trade imperialism."[97]

French military interventions in Madagascar, in 1819–20, 1829–31, and
1883–5, formed exceptions to the general rules of French foreign policy. The
1818–19 Madagascar expedition, financed by Portal, Minister of the Marine,
collapsed with his fall from government in 1821.[98] That of 1829, launched
by the pro-imperialist Charles X, was withdrawn following the July 1830

---

[94] Jean Stengers, "The Beginning of the Scramble for Africa" in Robert O. Collins (ed.), *The
Partition of Africa. Illusion or Necessity* (New York, 1969), 74–5, 77; A. S. Kanya-Forstner,
"French expansion in Africa: the mythical theory" in Owen & Sutcliffe (eds.), *Studies in the
Theory of Imperialism*, 287–92.

[95] The *entente* was reached when François Guizot was prime minister and foreign minister (1841–
8). See Brunschwig, "Anglophobia and French African Policy," 6–7, 16, 20–1, 23; Sanderson,
"European Partition of Africa," 19; Fieldhouse, *Economics and Empire*, 20; Louis Nicolas,
Histoire de la Marine Française (Paris, 1949), 89.

[96] Robinson & Gallagher, *Africa and the Victorians*, 45; Norman R. Bennet, "France and Zanzibar"
in *idem* et al. (eds.), *Eastern African History* (New York, 1969), 162–4; Sanderson, "British
Informal Empire," 189; *idem*, "European Partition of Africa," 20; Deschamps, *Méthodes et
doctrines coloniales*, 109–12; Brown, *History of Madagascar*, 161–3, 198; Power, *Jules Ferry*,
116.

[97] Gallagher & Robinson, "Imperialism of Free Trade" *Economic History Review* 6 (1953).

[98] Wastell, "British Imperial Policy," 128–30; *GH* vol. V.III (1958), 107–8; Oliver, *Madagascar* vol. I, 148; Nicolas, *Histoire de la Marine Française*, 88; Georges Hardy, *Histoire de la
colonisation française* (Paris, 1943), 160.

Revolution, when Louis Philippe (1830–48) sought, in the face of the recent French occupation of Algiers, to appease hostile British sentiment. Subsequently, the only French acquisitions in the area were small offshore islands and Diego Suarez.[99] Indeed, when in 1854, at the time of Franco–British cooperation in the Crimea, a group led by Rakoto Radama, heir apparent to the Merina throne, invited the French to establish a protectorate, Napoleon III informed the British who, according to Kent, passed the information on to Ranavalona I, who in turn promptly expelled French subjects from the island.[100]

The 1883–5 war was a rare example of successful naval–Réunionnais opportunism.[101] In July 1882, the French parliament rejected a vote of credit to join Britain in offering armed protection of the Suez Canal, and the ministry resigned.[102] Unilateral British intervention in Egypt created an anglophobic atmosphere in France, which Jauréguiberry used, when he moved from the Ministry of the Marine to temporarily assume the premiership, to adopt an aggressively anti-British line in Madagascar.[103] A shooting incident on the island's northwest coast was the pretext for demanding an indemnity, and the French government expelled a Merina embassy from Paris.[104] On 15 February 1883, three days before the cabinet dissolved, François de Mahy, a Réunion deputy and minister of commerce, who in early 1883 temporarily filled the post of minister of the marine, ordered Rear-Admiral Pierre to enforce French claims. In April, the new government under Jules Ferry assured Britain that military action in Madagascar had not been authorized. However, Brun, the

---

[99] In the 1829 attack, 68 Merina and 26 French soldiers were killed – Baker to Stanley, "Memorial" [Antananarivo, 1832], *SOAS/LMS-MIL* B3.F4.JC; E. Vidal, *Madagascar. Situation actuelle* (Bordeaux, 1845), 10; Guillain à M. L'Ordinateur de l'Île Bourbon, Nosy-Be, 1842, C8e, *AHVP*; Prud'homme, "Observations," 424; Wastell, "British Imperial Policy," 224–6, 232, 271, 277–8; former Resident, *Madagascar and the United States*, 7; Raymond Decary, *L'Ile Nosy Bé de Madagascar. Histoire d'une colonisation* (Paris, 1960), 20–1; M. L. G. Gourraigne, "Les relations de la France avec Madagascar pendant la première moitié du XXe siècle," *Conférence de l'Ecole Coloniale* (28 janvier 1909), 20; Georges Spillmann, "L'anticolonialisme en France du XVIIe siècle à nos jours," *L'Afrique et l'Asie* 101 (1974), 9; Brunschwig, "Anglophobia and French African Policy," 4; Fieldhouse, *Economics and Empire*, 107.

[100] Thureau, "Des intérêts français à Madagascar" *Chronique de la Quinzaine* (1856), 462, 464; Kent, "How France acquired Madagascar," 16; Brunschwig, "Anglophobia and French African Policy," 16, 20–1, 23; Sanderson, "European Partition of Africa," 19; M. E. Chamberlain, *British Foreign Policy in the Age of Palmerston* (UK, 1984), 68–73; Spillmann, "L'anticolonialisme en France," 10–11; Deschamps, *Méthodes et doctrines coloniales*, 103; Fieldhouse, *Economics and Empire*, 108; Nicolas, *Histoire de la marine française*, 94–6.

[101] Réunion was represented in the French parliament by two deputies and one senator – Power, *Jules Ferry*, 116. See also *ibid*, 121–2.

[102] Oliver, *Madagascar* vol. II, 297.

[103] Sanderson, "European Partition of Africa," 24; Cain & Hopkins, *British Imperialism*, 367–8.

[104] Anon, "Brief Summary of Important Events in Madagascar during 1884," 118.

new minister of the marine and the colonies, endorsed de Mahy's action and, on his orders, Pierre shelled and dislodged Merina garrisons on the northwest coast of Madagascar and seized Mahajanga and Toamasina. The Marine and Réunionnais interests had effectively hijacked the French government into war with the Merina.[105]

A 75-year-old desire by the French navy to possess a major port in the Indian Ocean was satisfied when naval bases were established in 1885 at Obock, in Somaliland, and in 1886 at Diego Suarez.[106] However, by then the tide of public and political opinion in France had swung against expansion in Madagascar, in favor of consolidating a French empire in West and North Africa. It was on these latter areas that the colonial group focused. This body, which emerged in the 1880s, possessed a small, largely professional, membership but claimed significant support in French administrative and political circles. Its leadership included Paul Leroy-Beaulieu and Eugene Etienne, the "Notre Dame des coloniaux." Etienne, like de Mahy an annexionist deputy from an overseas territory (Oran), was undersecretary in the Colonial Department in 1887 and 1889–92. The colonial grouping also gained considerable support from within the ranks of the specialized nonmilitary colonial administration that developed with the burst of French imperial expansion in the 1880s, notably from 1887 when a Colonial Administration Corps was established.[107]

The group's links with, and influence upon, government were strengthened from mid-1892, at the height of Franco–British rivalry, with the formation in parliament of a colonial party led by Etienne. Backed by the Ministry for the Colonies, it rapidly became the most powerful pressure group in the Chamber

---

[105] Pierre and Baudais (the French consul in Madagascar) demanded recognition of a French protectorate north of latitude 16°S, freehold possession of land for foreigners, and an indemnity of 1 million francs: Oliver, *Madagascar* vol. II, 314–22; Brown, *History of Madagascar*, 207–8; Sanderson, "European Partition of Africa," 23–5; Raminosoa, "La Maison 'Wm O'Swald & Co.,'" 174–5; Cooke, *New French Imperialism*, 14–15. The French forward movement in Senegal similarly owed much to the promotion in 1879 of Admiral Jauréguiberry, a former governor of Senegal, to the position of Minister of the Colonies – see Power, *Jules Ferry*, 79, 83, 121–2, 195–6.

[106] Admiral Galiber had played a major role in Madagascar during the naval campaign of 1883–4 – Cooke, *New French Imperialism*, 23. See also C. M. Andrew & A. S. Kanya-Forstner, "The French 'Colonial Party': Its Composition, Aims and Influence, 1885–1914" *Historical Journal* 14.1 (1971), 99–100; Power, *Jules Ferry*, 123–30. At the time, coaling stations were vital as warships could only carry a fortnight's supply of coal – *ibid*, 178–9, 192.

[107] In 1881, responsibility for colonial administration moved from the Ministry of the Marine to the Under Secretary of State for the Colonies, and again in 1890 to the Ministry for Colonies. The Colonial Administration Corps was later serviced by graduates from a Colonial School established in 1889 – see Andrew & Kanya-Forstner, "The French 'Colonial Party,'" 102, 105; *idem, France Overseas*, 24; Deschamps, *Méthodes et doctrines coloniales*, 140, 151.

of Deputies, providing five of the seven colonial ministers who served in the period 1894–9.[108] Additional backing for the pro-colonial movement was provided from the late 1870s by newly founded geographical societies. In this circle, Alfred Grandidier was a powerful exponent of French interests in Madagascar.[109]

However, the first formal pro-imperial pressure groups, the Comité de l'Afrique française and the Union Coloniale, founded in 1890 and 1894 respectively, concentrated upon the traditional areas of French imperial interest in West and North Africa.[110] Indeed, until the mid-1890s, the Réunion deputy, de Mahy, was almost the sole voice calling for France to transform a nominal into an actual protectorate in Madagascar.[111] Only when the colonial grouping was strengthened following the August 1893 elections did pressure mount on the new foreign minister, Casimir-Périer, to act on Madagascar. French public opinion was then firmly behind the French forward movements in Thailand and Egypt, which were seen in terms of rivalry with Britain. It was in this context that Le Myre de Vilers, the French resident in exile, backed a parliamentary speech in 1894 by Brunet, a deputy for Réunion, calling for a final showdown with the Merina. When an ultimatum to the Merina was rejected in November 1894, parliament voted to finance an expedition. A Comité de Madagascar, under the presidency of Grandidier, only formed in 1895, after the start of the decisive French forward movement in Madagascar. However, it helped to push for the protectorate to be transformed in 1896 into a colony ruled directly from Paris.[112]

The Crisis of the Indigenous Aristocracy

Scholars such as D. K. Fieldhouse argue that, ultimately, the decision on formal incorporation of regions into a European empire was taken in Europe.[113] They

---

[108] *Parti colonial* members included the president of the *Comité de Madagascar*, Jean Charles-Roux, and Le Myre de Vilers, former French Resident General in Madagascar – Andrew & Kanya-Forstner, "The French 'Colonial Party,'" 61, 101, 103, 107–9, 150–1.

[109] Agnes Murphy, The Ideology of French Imperialism, 1871–1881 (Washington DC, 1948), 5, 25–30, 48–9; Henri Brunschwig, *French Colonialism 1871–1914. Myths and Realities* (London, 1966), 24–5.

[110] Schmidt, "Prelude to Intervention," 719; Andrew & Kanya-Forstner, "The French 'Colonial Party,'" 101, 103, 107–9.

[111] Andrew & Kanya-Forstner, "The French 'Colonial Party,'" 108–9; *CdM* (2 février 1892).

[112] Kanya-Forstner, "French expansion in Africa," 282–3; Andrew & Kanya-Forstner, "The French 'Colonial Party,'" 101, 103, 107–9; *idem, France* Overseas, 29–30, 33; Deschamps, *Méthodes et doctrines coloniales*, 150; *idem, histoire de Madagascar*, 227–9; Pierre Randrianarisoa, *La Diplomatie malgache face à la politique des grandes puissances (1882–1895)* (Antananarivo n.d.), 181–94; see also Marcel Dubois et Auguste Terrier (eds.), *Les colonies françaises* (Paris, 1902), 716–18; Schmidt, "Prelude to Intervention," 729–30.

also underline the importance in the late nineteenth century of developments that effectively brought geographically distant regions of the globe within striking distance of Europe and which dramatically altered the power relationship between European and non-European peoples, enabling the former to impose their will on the latter. Such developments stemmed essentially from technological innovations of the Industrial Revolution, notably the application of steam to transport, the invention of the Gatling gun, and the widespread adoption of quinine – which enabled Europeans to permanently settle malarial regions of the Tropics.[114] Also, some historians have argued that the slave export trade and increasing European intervention in Africa upset a fragile balance between population and resources to the degree that it triggered an unparalleled series of diseases and ecological disasters, leading to famine and population decline, which weakened African resistance and facilitated colonial takeover.[115].

However, the most striking development in sub-Saharan Africa in this era was European settlement not in tropical areas, but in semi- or nontropical regions on the north African littoral or in southern Africa south of the river Limpopo.[116] In Madagascar, there was relatively little European settlement: By 1913, Algeria accounted for over 70 percent of the 855,000 French people settled in the empire while in 1921, the French inhabitants of Casablanca, in Morocco (26,000), were more than treble those in Madagascar (8,000).[117] Similarly, technological advantage played an extremely limited role in the French conquest of Madagascar, while disease, rather than undermining Merina resistance, nearly defeated the French invasion force single-handedly. The French expedition was characterized by poor planning, inadequate medical and other supplies, and incompetent management. It did not possess the transport capable of quickly forging a way along the rough and unmaintained routes from the coast to the plateau, and it failed to provide troops with the quinine vital to their survival in a malarial environment. Thus, of the 6,725 fatalities during the French expedition, only 25 were due to battle wounds – the remainder were caused by malaria (72 percent) and typhoid (12 percent).[118] As one French officer commented,

"errors were committed in the planning and organisation of the Madagascar expedition, which made it so costly in terms of human lives that it was the deadliest [military] campaign of the nineteenth century."[119]

[113] Fieldhouse, *Economics and Empire*, 82–3.

[114] Fieldhouse, *Economics and Empire*, 78.

[115] See, e.g., Catherine Coquery-Vidrovitch, *Africa. Endurance and Change South of the Sahara* (Berkeley, 1988), 7–29.

[116] Fieldhouse, *Economics and Empire*, 92.

[117] Andrew & Kanya-Forstner, *France Overseas*, 18; Cros, *Madagascar pour tous*, 26.

[118] Reibell, *Le Calvaire de Madagascar*, annexe IV; Deschamps, *histoire de Madagascar*, 228.

[119] Reibell, *Le Calvaire de Madagascar*, 57.

The expedition succeeded only due to the use of Senegalese colonial troops in a rapid push to the plateau interior. Even then, had any real resistance been offered by imperial Merina troops, the likelihood is that the expedition, a costly and therefore increasingly unpopular affair in France, would have collapsed and the troops been withdrawn. The British-trained Merina army comprised 13,000 soldiers equipped with modern rifles and Armstrong cannons.[120] Given the extensive logistical mistakes made by the French commanders and the ravages of disease, the Merina government would in all likelihood have been able to repulse the French advance of 1895 had its soldiers not deserted en masse.[121]

Indeed, the critical factor guaranteeing the success of the French attack of 1895 was the collapse of the Merina empire. Hopkins has argued for West Africa that economic factors, namely the 1880s depression, during which prices of both import and export staples declined, coupled with the structural adjustments following the end of the slave trade, provoked a crisis of the indigenous aristocracy. Attempts by the latter to tighten their control over the local economy resulted in conflict with European traders that helped to precipitate European military intervention and colonization.[122] For Madagascar, a number of historians have stressed that the cost of the 1883–5 war, and the French-imposed indemnities, takeover of imperial customs, and concessions, provoked the bankruptcy of the Merina regime. In addition, Bernard Schlemmer and Guy Jacob have argued that the price of Malagasy staples fell sharply during the 1880s' world depression. This imposed an unequal exchange between the West and Madagascar that deprived the Merina regime of its due revenue and led to the domination of Madagascar by French finance capitalism. At the same time, French manufactured imports, notably cloth, ironmongery, and alcohol, undermined local production.[123]

The 1883–5 war did damage French and official east coast trade. However, the evidence points to a brisk clandestine and unofficial foreign trade with Imerina via unauthorized ports on the east and west coast throughout the war years.[124] Moreover, during the 1880s, the price of Malagasy export staples – like those of East Africa in general – remained buoyant, despite occasional sharp price falls (as for Malagasy hides, rubber, and sugar in the U.S. market

[120] Vérin, *Madagascar*, 148.
[121] See, e.g., Esoavelomandroso, "Rainilaiarivony," 247–8.
[122] Hopkins, *Economic History of West Africa*, Ch. 4.
[123] Jacob, "Influences occidentales"; Schlemmer, *Le Menabe*, 35; see also Esoavelomandroso, "Rainilaiarivony" 232–3; Ellis, "The Malagasy Background"; Vérin, *Madagascar*, 146–8.
[124] W. Clayton Pickersgill, "The Trade and Commerce of Madagascar" *AAMM* (1885), 221–9; see also earlier remarks on the Natal trade in this chapter and Chapters 7–10.

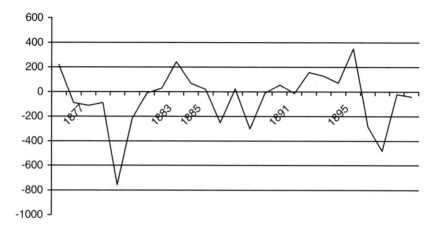

Figure 22. *Madagascar: Balance of Visible Direct Trade with Britain, 1875–99* ($000 Malagasy).
Source: Parliamentary Papers (1876–1900).

in 1884 and 1891).[125] Analysis of direct visible trade between Madagascar and Britain, its major trading partner, neither confirms nor undermines the depression thesis. However, it suggests that the price of manufactured goods fell more sharply than those of Malagasy staple exports, that the terms of trade were unfavorable to Britain for much of the period 1875–95, and that the trade balance was in Madagascar's favor for a considerable part of that period (1882–5, 1887, 1890, 1892–5).[126] More specifically, the argument that foreign cloth, by far the most important import into imperial Madagascar, undermined the local textile industry critically fails to distinguish between types of fabric – both imported and manufactured locally – or to analyze their uses. Indeed, the evidence indicates that imported cloths supplemented, rather than replaced, local cloth production[127] (Figure 22).

There was some French investment – notably in sugar plantations, the Suberbie gold mines, and in a loan to the Merina government – but insufficient to back claims that it rendered the Merina regime subservient to French financiers. Indeed, little French capital was exported to the Tropics. From 1882

[125] Dawson to Ropes, Emmerton & Co, and Arnold, Hines & Co, Port Louis, Mauritius, 29 Jan. 1884; Blyth Bros. to Ropes, Emmerton & Co, Mauritius, 8 July 1884; Ropes, Emmerton & Co, to J. Orme Ryder, Salem, 23 May 1884; Whitney to Ropes, Emmerton & Co, Tamatave, 27 April 1891 – *REC/CR-MZL*.

[126] Campbell, "Toamasina (Tamatave) and the Growth of Foreign Trade."

[127] Jacob, "Influences occidentales," 227; *GH* (1908), 174–5; Mack, *Malagasy Textiles*; also see Chapter 4.

to 1902, one quarter of French foreign investment flowed to Russia and a further 13 percent to Latin America. Far less capital was attracted to Africa. The main fields of French investment there were either Algeria, a colony since 1830, or regions such as the South African diamond and gold mines – where substantial French financial interest in the 1870s and 1880s did not stimulate calls for French political intervention.[128]

Nevertheless, Madagascar did experience a crisis of the indigenous aristocracy that contributed to French colonization in 1895. First, while there is considerable evidence that monopolies and other commercial policies of the Merina court restricted foreign trade and helped accentuate problems of money supply within the Merina empire, most of western and southern Madagascar remained independent of Merina rule. There, growing foreign trade fueled the capacity of local peoples, notably the Sakalava and Bara, to resist Merina imperial pretensions and, especially from the 1883–5 war, launch raids for cattle and slaves into the imperial heartland.[129] In addition, the system of imperial *fanompoana* proved extremely unpopular, notably from 1828 to 1853 and 1880 to 1895, when it was applied in full rigor. Popular reaction against it was one of the chief reasons for the failure of the industrial experiment in the first half of the nineteenth century,[130] while the 1888 Maevatanana rebellion was ascribed to the "unbearable labour connected with the working for gold" of *Masombika* there.[131] *Fanompoana* caused many imperial subjects to flee their homes and join brigand bands that cooperated with the Sakalava in attacks upon Merina convoys and installations.[132]

---

[128] Francois Caron, *La France des patriotes* (Paris, 1985), 318; Hebert Feis, *Europe, the World's Banker, 1870–1914* (New York, 1965), 37–59; Jean Jacques van Helten, "La France et l'or des Boers." Some aspects of French investment in South Africa between 1890 and 1914" *African Affairs* 84.335 (1985), 247–63; Fieldhouse, *Economics and Empire*, 60; Jacques Marseille, "The Phases of French Colonial Imperialism: Towards a New Periodization," *Journal of Imperial and Commonwealth History* 13.3 (1985), 127; André Broder, "Le commerce extérieur: L'échec de la conquête d'une position internationale" in Fernand Braudel & Ernest Labrousse (eds.), *Histoire sociale et économique de la France. TIII 1789–1880* (Paris, 1976), 333–4.

[129] Campbell, "History of Nineteenth Century Madagascar."

[130] Chauvin, "Jean Laborde," 33, 44; Chapus, *Quatre-vingts années*, 207; Ransome, "The river Antanamalana," 230; Raombana, "Manuscrit," 4; Fontoynont et Nicol, *Les traitants français*, 27.

[131] R. Baron, in LMS, *Ten Years' Review (1880–1890)* (Antananarivo, 1890), 12; see also Campbell, "Madagascar and the Slave Trade"; Henri Rusillon, *Le Boina* (Paris, 1926), 152; Sewell, *Remarks on Slavery*, 13.

[132] Knight, *Madagascar in war time*, 157–8; H. Hanning, "Lanihay in North-East Madagascar" *AAMM* 20 (1896), 480–1, 483; Robequain, *Madagascar*, 278; Thorne to Wardlaw Thompson, Antananarivo, 19 July 1889, IDC Letterbook (1875–91), 929–30; LMS, *Ten Years' Review (1880–1890)*, 12; Edmund Sturge, "letter," Charlebury, 13 Sept., 1888, in *ASR* (September & October 1888); Knott to Dumford, Morondava, 3 Jan. 1897, "Correspondence of the British

Also damaging to the imperial economy was the erosion of the traditionally strong Merina artisan class upon which, by 1837, the crown had imposed permanent *fanompoana* that deprived its members of the wages and leisure which, in a free labor market, would have been greater than for unskilled laborers. *Fanompoana* crushed individual enterprise and pushed artisans into abandoning their trades.[133] Furthermore, the opportunity cost of imperial labor policies undermined agricultural production through a hemorrhage of labor drafted into, or fleeing from, *fanompoana*. For instance, Lastelle's attempt to establish vanilla plantations at Mananjary on the east coast in the early nineteenth century collapsed because the local population vanished during the recruitment period.[134] On the plateau, where *fanompoana* peaked during periods of industrial exploitation from 1825 to 1861 and 1883 to 1895, its impact was cumulatively more destructive because highland riziculture, in contrast to that practiced on the coast, required a constant and heavy labor input. Thus, the opportunity cost of the *fanompoana* system was high – measured by the flight or transfer of labor and the consequent undermining of the irrigated riziculture base of the Merina economy.[135]

Although *fanompoana* impositions slackened from 1853 to 1880, they intensified in the 1880s.[136] Moreover, increased *fanompoana* during and after the 1883–5 Franco–Merina War swelled the number of brigands – termed *fahavalo* or "enemies" by the Merina court. By the early 1890s, brigand bands were virtually unopposed as they preyed off villages, taking food and cattle and enslaving local people – thus accentuating the cycle of impoverishment, abandonment of the land, and famine.[137] In 1893, *fahavalo* forced the

---

ViceConsul in Majunga, 1894–97" copy in *AM*; see also Anon, "Gold in Madagascar," 69–70; "letter" from Antananarivo, in *ASR* (Sept. and Oct. 1888), 181; Bachelder to Ropes Emmerton & Co, Mojanga, 23 Jan. 1889, Bx.45 F2 (Nov. 1888, April 1889), *REC/CR-MZL*.

[133] *HR* vol. I, 164, 2534, 303; vol. II, 596; vol. III, 885; vol. V, 1158; *GH* (1908), 249, 370 and (1928), 166, 175; Freeman and Johns, *A Narrative*, 78; A Resident, *Madagascar*, 57, 60, 62; Raombana, B2 Livre 13, 29; [Finaz], "Tananarive" (1855–7), 109 – *AHVP*.

[134] Ellis, *History of Madagascar* vol. I, 337 and vol. II, 521–2; *HR* vol. V, 1167; Deschamps, *histoire de Madagascar*, 191–2; Chapus, *Quatre-vingts années*, 33; Oliver, *Madagascar* vol. II, 810; Lyall, "Journal," 186–7; Chauvin, "Jean Laborde," 415, 912; M. Desiré Charnay, "Madagascar à vol d'oiseau" *Le Tour du Monde* (1864), 21–56; Fontoynont et Nicol, *Les traitants français*, 11–12, 21, 24–6, 29–30.

[135] Gwyn Campbell, "The State and PreColonial Demographic History: The Case of Nineteenth Century Madagascar," *JAH* 32.3 (1991); *idem*, "Slavery and *Fanompoana*"; *idem*, "Role of the London Missionary Society" vol. II, 263, 332; Finaz, "Journal" (1855–7), 113 Diaires II.20, *AHVP*; see also *idem*, 31; Raombana Livre 12 C.1, 489; *RA*, 247; see also Chapter 6.

[136] Campbell, "Crisis of Faith."

[137] Campbell, *Brigandry and Revolt*.

abandonment of Suberbie's Maevatanana gold works[138] and in 1894 disrupted the Maevatanana mine railway and launched raids on the neighboring Andranomiangana and Ambalamamoko gold works.[139] Brigand activity also expanded in Imerina, a foreign trader noting as early as March 1891 that "throughout the districts 40 to 100 miles [64–160 km] North, West and South of that centre [Antananarivo], numerous bands of robbers are operating extensively to the great detriment of trade."[140]

Indeed, *fanompoana* was the most important causative factor in the collapse of the imperial Merina economy in the early 1890s. It thus indirectly laid the basis for the French takeover. More directly, desertion from the imperial army – itself a form of *fanompoana* (always unremunerated), guaranteed the success of the French troops in 1895.[141] Moreover, when the French declared a protectorate that maintained a highly unpopular Merina regime, a massive revolt erupted in which one of the key rebel targets was not the French, but the state church structure through which imperial *fanompoana* had been enforced.[142]

Summary

Most explanations for the French conquest of Madagascar have concentrated on French historical claims to the island and Merina resistance to those claims. However, French military intervention in Madagascar in the nineteenth century occurred in the rare moments when the Ministry of the Marine directed French foreign policy, the general principle of which, in the wake of defeat in the Napoleonic Wars, was to promote French interests only if they did not offend British government sensibility. IOA, including Madagascar, was recognized by the French government as an area of British influence. Although insignificant in international terms, Madagascar formed a significant part of the intraregional economy, forging commercial links with the Mascarenes, India, the Swahili

---

[138] Devred, "Les mines"; Hanning, "Lanihay," 4801, 483; Knight, *Madagascar in war time*, 1578.

[139] *CdM* 38 (13 Sept. 1892), 128 (30 jan 1894), 140 (24 avr 1894), 143 (15 mai 1894), 156 (14 août 1894); Decary, "L'ancien régime de l'or," 90; Defoort, *Étude historique*, 78; Colville, *Around the Black Man's Garden*, 190, 1923, 1962. Many of the *Menalamba* rebels from 1895–7 were ex-gold workers, *fahavalo* attacks continuing to plague gold production under the French until 1905 – Campbell, "Missionaries, Fanompoana and the Menalamba Revolt."

[140] Whitney to Ropes, Emmerton & Co, Tamatave, 27 March 1891, *REC/CR-MZL*; Rosaas to PM, Antsirabe, 10 Septembra 1890, HH6, *ANM*; Minute Book of the English Church Mission in Madagascar (4 Jan. 1890).

[141] See, e.g., Campbell, "Missionaries, Fanompoana and the Menalamba Revolt"; Esoavelomandroso, *La province maritime oriental*, 347–50.

[142] Campbell, "Missionaries, Fanompoana and the Menalamba Revolt."

coast, Mozambique, and South Africa. By the 1870s, British subjects dominated the foreign trade of Madagascar, and the 1883–5 war bolstered British and weakened French economic and political influence in the island. Indeed, from 1886, the French government became disinterested in pressing its colonial claims to the island.

In the context of a general British forward movement in IOA from the 1870s, an explanation must be sought for why Madagascar became a French and not a British colony. There appear to have been three principal reasons. First, Britain's paramountcy in Africa came under increasing pressure from European rivals from the late 1870s. By 1890, it decided to concentrate upon those regions deemed essential to its wider imperial interests – notably Egypt, South Africa, and East Africa. Britain granted France a free hand in Madagascar in return for acceptance of British dominance in Zanzibar. In reality, the French had little authority in Madagascar or desire to enforce its claims there until 1894–5, when popular hostility to British moves in Egypt and Thailand permitted the pro-colonial grouping to push the government into action. Even then, the expeditionary force was almost defeated by military incompetence and disease. Had the opposing forces put up any fight, the French would have been forced to withdraw.

Focus thus falls on the mass desertion of Merina soldiers as the main reason for the French success. Desertion is in turn explicable in terms of autarkic policies, adopted in the 1820s, that not only failed to stimulate an industrial revolution, but also through excessive forced labor resulted in the flight of ordinary farmers from the land, as well as in famine and brigandry. The cumulative effects of this had, by the early 1890s, critically undermined the economy and alienated the mass of people from the Merina court, thus precipitating a crisis of the indigenous aristocracy. Merina soldiers deserted en masse so that when Senegalese troops finally relieved the malaria stricken French expeditionary force of 1894, their passage to the Merina capital was virtually unopposed.

Epilogue: The Rise and Fall of Imperial Madagascar

Since independence in 1960, Madagascar has been troubled by interethnic enmity, specifically against the Merina of the central highlands. Historians of the dominant Nationalist school have tended to either downplay such divisions or cite them as a product of French colonial tactics of divide and rule. They choose rather to extol a precolonial regime which, unique in nineteenth-century Africa, forged a progressive nation state unjustly undermined by a combination of French colonial aggression and Western capitalist forces.

This study, the first comprehensive economic history of precolonial Madagascar, challenges conventional historiography. It reveals a Merina regime that countered British and French imperial ambitions by attempting to create an autarkic empire in Madagascar – an island considerably larger than France. Rejecting external investment, the Merina court pushed for rapid economic modernization and self-sufficiency, including an industrial revolution, through the exploitation of the island's natural and human resources. Underpinning this effort was *fanompoana*, unremunerated forced labor imposed on free subjects. This, rather than the slavery highlighted by scholars of the Nationalist school, formed the basis of the imperial Merina economy.

Conventional explanations of the French colonial takeover grossly overestimate the strength of French colonial and Western capitalist forces in Madagascar and underestimate the destructive impact of internal forces, notably Merina imperialism and *fanompoana*. The drive to forge an island empire created enduring enmity among the peoples brutalized by Merina armies, settlers, and colonial administrators. Ultimately, Merina forces established firm rule over only one-third of the island. Henceforth, Madagascar was characterized by a dual economy, that of the Merina empire in the center and east and that of the vast western plains and the deep south, which remained largely independent.

340

The foreign trade of the independent region, which incorporated it in a regional economy that embraced the western Indian Ocean from Natal to Zanzibar to Oman to Bombay, was dominated by British Indians. Independent Madagascar was deeply hostile to and the base for armed incursions into the Merina empire, where highland cattle were seized and villagers enslaved.

Independent Madagascar posed a steadily increasing threat to the imperial court, but *fanompoana* was its Achilles' heel. By making unremunerated forced labor the principle of the imperial economy, the Merina regime alienated the vast bulk of its subjects. Artisans, often drafted into permanent *fanompoana*, relinquished their crafts. The drafting of ordinary cultivators, often for lengthy periods, undermined agricultural production. Increasingly, skilled and unskilled labor responded to *fanompoana* by flight. This ensured the collapse of the promising industrial experiment. It further eroded agricultural production as the fugitives often joined brigand bands that survived by raiding villages. The Merina regime responded by enlarging the system: from the 1880s, it used missionary schools and churches to recruit and sometimes supervise *fanompoana* and drafted children as well as adults.

In 1895, the French expeditionary force, ravaged by disease and plagued by military incompetence, took Madagascar by default. Imperial Merina troops, all of whom were *fanompoana* conscripts, simply refused to back a highly unpopular regime. They deserted, thus enabling the French to snatch victory and replace an indigenous imperial system with their own.

Appendices

Appendix A. French Claims to Madagascar

Date	Result
1642–54	Compagnie française de l'Orient colony at Fort Dauphin – abandoned due to disease and local hostility
1665–76	Compagnie française de l'Orient colony at Fort Dauphin – failed due to metropolitan neglect, internecine conflict, malaria, and local hostility
163[?]–9	Trading post in Antongil Bay – abandoned following massacre by Malagasy
1745–61	Compagnie des Indes colony, Fort Dauphin and Nosy Boraha – abandoned due to malaria and local hostility
1768–70	Colony at Fort Dauphin – abandoned due to lack of support from Mauritius and France
1774–6	Colony in Antongil Bay – abandoned due to opposition from Mauritius and France
1777–81	Morice's treaty with Kilwa establishing French pretensions to Madagascar – not ratified by Paris
1784–6	U.S. colony in Antongil Bay – expelled by French forces from Mauritius
1804	Colony at Fort Dauphin – abandoned due to local hostility
1806/7–11	Trading posts at Toamasina and Mahavelona
1818–22/5	French posts on east coast: Tintingue (expelled 1822) and Fort Dauphin (expelled 1825)
1818–	French settlement at Nosy Boraha

1829–31	French occupy Tintingue and attack Toamasina and Mahavelona (68 Merina and 26 French soldiers killed) – French withdraw July 1831
1841	French declare protectorates over offshore islands (Nosy Be, Nosy Faly, Nosy Mitsio, Nosy Komba) and Mayotta
1845	Franco–British naval attack on Toamasina repulsed
1883–5	Franco–Merina War; expulsion of French nationals. Hostilities end in cession of Diego Suarez to France and nominal French Protectorate in Madagascar
1887–	French control customs of main Merina ports
1895	French conquest and declaration of protectorate
1896	Madagascar declared a French colony

Source: Gwyn Campbell, "Imperial Rivalry in the Western Indian Ocean and schemes to colonise Madagascar, 1769–1826" in Lawrence Marfaing & Brigitte Reinwald (eds.), *Africanische Beziehungen, Netzwerke und Räume* (Münster: Lit Verlag, 2001), 111–30.

Appendix B. British Imperial Influence in Madagascar

1645–6	Courteen Association colony in St Augustin Bay – abandoned due to malaria and local hostility
1649–50	Colony on island [Nosy Komba?] near Nosy Be – abandoned due to disease and local hostility
1680–1720	Mainly British pirates settle east coast, notably Nosy Boraha
1811	Seized French trading posts at Toamasina and Mahavelona – abandoned due to malaria
1814–15	Mauritian colony in Antongil Bay – massacred by Malagasy
1815	Temporary occupation of Toamasina and Mahavelona
1815–16	Unsuccessful attempt by Mauritian settlers to establish plantations near Toamasina
1816	Mauritian colony in Antongil Bay – abandoned due to malaria
1817	Treaties establish British presence in Imerina – General Hall on Mauritius refuses ratification
1820	Treaty establishes British informal dominance in Imerina and right of settlement in Madagascar to British subjects
1820–5	British-trained Merina army expels French from mainland Madagascar (east coast) and occupies Mahajanga (west coast)
1820–36	British (LMS) mission established – expelled 1835/6
1838–9	– Seyyid Said accepts Sakalava offer of Zanzibari sovereignty over Iboina and Antankarana in northwest Madagascar,

	establishes fort at Ambavatoby Bay, and in early 1839 defeats Merina force, but subsequently withdraws.
	– British naval bombardment of Toamasina averted only by Merina payment of indemnity and promise to provide free trade and security for British merchants
1845	Franco–British naval attack on Toamasina repulsed
1869–95	State church established with British LMS missionaries in leading position
1881	British navy visits west coast of Madagascar to reinforce Merina and deter French claims
1883–5	Franco–Merina War: French nationals expelled – British missionaries and consular agents help finance Merina war effort
1885–95	– Foreign (non-French) consuls including Britain continue to demand *exequaturs* from and otherwise accept Merina sovereignty in Madagascar.
	– British army officers train Merina army

Source: Campbell, "Imperial Rivalry."

Appendix C. Population References

James Sibree, *Madagascar and its People*, 272–3; *idem*, "The Arts and Commerce of Madagascar, its recent progress and its future prospects" *Journal of the Society of Arts* (4 June 1880), 625; Slawecki, *French Policy Towards the Chinese* (1971), 78; J. C. Thorne, "Elementary Education in Madagascar" *AAMM* 9 (1885), 47; Thureau, "Des intérêts français," 459; Vidal, *Madagascar*, 31; Richard Lovett, *History of the London Missionary Society* vol. I (London, 1899), 754; Griffiths, *Hanes Madagascar*, 14; GH (1908), 160, 291–3, 299, 316, 319–21, 321 and (1928), 299; *idem*, "Souvenirs," 32; Robert Griffith, *Madagascar. Century of Adventure* (London, 1919), 11; Keller, *Madagascar*, 70, 147–8; Knight, *Madagascar in War Time*, 122, 135; de Lacombe, *Voyage à Madagascar*, 6, 24; Leminier, "Notes" (1825), 795; Little, *Madagascar*, 134; E. O. McMahon, "The Population of Madagascar: Does it Increase or Decrease?" *AAMM* 17 (1893), 90; *Les Missions Catholiques* 180 (1872), 662; 555 (1880), 71; 555 (1880), 71; *Le Temps* (16 octobre 1896); Mullens, *Twelve Months*, 17, 67, 172; Pfieffer, *Last Travels*, 143; Prout, *Madagascar*, 1; Rahamefy, "L'église du palais," 406; Rasoamiaramanana, "Aspects économiques," 8, 10; Ravelomanana, "La vie religieuse à Ambositra," 151;

Razi, "Sources d'histoire malgache," 59, 61–2, 70; Richardson, "Dr. Mullens," 72–4; Samat, "Notes" (1852), 57; E. W. Dawson, *Madagascar: Its Capabilities and Resources* (London, 1895), 79; de Contessouze, "Etablissements français," 248; Crémazy, *L'Île de la Réunion*, 26; W. E. Cousins, "The Great Hova City" *AAMM* 15 (1891), 372; Catat, *Voyage à Madagascar*, 15–16, 289; Ellis, *History of Madagascar* vol. I, 67, 96–7, 113–14; *idem, Martyr Church*, 3; *idem, Three Visits*, 1, 36; *idem, Madagascar Revisited*, 403; Deschamps, *Histoire de Madagascar*, 215–16; Freeman, in *South African Commercial Gazette* (6 Nov. 1830); *idem* & Johns, *A Narrative*, 84–5; FFMA, *Review of the Work of the Friends Foreign Mission Association in Madagascar, 1867–1880* (Antananarivo, 1880), 98; Esoavelomandroso, *Problèmes de police*, 21; Nigel Heseltine, *Madagascar* (London, 1971), 148; Robequain, "Une capitale montagnarde," 279; Oliver, *Madagascar* vol. I, 38, 243–4, 436; Sémerville, "Souvenirs" (1824), 37; Nordhoff, *Stories of the Island World*, 34; *The Madagascar Times* (9 April 1884); Former Resident, *Madagascar and the United States*, 5; Beehler, *Cruise of the Brooklyn*, 200; T. T. Mathews, *Thirty Years in Madagascar* (London, 1904), 235; Maude, *Five Years in Madagascar*, 29, 235; Marius Chabaud, *La Réunion et Madagascar* (Paris, 1892), 16; Browne, *Etchings*, 239; Putnam, "A Cruise" (1848–50); Decary, "population de Madagascar," 29–47; Duhaut-Cilly, "Notice" (1825), 237; Lloyd, "Memoir on Madagascar," 64; Lewis, "Account of the Ovahs," 231; Peill, "Historical Sketch," 253; Marriot, "Report" (1905), 7; anon, "Madagascar et la côte orientale d'Afrique" (1860), 6; Ravis, "Projet de systeme de conquête" (1852); anon, *Notices statistiques*, 29; Le Sage, "Mission to Madagascar" (1816), 26–7, 60; Hastie, "Diary" (1820), 467; *idem*, "Diary" (1824); Mayeur, "Voyage au pays d'ancove" (1777), 179–80; *idem*, "Voyage au pays d'ancove" (1785), 226; Dumaine, "Voyage à la côte de l'ouest" (1793), 297; Hugon, "Aperçu" (1808), 17; *Church Quarterly Review* 6 (1878), 391; *ALGC 19157E* – David Griffiths to William Griffiths [1821]; Hastie to Griffiths, Port Louis, 18 Feb. 1821; *SOAS/LMS-MIL* – Griffiths, "Journal" (1821); Johns to LMS, Antananarivo, 8 Nov. 1826, B2.F3.JC; Freeman to Orme, Port Louis, 14 June 1830, B3.F3.JB; Philips and Freeman, "Memorial to the French Government" (Cape Town, 24 Nov. 1830), B3.F4.J.B; Freeman to Philip, Antananarivo, 11 Feb. 1832, B4.F2.JB; *US* – Robinson to Hunter, Tamatave, 22 Sept. 1879; Robinson to Payson, Tamatave, 2 Aug. 1880, 2 Oct. 1880 and 9 June 1881; Robinson to 3rd Asst. Sec. of State, Tamatave, 2 June 1885; *FJKM* – "*IDC* Letter Book (1875–1891)," 821–2; Thorne to Wardlaw Thompson, 25 May 1887; *AHVP* – Ph. Samat à M le Contre-Amiral Desfossès, St Denis, 28 mai 1848, Carton dossier lld; Dalmond à son frère, St Denis, Bourbon, 21 avril 1837, in "Lettres de M Dalmond à ses parents etc, 1826–1846," C47; Cazet, "Esclavage à Madagascar" (1 mars 1890), 22, D63;

Dalmond "Mission apostolique de Madagascar, 1837–1847," 41–2, Diaires sect.II 1; [Finaz], "Tananarive" (1855–7), 1; L. Maillard au R. P, Lyons, 28 octobre 1850, Correspondance C35; see also D. Ian Pool, "A Framework for the analysis of West African Historical Demography" in *AHD* vol. I, 50–1; Miller, "Demographic History Revisited," 93–6; Cordell and Gregory, "Historical Demography," 396–404.

Bibliography

Archival Material

Académie Malgache, Tsimbazaza, Antananarivo – AAM
– Correspondence of the British Vice-Consul in Majunga, 1894–7 – copy.
– Raombana. 1853a. "Histoires." – *RH*.
  • 1853b. "Annales." – *RA*.
  • B2 Livre 13 – ms.
  • Livre 12 C1 – ms.
  • vol. 8 B.1 – ms.

Anglican Church Mission in Madagascar, Antananarivo – ACM
– Minute Book of the English Church Mission in Madagascar (1884).
– Accounts Books, 1877–1903.
– F. A. Gregory, "Annals of St. Paul's College, Ambatoharanana."
– Letterbook, 1876–84.

Archifdy Llyfrgell Genedlaethol Cymru (Archives of the National Library of Wales), Aberystwyth – ALGC
– Griffiths, David. [1821] "letter" to William Griffiths. 19157[E]
– Hastie to Griffiths, Port Louis, 18 Feb. 1821. 19157[E]

Archives historiques de la Vice-Province Société de Jésus de Madagascar, Antananarivo – AHVP
– Anon. 1860. "Madagascar et côte orientale d'Afrique." Cllg.
– Anon. 1840. "Notices statistiques sur les colonies françaises. IV" (Paris) M.71126.
– Cartier. 1839–40. "notes sur Madagascar." Clla.
  • 1843. "renseignements." Cllb.
– Cazet. 1890. "Esclavage à Madagascar" (1 mars). D63.
– Dalmond, "Mission Apostolique de Madagascar, 1837–1847." Diaires. sect. II.
  • "Lettres à ses parents entre 1826 et 1846." C47.

– Finaz, "Tananarive, Capitale de Madagascar. Séjour d'un missionnaire Catholique en 1855, 56 et 57." sect. II. Diaires. no. 20.
  • 1855–7. "Journal." Diaires II.20.
  • "Journal" II. section II. Diaires 21.
  • 1876. "Mémoires sur le commencement de la mission dans la province du Betsileo." Diaires II no. 24.
– Denieu, "Lettre," Toulia, 4 septembre 1847. C35.
– Jouen, "Correspondence 1859–1869" C52.
– Lacombe, "Histoire de la mission de Tamatave," II.
– "Lettres du gouvernement et de la Reine, 1852–1859," Carton section II c.12.
– de Ravis, Tentor 1852. "Projet de système de conquête, colonisation et civilisation de l'Île de Madagascar," St. Denis (15 août). Carton dossier 11ᵉ.
– Samat, P, "lettre" à M. le Contre-Amiral Desfossès, St. Denis, 28 mai 1848, Carton Dossier 11d.
– Taix, P. "Tamatave: notes historiques" IV.I.

Archives Nationales de Madagascar, Antananarivo – ANM
– "Registre de Rabezandrina"

Archives de Port Louis
– Gazette du Maurice.
– Farquhar. 1816. "Instructions to Lieutenant Le Sage" (20 April). F.7 no. 2.

Baker Library, Graduate School of Business Administration, Harvard University, Massachusetts – BLHU
– "Invoice of Merchandise Shipped by William Hunt on Board the Brig Shaumut – James Emerton Master," Invoices, Bills of Lading, Bills, 1816–1835, James and Ephraim Emerton, File 2, mss.1816–35 E63 v. 6 E & J. Emerton, Shipping.

Barlow Rand Archives, Johannesburg – BRA
– Hugh Marriot. 1905. "Report on the Golf Resources of Madagascar with special reference to the properties of the Lecompte Madagascar Gold, Hanning's Concessions, Harrison Smith's Concessions, Cie.Coloniale, Cie. Lyonnaise." Johannesburg (22 September). HE Record Department F.10. No. 9. "Private Papers."
– Smith, C. G. "Journal," Tulear, Madagascar, 5 September 1902,' in "Notes Taken by C.G.S. on Trip to Madagascar in 1902."

British Library – BL
– Anon. [1790]. "Mémoire historique et politique sur l'Isle de Madagascar." BL Add.18126.
– Anon. 1811. "Instructions sommaires qu'il est convenable d'adresser aux agens du gouvernement à Tamatave et à foulepointe, Isle de Madagascar." BL.Add.18136.
– Anon. (1816). "Essai sur Madagascar." BL, Add.18135.
– Capmartin. [1815]. "Notes sur la Baye St. Augustin (Côte occidentale de Madagascar)." BL Add.18135.
– Chardenoux. 1816. "Journal du voyage fait dans l'intérieure." BL Add.18129.
– Chazal. [1815] "Réflexions . . . sur Madagascar et autres mémoires." BL Add.18135.
  • 1816. "Notes." BL Add.18135.

– de Cossigny. 1800. "Réflexions sur l'îsle de Madagascar." BL Add.18126.
– Dumaine. 1790. "Voyage au pays d'ancaye, autrement dit des Bezounzouns, Isle de Madagascar." BL Add.18128.
• 1793. "Voyage à la côte de l'ouest, autrement dite pays des Séclaves." BL Add.18128.
– Hugon. "Aperçu de mon dernier voyage à ancova de l'an 1808." BL Add.18137.
– Legentil. 1781. "Voyage à Madagascar." BL Add.18126.
– Lescalier. 1792. "Voyage à l'isle de Madagascar." BL Add.18128.
– Mayeur. 1774. "Voyage au pays des Séclaves, côte de Madagascar." BL Add.18128.
• 1775. "Voyage dans le nord de Madagascar." BL Add.18128.
• 1777. "Voyage au pays d'ancove, autrement dit des hovas ou Amboilamba dans l'intérieur des terres, Isle de Madagascar." BL Add.18128.
• 1785. "Voyage au pays d'ancove, par le pays d'ancaye autrement dit des Baizangouzangoux," related by Dumaine. BL Add.18128.
• 1802. "Réflexions sur l'établissement et l'amélioration du commerce de Madagascar." BL Add.18136.
– Des Milices. 1780. "Mémoire sur les moyens de former pour le Roi dans l'isle de Madagascar un établissement de culture, de commerce, et d'entrepôt général pour l'Europe, l'Asie, et l'Afrique." BL Add.18136.
– Morice. 1777. "Mémoire sur la côte oriental d'Afrique." Isle de France (15 juin). Ed. de Cossigny 1790. BL Add.18126.
– La Salle. 1816. "Notes sur Madagascar." BL Add.18135.

Council of World Mission (CWM) Archives, School of Oriental & African Studies, London – SOAS/LMS
– Griffiths, David. "Journal" (Port Louis, 4 March–4 May 1821), Madagascar Journals, Madagascar and Mauritius.1 (1816–24).
– Hastie. "Extract" in 'Report of the Examination of the Schools' (17 March 1825), B2 F2 JA – LMS, Committee Minutes, Africa and Madagascar Bk.I (1826–32): Minutes of the Southern Committee (1828–31).
– Madagascar Incoming Letters (*MIL*)

Essex Institute, Salem, Massachusetts
– John Bertram Papers Bx.2 F5.
– Thomas D. Brace (captain), *Logbook of the Brig Susan from Salem* (24 March 1828–2 January 1829).
– *Emmerton & Co., and Arnold, Hines & Co., Partner and Agency Records – REC/CR MZL:*
• Correspondence and Accounts, 1867–70.
• John Bertram Papers. Agency Records. Tamatave. Bx.2 F5.
• Correspondence, January–July 1893. Bx.46 F1.
• Correspondence Sent. Letterbook, 1889–90 (May 1891–April 1892), ms.103, B46 F3 – Partner & Agency Records, Madagascar Agencies.
• Correspondence Received. Madagascar and Zanzibar Letterbook, 1883–5 in Ropes, Emmerton & Co. Records (1873–1902), Bx.42 F4.
• Madagascar Agencies. Correspondence Sent. 1884–7.
• Tamatave Accounts (May–October 1893), Bx.52 F2.
– Manuscript Collection Register y.III.

– Putnam, Horace P. "A Cruise to the Indies and a Life on Shore" in La Plata, Bark, *Seaman's Journal* (December1848–January 1850), Log 1847 W3 (B15).
– "Private Journal on the bark 'Emily Wilder,' McFarland master, voyage from Salem to the East Indies." m.656 184 E.

Archives of the Fiangonana Loterana Madagaskara/ Norwegian Missionary Society, Isoraka, Antananarivo, Madagascar – FLM/NMS
– Anon, "Sombintsombin'ny Tantaran'ny Sosieten'ny Misiona Norveziana Tanatin'ny 100 Taona, 8 août 1842 – 8 août 1942." ms. Boks.56f.
– Nilsen, John A. "Ny tantaran'ny distry Fianarantsoa, 1878–1943." ms. 57H.

Fiangonana Jesosy Kristy aty Madagascar, Antananarivo – FJKM
– Betsileo District Committee Letterbook 1896–1900.
– Cameron, "Newspaper Cuttings describing Recent Events in Madagascar" (1883) File X.
– *LMS Letterbook, 1868–75.*
– Commercial Correspondence from Procter.
– Correspondence with the SPG, 1870–1926.
– Correspondence from the Secretary to Missionaries and Committees, 1888–99.
– file, "LMS, Local, T & F, D & E."
– file M, "Local, Commercial, Transport."
– "Letters to Government," Folder 1.7.
– "Statement to Prime Minister." 1894. in "LMS Letters to Government," Folder 1.7.

Imerina District Committee (IDC).
• Letterbook 2.
• IDC Letterbook, 1875–97.
• Letters to the Treasurer, 1886–97, B.7.

Natal Archives
– ms: 722/4521 (1879); 723/4636 (1879); 723/4679 (1879); 724/4750 (1879); 726/4955(1879); 733/5626 (1879); 1236/5851 (1889); 1352/6003 (1892).

Peabody Museum, Salem, Massachusetts
– John Bartlett. "Journal to the N.W. Coast and China 1790 on the ship *Massachusetts,"* M.656 1790M.
– Hathorne, H. "'letterbook' to Arnold, Hines & Co., New York and John Bertram, Salem, 1877–79 and 1878–1880," "Letterbook." acc.11.584.
– Richard P.Waters, 'Papers' (1831–87). mss. MH-14

Public Record Office, Kew, London – PRO
– Farquhar, "Minute" on Madagascar (Port Louis, August 1822), *PRO.CO* 167/63.
– Hastie, James. 1817. "Diary." *PRO.CO* 167/34.
• 1820. "Diary." *PRO.CO* 167/50.
• 1822. "Diary." *PRO.CO* 167/63.
• 1822–3. "Diary." *PRO.CO* 167/66.
• 1825. "Diary." *PRO.CO* 167/78 pt. II.
• 1824a. "Report on Missionary Instruction in Ovah" (17 March). *PRO.CO*.167/78, pt. II.

- 1824b. "Report on the Schools superintended by the Missionaries at Tananarive" (19 April). *PRO.CO* 167/78, pt. II.
- 1824–5. "Diary." *PRO.CO* 167/78.
- 1825. "Report on Missionary Instruction in Ovah" (17 March), *PRO.CO* 167/78, pt. II.
- Polignac, de. 1821. "The Slave Ship Success" (4 October), *PRO.CO* 167/77.
- Pye, Thomas. 1817. "Summary of the Proceedings at Madagascar from the 6th June to the 14th June 1817," *PRO.CO* 167/34.
- "Report on the Slave Trade," Cape Town, 25 April 1844, *PRO.CO*, 84/515 ERD/1144 no. 29.
- Le Sage. 1816. "Mission to Madagascar." *PRO.CO* 167/34.
- Samat, A. 1844. "Rapport" in "Report on the Slave Trade," Cape Town (25 April). *PRO.CO*, 84/515 ERD/1144 n. 29.

Staatsarchiv Hamburg
- Firma Wm. O'Swald & Co.

United States National Archives, Washington, DC
- Despatches of United States Consuls in Tamatave, 1853–1906.
- Despatches of United States Consuls in Mozambique, 1854–98.

Printed Primary Sources

Anderson, J. 1858. *Descriptive Account of Mauritius, Its Scenery, Statistics, etc. with a brief Historical Sketch* (Mauritius).
Anon. 1966. "Etat de l'approvisionnement des marchandises de France destinées à faciliter les traites de nègres à l'isle de Madagascar," ms. (1768), in Decary, Raymond. *Coutumes guerrières et organisation militaire chez les anciens malgaches* vol. I.
Anon. 1826. "Instruction of the Rising Generation" in *The Missionary Register*.
Anon. 1840. *Notices statistiques sur les colonies françaises. IV: Madagascar* (Paris).
Anon. 1876. "Ny Toaka avy tany Morosy" in *Ny Gazety Malagasy* I.4 (2 August).
Anon. 1889. "Report," Tamatave (9 December 1888), in *Anti-Slavery Reporter* (January & February).
Anon. 1893. "letter," Madagascar (21 March 1893), in *Anti-Slavery Reporter* (March & April).
Avine, Grégoire. 1958. "Notes de voyage à Fort Dauphin" (1804) in Raymond Decary, "Le voyage d'un chirurgien philosophe à Madagascar," *Bulletin de l'Académie Malgache* 36.
   1961. "Voyages aux isles de France d'Anjouan de Madagascar, de Mosambique, de Zanzibar et de la côte Coromandel" (1802) *Mauritius Archives Publications* 5 (Paris).
Barnard. 1848. *A Three Years' Cruise in the Mozambique Channel for the Suppression of the Slave Trade* (London).
Bates, William. 1965. "Journal and Observations, 8th Voyage, Brig Richmond" (1845) in Bennett and Brooks, *New England Merchants in Africa* (Boston).
Beehler, W. H. 1885. *The Cruise of the Brooklyn* (Philadelphia).
Bergsten, Nils. 1966. "Mémoire sur les moyens d'augmenter à Madagascar les revenus du gouvernement" (1825) in Jean Valette (ed.), *Bulletin de l'Académie Malgache* 44.

Besson, L. 1894. *Voyage au pays des Tanala Indépendants de la région d'Ikongo* (Paris).

Bojer. 1963. "Journal," in Jean Valette (ed.), "L'Imerina en 1822–1825 d'après les journaux de Bojer et d'Hilsenburg," extrait du *Bulletin de Madagascar* (avril-mai).

Borchgrevink. 1871. "letter," Morondava (27 September 1870) in *Norsk Missionsytilande*.

Browne, J. Ross. 1846. *Etchings of a Whaling Cruise with notes of a sojourn on the island of Zanzibar* (New York).

Callet, R. P. 1974. *Histoire des Rois* vols. I-IV (Tananarive).

    1978. *Histoire des Rois* vol.V (Tananarive).

Cameron, James. 1874. *Recollections of Mission Life in Madagascar in the early days of the LMS Mission* (Antananarivo).

Campbell, Charles Mackenzie. 1963. "Journal" in Jean Valette (ed.), "Le Journal de Campbell" (1840), *Studia* II.

Chapelier. 1904. "Lettres en mission à Madagascar de décembre 1803 en mai 1805" ed., M. Jully. *Bulletin de l'Académie Malgache.*

    1905–6. "lettres adressées au citoyen préfet de l'île de France, de décembre 1803 en mai 1805," *Bulletin de l'Académie Malgache* IV.

    1940. "manuscrits" ed. Henri Poisson. In Académie Malgache, *Collection de documents concernant Madagascar et les pays voisins* vol. II (Tananarive).

Charnay, M. Desiré. 1864. "Madagascar à vol d'oiseau" *Le Tour du Monde.*

Clark, H. E. 1884. "How We Travel in Madagascar," *Antananarivo Annual and Madagascar Magazine* 8.

Coignet, M. 1884. "Madagascar. Its Trades and Resources" (1862), *The Madagascar Times* II.41 (15 October).

Colin et Suau. 1896. "Album Malgache – Les borizanos," *Les missions catholiques.*

Colomb, P. 1968. *Slave Catching in the Indian Ocean* (1873) (London, reprint).

Colony of Natal Statistical Year Book.

Colville, Zélie. 1893. *Around the Black Man's Garden* (Edinburgh).

Contessouze, A. de. 1860. "Etablissements français à Madagascar," *Correspondant* (31 mai).

Copland, Samuel. 1822. *A History of Madagascar* (London).

Correspondence Respecting Madagascar relating to the Mission of Hova Envoys to Europe in 1882–83. 1883. (London).

Crémazy. 1822. *L'île de la Réunion et Madagascar* (London).

Crosfield, A. J. & G. A. n.d. *Man in Shining Armour. The Story of the Life of William Wilson, M.R.C.S. and L.R.C.P., Missionary in Madagascar, Secretary of the Friends' Foreign Missionary Association* (Antananarivo).

Cousins, George. 1884. "Christian rule in Madagascar," *The Sunday Magazine* (April).

Cousins, W. E. 1886. *Madagascar of Today* (London).

    1891. "The Great Hova City," *Antananarivo Annual and Madagascar Magazine* 15.

    1896. "The Abolition of Slavery in Madagascar," *Antananarivo Annual and Madagascar Magazine* 20.

Dawson, E. W. 1895. *Madagascar: Its Capabilities and Resources* (London).

Duhaut-Cilly. 1968. "Notices sur le royaume d'Emirne, sur la capitale de Tananarivou et sur le gouvernement de Rhadama" in Jean Valette, "Deux documents français sur Madagascar en 1825; les rapports Duhaut-Cilly et Frère," *Bulletin de l'Académie Malgache* 16/I–II.

Ellis, Mrs. 1863. *Madagascar: Its Social and Religious Progress* (London).

Ellis, William. 1838. *History of Madagascar*, 2 vols. (London).

1859. *Three Visits to Madagascar during the years 1853–1854–1856* (London).

1867. *Madagascar Revisited* (London).

1870. *The Martyr Church* (London).

Emmerton, Ephraim. 1965. "A Visit to Eastern Africa" (1843–4) in Bennett and Brooks (eds.), *New England Merchants Africa* (Boston).

FFMA. 1880. *Review of the Work of the Friends Foreign Mission Association in Madagascar, 1867–1880* (Antananarivo).

FJOD. 1886. "South West Coast," *The Madagascar Times* (27 November).

Frappaz. 1820. "Notice sur les vents, les courans, et les atterrages de la côte sud-est de l'ile de Madagascar," *Annales maritimes et coloniales* vol. II.

Frère, Louis Armand. 1968. "Situation politique et morale de Madagascar" (1826) in *Bulletin de l'Académie Malgache* 46/I–II.

Freeman, J. J. & Johns, David. 1840. *A Narrative of the Persecution of the Christians in Madagascar* (London).

Frere, Bartle. 1873. "Correspondence Respecting Sir Bartle Frere's Mission to the East Coast of Africa, 1872–73," *House of Commons Parliamentary Papers* (London).

Gore-Jones, W. 1881. *Report* (London).

Grandidier, Alfred. 1916. "Souvenirs de voyages, 1865–1870" in *Documents anciens sur Madagascar*, vol. VI (Tananarive, n.d.)

Griffiths, David. 1841. *The Persecuted Christians of Madagascar* (London).

1843. *Hanes Madagascar* (Machynlleth).

Guerret. 1883. *Trois mois autour de Madagascar* – ed. E. Genin (Douai).

Hall, W. H. 1844. *Narratives of the Voyages and Services on the Nemesis* (London).

Hanning, H. 1896. "Lanihay in North-East Madagascar," *Antananarivo Annual and Madagascar Magazine* 20.

Hastie, James. 1831. "Diary" in Daniel Tyerman and George Bennett, *Journal of Voyages and Travels, 1821–1829*, ed. James Montgomery. Vol. II (London).

1902. "Journal," in James Sibree and A. Jully, eds. "Le voyage de Tananarive en 1817–18 – manuscrits de James Hastie," *Bulletin de l'Académie Malgache* 2.

Hilsenburg. 1963. "Journal," ed. Jean Valette. *Bulletin de Madagascar* (avril-mai).

Horn, Alfred. 1928. *Trader Horn in Madagascar* (London).

1932. *The Waters of Africa* (London).

House of Commons Parliamentary Papers (HCPP):

– (1821); (1828); 47 (1837–8); *Africa* 1 (1883).

– "Expenses incurred by the Government of Mauritius on account of Madagascar" in *Foreign Office Correspondence Relating to the Slave Trade* (London, 1873 and 1880).

– "Treaty between Radama and Governor Farquhar," Tamatave, 23 Oct. 1817, in *Papers relating to the Abolition of the Slave Trade in the Mauritius, 1817–1829*.

Ives, Edward. 1898. "Extract" from "A Voyage to India" (1754), *Antananarivo Annual and Madagascar Magazine* 22.

Jeffreys, Keturah. 1827. *The Widowed Missionary's Journal* (Southampton).

Johns, David – see Freeman, J.

Jones, David. "Journal," *Quarterly Chronicle* (1821–4).

Jully. 1903. "Mission en extrême-orient," *Bulletin de l'Académie Malgache* II.2.

Kirk, John. 1865. "Notes on Two Expeditions up the River Rovuma, East Africa," *Journal of the Royal Geographical Society* 35.

Knight, E. F. 1895. "From Fort Dauphin to Fianarantsoa," *Antananarivo Annual and Madagascar Magazine* 19.

1896. *Madagascar in War Time* (London).

Knott. 1888. "letter" to Aitken, Mojanga (21 March 1888), in *Anti-Slavery Reporter* (November & December).

De Lacombe, Leguéval. 1840. *Voyage à Madagascar et aux Îles Comores (1823 à 1830)* (Paris).

Landmark, N. 1899. *Det Norske missionsselskab* (Kristiania).

Larsen, Ludvig. 1894. *Livet for Doden* (Christiania).

Leminier. 1970. "Notes sur une excursion faites dans l'intérieur de l'ile de Madagascar" (1825) in *Bulletin de Madagascar* 292.

Lewis, Locke. 1835. "An Account of the Ovahs, a race of people residing in the Interior of Madagascar: with a Sketch of their Country, Appearance, Dress, Language, &c," *Journal of the Royal Geographical Society* 5.

Little, Henry W. 1884. *Madagascar, Its History and People* (London).

Lloyd, J. A. 1851. "Memoir on Madagascar" (10 December 1849), *Journal of the Royal Geographical Society* 20.

London Missionary Society (LMS). 1871. *A Brief Review of the LMS Mission in Madagascar from 1861 to 1870* (Antananarivo).

1880. *Ten Years' Review of Mission Work in Madagascar 1870–1880* (Antananarivo).

1890. *Ten Years' Review of Mission Work in Madascar 1880–1890* (Antananarivo).

Lyall, Robert. 1954. "Journal," eds. Chapus, G. S. & Mondain, G. in Académie Malgache, *Collection de documents concernant Madagascar et les pays voisins* 5 (Tananarive).

McFarland. 1965. "List of goods suitable for Nos Beh, Mayotta, &c," in Bennett and Brooks (eds.), *New England Merchants in Africa* (Boston).

McMahon, E. O. 1890. "The Sakalava and their Customs," *Antananarivo Annual and Madagascar Magazine* 4.

1891. "First Visit of a European to the Betsiriry Tribe," *Antananarivo Annual and Madagascar Magazine* 15.

1893. "The Population of Madagascar: Does it Increase or Decrease?" *Antananarivo Annual and Madagascar Magazine* 17.

Malzac. 1902. "Dernières recommandations d'Andrianampoinimerina (1810) d'après un ma nuscrit du P. Callet," *Bulletin de l'Académie Malgache* 1.

Mathews, T. T. 1904. *Thirty Years in Madagascar* (London).

Maundrell, H. 1867. "A Visit to the North-East Province of Madagascar," *Journal of the Royal Geographical Society* 37.

Mayeur. 1896. "Imerina and Antananarivo" (ed. James Sibree), *Antananarivo Annual and Madagascar Magazine* 20.

1912. "Voyages, 1774–1776," *Bulletin de l'Académie Malgache* 10.

1913. "Voyages" (1777) *Bulletin de l'Académie Malgache* 12/I.

Morice. 1965a. "Plan for a Trading Centre on the East Coast of Africa" (Île de France, 24 September 1777) in G. S. P. Freeman-Grenville, *The French at Kilwa Island* (Oxford).

1965b. "Plan of Operation for the Trade of the Coast of East Africa" in G. S. P. Freeman-Grenville, *The French at Kilwa Island* (Oxford).

Mullens, Joseph. 1875. *Twelve Months in Madagascar* (London).

Natal Blue Books

Nordhoff, Charles. 1857. *Stories of the Island World* (New York).

O'Neil. 1883. "Journey in the District West of Cape Delgado Bay, September–October 1882," in *Anti-Slavery Reporter* (July).

Owen, W. F. W. 1833. *Narrative of Voyages to . . . Africa, Arabia, and Madagascar*, vol. II (London).

Parliamentary Papers (1876–1900)

Pfeiffer, Ida. 1861. *The Last Travels of Ida Pfeiffer* (London).

1981. *Voyage à Madagascar (1857)* (Paris).

Pickersgill, S. 1893. "North Sakalava-land," *Antananarivo Annual and Madagascar Magazine*.

Pickersgill, W. Clayton. 1885. "The Trade and Commerce of Madagascar," *Antananarivo Annual and Madagascar Magazine*.

Prout, E. 1863. *Madagascar: Its Mission and Its Martyrs* (London).

Raombana. 1930. "Manuscrit écrit à Tananarive (1853–1854)," trans. J. F. Radley, *Bulletin de l'Académie Malgache* 13.

1976. "texts" in Simon Ayache (ed.), *Raombana (1809–1855) l'Historien* II (Fianarantsoa).

Rees, D. M. 1898. "Y 'Safo-tany' na 'Raporapo,'" *Y Cronicl*.

Reibell. 1935. *Le Calvaire de Madagascar. Notes et souvenirs de 1895* (Paris).

Resident, A [Baker]. 1847. *Madagascar Past and Present* (London).

Resident. 1883. A former Resident of the Island, *Madagascar and the United States* (New York).

Rochon, Alexis. 1890. "An Account of the Island of Madagascar" (1768) in S. P. Oliver (ed.), *Madagascar* (London).

Rondeaux. 1966. "Mémoire" (1809) in Jean Valette, "Un mémoire de Rondeaux sur Madagascar (1809)," *Bulletin de l'Académie Malgache* 44/II.

Rostvig, L. 1886. *Sakalaverne og deres land* (Stavanger).

Samat, Edmont. 1932. "Notes: La côte ouest de Madagascar en 1852," *Bulletin de l'Académie Malgache* 15.

Schneider. 1928. Archives Coloniales (1818) in Alfred and Guillaume Grandidier, *Histoire physique, naturelle et politique de Madagascar* (Paris).

Sémerville. 1933. "Souvenirs de Sainte-Marie" (1824) (ed. Raymond Decary) in *Bulletin de l'Académie Malgache* 16.

Sewell, Joseph. 1875. *The Sakalava. Being Notes of a Journey made from Antananarivo to some Towns on the Border of the Sakalava Territory, in June and July 1875* (Antananarivo).

1876. *Remarks on Slavery in Madagascar* (London).

Shaw, G. 1885. *Madagascar and France* (London).

Shipton, Samuel. 1848. "Madagascar" in *Sentinelle de Madagascar* (9 juin).

Smith, A. 1883. "From Zanzibar to Nosibe," *Antananarivo Annual and Madagascar Magazine* 7.

Sonnerat. 1782. *Voyage aux Indes Orientales et à la Chine (1774–1781)*, vol. II (Paris).

Street, L. 1877. "letter" in *The English Independent* (15 and 22 November).

Sturge, Edmund. 1888. "letter," Charlebury, 13 Sept. 1888, in *Anti-Slavery Reporter* (September & October).

Suau – see Colin.

Third Report of the Commission on Scale and Stock Diseases, 1894–95 (Pietermaritzburg, 1895).

Thiriot. 1882. *L'Ile Maurice, La Réunion et les productions de l'Inde, 1785* – ed. E. Génin (Douai).

Thorne, J. C. 1885. "Elementary Education in Madagascar," *Antananarivo Annual and Madagascar Magazine* 9.

Toy, R. 1878. "Remarks on the Meteorology of Antananarivo and the Neighbourhood," *Antananarivo Annual and Madagascar Magazine* 2.

Tyerman, Daniel and Bennet, George. 1831. *Journal of Voyages and Travels, 1821–1829* (ed. James Montgomery), vol. II (London).

Wills, J. A. 1885. "Native Products used in Malagasy Industries," *Antananarivo Annual and Madagascar Magazine* 9.

Journals & Newspapers etc.

Annales maritimes et coloniales II.46 (1831)

Antananarivo Annual and Madagascar Magazine – AAMM

Anti-Slavery Reporter – ASR

Bulletin de l'Académie Malgache – BAM

Church Quarterly Review 6 (1878)

Le courrier de Madagascar (1892–94) – CdM

La feuille hebdomadaire (1819–32)

Ny Gazety Malagasy (1875)

Le Journal (1895)

Juvenile Missionary Magazine (1886)

The Madagascar Times (1882–88) – MT

Missionary Register (1821)

Les Missions Catholiques (1872–7)

The Madagascar Mail (1894)

Notes, reconnaissances et explorations

Quarterly Chronicle (1821–4)

South African Commercial Gazette (1830)

Le Temps (1896)

Secondary Sources

Abu-Lughod, Janet L. 1989. *Before European Hegemony. The World System A.D. 1250–1350* (New York & Oxford).

Ader, R. L. 1970. "Les traitants de Nosy-Vé, Tulear à la fin du XIXe siècle," *Etudes Tuléariennes* 2 (décembre).

African Historical Demography, 2 vols. (Centre of African Studies, University of Edinburgh, 1978 & 1981).

Agence économique du gouvernement général de Madagascar, *Madagascar "La Grande Ile"* (Paris, n.d.).

Agnew, John. 1987. *The United States in the World-Economy* (Cambridge).

Agnew, Swanzie. 1978. "Factors Affecting the Demographic Situation in Malawi in Pre-colonial and Colonial Times," *African Historical Demography* vol. I (Edinburgh).

Aldrich, Robert. 1987. "Late-Comer or Early-Starter? New Views on French Economic History," *Journal of European Economic History* 16.1.

Alexandre, Valentim. 1979. *Origens do Colonialismo Portugues moderno (1822–1891)* vol. II (Lisboa).

Allen, Richard B. 1999. *Slaves, Freedmen and Indentured Laborers in Colonial Mauritius* (Cambridge).

    2001. "Licentious and Unbridled Proceedings: The Illegal Slave Trade to Mauritius and the Seychelles during the early Nineteenth Century," *Journal of African History* 42.

    2003. "The Mascarene Slave Trade and Labour Migration in the Indian Ocean during the Eighteenth and Nineteenth Centuries" in Gwyn Campbell (ed.), *The Structure of Slavery in Indian Ocean Africa and Asia* (London).

Alpers, E. A. 1967. "The French Slave Trade," *Historical Association of Tanzania* paper 3.

    1975. *Ivory and Slaves in East and Central Africa to the Later Nineteenth Century* (London).

Anderson, M. S. 1978. *The Eastern Question 1774–1923* (London).

André, E. C. 1899. *De l'esclavage à Madagascar* (Paris).

Andrew, C. M. & Kanya-Forstner, A. S. 1971. "The French 'Colonial Party': Its Composition, Aims and Influence, 1885–1914," *Historical Journal* 14.1.

    1974. "Gabriel Hanotaux, the Colonial Party & the Fashoda Strategy," *Journal of Imperial & Commonwealth History* 3.1 (1974).

    1981. *France Overseas. The Great War and the Climax of French Imperial Expansion* (London).

Anon. 1884. "Brief Summary of Important Events in Madagascar during 1884," *Antananarivo Annual and Madagascar Magazine* 8.

Anon. 1890. "Gold in Madagascar," *Anti-Slavery Reporter* (March and April)

Anon. 1896. "Dr Forsyth Major's Expedition in Madagascar," *Antananarivo Annual and Madagascar Magazine* 20.

Anon. 1897. "Les études de colonisation, district de Mahanoro, district de Vatomandry," *Notes, reconnaissances et explorations* 2.

Anon. 1897. "Les études de colonisation (province de Tamatave)," *Notes, reconnaissances et explorations* 3.

Anon. 1898. "Natural history notes," *Antananarivo Annual and Madagascar Magazine* 22.

Anon. 1898. "Some Betsimisaraka folk-tales and superstitions" (trans. J. Sibree), *Antananarivo Annual and Madagascar Magazine* 22.

Anon. 1954. "Travaux du service géologique," *Bulletin de Madagascar* 97.

Anon [1999/200?], *Indray Andro Hono Nisy Nosy Anankiroa. A Tale of Two Islands*.

Archer, Léonie (ed.). 1988. *Slavery and Other Forms of Unfree Labour* (London & New York).

Ashworth, William. 1981. *A Short History of the International Economy since 1850* (UK).

Athenas, Georges. 1947. "Ethnographie [de la Réunion]" in Marcel de Coppet (ed.), *Madagascar*, vol. I (Paris).

Aujas, L. 1905–6. "Notes sur l'histoire des Betsimisaraka," *Bulletin de l'Académie Malgache* 4.

Austen, Ralph. 1986. "Social bandits and other heroic criminals. Western models of resistance and their relevance for Africa" in Crummey (ed.), *Banditry, Rebellion and Social Protest in Africa* (London).

1987. *African Economic History* (London).

1989. "The 19th Century Islamic Slave Trade from East Africa (Swahili and Red Sea Coasts): A Tentative Census" in William Gervase Clarence-Smith (ed.), *The Economics of the Indian Ocean Slave Trade in the Nineteenth Century* (London).

Axelson, Eric. 1967. *Portugal and the Scramble for Africa* (Johannesburg).

Ayache, Simon. 1975. "Esquisse pour le portrait d'une reine: Ranavalona 1ère," *Omaly sy Anio* 1–2.

1976a. ed. *Raombana (1809–1855) l'Historien*, 2 vols. (Fianarantsoa).

1976b. – see Munthe, Ludvig (1976).

Ballard, Charles. 1896. "Drought and Economic Distress: South Africa in the 1800s," *Journal of Interdisciplinary History* 17.2.

Baré, Jean-François. 1983. "Remarques sur le vocabulaire monarchique sakalava du nord" in Raison-Jourde (ed.), *Les souverains de Madagascar* (Paris).

Barnwell, P. J. and Toussaint, Auguste. 1949. *A Short History of Mauritius* (London).

Baron, R. 1884. "Ranavalona II, the Christian Queen of Madagascar," *The Sunday Magazine* (January).

1890. "Malagasy Terms of Monetary Values," *Antananarivo Annual and Madagascar Magazine* 14.

1898. "Notes on the economic plants of Madagascar," *Antananarivo Annual and Madagascar Magazine* 22.

Beachey, R. W. 1976. *The Slave Trade of Eastern Africa* (London).

1978. "Some Observations on the Volume of the Slave Trade of Eastern Africa in the Nineteenth Century," *African Historical Demography*, vol. I (Edinburgh).

Beinart, William. 1982. *The Political Economy of Pondoland 1860 to 1930* (Cambridge).

Beltran, Alain & Griset, Pascal. 1988. *La Croissance économique de la France 1815–1914* (Paris).

Bennett, Norman R. 1962. "Americans in Zanzibar: 1865–1915" in *Essex Institute Historical Collection* 9.

1963. "Americans in Zanzibar: 1865–1915" in *Studies in East African History* (Boston).

1965. with Brooks, George E. (eds.), *New England Merchants in Africa* (Boston).

1969. "France and Zanzibar" in Bennett, Norman et al. (eds.), *Eastern African History* (New York).

Berg, Gerald M. 1979. "Royal Authority and the Protector System in Nineteenth Century Imerina" in Raymond Kent (ed.), *Madagascar in History* (Berkeley).

1988. "Sacred Acquisition: Andrianampoinimerina at Ambohimanga, 1777–1790," *Journal of African History* 29.

Berlioux, E. T. 1971. *The Slave Trade in Africa in 1872* (London).

Berman, Edward. 1969. "Salem and Zanzibar: 1825–1850. Twenty-Five years of Commercial Relations," *Essex Institute of Historical Collections* 105.4.

Berthier. 1908. "La tribu des Hova," *Conférence à l'école coloniale* (Paris, décembre).

Bhana, Surendra. 1985. "Indian Trade and Trader in Colonial Natal" in Bill Guest and John M. Sellers (eds.), *Enterprise and Exploitation in a Victorian Economy. Aspects of the Economic and Social History of Colonial Natal* (Pietermaritzburg).

Birkeli, F. 1946. "Sur les projets maritimes de l'ancien gouvernement hova," *Bulletin de l'Académie Malgache* 27.

Birmingham, David and Martin, Phyllis M. (eds.). 1986. *History of Central Africa*, vol. II (London).

see also Gray

Bloch, Maurice. 1971. *Placing the Dead: Tombs, Ancestral Villages and Kinship Organisation in Madagascar* (London).

1980. "Modes of production and slavery in Madagascar" in James L. Watson (ed.), *Asian and African Systems of Slavery* (Oxford).

1983. "La séparation du pouvoir et du rang comme processus d'évolution. Une esquisse du développement des royautés dans le centre de Madagascar" in Raison-Jourde (ed.), *Les souverains de Madagascar* (Paris).

1986. *From Blessing to Violence* (Cambridge).

Bohannan, Paul and Dalton, George (eds.). 1962. *Markets in Africa* (Evanston).

Boomgaard, Peter. 2004. "Human Capital, Slavery and Low Rates of Economic and Population Growth in Indonesia, 1600–1910" in Gwyn Campbell (ed.), *The Structure of Slavery in Indian Ocean Africa and Asia* (London).

Boucabeille. 1897. "De Tananarive à Diego-Suarez (suite et fin)," *Notes, reconnaissances et explorations* 2.

Boudou, Adrien. 1942. *Les Jésuites à Madagascar*, 2 vols. (Paris).

Bousserand. 1947–8. "Notice sur les tribus Tanala et Sakalava" in M. E. Fagereng, "Histoire des Maroserana du Menabe," *Bulletin de l'Académie Malgache* 28.

Brady Jr., Cyrus T. 1959. *Commerce and Conquest in East Africa with particular reference to the Salem Trade with Zanzibar* (Salem).

Braudel, Fernand & Labrousse, Ernest (eds.). 1976. *Histoire sociale et économique de la France*, vol. III *1789–1880* (Paris).

Bray, J. 1969. "The economics of traditional cloth production in Iseyin, Nigeria," *Economic Development and Cultural Change* 17.

Broder, André. 1976. "Le commerce extérieur: L'échec de la conquête d'une position internationale" in Fernand Braudel & Ernest Labrousse (eds.), *Histoire sociale et économique de la France*, vol. III *1789–1880* (Paris).

Brygoo, E. R. 1971. "Les débuts del'enseignement médical à Madagascar. Un siècle d'expérience," *Bulletin de l'Académie Malgache* 49.1.

Brooks, Alexander – see Deerr, Noel.

Brooks, George E. – see Bennett, Norman.

Brown, Mervyn. 1977. "Ranavalona I and the Missionaries, 1828–1840," *Omaly sy Anio* 5–6.

1978. *Madagascar Rediscovered* (London).

1995. *A History of Madagascar* (London).

Brown, Michael Barratt. 1974. *The Economics of Imperialism* (UK).

Browne, J. Ross. 1846. *Etchings of a Whaling Cruise with notes of a sojourn on the island of Zanzibar* (New York).

Bruce-Chwatt, Leonard Jan. 1980. *Essential Malariology* (London).

Brunschwig, Henri. 1966. *French Colonialism 1871–1914. Myths and Realities* (London).

1971. "Anglophobia and French African Policy" in Prosser Gifford & William Roger Louis (eds.), *France and Britain in African Imperial Rivalry and Colonial Rule* (New Haven).

Buchenssenschutz, P. 1938. *La mission luthérienne à Madagascar* (Tananarive).

Burroughs, Peter. 1976. "The Mauritius Rebellion of 1832 and the Abolition of British Colonial Slavery," *Journal of Imperial and Commonwealth History* 4.3.

Cain, P. J. and Hopkins, A. G. 1986. "Gentlemanly Capitalism and British Expansion Overseas vol. I. The Old Colonial System, 1688–1850," *Economic History Review* 39.4.

1993. *British Imperialism. Innovation and Expansion, 1688–1914* (London).

Caldwell, J. C. 1978. "Major Questions in African Demographic History." *African Historical Demography*, vol. I (Edinburgh).

Cameron. 1888. "Cardinal Lavigerie and the Anti-Slavery Crusade," *Anti-Slavery Reporter* (September & October).

Campbell, Gwyn. 1980. "Labour and the Transport Problem in Imperial Madagascar, 1810–1895," *Journal of African History* 21.

1981. "Madagascar and the Slave Trade, 1810–1895," *Journal of African History* 22.

1986a. "Toamasina (Tamatave) and the Growth of Foreign Trade in Imperial Madagascar, 1862–1895" in G. Liesegang, H. Pasch, & A. Jones (eds.), *Figuring African Trade* (Berlin).

1986b. "The monetary and financial crisis of the Merina empire, 1810–1826," *South African Journal of Economic History* 1.1.

1987a. "The Role of the Merina State in the Decline of the Imperial Merina Economy, 1875–1895" in Clive Dewey (ed.), *The State and the Market* (New Delhi).

1987b. "The Adoption of Autarky in Imperial Madagascar, 1820–1835," *Journal of African History* 28 (1987).

1988a. "Slavery and Fanompoana: The Structure of Forced Labour in Imerina (Madagascar), 1790–1861," *Journal of African History* 29.

1988b. "Missionaries, Fanompoana and the Menalamba Revolt in late nineteenth century Madagascar," *Journal of Southern African Studies* 15.1.

1988c. "The East African Slave Trade, 1861–1895: The 'Southern' Complex," *International Journal of Southern African Studies* 21.4.

1988d. "Currency Crisis, Missionaries and the French Takeover in Madagascar, 1861–1895," *International Journal of African Historical Studies* 21.2.

1988e. "Gold Mining and the French Takeover of Madagascar, 1883–1914," *African Economic History* 17.

1989a. "Madagascar and Mozambique in the Slave Trade of the Western Indian Ocean, 1800–1861" in W. G. Clarence-Smith (ed.), *The Economics of the Indian Ocean Slave Trade in the Nineteenth Century* (London).

1989b. "The East African Slave Trade, 1861–1895: The "Southern' Complex," *International Journal of African Historical Studies* 22.1.

1990–1. "Disease, Cattle, and Slaves: The Development of Trade between Natal and Madagascar, 1875–1904," *African Economic History* 19.

1991a. "The State and Pre-Colonial Demographic History: The Case of Nineteenth-Century Madagascar," *Journal of African History* 32.3.

1991b. "An Industrial Experiment in –re-colonial Africa. The Case of Imperial Madagascar, 1821–1861," *Journal of Southern African Studies* 17.3.

1992. "Crisis of Faith and Colonial Conquest: The Impact of Famine and Disease in late nineteenth-century Madagascar," *Cahiers d'Études Africaines* 32 (3), 127.

1993a. "Indians and Commerce in Madagascar, 1869–1896," University of the Witwatersrand *African Studies Seminar Paper* 345 (23 August).

1993b. "The Structure of Trade in Madagascar, 1750–1810," *International Journal of African Historical Studies* 26.1.

1994. "The History of Nineteenth Century Madagascar: 'le royaume' or 'l'empire'?" *Omaly sy Anio* 33–6.

1996a. "'Out of Africa': Madagascar and South Africa since the 1820s" in Chris Alden et Jean-Pascal Daloz (eds.). *Paris, Pretoria and the African Continent. The International Relations of States and Societies in Transition* (London).

1996b. "The Cocoa Frontier in Madagascar, the Comoro Islands and Réunion, c.1820–1970" in William Gervase Clarence-Smith (ed.), *Cocoa Pioneer Fronts since 1800* (London).

1996c. (with R. Hewitt, A. Krause, A. Goldman, & T. Jenkins), "ß-Globin Haplotype Analysis Suggests that a Major Source of Malagasy Ancestry Is Derived from Bantu-Speaking Negroids," *American Society of Human Genetics* 58 (1996).

2000. "Madagascar and the Slave Trade in the south west Indian Ocean" in Sandra J. T. Evers & Vinesh Y. Hookoomsing (eds.), *Globalization and the South West Indian Ocean* (Leiden & Mauritius).

2001. "Imperial Rivalry in the Western Indian Ocean and Schemes to Colonise Madagascar, 1769–1826" in Lawrence Marfaing & Brigitte Reinwald (eds.), *Africanische Beziehungen, Netzwerke und Räume* (Münster).

2002. "Larceny in the Highlands of Madagascar" review article, *Slavery and Abolition* 23.1.

2003. "Coffee production in Madagascar" in Steven Topik & William Gervase Clarence-Smith (eds.), *Coffee under Colonialism and Post-Colonialism: The Global Coffee Economy in Africa, Asia, and Latin America, c1800–c1960* (Cambridge).

2004a. "Madagascar" in *Encyclopaedia of World Environmental History* (London) vol. 2.

2004b (ed.), *The Structure of Slavery in Indian Ocean Africa and Asia* (London).

2004/5a (ed.), *Abolition and Its Aftermath in Indian Ocean Africa and Asia* (London).

2004/5b. "Unfree Labour and the Significance of Abolition in Madagascar, circa 1825–1897" in *idem* (ed.), *Abolition and Its Aftermath in Indian Ocean Africa and Asia* (London).

forthcoming. *Brigandry and Revolt in Pre-Colonial Africa: Imperial Madagascar, 1750–1900.*

Capela, Jose. 1987. "The Mujojos Slave Trade in Moçambique, 1830–1902," paper presented at the *Workshop on the Long-Distance Trade in Slaves across the Indian Ocean and Red Sea*, SOAS, London (December).

Caron, François. 1979. *An Economic History of Modern France* (London).

1985. *La France des patriotes* (Paris).

Castel, Rémy – see Decary, Raymond (1941).

Catat, Louis. 1895. *Voyage à Madagascar, 1889–90* (Paris).

Chabaud, Marius. 1892. *La Réunion et Madagascar* (Paris).

Chamberlain, M. E. 1984a. *British Foreign Policy in the Age of Palmerston* (UK).

1984b. *The Scramble for Africa* (UK).

Chapus, G. S. 1925. *Quatre-vingts années d'influences européennes en Imerina (1815–1895)* (Tananarive).

1944–5. with Birkeli, E. "Historique d'Antsirabe jusqu'en l'année 1905," *Bulletin de l'Académie Malgache* 26.

1951–2a. "le soin du bien-être du peuple sous le règne d'Andrianampoinimerina," *Bulletin de l'Académie Malgache* 30.

1951–2b. with Dandouau. "Les anciennes industries malgaches," *Bulletin de l'Académie Malgache*. 30.

1951–2c. with Mondain, G. "Un chapitre inconnu. Des rapports de Maurice et de Madagascar," *Bulletin de l'Académie Malgache* 30.

1953. *Rainilaiarivony: un homme d'état malgache* (Paris).

Chaudhuri, K. N. 1985. *Trade and Civilisation in the Indian Ocean. An Economic History from the Rise of Islam to 1750* (Cambridge).

1992. *Asia Before Europe. Economy and Civilisation of the Indian Ocean from the Rise of Islam to 1750* (Cambridge).

Chauvicourt, J. et S. 1968. "Les premières monnaies de Madagascar," *Bulletin de Madagascar* 261.

Chauvin, J. 1939. "Jean Laborde, 1805–1878," *Mémoires de l'Académie Malgache* 29 (Tananarive).

Cheffaud, M. 1931. "L'artisanat indigène à Madagascar," *Exposition coloniale internationale de Paris*.

Chelin, Antoine. 1973. *Une île et son passé: Ile Maurice, 1507–1947* (Mauritius).

Chilver, E. M. – see Harlow, V.

Chrétien, J-P. 1987. "Démographie et écologie en Afrique orientale à la fin du XIXe siècle: une crise exceptionnelle?" *Cahiers d'Études Africaines* 27.105–6.

Ciolina, F. 1947. "Café" in Marcel de Coppet (ed.), *Madagascar*, vol. I (Paris).

Clarence-Smith, W. G. 1986. "Portuguese Trade with Africa in the 19th century: An economic imperialism" in Liesegang, G., Pasch, H., & Jones, A. (eds.), *Figuring African Trade* (Berlin).

1989 (ed.). *The Economics of the Indian Ocean Slave Trade* (London).

Clendenen, Clarence – see Duignan, Peter.

Cockburn, T. Aidan. 1977. "Infectious Diseases in Ancient Populations" in David Landy (ed.), *Culture, Diseases and Healing* (New York).

Cohen, William B. 1983. "Malaria and French Imperialism," *Journal of African History* 24.1.

Coleman, D. C. 1983. "Proto-Industrialization: A Concept Too Many," *Economic History Review* 36.3.

Cooke, James J. 1973. *New French Imperialism 1880–1910: The Third Republic and Colonial Expansion* (Newton Abbot).

Cobban, Alfred. 1972. *A History of Modern France. Vol. III: France of the Republics, 1871–1962* (England).

Coppet, Marcel de (ed.). 1947. *Madagascar*, vol. II (Paris).

Coquery-Vidrovitch, Catherine. 1988. *Africa. Endurance and Change South of the Sahara* (Berkeley).

Cordell, Dennis D. 1980. with Gregory, Joel W. "Historical Demography and Demographic History in Africa: Theoretical and Methodological Considerations," *Canadian Journal of African Studies* 14.3.

　　1987. with Gregory, Joel W. and Pich, Victor. "African Historical Demography. The Search for a Theoretical Framework" in Dennis D. Cordell and Joel W. Gregory (eds.), *African Population and Capitalism* (Boulder).

Cornevin, Robert et Marianne. 1990. *La France et les Français outre-mer* (Paris).

Couland, Daniel. 1973. *Les Zafimaniry, un groupe ethnique de Madagascar à la poursuite de la forêt* (Tananarive).

Coupland, R. 1939. *Exploitation of East Africa* (London).

　　1956. *East Africa and Its Invaders* (Oxford).

Crafts, N. F. R. 1983. "British Economic Growth, 1700–1831: A Review of the Evidence," *Economic History Review* 36.2.

Crisp, Olga. 1978. "Labour and Industrialisation in Russia" in *Cambridge Economic History of Europe* 7.2 (Cambridge).

Cros, Louis. [1922]. *Madagascar pour tous* (Paris).

Crummey, Donald (ed.). 1986. *Banditry, Rebellion and Social Protest in Africa* (London).

Curtin, P. D. 1970. *The Atlantic Slave Trade: A Census* (Madison).

　　1984. et al. *African History* (London).

Dahle, L. 1876. "The influence of Arabs on the Malagasy Language," *Antananarivo Annual and Madagascar Magazine* 2.

Dahle, O. C. (ed.). 1924. *Atopazy ny Masonao* (Antananarivo).

Daruwala, Rusi J. 1986. *The Bombay Chamber Story* (Bombay).

Davidson, Basil. 1985. *Africa in Modern History* (New York).

Dawson, Marc H. 1981. "Disease and Population Decline of the Kikuyu of Kenya, 1890–1925," *African Historical Demography*, vol. II (Edinburgh).

Decary, Raymond. 1930. "Documents historiques relatifs à l'établissement française de Sainte-Marie sous la restauration," *Bulletin de l'Académie Malgache* 13.

　　1932. "La reddition de Tamatave à l'Angleterre en 1811," *Bulletin de l'Académie Malgache* 15.

　　1933. "Le voyage du lieutenant de vaisseau de Sémerville à L'île Sainte-Marie en 1824," *Bulletin de l'Académie Malgache* 16.

　　1935. "Mœurs maritimes au XVII siècle," *Bulletin de l'Académie Malgache* 18.

　　1937. *L'établissement de Sainte-Marie sous la Restauration et le rôle de Sylvain Roux* (Paris).

　　1941. with Castel, Rémy. *Études démographiques. Modalités et conséquences des migrations intérieures récentes des populations malgaches* (Tananarive).

　　1947–8. "La population de Madagascar," *Bulletin de l'Académie Malgache* 28.

　　1953. "Contribution à l'histoire de la France à Madagascar," *Bulletin de l'Académie Malgache* 31.

　　1957. "Poids et mesures d'autrefois," *Bulletin de l'Académie Malgache* 35.

　　1958. "Le voyage d'un chirurgien philosophe à Madagascar," *Bulletin de l'Académie Malgache* 36.

　　1960. *L'île Nosy Bé de Madagascar. Histoire d'une colonisation* (Paris).

　　1962. "L'ancien régime de l'or à Madagascar," *Bulletin de l'Académie Malgache* 40.

　　1966. *Coutumes guerrières et organisation militaire chez les anciens malgaches*, 2 vols. (Paris).

Deerr, Noel. 1940. with Brooks, Alexander. *Early Use of Steam Power in the Sugar Cane Industry* (London).

1949–50. *The History of Sugar*, 2 vols. (London).

Defoort, E. 1905. *Étude historique et ethnologique sur le secteur d'Ambato-Boeni (cercle de Maevatanana)* (Tananarive).

Delivré, Alain. 1974. *L'histoire des rois d'Imerina. Interprétation d'une tradition orale* (Paris).

Delmont, Jean. 1982. "Paludisme et variations climatiques saisonnières en savane soudanienne d'Afrique de l'Ouest," *Cahiers d'études africaines* 22.85–6.

Delval, Raymond. 1972. *Radama II: prince de la renaissance malgache 1861–1863* (Paris).

Deschamps, Hubert. 1949. *Les pirates à Madagascar* (Paris).

1953. *Méthodes et doctrines coloniales de la France* (Paris).

1959. *Les migrations intérieures à Madagascar* (Paris).

1972. *L'histoire de Madagascar* (Paris).

1976. "Tradition and change in Madagascar, 1790–1870," *Cambridge History of Africa*, vol. V (Cambridge).

Devred. 1947. "Les mines" in Marcel de Coppet (ed.), *Madagascar*, vol. II (Paris).

Dewey, Clive & Hopkins, A. G. (eds.). *The Imperial Impact: Studies in the Economic History of Africa and India* (London).

Dez, Jacques. 1962a. "Développement économique et tradition à Madagascar," *Cahiers de l'institut de science économique appliquée* supplément 129, série V.4.

1962b. "Considération sur les prix pratiqués à Tananarive en 1870," *Bulletin de l'Académie Malgache* 40 (1962).

1963. "Le fokonolona malgache : institution désuète ou cellule de développement?" *Cahiers de l'ISEA : économie et sociologie rurales* (avril), 189–252.

1970a. "Éléments pour une étude de l'économie agro-sylvo-pastorale de l'Imerina ancienne," *Université de Madagascar: École nationale supérieure agronomique* 8.

1970b. "Monnaie et structure traditionnelle à Madagascar," *Cahiers Vuilfredo Pareto – Revue européenne des sciences sociales.*

1970c. "Éléments pour une étude sur les prix et les échanges de biens dans l'économie mérina ancienne," *Bulletin de l'Académie Malgache* 48/1–2.

1971. "La monarchie mérina et le développement agricole," *Terre Malgache* 10.

Domenichini-Ramiaramanana, B. and Domenichini, J. P. 1980. "Questions relatives à l'esclavage en Imerina d'après les édits des souverains," paper presented at the Colloque d'Histoire, Université de Madagascar (Mantasoa).

Dubois, H. M. 1927. "Les Origines des Malgaches," *Anthropos* 22.

1938. *Monographie des Betsileo (Madagascar)* (Paris).

Dubois, Marcel et Auguste Terrier (eds.). 1902. *Les colonies françaises* (Paris).

Duffy, J. A. 1967. *Question of Slavery* (Oxford).

Duignan, Peter and Clendenen, Clarence. 1963. *The United States and the African Slave Trade, 1619–1862* (Stanford).

Durand, J. P. et J. 1978. *L'île Maurice et ses populations* (Bruxelles).

Eastman, Carol M. 1988. "Women, Slaves and Foreigners: African Cultural Influences and Group Processes in the Formation of Northern Swahili Coastal Society," *International Journal of African Historical Studies* 21.1.

Ellis, Stephen. 1985. *The Rising of the Red Shawls: A Revolt in Madagascar, 1895–1899* (Cambridge).

    1986. "The Malagasy Background II: The nineteenth century" in Finn Fuglestad & Jarle Simensen (eds.), *Norwegian Missions in African History, vol. 2: Madagascar* (Oslo).

Echalier. 1909. "Betsileo et ses habitants," *Conférence de l'école coloniale* (15 février).

Eno, Omar. 2004/5. "The Abolition of Slavery and the Aftermath Stigma: the Case of the Bantu/Jareer People on the Benadir Coast of Southern Somalia" in Gwyn Campbell (ed.), *Abolition and Its Aftermath in Indian Ocean Africa and Asia* (London).

Escande, E. 1923. *La Bible à Madagascar* (Paris).

Esoavelomandroso, F. V. 1979. "Rainilaiarivony and the Defence of Malagasy Independence at the End of the Nineteenth Century" in Raymond K. Kent (ed.), *Madagascar in History. Essays from the 1970s* (Albany, CA).

Esoavelomandroso, Manassé. 1974. *Problèmes de police et de justice dans le gouvernement de Tamatave à l'époque de Rainandriamampandry, 1882–1895* (Antananarivo).

    1979a. *La province maritime orientale du "Royaume de Madagascar" à la fin du XIXe siècle (1882–1895)* (Antananarivo).

    1979b. "La région du Fiheregna à la veille de la conquête française," *Colloque d'histoire* (Université de Madagascar).

Evers, Sandra. 1995. "Stigmatization as a Self-Perpetuating Process" in *idem* and Marc Spindler (eds.), *Cultures of Madagascar* (Leiden).

    1996. "Solidarity and Antagonism in Migrant Societies on the Southern Highlands" in François Rajaoson (ed.), *Fanandevozana ou Esclavage* (Antanarivo).

Fage, J. D. 1969. "Slavery and the slave trade in the context of West African History," *Journal of African History* 10.3.

Fagereng, M. E. 1947–8. "Histoire des Maroserana du Menabe," *Bulletin de l'Académie Malgache* 28.

Fairburn, William. 1945–55. *Merchant Sail*, vol. V (Lovell).

Faymoreau D'Arquistade, A. de. [1897?]. "Les Grandes Cultures à Madagascar" in E. Caustier, A. Milne-Edwards, De Faymoreau, L. Suberbie, G. Foucart, Lacaze, and L. Olivier (eds.), *Ce qu'il faut connaître de Madagascar* (Paris).

Feis, Herbert. 1965. *Europe, the World's Banker, 1870–1914* (New York).

Ferrand, Gabriel. 1908. "L'origine africaine des malgaches," *Journal Asiatique* 10.11.

Feugeas, Yves. 1979. *Le marché du riz pendant la période coloniale à Madagascar (1905–1940)* (Antananarivo).

Fieldhouse, D. K. 1973. *Economics and Empire 1830–1914* (London).

Filliot, J. M. 1974. *La traite des esclaves vers les Mascareignes* (Paris).

Fisher, A. G. E. and H. J. 1970. *Slavery and Muslim Society in Africa* (London).

Flint, J. E. 1966. "Chartered Companies and the Scramble for Africa" in Joseph C. Anene & Godfrey Brown (eds.), *Africa in the Nineteenth and Twentieth Centuries* (London).

Fontoynont et Nicol. 1940. *Les traitants français de la côte est de Madagascar de Ranavalona I à Radama II* (Tananarive).

Foreman-Peck, James. 1983. *A History of the World Economy* (Brighton).

Förster, Stig. 1988. with Wolfgang J. Mommsen & Ronald Robinson (eds.). *Bismarck, Europe and Africa. The Berlin Africa Conference 1884–85 and the Onset of Partition* (Oxford).

Foucart, G. [1897?]. "L'Etat du commerce à Madagascar" in E. Caustier, A. Milne-Edwards, de Faymoreau, L. Suberbie, G. Foucart, Lacaze, and L. Olivier (eds.), *Ce qu'il faut connaître de Madagascar* (Paris).

Frank, Andre Gunder. 1998. *ReORIENT: Global Economy in the Asian Age* (Berkeley, Los Angeles, & London).

Fremigacci, Jean. 1975. "Mise en valeur coloniale et travail forcé: la construction du chemin de fer Tananarive-Antsirabe (1911–1923)," *Omaly sy Anio* 1–2.

    1976. "La colonisation à Vatomandry-Mahanoro – Espérances et désillusions (1895–1910)," *Omaly sy Anio* 3–4.

    1982. "Les colons de la côte-est centrale de Madagascar, de la prospérité à la crise (1924–1939)," *Omaly sy Anio* 15.

    1985. "Les difficultés d'une politique coloniale: le café de Madagascar à la conquête du marché, français (1930–1938)," *Omaly sy Anio* 21–2.

Freund, William. 1986. "Theft and social protest among the tin miners of northern Nigeria" in Crummey, Donald (ed.), *Banditry, Rebellion and Social Protest in Africa* (London).

Fuglestad, F. & Simensen, S. (eds.). 1986. *Norwegian Missions in African History*, vol. II, *Madagascar* (Oslo).

Fuglestad, F & K. Lode. 1986. "Norwegian Missionaries in Vakinankaratra and Betsileo: The Rise and Partial Demise of a New Power Group in Malagasy Politics" in F. Fuglestad & J. Simensen (eds.), *Norwegian Missions in African History*, vol. II, *Madagascar* (Oslo).

Gallagher, J & R. E. Robinson. 1953. "The Imperialism of Free Trade," *Economic History Review* 6.

    see also Robinson, Roland.

Galloway, J. H. 1989. *The Sugar Cane Industry. An historical geography from its origins to 1914* (Cambridge).

Gautier, Émile F. 1898. "Western Madagascar: its geology and physical geography," *Antananarivo Annual and Madagascar Magazine* 22.

Gerbeau, Hubert. 1979. "Quelques aspects de la traite illégale des esclaves à l'Ile Bourbon au XIXe siècle" in *Mouvements de populations dans l'océan indien* (Paris).

Girardet, Raoul. 1972. *L'idée coloniale en France de 1871 à 1962* (Paris).

Goodrich, Lawrence C. 1883. "France and the Slave Trade in Madagascar," *The Nineteenth Century* (August).

Goody, Jack. 1974. "The evolution of the family" in Peter Laslett and Richard Wall (eds.), *Household and Family in Past Time* (Cambridge).

Gourraigne, M. L. G. 1909. "Les relations de la France avec Madagascar pendant la première moitié du XXe siècle," *Conférence de l'Ecole Coloniale* (28 janvier).

Gow, B. A. 1979. *Madagascar and the Protestant Impact* (London).

Graham, Gerald S. 1967. *Great Britain in the Indian Ocean, 1810–1850* (Oxford).

Grandidier, Alfred. 1885–1928 and 1958. with Grandidier, Guillaume. *Histoire physique, naturelle et politique de Madagascar*, vols. I-IV (Paris) and V (Tananarive 1958).

    1898. "Property among the Malagasy" (trans. James Sibree), *Antananarivo Annual and Madagascar Magazine* 22.

Graveson, Samuel. 1935. "British Inland Mail Stamps of Madagascar," *The Raconteur and Philatelist* (October).

Gray, J. R. 1966. "The Partition of East Africa" in Joseph C. Anene & Godfrey Brown (eds.), *Africa in the Nineteenth and Twentieth Centuries* (London).

Gray, R. & Birmingham, David. (eds.). 1970. *Pre-Colonial African Trade* (Oxford).

Green, M. S. 1958. *The Making of South Africa* (Cape Town).

Gregory, Joel W. & Pich, Victor. 1986. "Démographie, impérialisme et sous développement: le cas africain" in D. Gauvreau et al. (eds.), *Démographie et sous-développement dans le Tiers-Monde* (McGill University).

  see also Cordell.

Griffith, Robert. 1919. *Madagascar. Century of Adventure* (London).

Guest, Bill & Sellers, John M. (eds.). 1985. *Enterprise and Exploitation in a Victorian Economy. Aspects of the Economic and Social History of Colonial Natal* (Pietermaritzburg).

Guillain. 1845. M *Documents sur l'histoire, la géographie et le commerce de la partie occidentale de Madagascar*, 2 vols. (Paris).

Hagan, Jim, Castle, Robe, & Wells, Andrew 2001. "'Unfree' Labour on the Cattle Stations of Northern Australia, the Tea Gardens of Assam, and the Rubber Plantations of Indo-China, 1920–1950," paper presented at the international conference on "Unfree Labour, Brigandry and Revolt in the Indian Ocean and Asia," Avignon.

Hallett, Robin. 1975. *Africa since 1875*, vol. 2 (London).

Hardy, Georges. 1943. *Histoire de la colonisation française* (Paris).

  1966. "The Scramble: Preconditions and postconditions in Africa" in Raymond F. Betts (ed.), *The "Scramble" for Africa. Causes and Dimensions of Empire* (Lexington, MA).

Hargreaves, John D. 1966. *Prelude to the Partition of West Africa* (London).

Harlow, V. and Chilver, E. M. (eds.). 1965. *History of East Africa* (Oxford).

Harries, Patrick. 1981. "Slavery, incorporation and surplus extraction; the nature of free and unfree labour in South-East Africa," *Journal of African History* 22.

  1994. *Work, Culture, and Identity. Migrant Laborers in Mozambique and South Africa, c.1860–1910* (Portsmouth, NH, Johannesburg, & London).

  2000. "Culture and Classification: A History of the Mozbieker Community at the Cape," *Social Dynamics* 26.2, 29–54.

Hervey. 1785. *Hervey's New System of Geography* I (London).

Heseltine, Nigel. 1971. *Madagascar* (London).

Hewlett, A. M. 1887. "Mantasoa and its Workshops; a page in the History of Industrial Progress in Madagascar," *Antananarivo Annual and Madagascar Magazine* 11.

Heydenrych, Hein. 1985. "Railway Development in Natal to 1895" in Bill Guest & John M. Sellers (eds.), *Enterprise and Exploitation in a Victorian Economy. Aspects of the Economic and Social History of Colonial Natal* (Pietermaritzburg).

Hieke, Ernst. 1939. *Zur Geschichte des deutschen Handels mit Ostafrika 1: 1831–1870* (Hamburg).

Hobsbawn, E. J. 1970. *Industry and Empire* (UK).

  1987. *The Age of Empire 1875–1914* (London).

Hogendorn, Jan & Johnson, Marion. 1986. "The Cowrie Trade to West Africa from the Maldives in the 19th century" in Liesegang, G., Pasch, H., & Jones, A. (eds.), *Figuring African Trade* (Berlin).

  1986. *The Shell Money of the Slave Trade* (Cambridge).

Hopkins, A. G. 1977. *An Economic History of West Africa* (London).

see also Cain, P. J. and Dewey, C.

Houlder, J. A. 1930. *Ohabolana or Malagasy Proverbs* II (Antananarivo).

Howe, Sonia. 1936. *L'Europe et Madagascar* (Paris).

Hunt, Nancy Rose. 1988. "'La Bebe En Brousse': European Women, African Birth Spacing and Colonial Intervention in Breast Feeding in the Belgium Congo," *International Journal of African Historical Studies* 21.3.

Hurd, Archibald. 1921. *The Sea Traders* (London).

Hynes, William G. 1979. *The Economics of Empire. Britain, Africa and the New Imperialism 1870–95* (UK).

Iliffe, John. 1989. "The Origins of African Population Growth," *Journal of African History* 30.1.

Immelman, R. F. M. 1955. *Men of Good Hope, 1804–1954: The Romantic Story of the Cape Town Chamber of Commerce* (Cape Town).

Inikori, J. E. 1981. "Under-Population in nineteenth century West Africa: the role of the export slave trade," *African Historical Demography*, vol. II (Edinburgh).

Isaacman, Allen. 1972. *Mozambique. The Africanisation of a European Institution. The Zambesi Prazas, 1750–1902* (University of Wisconsin).

1976. *The Tradition of Resistance in Mozambique* (London).

Jackson, Mable V. 1967. *European Powers and Southeast Africa, 1796–1856* (London).

Jacob, Guy. 1977. "Influences occidentales en Imerina et déséquilibres économiques avant la conquête française," *Omaly sy Anio* 5–6.

1989. "La révolution industrielle et l'Imerina au XIXe siècle ou l'impossible transfert," *Colloque International d'histoire Malgache* (Antananarivo, 31 juillet – 5 août).

Jeannin, Pierre. 1980. "La proto-industrialisation: développement ou impasse? (Note critique)," *Annales – économies – sociétés – civilisations* 35.1.

Jeeves, Alan H. 1985. *Migrant Labour in South Africa's Mining Economy. The Struggle for the Gold Mines' Labour Supply* (Kingston and Montreal).

Jenkins, T. – see Nurse.

Johnson, H. T. 1900. "Betsileo, Past and Present, a twenty years' review," *Antananarivo Annual and Madagascar Magazine* 24.

Johnson, M. 1978. "Technology, Competition and African Crafts," in C. Dewey and A. G. Hopkins (eds.), *The Imperial Impact: Studies in the Economic History of Africa and India* (London).

Jones, A. (see Liesegang, G.)

Jones, Richard – see McEvedy

Jordaan, Bee. 1969. *Splintered Crucifix. Early Pioneers for Christendom on Madagascar and the Cape of Good Hope* (Cape Town).

Jumelle, H. 1900. *Le cacaoyer, sa culture et son exploitation dans tous les pays de production* (Paris).

Kalinga, Owen. 1980. "The Karonga War: Commercial Rivalry and the Politics of Survival," *Journal of African History* 21.

Kanya-Forstner, A. S. 1972. "French expansion in Africa: the mythical theory" in Roger Owen & Bob Sutcliffe (eds.), *Studies in the Theory of Imperialism* (London).

see also Andrew, C. M.

Katzenellenbogen, Simon. 1975. "British businessmen and German Africa, 1885–1919" in Barrie M. Ratcliffe (ed.), Great *Britain and Her World 1750–1914; Essays in honour of W O Henderson* (Manchester).

Kea, Ray A. 1986. "'I am here to plunder on the general road': Bandits and banditry in the pre-nineteenth century Gold Coast" in Donald Crummey (ed.), *Banditry, Rebellion and Social Protest in Africa* (London).

Keale, B. B. [1924/5]. *Coffee from Grower to Consumer* (London).

Kellenbenz, Hermann. 1981. "Zanzibar et Madagascar dans le commerce allemand, 1840–1880," *Colloque d'histoire de Madagascar* (Université de Madagascar, Mahajanga).

Keller, C. 1901. *Madagascar, Mauritius and the Other East African Islands* (London).

Kent, Raymond K. 1969. "How France acquired Madagascar," *Tarikh* 2.4.

    1970. *Early Kingdoms in Madagascar, 1500–1700* (New York).

    1979. ed. *Madagascar in History. Essays from the 1970s* (Berkeley).

Kenwood, A. G. & Lougheed, A. L. 1992. *The Growth of the International Economy 1820–1990* (London).

Kim, Bok-Rae. 2004. "'Nobi,' a Korean Slave System" in Gwyn Campbell (ed.), *The Structure of Slavery in Indian Ocean Africa and Asia* (London).

Kitching, Gavin. 1983. "Proto-industrialisation and Demographic Change: a Thesis and some possible African Implications," *Journal of African History* 24.2.

Kjekshus, Helge. 1977. *Ecology Control and Economic Development in East African History* (London).

    1978. "The Population Trends of East African History: A Critical Review," *African Historical Demography*, vol. I (Edinburgh).

Klein, Martin A. 1987. "The Demography of Slavery in Western Soudan. The Late Nineteenth Century" in Cordell & Gregory (eds.), *African Population and Capitalism*.

    1993. (ed.), *Breaking the Chains. Slavery, Bondage and Emancipation in Modern Africa and Asia* (Madison, Wisconsin).

Koponen, Juhani. 1988. "War, Famine and Pestilence in Late Precolonial Tanzania: A Case for a Heightened Mortality," *International Journal of African Historical Studies* 21.4.

Kriedte, Peter, Medick, Hans, and Schlumbohm, Jurgen. 1981. *Industrialization Before Industrialization* (Cambridge).

Labrousse, Ernest (see Braudel, Fernand).

Lacroix, Louis. [1939]. *Les derniers négriers* (Paris).

Larson, Pier. 2000. *History and Memory in the Age of Enslavement* (Portsmouth).

Lebon, André. 1901. *La Politique de la France en Afrique, 1896–1898* (Paris).

Lefevre, Daniel. 1975. *Saint-Pierre de la Réunion* (Réunion).

Lenin, V. I. 1970. *Imperialism, the Highest Stage of* Capitalism (Moscow).

Letcher, Owen. 1936. *The Gold Mines of Southern Africa* (Johannesburg).

Lewis, W. A. 1978. *Growth and Fluctuations 1870–1914* (London).

Liesegang, G. Pasch, H. & Jones, A. (eds.). 1986. *Figuring African Trade* (Berlin).

Liesegang, Gerhard. 1986. "A First Look at the Import and Export Trade of Mozambique, 1800–1914" in *idem*, H. Pasch and A. Jones (eds.), *Figuring African Trade* (Berlin).

Lindsay. 1888. "How to Fight the Slave Trade in East Africa," *Anti-Slavery Reporter* (July and August).

Lloyd, Christopher. 1968. *The Navy and the Slave Trade* (London).

Lode, K. – see Fuglestad.

Lombard, Jacques. 1973. *La royauté Sakalava: Formation, développement et effondrement du XVIIe au XXe siècle* (Tananarive).

Lopez, R. S. 1971. *The Commercial Revolution of the Middle Ages, 950–1350* (New Jersey).

Lougnon, Albert. 1940. "Vaisseaux et traites aux îles depuis 1741 jusqu'à 1746," *Recueil de documents et travaux inédits pour servir à l'histoire de la Réunion* 5.

1956. *L'Ile Bourbon pendant la Régence – Desforges Boucher. Les Débuts du Café* (Nevac).

Louis, William. 1967. "Great Britain and German Expansion in Africa, 1884–1919" in P. Gifford & William Louis (eds.), *Britain and Germany in Africa* (New Haven).

Lovejoy, Paul E. 1983. *Transformations in Slavery. A History of Slavery in Africa* (Cambridge).

Lovett, Richard. 1899. *History of the London Missionary Society*, 2 vols. (London).

Lyons, Maryinez. 1985. "'From Death Camps to Cordon Sanitaire': The Development of Sleeping Sickness Policy in the Uele District of the Belgian Congo, 1903–1914," *Journal of African History* 26.1.

McClellan, Charles W. 1980. "Land, Labor, and Coffee: The South's Role in Ethiopian Self-Reliance, 1889–1935," *African Economic History* 9.

McEvedy, Colin & Jones, Richard. 1978. *Atlas of World Population History* (London).

McNeill, William H. 1976. *Plagues and People* (New York).

Machado, Pedro. 2004. "A Forgotten Corner of the Indian Ocean: Gujarati Merchants, Portuguese India and the Mozambique Slave Trade, c.1730–1830" in Gwyn Campbell, *The Structure of Slavery in Indian Ocean Africa and Asia*, (London).

Mack, John. 1989. *Malagasy Textiles* (Aylesbury).

Mackenzie, J. M. 1983. *The Partition of Africa 1880–1900* (London).

Maestri, Edmond. 1989. "Naissance et premiers développements d'un outil économique: le chemin de fer de la Réunion" in Claude Wanquet (ed.), *Fragments pour une histoire des économies et sociétés de plantation à la Réunion* (St. Denis).

Manning, Patrick. 1981. "A Demographic Model of African Slavery," *African Historical Demography*, vol. II (Edinburgh).

1983. "Contours of Slavery and Social Change in Africa," *American Historical Review* 88.4.

Mannix, Daniel P. 1962. *Black Cargoes. A History of the Atlantic Slave Trade, 1518–1865* (New York).

Mantaux, Christian G. 1971. "Journal de Berube-Dudemene Capitaine du Bougainville à Madagascar en 1774," *Bulletin de l'Académie Malgache* 49 II.

Marcuse, Walter. 1914. *Through Western Madagascar in Search of the Golden Bean* (London).

Marseille, Jacques. 1984. *Empire colonial et capitalisme français* (Paris).

1985. "The Phases of French Colonial Imperialism: Towards a New Periodization," *Journal of Imperial and Commonwealth History* 13.3.

Martin, Phyllis M. – see Birmingham.

Martineau, A. n.d. *Madagascar en 1894* (Paris).

Maude, Francis Cornwallis. 1895. *Five Years in Madagascar* (London).

Mendels, Franklin F. 1972. "Proto-industrialization. The First Phase of the Industrialization Process," *Journal of Economic History* 32.1.

Michel, Louis. 1957. *Mœurs et coutumes des Bara* (Tananarive).

Miller, Joseph C. 1982. "The Significance of Drought, Disease and Famine in the agriculturally marginal zones of West-Central Africa," *Journal of African History* 23.1.

1984. "Demographic History Revisited," *Journal of African History* 25.

Mirzai, Behnaz. 2004. "The 1848 Abolitionist *Farmān*: a Step Towards Ending the Slave Trade in Iran" in Gwyn Campbell (ed.), *Abolition and Its Aftermath in Indian Ocean Africa and Asia* (London).

Modelski, George and Thompson, William R. 1996. *Leading Sectors and World Powers. The Coevolution of Global Economics and Politics* (Columbia).

Molet, Louis. 1953. "Le bœuf dans l'Ankaizinana: son importance sociale et économique," *Mémoire de l'institut scientifique de Madagascar* série C, T.II.

1955. 'Présence d'éléments Makoa à Sainte-Marie de Madagascar,' *Bulletin de l'Académie Malgache* 33.

1962. "Les monnaies à Madagascar," *Cahiers de l'institut de science économique appliquée* supplt.129.V.

Mollet, Michel. 1971. "Les relations de l'Afrique de l'est avec l'Asie: essaie de position de quelques problèmes historiques," *Cahiers d'historique mondial* 13.2.

Mommsen, Wolfgang J. – see Förster, Stig.

Mondain, G. 1905–6. "Notes sur la condition sociale de la femme hova," *Bulletin de l'Académie Malgache* 4.

also see Chapus.

Mourba, Suresh. n.d. *Misère noire: ou réflexions sur l'histoire de l'île Maurice* (Mauritius).

Munro, J. Forbes. 1976. *Africa and the International Economy 1800–1960* (London).

1984. *Britain in Tropical Africa 1880–1960. Economic Relationships and Impact* (London).

Munthe, Ludvig. 1969. *La bible à Madagascar. Les deux premières traductions du Nouveau Testament Malgache* (Oslo).

1976. with Ravoajanahary, Charles et Ayache, Simon. "Radama I et les Anglais. Les négociations de 1817 d'après les sources malgaches ('sorabes') inédits," *Omaly sy Anio* 3–4.

1977. 'La tradition Arabico-Malgache' *CRASOM* 37. 2.

Murphy, Agnes. 1948. *The Ideology of French Imperialism, 1871–1881* (Washington, DC).

Mutibwa, P. M. 1974. *The Malagasy and the Europeans* (London).

Neill, Stephen. 1975. *A History of Christian Missions* (England).

Nèple. 1899. *Guide de l'Immigrant à Madagascar*, vol. II (Paris).

Newbury, Colin W. 1968. "The Protectionist Revival in French Colonial Trade: The Case of Senegal," *Economic History Review* 2.

Newitt, M. D. D. 1972. "Angoche, the Slave Trade and the Portuguese, c.1844–1912," *Journal of African History* 13.4.

1973. *Portuguese Settlement on the Zambesi* (London).

Nicol – see Fontoynont.

Nicolas, Louis. 1949. *Histoire de la Marine Française* (Paris).

Nightingale, P. 1985. "The Evolution of Weight Standards and the Creation of New Monetary and Commercial Links in Northern Europe from the Tenth to the Twelfth Century," *Economic History Review* 38.

Noel, Vincent. 1843. "Ile de Madagascar: Recherches sur les Sakalava," *Bulletin de la société de géographie*.

Norby. 1967. "Norwegian 'local' stamps – on Madagascar," *The Posthorn* 24.3 (July).

North-Coombes. 1971. *The Island of Rodrigues* (Mauritius).

Nurse, G. T., Weiner, J. S., & Jenkins, T. 1985. *The Peoples of Southern Africa and Their Affinities* (Oxford).

Nutting, Anthony. 1970. *Scramble for Africa* (London).

Oliver, Roland & Mathew, Gervase (eds.) 1963. *History of East Africa* I (Oxford).

Oliver, Samuel Pasfield. 1866. *Madagascar and the Malagasy* (London).

    1886. *Madagascar. An Historical and Descriptive Account of the Island and Its Former Dependencies*, 2 vols. (London).

    1888. "General Hall and the export slave trade from Madagascar. A Statement and a Vindication," *Antananarivo Annual and Madagascar Magazine* 12.

    1890. (ed.) *Madagascar* (London).

    1891. "Sir Robert Townsend Farquhar and the Malagasy Slave Trade," *Antananarivo Annual and Madagascar Magazine* 15.

Ottino, Paul. 1963. *Les économies paysannes malgaches du Bas-Mangoky* (Paris).

    1974. *Madagascar, les comores, et le sud-ouest de l'Océan Indien* (Tananarive).

Owen, Roger. 1972. *The Middle East in the World Economy 1800–1914* (London).

    1981. with Bob Sutcliffe (eds.). *Studies in the Theory of Imperialism* (London).

Ozoux, Léon. 1926. *Vieux principes d'économie rurale malgache* (Paris).

Paillard, Yvan-Georges. 1987. "Les recherches démographiques sur Madagascar au début de l'époque coloniale et les documents de "l'AMI"," *Cahiers d'Études Africaines* 27.

Pankhurst, Richard. 1968. *Economic History of Ethiopia, 1800–1935* (Addis Ababa). ˙

Parkinson, C. Northcote. 1937. *Trade in the Eastern Seas, 1793–1813* (Cambridge).

Pasch, H. – see Liesegang, G.

Utsa Patnaik and Manjari Dingwaney (eds.). 1985. *Chains of Servitude, Bondage and Slavery in India* (Hyderabad).

Peill, J. 1909. "Historical sketch in memorial to W. W. Wilson" in Crosfield, *Man in Shining Armour*.

Pélissier, René. 1984. *Naissance de Mozambique*, vol. I (Orgeval).

Peltier, Louis. 1903. "La traite à Madagascar au XVIIe siècle," *Revue de Madagascar*.

Phillips, Rod. 2000. *A Short History of Wine* (London).

Piché, Victor – see Cordell and Gregory.

Piolet, J. B. 1896. *De l'esclavage à Madagascar* (Paris).

Polyansky, F. n.d. *An Economic History. The Age of Imperialism 1870–1917* (Moscow).

Pool, D. Ian. 1978. "A Framework for the analysis of West African Historical Demography," *African Historical Demography*, vol. I (Edinburgh).

Porter, Andrew. 1986. *Victorian Shipping, Business and Imperial Policy. Donald Currie, the Castle Line and Southern Africa* (Woodbridge & New York).

Porter, Bernard. 1975. *The Lion's Share. A Short History of British Imperialism 1850–1970* (London).

    1983. *Britain, Europe and the World 1850–1982: Delusions of Grandeur* (London).

Power, Thomas F. 1944. *Jules Ferry and the Renaissance of French Imperialism* (New York).

Profita, Pietro. 1975. "Présence des originaires malgaches dans la population générale de Maurice," *Bulletin de l'Académie Malgache* 53, 1–2.

Price, Roger. 1981. *An Economic History of Modern France, 1730–1914* (London).

Prud'homme. 1900a. "Considérations sur les Sakalaves," *Notes reconnaissances et explorations* 6.

1900b. "Observations on the Sakalava," *Antananarivo Annual and Madagascar Magazine* 24.

1931. "Contribution à l'histoire de l'Imerina" in "Notes d'histoire malgache," *Bulletin de l'Académie Malgache* 14 (1931).

Prunières, André. 1934. *Madagascar et la crise* (Paris).

Quin, P. J. 1959. *Foods and Feeding Habits of the Pedi* (Johannesburg).

Rabary. 1930. *Ny Daty Malaza*, vol. I (Tananarive).

Rahamefy, Henri. 1954. "L'Église du Palais à Madagascar," *Le monde non-chrétienne* 32.

Raharijaona and Raveloson. 1954. "Andriamazanoro, prince Antaimoro de Vohipeno," *Bulletin de l'Académie Malgache* 32.

Raison, J. P. 1977. "Perception et réalisation de l'espace dans la société merina," *Annales, économies, sociétés, civilisations* 32.

Raison-Jourde, Françoise. n.d. "Un tournant dans l'histoire religieuse Merina du XIXe siècle: La fondation des temples protestants à Tananarive entre 1861 et 1869," *Annales de l'Université de Madagascar. Série lettres et sciences humaines* 11.

1976a. "L'échange inégal de la langue. La pénétration des techniques linguistiques au sein d'une civilisation de l'oral (Imerina, début du XIXe siècle)," *Revues annales ESC* (février).

1976b. "Les Ramanenjana. Une mise en cause populaire du christianisme en Imerina, 1863," *ASEMI* 7/2–3.

1983. "Introduction" in *idem* (ed.), *Les souverains de Madagascar* (Paris).

1991. *Bible et pouvoir à Madagascar au XIXe siècle* (Paris).

Rajaoson, François (ed.). 1996. *Fanandevozana ou Esclavage* (Antanarivo).

Ralaikoa, Albert. 1987. *Fiscalité, administration et pression coloniales dans le sud Betsileo (1895–1918)* (Antananarivo).

Ralinoro. 1954. "Le problème démographique dans la circonscription médicale de Fianarantsoa," *Bulletin de Madagascar* 99.

Raminadrasoa, F. and Ratsivalaka, Gilbert. 1979. "De l'usage du concept 'ethnie' dans l'historiographie de Madagascar. L'exemple des Bezanozano au XVIIIe siècle," *Colloque d'histoire, Université de Madagascar* (Toliara).

Randrianarisoa, Pierre. n.d. *La Diplomatie malgache face à la politique des grandes puissances (1882–1895)* (Antananarivo).

Ransome, L. H. 1890. "The river Antanamalana," *Antananarivo Annual and Madagascar Magazine* 14.

Rantoandro, Gabriel. 1981. "Une communauté mercantile du nord-ouest: Les Antalaotra," *Colloque d'histoire de l'Université de Madagascar* (Mahajanga).

Rasoamiaramanana, Micheline. 1983. *Aspects économiques et sociaux de la vie à Majunga entre 1862 et 1881* (Antananarivo).

Ratsivalaka, Gilbert – see Raminadrasoa, F.

Ravoajanahary, Charles – see Munthe, Ludvig.

Razafintsalama, Adolphe. 1983. "Les funérailles royales en Isandra d'après les sources du XIXe siècle" in Françoise Raison-Jourde (ed.), *Les souverains de Madagascar* (Paris).

Razi, G. M. 1977. "Sources d'histoire malgache aux Etats-Unis, 1792–1882," Communication présentée le 6 septembre au Colloque des Historiens et Juristes lors du 75ème anniversaire de l'Académie malgache (6 septembre).

Rennemo, O. 1986. "The Menalamba Uprising in the Norwegian Mission Districts" in Finn Fuglestad & Jarle Simensen (eds.), *Norwegian Missions in African History vol. 2: Madagascar* (Oslo).

Rey, Claude. 1965. "A propos d'une lettre de Jean Laborde," *ORSTOM* 25.

Rice, C. Duncan. 1975. *The Rise and Fall of Black Slavery* (London).

Richardson, J. 1876a. "Tanala Customs, Superstitions and Beliefs," *Antananarivo Annual and Madagascar Magazine* 2.

　1876b. "Dr Mullens and the Population of Antananarivo," *Antananarivo Annual and Madagascar Magazine* 2.

　1877. *Lights and Shadows* (Antananarivo).

Richardson, Peter. 1985. "The Natal Sugar Industry, 1849–1905" in Guest & Sellers (eds.), *Enterprise and Exploitation in a Victorian Economy. Aspects of the Economic and Social History of Colonial Natal* (Pietermaritzburg).

Robequain, Charles. 1949. "Une capitale montagnarde en pays tropical: Tananarive," *Revue de géographie alpine* 37.2.

　1958. *Madagascar et les bases dispersées de l'union française* (Paris).

Roberts, Stephen H. 1929. *History of French Colonial Policy (1870–1925)*, vol. II (London).

Robinson, Ronald. 1965. with Gallagher, John. *Africa and the Victorians* (London).

　1966. "The Scramble: Effect of British Egyptian Policy" in Raymond F. Betts (ed.), *The "Scramble for Africa." Causes and Dimensions of Empire* (Lexington, MA).

　1972. "Non-European foundations of European imperialism: sketch for a theory of collaboration" in Roger Owen & Bob Sutcliffe (eds.), *Studies in the Theory of Imperialism* (London).

　see also Förster, Stig; Gallagher, J.

Ross, Robert. 1978. "Smallpox at the Cape of Good Hope in the Eighteenth Century," *African Historical Demography*, vol. I (Edinburgh).

Rusillon, Henri. 1926. *Le Boina* (Paris).

Ruud, Jorgen. 1960. *Taboo. A Study of Malagasy Customs and Beliefs* (Oslo).

Sahlins, Marshall. 1974. *Stone Age Economics* (London).

Saint-Ours, Jaques de. 1955. "Étude des feuilles Tsaratanana et Marovato," *Bulletin de Madagascar* 107.

Sanderson, G. N. 1974. "The European Partition of Africa: Coincidence or Conjecture?" *Journal of Imperial and Commonwealth History* 3.1.

　1988. "British Informal Empire, Imperial Ambitions, Defensive Strategies, and the Anglo-Portuguese Congo Treaty of February 1884" in Stig Förster, Wolfgang J. Mommsen, & Ronald Robinson (eds.), *Bismarck, Europe, and Africa. The Berlin Africa Conference 1884–85 and the Onset of Partition* (Oxford).

Savaron, C. 1931. "notes d'histoire malgache," *Bulletin de l'Académie Malgache* 14.

Scarborough, E. & Fuglestad, F. 1986. "A Note on the History of Education in Vakinankaratra and Neighbouring Regions, 1870–1907" in Finn Fuglestad & Jarle Simensen (eds.), *Norwegian Missions in African History vol. 2: Madagascar* (Oslo).

Scherer, André. 1966. *Histoire de la Réunion* (Paris).

Schlemmer, Bernard. 1983. *Le Menabe, histoire d'une colonisation* (Paris).

Schmidt, Martin E. 1972. "Prelude to Intervention: Madagascar and the Failure of Anglo-French Diplomacy, 1890–1895," *Historical Journal* 15.4.

Sédillot, René. 1958. *Histoire des colonisations* (Paris).

Segre, Dan. 1969. "Madagascar: An Example of Indigenous Modernisation of a Traditional Society in the Nineteenth Century," *St. Antony's Papers* 21.

Sellers, John M. (see Guest, Bill).

Shannon, Richard. 1976. *The Crisis of Imperialism 1865–1915* (UK).

Shaw, George. 1877. "The Betsileo: Country and People," *Antananarivo Annual and Madagascar Magazine* 3.

   1883. "The Future Prospects of Madagascar," *Contemporary Review* (January).

   1885. A *Madagascar and France* (London).

Shaw, Thurstan. 1978. "Questions in the Holocene Demography of West Africa," *African Historical Demography*, vol. I (Edinburgh).

   1981. "Towards a Prehistoric Demography of Africa," *African Historical Demography* II (Edinburgh).

Shepherd, Gill. 1980. "The Comorians and the east African Slave Trade" in James L. Watson (ed.), *Asian and African Systems of Slavery* (Oxford).

Sheriff, Abdul. 1986. "Ivory and Commercial Expansion in East Africa in the Nineteenth Century" in G. Liesegang, H. Pasch, & A. Jones (eds.), *Figuring African Trade* (Berlin).

   1987. *Slaves, Spices and Ivory in Zanzibar* (London).

   1989. "Localisation and Social Composition of the East African Slave Trade, 1858–1873" in William Gervase Clarence-Smith (ed.), *The Economics of the Indian Ocean Slave Trade in the Nineteenth Century* (London).

   2004/5. "The Slave Trade and its Fallout in the Persian Gulf" in Gwyn Campbell (ed.), *Abolition and Its Aftermath in Indian Ocean Africa and Asia* (London).

Sibree, James. 1870. *Madagascar and Its People. Notes of a Four Years' Residence* (London).

   1880. "The Arts and Commerce of Madagascar, its recent progress and its future prospects" *Journal of the Society of Arts* (4 June).

   1883. "England, France and Madagascar," *Contemporary Review* (January).

   1898. "Industrial Progress in Madagascar," *Antananarivo Annual and Madagascar Magazine* 22.

   1915. *A Naturalist in Madagascar* (London).

   1924. *Fifty Years in Madagascar* (London).

Slawecki, Leon M. S. 1971. *French Policy Towards the Chinese in Madagascar*.

SPG. 1893. *SPG Records 1701–1892* (London).

Spillmann, Georges. 1974. "L'anticolonialisme en France du XVIIe siècle à nos jours," *L'Afrique et l'Asie* 101.

Stengers, Jean. 1966. "The Scramble: Effect of French African Activity" in Raymond F. Betts (ed.), *The "Scramble" for Africa. Causes and Dimensions of Empire* (Lexington, MA).

   1969. "The Beginning of the Scramble for Africa," in Robert O. Collins (ed.), *The Partition of Africa. Illusion or Necessity* (New York).

Stone, Orra L. 1930. *History of Massachusetts Industries* I (Boston-Chicago).

Sundström, Lars. 1974. *The Exchange Economy of Pre-Colonial Tropical Africa* (London).

Swindell, Kenneth. 1981. "Domestic Production, labour mobility and population change in West Africa, 1900–1980," *African Historical Demography*, vol. II (Edinburgh).

Terrier, Auguste (see Dubois, Marcel).

Theal, George. 1964. *Records of South-Eastern Africa* 9 (Cape Town).

Thompson, Alvin. 1974. "The role of firearms and the development of military techniques in Merina warfare c.1785–1828," *Revue française d'histoire d'outre-mer* 61.224.

Thorel, Jean. 1927. *La mise en valeur des richesses économiques de Madagascar* (Paris).

Thornton, John. 1980. "The Slave Trade in Eighteenth Century Angola: Effects on Demographic Structure," *Canadian Journal of African Studies* 14.3.

   1981. "The Demographic Effect of the Slave Trade on Western Africa, 1500–1850," *African Historical Demography*, vol. II (Edinburgh, 1981).

Thureau. 1856. "Des intérêts français à Madagascar," *Chronique de la Quinzaine*.

Toussaint, Auguste. 1966. "Le trafic commercial entre les Mascareignes et Madagascar de 1773 à 1810," *Annales de l'Université de Madagascar*.

   1967. *La route des îles – contribution à l'histoire maritime des Mascareignes* (Paris).

   1971. *Histoire de l'île Maurice* (Paris).

   1972. *Histoire des îles Mascareignes* (Paris).

   1975. "Les Lyonnais à l'île de France (île Maurice) 1721–1810," *Cahiers d'Histoire* 20.

   see also Barnwell.

Vail, Leroy and White, Landeg. 1980. *Capitalism and Colonialism in Mozambique* (London).

Valette, Jean. 1961. "Quelques renseignements sur Madagascar en 1843," *Bulletin de Madagascar* 183.

   1962. *Etudes sur le règne de Radama I* (Tananarive).

   1963. (ed.) "L'Imerina en 1822–1825 d'après les journaux de Bojer et d'Hilsenburg," extrait du *Bulletin de Madagascar* (avril-mai).

   1966a. (ed.) *Le préfet Legèr à Madagascar* (Tananarive).

   1966b. "Un mémoire de Rondeaux sur Madagascar (1809)," *Bulletin de l'Académie Malgache* 44.II.

   1966c. "Un plan de développement de Madagascar. Le projet Bergsten" (1825), *Bulletin de l'Académie Malgache* 44.II.

   1966d. "Notes sur la géographie médicale de l'Imerina à la fin de la monarchie (1889–1893),' *Bulletin de Madagascar* 246.

   1967. (ed.) "Correspondance de Jean René et Sir Robert Farquhar," *Bulletin de l'Académie Malgache* 45.

   1968a. "Documents pour servir à l'étude des relations entre Froberville et Mayeur," *Bulletin de l'Académie Malgache* 16/I–II.

   1968b. "Deux documents français sur Madagascar en 1825; les rapports Duhaut Cilly et Frère," *Bulletin de l'Académie Malgache* 16/I–II.

   1970. "Rainandriamampandry, historien de Jean René," *Bulletin de l'Académie Malgache* 48/I–II.

   1972. "Nouvelle note pour servir à l'étude des exportations de bœufs de Fort Dauphin à Bourbon (1820)," *Bulletin de l'Académie Malgache* 50 II.

1979. "Radama I, the Unification of Madagascar and the Modernisation of Imerina (1810–1828)" in Raymond K. Kent (ed.), *Madagascar in History. Essays from the 1970s* (Berkeley).

Van Helten, Jean Jacques. 1985. "'La France et l'or des Boers." Some aspects of French investment in South Africa between 1890 and 1914," *African Affairs* 84.335.

Vandenbroeke, Christian. 1987. "The Regional Economy of Flanders and Industrial Modernization in the Eighteenth Century: a Discussion," *Journal of European Economic History* 16.1.

Vansina, J. 1981. "Long-Term Population History in the African Rain Forest," *African Historical Demography*, vol. II (Edinburgh).

Vérin, Pierre. 1990. *Madagascar* (Paris).

Vidal, E. 1845. *Madagascar. Situation actuelle* (Bordeaux).

Vidler, Alec R. 1978. *The Church in an Age of Revolution* (London).

Voas, David. 1981. "Subfertility and Disruption in the Congo Basin," *African Historical Demography*, vol. II (Edinburgh).

Von Wissman. 1891. "From the Congo to the Zambesi," *Anti-Slavery Reporter* (November and Decemebr).

Walvin, James. 1983. *Slavery and the Slave Trade* (London).

Wanquet, Claude. 1989. *Fragments pour une histoire des économies et sociétés de plantation à la Réunion* (Réunion).

Watson, James (ed.). 1980a. *Asian and African Systems of Slavery* (Oxford).

　1980b. "Introduction. Slavery as an Institution, Open and Closed Systems" in *idem* (ed.), *Asian and African Systems of Slavery*.

　1980c. "Transactions in People: The Chinese Market in Slaves, Servants, and Heirs" in *idem* (ed.), *Asian and African Systems of Slavery*.

Weber, Jacques. 1987. "Les relations commerciales entre les établissements français de l'Inde et 'île de la Réunion dans la première moitié du XIXe siècle, au temps de l'exclusif" in *Les relations historiques et culturelles entre la France et l'Inde XVIIe-Xxe siècles* vol. 2 (Sainte Clotilde).

Webster's *New International Dictionary* (1928).

Weiner, J. S. – see Nurse.

White, Landeg – see Vail.

Williamson, James. 1946. *Great Britain and the Empire* (London).

Willis, R. G. 1978. "Comment on Dr. Kjekshus' paper," *African Historical Demography*, vol. I (Edinburgh).

Wilson, Francis. 1971. "Farming, 1866–1966" in Monica Wilson & Leonard Thompson (eds.), *Oxford History of South Africa*, vol. II (Oxford).

　1972. *Migrant Labour in South Africa* (Johannesburg).

Wink, André. 1996, 1997. *Al-Hind. The Making of the Indo-Islamic World*, 2 vols. (Leiden, New York, Köln.)

Wolf. 1833. "Analysis" of *Narrative of Voyages to Explore the Shores of Africa, Arabia, and Madagascar*, *Journal of the Royal Geographical Society* 3.

Wolfe, Martin (ed.). 1972. *The Economic Causes of Imperialism* (New York).

Woodruff, William. 1958. *The Rise of the British Rubber Industry during the Nineteenth Century* (Liverpool).

Worden, Nigel. 2003/4. "Indian Ocean Slavery and its Demise in the Cape Colony" in Gwyn Campbell (ed.), *Abolition and its Aftermath in Indian Ocean Africa and Asia* (London).

Wrigley, Christopher. 1981. "Population and History: Some Innumerate Reflexions," *African Historical Demography*, vol. II (Edinburgh).

Theses

Andriamarintsoa. 1973. "Le gouvernement de Tamatave de 1845 à 1865; développement économique," Université de Madagascar.
Campbell, Gwyn. 1985. "The Role of the London Missionary Society in the Rise of the Merina Empire, 1810–1861," Ph.D., University of Wales.
Evers, Karl. 1986. "Das Hamburger Zanzibarhandelshaus Wm. O'Swald & Co. 1847–1890. Zur Geschichte des Hamburger Handels mit Ostafrika," Ph.D., University of Hamburg.
Fernyhough, Timothy Derek. 1986. "Serfs, Slaves and Shefta: Modes of Production in Southern Ethiopia from the late nineteenth century to 1941," Ph.D., University of Illinois Urbana-Champaign.
Hafkin, N. 1973. "Trade, Society and Politics in Northern Mozambique c.1753–1913," Ph.D., Boston University.
Raminosoa, Beby Soa Saholy. 1987–8. "La Maison 'Wm O'Swald & Co.' dans les relations Germano-Malgache à la fin du dix-neuvième et au début du vingtième siècle," Université de la Sorbonne Nouvelle, Paris III.
Rantoandro, Gabriel. 1973. "Le gouvernement de Tamatave de 1845 à 1865; développement économique," Université de Madagascar.
Rasoamiaramanana, Micheline. 1973. "Aspects économiques et sociaux de la vie à Majunga entre 1862 et 1881," Université de Madagascar.
Ravelomanana, Jacqueline. 1971. "La vie religieuse à Ambositra, 1880–1895," Université de Madagascar.
Wastell, R. E. P. 1944. "British Imperial Policy in relation to Madagascar, 1810–96," Ph.D., London University.

Glossary

ambatry	pigeon pea shrub on which silkworm were reared, which gave its name to the *eranambatry*
amberivatry	shrub (*ambrevade* on Mauritius) on which silkworm were reared
amboninzato	local leader and term for commander of 100-strong *fanompoana* labor gang
Andriana	royal caste
angady	long-handled Malagasy spade
Antalaotra	generic term for Muslims of Swahili–Arab descent
ariary	Malagasy unit of account, theoretically weighing 27 grams. Based on the Spanish silver dollar, it was also the term given to the French five-franc piece and U.S. dollar.
azo sakelehina	lit. "what could be easily carried under one arm" – between 2 and 3 kg
boribory	lit. "circular" – and the name for a variety of tree from which potash was extracted
borizano	generic term for porters (also term for Merina civilians who were theoretically subject to irregular civilian *fanompoana*)
deka	aide in imperial Merina army or administration
efitra	no-man's land between areas under firm imperial rule and independent or semi-independent regions
engagés	French for contract workers – the *engagé* system often disguised a continued slave trade to the French islands of the western Indian Ocean

eranambatry	cut coin weighing 0.375 grams – equivalent to $0.0139
fahavalo	lit. "enemy" – term for brigands or those opposed to the Merina imperial regime
Fandroana	Merina New Year festival
fanjakana ifanoavana	supreme kingship and vassalage – a concept linked to *fanompoana*
fanompoana	unremunerated forced labor in the Merina empire
farasila	standard weight in northeast Madagascar, equivalent to 15.9 kg (35 pounds)
farasisa	Malagasy term for all chronic diseases with cutaneous symptoms
fatidra	blood brotherhood
fihaonana	meeting place (old Malagasy term for marketplace)
filanzana	palanquin
fitonjatolahy	lit. the "seven hundred" – a large *fanompoana* unit formed in Vakinandiana, east of Antananarivo, specifically to erect construction timber for royal buildings
foko	territorially based groupings in Imerina
fokon'olona	local village councils
foloroazato	lit. "the 1,200" – woodcutter *fanompoana* whose numbers grew in the nineteenth century from 1,200 to 2,000
fotsy	"pure" or "white" – a concept linked to a nonslave
gadralava	people originally of free status convicted for crimes including debt, sorcery, and sedition
hafotra	small trees and shrubs, the fiber of which was used to manufacture rope
harangy	variety of west coast Malagasy rubber
hasina	ritual purity (also a term for the one *piastre* tribute paid to sovereign)
hazo	Malagasy for wood and the term used for the dense tropical rainforest of East Madagascar
hazondrano	a kind of rush used in the manufacture of mats and baskets
herana	a sedge commonly used to thatch houses
Hova	Merina caste second in status to the *Andriana* – often used by Europeans as a generic term for all Merina officials of the Merina court
irak'Andriana	

Karana	generic term for Indians in Madagascar – also called *Karany*
Karany	see *Karana*
lamba	a kind of toga, generally of cotton or silk
lokanga	a Malagasy guitar
loso	traditional weight equivalent to 13.5 grams
Mainty	"black" – a reference to the third and inferior (slave) caste
maloto	"impure" – a concept linked to "*Mainty*"
manampaka	traditional standard weight on west coast of about 34 kg (75 pounds)
maromita	traditional term for a (Betsimisaraka) porter
Masombika	generic term for slaves imported from Africa. On the west coast, they were more commonly known as *Makoa* – a reference to the Makua people of Northern Mozambique – a major slave source.
Menalamba	lit. "red cloth" – also the name given to the rebels and rebellion from 1895–7
mizana	iron or brass scales
mpaka entana	freight-carrying porter
mpanakalo-vola	moneychanger
mpanana	lit. "rich" – a group of professional money-lenders that emerged in Imerina early in the nineteenth century
mpanantatra	a group of headman charged by the crown with responsibility for extending *santatra* to the provision by freeman of more general public works *fanompoana*
mpiambinjia	lit. "watchers on the sand" or shore hunters of turtles
mpilanjana	lit. "carrier on the shoulder" or transporter of *filanjana*
mpirehy rano	lit. "rowers on water" or marine fishermen
mpitondra entana	see *mpaka entana*
nanto	a hard red mahogany-like wood
piastra	see *ariary*
pinky	variety of quality rubber from northeast Madagascar
refy	measurement of one arm's length (from 1.68 to 1.83 meters or 5.5 to 6 feet)
salaka	loincloth

sangongo	tumescent lump that characteristically formed on the shoulders of *mpaka entana*
santatra	ritual task performed as a part of *fanompoana*
saonjo	species of edible arum
satrana	palm plant, the seed of which was used in distilling alcohol
Silamo	term for Muslims of Arab–Swahili and Indian descent (*Antalaotra* and *Karany*)
somangy	a tree, the bark of which is used in the manufacture of a blue dye
sorabe	the oldest known form of Malagasy script (Arabic characters)
sorondany	military personnel who formed a permanent *fanompoana* category from the time of Radama I
tangena	poison ordeal (poison extracted from nut of same name)
tanin'ketsa	wet rice nursery beds
tany-ravo	high quality kaolin found in Imerina
tapia	bush upon which silkworm reared
taratasy	a "letter" or "paper" – the early-nineteenth-century meaning was wider – "reading and writing"
tavaiky	coin printed by Andriambelomasina (c. 1730–70)
tavo	species of edible arum
tavy	swidden or slash and burn (dry rice) cultivation
tazo	Malagasy for (malarial) fever
toaka-gasy	locally produced Malagasy rum
toko	regional groupings of *foko* – six *toko* were formed in Greater Imerina
torotorombola	see *vakim-bola*
tsena	market
Tsimandao	see *Tsimandoa*
Tsimandoa	lit. "Will not forsake" – members of a special state courier service selected from the *Tsiarondahy*, a royal servant caste
Tsimioty	seven-year famine in Imerina at the start of eighteenth century (c.1708–16)
vakim-bola	lit. "cut money" – fractions of a coin cut and sold by the *mpanakalo-vola*

Vakok'Andriamasi navalona	lit. "the great silver chain of Andriamasinavalona" – a dyke bordering the river Ikopa in central Imerina
varongy	a tree, the wood from which is commonly used to construct houses and canoes
vary	rice
vary aloha	secondary plateau rice crop harvested from December to February
vary-iray	*vata* (which see)
vary vaky ambiaty	main plateau rice crop harvested from May to June
vata	measure of rice equivalent to 120 liters or 3.3 bushels
vata-menalefona	measure of rice equivalent to 22 liters or 0.6 bushels
vatsy	money, separate from wages, given by employers to workers for daily provisions
vazaha	generic term for white foreigners
voanemba	species of bean
voanjo	species of peanut and term for Merina soldier colonies
vola kely	lit. "a little money" – small change
vola madio	unadulterated money – "good money"
zazamadinika	lit. "little children" – the 5,000-strong workforce formed by Laborde at Mantasoa
zozoro	reed used in the manufacture of coarse cloth and basketry

Index

mints, 47, 288, 291, 300
missionaries (*see also* LMS), 2, 3, 4, 10, 13,
    14, 15, 16, 59, 92, 110, 115, 131, 149,
    162, 195, 207, 242, 247, 248, 264, 265,
    268, 281, 285, 298, 341
  credit system, 298–300, 304
  mail service, 265, 266
  expulsion of, 89, 248
  use of *fanompoana* labor, 101, 131–132,
    133, 248–249, 264
Mocha, 99, 195
Moçimboa, 219, 221
Mogadishu, 195
Mohammed Ali, ruler of Egypt, 8
Moma, 221
Mombasa, 191, 307
money (*see also* coinage, commodity monies,
    piastres), 9, 47, 57, 69, 76, 116, 117, 120,
    161, 200, 201, 222, 233, 254, 255, 256,
    273, 276–304
moneychangers, 285, 287
moneylenders, 295, 296
money supply, 65, 70, 71, 75, 169, 258, 280,
    282, 285–292, 295–304, 336
monopolies, 113, 177, 202, 260, 261, 325
  granted foreign traders, 166, 170, 186, 190,
    192, 198, 249
  of Ambohimalaza cartel, 169
  of *East India Company*, 313
  of Indian traders, 177, 179, 294
  of *La Compagnie des Indes*, 63
  of members of the Merina court, 91, 117,
    179, 184, 277, 280, 296, 299, 336
  of Merina crown, 10, 70, 71, 83, 86, 89, 90,
    103, 106, 107, 113, 162, 165, 166, 170,
    181, 192, 193, 194, 195, 209, 212, 215,
    216, 278, 284, 291
  of porters, 85
monsoons (*see* wind)
Moramanga valley, 22
Moresby Treaty (1822), 239
Morice, 64, 342
Morocco, 333
Moromaniry, 84
Morombe, 231
Morondava, 51, 57, 162, 176, 200, 205,
    210, 221, 231, 248, 267, 268, 282, 300,
    315
Moriandro, 25
mortality, 10, 16, 42, 76, 102, 118, 136, 144,
    145–156, 239, 311, 333, 343
mortality rate, 134, 135, 140, 142, 144,
    145–156, 163, 216, 217, 236, 240

mortgages, 294, 296
motor vehicles, 269
mountains, 22, 24, 80, 81
Mozambique (*see also* Mozambique Island),
    216, 224, 306, 321, 326–327, 328, 329
  coast, 6, 38, 43, 64, 174, 182, 205, 219, 220,
    222, 224, 226, 228, 230, 236, 239, 285
  commerce, 6, 7, 15, 49, 171, 174, 175,
    178–179, 182, 187, 190, 191, 194, 205,
    214, 218, 219, 220, 224, 226, 228, 230,
    232, 235, 236, 239–240, 270, 277, 294,
    310, 311, 312, 313, 314, 339
  Portuguese settlement, 49, 179
  slaves in Madagascar, 131, 226, 233, 235,
    336
Mozambique Channel, 18, 38, 50, 213, 221,
    223–229, 235, 293, 307
Mozambique Island, 56, 174, 218, 219, 221,
    239
mpaka entana, 251–252, 254, 267, 271–272
mpanantatra, 122
mpilanjana, 251, 252, 254, 271, 272
mules, 74
Mullens, Joseph (LMS director), 165, 257
Munroe Doctrine, 321
Muscat, 329
muskets, 37, 42, 47, 50, 51
  production, 93, 96, 97
  trade, 47, 55, 57, 63, 91, 153, 173, 203, 205,
    206, 279
Myre de Viliers (French Resident in
    Madagascar), 311, 332

nails, 36
Namehana, 246
Namorona river, 37
Napoleon I (French Emperor, 1804–14,
    1814–5), 290
Napoleon III (French Emperor, 1852–70), 330
Napoleonic Wars, 4, 51, 61, 209, 215, 225,
    278, 307, 313, 328, 338
Narinda, 221
Natal, 260, 271, 305–306
  commerce, 11, 15, 175, 179, 180, 185, 186,
    187, 203, 205, 207, 211, 268, 270, 285,
    310, 311, 312, 313, 314, 315–316, 341
  postal service, 266, 268, 269
  shipping, 266, 268, 269, 311, 312, 315, 322
  sugar cane industry, 317
Natal Bank (Durban), 297
nationalism, 4, 305–306
natural disasters, 140, 185, 236, 316, 333
needles, 36, 42

(continued from page iii)